Storytellers

Storytellers

A Biographical Directory of 120 English-Speaking Performers Worldwide

by CORKI MILLER *and*
MARY ELLEN SNODGRASS

McFarland & Company, Inc., Publishers
Jefferson, North Carolina, and London

Front cover: Mary Carter Smith.

Back cover (clockwise from top right): Robin Moore, Linda Goss,
Sosha Goren, Adisa Bankole.
(All photographs courtesy of the artists.)

British Library Cataloguing-in-Publication data are available

Library of Congress Cataloguing-in-Publication Data

Miller, Corki, 1952–
    Storytellers : a biographical directory of 120 English-speaking
performers worldwide / by Corki Miller and Mary Ellen
Snodgrass.
        p.   cm.
    Includes bibliographical references and index.
    ISBN 0-7864-0470-1 (case binding : 50# alkaline paper) ∞
    1. Storytellers — Biography — Directories.   2. Folklorists —
Biography — Directories.   I. Snodgrass, Mary Ellen.   II. Title.
GR50.M54   1998
398.2'092'273 — dc21
    [B]   97-49075
                                                                                   CIP

Manufactured in the United States of America

*McFarland & Company, Inc., Publishers
  Box 611, Jefferson, North Carolina 28640*

To Dad and Mom, Jack and Thelma Chandler.
Most tellers talk about Jack —
I grew up with him.

— C.M.

Acknowledgments

Our thanks to all the tellers who have deluged us with résumés, photos, tapes, books, CDs, articles, interviews, and news clippings. Many have interrupted their itineraries to phone, fax, email, and meet us in person to provide details of their careers. Particular recognition goes to tellers Michael Parent, Doc McConnell, Milbre Burch, and Donald Davis, Jason Maynard of August House, Barbara Ittner and Debby Mattil of Libraries Unlimited, and the staffs of H. W. Wilson, Rounder Records, Peachtree Publications, Yellow Moon Press, National Storytelling Association, Smithsonian Folkways, and the Cloister Book Store in Barbados. We owe our gratitude to private collectors of storytelling books, journals, and tapes and to the library staffs at Appalachian State University, Boone, North Carolina; San Francisco Public Library; East Tennessee State University, Johnson City, Tennessee; Chicago Public Library; Catawba County Library, Newton, North Carolina; and Elbert Ivey Memorial Library, Hickory, North Carolina, and to the staff of the Jonesborough *Herald & Tribune*. Finally, heartfelt thanks to Kathy Duffy, who introduced me to storytelling.

— C.M.

Table of Contents

Preface

While compiling this directory of contemporary storytellers, Corki and I met and interviewed the world's most talented English-speaking tellers of tales. Our letters reached them in Israel, Tobago, Barbados, Australia, Canada, England, Scotland, Austria, and France, and in most states in the Union. Although some of those contacted chose not to participate, most tellers were gracious and enthusiastic about sharing their lives and careers with us. We found them traveling from town to town, writing poetry and children's books, working in libraries, attending powwows, teaching school, preaching, counseling, protecting the environment, producing television programs and films, acting, performing in halls and conference centers, and serving their neighbors wherever a group of listeners need and want stories.

Some storytellers intersperse the history and lore of many cultures, faiths, and languages to bridge the soul-killing divisions that isolate and alienate. Others move hands, bodies, and faces to create kinetic word pictures. Many play musical instruments, sing, dance, juggle, and tell jokes along with their stories. A few interpret stories with sign language for the deaf or perform in a blend of indigenous languages.

Overall, storykeepers share with grace and spontaneity their past, their families, tales and morals of old, modern quandaries, and the generous outpourings of wit and humor that keep the world sane. This book preserves in little the great-heartedness of them all.

The plan of this book is to present essential personal and professional information about storytellers, their art, and their publications. Entries, listed alphabetically, provide pronunciations of unfamiliar names, addresses, delineations of style and target audience, and any props, costumes, or musical instruments that enhance performance.

Photographs capture tellers in action, many in costume or miming or playing instruments. Biographies delineate where and how tellers got their start, what influenced and guided their careers, and where they have achieved satisfying interaction with listeners, students, and workshop participants.

Listings of articles, published stories and books, audiocassettes, and videotapes precede a chronological arrangement of awards and honors. Source material offers names of publications from which the entries derive and from which folklorists and researchers can learn more about each teller. The work concludes with a list of performers broken down by home state and country of origin, and a glossary of such foreign and unfamiliar terms and acronyms as *seanachie, mbira,* Kabala, jataka tale, and NAPPS. A bibliography lists works that storytellers mention most frequently as influencing their careers. An index directs readers to specific styles, performers, and genres.

All in all, the work presents to the re-searcher, teacher, librarian, promoter, media, or lover of stories a belated tribute to story-telling, the world's oldest and most resilient form of literature.

—M.E.S.

Introduction

Storytelling wears many faces: the parent quietly reciting "The Three Bears" to a sleepy toddler at bedtime, an elaborate musical production of "Peter and the Wolf," a minister offering a parable from the pulpit, or a therapist citing hypothetical examples to help a patient cope with trauma or despair. For whatever purpose, the act of storytelling dates back to early human beings who chose to pass along family history, personal recollections, participatory games, or ritual chant.

With the first spoken word, the first bold gesture, glinting eye, and crimping of the brow, came the rudiments of the teller's art. More than a casual exchange or momentary diversion for children, the work of the folksayer is both ephemeral and eternal — as integral to verifying, collecting, and preserving group identity and achievement as that of the sculptor, painter, architect, or singer.

Throughout history, Greek poet-tellers, Celtic bards and *seanachies*, English scops and gleemen, European troubadours and jongleurs, Polynesian and native American tribal mythkeepers, and African, Caribbean, and Atlantic sea island griots have maintained the teller's aim to honor the events, beliefs, accomplishments, morals, and values embedded in traditional folk texts.

In the last half of the twentieth century, a worldwide storytelling renaissance has rejuvenated the enduring spoken art by countering impersonal electronic transmissions that spew a myriad of words and images from an amplifier or screen to an unseen audience. Unlike the anonymous entertainments that permeate society, the professional teller has revived a neglected job by conveying a stock of tales one audience at a time and continues a folk-blessed practice as old as mouths to speak and ears to hear.

The stimulation of oral performance is self-replicating: it impels listeners to spread a lively anecdote, rephrase a pungent bit of humor, recite a romance, or punch up a spook tale or jump story. This urge to communicate in story form is as indigenous to human existence as the need to eat, sleep, or reproduce and protect young.

The oral tradition is one of the primeval qualities that sets human apart from beast. Its one requirement is the will to exchange a worthwhile body of lore for the listener's attention. As Franco-American raconteur Michael Parent reminds his listeners: "Tell me a story. I'll give you a nickel. Then you, too, will be a professional storyteller."

— C.M. and M.E.S.

1

The Storytellers

DAVID ALEXANDER

Address: Desk Top Publishers
P. O. Box 4931, Topeka, Kansas
66604-0931
phone 785-232-4810 or 785-357-0481
toll-free 1-888-232-4812
email 72640.3045@compuserve.com
or dalex@dtoppub.com
website www.dtoppub.com

Focus: humorous stories of coming-of-age, college, travel, and personal experience; worldwide folktales and fairy tales; after-dinner entertainment.

Audience: all ages.

Style: a versatile blend of humanistic and multicultural musings on unusual topics with emphasis on personal and community values.

Storyteller David Alexander, who heads his own production company, combines the talents of performer, teacher, writer, and producer. As a teacher of grades 6–12 and a school counselor, Alexander has taught in the United States, Ethiopia, Pakistan, Australia, Thailand, and Indonesia. He maintains an informative website on storytelling and has published two children's picture books. The adopted son of a traditional 1950s-style family, he came of age in Topeka, Kansas, and draws material for a broad repertoire from his Midwestern middle school and high school experiences and from imitation of stand-up comedians. While attending Kansas State University, he studied creative dramatics under communications specialist Mike McCarthy. Other of Alexander's mentors include veteran tellers Donald Davis, Chuck Larkin, and Bev Twillmann.

Alexander launched his freelance career in

1970. To prepare for the profession of griot, he recorded a tape, attends storytelling events in his area as well as professional meetings of the Kansas Reading Association and conventions for counselors, and shares his recorded stories with Kansas schools and family gatherings. Following his debut as a full-time professional storyteller in 1996, he began conducting "Storytelling in the Classroom," a practical one-hour teacher workshop on turning students into storytellers. One of his methods of drawing students into the narrator's role is to begin a story and leave it for participants to finish in their own style. A student workshop, "Storytelling: The Literature Connection," inspires listeners to write entertaining tales that draw on originality and the full panoply of language skills. He has performed at the Tejas Storytelling Festival, Sun Fest, Nebraska Storytelling Festival, St. Louis Storytelling Festival, and Florida Storytelling Camp. At his most memorable festival, the Big South Fork National Park in Tennessee, he related an original narrative, "The Haunting of the Hills."

Bibliography

Jack Becomes a Giant, Desk Top Publishers, 1994.

The Little Wide Mouth Gecko, Desk Top Publishers, 1996. A traditional tale for primary readers illustrated by Yoes Rizal, an Indonesian artist.

To Your Good Health, Your Majesty!, Desk Top Publishers, 1996. A picture book retelling an ancient Russian tale for elementary readers; illustrated by Emmanuel Laumonier, an eighth-grader from France in Alexander's class.

Audiography

World Journeys (audiocassette), Desk Top Publishers, 1996. A reprise of *The Little Wide Mouth Gecko* and *To Your Good Health, Your Majesty!* along with Alexander's memoir of the search for his birth family.

Awards

1997 Kansas Arts Commission Tour.

Opposite: **Charlotte Blake Alston.**

Source

"Bumbershoot '94: Who's Where at Arts Festival," *Seattle Times*, 1997.

CHARLOTTE BLAKE ALSTON

Address: Five Corners Music
P. O. Box 3580
Silver Spring, Maryland 20918
phone 301-588-1618
fax 301-588-7270

Focus: traditional Hebrew, African-American, and native American stories; history and biography; participation stories; rap; monologue; rhyme; hymns and spirituals; call and response; beast fables; morality stories.

Audience: student groups; general.

Style: narration in the griot tradition; humor; kinetic movement, gesture, facial expression, accents; performs solo and with the John Blake Jazz Quartet, the Carolyn Dorfman Dance Company, and the jazz duo of violinist John Blake and percussionist Horace Arnold.

Instruments/Props: robes, headdresses, jewelry; drums, shakere.

A keeper and transmitter of village traditions, Charlotte Blake Alston was a second-grade teacher for 20 years before devoting her talents to performing, recording, researching, and developing stories for platform presentation. In her role as educator she presided over "Keepers of the Culture," Philadelphia's Afrocentric storytelling group, at its 1996 gathering entitled "In the Tradition — A National Festival of Black Storytelling." She presents programs of poems by Nikki Giovanni, Countee Cullen, Gwendolyn Brooks, and other black poets as models of decorum and symbols of hope to young listeners. Her interest in literacy and child development grew organically from experience. A daddy's girl born in Philadelphia in 1949, she heard her father, a Philadelphia mail carrier, recite verse and read aloud to her when she was small, choosing sonorous prose and the dialect verse of Paul Lawrence Dunbar as a treat. To her, these oral gifts had the value of pearls and jewels, for they validated black experience during a period of racism and isolation. She and her father formed a duo on the church banquet and tea circuit as reciters of great literature. She values the nurturance and recognition of her South Philadelphia community and congregation of Holy Trinity Baptist Church and looks back on a second-grade teacher, Dr. Wilma Mitchell, as an impetus to her career in platform narrative.

Alston's mid-life crisis was a blossoming rather than a wilting. At Friends Select School in Philadelphia in 1990, she experienced a lift while telling her class "Who's in Rabbit's House," a traditional Ashanti story. The dramatization and response encouraged her to make a career of storytelling. With her brother, jazz violinist John Blake, she recorded "How Raccoon Got His Dinner" and "The Ant and the Crumb," both traditional beast fables. She chose prestigious and humanistic mentors: writers Paul Laurence Dunbar, Langston Hughes, and Zora Neale Hurston, and tellers Mary Carter Smith, Donald Davis, Baba Jamal Chlonesu "Storyman" Koram, and Jackie Torrence, America's Story Lady. Alston appears annually with the Philadelphia Orchestra for sell-out performances and on Philadelphia radio for *Kids' Corner*, National Public Radio's *Crossroads*, and "New York Kids," over WNYC-FM, New York public radio, co-hosted by storyteller David Gonzalez. Her bookings are supported in part by Arts Midwest, Mid-Atlantic Arts Foundation, Lila Wallace-Readers Digest Fund, Meet-the-Composer, and individual Pennsylvania arts agencies.

Alston's stage presence is issue-oriented, dramatic, and memorable. She encourages reading and literacy while offering young viewers a model of good grooming, erect posture, and lessons on self-esteem, coping with loss, and conflict resolution. She was featured teller at Mansfield University's Storytelling '96 and has appeared at the University of Massachusetts, Carnegie Hall, Rose Lehrman Arts Center, Annenberg Center, Princeton Art Museum, Kennedy Center for the Performing Arts, Henry Street Settlement, Kahn's African Culture Fest, Oshkosh Opera House, Longwood Gardens, Fels Planetarium, and the Presidential Jazz Fest, where she presented signature songs — "There's Always Something You Can Do," "Get Your Stereotypes Off Me," "The Kindergarten Blues," "Make Your Own Decision," "Sing for King," and "Talk It Out." Her program topics include "Stories for Life and Life Stories" and "History as Told in Story and Poem," covering prominent African-American figures — Harriet Tubman, Sojourner Truth, and Langston Hughes. In collaboration with Carolyn Dorfman's dance troupe, Alston recites such values-enriched stories as "The Silent Debate," "The Lion's Whiskers," "The Tall, Tall Tale," and "The Yam Story." With the discernment and rapport of a classroom teacher, she leads call-and-response in "Did You Feed My Cow?," "Hambone," "The Song of the Underground Railroad," "Shoo Turkey," "Today Is Monday," "All Hid," and "Kye Kye Kule," and summons children to participate in "Charlotte's Rock," "Martin Luther King Rap," "The Story of Anniko," "The People Could Fly," and "Raccoon and Other Tales." Her monologues include "Grandma," "Elizabeth Eckford," "Harriet Tubman," and "Ain't I a Woman?," a feminist speech delivered by Sojourner Truth at the 1851 suffragist convention in Akron, Ohio. Alston has also narrated "Soldier of the Cross: Richard Allen and the Founding of the AME Church" at the Smithsonian Institution's Museum of American History and performed at orchestral presentations of Sergei Prokofiev's "Peter and the Wolf," Camille Saint-Saens's "Carnival of the Animals," and Benjamin Britten's "Young Person's Guide to the Orchestra." Annually, she presents holiday programs on black history, women's history, Kwanzaa, and Martin Luther King's birthday.

Bibliography

"Introducing African Storytelling," in *Tales as Tools: The Power of Story in the Classroom,* National Storytelling Press, 1994, 174–175.

Awards

1994 Pew Charitable Trust Fund Arts Fellowship of $50,000.

Source

Belluck, Pam, "A Storyteller Beats Drum, Teaches Some," *Philadelphia Inquirer*, February 9, 1992, B1, B2.

"Charlotte Blake Alston," *The African-American Journal*, December 1993, 1, 29, 34.

"Charlotte Blake Alston Narrates and Introduces Snoopy and Charles Schulz," *The Washington Post*, March 16, 1997, Section 2, Page 1.

Demaline, Jackie, "Pearls from My Own Culture," *Cincinnati Enquirer*, January 12, 1996.

"Fabulous Fables," *Washington Post*, February 23, 1992.

Heimel, Paul W., "Sending a Musical Message," *Storytelling Magazine*, Fall 1993, 36.

Klein, Julia M., "Sixteen Selected for Pew Arts Fellowships," *Philadelphia Inquirer*, June 14, 1994, E1, E5.

Martin, Kay, "Book Giveaway Sells Students on Reading," *Sun Gazette*, January 14, 1993.

"Reason for Rhyme," *Philadelphia Inquirer*, March 1, 1991, 1.

Stamler, Gayle, "People: Charlotte Blake Alston," *Inside Arts*, March 1992.

Sudol, Valerie, "Dorfman Troupe to Perform African Tales," *Star Ledger*, January 15, 1995.

BRENDA WONG AOKI

[Ay • oh' • kee]

Address: 41-A Parsons Street
San Francisco, California 94118
phone 415-221-0601
fax 415-221-2558

Focus: multicultural dance/theater and storytelling; traditional Chinese and Japanese ghost stories; comedy.

Audience: students and adults.

Style: noh and kyogen song/dance/drama; talking jazz.

Instruments/Props: accompaniment by koto, sho, and Polynesian percussion; costumes and masks; three-dimensional lighting.

A true American amalgam of Chinese, Japanese, Spanish, and Scots descent, Brenda Wong Aoki was born in Salt Lake City, Utah, raised in Los Angeles County, and currently lives in San Francisco. Before becoming a full-time performer, she worked as a community organizer, teacher, and youth gang counselor. The eldest of six children, she grew up in the multicultural community of the Long Beach Naval Shipyards. She and her sisters helped out at her parents' mom & pop store. While conducting business on the barter system, she learned the importance of *ohana* (family) and laughter.

In college, Aoki studied music composition and modern dance. After graduating, she co-founded the Dell'Arte Players Company, a Humboldt, California, troupe performing *commedia dell'arte*. Moving to San Francisco, she danced with the Asian American Dance Collective and with Bacchanal, a Brazilian samba company. She also sang and played keyboards in several jazz bands. To solve the dilemma of a dancer who wanted to sing, an actor who wanted to move, and a musician who wanted to dance, she began to study noh and kyogen, traditional Japanese theater in which music, dance, and acting form integral parts of a performance. For seven years, she studied with Yuriko Doi of San Francisco's Theater of Yugen and with Cultural Intangible Properties in Japan under Nomura Shiro and Nomura Mansaku. One day, while sitting with Shiro-Sensei at the Cliff House in San Francisco, she was depressed that she would never become an artist. Shiro Sensei advised, "Aoki-San, you must not get discouraged. The world is a very small place and people like you are now being born every day. How lucky! You are a new people." He predicted that the new people would have their own stories and art forms and urged, "Take what I teach you and make them your own." Since that time, Aoki has dedicated her work to creating for and about the new people.

Directed by Shiro-Sensei's wisdom, Aoki blends Japanese noh and kyogen with Italian *commedia dell'arte*, modern dance, and everyday experience. She creates contemporary folklore with an edge. As she discovered, "The more painfully personal I become, the more universal the work. Personal stories go beyond race and gender to become simply human."

Her full-length one-woman shows include: "Random Acts of Kindness," "Obake!," "Some Japanese Ghosts," "Tales of the Pacific Rim," and "The Queen's Garden," which won four 1992 Dramalogue awards and a San Diego Critics Circle Award. Her latest work, "Mermaid," premiered in 1997 with the Berkeley Symphony Orchestra, conducted by Kent Nagano.

Aoki has earned commissions and fellowships from the Rockefeller Foundation, National Endowment for the Arts, California Arts Council, San Francisco Museum of Art's "Tokyo Form and Spirit" exhibit, and Long Beach Museum of Art's "Whisperings." She is currently working on a Redress and Reparations United States Civil Liberties Public Education Grant to create "Uncle Gunjiro's Girlfriend," a story about her great-uncle's love affair and illegal marriage to a white woman under the anti-Asian laws of the early 1900s. She has performed in Japan and Austria and throughout North America in such venues as the Kennedy Center in Washington, D.C., the Vancouver Folk Festival, and New Victory Theater on Broadway.

In 1996, *Avenue* Magazine named Aoki one of the 500 most influential Asian Americans. She received a U.S. Pan Asian Chamber of Commerce Excellence 2000 Award and the 1996 Woman Warrior Award, and performed at the Smithsonian Institution before the 1996 National Asian American Congressional Caucus. She teaches and lectures at colleges across the country; her plays have become standard college curriculum. She is the artistic director of First Voice, an arts organization dedicated to creating stories and music based on the experience of intracultural people, and serves on the theater arts faculty at the University of California at Santa Cruz.

Bibliography

"The Bell of Dojoji," in *More Best-Loved Stories Told at the National Storytelling Festival*, August House, 1992.

"Black Hair," in *Best-Loved Stories Told at the National Storytelling Festival*, August House, 1991.

Obake! Tales of Spirits Past and Present, Pele Productions, 1991. Chinese and Japanese ghost stories, including "The Bell of Dojoji," "Black Hair," "Dancing in California," and "Havoc in Heaven."

"The Queen's Garden," *Contemporary Plays by Women of Color*, Routledge, 1995. A one-woman play about a Hawaiian prince and a mainland girl.

Random Acts of Kindness, Pele Productions, 1994. A one-woman show.

Videography

Layin' It on the Line, Jefferson Starship, 1985.

Living on Tokyo Time (director Steven Okazaki), 1987

No Way Out, Jefferson Starship, 1984.

Oral Tradition Through Time (videodisc and textbook), McDougal Littell, 1996.

Soul of the Great Bell (composer Mark Izu), Pacific Film Archives, 1995.

Audiography

"Aunti Anna," on *Rainbow Tales* (CD), Rounder Records, 1997.

Black Hair: Some Japanese Ghosts (audiocassette), Pele Productions, 1997. Features the title story plus "Dancing in California," "The Bell of Dojoji," and an interview with Aoki on story origins.

Dreams and Illusions: Tales of the Pacific Rim (audiocassette and CD), Rounder Records, 1990.

The Queen's Garden (audiocassette), Asian Improv Records, 1997.

Awards

1997 Golden Rings Award

1997 New America Playwrights Festival

1997 Civil Liberties Public Education Fund Award

1997 *Avenue* Magazine 500 Most Influential Asians Award

1996 U.S. Pan Asian Chamber of Commerce Excellence 2000 Award

1996 National Storytelling Champion

1996 United States Pan Asian Chamber of Commerce Excellence 2000 Award

1996 Pacific Asian American Women Bay Area Coalition Woman Warrior Award

1994–1995, 1997 National Endowment for the Arts Presenting and Commissioning Award

1994, 1991 National Endowment for the Arts Solo Theater Fellowship

1994–1996 Ruth Mott Fund
1992–1993 Rockefeller Foundation Multi-Arts Production Award
1992 Dramalogue Award for Best Performance, Music, Lighting, and Writing for *The Queen's Garden*
1992 San Diego Critic's Circle Award for *The Queen's Garden*
1991–1994, 1996 Zellerbach Family Fund Award
1991 New Langton/Multicultural Arts Award
1990 NAIRD Indie Award for Best Spoken Word Album for *Dreams and Illusions: Tales of the Pacific Rim*
1988–1997 California Arts Council Touring Roster

Source

"Arts and Design," *Avenue*, Vol. 20, No. 11, 1996-1997.

Churnin, Nancy, "Memories of the Gang Trap," *Los Angeles Times*, November 6, 1992.

"Interview," *San Diego Repertory Theatre*, November-December 1992, 1, 6–7.

Manuel, Diane, "Activist Artist Aoki: Standing Up and Speaking Up," *Stanford Report*, February 7, 1996.

North, Cheryl, "It's a Scream at Berkeley Symphony," *Oakland Tribune*, CUE-1–5.

Timeless Voices: Images of the National Storytelling Festival. Jonesborough, Tenn.: National Storytelling Press, 1997.

Weeks, Jerome, "Storyteller Cooks Up Rich Multicultural Stew," *Dallas Morning News*, June 17, 1994.

Weinberg-Harter, George, "Theatre Reviews: Obake!," *Drama-Logue*, November 12–18, 1992.

LLOYD ARNEACH
[Ar•neech']

Address: P. O. Box 861
        Cherokee, North Carolina 28719
    phone 828-497-5172

Focus: native Cherokee history and lore; historic speeches by great Indian leaders; vision stories and creation myths; contemporary stories; tall tales and humor.
Audience: all ages.
Style: traditional.
Instruments/Props: Cherokee ribbon shirt, hat, moccasins; artifacts.

Of all his lifetime achievements, Lloyd Arneach values most his credentials as an Eastern Cherokee teller. Born and reared on the Cherokee Indian Reservation in the Great Smoky Mountains of Cherokee, North Carolina, he values storytelling as an integral part of his youth and explains that, in the old days, Cherokee parents and elders told stories as a form of discipline. Children gain wisdom from the non-threatening parables that explain elements of morality, courtesy, and self-awareness. From two uncles, George and David Owl, he learned history and tribal stories, including the legend of Spearfinger and the story of a cannibal monster who preyed on Cherokee. A friend and mentor, Mary Chiltosky, pushed Arneach to share his learning with the younger generation, who needed someone to introduce them to tribal oral tradition. His most prized audience was with First Lady Eleanor Roosevelt. While visiting Billy Mills, the native American gold medal-winning runner who set a new world's record in the 10,000-meter run at the 1964 Olympics in Tokyo, Lloyd gathered more incidents and added to his repertory by interviewing actor Floyd Red Crow Westerman, who played Ten Bears in Kevin Costner's 1990 Oscar-winning film, *Dances with Wolves*. Arneach's movie career includes a small speaking role as a Cherokee chief in the PBS-TV movie, *Voices in the Wind*, as well as parts in industrial films for the Smithsonian Institution and safety films on snakes for AT&T. He has also narrated videos for Qualla Arts and Crafts Co-op and the Cherokee Historical Association.

Before becoming a teller, Arneach served in the U.S. Air Force, married, and moved to Atlanta, where he worked for AT&T from 1971 to 1993. The late 1980s brought hardship during his wife's illness and death. He sought activities to fill his time and wrote a children's book, *Animal's Ball Game*. After addressing a Girl Scout troop studying Indian lore, he

eth anniversary festival of the National Storytelling Association in Jonesborough, Tennessee, even though they had never heard him tell before and had to shorten their platform appearances to allow him time to perform. Arneach was proud to be the only teller who did not require an audition and approval for inclusion on the program.

After his retirement as data processing associate for AT&T and initiation of a full-time platform career, Arneach developed a large repertory, including an account of a Cree girl with no stories to tell, the postmaster at a Papago reservation, and the Trail of Tears, General Andrew Jackson's forced removal of Cherokees, Creeks, and Choctaws from their eastern homeland. Arneach also tells tall tales, animal fables, and his favorite, the arrest of Chief Joseph, a Nez Percé leader who was arrested in 1877 in flight to Canada and who sadly promised his captor, General Miles, "I will fight no more forever." Arneach culti-

began traveling the Southeastern United States to lecture on Cherokee history and culture, and visited Mississippi State, Emory, Georgia State, Georgia Tech, University of North Carolina at Asheville, Spelman College, and Northwestern University. After a Georgia State professor, Dr. John Burrison, wrote a chapter on Lloyd in *Storytellers: Folktales and Legends from the South*, a book about storytellers, Lloyd appeared at book signings and received an invitation to a storytelling festival in Atlanta, the first of his career. The event was the beginning of many professional engagements, which include the Northwestern Festival, Merry Olde Christmas, and the Mississippi State Festival. A surprise request from veteran tellers Gayle Ross, Joseph Bruchac, and Johnny Moses brought him out of the audience to the platform at the twenti-

vates a balanced program of creation myths, heroic deeds, and his teasing "Naked Lady" yarn, which identifies an enticing sunbather as an eye-catching eastern diamondback rattler.

Arneach observes a ritual that prepares him for each telling or workshop on oral tradition. In native style, he plants his feet on bare earth and "smudges," a native term for the cleansing of the spirit with prayer and a brief inhaling of smoke from burning sweet grass, a ceremonial herb. He commented to *Focus* magazine that he makes this ritual gesture "so the old ones [spirits of the dead] are more inclined to sit at my shoulder while I do my stories" (Jundos, 1993, 36). His appearances have been close to home: the President Carter Center, Atlanta Storytelling Festival, Cherokee Rose Storytelling Festival, Atlanta Arts

Festival, National Storytelling Conference, Radnor State Park, Veteran's Powwow, Memorial Day Powwow, Asheville Storytelling Festival, Albany and Lawrenceville Powwows, Raccoon Mountain, Cherokee Fall Festival, Atlanta High Museum, Atlanta History Center, Columbus Museum, Anniston Museum, Rocky Mount Storytelling Festival, Mount Airy Storytelling Festival, Appalshop in Whitesburg, Kentucky, Laurel Theater in Knoxville, Tennessee, New Echota State Park, Gwinnett County Historical Society, Cobb County Historical Society, Columbus College, Clark College, Georgia Southern College, and Habitat for Humanity benefit in Kentucky. In addition, he has co-chaired the Eastern Band of Cherokee Indians Constitution Committee and lectured at theaters, camps, churches, schools, and informal venues; his telling on Georgia Public Television has spread Cherokee lore.

Bibliography
Animal's Ball Game, Children's Press, 1992.

Awards
1996 Senior Native American adviser for "Festival of Fires" at the 1996 Olympics.

1992 Elected chair of the Georgia Governor's Council for Native American Concerns.

Source
Burrison, John A. *Storytellers: Folktales and Legends from the South*. Athens: University of Georgia Press, 1989.

Jundos, Elaine M., "Telling It Like It Is," *Focus*, March/April 1993, 36–37.

"Lloyd Arneach," http://www.wnc.com/cherokee/nativeam.htm, June 11, 1997.

Thrasher, Paula Crouch, "Southern Storytelling Festival the Main Event," *Atlanta Journal-Constitution*, April 29, 1995.

PATRICK BALL

Address: 2100 Schaeffer Road
        Sebastopol, California 95472
    phone and fax 707-823-2923
    email celt@monitor.net

Focus: traditional, humorous, and imaginative Irish tales, history, and music.

Audience: principally adults.

Style: witty, imaginative presentation of music and story presented in authentic native idiom to entertain and give a sense of place and belonging.

Instruments/Props: Celtic harp, a traditional Irish brass-strung instrument played with fingernails. The harp was popular from the eighth to the eighteenth centuries, when metal strings gave place to gut strings. The beguiling, bell-like tones, once a favorite of kings and chieftains, earned players honor and celebration for soothing and mesmerizing listeners with graceful, resonant melodies known as the sound of Ireland.

Following the style of the peripatetic bard, Patrick Ball combines narration with music and history, an amalgam that reflects the Irish love of wordcraft, laughter, and the celebration of tradition. Tower Records' *Pulse Magazine* proclaims him the leading American practitioner of the art perfected by O'Carolan, Ireland's classic harper. A native of California, Ball considered following his father into the legal profession. Instead, he developed a flair for musical expression in college, where he played the tin whistle, in part to annoy his roommate. The college experience brought to the surface a love of musical words, a gift of his Irish forebears, and produced an immersion in Ireland's lyrical, turbulent history. After his father's death, Ball pursued an M.A. in Irish history at Dominican College. While visiting Ireland, he recognized the calling that became his destiny — playing the Celtic harp while telling stories in the Irish style.

Establishing a career in the area of Celtic culture proved difficult for Ball. After abandoning unrewarding jobs, he hitchhiked around the United States and worked for two years as groundskeeper at Penland School of Crafts in North Carolina's Blue Ridge Mountains. Local Scotch-Irish traditions appealed to him, as did the Appalachian penchant for tale-telling. Following a second trip to Ireland to acquire material, he returned to his home state to renew a search for the right form and style for a career in Celtic music and lore. He

commissioned Jay Witcher, a master harper in Houlton, Maine, to craft an authentic Celtic harp of 32 brass strings set in a maple frame. Ball set to music the Druidic words and history he longed to tell. In tours about the United States and Canada, he has been acclaimed a premier Celtic harper and interpretive storyteller. His versatile programs combine English literature, folklore and mythology, theater and storytelling, music, and the culture of Ireland and Appalachia. He provides teachers a list of traditional stories and books suited to grade level to enhance classroom follow-up that encourages students to retell the tales or write them down. His attendance at folk, jazz, and storytelling festivals has taken him to most of the United States, Canada, Scotland, England, and Wales. He has performed at numerous colleges and universities, festivals, history and arts centers, museums, educational foundations, theaters, and music halls. He was featured teller at the Forest Storytelling Festival in Port Angeles, Washington, and at the National Storytelling Festival. His six instrumental and two spoken albums have sold over a half million copies.

Ball is best known for solo performances of O'Carolan's Farewell to Music, a play he composed in collaboration with Peter Glazer, writer and director of Woody Guthrie's American Song. The musical theater piece is an amalgam of the life, background, and performances of Turlough O'Carolan (1670–1738) of County Meath. The revered Gaelic itinerant harper and composer, known as "the last of the Irish bards," illustrates the upheaval wrought by social and political dominance of the Irish by English overlords. Fourteen original tunes accompany the narration of the character, poet and harper Charles MacCabe, the master's friend and traveling companion. The nostalgic theme reflects the displacement of the itinerant bardic order after the English supplanted Irish home rule. The £50 Irish note, which bears O'Carolan's portrait, is a sign of the nation's respect and admiration.

Audiography

Celtic Harp I: The Music of Turlough O'Carolan (audiocassette), Fortuna, 1983.

Celtic Harp II: From a Distant Time (audiocassette), Fortuna, 1983.

Celtic Harp III: Secret Isles (audiocassette), Fortuna, 1985.

Celtic Harp IV: O'Carolan's Dream (audiocassette), Fortuna, 1989.

The Christmas Rose (audiocassette), Fortuna, 1990.

Finnegans Wake (audiocassette), Celestial Harmonies, 1997.

Fiona (audiocassette), Celestial Harmonies, 1993.

Storyteller/Gwilan's Harp and Other Celtic Tales (audiocassette), Celestial Harmonies, 1995.

The Ugly Duckling (audiocassette), Windham Hill, 1987. A classic fairy tale by Hans Christian Andersen; performed with Cher.

Awards

1995 NAIRD Indie Award for *The Christmas Rose*.

1995 NAIRD Indie Award for Best Spoken Word Recording for *Storyteller/ Gwilan's Harp and Other Celtic Tales*.

Source

"Make Your Splash: Suit Yourself with a Range of Festivals," *Chicago Tribune*, May 24, 1992.

LINDA BANDELIER

Address: 30 Newhaven Road
        Edinburgh, Scotland EH6 5PY
    phone 0131-554-8771
    fax 0131-558-3550
    email lbandelier@cableinet.co.uk

Focus: tales of the wild American West; Scottish lore and songs; stories of faith and love; myths; original songs and anecdotes; tales from science and nature.

Audience: all ages; pubs to church congregations.

Style: solo; collaborates with David Campbell and other tellers.

Instruments/Props: guitar, harmonica.

An immigrant to the British Isles, registered with the Scottish Arts Council's Writers in Public Schools, Linda Bandelier has appeared in pubs, schools, libraries, and churches in the United Kingdom, South Africa, Germany, India, Holland, Israel, and the United States. She has combined her talents of singing, songwriting, and storytelling with David Campbell, but confides that she's been telling tales longer than he. Raised in Dillon, Montana, she came to storytelling by way of the Methodist ministry. During her theological training she attended Sharing the Fire Storytelling Congress workshops at Lesley College, Cambridge, Massachusetts, where she conquered her fear of public speaking through storytelling and marrying the tenets of her faith with the skills of a storyteller. This inspiration, along with meeting and collaborating with colleague Elizabeth J. Davis, reshaped her career. Together they founded the Lost and Found Storytellers in 1985 and, responding to widespread demand, successfully toured their program of *Women in the Bible* throughout New England.

The year 1987 opened a new chapter in the story. Bandelier met and married a Scotsman and crossed the ocean to Edinburgh. While Scottish congregations were unprepared for this American-style storytelling, Linda was equally astonished to discover that sharing stories in Scotland of an evening is as normal as ordinary conversation. Meeting and working with such master storytellers as Duncan Williamson and Stanley Robertson, she absorbed the relaxed mode of an ancient tradition. She acquired their skill by a process of osmosis, "eye to eye, mind to mind, heart to heart." With this new expertise, she overcame her apprehensions and began working with children. Her repertoire rapidly expanded from Bible stories to include Scottish tales and songs. She found young audiences particularly responsive to native Wild West tales of outlaw sheriffs, homesteaders, natives, prostitutes, prospectors, gamblers, missionaries, and lonely pioneer women. Her three-month storytelling sabbatical in India added rich and colorful tales from ancient Asian traditions.

Bandelier is at the forefront of an artistic renaissance among Christian communities in the United Kingdom. A significant landmark was her recognition and appointment by the British Methodist Conference on September 1, 1997, as the first minister in storytelling. Church work takes her throughout Britain and includes performances in church settings, leading retreats, and running training sessions for youth workers, lay speakers, ministers, and pastoral care workers and counselors. As an associate of the Netherbow Centre, the arts outreach of the Church of Scotland, she joined Dr. Donald Smith, the artistic director, in compiling and editing the *Act and Image Directory of the Arts*, a guide to arts resources for local parishes. Now in its fifth edition, the directory regularly adds new artists as interest grows in the use of performance arts in worship.

Bandelier's travels, research, and drive for excellence in the art combine to mold her style and sense of purpose. She frequently collaborates with other tellers and musicians on commissioned programs in environmental studies and history. *Unlocking the Waterways*, the story and songs of the Scottish lowland canals for British waterways, and *The Mystery of Rookery Wood*, a study of a woodland site for Scottish Natural Heritage, are pioneering work in Scotland combining science, the arts, storytelling, and environmental education. *An Evening with Robert Burns* and *The Life of Mary Stewart* form part of an extensive repertoire of historical Scottish characters. Bandelier teaches *Women in Scottish History* for Elderhostel, presenting famous, infamous, and ordinary women's lives through narrative and song. These multidisciplinary studies call for imaginative research into science, history, and human nature. Platform narrative highlighted with music and song bring these topics and characters to life in the imagination. For Bandelier, that synthesis is the great gift of storytelling.

Bibliography

The Mystery of Rookery Wood (co-writer Kate Ainsworth), Scottish Natural Heritage.

The Three Donalds (co-written with David Campbell), Scottish Children's Press 1997. A children's story in which three identical children from three different families are rescued by tartan.

Audiography

Joukerie Pawkerie (co-tellers David Campbell and Alison Millen) (audiocassette), Scottish Traditional Storytellers, 1995.

Tales from the Fire (co-producers David Campbell, Paraig MacNeil, and Alison Millen) (audiocassette), Scottish Traditional Storytellers, 1993. Folk stories and songs from Scotland and the American West.

Woman at the Well (audiocassette), Scottish Traditional Storytellers, 1993. Stories and songs of women in the Bible.

Source

Act and Image Directory for the Arts, Neterbow Art Centre, 43/45 High Street, Edinburgh, Scotland EH1 1SR.

Scottish Storytellers Directory, Scottish Storytelling Centre, 43/45 High Street, Edinburgh EH1 1SR.

See also David Campbell.

ADISA BANKOLE
[ah•dee•sah' ban'•koh•leh]

Address: 381 Garibaldi Avenue, #11
Lodi, New Jersey 07644
phone 974-614-8671

Focus: original educational stories with African diaspora motifs.

Audience: children and adults.

Style: kinetic, dynamic, and culturally liberating.

Instruments/Props: traditional African wear, bare feet; drums and other accompanying instruments.

Griot-warrior Adisa Olubayo Bankole follows the path of the ancient African folksayer and bills himself as a griartist, an Afrocentric educational soldier. With humility, he declares that he serves African deities and his ancestors as a carrier of messages. His program "In the Spirit of Our Ancestors: Recapturing the Dreams" was well received at a choreopoetry presentation for a Brooklyn school. Bankole learned the wisdom of stories from his great-grandmother, keeper of family history, from his father's original tales, and from Papa Slim, an elderly family friend who shared his adventures. Bankole and his brother created their own stories together and acted out original plots as play. In 1972, while Bankole was studying theater at Onandaga Community College in Syracuse, New York, he learned the elements of the theatrical profession — acting, directing, and playwrighting — and has applied his enthusiasm to stage and film. After obtaining a B.A. in theater from State University of New York at Albany, he appeared on and behind the stage in California and New York in the Globe Playhouse, Empire State Youth Theater, and New Federal Theater, and acted in two feature films, *The Saint of Fort Washington* and *Williamstowne* (not yet released). In addition to composing verse, he wrote two plays and began creating choric poetry presentations. At the Hamilton Art Center he created "Ebo: How the Lion Got His Roar" as a lesson in listening. With a drum and poetry troupe, the Guardians Drummers and Poets, he staged verse drama in the Albany/Schenectady area. From there, he advanced as a professional performing artist and workshop conductor for the Adopt-a-School project at the Paper Mill Playhouse in Milburn, New Jersey.

Bankole validates the experience of African people by informing listeners and by inspiring them to a greater Africultural sensitivity. He dedicates such original works as "Binsee

Bee" and "Elika the Elikoo Bird" to advance storytelling to greater respect among the arts and to promote African ideals and history as lessons from the past. As one of the featured tellers at the 1997 National Black Storytellers Festival, he profited from the examples of veteran performers Granddaddy Junebug, Baba Jamal Koram, and Sister Carolees Reed, and has honed his performance as artist-in-education. In addition to writing for the *National Black Storyteller's Newsletter*, he was guest artist on *Illuminations*, where he discussed the meaning of cultural identity through the art of storytelling and what it means to be a "griartist" and "Afrocentric educational soldier." He appeared on *Third World Children's Story Hour* on PBS-TV, a show dedicated to bringing stories from other worlds besides Euro-America, and performed on *A World of Difference* for WTEN-TV. He has presented his art at the Queens Borough Library for the Tenth Annual Langston Hughes Kwanzaa Celebration, Walt Whitman Cultural Arts Center, Museum for Arts and Sciences, New Jersey Educational Theater, Harbor Musical Festival, Museum for African Art, and schools and events along the Eastern seaboard. He has conducted workshops in drumming/storytelling at the Caribbean Cultural Center, New Jersey State Museum, and Borders Book and Music Store. He has also served as contributing editor for his hometown newspaper, *South End Scene*, and as editor trainee for the African Writer's Collection.

Bibliography

"Afrika's Melanin Melody," *National Black Storytellers Newsletter*, Fall 1996, 3.

Awards

State University of New York Dean's List for academic achievement.

Source

"Adisa Olubayo Bankole," *National Storyteller's Direction*, http://www.storynet.org.

Barker, Allen C., "Albany Black Theatre — Asleep or Dead?" *South End Scene*, September 1982.

_____, "Drama: Crossing the Line," *Getting Off*, February 1983.

"Black Roots Lay in Africa," *South End Scene*, February 1985.

"Casting in New York," *South End Scene*, May 1985.

BOB BARTON

Address   58 Sparkhall Avenue
              Toronto, Canada M4K 1G6
       phone 416-469-3818
       fax 416-469-5771
       email bbarton@ilap.com

Focus: traditional world tales; beast fables; wonder tales.

Audience: children and adults.

Style: vivid pictographic work portraits.

Writer and storyteller Bob Barton is a natural with children after 32 years as a teacher and Ministry of Education employee. He debuted in storytelling at Artpark in Lewiston, New York, in 1979. A regular on the professional platform, he was keynote speaker in 1987 at the First Congress on Storytelling in St. Louis, Missouri, and featured teller at the Northern Appalachian Festival '96. He has led courses for the Centre for Language in Primary Education in London and for the National Storytelling Association in Jonesborough. His performances have enlivened the North Atlantic Festival, New Brunswick Storyfest, International Children's Festival, Detroit Storytelling Festival, Stories from the Heartland, Dromkeen Centre for Children's Literature, Magic Fire, Battersea Arts Centre, World Conference on Reading, Northern Appalachian Festival, and the National Storytelling Festival. An undemonstrative performer, he uses a sensible, pragmatic approach that relies on imaginative diction and style. He prefers to stress words rather than props or costumes, and remains behind the scenes as the transmitter of the action rather than a participant. He bases his approach to workshops on Dorothy Heathcote's philosophy that teachers should lengthen the period of incubation by expanding a storytelling experience with retelling, drawing, changing the point of view, dramatizing and interpreting, creating a tableau, or interviewing the teller about details from the action. Barton advises new tellers to select a story that requires an enthusiastic telling to tap the listeners' skill at picturing the action in their minds.

A native of Hamilton, Ontario, Barton recalls the influence of World War II on his childhood. At age three, he was a regular patron of the Hamilton Public Library, where his family obtained ration tickets for butter and sugar. From the line for coupons, each week, his family took him to the children's section to select three books. He learned to love Randolph Caldecott's visual storytelling in *Three Jovial Welshmen* and *The Queen of Hearts,* a style that has stayed with Barton for a lifetime. He completed his education at Hamilton Teachers' College and McMaster University. As a storyteller in adulthood, he continues to paint detailed word portraits and takes as models English teller Ben Haggarty and Canadians Joan Blodger, Dan Yashinsky, Helen Porter, and Alice Kane. He adapts techniques his mother used in Sunday School classes while teaching Old Testament stories on a flannel board and performing stories from the King James Bible, which influence his phraseology and diction. He comments in

his résumé, "The *sounds* of the language were very much a part of shaping my love of words."

Barton's father was an amateur trumpeter who played in four military bands. Barton learned to love pageantry while hearing performances of the Six Nations Reservation Band in Brantford, Ontario, on Queen Victoria's birthday. The concerts ended with the traditional distribution of bread and cheese initiated by the Queen. The sound and rhythm of trumpet music, which his father played at church and with his own dance band, still influence Barton, who often slips a story into keynote speeches. He believes that inclusion of tales is a pleasant surprise for people who would not seek out a storytelling event. He recalls telling a story in an L-shaped banquet hall and having to pause while an ailing diner out of his line of vision was hauled out on a stretcher. Barton, who is accustomed to adapting to a variety of physical settings, continued his telling. He admits that multiple sessions drain him of energy because he works alone and must create all the magic for a variety of widely different story worlds. To stay in shape, he enjoys cross-country skiing.

The co-founder of the Storytellers School of Toronto, Barton works full-time telling stories at schools, libraries, churches, and parks, and makes an annual pilgrimage to New York's Central Park Storyhour to tell a tale at the foot of the Hans Christian Andersen statue. His career as a professional narrator began in 1990 and is based on a straightforward faith in listeners. He believes that children need to see and hear adults telling stories and considers it time well spent. He maintains that the experience of hearing and seeing the storyteller is more powerful than listening to a reader or hearing tapes. To assist parents in enjoying stories with their families, he has collaborated with the BBC to produce a series of books and companion radio programs for young listeners to share with adults.

Barton specializes in ancient stories. He admires a 2,000-year-old Jataka tale about 500 monkeys who discovered the drinking straw while sipping from a lake through hollow reeds to avoid being eaten by a water monster. From his childhood reading he selected the tale "The Storm Wife," a text derived from a collection of Siberian stories, which he reinterpreted with a subtle contemporary edge. He has also performed in storytelling theatre with shows such as "Mainly Under Moonlight," "Destinations of the Heart," and "My Mother the Merwoman of Donegal." His published works are available in the United States, Canada, Great Britain, and Australia.

Barton's career has not ended his affiliation with educators. He maintains his interest in children's literature, early literacy, and drama in education. He has acted as a school board consultant in English and drama and teacher educator and adviser on TV Ontario and the National Film Board of Canada. He has made in-depth studies of drama in the classroom and curriculum writing, and leads workshops for parents on early literacy in the home and addresses American and Canadian education conferences. He has hosted Canadian Broadcasting Corporation Radio School series for children and was featured at the International Reading Association conferences in Chicago, Anaheim, New Orleans, San Antonio, Toronto, and Orlando. His essays have appeared in *Spelling Links, Literacy Across the Curriculum, Children's Voices, The Drama Theatre Teacher, Language Matters, Primary Teaching Studies*, and *Reading in Virginia*.

Bibliography

Best and Dearest Chick of All, Red Deer, 1994.

Brown Is the Back of a Toad; Yellow Is a Lemon Tart; Red Is the Nose of a Clown (co-author David Booth), Longman, 1976.

The Honest Penny, Quarry, 1997.

Mother Goose Goes to School (co-author David Booth), Pembroke, 1995.

Nobody in the Cast (co-authors David Booth et al.), Longman, 1972.

Primary Teaching Studies (co-author David Booth), University of North London Press, 1993.

The Reindeer Herder and the Moon, Longman/BBC, 1991.

Stories in the Classroom (co-author David Booth), Pembroke, 1991.

Stories to Tell, Pembroke, 1992.

The Storm Wife, Quarry, 1993.

Tell Me Another: Storytelling and Reading Aloud at Home, at School and in the Community, Heinemann, 1986. A handbook on selecting, personalizing, reading, telling, and teaching stories; contains numerous models from a variety of sources.

The Twelve Days of Christmas, Somerville House, 1997.

Awards

1990 International Reading Association's Jennie Mitchell Celebrate Literacy Award.

1989 Fabian Lemieux Memorial Award for Contribution to the Arts in Ontario Schools.

1985 Ginn Reading Award.

Source

Alvarado, Monsy, and Steven C. Johnson, "Antiques, Tales, and Cherry Pie," *Northern New Jersey Record*, September 8, 1996, 3.

Aylwin, T. *Traditional Storytelling and Education*. University of Greenwich, 1993, 28–29.

Goudie, Marlene, and Sharon Morgan, "Kateri Students Enjoy Author's Visit," *Weekender*, March 5, 1994, 6.

Granfield, Linda, "Introducing Bob Barton," *CANSCAIP News*, Spring 1991, 1–2.

Lloyd, Leslie, "Tellers of Tales Meet Again in Storied Tennessee Community," *Memphis Commercial Appeal*, October 4, 1992, B8.

Sambrano, Marilynn, "Storytellers Bring Their Art to Detroit," *Detroit Free Press*, June 28, 1987, 1K.

JOHN BASINGER

Address: 133 Lincoln Street
Middletown, Connecticut 06457
phone 860-346-3262
fax 860-685-2221

Focus: mainly reciting John Milton's *Paradise Lost*; tells about his character Chester Behnke using humorous anecdotes and verse adapted from daily life, observations, and personal and family events.

Audience: older children and adults.

Style: conversational and dramatic narration interspersed with sign language.

Instruments/Props: harmonica and other musical instruments.

John Peter Basinger's early years precede a lifetime of traveling, which has taken him to the top of Mt. Kilimanjaro, by kayak down the Connecticut River, and on foot from Minnesota to San Francisco. A student at Haugen and LaSalle elementary schools in Chicago, he attended high school in Mountain Lake, Minnesota, and Bluffton College in Bluffton, Ohio, where he earned a B.S. in mathematics. Subsequent training came from summer school at Mankato State University, Mankato, Minnesota, night school at the University of Southern California, summer school at the University of Chicago, and Wesleyan University in Middletown, Connecticut, and diversified his skills, which include proficiency in German and Swahili. From all this training, he winnowed out an M.A.T. in mathematics and biology and an M.A. in theater, both from Wesleyan. In an equally varied employment history, he worked as research engineer at North American Aviation, in a glue factory, and in men's underwear at Chicago's Marshall Field, and as a computer programmer and in Air Force intelligence. He parked cars in San Francisco and taught biology at the Government African Secondary School in Kakamega, Kenya, and English and math at the Martin Luther King, Jr., Medical Care Center. Other teaching stints have taken him to Texas Southern University and Woodrow Wilson

High School. By 1968, he was acquiring experiences that led to a career in narrative: actor and musician at the National Theatre of the Deaf, teacher of drama and sign language at Mohegan Community College, National Slam Poetry Competition, engagements at the Long Wharf Theater and Hartford Stage Company, actor in Paramount Pictures' 1986 feature film, *Children of a Lesser God*, and drama teacher at the National Theatre Institute and University of Rhode Island and Three Rivers Com-Tech College in Norwich, Connecticut, from which he retired in 1992.

As a storyteller, Basinger has led workshops for the National Storytelling Association and has performed at the National Folktale Institute, Corn Island Festival, Whitney Museum, and the Mark Twain House in Hartford, Connecticut, as well as numerous festivals through the East and Midwest. He has worked in American Sign Language with deaf tellers in the Manhattan Theatre Club, Omega Institute, Boston Museum of Fine Arts, and American Museum of Natural History, and has performed on seven occasions at the Hudson Clearwater Revival, where he now programs storytellers along with Louise Kessel and Davis Bates. In May 1997 he was a featured performer at Folke Tegetthoff's "Lange Nacht of Storytelling" at the Graz Erzählt Festival in Austria, along with Susan Klein, Laura Simms, Dan Yashinsky, Michael Parent, Milbre Burch, and Shosha Goren. His repertoire centers on one character at different stages of his life for six main situations: "Chester Behnke Goes Hunting," "Chester Behnke Meets Ada Harper," "Chester Behnke Meets Robert Frost," "Chester Behnke, the Birth of a Poet," "Chester Behnke in Iowa," and "Chester Behnke Keeps Christmas." He co-authored and directed *Mountain Sweet Talk*, a two-act storytelling play that ran for eight seasons at the Folk Art Center on the Blue Ridge Parkway outside Asheville, North Carolina, and helped stage *First Times and Forgotten Toys* for veteran tellers Lee Ellen Marvin, Judy Black, Doug Lipman, Elizabeth Dunham, and Jay O'Callahan.

Basinger enjoys spontaneous performance rap and has recited long narrative verse by American authors Henry Wadsworth Longfellow, Sidney Lanier, and Robert Nathan. An unusual accomplishment is Basinger's performance of books I through VIII of John Milton's Bible-based epic, *Paradise Lost*, which he has told at the Asheville Poetry Festival and the Connecticut Poetry Festival. He plans to memorize the entire work for a grand telling by the millennium. Currently composing his seventh play, *Benedict Arnold: A Brave Revenge*, he draws on the burning of New London and the September 6, 1781, Battle of Groton Heights, where 2,000 British regulars and units of loyalists and Hessians attacked the area during the Revolutionary War. Basinger intends to present Arnold's story as an outdoor historical pageant drama in southeastern Connecticut at an amphitheater built for summer shows.

Bibliography

Caleb's Story, Caleb's Dream, self-published, 1983.

The Cauldron, self-published, 1986.

Egon Reese, self-published, 1987.

"Chester Behnke Goes Hunting," in *More Best-Loved Stories Told at the National Storytelling Festival*, August House, 1992.

Indian Hill, self-published, 1985.

Mountain Sweet Talk (co-author), The Folktellers, 1986.

The White Hawk, self-published, 1981.

Video

Children of a Lesser God (actor), Paramount Pictures, 1986.

The Teller and the Tale (participant), CBS-TV. A storytelling series aired in New Hampshire.

Awards

1988–1989 Yale University's Mellon Fellow in theater.

1986 Merit Award for Excellence in Teaching.

Source

Brown, Tony, "Two Tell Tall Tales: Storytelling Cousins Blend Differing Perspective of Their Appalachian Heritage as They Spread Joy from Asheville to Asia," *Charlotte Observer*, March 1, 1989, 1D.

Kiss, Tony, "Playwright Memorizes Part of Milton's 'Paradise Lost,'" *Asheville* (North Carolina) *Citizen-Times*, June 24, 1994, 8C.

Mills, Marja, "Many a Yarn to Be Spun at Festival," *Chicago Tribune*, July 24, 1989, 2.

_____, "Storytellers Bring Their Tales to Life," *Chicago Tribune*, July 31, 1989, 1.

Osborne, Linda, "The Wisdom of Nations," *World & I*, May 1993.

See also Connie Regan-Blake.

JEANNINE PASINI BEEKMAN

Address: 10606 Clematis Lane
        Houston, Texas 77035
   phone 713-728-3655
     P. O. Box 562
     Benton, Louisiana 71006
   phone 318-965-9984

   Focus: diverse world folklore; multicultural Texas stories.
   Audience: all ages.
   Style: lively, dramatic narrative.
   Instruments/Props: costumes when venue necessitates.

Storyteller Jeannine Pasini Beekman draws energy from history, myth, and her love of travel and dancing. The daughter of Ward Robert and librarian Lucille Hanks Pasini, Beekman was born May 14, 1951. She grew up among storytellers and agrees with the Southern Edwardian belief of Nana, her maternal grandmother, that one should know the stories of one's people. Beekman recalls sitting in the porch glider and listening to the talk of visiting women. The day before Nana's death, she summoned her six-year-old granddaughter and spent a whole day relating stories. Beekman remarks in her résumé, "With mentors like these I had no choice but to turn out the way that I did."

A student of drama, Beekman attended the College of Fine Arts of the University of Texas, where she studied folklore with a student of national legend, Frank Dobie, America's premier collector of cowboy songs and Southwestern lore. Married to opera singer Robert Anthony Beekman in 1971, Beekman worked in the Children's Room of the Houston Public Library and facilitated community programs. While holding a picture book for the umpteenth storytelling session, she decided to put it down and tell her own story. She recalls, "The effect was so magical and transformative that I wanted more. And so did the public."

From her platform debut in 1974, Beekman developed into a popular teller lauded by the Gulf Coast media. Six years later, she gained a colleague in internationally known teller Laura Simms, followed in 1986 by collaboration with Texas storytellers Elizabeth Ellis and Gayle Ross. Beekman summarizes, "Without these extraordinary women — my mama, my Nana, and my three sisters in story — I would never have had such a remarkable journey nor found this life's work." In addition, she credits Charlotte Blake Alston, Carol Birch, Milbre Burch, Donald Davis, Gay Ducey, Dan Keding, Susan Klein, David Novak, Jon Spelman, and Kathryn Windham with influencing and sustaining her love of language and narration.

Beekman has appeared at the National Storytelling Festival, Disney Institute, Mark Taper Theater in Los Angeles, and Sisters of Charity Leadership Symposium, and has performed with the Houston Symphony. She has developed collaborative arts projects with the Smithsonian Institution, American Library Association, and Opera America, and has received funding from the National Endowment for the Humanities and the National Endowment for the Arts. A spirited joiner who belongs to the National Storytelling Association, Tejas Storytelling Association, and National Speaker's Association, she helped found the Houston Storytellers Guild and currently assists Baylor College of Medicine in a *Healing Arts Project*, which uses storytelling to determine brain function in children.

Bibliography

"Mr. Cramer: A True Ghost Story of Houston," in *Best Stories from the Texas Storytelling Festival*, August House, 1995.

Audiography

In Your Ear, a 1997 in-flight audio series, P. O. Box 781175, San Antonio, Texas 78278-1175.

One Texan's Tales (audiocassette), Spellweaver Productions, 1989. Includes "Master Frog," "The Legend of the White Buffalo," "Pedro and the Devil," and "Mr. Cramer"; for ages 10 to adult.

"Riccitello and Riccitella," on *Rainbow Tales, Vol. 1* (CD), Rounder Records, 1997.

Turn Up Your Imagination (audiocassette), Spellweaver Productions, 1995. Includes "A Fox in One Bite," "How Anansi Got His Bald Head," "The Turnip," and "When the Rooster Was King of the Cats"; for ages 3–10.

Under a Texas Sun (audiocassette), Spellweaver Productions, 1995. Multicultural beast tales reflecting Texas diversity in "The Talking Turtle," "Hermano Coyote and Señor Yellow Jacket," "Why Rattlesnake Always Warns Us," and "How Sun Came to Be in the Sky"; for all ages.

Videography

Power of Storytelling Series, a 12-part series for HCCA-T, 1996.

Awards

1996 Parent's Choice Award for *Turn Up Your Imagination*.

1992 Ann Martin Book Award (CLA) for outstanding contributions to literacy.

1991 John Henry Faulk Award for outstanding contributions to storytelling.

1990 Tejas Storytelling Association Award for outstanding contribution to the art and folkway of storytelling.

1989 Unsung Hero of the Arts Community from *Houston Metropolitan* magazine.

Source

Ballew, Cheri, "Storyteller Can Weave a Yarn That Will Enchant Young and Old," *Huntsville Item*, April 22, 1989.

Bennett, Elizabeth, "Did You Hear the One About…," *Houston Post*, December 2, 1986.

Farrar, Foss, "Guild Helps Revive Art of Storytelling," *Houston Chronicle*, November 26, 1989.

Karkabi, Barbara, "A Mouthful," *Houston Chronicle*, May 10, 1987.

_____, "Tell Me a Story: The Old Tales Are Told Again," *Houston Chronicle*, January 20, 1985.

Lloyd, Leslie, "Telling of Stories Lives On at Festival," *The Birmingham News*, October 16, 1995.

Long, Sandra, "Storytellers Use Different Techniques to Capture Children's Imaginations," *Kid Times*, November 1986.

McVicker, Steve, "Ghostly Tales of Texas," *Houston Press*, October 1994.

Parker, Dan, "Festival Salutes Art of Storytelling," *Corpus Christi Caller Times*, November 3, 1996.

Strickler, Jeff, "Tell Me a Story," *Minneapolis Star Tribune*, June 24, 1990.

JOEL BEN IZZY

Address: 1715 La Loma Avenue
              Berkeley, California 94709
       phone 510-883-0883
       fax 510-883-0888
       website www.storypage.com.

Focus: world folktales collected in his travels; the wise men of Chelm and other Yiddish and Hasidic folktales; tall tales; ghost stories; personal reflection and family memories.

Audience: all ages.

Style: conversational and dramatic narration laced with mime.

Instruments/Props: gray fedora.

A cheery, handsome platform narrator, Joel ben Izzy first donned his gray fedora and hit the road as a traveling storyteller in 1983. Since then, his travels have taken him to performances in the marketplace of Jerusalem, the subways of Tokyo, and from ancient amphitheaters in Italy to high-rises in Hong Kong. While growing up in the San Gabriel Valley, a suburb of Los Angeles, California, he saw his horizons diminished because of his father's ill health and failing insurance business and the heavy financial responsibility that fell to his mother. He recalls that his grandfather Izzy told stories, but his father was too preoccupied to impart his memories. His mother, while busily driving her family in the station wagon, tossed out only scraps of tales along the way. Craving wonder and a knowledge of life beyond his limited valley, ben Izzy played with puppets in nursery school. In his early teens, he chose Houdini as a hero—a Jewish kid who escaped Wisconsin by eluding chains, trunks, and water torture chambers. While learning magic on his own, ben Izzy met and studied the repertoire of Professor Presto, who made an annual visit to the local temple and demonstrated how to perform onstage. The cachet of local amateur magician followed ben Izzy to school and around the neighborhood. However, while performing at the Magic Castle in Hollywood Hills, he saw his stage act as fakery, grew disillusioned and abandoned magic.

While reading J. R. R. Tolkien's *The Hobbit*, ben Izzy settled on fiction as a better form of magic. In 1980, he dropped out of creative writing classes at Stanford University and flew to Paris, where he walked the Latin Quarter and kept a journal. He talked with other writers, but wrote no books. His one submission to a publisher returned with a rejection slip. Again discouraged, he gave up writing to take up mime and read the lives of the great silent performers — Marcel Marceau and Charlie Chaplin. Ben Izzy's venue consisted of entertaining drivers stuck in traffic, until gendarmes escorted him out of the thoroughfare. On his return to the United States he and a friend formed "The Real World Mime Troupe" and drove toward Chicago, where a car accident wrecked his hip and destroyed the fluid body movements that were essential to mimetic performance. The unforeseen end to his act answered a question that had been bothering him — how to talk in a world of silence.

As ben Izzy's dad had observed, "People make plans and God laughs." On return to California in 1982, the year of heavy rains, ben Izzy, still on crutches, enrolled in the English department at the University of California in Santa Cruz. He was moping in his apartment over a failed love match when a newspaper headline caught his attention: "Storytelling Center Helps Young Storytellers." A tutor named Ruthmarie listened to his stories and gave pointers on technique. He explored library stocks of tales, which he added to the unfinished stories of his father and mother. He admired the work of some of the best in the business — Ed Stivender, Angela Lloyd, Michael Parent, Rex Ellis, Donald Davis, Steve Sanfield, Gay Ducey, Paddy O'Brien, and Eddie Lenihan. The magic returned to ben Izzy's life as he honed his style. He returned to Stanford, got a degree in narration, and graduated. The shift set him on the path to success as a platform raconteur.

A world traveler who speaks German, French, Italian, Spanish, and Hebrew, ben Izzy has met his counterparts in a Hasidic *maggid*, a Hawaiian story-talker, and an Irish *seanachie*. He collects material from books and sojourns along the way, whether in Cardiff, Athens, Zurich, Honolulu, or Paris. As an antidote to a too-technical world, he passes on the warmth and pathos of stories by weaving the material into performances and workshops tailored for schools and universities, synagogues and churches, theaters, libraries, and radio and television. Festival appearances have included the Cape Clear International Storytelling Festival in Ireland, Bankoh Talk Story Festival in Hawaii, International Schools

Theater Association Festival in Switzerland, and the Bay Area Storytelling Festival in California. Among Catholics at the Cape Clear International Storytelling Festival in Cork, Ireland, he stood out as the rare Jew and transcended prejudice with marathon stories. He makes his home in Berkeley, California, just behind the university, and lives with wife Taly Rutenberg and their children, Elijah Lev and Michaela, in a hundred-year-old redwood house. In addition to teaching at Dominica College in San Rafael, California, he serves as resident teller at East Bay School of the Arts. He has won audiences over BBC radio and at Hillel in Santa Barbara, the Zionist Confederation House and the Israel Centre in Jerusalem, the American school in Tokyo, and oral interpretation classes at the University of California at Berkeley.

Bibliography

"On Crossing Borders with Stories: Notes of a Traveling Storyteller," *National Storytelling Journal*, Spring 1987, 9–12.

"An Orange," in *Jewish Chicken Soup for the Soul*, projected 1997.

"An Orange," in *Many Voices: True Tales from America's Past*, National Storytelling Association 1995.

"A Story from the Jewish Cemetery in Japan," in *Stories Told by Jewish Storytellers*, Jason Aronson, 1995.

"The Tale of a Storyteller," *Washington Post*, December 8, 1996, 19, 22.

Audiography

The Beggar King and Other Tales from Around the World (audiocassette and CD), Old City Press, 1993. Contains "The King's Riddles," "Stories of the Fools of Chelm," "Be Polite," "The Pickpocket: Tales About Babies," "The Field of Two Brothers: Tales from the Old City of Jerusalem," and the title story; a blend of traditional klezmer, Romanian hora, Gypsy czardas, Irish jig, and other music.

Buried Treasures — A Storyteller's Journey (audiocassette), Old City Press 1996. Contains stories about Hershel the Trickster, a Haitian story about the theft of the Elephant King's drum, and remembrances of ben Izzy's father.

Chanukah in Chelm and Other Tales (audiocassette and CD), Old City Press, 1997. Accompanied by klezmer variations of traditional Chanukah tunes.

The Green Hand and Other Ghostly Tales from Around the World (audiocassette and CD), Old City Press, 1996. Features "Creepy Car Tales," "How I Got Bill the Chicken," "The Cremation of Sam McGee," "King Solomon and Death/The Graveyard in Safed," and the title story.

How I Learned to Love Liver and Other Tales Too Tall to Tell (audiocassette and CD), Old City Press, 1997. Features the title story plus "Watermelon Stories," "Hi, Mom!," "The Hobo's Story," "Cookies in the Train Station," and "The *True* Story of Paula Bunyan"; accompanied by silent movie-style tunes composed by Joshua Raoul Brody.

Stories from Far Away (audiocassette), Old City Press 1991. Contains "King Solomon and the Smell of the Bread," "A Tale from Jerusalem," "Tokyo Stories of Nasrudin the Trickster," "A Tale of Curses, Blessings, and Bee Stings," "Stories of the Fools of

Chelm," and "The Old King and His Daughters"; klezmer clarinet accompaniment by David Julian Gray

Awards

1996 Booklist Editor's choice Award for *Buried Treasures — A Storyteller's Journey.*

1994 National Endowment for the Arts Travel Grant.

1993 Parent's Choice Gold Award for *The Beggar King and Other Tales from Around the World.*

1991 American Library Association Notable Recording for *Stories from Far Away.*

1991 Parent's Choice Award for *Stories from Far Away.*

1991 Chapter One Grant.

1986 Chapter Two Grant.

1984 San Francisco Education Fund Grant.

Source

"Audio: Top Choices for Kids," *Los Angeles Times*, November 28, 1992.

Flocken, Corinne, "What's Your Story?: Everybody Has Something to Tell at the Third Annual Festival Tales," *Los Angeles Times*, October 7, 1993, 3.

Guthartz, Norm, "Ties and Tales," *The Jerusalem Post*, October 17, 1986, 1.

Heffley, Lynn, "'Treasures' Tales Pay a Loving Tribute to Dad," *Los Angeles Times*, August 8, 1996.

"Joel ben Izzy from the US," *The Cork Examiner*, September 5, 1994, 1.

Kaplan, Karen, "Learning Curve: Anecdotal Evidence," *Los Angeles Times*, January 23, 1996, 6D.

"Review," *Washington Post Book World*, September 1, 1996.

Ziaya, Christine, "Learn to Spin Yarn from the Masters at This Festival of Jewish Storytelling," *Los Angeles Times*, October 27, 1989, 25A.

LaDoris Bias-Davis

Address   2870 Valley Ridge Drive
Decatur, Georgia 30032
phone 404-288-2759

Focus: personal reflections; multicultural folktales; farm tales; Bible stories; seasonal material; Gullah tales; participatory stories; spirituals.

Audience: children and adult groups.

Style: griot tradition; call and response; animated actions and voices.

Instruments/Props: costumes and props.

A native Southerner, LaDoris Bias-Davis speaks of her background in *Me and Mississippi*, a collection of anecdotes from her home state. One of eleven children who learned at home how to embellish a good story, she learned from her father, who could perk up family ears with his yarns. In her platform career, she reflects on growing up on a farm as well as on material from the Bible and folklore. As a docent at the Tullie Smith historical site, she tells a tale while displaying an old quilt, iron, and ingredients for rabbit or possum stew. To fervid audiences she asks, "Can I get an Amen?"; to children, she reels off the sacred ingredients of Grandma's biscuits as part of a favorite story, "Sodie Sally Rytus." For Kwanzaa, she lights the kinara candles and

explains the seven holiday principles of unity, self-determination, collective work and responsibility, cooperative economics, purpose, creativity, and faith. At the annual ALA Read-in, she interprets stories to encourage reading and listening. Professional activities include membership in the Southern Order of Storytellers, Atlanta History Center Guild, Decatur Storytellers, Kuumba Storytellers of Georgia, and Peachseed Youth Storytellers Guild, which she serves as member of the advisory board. Her fairytale workshops assist students in updating familiar tales. Her voice is familiar to listeners of *The Voice of Choice* and *Telling Tales — Folklore of the South* on Georgia Peach Radio and *Read to Me* on Florida television.

Bias-Davis brings to her career in platform narrative an educational background rich in creative skills. She majored in speech, theater arts, and sociology at William Carey College in Hattiesburg, Mississippi, and completed her education with advanced studies in creative writing and computer skills at Emory University, in Atlanta, Georgia, EPI at Chapel Hill, and DeKalb Community College, where Professor Jane Zanca nurtured her talents and referred her to the Southern Order of Storytellers. Influenced by veteran tellers Bobby Norfolk and B. J. Abraham, she turned voracious reading and observation to her advantage for an initial performance at the Dunbar Community Center Family Social Day. Past jobs have ranged from director of education at Dixie Hills Baptist Church to editor and writer for the Cambridge Academy newsletter, owner of Davis Love & Care, writer and director at the Cathedral of the Holy Spirit, and coordinator of Atlanta's Save the Children.

In addition to private coaching for beginning tellers, Bias-Davis provides a number of programs to professional groups. Her focus centers on child care programs, training for child care professionals and youth ministers, creating and producing children's theatrical exercises and puppet drama, implementing setting and costuming, and performing for motivational assemblies, camps, family reunions, PTA assemblies, and Kwanzaa and Black History Month. She has broadened her range from local schools, libraries, camps, bookstores, and churches to Dekalb Mental Health, YMCA, Spruill Arts Center, Egleston Hospital, Georgia Special Olympics, Pickneyville Arts Center, and American Business Women. Her festival experience covers Georgia Writers, Southern Storytelling, SOS Olde Christmas, Lake Lanier Islands Fiddlin' Fish, Atlanta Dogwood, Atlanta History Center Harvest and Folklife, Georgia Peanut, and Peachseed Youth.

Bibliography

"Blood Journey," *Zebulon Speaks*, 1993.

"Forlorn," *Zebulon Speaks*, 1993.

"A Home for Writers and Writers," *The Write Margin*, Spring 1991, 6.

"Tot Telling Tips," *SOS Newsletter*, Spring 1995, 3.

Source

"Big Read-in at Hightower," *Kaleidoscope*, Winter 1997, 2.

"Guest Storyteller," Nashville, Georgia, *Berrien Press*, June 18, 1997, 7.

Helton, Charmagne, "Yarn-Spinners Weave Magic Web," *City Life*, July 27, 1995, JD8.

Johnson, Morieka, "La Doris Bias-Davis," *Eye on Women*, November/ December 1996, 2, 12, 15.

Richards-Kreiner, Hadley, "Libraries Offer Funds, Tales and Crafts for Kids," *Atlanta Journal-Constitution*, July 17, 1997, JK7.

"Storyteller Will Lead Celebration at Library," *On Common Ground*, December 1996, 26.

"Summer Reading Club," Nashville, Georgia, *Berrien Press*, June 25, 1997, 7.

"Tell Me a Story," *Sarasota Herald-Tribune*, June 26, 1996.

"Telling the Story," *Tifton Gazette-Entertainment*, June 14, 1997.

Thrasher, Paula Crouch, "Have They Got a Story for You," *Atlanta Journal-Constitution*, April 29, 1995, 4.

CAROL BIRCH

Address: P. O. Box 32
Southbury, Connecticut 06488
phone 203-264-3800

Focus: imaginative stories.
Audience: all ages.
Style: dynamic.

Librarian and platform performer Carol L. Birch emerged as a platform performer during the storytelling renaissance. A student of storyteller and folklorist Dr. Ellin Greene at Rutgers University, Birch profited from classroom exposure to Greene's scholarly approach to narrative and literature for children. During the final semester of her master's degree, her selection of the storytelling course was serendipitous: in the early 1970s, she signed up on the advice of a nurse, who urged Birch to apply for the librarian's job at a reformatory for young boys. In lieu of a course in organizing government documents, Birch chose a study of oral narrative. From the second class meeting she was hooked on stories and told her husband, "The most wonderful thing happened to me today. I found out who I am." She elaborates on the experiences as "a bass note sounding inside me. I just recognized it as my art form." As though stories were paintings and she the painter, she declares that Dr. Greene handed her the brush and pointed to a lifetime of canvas.

Against images of isolation in modern art, the hate and suspicion of those who opposed the civil rights movements, and the war-mongering of the late 1960s and early 1970s, Birch and her generation chose the ancient verities found in folk music, pottery, and storytelling. Not only like musicians Rosalie Sorrels and Gamble Rogers, but other influential tellers like Kathryn Windham, Donald Davis, Jon Spelman, Rafe Martin, Jim May, Syd Lieberman, Susan Klein, Heather Forest, Alice McGill, and Elizabeth Ellis, Birch joyed in the possibilities for human connection. She describes her career choice as a search for identity, voice, and meaning at a time when the world seemed engulfed in clangor. For years images of death dominated the news from the Vietnam War, Cambodian bombings, Kent State shooting, and the assassinations of John and Bobby Kennedy and Martin Luther King. She felt the urge to create a tangible, life-giving art that transcended the despair and materialism of the times.

Birch claims a quarter century of experience. A baby boomer born in 1946, she reflects on her outspoken family, who made no effort to hide their desires or intentions. Her development of unsubtle gesture and expression proved useful to platform narrative. Experience with piano and voice in preparation for a career as a choir director armed her with a sense of phrasing and timing, also adjuncts to the raconteur. After she earned degrees from Saint Olaf College and Rutgers University, and completed all but her dissertation for a doctorate in communication from the University of Southern California, she served faculties on both coasts. In California, she taught at Loyola-Marymount, the universities of Southern California and California at Los Angeles, and Long Beach City College. In Connecticut, she has continued teaching at Wesleyan and Southern Connecticut State University. In addition to library posts in Chappaqua, New York, Woodbridge and Mercer County, New Jersey, she has lectured at 45 universities, directed audiocassette projects, chaired the Anne Izard Storyteller's Choice Award, and co-authored *Who Says? Essays on Pivotal Issues in Contemporary Storytelling*, a widely acclaimed study of the medium. The excellence of her work caught the attention of media production companies. National recognition of her work has resulted in appearances on special half-hour programs for *The Story Channel*, *ABC's Nightline*, *CBS This Morning*, National Public Radio's *Good Evening, America*, and on the Emmy-winning program for children, *A Likely Story*, as well as in *Glamour* magazine and the *New York Times*.

A four-time veteran of the National Storytelling Festival in Jonesborough, Tennessee, Birch has earned the praise of fellow tellers Elizabeth Ellis, Michael Parent, Donald Davis, and Heather Forest, and receives top billing at performances across the United States and in Australia, Canada, Germany, Norway, and Singapore. Renowned for skillful audio production, she has developed audio packages for Samuel Babbitt, Milbre Burch, Donald Davis, Heather Forest, Jean Fritz, Joe Hayes, Sonia Landes, Rafe Martin, Michael Parent, Jackie Torrence, and Jean Yolen. The National Storytelling Association hired her to index the archives of live-performance tapes from the first 15 years of the National Storytelling Festival. From that experience, she was equipped to select, edit, and arrange 75 stories from thousands told at the festivals into nine audio anthologies: *A Storytelling Treasury: Stories Told at the Twentieth National Storytelling Festival, Vols I–VI*; *Tales of Humor and Wit: Wise Men and Simpletons*; and the first two volumes of *Best Loved Stories Told at the National Storytelling Festival*. In addition, she has directed Heather Forest for August House, Arlo Guthrie for Lightyear, and independent productions for Milbre Burch and Marianne McShane. Her productions have won both the Parents' Choice Gold Award and a *Storytelling World* honor tape award.

A visionary of the storytelling wing of spoken arts, Birch demonstrates philosophy, technique, and the art itself. Her workshop topics — "Who Says?," "The Trouble with Princesses (And Other Royal Figures)," "And Then What Happened," and "When Pigs Were Swine" — cover the essentials of fictional point of view, characterization, sequencing, and setting. She projects sound educational goals, including facility with language, creative and

empathetic imagery, treasuring the past, deepening the understanding of humanistic truths, celebrating diverse cultures, and reinforcing literary skills. Her adult concerts — *Myth America: Summer, 1928, Will We Ever See Their Likes Again?, A Delicate Balance, Happily-Ever-After Love Stories … More or Less* — mine the stories in Ray Bradbury's *Dandelion Wine*, celebrate immigrants, recount tales of conflicted women, and reconstruct the paths by which love travels. For adults she presents workshops through lecture and demonstration of *Do Tell! The Art of Storytelling*; *IMAGE-ination: The Heart (And True Art) of Storytelling*; *Three-Part Harmony: Voices of Parallel Peoples*; *A Storyteller's Passionate Virtuosity*; and *Who Says?*

She has practiced her art at conferences in Tennessee, Texas, Connecticut, Maine, California, Alabama, Georgia, New York, Illinois, North Carolina, Missouri, Massachusetts, South Carolina, Michigan, Oklahoma, New York, Indiana, Minnesota, Utah, Florida, and Virginia. Her appearances have graced stages at McCabe's Coffee House, Perth Symphony Center, Mark Taper Forum, Lincoln Center, and Busch Gardens as well as 5 cruises for Holland America, five corporations, 19 professional associations, and 53 storytelling festivals around the world.

Bibliography

"The Boy with a Keg," in *More Best-Loved Stories Told at the National Storytelling Festival*, August House, 1992, 13–16.

"Bracelets," in *Joining In*, Yellow Moon Press, 1988.

"Bracelets," in *Stories in My Pocket*, Fulcrum, 1997, 75–78.

"Building Bridges with Stories," *Storytelling Encyclopedia*, Oryx, 1997.

"Choreographing a Story" and "The Voyage of the Wee Red Cap," in *Storytelling: Art and Technique*, Bowker, 1996.

"A Fisherman and His Wife," in *Best-Loved Stories Told at the National Storytelling Festival*, August House, 1991, 168–171.

"Pecos Bill," *The Five Owls*, September/October 1986, 8.

Stories in My Pocket, Fulcrum, 1996.

"Storytelling: Practice and Movement," *Teach-*

ing Oral Traditions, Modern Language Association 1997.

"Storytelling Programs Between Schools and Public Libraries," Libraries Love Storytelling, National Storytelling Press, 1997.

"Storytelling Programs for the Family," National Storytelling Journal, Summer 1984, 14–18.

Teaching Oral Traditions (contributor), Modern Language Association.

"Those Three Wishes," in Ready to Tell Tales, August House, 1994, 132–135.

"Weston Woods: A Commitment to Excellence," Top of the News, Summer 1985, 326–332.

Who Says? Essays on Pivotal Issues in Storytelling (co-editor Melissa A. Heckler), August House, 1996. Contains Birch's "Who Says? The Storyteller as Narrator" plus essays by Rafe Martin, Peninnah Schram, Joseph Bruchac, Bill Harley, and six other tellers, folklorists, anthropologists, literary theorists, and educators; annotated.

Filmstrips

Red Riding Hood (illustrator Edward Gorey), Weston Woods, 1985.

Videography

Carol Birch at the Storytelling Cafe, projected 1997. Features "Toby Boyce" and "The Easy Reader Version of Jane Eyre."

"Interview," The Twentieth Anniversary of the National Storytelling Festival, Hometown Entertainment, 1994.

Storytelling (contributor), McFeely-Rogers, 1996.

"Tayzanne," in American Storytelling Series, Vol. VII, H. W. Wilson, 1986.

Audiography

Careful What You Wish For (audiocassette), Frostfire, 1993. Contains "Those Three Wishes," "Peter Kagan and the Wind," "The Fisherman and His Wife," "Careful Wishing," and "Wee Meg Barnileg and the Fairies."

Happily-Ever-After Love Stories ... More or Less (audiocassette), Weston Woods, 1987. Features "The Porcelain Man," "Tayzanne," "Who Will Wash the Pot?," and "The Wooing of the Maze."

"How the Rhinoceros Got Its Skin," in Tales of Humor and Wit (contributor) (audiocassette), National Storytelling Press, 1992.

Image-ination: The Heart (And True Art) of Storytelling (audiocassette), Frostfire, 1992. Includes guided imagery exercises to shape character and setting.

Nightmares Rising (audiocassette), Frostfire. 1984. Contains "Mary Culhane and the Dead Man," "Mr. Fox," "The Boy with the Keg of Beer," and "Caryn's Story."

Awards

1997 NAPPA Gold award.

1996 Storytelling World's special award honor book for Who Says?

1987 American Library Association Notable Recording for Happily-Ever-After Love Stories ... More or Less.

1984 New York Public Library Best Recording for Nightmares Rising.

Source

"Carol Birch, the Storyteller," The Story Channel, December 24, 1996.

"Festival's Tents Are Multistoried," Chicago Tribune, July 30, 1995.

Kellogg, Steven, "Review of 'Pecos Bill,'" The Five Owls, September/ October 1986, 8.

Mooney, Bill, and David Holt. The Storyteller's Guide. Little Rock, Ark.: August House, 1996.

"A Quick Look at Featured Storytellers," Jonesborough, Tennessee. Herald & Tribune, September 29, 1993.

Ruiz, Ben, "Review," Tale Trader, November 1996, 14.

Timeless Voices: Images of the National Storytelling Festival. Jonesborough, Tenn.: National Storytelling Press, 1997.

"Women Right Now," Glamour, May 1990.

JUDITH BLACK

Address: 33 Prospect Street
Marblehead, Massachusetts 01945
phone 617-631-4417

Focus: American history; contemporary life and relationships; humor; tales for young people and their families to grow on.

Born in Pittsburgh, Pennsylvania, October 2, 1951, she is the third of four children. Her father was a linen supplier, her mother a housewife. Black earned a degree in early childhood development from Wheelock College. Grounded in educational theory, she taught elementary school for three years, but suffered recurrent headaches. Her malady disappeared during evening theater rehearsals with a downtown company. To rid herself of pain, she studied theater in the United States and at the Royal Academy of Dramatic Arts in London. She found roles such as Golda in *Fiddler on the Roof* too self-limiting. From two years of acting with the Little Flags Theater Company and an evening in 1976 watching Jay O'Callahan perform, she developed into a storyteller, which in her words is "the only job I could do that left me with more energy than I started with." From telling stories in local bookstores and at weddings and engagement parties, she expanded to a broad array of audiences, including the Smithsonian Institution's National Museum of American History, Hillel International Leaders Assembly, National Trust for Historic Preservation, and Annual Institute of Alcohol and Drug Studies. In the early 1990s, she collaborated with Boston tenor Walter Boyce to produce *Peter and Magelone*, an introduction to classical music.

Audience: children and adults.

Style: dramatic, uninhibited involvement of the audience through recreated lives of real people in demanding situations.

Instruments/Props: costumes if needed.

A four-time presenter at the prestigious National Storytelling Festival as well as at universities and area festivals, including gatherings in Indianapolis and Las Vegas and the Montreal Comedy Festival, Judith Black is a 20-year veteran and co-founder of Three Apple Storytelling Festival who draws on lively stories that reflect a middle-class, Jewish background. She serves as workshop leader and teacher in related fields, most recently for the Texas Commission on Alcohol and Drug Abuse.

Black's stories center on one of three themes: American history, stories woven from contemporary life and relationships, and humor. When drawing on her own life, she utilizes Steve Allen's famous formula, pain + time = comedy, shaping very personal experiences into stories that resonate with truth and humor. Other favorite topics include figures from union history, particularly Mother Jones, a labor organizer for the I.W.W., a focal character in her series called *History Stories*. To give the program flow, Black concentrates on the thematic bridges that ally different segments of the presentation, but rejects over-refinement to keep the human elements at the forefront. Her tellings suit the needs of a number of library and literacy conferences and historic societies, a flexibility that she calls the *sine qua non* of telling. She has soloed with the North Shore Philharmonic Orchestra and at the Boston Conservatory and produced "Hell for a Picnic" for the U.S.S. *Constitution* Museum. She has written and directed a musical comedy about reducing waste and developed *Pinching the Giants*, a television series on tricksters from around the world. Her published articles have appeared in *Storytelling Magazine, Yarnspinner, Journal of Reading, Inside Story, Story Bag*, and *Storytelling World*, and in collections published by August House, Jason Aaronson, Random House, and the National Storytelling Press. She has addressed the Wheelock College Alumni Forum on multicultural education and delivered a paper on censorship at the National Congress on Storytelling.

With a grant from the Department of the Interior, Black taped *From Her Arms to His*, a World War II story of women ordnance workers at the Springfield Armory, and has given one-woman performances depicting sweatshop working conditions, lives of recent U.S. immigrants, and the results of racism. She has performed for a gathering of Hollywood screenwriters and developed middle-school curriculum exploring links between the Holocaust and scapegoating and peer pressure. As the featured presenter for the Hebrew College Masters Performance Series, she premiered *Looking for G-d's Doorbell*, an exploration of Judaism that grew out of her son Solomon's disinclination to study for his bar mitzvah. On a grant from National Public Radio, she taped *Adult Children of ... Parents*, which debuted at Israel Horowitz's Gloucester Stage Company. The Boston *Phoenix* named her show "Banned in the Western Suburbs" as one of the year's top ten small theater productions. A faculty member of Leslie College's Art Institute, Black has taught narrative arts at Boston

University Law School, the National Institute on Storytelling, Annual Institute of Alcohol and Drug Studies, Boston Museum of Fine Arts, and National Congress on Storytelling, and she joins Doug Lipman annually for a course entitled "Telling Stories to Children."

Bibliography

"Creating the History Story" and "Bread and Roses," *Storytelling World*, Summer/Fall 1992, 3–6.

"Cynthia the Caterpillar," in *Storytelling World*, Winter/Spring 1995.

Home Grown Stories for Kids, National Storytelling Association, 1995.

"The King's Child," in *Ready-to-Tell Tales*, August House, 1994.

"Noah's Wife," in *Chosen Tales*, Jason Aronson, 1995.

"Rosie the Riveter," in *Many Voices, True Tales from the American Past*, National Storytelling Press, 1995.

Video

From Her Arms to His, Connecticut Valley Historic Society, 1996. An original story of female factory workers at the M-1 rifle plant in Springfield during World War II.

Audiography

Adult Children of ... Parents (audiocassette), Tidal Wave Productions, 1995. A comedic saga about the onset of middle age; for ages 14 and up.

Banned in the Western Suburbs: Stories about Adult Passions, Choices and Relationships (audiocassette), Tidal Wave Productions. Adult entertainment, including "The Aerobics of Life" and "Deborah and Simon," who meet at an adult education lecture on death; for ages 16 and up.

Glad to Be Who I Am (audiocassette), Tidal Wave Productions, 1988. Stories and songs celebrating empowerment for age 4 and up, containing "Molly Whoopie" and "Three Billy Goats Gruff."

Hell for a Picnic (audiocassette), Tidal Wave Productions. An adventure story of an 11-year-old who goes to sea aboard the U.S.S. *Constitution* during the War of 1812 in search of the father who left him in an orphanage.

The Home Front (audiocassette), Tidal Wave Productions. Stories of working women during World War II, featuring "Rosie the Riveter" and "From Her Arms to His"; for ages 12 and up.

"Mother Jones," on *Rainbow Tales* (CD), Rounder Records, 1997.

Oops Ma!: Songs and Stories of Family Life (audiocassette), Tidal Wave Productions. A set of seven stories and songs by Victor Cockburn and Judith Black reflecting how parents and children can survive daily rituals; for ages 4 and up.

Waiting for Elijah (audiocassette), Tidal Wave Productions. A collection of traditional, literary, midrashic, and original stories about Judaism; for ages 6 and up.

Awards

1996 Cable Ace Award nomination for performing arts.

1996 Emmy Award nomination for *From Her Arms to His.*

1996 New England Emmy nomination for outstanding actor/performer.

1996 Springfield Cable Endowment Ace Award for *From Her Arms to His.*

1996 Springfield Cable Endowment for programming excellence.

1995 *Boston Globe* National Honor Tape for *Adult Children of ... Parents.*

1995 *Storytelling World* award for *Adult Children of ... Parents.*

1989 Wheelock College Centennial Alumni award.

1988 *Parents' Choice* Gold Medal for *Glad to Be Who I Am.*

1987 *Boston Parents* Gold Medal Family Entertainer of the Year.

1985 WBZTV Rising Star of New England.

Source

Bach, Lisa Kim, "Storytelling Festival Headed by Renowned Tale-Spinners," *News-Sentinel*, June 18, 1993, 11A.

"Jonesborough's National Storytelling Festival Attracts Thousands to Annual Three-Day Event," *The Loafer*, October 1, 1996, 19, 21.

Katz, Debra, "Tell Me a Story: Spinning Tales to Entertain Your Children Is a Way to Connect with Them," *Tallahassee Democrat*, June 4, 1996, 3D.

Keva, Bette Wineblatt, "The Many Faces of Judith Black," *Jewish Journal*, January, 1997, 17.

Mooney, Bill, and David Holt. *The Storyteller's Guide.* Little Rock, Arkansas: August House, 1996.

Richardson, Peggy Hemlich, "The Texas Storytelling Festival, 1997," http://members.aol.com/storypage/news/97texas.htm.

"Storyteller Gets Emmy Nomination," *Storytelling Magazine*, July 1996, 6.

"Storytellers to Weave Their Special Magic During the First Week of October," Jonesborough, Tennessee, *Herald & Tribune*, October 2, 1996, 3C–5C.

Timeless Voices: Images of the National Storytelling Festival. Jonesborough, Tenn.: National Storytelling Press, 1997.

See also Doug Lipman.

BROTHER BLUE
(pseudonym of Dr. Hugh Morgan Hill)

Address: P. O. Box 381315
Cambridge, Massachusetts 02238-1315
phone 617-496-8340

Focus: original tales; *Panchatantra* and Jataka tales; traditional Western lore from Aesop, the Brothers Grimm, and Hans Christian Andersen; folk stories, legends, rap, and chant; Asian and African spirituals; one-man street versions of Shakespeare's plays, Greek mythology, sacred literature, and world classics.

Audience: all people.

Style: energized fantasy figure; the tone and purpose of a religious missionary.

Instruments/Props: tambourines, harmonica, saxophone, umbrella, fool's bells, balloons, ribbons, banner, finger puppet mouse named "Just-One-of-Those-Things the Third," hand-made dragon named Almara, slave chains; tells in his bare feet and wearing face and hand decorations in rainbow colors to represent segments of the human race; butterflies symbolize the soul emerging from the flesh.

Treasured and lauded in the *Boston Globe* and *Wilson Library Bulletin*, on WGBH-TV, in the *Philadelphia Inquirer, Episcopal Times, Newsweek, Village Voice, Toronto Star,* and *Harvard Summer Times*, Brother Blue seems touched by divine madness. One of storytelling's most innovative journeymen and the official storyteller for both Boston and Cambridge, he refers to himself as God's clown, the "Storytellin' Fool of New England." He has a broad-based appeal. His stories and poems range from "Peek-a-Boo" and "Muddy Duddy" to "Po' Caterpillar," "Othello," "The King of the Golden Deer," and "Ugly Duckling Number Two." He has earned over $1,000 an hour and regularly performs free at daycare centers, prisons, saloons, street corners, and homeless shelters. He addresses birds and animals as well as street derelicts; he once demonstrated for world hunger by telling for 72 hours nonstop. He disdains money and lives like Jesus, Moses, and St. Francis. His wife, Ruth Hill, supports the family with her work at Radcliffe's Schlesinger Library on a Rockefeller grant as coordinator of an effort to record the oral history of elderly black American women.

For over four decades, Brother Blue has car-

ried his art to varied venues: the National Festival of Black Storytelling, New York Folk Festival, UNICEF pavilion at the 1984 World's Fair, Academy of American Psychotherapists, Sacred Dance Guild, Baltimore Artscape, American Imagery Conference, and college and university classrooms. Known formally as Dr. Hugh Morgan Hill, he has created stories as bread for the mind, imagination, heart, and soul. While an honor graduate of Harvard, he earned an M.F.A. in playwriting from Yale and a doctorate in African-American and third world poetry from Union Graduate School. His thesis was a presentation of "Soul Shout," a storytelling concert for prisoners, who provided musical accompaniment. Welcomed in churches, libraries, schools, conference halls, parks, and radio and television studios throughout North America, Europe, and the Caribbean, he has also starred as official storyteller for the 1976 United Nations Habitat Forum in Vancouver, Westinghouse's *Playmates/Schoolmates* on national television, New Orleans's Bourbon Street at midnight, and National Storytelling Festival in Jonesborough, Tennessee.

Brother Blue, a native of Cleveland, Ohio,

brother Tommy produced a call to heal broken hearts and trumpet love to others. Profoundly retarded, Tommy couldn't dress himself or read and write. His death in an institution traumatized Brother Blue, who determined to rescue others who are immured in harsh circumstances. After the army discovered Blue's high IQ, he had no difficulty getting into Harvard and becoming an ordained minister. While living in Pittsfield, Massachusetts, he began touching souls by telling stories. The death of Dr. Martin Luther King, Jr., occurred in 1968 while Brother Blue was in divinity school. Moved to laud his hero's life, he created a requiem, "O Martin, O King," and joined guitarist Lee Riethmiller, Pastor Doug Koch, and the founder of Project Place in spreading King's story to churches and schools. Alone, he created Soul Theater by setting improvisational Bible stories and worship to music for prisoners and worked as a field education supervisor for divinity school students. He has presented his sacred art in Italy, Switzerland, Russia, and Canada. To remind himself of his purpose, he carries chains from a former slave in his bag and uses them in stories that remind listeners of America's history of oppressing blacks. Among his aims, he hopes to create a simple, unrehearsed television show of storytellers.

adopted his new first name after a child rhymed Hugh with Blue. He sees himself as a member of the poor, hungry, and lost everywhere. Blue was born in the 1920s to a gruff out-of-work bricklayer who roughed him up and a mother who had no time to give him attention. Feeling neglected, he wept in school and did poor work in arithmetic. The turning point in his life came at age eight, when he found inspiration in a teacher who believed that everyone is born for a purpose. Uplifted, he moved beyond sadness to a new identity. He discovered that unconditional love brought out the best in him and declares that his teacher saved his life. As a professional teller, he immortalized her in his signature tale, "Miss Wunderlich."

According to Brother Blue's childhood memories, his relationship with his disabled

Bibliography

"The Butterfly," in *Talk That Talk*, Simon & Schuster, 1989.

"Miss Wunderlich," in *Homespun: Tales from America's Favorite Storytellers*, Crown, 1988.

"no title," http://www.ke.ics.saitama-u.ac.jp1_dh95/cgi-bin/article6-e.html, June 2, 1997.

"The Rainbow Child," in *Spinning Tales, Weaving Hope: Stories of Peace, Justice, and the Environment*, New Society, 1992.

Videography

Brother Blue, Mark Saltveit, Harvard College, 1983.

Brother Blue, Melvin McCray, 1983.

Knightriders, George Romero, 1981. Brother Blue in the role of Merlin.

"Miss Wunderlich" in *American Storytelling Series, Vol. 6*, H. W. Wilson, 1987.

Storytelling, Kay Armatage, 1983.

Audiography

"Ahhh," on *Rainbow Tales, Vol. 2* (audiocassette), Rounder Records, 1997.

"America *Be* Beautiful," on *Getting It All Together* (audiocassette), Outrageous Records, 1977.

"Miss Wunderlich," on *Rainbow Tales, Too, Vol. 1* (audiocassette), Rounder Records, 1997.

Street Car (audiocassette), Out of the Blue Records, 1992.

Awards

1996 National Storytelling Association Circle of Excellence.

1982 Best of Boston Award for street performance.

1976 Walt Whitman International Media Competition for Poetry on Sound Tape for *Malcolm X*.

1975 Corporation for Public Broadcasting Local Programming Award. Outstanding Solo Performance on Public Radio Special Citation for "Miss Wunderlich."

Zora Neale Hurston Award.

Source

An American Portrait (video), CBS-TV, October 4, 1985.

Bloom, Connie, "Singing the Blues," *Akron Beacon Journal*, October 4, 1976, A8.

"Brother Blue," http://nsn.bbn.com/community/bl_hist/brother_blue_intro.shtml, June 2, 1997.

Cech, John, "Breaking Chains: Brother Blue, Storyteller," *Children's Literature*, Vol. 9, 1981, 151–177.

Chum, Diane, "You Can Call Me Blue," *Gainesville Sun*, February 1, 1980, 23.

El-Mohammed, Fatima Cortez, "Visit from Planet Blue," *Afro-American Cultural Center Newsletter*, University of Connecticut, October 1976, 5.

Johnson, Doris, "Butterflies Are Free Inside Brother Blue," *Boston Herald American*, July 31, 1976, 7.

Lehrer, Warren. *Brother Blue*. Albany, Calif.: Bay Press 1995.

Marion, John, "A Spoleto Retrospective," *Columbia (S.C.) Osceola*, June 22, 1978, 16.

Mason, Marilynne S., "Telling Stories Isn't Just Kid Stuff," *Christian Science Monitor*, December 23, 1993, 12.

Noah, Timothy, "Brother Blue," *Harvard Magazine*, January-February 1979, 87.

Pothier, Dick, "Let Brother Blue Put a Story on You," *Philadelphia Inquirer*, May 18, 1979, 4.

Precopio, Joseph S., "Brother Blue: His Own Story," *Berkeley Beacon*, September 27, 1978, 6.

Search of Joy (video), Two Loons, 1991.

Serino, Michael. *Brother Blue* (film), Emerson College, 1973.

Shanta, "Brother Blue," *Bloomsbury Review*, Winter 1996.

"The Story Behind Brother Blue," *Boston Globe*, July 10, 1991, 51, 54.

Zevin, Dan, "Talespinner," *Travel & Leisure*, March 1990, 219–221.

ROBERTA BROWN

Address: P. O. Box 43745
Louisville, Kentucky 40253-0745
phone 502-244-1291

Focus: scary stories; personal anecdotes.
Audience: general.
Style: traditional.
Instruments/Props: none.

A resident of Louisville, Roberta Simpson Brown grew up in the South's traditional storytelling training grounds — in the foothills of the Appalachians at Russell Springs near Lake

Cumberland, Kentucky. From early childhood, she heard neighbors entertain each other with scary tales. Her parents, Tom and Lillian Simpson, especially influenced her with stories. At age 7, she was caught in a storm on her way home from Pleasant Point School and was protected from a tornado by the recently deceased spirit of a friend named Jim. In her middle school years, she valued teachers of history and health who used stories to liven their teaching. Throughout her life, Brown has valued local lore and, after entering Berea College, made a point of preserving and passing it along. She introduced stories to her language arts classes, grades 6–12, which she has taught for 30 years in the inner city at Louisville's Southern Middle School. Students use the tales as examples of literary structure and technique for writing and oral delivery. Brown serves as a model to other teachers and encourages the use of oral narrative as a means of lengthening attention span and bolstering learning skills across the curriculum.

Affectionately known as "Queen of the Cold-Blooded Tales," Brown claims horror specialists Stephen King and Edgar Allan Poe and tellers Mary Hamilton, David Holt, and Lee Pennington as influences on her work. More important is the influence of her sister Fatima, teacher Myrtie Gaskins Sullivan, and husband Lonnie, to whom she assigns most of the credit for her success. She sets her material in a variety of locales, from a camping trip to banks of school lockers and an Easter egg hunt. Each original tale bears a catchy title, such as "Storm Walker," "Snowman," "Ghostland," and "Rain Thing." The plots focus on terror with a twist, not just to entertain listeners, but to teach them to live comfortably with fears and phobias. She intends to instruct parents, teachers, and children in talking over and coping with fears.

Brown credits Lee and Joy Pennington with involving her in the profession of platform narrative, which she began in 1983. She has published over 200 stories, which have won awards and praise from *Kirkus Review, Publisher's Weekly*, and *Booklist* and are listed in the National Public Radio audio catalog. In her coast-to-coast lineup of appearances, she has led workshops and performed stories at parks, libraries, and schools, including the University of Louisville School of Education. Festival performances and book signings have taken her to Corn Island, Kentucky Book Fair, and the National Storytelling Festival. In 1997, she was featured teller at the Southern Festival of Books in Nashville, Tennessee. She has also appeared on *Louisville Tonight* over WHAS-TV as well as the "Milton Metz Show" and "Jane Norris Show" on WHAS-radio and *Voice of America*, broadcast in Western Europe.

Bibliography

"Earthbound," in *The Young Oxford Book of Ghost Stories*, British Library, 1994.

The Queen of the Cold-Blooded Tales, August House, 1993. Twenty-three original horrific tales of vengeful spirits, featuring "Skin Crawlers."

Scared in School, August House, 1997. Scary tales from the 13th Street School, featuring *The Walking Trees* and *Queen of the Cold-Blooded Tales;* for ages 10–13.

The Walking Trees and Other Scary Stories, August House. 1991. Short, creepy, original stories, including "Earthbound" and "Night Catch."

Videography

Many Voices, One Heart, Euphoria Productions, Hollywood, 1987.

Audiography

The Scariest Stories Ever (audiocassette), August House, 1992. Six stories, featuring "Lockers," a story about the school where Brown teaches.

Scary Stories for All Ages (audiocassette), August House 1992. For all ages.

Awards

1997–1990 Jefferson County Board of Education Outstanding Staff awards.

1994 Certificate of Recognition for Storytelling contribution to the City of Memphis by Mayor W. W. Herenton.

1994 Proclamation for Outstanding Service to Friends of the Library in Memphis from Tennessee Congressman Harold Ford, U.S. House of Representatives.

1992 Ashland Oil's Golden Apple Award for Teaching.

1992 Parents' Choice Award nomination for *The Walking Trees and Other Scary Stories.*

Source

Contemporary Authors. Detroit: Gale Research, 1996.

Crawford, Byron, "A Ghost of a Summer Past Holds Pupils Rapt," *Courier-Journal,* December 13, 1996.

Eaton, Yvonne, "Ghost Writer Casts Spell," *Courier-Journal,* May 29, 1996, 1, 2.

Mooney, Bill, and David Holt. *The Storyteller's Guide.* Little Rock, Arkansas: August House, 1996.

Pike, Bill, "Frightening Writing: Southern Middle Teacher Has Scary Stories Published," *Courier-Journal,* January 18, 1995.

Roberta Brown

JOSEPH BRUCHAC III
[broo'•shak]

Address: P. O. Box 308
Greenfield Center, New York
12833
phone 518-583-1440
fax 518-583-9741

Focus: entertaining, moral, and instructive nature and culture stories that encourage expression of native traditions, foster harmony with nature, strengthen native literature and literary organizations, and reaffirm native identity and lore in a Europeanized society.

Audience: all ages.

Style: has appeared with his two sons, James Edward and Jesse Bowman Bruchac, and Joseph's sister, Marge Bruchac, in an ensemble called the Dawn Land Singers.

Instruments/Props: hand drum, rattle.

A resilient pro at storytelling and an inspiration to tellers of all nationalities, Dr. Joseph Bruchac III believes that stories are living entities that require respect. Growing from traditions that date to the beginnings of human life, his narratives are a worthy use for words that are meant to instruct humanity about the intricacies and significance of culture. A gentle, unassuming celebrity, he follows the calling of the Learning Circle, which impels all to listen, observe, remember, and share. His personal method requires him to be sensitive to motion, sound, and nature, which he calls "the circle of life." His philosophy impels him to select stories appropriate to the audience and to ally the hearer with the land. His leanings toward family, environment, community, and storytelling derive from native American traditions, which Bruchac claims are basic human values.

Since his first reading at an elementary school in 1976 turned into a storytelling session, Bruchac has kept up a schedule of over 100 appearances per year, at which he performs chants, legends, and drum songs. Highlights of his itinerary are the National Storytelling Festival, Three Apples Festival, British Storytelling Festival, Bay Area Storytelling Festival, Stone Soup, American Library Association, National Geographic, Smithsonian Institution's Discovery Theater, Institute of

ily's secret, Bruchac envisioned himself as a park ranger guiding tourists through natural reserves.

After learning his lineage, Bruchac became a diligent researcher and edited a literary journal, *The Greenfield Review*. In the mid–1960s, when he began publishing his writings, he immersed himself in native lore and developed into an eloquent "wampum keeper" or storyteller. He holds degrees in literature and creative writing from Cornell and Syracuse universities and a Ph.D. in comparative literature from Union Institute of Ohio. During his college years, he took part in the civil rights and anti-war demonstrations of the 1960s. For three years, he taught English at the Keta Secondary School in Ghana. Upon his return home, he and Carol settled in his boyhood home with Grampa Jesse. He has

Alaska Native Arts, Onondaga Nation School, and National Museum of the American Indian. He claims as colleagues Gayle Ross, Dovie Thomason, Johnny Moses, Bill Smith, Len Cabral, Judith Black, Steve Sanfield, Wolf Song, and John Stokes. In 1971, Carol Worthen Bruchac, his wife and partner, helped him found their own publishing house, Greenfield Review Press, which fosters works by America's ethnic and regional authors.

Audiences are surprised to learn that Bruchac did not grow up in a native atmosphere. Born October 16, 1942, in Saratoga Springs, New York, the son of taxidermist Joseph E. and Flora Bowman Bruchac, he was reared by his maternal grandparents, who kept a general store where people sat around swapping Adirondack stories. His ancestry is Slovak-English-Abenaki, but he spent his childhood in the Adirondacks with no knowledge of his native American forebears because his Grandpa Jesse tried to protect him from the label of half-breed. Before learning his fam-

worked as visiting scholar at Hamilton College, Columbia University, and the State University of New York at Albany and taught at Skidmore College and the Great Meadows Institute, which he founded at Comstock, a maximum-security prison, where he established *Prison Project Newsletter* as an outlet for inmate writings.

A man of multiple interests, Bruchac is a leader of a native American renaissance, which has introduced native lore to Indians and non–Indians. His spirited activism befits an animist bearing the Onondaga name Gah ne goh he yoh, which translates as "the Good Mind." In 1992, his example influenced "Returning the Gift," an Oklahoma-based international literary-heritage project which spawned the Wordcraft Circle and the Writers' Circle of the Americas and encouraged the development of the Directory of Native Writers of the Americas and the North American Authors Distribution Project. Inspired by a force he calls the Owner Creator, he has written novels, verse, and stories, judged the National Book Awards, and edited *Prison Writing Review, Kite, Nickel Review,* and *Studies in American Indian Literature.* The popular "Keeper" series, which has sold over half a million copies, he co-wrote with ecologist Michael J. Caduto. As a storyteller, Bruchac has appeared in Africa, Canada, Europe, and all 50 of the United States. He assists son Jim in the Ndakinna Native American Interpretive Center at Greenfield Center, where native enrichment materials range from books and periodicals to deer hide garments, longhouse beds, the beginnings of an Indian museum, and a garden tilled with native tools. His writings number over 50 titles, and articles by or about him have appeared in 500 publications.

Articles

"Combing the Snakes from Atatarho's Hair," *Parabola,* XIV:4, 59–65.

"Digging into Your Heart," *Parabola,* XIX:4, 36–41.

"Families Gathered Together," *Parabola,* XVIII:4, 36–39.

"Stealing Horses," *Parabola,* IX:2, 54–59.

"Storytelling and the Sacred: On the Uses of Native American Stories," in *Tales as Tools: The Power of Story in the Classroom,* National Storytelling Press, 1994, 167–173.

"The Storytelling Seasons," *Parabola,* XIV:2, 87–92.

"Striking the Pole: American Indian Humor," *Parabola,* XII:4. 22–29.

"Two Poems," *Parabola,* VII:3, 76–77.

"Waw Giwulk: Center of the Basket," *Parabola,* XVII:2, 52–53.

Who Says? Essays on Pivotal Issues in Storytelling (contributor), August House, 1996.

"Why People Speak Many Languages," in *Spinning Tales, Weaving Hope: Stories of Peace, Justice, and the Environment,* New Society, 1992.

Bibliography

Ancestry, Great Raven, 1980.

Between Earth and Sky (co-author Thomas Locker), Harcourt Brace, 1996.

"Birdfoot's Grandpa," http://wasatch.uoregon.edu/~adam/poetry/ birdfoots_grampa.html, March 1, 1997.

Bowman's Store: A Journey to Myself, Dial, 1997.

A Boy Called Gluskabe and the Four Wishes, Cobblehill, 1995.

A Boy Called Slow: The True Story of Sitting Bull (illustrator Rocco Baviera), Children's Forecasts, 1996.

The Boy Who Lived with the Bears and Other Iroquois Stories, HarperCollins, 1995. Six stories dating to tellings around the fire of an Iroquois longhouse.

Breaking Silence (editor), Greenfield Review, Press 1984.

The Buffalo in the Syracuse Zoo, Greenfield Review Press, 1972.

Children of the Longhouse, Dial, 1996.

The Circle of Thanks: Native American Poems and Songs of Thanksgiving, Bridgewater, 1996.

Dawn Land, Fulcrum, 1993.

Dog People: Native Dog Stories, Fulcrum, 1995. Native American stories about the relationship between dogs and children; for junior readers.

The Dreams of Jesse Brown, Cold Mountain Press, 1977.

"The Earth and the People Are One," *Storytelling Magazine,* March 1997, 11–14.

The Earth Under Sky Bear's Feet (illustrator Thomas Locker), Philomel, 1995.

Editor's Choice (contributor), Spirit That Moves Us, 1981.

Entering Onondaga, Cold Mountain Press, 1978.

The Faithful Hunter, Bowman, 1988.

The First Strawberries, Dial, 1993.

Flow, Cold Mountain Press, 1975.

Flying with the Eagle, Racing the Great Bear, Bridgewater, 1993.

Four Ancestors: Stories, Songs and Poems from Native North America, Bridgewater, 1996.

Fox Song (illustrator Paul Morin), Philomel, 1997.

From A to Z: 200 Contemporary Poets (contributor), Swallow Press, 1981.

From the Belly of the Shark: A New Anthology of Native Americans (contributor), Vintage, 1973.

The Girl Who Married the Moon (co-author Gayle Ross), Bridgewater, 1994.

"Gluskabe and Dzidziz," *The Tale Trader,* May 1996, 11.

Gluskabe and the Four Wishes, Cobblehill Books, 1995.

The Good Message of Handsome Lake, (translator) Unicorn Press, 1979.

"Grandmother Woodchuck's Children: Abenaki Storytelling Today," *Tale Trader*, May 1996, 1, 4.

The Great Ball Game, Dial, 1994.

Hoop Snakes, Hide-Behinds and Side-Hill Widners: Tall Tales from the Adirondacks, Crossing Press, 1991.

Indian Mountain and Other Poems, Ithaca House, 1971.

Iroquois Stories: Heroes and Heroines, Monsters and Magic, Crossing Press, 1985.

Keepers of Life (co-author Michael Caduto), Fulcrum, 1994.

Keepers of the Animals (co-author Michael J. Caduto; illustrator John Kahionhes Fadden), Fulcrum, 1990. Contains stories of creation, celebration, vision, feathers and fur, scales and skin, and survival.

Keepers of the Earth: Native American Stories and Environmental Activities for Children (co-author Michael J. Caduto; illustrators John Kahionhes Fadden and Carol Wood), Fulcrum, 1988. Contains stories of creation, fire, earth, wind and weather, water, seasons, plants and animals, life, death, and spirit, and unity of earth.

Keepers of the Night: Native American Stories and Nocturnal Activities for Children (co-author Michael Caduto), Fulcrum, 1994. Native stories that develop stewardship with the earth

The Light from Another Country, Greenfield Review Press, 1983.

"Little Hare and the Pine Tree," in *Ready-to-Tell Tales*, August House, 1994.

Long River, Fulcrum Books, 1995.

Native American Animal Stories, Fulcrum, 1993.

Native American Gardening (co-author Michael Caduto), Fulcrum Press, 1996.

Native American Stories (co-author Michael J. Caduto; illustrator John Kahionhes Fadden), Fulcrum, 1991. Contains "The Coming of Gluscabi" plus other stories on creation, fire, earth, wind and weather, water, sky, seasons, plants and animals, life, death, and spirit, and unity of earth.

The Native American Sweat Lodge, Crossing Press, 1993.

Native Plant Stories, Fulcrum, 1995. Myths drawn from *Keepers of Life*.

Native Wisdom, San Francisco: Harper, 1995.

Near the Mountains, White Pine, 1987.

New Campus Writing (contributor), McGraw, 1966.

No Telephone to Heaven, Cross-Cultural Communications, 1984.

Our Only Hope Is Humor: Some Public Poems (contributor), Ashland Poetry Press, 1972.

Peace Is Our Profession, East River Anthology, 1981.

The Poetry of Pop, Dustbooks, 1973.

The Pushcart Prize Anthology, 1980–1981, Pushcart Press, 1981.

The Remembered Earth (contributor), University of New Mexico, 1979.

Remembering the Dawn, Blue Cloud, 1983.

Return of the Sun, Crossing Press, 1989.

The Road to Black Mountain, Thorp Springs Press, 1976.

Roots of Survival: Native American Storytelling and the Sacred, Fulcrum, 1996.

Songs from This Earth on Turtle's Back (editor), Greenfield Review Press, 1983.

Stone Giants and Flying Heads: More Iroquois Folk Tales, Crossing Press, 1978.

The Story of the Milky Way, Dial, 1995.

Survival This Way: Interviews with American Indian Poets, University of Arizona Press, 1987.

Syracuse Poems, 1963–1969 (contributor), Syracuse University Press, 1970.

Tell Me a Tale, Harcourt Brace, 1997. About storytelling, for ages 10 and up.

There Are No Trees Inside the Prison, Blackberry Press, 1978.

Thirteen Moons on Turtle's Back (co-author Jonathan London; illustrator Thomas Locker), Philomel, 1992.

This Earth Is a Drum, Cold Mountain Press, 1977.

Translator's Son, Cross-Cultural Communications, 1981.

Turkey Brother and Other Iroquois Folk Tales, Crossing Press, 1976.

Turtle Meat and Other Stories, 1992

The Wind Eagle and Other Abenaki Stories, Bowman Books, 1997.

Words from the House of the Dead: An Anthology of Prison Writings from Soledad (ed. with William Witherup), Greenfield Review Press, 1971.

Audiography

Abenaki Cultural Heritage Days (audiocassette), Good Mind Records, 1992. Music and storytelling with the Dawn Land Singers and Wolf Song.

Alnobak (audiocassette and CD) (accompanied by Awassos Signan drum group), Jesse Bruchac, 1993.

The Boy Who Lived with the Bears and Other Iroquois Stories (audiocassette), Caedmon/Parabola, 1992.

Dawn Land (audiocassette), Fulcrum, 1993.

"Gluscabi and the Wind Eagle," in *More Best-Loved Stories Told at the National Storytelling Festival* (audiocassette), August House, 1992.

Gluskabe Stories (audiocassette), Yellow Moon Press, 1990. Contains "Gluskabe and the Creator," "Gluskabe's Game Bag," "Gluskabe and Dzidziz," "Gluskabe and Tobacco," "The Wind Eagle," and five more stories.

Iroquois Stories (audiocassette), Good Mind Records, 1988.

Keepers of Life (two audiocassettes), Fulcrum, 1994.

Keepers of the Animals (two audiocassettes), Fulcrum, 1992.

Keepers of the Earth (two audiocassettes), Fulcrum, 1991.

Video

Stories of North America, Part II, National Geographic Video, 1994.

Storytellers (four cassettes), Acorn Media 1991. Contains stories by Alice McGill, John Spelman, and Olga Loya. Cassettes are labeled "Tall Tales, Yarns, and Whoppers," "Animal Stories," "Magic Tales," and "Scary Stories."

Awards

1997 Amelia Frances Howard-Gibbon award for *Fox Song.*

1997 Bank Street College Child Study Book of the Year for *Fox Song.*

1996 American Folklore Society Aesop Accolade for *The Story of the Milky Way.*

1996 New York Library Association Knickerbocker Award for Juvenile Literature.

1996 Bank Street College Child Study Book of the Year for *The Earth Under Sky Bear's Feet.*

1996 PLA/ALLS Top Title for Adult New Readers for *The Earth Under Sky Bear's Feet.*

1996 Kansas State Reading Circle Title for *The Earth Under Sky Bear's Feet.*

1996 *Body Mind Spirit* Book award for *The Earth Under Sky Bear's Feet.*

1996 Mountains and Plains Booksellers Association's Regional Book Award for *A Boy Called Slow.*

1996 Bank Street College Study Children's Book of the Year for *A Boy Called Slow.*

1996 NCSS Notable Children's Trade Books in the Field of Social Studies for *A Boy Called Slow.*

1996 Kansas State Reading Circle Title for *A Boy Called Slow.*

1996 Heart of Texas Literature Best of the Best for *A Boy Called Slow.*

1996 American Library Association Notable Book for *A Boy Called Slow.*

1995 Scientific American Young Readers Book award for *The Story of the Milky Way.*

1995 Parents' Choice Award for *Dog People.*

1994 Skipping Stones Multicultural Award for *With the Eagle, Racing the Great Bear.*

1993 Notable Children's Book in the Language Arts Award for *Thirteen Moons on Turtle's Back.*

1993 Benjamin Franklin Person of the Year from the Publishers Marketing Association.

1992 Benjamin Franklin award for *The Boy Who Lived with the Bears and Other Iroquois Stories.*

1993 Bank Street College Child Study Children's Book of the Year for *Thirteen Moons on Turtle's Back.*

1992 IRA Teachers' Choice for *Thirteen Moons on Turtle's Back.*

1992 NCSS Notable Children's Trade Books in the Field of Social Studies for *Thirteen Moons on Turtle's Back.*

1992 NCTE Notable Book in Language Arts for *Thirteen Moons on Turtle's Back.*

1992 NSTA Outstanding Science Trade Book for Children for *Thirteen Moons on Turtle's Back.*

1992 *Reading Rainbow* choice for *Thirteen Moons on Turtle's Back.*

1992 Association of Children's Booksellers Choice Award.

1990 Art and Literary Award from the New York State Outdoor Education Association for the "Keeper" series.

1982-1983 Rockefeller Foundation Humanities Fellowship.

1980 Coordinating Council of Literary Magazines Fellowship.

1974 National Endowment for the Arts Poetry Fellowship.

1973, 1982 New York State CAPS Poetry Fellowship.

1972 Vermont Arts Council Grant.

1972 Poetry Society of America Prize.

1972 New York State Arts Council Grant.

Source

Alderdice, Kit, "Joseph Bruchac: Sharing a Native-American Heritage," *Publishers Weekly*, February 19, 1996, 191–192.

Baker, Will, "Feisty Words from Native American Poets," *San Francisco Examiner and Chronicle*, June 25, 1989.

Bodin, Madeline, "Keeping Tradition Alive," *Publishers Weekly*, December 14, 1993, 23.

Bogenschutz, Debbie, "Review of 'Dawn Land,'" *Library Journal*, May 1, 1993, 114.

Burchfield, Linda, "This Is the World's Biggest Reunion for Storytellers," *Herald & Tribune*, October 2, 1996, 7-C.

Caudell, Robin, "Telling Tall Tales: A Family Tradition," Plattsburgh (N.Y.)

Contemporary Authors (CD-ROM). Detroit: Gale Research, 1994.

DISCovering Authors (CD-ROM). Detroit: Gale Research, 1993.

Di Spoldo, Nick, "Writers in Prison: The Story of an Unusual Professor and His Unusual Project," *America*, January 22, 1983, 50–53.

Grossmann, Mary Ann," American Indian Author Stresses Authenticity," *St. Paul Pioneer Press-Dispatch*, October 22, 1989.

Hauprich, Ann, "Native Ways," *Grit*, December 31, 1995, 1, 18.

"Joseph Bruchac," http://www.mcdougallittell.com/lit/brucha.html, May 13, 1997.

Jr. DISCovering Authors (CD-ROM). Detroit: Gale Research, 1994.

"Kids Konnection: Who Is Joseph Bruchac?,"

http://wicomico.me.us/konnect/kask4.html, May 13, 1997.

Native North American Almanac. Detroit: Gale Research, 1994.

Osborne, Linda, "The Wisdom of the Nations," *World & I*, May 1, 1993.

"Review," *Publishers Weekly*, June 30, 1989, 106.

"Review of 'Dawn Land,'" *Publishers Weekly*, March 15, 1993, 68.

"Review," *School Library Journal*, December 1992, 137.

"Review," *School Library Journal*, March 1993, 161.

Sokoll, Judy, "Review of 'Dawn Land,'" *School Library Journal*, August 1993, 205.

Something About the Author. Vol. 42. Detroit: Gale Research, 1986.

Zad, Martie, "'Storytellers' Captives: Kids of All Ages," *Washington Post*, October 20–26, 1991.

MILBRE BURCH

Address: 582 Eldora Road
Pasadena, California 91104
phone 626-797-6817
fax 626-798-3064
email kindcrone@aol.com

Focus: variety of world folktales; original monologues and stories; contemporary literature.

Audience: from preschool to prisons and Elderhostel.

Style: dynamic, theatrical.

Instruments/Props: occasional costumes or props.

Milbre Burch, who claims to be a "carport theatrical producer" from childhood, grew up in Atlanta and is a 1971 alumna of Westminster High School in Atlanta, Georgia. A reader like everyone in her family, she came to stories through written texts, often located in the 398.2 section of the library, or culled from hours of television-watching. Unlike platform narrators who observed storytellers in infancy, she learned to appreciate oral lore much later

in adulthood and trusted to instinct in the selection of the best plots. She acquired polish in delivery from study of theater, film, modern dance, and mime. A 1975 *cum laude* graduate of Duke University, majoring in political science and film production, she worked in independent film production, but was never completely at home behind a camera. She decided to join the mime and modern dance troupe of Meli Kaye, a protégé of dancer Doris Humphrey. In 1978, Burch studied in Maine under Tony Montanaro before completing a mime and creative drama artist-in-residency for the South Carolina Arts Commission. With Montanaro's assistance, she developed her talents in characterization and narrative.

In 1980, Burch helped to establish the Heart of Gold Vaudeville Company in Providence, Rhode Island, which she served as mime/storyteller. In explanation of the title, she declared herself a mime who wearied of quiet. She named her production company Kind

Crone after a line in Gwyn Jones's *Scandinavian Legends and Folk Tales*. While searching out library sources for likely stories, she recalls, there came a confrontation with serendipity when a volume on the children's shelf literally fell at her feet. The work of young adult writer Jane Yolen, *Sleeping Ugly*, entered Burch's repertory. After several months of using the story, she met Yolen and confessed that the book was living an independent life as a platform performance. Yolen conferred her blessing on Burch's career and autographed a well-thumbed copy of *Sleeping Ugly*.

Like a well rehearsed stage performer, Burch works at gesture, imagination, diaphragm breathing, and body language, all elements of her kinetic style. She streamlines performances by weeding out ambiguity, superfluous characters, and secondary plots. To get at the organic gist of a story, she sometimes choreographs it, itemizing it detail by detail to understand its physicality. At other times, she smoothes action by videotaping or blocking, as though setting a stage for action, so that she can command the space around her and pull the audience into the telling. She edits ruthlessly, tailoring written stories to the requirements of telling, varying comic motifs with surprise. The result is a seamless delivery that has become her trademark.

Burch has supported herself through residencies for four state arts councils and has toured with Heart of Gold. She makes the rounds of festivals, covering North Carolina, Virginia, Texas, Georgia, Alabama, and Florida in the South, west to Hawaii, Nevada, California, and Utah, into the American heartland in Indiana, Illinois, Missouri, and Kentucky, north to Michigan, and northeast to Massachusetts, New York, and Rhode Island. She has been featured at the Washington, D.C., Storytellers' Theatre, Cal Plaza Presents, Del Norte Association for Cultural Awareness, Los Angeles Women's Theater Festival, Monterey Public Library, Lincoln Center Institute, Saddleback College High School Theatre Festival, Sushi Performance and Visual Art's Solo Visions Festival, and three times at the National Storytelling Festival. In 1995, she toured twelve cities in Austria and Slovenia with Folke Tegetthoff's "Lange Nacht of Storytelling" at the Graz Erzählt Festival in Austria. In May 1997, she was again a featured presenter at Graz Erzahlt!, where she appeared along with Shosha Goren, Laura Simms, Dan Yashinsky, Michael Parent, Susan Klein, and John Basinger. A September appearance at the 1997 Corn Island Storytelling Festival joined her talents with tellers Jackie Torrence and Jim May.

She has taught at the Storytellers' Theatre, National Storytelling Conference, Wasco State Prison, Pasadena Public Library, Hollywood Literary Retreat, Pacific School of Religion, New England Storytelling Conference, Trinity Repertory, Providence Public Library, and at Occidental College and Phoenix, Mercer, and South Carolina universities. Residencies have placed her before audiences at Walden School, Marianne Frostig Center, Park Century School, Multnomah School, and Livermore Unified School District in California; Zambrano Hospital, University of Rhode Island, Rhode Island College, School One High School, Edgewood-Highland Middle School in Rhode Island; Lee County Primary School and Annandale Village in Georgia; and the Hyatt Park Elementary and Beaufort County Schools in South Carolina. Fully committed to storytelling, she has served six years on the board of directors of the National Storytelling Association and has produced six seasons of *By Word of Mouth*, a Pasadena-based adult storytelling series.

The wife of editor and writer Berkley Hudson and mother of daughters Katy Blake and Elizabeth Travis, Burch maintains a balance between parenting and work and has taken both girls on tour. The expansion of performances to one-woman shows began in 1991, when she created sets, props, and staging for *Theatre of the Spoken Word*. Her performances have found sponsors at Caltech, Atlanta's 14th Street Playhouse, Monterey Public Library, Indianapolis Art Museum, Occidental College, the Washington, D.C., Storytellers Theatre, University of San Diego, and Western Montana College.

Articles
"Finding and Learning Stories," *Storytelling Magazine*, May 1994.
"A Storytelling Artist at Work," *Storytelling World*, Summer/Fall 1996, 17–21.

Bibliography
"Abe Zaccheus," *The Providence Journal Magazine*, January 22, 1989.
"The Huntsman," in *Ruby Slippers, Golden Tears*, Avon-Nova Books, 1995.
"Little Burnt Face," in *Ready-to-Tell Tales*, August House, 1994.
"Meeting Martin," *The Providence Journal Magazine*, November 6, 1988.
"Metamorphosis," *Xanadu 2*, St. Martin's Press, 1994.
"Morgan and the Pot o'Brains," *Best-Loved Stories Told at the National Storytelling Festival*, National Storytelling Press, 1992.
"Push Comes to Shove," in *Ruby Slippers, Golden Tears*, Avon-Nova Books, 1995.
"Wilbern's Story," *The Providence Journal Magazine*, July 23, 1989.

Videography
"The Lindworm," in *Tell Me a Story, Vol. 2*, Hometown Entertainment, 1995.

Audiography
In the Family Way (audiocassette), Kind Crone, 1993. Contains "A Mismatch," "The Grandfather and His Grandson," "Twins," "Ona, My Darling, Come to Mama," "Atalanta," "It's in Your Hands," "Mother of the Waters," "The Cow-tail Switch," and "In Blackwater Woods."

Mama Gone and Other Stories to Trouble Your Sleep (audiocassette), Kind Crone, 1997. Features the title story plus "Mr. Fox," "Short Story," "Drink My Blood," "The Wife's Story," "After Push Come to Shove," and "Mr. Death and the Red-Headed Woman."

The Mary Stories (audiocassette), Kind Crone, 1991. Contains "Waiting for the Wonder," "The Visitation," "Treasures in Her Heart," and "Coming Back from Calvary."

Metamorphosis and Dragonfield (audiocassette), Kind Crone, 1988. Contains an original story, "Metamorphosis," and "Dragonfield," adapted from a novella by Jane Yolen.

The Ready Heart-More Jane Yolen Stories (audiocassette), Kind Crone, 1994. Contains "'Once Upon a Time,' She Said," "The Moon Ribbon," "Knives," "The Boy Who Had Wings," "Beauty and the Beast: An Anniversary," "Good Griselle," "Ballad of the White Seal Maid," "The Fisherman's Wife," "Undine," "Silent Bianca," "The Faery Flag," and "The Storyteller."

Saints and Other Sinners (audiocassette), Kind Crone, 1991. Contains "Abe Zaccheus," "The Rabbi Spoke in Stories," "St. Aloya, the Blacksmith," "Odilia and Aldaric," "St. Clare Blesses the Bread," "Wilbern's Story," "The Giant at the Ford," "How Come Christmas," and "Meeting Martin."

Touch Magic ... Pass It On! Jane Yolen Stories (audiocassette), Kind Crone, 1987. Contains "The Ballad of the Mage's Birth," "The Cat Bride," "Sans Soleil," "Sleeping Ugly," "Princess Heart O'Stone," "The King's Dragon," "The Lady and the Merman," and "L'Envoi."

The World Is the Storyteller's Village (audiocassette), Kind Crone, 1994. Contains "The Smart Parrot," "Morgan and the Pot of Brains," "Grandmother Spider," "Why Mosquitoes Buzz," "The Mirror," "The Purchased Miracle," "Sweet Misery," "Boreguita and Coyote," "Strength," "Pine Trees for Sale," "Little Burnt Face," and "Bye Bye."

Awards
1995 Parent's Choice Gold Award for *The Ready Heart.*

1995 City of Pasadena Arts Division fellowship.

1991 City of Pasadena Arts Division fellowship.

1991 NAIRD Indie Award Finalist for *Saints and Other Sinners.*

1989 City of Pasadena Arts Division Grant-in-Aid.

1978–1980 South Carolina Arts Commission Resident Artist.

Source
"Alumna Mimes at Coffeehouse," Durham, North Carolina *Duke Chronicle*, September 17, 1984.

"Annandale Storyteller Uses Tricks of Trade," Gwinet, Georgia *Daily News*, January 16, 1984.

"Annandale Villagers Find Hard Work Part of Acting," Gwinet, Georgia *Daily News*, March 1984.

"Farewell Tale — Storyteller Milbre Burch Heads West," Providence, Rhode Island *NewPaper*, March 2–9, 1988.

"For Book Lovers," *Sierra Madre News*, January 13, 1990.

"Last Laugh," *Mother Earth News*, January 1985.

"A Life in the Theatre: Milbre Burch," Providence, Rhode Island *NewPaper*, May 2–9, 1984.

"Local Storyteller Helps Preserve Oral Tradition," *San Gabriel Valley Tribune*, September 1991.

"Master Mime, Storyteller to Perform Here Tonight," *Atlanta Constitution*, May 16, 1986.

"Milbre Burch — A Creative Journey," *Artworks*, Summer 1991.

"Miming Tales of Magic, Morals," Jamestown, Rhode Island *Standard-Times*, April 19, 1984.

Mooney, Bill, and David Holt. *The Storyteller's Guide*. Little Rock, Ark.: August House, 1996.

"Second Annual Vineyard Storytelling Festival Will Be Staged This Weekend in Oak Bluffs," Martha's Vineyard, Massachusetts *Gazette*, June 20, 1989.

"A Storied Affair," *Los Angeles Times*, May 6, 1991.

"Storyteller Mesmerizes Waterman Kindergartners," Providence, Rhode Island *Journal-Bulletin*, January 20, 1986.

"Storyteller's Enchantment Has Educational Purpose," Providence, Rhode Island *Journal-Bulletin*, March 15, 1985.

"A Storytelling Artist at Work," *Storytelling World Magazine*, East Tennessee State University, Summer/Fall 1996.

"Storytelling Art Revived 'By Word of Mouth,'" *San Gabriel Valley Tribune*, January 7, 1989.

"Storytelling Festival," *Narragansett* (R. I.) *Times*, September 19, 1990.

"Storytelling Opens a Whole New World for Kids," Livermore, California *Valley Times*, January 1990.

"Storytelling Takes Center Stage at the Ark This Weekend," Ann Arbor, Michigan *News*, December 9, 1988.

"Story Time — Milbre Burch Has a Tale to Tell Pasadena Audiences," *Pasadena Weekly*, January 12, 1989.

"A Tale to Be Told," Providence, Rhode Island *Eagle*, January 24, 1985.

"Telling a Story Isn't Just Kid Stuff," *Pasadena Star-News*, January 11, 1989.

"Telling Tales in Tennessee," *New York Times*, September 1985.

"Tell Me a Story," *Pasadena Weekly*, April 13, 1991.

"Theatre," Providence, Rhode Island *Journal-Bulletin*, January 8, 1985.

"Using Mime and Mimicking, Storyteller Fires Up Young Audience's Imagination," Providence, Rhode Island *Journal-Bulletin*, July 24, 1985.

"Vineyard's Second Annual Storytelling Festival Gathers Masters to Spin Wonderful Tales," Martha's Vineyard, Massachusetts *Gazette*, June 27, 1989.

Welsh, Anne Marie, "Performance Review," *San Diego Union-Tribune*, September 16, 1995.

LEN CABRAL
[kuh•brahl']

Address: 30 Marcy Street
Cranston, Rhode Island 02905
phone 401-781-0019
fax 401-781-0020

Focus: Cape Verdean, African, and Caribbean folktales as well as world folklore; original stories; humorous tales; inspirational stories.

Audience: all ages.

Style: uses mime, dance-like movement, poetry, song, humor, repetition, participation, and vivid characterizations.

The great-grandson of a whaler who emigrated from Cape Verde to the United States in the early twentieth

Len Cabral

century, Len Cabral profited from the Creole spirit that vibrated in songs and games heard and played in his home throughout his childhood. While working as a teacher at a day care center in Providence, Rhode Island, in 1972, he discovered the art of storytelling as a method of personalizing and engaging fifteen rambunctious young children. His success led to study in mime, children's theater, and creative dramatics. After performing children's theater, he co-founded the Sidewalk Storytellers, performing at local schools, libraries, museums, and festivals. In addition to telling stories from literature through creative drama, he co-developed commissioned shows on nutrition, anti-smoking, and environmental issues. His dramatic style led to solo storytelling performances. Twenty years later, he has become a nationally acclaimed, award-winning storyteller and author who travels the United States and Canada sharing a unique, personable style. In addition to performing, he provides keynote addresses and creates workshops for educators and students from elementary grades through college.

Cabral's material focuses on humanism. At his teacher workshop he advises participants to weave children's names into stories to combat alienation, a discounting of human worth that fragments society. Inspirational stories provide audiences with alternatives for promoting self-esteem. Len sees storytelling as a way for people to connect, to share collective wisdom and to stir imaginations that have sometimes been dulled by television and other electronic media. He has appeared at President Clinton's Inaugural Reunion on the Mall Festival, Black Storytellers in Concert Series, National Storytelling Festival, Kennedy Center Theater, Smithsonian Institution Discovery Theater and Folklife Festival, St. Louis Storytelling Festival, and Sierra Storytelling Festival.

Cabral's name appears in numerous venues. He is featured in textbooks by Houghton-Mifflin and Silver Burdett & Ginn and is also a co-founder of Spellbinders, Rhode Island's storytellers' collective. Cabral has advised the Rhode Island State Arts Council, National Storytelling Association, Rhode Island's First Night Festival, and Providence Inner City Arts Association. By valuing the spoken work, he has inspired educators, service providers, and entertainment managers to consider the effectiveness of telling a good story. Some recent appearances include the International Heifer Project Conference, National Headstart Conference, Teen Institute Conference, and Core Knowledge Foundation Conference.

Bibliography

Anansi's Narrow Waist (easy reader in English and Spanish), Addison-Wesley, 1994.

"Ananzi's Narrow Waist" and "Ananzi and Common Sense," in *African-American Folktales for Young Readers*, August House 1993.

Len Cabral's Storytelling Book, Neal-Schuman, 1997. Contains 22 participation stories from around the world plus a telling guide and teaching guide.

"The Lion's Whisker," in *Ready to Tell Tales* , August House 1994.

"The Lion's Whisker," in *Teacher's Read Aloud Anthology*, Macmillan/McGraw-Hill, 1993.

"Nho Lobo," in *Jump Up and Say: A Collection of Black Storytelling*, Simon & Schuster, 1995.

Audiography

Ananzi Stories and Others, Story Sound Productions 1988. Contains "Ananzi's Narrow Waist," "Ananzi and Common Sense," "Three Little Pigs" (modern version), "The Beggar Boy and the King's Daughter," and "The Little Girl and the Gunnywolf"; for ages 5 and up.

It's How You Say It, Story Sound Productions, 1996. Contains the title story plus "Pat Divers the Fixer," "Coyote Dances with the Stars," "What Is Strength?," "Old Man Winter," "Three Heavenly Gifts," "Two Frogs," "Miles Away and Dr. Seuss on the Loose," and "Wha-Sup?," a hip version of an old folktale; for ages 10 and up.

"Nho Lobo," on *Rainbow Tales* (CD), Rounder Records, 1997.

Nho Lobo and Other Stories (sung with Bill Harley), Story Sound Productions, 1984. Features the title story plus "Wiley and the Hairy Man," "The Lion's Whisker," "How the Rabbit Lost His Tail," "That's What Friends Are For," and "So Sabe," a Cape Verdean folk song; for ages 6 and up.

Stories for the Wee Folk, Story Sound Productions. Contains "Grandmother Spider," "Coconut and the Monkey's Face," "Ananzi's Riding Horse," "Two Frogs," "The Old Woman and the Pumpkin," "Bubbles or Why the Cat Washes After Eating and Not Before," and "Coyote Dances with the Stars"; for ages 4–12.

"Why the Sky Is Far Away," on *A Storytelling Treasury*, National Storytelling Association, 1993.

Awards

1997 NAPPA Gold Award (National Association of Parenting Publishers Award) for *Ananzi Stories and others*.

1997 NAPPA Silver Award for *Nho Lobo and other stories*.

1996 Parents' Choice Silver Award for *It's How You Say It*.

1995 Rhode Island's Remarkable People Award.

1994 Rhode Island Business Volunteers for Arts Gilbert Stuart Award.

1987 *New England Monthly* Magazine's Local Hero.

1984 Rhode Island's Jefferson Award for Outstanding Citizenship.

Source

"All About Storytelling," *Country Journal*, April 1990.

Burchfield, Linda, "Len Cabral to Make Storytelling Festival a Family Affair," Jonesborough, Tennessee *Herald & Tribune*, October 2, 1996, 4-C.

"Focus on Fatherhood," *Rhode Island Parent's Paper*, June 1993.

Gaines, Judith, "He Spins Tales That Entertain and Teach," *Boston Globe*, January 17, 1993.

"Jonesborough's National Storytelling Festival Attracts Thousands to Annual Three-Day Event," *The Loafer*, October 1, 1996, 19, 21.

"Len Cabral: Teller of Tales," *Kennedy Center Playbill*, February 1997, 20–21.

Literature Works. Silver Burdett & Ginn, 1997, 146–147.

McClure, John, "The Narrative Function of Preaching," *Liturgy, Journal of the Liturgical Conference*, 1989, 49.

Mooney, Bill, and David Holt. *The Storyteller's Guide*. Little Rock, Arkansas: August House, 1996.

Mulligan, John, "Master Storyteller Turns Talent to Mission," *Providence Journal*, February 3, 1997, 1, 6.

"Offbeat Job — Len Cabral: Storyteller," *Career World*, May 1985, 32.

"Once Upon a Time," *New England Monthly*, September 1987, 61.

O'Neill, James, "On Eve of Inaugural, Clinton Celebrates; Rhode Islander Glad to Perform at a New Kind of Party in DC," *Providence Journal*, November 1993.

Reed, Leonard, "Honestly, a Good Story Need Not Be the Truth," *Los Angeles Times*, March 2, 1995, 21.

Share: Invitations to Literacy, Houghton Mifflin, 1994, 86–87.

"The Storyteller," *Rhode Island Monthly*, November 1989, 43–44.

"Storyteller Len Cabral: A Tour Guide to the Imagination," *Boston Parents Paper*, February 1997, 20.

"Storytellers to Weave Their Special Magic During the First Week of October," Jonesborough, Tennessee *Herald & Tribune*, October 2, 1996, 3C–5C.

Timeless Voices: Images of the National Storytelling Festival. Jonesborough, Tenn.: National Storytelling Press, 1997.

"A Unique Effort in Humane Education," *Human Education*, December 1983, 5–7.

Watson, Bruce, and Tom Raymond, "The Storyteller Is the Soybean ... the Audience Is the Sun," *Smithsonian*, March 1997, 60–67.

DAVID CAMPBELL

Address: 33 Dundas Street
Edinburgh, Scotland EH3 6QQ
phone 0131-556-1526
fax 0131-558-3550

Focus: traditional Celtic tales and love stories; fairy tales; contemporary anecdotes and humor.

Audience: all ages.

Style: solo; collaborates with Linda Bandelier, who plays the guitar and sings, and with other storytellers and musicians.

Instruments/Props: traditional Scottish kilt, plays harmonica.

A native of Edinburgh, storyteller David Campbell is acclaimed throughout the U.K. and in Holland, Germany, South Africa, Israel, New Zealand, Canada, Iceland, and the United States. His repertoire of Celtic legends, fairy tales, folklore, comic anecdotes, and contemporary Scottish tales suits his philosophy:

"Inside everyone is a child waiting to hear a story and to tell one!" Rotterdam *Dagblad* calls him an "absolute star" of a medium more in keeping with community entertainment than television or film. His workshops offer narrative art and practice in listening and telling skills, fun, comfort before an audience, and "bridging the gaps." He is the past chair of the Scottish Storytelling Forum and has taken part in the Scottish International Storytelling Festival and the "Guid Crack Club," which he founded.

Campbell, who was born in 1935, grew up in the fishing village of Fraserburgh and absorbed Scottish songs, stories, and lore from varied sources, including famed ballad singer Jeannie Robertson. From age three, he loved telling stories to his visiting aunt and eavesdropping on his father's bedtime stories for a younger brother. In his pre-teens, he broadcast ghost stories on a homemade radio set. He was educated at George Heriot's School (which was founded in 1625), where he gained a worthy background in Scottish verse, drama, and speech and was sports captain and athletics champion. He graduated with honors in English literature from Edinburgh University and taught English at Royal High School in Edinburgh. As a radio producer of imaginative story, drama, and educational programs, he served the BBC for sixteen years. Simultaneously, he updated and revolutionized the Scottish Religious Service for Schools, a series of Old and New Testament stories aimed at listeners aged 7–12, and wrote articles, drama and book reviews, and poetry for national publications.

Campbell moved from producer to storyteller after meeting and broadcasting with Duncan Williamson, the famed itinerant Scottish story master known to possess a repertoire of 3,000 stories. Campbell traveled and studied with Williamson and was invited to perform for audiences of all types. In New Zealand, while performing at the Glistening Waters Storytelling Festival, he met "my brother from across the sea," Jay O'Callahan, and subsequently performed with his brother in story in the Scottish International Storytelling Festival. In 1995-1996, Campbell extended his audience through stories on the Ken Fyne television show and a Scottish ghost stories program for Channel 4 television. Campbell treasures the memory of the Yukon Midsummer Festival and declares that such gatherings unite the world by healing, mending, and summoning courage and laughter, medicines for the mind, heart, and soul.

Bibliography

Tales to Tell (co-authored with other Scots), Saint Andrew Press, 1986. Biographical stories of men and women of faith, modern-day parables, contemporary folktales of faith and love.

Tales to Tell II, Saint Andrew Press, 1994.

The Three Donalds (co-author Linda Bandelier), Scottish Children's Press, 1997. A children's story in which three identical children from three different families are rescued by tartan.

Audiography

A Burns Supper (audiocassette), Whigmaleerie, 1986.

A Celebration, Robert Burns (audiocassette), Cannongate, 1997. Includes Robert Burns's "Selkirk Grace," "Address to the Haggis," and toasts, replies, stories, poems, and songs of a traditional Burns supper.

Joukerie Pawkerie (co-producers Linda Bandelier and Alison Millen) (audiocassette), Scottish Traditional Storytellers, 1995.

Tales from the Fire (co-producers Linda Bandelier, Alison Millen, and Paraig MacNeil) (audiocassette), Scottish Traditional Storytellers, 1993. Folk stories and songs from Scotland and the American West.

Tales to Tell II (audiocassette), Pathway Productions, 1994.

Woman at the Well (co-producer Linda Bandelier) (audiocassette), Scottish Traditional Storytellers, 1993. Stories and songs of women in the Bible.

Awards

1996 Edinburgh International Festival Fringe "International Yarnspinning Competition" champion.

Source

Act and Image Directory for the Arts, Netherbow Art Centre, 43/45 High Street, Edinburgh, Scotland EH1 1SR.

Jinks, Peter, "Telling Tales Out of School," Edinburgh, *The Scotsman*, October 25, 1994.

Scottish Storytellers Directory, Scottish Storytelling Centre, 43/45 High Street, Edinburgh EH1 1SR.

See also Linda Bandelier.

SAM YADA CANNAROZZI
[yah'•dah kan•nuh•raht'•zee]

Address: 76 Rue Neyret
01600 Parcieux, France
phone and fax 33 4 78 98 35 85

Focus: universal themes and stories.
Audience: all ages.
Style: visual and kinetic.
Instruments/Props: an innovative blend of Amerindian sign language, string figures, origami, percussion instruments, and bright colored costumes.

Sam Yada Cannarozzi's kinetic style derives from a lifetime interest in stage performance and language and from his hobby, collecting ancient board games from Egypt, Africa, and the Middle East. His broad interests involve him in multilingual verse, which he has presented in Romania at the International Symposium on Haiku and has published in two dozen periodicals. He has resided in Europe since 1974 and been a part of the creative blend that has grown out of the European storytelling revival. He lives with his wife, Danish actress Margrethe Højlund, and their two children in Parcieux, near Lyons, France, where he participated in the Concert for 100 Cars at the Lyonese Art Bienniale in 1988.

A native of Chicago, Cannarozzi was born Salvatore Peter James Cannarozzi in 1951. Of second generation Sicilian-Yugoslavian heritage, he graduated from Marist Brothers High School, studied for a year at the Université in Dijon, France, and earned a B.S. in linguistics and languages with a major in French and minor in German from Georgetown University in Washington, D.C. He has conducted postgraduate studies at the Università di Sienna in Italy, Eurocentrum in Cologne, Germany, and Foreigner's Institut in Aarhus, Denmark. Extensive training in performance arts under Jerzy Grotowski, Eugenio Barba, Bob Wilson, and Karin Waehner has secured experience in dance, bio-energetics, yoga, martial arts, body expression, mime, and theater. Likewise important to his development are stints with the Bread and Puppet Theater, Schola Cantorum, and Washington Theater Laboratory.

Cannarozzi soloed in 1976, demonstrating the influence of radio broadcasts of veteran teller Jackie Torrence and of studies of Mimi Barthélémy, Hamed Bouzzine, and the late Ken Feit, billed as "The Fool." He has performed professionally since 1982, when he attended his first international festival and shared a stage with tellers from Sicily, Rajistan, and Egypt. Surrounded by professionals, he absorbed the music, rhythm, and performance zest of varied stories told in tongues unknown to him. He has toured over a dozen countries and maintains twelve hours of material in his repertory. He has presented eleven offerings of "Head in the Stars," a series performed in a simulated skylab and featuring star lore of East Africa, the Pacific, and the Americas, including the Inuit of Alaska. His outstanding performances include the West African Kuma Ba Festival, Rotterdam's Dunya Festival, Novena Storytelling Festival in Celard, France, and Folke Tegetthoff's "Lange Nacht of Storytelling" at the Graz Erzählt Festival in Austria, where he enjoyed the camaraderie of Tegetthoff, Shosha Goren, and Huda Al Hilali. In addition to platform performances, Cannarozzi contributes articles to England's Society for Storytelling, *Dire*, the French national review, *National Storytelling Magazine,* and *The Tale Trader.*

Bibliography
"Back in the Time When Tigers Smoked Pipes," in *Dans le Vivier du Contem*, December 1997.
"A Novena of Stories," *Works in Progress.*
"Pacala," in *Investigating Cultures and Their Stories*, Frank Schaeffer, 1996.

Videography
CAP Canal, cable TV for children, 1995. A television segment from the Rhone-Alps

region featuring Cannarozzi and Senegal-
ese storyteller Mamadou Diallo.

Picto-Stories, "Made in France" Studios, 1993.
A pilot program financed by the Regional
Cultural Affairs office in Lyons, France.

A River of Words, Après-Spectra, 1990. Features the Oralies de Haute Provence Festival.

Source

"Cons-TALE-ations Aboard Starlab," *Storytelling Magazine,* July 1996, 10.

YONA B. CHOCK
[yoh' nuh]

Address: 91-1064E La'aulu Street
Ewa Beach, Hawaii 96706-3217
phone 808-683-5262
fax 808-683-3217
email alchock@worldnet.att.net

Focus: Hawaiian lore; spooky ghost stories; traditional fairy tales.
Audience: children.
Style: traditional.
Instruments/Props: magic tricks, puppetry, origami, paper cutouts, and balloon sculpture.

Yona Chock — a professional clown, magician, balloon artist, puppeteer, and square dance caller — feels blessed to have grown up in a storytelling family. From her early childhood on an orange ranch in southern California, she lived in a world of information: her father was a rancher and postmaster and her mother a stringer for small-town newspapers. When the U.S. Navy drafted her father in 1942, her family traveled often, moving to the town nearest each of his home ports. Because he was experienced in Japanese and had lived in Japan, he was sent on a bombing survey of Nagasaki, which was seriously damaged by an atomic bomb dropped in August 1945. His inside information made him valuable to the government. He remained in the military after the war and took a position in the Central Intelligence Agency, where Chock worked for three summers. While living in Washington, D.C., she heard her father's exaggerated stories and tales told by her mother and Aunt Ruth as well as the housekeeper, Allie, who knew lore of Eastern Shore whites, blacks, and Indians.

Married to Hawaiian Al Chock, Yona Chock became a 4-H leader while her husband worked for the Environmental Protection Agency and the Food and Agriculture Organization of the United Nations. The Chocks and their three daughters have lived in Italy and Holland and retired to Hawaii in 1992. Their travels to the Middle East and the South Pacific and around Europe provided her with material for yarning, which she augments with research and original stories. At the age of forty, Chock, a college graduate with a degree in anthropology and a teacher of Hawaiian folklore at the University of Hawaii at Manoa, took her first performance-oriented course in storytelling. A favorite platform experience occurred in a Maryland television studio, where she warmed up the teenaged audience while waiting for a professional teller. At the end of her spiel, she realized that the crew was filming her performance.

Chock's circuit takes her to schools, camps, the Honolulu Zoo, and the Nature Center. For Boy Scout camps, she calls square dances and ends the evening with spooky ghost stories to prepare campers for sleep. As a designated teller-in-the-schools, she illustrates tales with magic tricks, puppetry, origami, paper cutouts, and balloon sculpture. For an updated version of "Rapunzel," she uses a handkerchief that changes color. She looks forward to the children's stage portion of the Hawaii Talking Island Festival. She publishes her own story tapes and has several stories in print. Twice each year, her company, Aardvark Adventures, takes her to the continental United States, where she teaches workshops, researches stories, and visits her children.

GLADYS COGGSWELL

Address: P. O. Box 56
Frankford, Missouri 63441
phone 573-784-2589
fax 573-784-2364
email gladcogg@nemonet.com

Focus: healing, learning, teaching, and self-validation through sharing a blend of multicultural folklore, history, myths, family legends, and animal stories infused with humor, animation, songs, drama, history, and life lessons.
Audience: all ages.
Style: educational, entertaining, lively, and unique facial expression; audience participation.

Instruments/Props: voice, drum, tambourine, shakere, hand puppets, artifacts, harmonica, sound effects.

Gladys Coggswell's story is one of survival and resilience. A native of Montclair, New Jersey, she learned about stories from her great grandmother, who disciplined her by telling moral parables. Coggswell grew up in Paterson, New Jersey. After being attacked by a gang of boys, she dropped out of the Paterson Eastside High School's tenth grade, feeling ashamed, lonely, and dejected. Years later, her husband, Truman Coggswell, Sr., the son of the Schaghticoke tribe's chief Pahei, helped her overcome self-abnegation by telling native American stories that rid her of nightmares. With his encouragement, she earned a G.E.D. and an associate degree in general education from St. Louis Community College at Forest Park. Of 800 students, she was chosen student of the year in 1979. She gave the commencement address and was instrumental in returning the cap and gown graduation tradition to the Forest Park campus.

Coggswell earned an academic scholarship to Washington University and earned a B.S. in psychology and certification with honors in journalism. She followed with an M.Ed. from the University of Missouri, St. Louis, with counseling as her area of concentration. Resettled in Frankford, Missouri, she says that for the first time in her life, she felt at home. She recalls a display of pride and love from her friends and neighbors, who organized a surprise "M.Ed. completion" celebration, which included a horse-drawn ride parading her around town to the tune of "For She's a Jolly Good Fellow" and ended with a Queen for a Day party. As an adjunct professor at Hannibal La Grange College in Hannibal, Missouri, she taught psychology and education of exceptional children and now serves as off-campus professor for two Missouri universities.

A proponent of the personal touch, Coggswell supports telling as a complement of the cool media — radio, television, film, video, and computer, the impersonal conveyors of culture. Her 20-page "color and keep" coloring book, "Why There Are No Dragons," depicts a kingdom in which various species live amicably together until the newly elected Queen Fumebreath threatens to eliminate all non-dragons. A story of the abuse of power, repentance, and conciliation, it encourages children to notice how people treat each other and to be aware of the connection between choices and consequences. The book has inspired young readers to think about their roles as potential leaders, friends, helpers, and responsible citizens.

One of Coggswell's stories, "The Possum, the Snake, and Mr. Man," demonstrates how a possum learns the hard way to respect his parents' warnings. She composed "The Ballad of the Three-Eyed Cat from Hannibal, Missouri," a fun song. Her column, "F. Y. I.," which advises storytellers, appears regularly in *Storylines*, the newsletter for the By Word of Mouth Storytelling Guild, of which the Coggswells are the founders. Her column has also appeared in the National Association of Black Storytellers newsletter.

Coggswell demonstrates a commitment to preserving the oral tradition in multiple media. She portrays Harriet, the wife of Dred

Scott, during the Lincoln-Douglas debates in Quincy, Illinois. The performance has aired on PBS and netted her a live interview on C-Span on October 9, 1994. She hosts, produces, and directs *Storytime*, a weekly KPCR-AM radio program of stories and songs from Bowling Green, Missouri. She involves guest storytellers for the broadcast and for the annual Oral and Moral Storytelling Conference and Festival, a By Word of Mouth retreat. She also coordinates the Storytelling Fiddle, Food, and Fun Fest in Frankford. Her career has earned her numerous newspaper articles and magazine covers. She is currently planning to join a National Storytelling Association educational expedition to China and to tour Africa with the St. Louis African Chorus.

Bibliography
"The Colored Women of Missouri," *Mid-Missouri Black Watch*, Spring 1996, 13.
"Goodbye Joe Louis," *People's Guide*, April 15, 1980.
"Why There Are No Dragons" (coloring book), Coggswell Communications, 1996.

Audiography
A Story, a Story (audiocassette), Huckleberry Sound, 1994. Features "Three-Eyed Cat," "Man in the Moon," "Why Eagles Are Bald," "How Dogs Lost Their Tails," "Grandfather Rattlesnake," "Mulkee Weesaak People," and "Uncle Buddy."
Well Shut My Mouth (audiocassette), Coggswell Communications, 1995. Contains "Foot Story," "Hissin' in the Pit," "The Washboard Story," "The Gossip Bench," "Granddaddy Meeschack," and "How the Tooth Fairy Came to Be."

Awards
1997 Fannie Griffin Art Club Woman of the Year.
1993–1995 St. Louis Continental Societies' Making a Difference Award.
1995, 1992–1993 Missouri Master Folk Artist Award.
1979 Phi Theta Kappa Honor Society Outstanding Leadership Award.

Source
Conover, Joseph I., "The Story-Telling Art," *The Quincy Herald-Whig*, November 5, 1996.

McCarty, Jim, "She's Got a Story to Tell," *Rural Missouri*, June 1996.

ESTELLE CONDRA

Address: 3027 New Natchez Trace
Nashville, Tennessee 37215
phone 615-383-1065
fax 615-383-0008
email econdra@dalcon.com
website www.dalcon.com/home/estelle/ehome.htm

Focus: Shakespearean plots and famous American and English short stories; South African folklore; audience participation.
Audience: youth and adults.
Style: kinetic performance with music, dance, and gestures; dramatic monologue; inspirational speaking; one-woman shows; collaboration with actor, singer, and guitarist Ray Dooley.
Instruments/Props: African artifacts, bright colored costumes and wigs, theatrical props.

A victim of retinitis pigmentosa, an inher-

ited disease, Estelle Condra is a blind performer who creates vision through words and imagination. She came to the United States from Johannesburg, South Africa, in 1973 to marry an American. Several of her programs — "Village Drums," "The Sacred Cave," "When Animals Could Walk and Talk Like People," "The Dating Game African-Style," and "On Safari We Will Go!" — relate scenes of her homeland through ritualistic song and dance and the biography of African women living out primal traditions of courtship, dowry, marriage, birth, and death. Another, "Magical Menagerie," creates characters from Russia, China, and Africa. Her "Literature Alive" program features works by William Shakespeare, Edgar Allan Poe, Guy de Maupassant, Somerset Maugham, Oscar Wilde, Stephen King, Charles Dickens, and William Thurber and children's Mother Goose rhymes. A popular one-woman show, "Caged: A Soliloquy About the Loss of Sight," details her struggles and triumphs over blindness; "Vibrations of Laughter," based on the life of Annie Sullivan, recounts the famous teacher's role in educating Helen Keller. "Mystery and Suspense" recreates horror stories by Edgar Allan Poe, Roald Dahl, and Alfred Hitchcock; "The Power of Love" tells of Elizabeth Barrett's failing health and romance with Robert Browning. A humorous sketch, "Blind People Shouldn't Vacuum," is a vehicle for her wit. She also presents a workshop, "There Are Fifty Ways to Tell a Story," featuring tips and demonstrations on story selection, composition, voice and body, conquering fear, and audience participation. Her signature keynote presentation on total quality management, "I'll Know It When I See It," probes motivation and inspiration, recreates aspects of corporate culture in ancient peoples, and finds the humor in blindness.

An actress, teacher, author, and entrepreneur, Condra learned the power of stories from her African nanny, who heard rhythmic stories while walking long distances with native companions, and from her mother, a weaver of tales who could make the ocean seem like an old man with a wavy white beard flecked with pearls and shells. The visualization method aided Condra, who began losing her sight at age four. The family attempted to rescue her from darkness, but eye specialists, soothsayers, faith healers, and tribal elders failed to alter the condition. In her one-woman dramatization of the fearful sentence of blindness, she acts out her attendance at a girl's school and the move to more medical experimentation and drama school in London. Condra's spunk is evident in her insistence on learning to ski.

Condra does not let visual handicap limit her ambitions. She uses a computer reader to narrate books to her several hours daily and can select from several voices, including Husky Betty, Handsome Harry, and Perfect Paul. She owns two businesses — Imagination Station, a studio of innovative thinking and creative drama for children, and Imagination Crossroads, a toy store for adults and children — in Georgia and Tennessee and serves on the board of Dalcon, a computer company. She has taught speech and drama in South Africa and similar classes in Georgia and Tennessee as after-school enrichment for students. In 1976, while living in Carrollton, Georgia, she wrote and produced a bicentennial drama, *White Warrior*. Upon her resettlement in Nashville in 1979, she worked as a teaching artist for the Nashville Institute for the Arts. For her WPLN radio program, "Ear to Ear with Estelle Condra" for *Talking Library*, she has presented over 400 original stories. She has performed her specialties for the Prime Minister of South Africa as well as at the Kennedy Center, Gallagher Financial Corporation, Institute for Self-Actualization, Tennessee Repertory Theater, Nashville Symphony, Summer Lights, Southwire Company, Nashville Chamber of Commerce, Hospital Corporation of America, Maine Storytellers Convention, Vanderbilt University, and the University of Alabama School of Optometry.

Videography

Stories for Christmas Eve, Scene Three Productions, 1992. Contains "Hey You" and a war story, "The Peace Angel."

Bibliography

Miracle in a Shoebox (co-author evangelist Franklin Graham), Thomas Nelson, 1995.

A story of children who fill a box with gifts for a Bosnian family.

See the Ocean (illustrator Linda Crockett-Blassinghame), Ideals Children's Books, 1994. A girl named Nellie experiences the sea with her mind.

Audiography

"African Tribal Tales" (three audiocassettes), self-published, 1986. Explores five ethnic groups.

Awards

1997 Peabody College Outstanding Educator.

1994 American Booksellers Association Pick of the Lists for *See the Ocean*.

1978 Outstanding Young Woman of the Year.

Source

"Estelle to Give Two Performances," *Times-Georgian*, October 16, 1994, 5B.

Hance, Mary, "Mom Helps Author See the 'Ocean,'" *Nashville Banner*, August 1994.

Hieronymus, Clara, "'Caged' Shows the Unleashing of Spirit," *Tennessean*, January 12, 1997.

Kanouff, Sara, "Condra Breathes Life into Storytelling Tonight," *Vail Daily*, August 21, 1995.

Rogers, Tom, "Making Worlds of Mere Words," *The Tennessean*, March 31, 1985, 1D–2D.

Soltes, Fiona, "Storytime: Yarn Spinners Enthrall Kids with Tales of Cats, Ghosts," *The Tennessean*, October 13, 1991.

Traylor, Vickie, "Condra Brings Storytelling Talent to Families at Library," *Times-Georgian*, October 20, 1994.

LORALEE COOLEY

Address: Storyspinning
         410 Buckler Avenue
         Pampa, Texas 79065
phone 806-665-7321
fax 806-665-4844

Focus: folklore of the United States with emphasis on Appalachia, the Midwest, Texas, and Arizona; stories from the British Isles, Germany, Bulgaria, and the Republic of Georgia; family and personal anecdotes, especially of the World War II era; poetry and music.

Audience: all ages.

Style: ranges from dramatic to reflective and quiet; emphasizes the story rather than the teller.

Instruments/Props: autoharp, penny whistle, piano.

Loralee Cooley began her work as a professional storyteller in 1977, when she and her husband Ed lived in Casa Grande, Arizona. When her public library job was no longer funded through a CETA grant and Ed's work at a federally funded vocational training program ended, she discovered storytelling, a portable and enjoyable type of work. At the time, she knew no other tellers and had to develop her own credibility and motivation. In the past two decades she has presented storytelling concerts, conducted artist-in-residencies, and taught workshops, seminars, and classes. While living in Atlanta, Georgia from 1979 until 1988, she also founded the Southern Order of Storytellers and enjoyed professional relationships with tellers Chuck Larkin, Cynthia Watts, Betty Ann Wylie, Fiona Page, and Carmen Deedy. Cooley has held a place on the South Carolina Arts Commission Artist Roster since 1986 and was accepted as a touring artist in 1996 by the Texas Commission on the Arts. Her work has taken her to twenty states, Scotland, and the Republic of Georgia.

Cooley's background prepared her well for her profession. She completed a B.A. from Eastern Illinois University in Charleston in 1965 with a major in piano performance and minors in theater arts and French. Her M.A. from Antioch University in 1994 emphasized storytelling. She completed independent study in cross-cultural communication, folklore, narrative theory, and storytelling coaching with professors at Clemson University, Erskine College, and the University of Georgia. Her master's thesis was titled "Storytelling: Marked for a Special Calling," a phrase borrowed from an essay based on an interview with master teller Ray Hicks.

During the 1980s, Cooley and her husband

worked as sound technicians for the National Storytelling Festival, where she met the nation's best storytellers. While directing the Olde Christmas Storytelling Festival from 1983 to 1989, she invited her colleagues to come to Atlanta and developed friendships and collegial ties with Kathryn Windham, Ed Stivender, Robert Bela Wilhelm, Donald Davis, Milbre Burch, Carol Birch, Michael Parent, Syd Lieberman, Jackie Torrence, Doc McConnell, Doug and Frankie Quimby, Jay O'Callahan, Gwenda LedBetter, Peninnah Schram, and David Holt. Some of Cooley's notable storytelling appearances have been as featured teller at the Corn Island Storytelling Festival, as teacher for the Folk Arts Week at Ghost Ranch Conference Center, as guest storyteller for Eastern Illinois University's Celebration of the Arts, and as artist-in-residence throughout South Carolina, Georgia, and Texas. She has conducted a seminar entitled "The Art of Storytelling" at Columbia Theological Seminary and taught at Callanwolde Fine Arts Center in Atlanta and with her husband in a seminar, "I Love to Tell the Story" at the Louisville Presbyterian Theological Seminary.

Articles

Three-part series on a tour of the Republic of Georgia, *Gwinnett Daily News*, December 17–19, 1989.

"The Upstarts of Callanwolde," *National Storytelling Journal*, Winter 1984, 24.

Videos

Elsie Piddock Skips in Her Sleep, Sound Investments, 1993. Based on the story by Eleanor Farjeon; taped at Callanwolde Fine Arts Center, Atlanta, Georgia.

Storyspinning, Vol. 1 & 2 (two videotapes), Atlanta Video Production Co., 1987. Features international folk material, poems, rhymes, and storytelling rap for all ages; taped live at Prater's Mill Country Store, Dalton, Georgia.

Audiography

American Miscellaneous (audiocassette), self-produced, 1984. Contains American folk tales, poems, historical and biographical stories from Appalachia to Arizona; taped live at Lanier Middle School, Buford, Georgia.

Awards

1995, 1996, 1997 listed in *Marquis Who's Who in the South and Southwest*.

1994 Most Admired Men and Women of the Year.

1993 listed in *5,000 Personalities of the World*.

1991 listed in *Dictionary of International Biography*.

1990 listed in *2,000 Notable American Women*.

1990 listed in *The World Who's Who of Women*.

1989, 1992, 1997 listed in *Marquis Who's Who in Entertainment*.

1988 listed in *Who's Who in Professional and Executive Women*.

1986 Southern Order of Storytellers' Seanachie Award.

1966 Miss Louisville pageant winner.

Source

Hedgepeth, William, "The Art of the Storyteller," *Southern Magazine*, October 1986, 59–65.

Knober, Valerie, "Pampa Woman Leaves Audiences Spellbound," *Amarillo Daily News*, September 23, 1996, 1A, 9A.

Nickens, Ernie, "A Legacy of Lore: The Art of Storytelling," *Wachovia Magazine*, Fall 1991, 9–13.

Schonbak, Judith, "The Tell Tale Art," *Arts Georgia*, March 1988, 12–13.

Ward, Bernie, "Tell Us a Story," *Sky Magazine*, September 1988, 116–122.

KEVIN CORDI

Address: 1183 Goleta Way
            Hanford, California 93230
phone 209-587-0309
email KCtells@aol.com
web site www.geocities.com/Broadway/1940

Focus: storytelling in public schools; worldwide folktales; legends; ghost stories; holiday and real world stories; programs for small listeners.

Audience: classroom students.

A national first, Kevin Cordi takes pleasure in being the only high school teacher of storytelling in the country. In his words, "Stories are a powerful way of sharing learning, especially when it comes from teenagers." His pedagogy teaches improvisation and story mapping and models and demonstrates the life of teens to help them face problems and understand difficulties inherent in their time of life. The enhancement of curriculum demonstrates how narration opens lines of communication between teachers and noncommunicative students. At East Bakersfield and Hanford High in Hanford, California, he teaches narrative and coordinates two award-winning troupes of tellers — Voices of Illusion I and II — among whom is Adam McGee, the 1997 winner of the National Youth Storytelling Olympics at East Tennessee State University. His students have tested their skills with "The Rough-Face Girl," "La Llorana," "The Last Puppy," "The Rattlesnake Adventure," Mark Twain's "The Celebrated Jumping Frog of Calavaras County," and "Hometown Tales," an adaptation of Geoffrey Chaucer's *Canterbury Tales*. His enthusiasm invigorates the Pioneer Middle

School Junior Voices of Illusion and has inspired new troupes in Harlem and central Australia. His classes were the first to organize a student-run Tellabration, which brought 160 performers to an audience of 350. The troupe is currently working with Chicken Soup for the Soul to make a video from their book, *Chicken Soup for the Teenage Soul*. In a retrospect of their work, Cordi comments, "They are truly dedicated to the art of storytelling."

With a B.A. in communications from Kent State University, a combination M.A. from East Tennessee State University/University of Akron in storytelling as a component of English and speech education, a certificate in teaching methods from Sheffield, England, and over twelve years' experience as a performer, Cordi applies both talent and training in leading students toward beneficial uses of narrative art. He has coordinated their performance in a video and audiocassette and led workshops in Tennessee, Kentucky, Ohio, North Carolina, and England. Offers from promoters in Las Vegas and Ohio have vied for his troupe, which began receiving requests a week after its debut and performed for the Kings County Storytelling Festival and at Yosemite National Park and the Saroyan Theater for California Teachers of English. Cordi and his classes have been featured in *Storytelling Magazine*, *Tale Trader*, *Laugh-Makers Magazine*, *Fresno Bee*, and *Sing Out!* National Storytelling Association has named Cordi a state liaison and is commissioning him to produce *Voices Across America*, a book on middle school and high school troupes and libraries.

Cordi wants to revive storytelling for youth across America by encouraging tellers to become teachers and by assisting in the formation of other youth troupes, which already have spread to thirty states, Canada, and Australia. He believes "It is long past time for the youth to join in the Storytelling Revival. What better gift to give than a story that stretches across the ages. Our youth are marvelous tellers and at last the youth storytelling renaissance has begun."

Bibliography

Catch the Connection: Teenagers Want to Tell Too, self-produced, 1997.

"Hanford Fields Second Storytelling Olympian," *Hanford (California) Sentinel*, March 27, 1997, 1B, 4B.
"Teenagers Want to Tell, Too," *Tale Trader*, May 1996, 7.
"Telling Stories in High School," *Storytelling World*, Winter/Spring 1994, 35.
"What Storytelling Means to Me," *Tale Trader*, November 1996, 3.

Audiography

Strength Through Stories: A Nonviolent Way Told by Teens (audiocassette), Teaching Tolerance, 1998.

Awards

1997 King County Storytelling Festival Award finalist.
1997 National Youth Storytelling Olympics champion.
1997 College of Sequoias Tech Prep Storytelling Expo winner.
1996 King County Storytelling Festival Award finalist.
1996 National Youth Storytelling Olympics finalist for Tennessee.

Source

"High Schoolers As Tellers," *Storytelling Magazine*, September 1996, 5.

KEN CORSBIE

Address: Crossbreed Productions
6 President's Drive, Apartment 4-A
Port Jefferson, New York 11777
phone and fax 516-473-2419
email kcorsbi@suffolk.lib.ny.us

Focus: Caribbean stories; personal experiences and anecdotes; folklore; oral/aural poetry, song, and adaptations from literature; workshops.
Audience: grades 3–12; adults.
Style: dynamic, personable, and expressive; blurs distinctions among song, verse, narration, and rhythm; audience participation.
Instruments/Props: masks, percussion, and audio/video where appropriate and viable for workshops.

A dynamo of action, drama, and voice, Ken Corsbie, dubbed an "Elder Statesman of the Caribbean Stage," draws on his heritage, a blend of Chinese, African, Portuguese, Scottish, Welsh, Amerindian, Guyanese, Trinidadian, and Barbadian lineage. The rhythms, power, grace, and images of the islands permeate his tellings, which critics proclaim to be some of the best of the region for a quarter century. An announcer and idea man for the Guyana Broadcasting Service, Caribbean News Agency, Guyana Cultural Foundation, and Caribbean Broadcasting Union, he has developed his talent for storytelling in broadcasts and presentations throughout the English-speaking Caribbean. Energetic productions of two radio series—"Project One," which explored culture and politics of the thirteen Caricom (Caribbean Common Market) territories, and "Arts Caribbean"—demonstrate his restless urge to create in a variety of media, as illustrated by the sets he created for Michael Gilkes's epic stage play *Couvade* for the Guyana Independence Celebrations in 1993 and for the TV docudrama, *Sargasso!*, from Jean Rhys's novel, *Wide Sargasso Sea*, produced by the University of the West Indies. A former stand-up comedian and stage, radio, and television dramatist with 45 years' experience, he co-wrote, narrated, and is marketing *Caribbean Eye*, a thirteen-week pan-Caribbean television series showcasing island culture, ranging from theater to music, ritual, carnivals, art, games, film, literature, Amerindian survivors, and women's cooperatives.

Born in Georgetown, Guyana, in 1930, Corsbie grew up in a family that valued "ol' talking." Before grade school, he advanced his own knack for narrative, as did his sister and two brothers, by listening to the give-and-take banter of their parents and friends. He embellishes his tales with "appropriate and necessary" exaggeration, invention, and recreation, all skills he honed as a teenager in "the Yard" of the neighboring Taitt family, with whom he acted, danced, sang, and played in a steel band. Steeped in the beehive of local cultures, the Yard produced athletes, musicians, artists, dramatists, and dancers, and introduced basketball to Guyana after local children saw the 1950 film of the Harlem

Globe Trotters, *Go Man Go*. Corsbie was a foundation member of the Theater Guild of Guyana, and his successful theater activities earned him a three-month State Department–sponsored exchange to community theaters in the United States. A British Council scholarship sent him to England's Rose Bruford College for Speech and Drama and the BBC television school from 1965 to 1968. The experience prefaced a three-year producer/announcer post at the Guyana Broadcasting Service and two years as a regional liaison officer with the fledgling Caribbean Broadcasting Union. In the early 1970s, Corsbie evolved his own "He-One," a solo show of Caribbean poetry, story, and song, which doubled in strength after storyteller and poet performer Marc Matthews joined him for "Dem-Two," and doubled again to "All-Ah-We" with the inclusion of musicians and two more storytellers. Over the years, he has performed variations of these shows hundreds of times throughout the Caribbean and North America. Corsbie readily admits that he has also been influenced by the mother of Caribbean dialect poetry and storytelling, Louise "Miss Lou" Bennett of Jamaica, and by master teller Paul "Tim-Tim" Keens-Douglas of Grenada.

Corsbie credits Lee and Joy Pennington for formally labeling him a storyteller when they first invited him to tell at their Corn Island Storytelling Festival in Louisville, Kentucky, where he was thrice a guest teller. A storyteller as well as a playwright, media specialist, actor, and educator, he embraces the power of telling as an offshoot of all these experiences, with the spoken word as "the central medium having the power to incite and excite in immediate terms more than the eternally static visual fine arts." His style, indigenous to the islands and laced with imaginative dialect idioms, he characterizes as "a mobile, elaborately gestured, and often loudly expressive spontaneity." Corsbie originated and directed the first Caribbean Storytelling Festival and Tellabration in the Caribbean, held in Barbados in 1994 and 1995. He was guest teller and workshop leader at the Toronto Storytelling Festival, Boston's Sharing the Fire, and the Connecticut Storytelling Festival. He has also presented many lecture-demonstrations of Caribbean poetry at educational institutions and universities including Maryland, Florida, New York, Virgin Islands, West Indies, SUNY at Stony Brook, and Sienna College, and for students of Baldwin-Wallace College and New Brunswick University during their study abroad in Barbados.

Corsbie is now resituated with his wife, Elizabeth Barnum, in Port Jefferson, New York, where she is assistant dean for international services at SUNY at Stony Brook. He describes himself as non-nationalist, or more accurately, a multiculturist, and continues promoting Caribbean island cultures, particularly through storytelling. His signature anecdote, "Singing in the Rain," explains with both wit and nostalgia why he emigrated from Barbados, his third island homeland, to the United States. It is one of a series of stories in his repertoire which chronicles and explains his experiences in both the Caribbean and North America. Among the stories which he gleaned from other Caribbean writers are history professor Jan Carew's short story "The Third Gift," a celebration of beauty, hard work, and imagination; his friend Marc Matthews's boyhood adventure of watching the trains pass a small Guyanan village; and the metaphorical folktale of good versus evil adapted from Nobel Prize winner Derek Walcott's musical play *Ti-Jean and His Brothers*. Corsbie also presents the vibrant oral/aural poetry of Jamaicans Mikey Smith and Louise Bennett, Guyana's Martin Carter, Barbadians Kamau Braithwaite and Bruce St. John, Grenadian Paul Keens-Douglas, and DeCoteau Malik. Corsbie's workshops, "Caribbean Voices I — Dig de Riddim, Sing de Korus" and "Caribbean Voices 2 — See de Tellers Hear De Tales," analyze and demonstrate social and cultural traditions through the chorus, rhythms, call-and response, songs, story-poems, dialects, and variety of styles adapted from his region's best writers and performers.

Media Productions

Arts Caribbean, Caribbean News Agency, Barbados, 1991. Seventy-two weekly programs.

Caribbean Drama, Guyana Broadcasting Service, 1969. Fifteen radio plays.

Caribbean Eye, Caribbean Broadcasting Union, 1991. Thirteen television documentaries.

Centre Stage, Nation Newspaper, 1984. Fifty-two weekly articles.

Project One, Caribbean Broadcasting Union, 1972. Thirty radio documentaries.

Bibliography

"Storytelling, Caribbean Style: First Caribbean Storytelling Festival," *Tale Trader*, November 1994, 9.

Theatre in the Caribbean, London: Hodder and Stoughton, 1983. Introductory text for high school.

Plays

Barbados, Barbados, Tourist Trade of Barbados, 1981.

My Name Is Slave, Theatre Guild of Guyana, 1969.

Secrets of the Brain Coral, Barbados Dance Theatre, 1985.

Audiography

Caribbean Voices (audiocassette), Crossbreed Productions, 1997. Features "Monkey Liver Soup," "11 O'Clock Goods Train," "Palm Tree King," "Bajan Directions," "6 O'Clock Feeling," "Rainbow," "Letter Anon," "Sunparrots," and "Quetzy the Savior."

Caribbean Voices 2 (audiocassette), Crossbreed Productions, 1997. Features "Singing in the Rain," "Ol' Higue," "Third Gift," "Pan Birth," "Kites," "West Indian Stereotype," and "Luv Lettah."

Marc Up (LP) Theatre Information Exchange, 1979. Features "6 O'clock Feeling," "Sugar George," "Dark Time," "Rites," "12:30 Is Life," "Breakfast Blues," "Portia Faces Life," "Lament of the Banana Man," and "Dear Mother."

Awards

1994 Organization of Caribbean Associations, Barbados, Earthworks award for lifetime contribution to storytelling.

1993 Government of Guyana's award for set design for Michael Gilkes's *Couvade*.

1992 University of West Indies Centre for Management award for outstanding lifetime contribution to developing the arts.

1991 Caribbean Publishing and Broadcasting Association's award to outstanding feature presenter on television.

1985 Theatre Guild of Guyana's best director and design award for Derek Walcott's *Pantomime*.

1980 Yoruba Yard, Barbados, Bussa award for *All-Ah-We*.

1970 Government of Guyana's Arrow of Achievement for outstanding lifetime contributions to theater.

Sources

"Four Take Pride of Place at Festival Gala," *Daily Nation*, July 6, 1994, 25A.

Gilkes, Kathy-Ann, "Region Unites Through Stories," *Advocate: Barbados*, August 1995.

Gill, Charmaine, "Eight Thrill with Chilling Tales," *FanFare*, July 10, 1994, 11.

Harris, Margaret A., "A Caribbean Man," *Caribbean Week*, July 13–26, 1991, 28–29.

Jackman, Oliver, "Something to Shout About," *Daily Nation*, August 15, 1991.

"Ken Brings 40 Years to Stage," *Daily Nation*, June 20, 1994.

Kinas, Roxan, "Caribbean Week," June 10–23, 1995, 48.

"Mr. Theatre," *BWIA In-Flight*, Spring 1993, 72–75.

"New Guild in Barbados," *Storytelling Magazine*, January 1996, 29.

PETER DARGIN

Address: P. O. Box 1014
Dubbo, New South Wales
Australia 2830
phone 02 6882 8880
fax 02 6882 5671
email dap@lisp.com.au

Focus: traditional Australian lore; Outback adventure tales; Jack the Jolly Swagman stories with versions of "Stone Soup"; some personal reflections, fantasy, and adaptations of world folktales. ·

Audience: children, community groups, and historical societies.

Style: dramatic narration, conversational, traditional.

Instruments/Props: puppets, models, visuals, maps, and props.

An accredited Australian storyteller, Peter Dargin and his wife Pat travel the island nation assisting children in becoming storytellers, writers, editors, and published authors, using Jack the Jolly Swagman to bring them into the story of "Swagman's Stone Soup." The children perform a minor miracle: they retell, write, illustrate in color, and publish fifty copies of their sixteen-page book in a day. Dargin is a former teacher and principal in the Australian Outback from 1960 to 1979. As editor and publisher of the Country Areas Program Western Readers Project from 1979 to 1985, he has published over 250 books written by children and their teachers. The "Outback Kids Series" was the most popular.

Since 1986, Dargin has been a consultant, trainer, writer, and publisher with Development and Advisory Publications of Australia.

Until 1993, he served as technical, training, and networking coordinator for Contact Children's Mobile, a mobile preschool operating in remote border areas of New South Wales and Queensland. It was funded by the Bernard van Leer Foundation (Netherlands). The daily radio program "Contact with Kids," on Outback Radio 2WEB, promoted the reading and telling of stories to young children.

It was presenting *The True Story of Waltzing Matilda*—a contentious look at the writing of Australia's national song, at the Henry Lawson Mateship Festival, Bourke—that really started Dargin on storytelling beyond the classroom. His Outback Heritage Project looks at the story in history. He has organized flying expeditions by DC3s into remote areas to retrace and re-enact some of the most fascinating happenings in Australian history. Storytelling 7000 feet above the Australian Outback is rare. Tracking Captain Starlight lends material to "The Three Bushrangers," while Howitt's Pigeon Post 1861 has become the popular story "Mobile Phones for Burke and Wills." A parallel is Aboriginal Heritage with its lore of how the sun, the Milky Way, the Darling River, and fossils were made.

Ngaka Ebsworth, an Aboriginal dingo trapper, told Dargin how the gold and red opal came to the Outback through the death of "Kabungada the Pelican."

As a professional platform narrator, Dargin performs for the Australian Storytelling Guild, New South Wales, and at storytelling cafes and workshops. Other venues of oral publishing include Cairns under the flight path, Darling Harbor for the Australian Reading Association, the Miles Franklin Festival in the Snowy Mountains, schools along the Murray River, Golden West Museums and Historical Societies, Orange Regional Library International Literacy Day, members' stand at Warren Racecourse, Noccundra Hotel in outback Queensland, and Tibooburra Outback School of the Air, a unique interactive performance with children in two states plus those in the studio. Dargin's workshop, "Australian Folklore," was featured at the 1997 National Storytelling Festival at Macquarie University. He also presents one-hour shows from his Australian Storytelling Project, making programs around his characters: Captain Pickles and the Wandering Jane, Jack the Jolly Swagman, the Three Bushrangers, Colin Cod, and Coffin Charlie. Simple photocopy collages, such as those portraying "The Six Wise Men and the Elephant," focus on visual aspects of story before "leading them by the ear." Dargin has also published in *Telling Tales, Network News, Newswrite, Wyuna*, and *FreeXpression*, for which he writes a monthly column entitled "Xpressions of Interest."

Articles

"Australian Folklore," *Telling Tales*, October-November 1995, 4–5.

"Crafts of Storytelling," *Telling Tales*, April-May 1996, 5.

"The Darling River: Fact, Fiction and Fantasy," *Network News*, December 1995, 8.

"It's Different When You're a Kid," *Weekend Liberal*, June 1980.

"Land — Language — Lore: A Grave Look at the Outback," *Traditions & Tourism: The Good, the Bad, and the Ugly*, National Centre for Australian Studies, Monash University, and the Victorian Folklife Association, 1996, 124–128.

"Outback Folklore: A Regional Development of Fact, Fiction, and Fantasy," *Literacy and Learning in the South Pacific*, Australian Reading Association Inc., 1987.

"Outback Heritage: Australia's Great Grey-Green Darling River," *Storytelling Magazine*, March 1996, 22–23.

"Outback Heritage: Fact, Fiction, Folklore in *The Possum Stirs,*" Australian Folk Trust and the Centre for Leisure and Tourism Studies, Kuring-gai College of Advanced Education, 1986.

"Publishing a Book in a Day!," *Wyuna*, October 1994, 10–11.

"The Swede's Shout," *The Land*, June 1989.

"The Trials of a Small School Teacher," *Wyuna*, October 1994, 13.

Bibliography

Aboriginal Fisheries of the Darling-Barwon Rivers (3rd edition), DAP, 1991. Aboriginal land, language, and lore with explorers' writing.

The Book Factory: Publishing a Book-in-a-Day, DAP, 1995.

Captain Pickles and the Wandering Jane (illustrator Noela Young), Jacaranda, 1981. The story of Captain George Pickhills is set in the mid-nineteenth century.

Making and Telling Stories, DAP, 1997.

Outback Kids: Writers in Their Own Write, Country Area Program, 1984.

P. S. Brewarrina: A Profile, DAP, 1997.

Snake at School, Country Area Program, 1982. An anecdote that launches the *Outback Kids* series.

Stone Soup, DAP, 1997.

Swagman's Stone Soup, DAP, 1997.

Why the Weather Goes Wrong, Disadvantaged Country Area Program, 1980. Adaptation of "The Old Woman Who Lived in a Shoe."

Writing and Publishing: Caxton to Computer, DAP, 1986.

The Yab in the Tub, Disadvantaged Country Area Program, 1981.

Videography

Around the Pubs, ABC-TV.

Awards

1997 First Giraffe Tall Tales Competition.

1997 Varuna Writers' Retreat Fellowship.

1996 Royal Australian Historical Society and New South Wales Heritage Small Grants Program.

1989 Henry Lawson Short Story Award.

1988 Henry Lawson Short Story Commendation.

1987 Henry Lawson Short Story Commendation.

1988 National Bush Yarn Spinning Competition runner-up.

1988 Bicentennial Yarn Competition runner-up.

1986 National Bush Yarn Spinning Competition runner-up.

1982 State Development Committee Award to attend Pacific Rim Conference on Reading.

Source

"Adventures Retrace Capt. Starlight Legend," *Weekend Liberal*, August 6, 1988, 1.

Crosby, Heather, "A Change for the Better," *Daily Liberal*, 1989.

_____, "Folk Life," *Sunday Mag*, July 10, 1994, 9.

_____. "Magic of Story Telling Translated to Children," *Weekend Liberal*, October 7, 1995, 11.

_____, "There'll Always Be a Tale to Tell Says

Local Writer," *Daily Liberal*, January 27, 1997, 7.

McFarland, Greg, "Promoting the Written Word," *Central Western Daily*, September 10, 1996, 2.

"Peter Dargin — Traveling Storyteller," *Network News*, September 1995, 21.

Scarff, Robert, "CARP Brings Alive History of Rugged Outback Areas," *Daily Liberal*, July 18, 1986, 8.

_____, "Peter Dargin Crusades with Children in Mind," *Daily Liberal*, May 1980.

Stone, Kathy, "'Pioneers' Recreate Burke and Wills Rescue," *Weekend Liberal*, September 27, 1986, 1.

"Traveling Writer's Trail," *Free Xpressions*, December 1996, 18–19.

JOHN DASHNEY

Address: 1932 Chemeketa N. E.
        Salem, Oregon 97301
        phone 503-364-5825

Focus: original fantasies, supernatural lore, nonsense, and traditional material by Charles Dickens and Thomas Hardy; verse and prose beast fables; warrior stories; morality tales; rhymes and tongue twisters.

Audience: small groups of school children, including physically and mentally handicapped students in the Northwestern United States.

Style: witty, lively, humorous, and theatrical.

For eighteen years, John Braden Dashney has compensated for blindness by telling stories. He holds an M.F.A. from the University of Oregon, but claims no mentor and no classroom training in the art. His teacher was sightlessness, an impairment that, in 1979, unexpectedly cast a light on his ability to spin a yarn. Because he couldn't read to his son Braden, a toddler demanding bedtime stories, he made up interesting plots. His imaginative stories range from "The Sortalike" and "The Mousiegator" to "Ishmael the Clam" and "Not Everybody Is Always Nice." From telling stories to one school group, he was passed on to other potential audiences. After turning his hobby into a business, he widened his repertoire to more than forty original and traditional tales and traveled to four continents to tell them. In annual visits that classes anticipate, he delights in adding odd rhymes and alliterated tongue-twisters and verbal gymnastics. He has told stories at libraries, schools, and five international festivals in North America and New Zealand, and promoted the use of storytellers in school and library reading programs.

Dashney is a purist who uses no props, puppets, costumes, or multimedia gimmicks. He relies on a powerful voice and an imposing stage presence. To impress images on the mind and imagination of the audience, he incorporates fantasy, memory, vocal variations, inflection, timing, and gestures. In recognition of his skill, he was featured performer at the Regional Showcase at the 1993 National Storytelling Conference. His greatest thrill was doing a two-man show with veteran teller Jay O'Callahan at the 1996 Glistening Waters Festival in New Zealand. In

addition, he has appeared at the Australian National Storytelling Festival, Vancouver Storytelling Festival, Stories by the Sea, Forest Storytelling Festival, Kuala Lumpur Storytelling Festival in Malaysia in 1994, and the Dunya Festival in Rotterdam, Holland, in 1966 and 1997.

Bibliography

The Adventures of Mishka the Mousewere, Storm Peak Press, 1995.

The Adventures of Walter the Weremouse, Storm Peak Press, 1992.

The Ballad of Big Ben's Boot and Other Tales for Telling (illustrator Sheila Somerville), Storm Peak Press, 1994. Includes "The Bear Hunters," "The Plain Princess," "Mr. Skink & Mr. Skunk," "The Fox and the Squirrel," "The Great Chicken Stampede," and "Sam Samson's Simulated Sheep."

The King of Messy Potatoes, Storm Peak Press, 1997.

Audiography

The Story Tree (four-volume CD), Storm Peak Press, projected 1998. Contains three original stories — "Nobody Loves a Rotten Snake and Other Stories in Verse," "Tales of Strange Critters," and "The Dark Door"; the fourth, "Traditions," is an adaptation.

Awards

1992 Arts International grant.

1987 Oregon Arts Commission fellowship.

1983 *Dialogue* Magazine's Best Story of the Year.

1982 American Council of the Blind Ned Freeman Literary Award.

Source

"Prose Is Always Assured and Rich," Salem, Oregon *Statesman-Journal*, July 7, 1994.

"Storyteller Stumbled on Talent," Invercargill, New Zealand *News*, October 31, 1996, 3.

DONALD DAVIS

Address: P. O. Box 387
Ocracoke Island, North Carolina
27960-0397

phone 919-928-3917
fax 919-928-2587

Focus: whimsical, unpredictable Jack Tale cycles; Welsh and Scottish folktales; wonder tales; trickster lore; folk humor, fool stories, and mountain culture characteristic of Appalachia and rural North Carolina; coming-of-age motif; nostalgia, and humanistic reminiscences in traditional Anglo-Saxon lore.

Audience: all ages.

Style: realistic personal experiences; intense characterization.

A student of the tradition of oral culture, novelist and raconteur Donald Davis, a native of Appalachia, lives his philosophy that setting contains the story. A vivid recreater of characters in specific locales, he delights in establishing the person within a context, then exploding his context with a new twist or unforeseen cataclysm. For his purpose, theater must turn upside down, with acting preceding scripting. He carefully crafts material orally before committing them to paper, but maintains that oral delivery is the natural medium. Like a swimmer negotiating choppy waters, he has mastered thinking on his feet by fitting stories to the audience's expectations and ability to understand. With their assistance, he performs characters in action. The organic wholeness of Davis and his listeners becomes a satisfying synergy.

Davis's gift derives from genes and family tradition. Born June 1, 1944, in Waynesville, North Carolina, he claims fourteen generations of Welsh-Scottish pioneer ancestors, who settled Haywood County in 1781. The Jack of Appalachian Jack tales was as familiar as a neighborhood rapscallion. From childhood, Davis gathered Jack tales, fairy stories, and oral Scots history of the rural Blue Ridge Mountains, which his family presented as an integral part of their lineage and culture, dating to the Clan Fergus in the Scottish Highlands. His kin were land-based people who never converted to urban living because they didn't trust jobs. The strongest family models were his maternal grandmother, Zephie Williams Walker, and Francis "Uncle Frank" Madison Davis, both natural raconteurs who were unaware of either method or influence and who never set aside a formal time and place for storytelling. In true folk tradition, Davis was singled out as the bearer of family and area lore. After graduating from Waynesville Township High School and earning a B.A. in English literature from Davidson College, where he made a formal study of the print collections of Grimm brothers' tales, Geoffrey Chaucer's *Canterbury Tales*, and Shakespeare's plays, he completed a masters of divinity degree with a concentration in biblical languages from Duke University Divinity School. While serving as minister to the United Methodist Church of Andrews, North Carolina, he reclaimed the oral tradition by collecting and polishing folk tales and initiating his son Doug into the family art.

Davis's role in the National Storytelling Revival of the 1970s took him to in-service workshops, college residencies, libraries, churches, schools, colleges, and universities for a total of 300 school performances and fifteen festivals annually. He first considered himself a teller in 1981, after he was invited to participate at the National Storytelling Festival at Jonesborough. Now a regular face in the throng of fellow journeymen, he contributes to professional events, including the Miami-Dade County Children's Literature Festival, Three Apples Festival, San Juan Capistrano Storytelling Festival, Denver Storytelling Festival, Bay Area Festival, Amherst Storytelling Festival, Timpanogos Festival, Clearwater Revival Festival, Merle Watson Festival, North Atlantic Festival of Storytelling, North Appalachian Storytelling Festival, Illinois Storytelling Festival, Sierra Storytelling Festival, National Festival of Storytelling, and gatherings in Edinburgh, Scotland; Jakarta, Indonesia; Montreal, Canada; and Sidney, Australia. He has performed for the National Conference on Storytelling and Religious Message, Tennessee Iris Festival, Washington Storytellers Theatre, National Cathedral, Dowagiac Dogwood Festival, Smithsonian Institution, and the 1982 Knoxville World's Fair. An influential member of the National Storytelling Association, he chaired the board from 1983 to 1989.

Currently, Davis lives on Ocracoke Island off the North Carolina coast and makes his living as a storyteller. He has written commentary for the Abingdon Press *Storytellers' Companion to the Bible* and leads whole language workshops for educators. His workshops tap experience and expertise to provide pointers to beginners. He has appeared on CNN and *Nightline* and has hosted American Public Radio's *Good Evening*. Since 1994, he has held an honorary doctor of human letters degree from LaGrange College. In August 1997, he led an eastern Caribbean storytelling cruise aboard the *Norway*, an Atlantic liner of the Norwegian Cruise Line. His wife Merle, who is a former grade school teacher and arts administrator, manages his business as storyteller.

Articles

"Inside the Oral Medium," *Storytelling Journal*, 1984, 7.

"To Ease the Heart: Traditional Storytelling" (co-author Kay Stone), *Storytelling Journal*, 1984, 3–6.

Bibliography

Barking at a Fox-Fur Coat, August House, 1991. Seventeen family stories about universal characters, including "Rainy Weather," "The Southern Bells," and "Old Man Hawkins's Lucky Day."

"The Crack of Dawn," in *Homespun: Tales from America's Favorite Storytellers*, Crown, 1988.

Jack ALWAYS Seeks His Fortune: Authentic Appalachian Jack Tales, August House, 1992. Traditional Jack tales and their influence on the storyteller.

Jack and the Animals: An Appalachian Folktale (illustrator Kitty Harvill), August House. 1995. A cumulative Appalachian tale about a boy, five animals, and a fortune.

"Jack's Biggest Tale," *Jack in Two Worlds*, University of North Carolina Press, 1994, 213–228.

Listening for the Crack of Dawn, August House, 1990. Humorous and bittersweet stories of youth in the Appalachia of the 1950s and '60s

"Miss Daisy," in *Homespun: Tales from America's Favorite Storytellers*, Crown, 1988.

My Lucky Day, Johnson Publishing, 1984.

"Rainy Weather," in *More Best-Loved Stories Told at the National Storytelling Festival*, August House, 1992.

See Rock City: A Story Journey Through Appalachia, August House, 1996. Sequel to *Listening for the Crack of Dawn;* for young adult readers of historical fiction.

Southern Jack Tales, August House, 1997. Thirteen Scotch-Irish tales from Davis's Haywood County home for ages 10 and up.

Telling Your Own Stories: A Resource for Family Storytelling, Classroom Story Creation, and Personal Journaling, August House, 1993. A resource for discovering and creating personal stories condensed from a popular workshop.

Thirteen Miles from Suncrest, August House, 1994. A novel on hardship and tragedy in the Appalachian tradition set on Close Creek, North Carolina, in 1910.

"The Time Jack Got the Silver Sword," in *Ready-to-Tell Tales*, August House, 1994.

"Uncle Frank and the Southern Bells," *Storytelling World*, Winter/Spring 1992, 11–14.

Videography

"The Crack of Dawn," in *American Storytelling Series, Vol. 8*, H. W. Wilson, 1986.

"Interview," *The Twentieth Anniversary of the National Storytelling Festival*, Hometown Entertainment, 1994.

Audiography

Christmas at Grandma's (audiocassette), August House, 1994. Three stories rich in seasonal nostalgia.

"The Crack of Dawn," in *Homespun Tales* (contributor) (audiocassette), National Association for the Preservation and Perpetuation of Storytelling, 1986.

"C-R-A-Z-Y," in *Best-Loved Stories Told at the National Storytelling Festival* (audiocassette), August House, 1991.

Dr. York, Miss Winnie, and the Typhoid Shot (audiocassette), August House, 1997. Also contains "Tonsils."

Favorites from Uncle Frank (audiocassette), self-published, 1983. Contains "Rainy Weather," "Run, Run, Run," "The Electronic Microphone," and "Why I Can't Read."

Grandma's Lap Stories (audiocassette), August House, 1997. Stories from Appalachian oral tradition for young children.

Jack and Grannie Ugly (audiocassette), August House, 1997. Contains "Something Old, Something New" and the title story, both about the theme of fate and filled with humor, drama, and suspense.

Jack's First Job (audiocassette), August House, 1993. Four Jack tales in the Appalachian oral tradition.

Listening for the Crack of Dawn (audiocassette), August House, 1990. Humorous and bittersweet stories of youth in the Appalachia of the 1950s and 1960s.

Meet the Jollies (audiocassette), self-published, 1982. Nostalgic stories of Aunt Laura, Uncle Frank, and the Jolly family.

Miss Daisy and Miss Annie (audiocassette), August House, 1986. Davis's classic stories, featuring "Miss Annie" and "Miss Daisy."

Miss Winnie (audiocassette), August House, 1996.

More Than a Beanstalk (audiocassette), Weston Woods, 1985.

Mrs. Rosemary's Kindergarten (audiocassette), August House, 1996.

Party People (audiocassette), August House, 1993. The story of a birthday party; a sequel to *Listening for the Crack of Dawn.*

Rainy Weather (audiocassette), August House, 1992. A tall tale about a legendary North Carolina foxhound.

See Rock City: A Story Journey Through Appalachia (audiocassette), August House, 1996. A sequel to *Listening for the Crack of Dawn;* for young listeners.

Southern Bells (audiocassette), August House, 1994. Nostalgic humor about the coming of telephone service and party lines.

Stanley Easter (audiocassette), August House, 1997. Contains a student bus-driver story and "Some Things Never Change."

Stanley, the Easter Bunny (audiocassette), August House, 1997.

"The Strongest Woman I Ever Knew," on *Rainbow Tales* (CD), Rounder Records, 1997.

Telling Old Testament Stories (two-volume record album), Graded Press, 1997.

Traditional Tales for Children (audiocassette), self-published, 1983.

Uncle Frank Invents the Electron Microphone (audiocassette), August House, 1992. Tall tales of Appalachian wit and wisdom.

Awards

1997 *Storytelling World* Winner for *See Rock City.*

1996 National Storytelling Association's Circle of Excellence.

1996 *Storytelling World* Award for Best Audio Recording for *Mrs. Rosemary's Kindergarten.*

1995 *Storytelling World* Award for Best Audio Recording for *Listening for the Crack of Dawn.*

1995 *AudioFile* Earphones Award for Best Audio Recording for *Listening for the Crack of Dawn.*

1995 Parents' Choice Honor Award for *Christmas at Grandma's.*

1994 American Library Association Notable Children's Recording for *Christmas at Grandma's.*

1992 Anne Izard Storyteller's Choice Award for *Jack ALWAYS Seeks His Fortune.*

1990 Anne Izard Storyteller's Choice Award for *Listening for the Crack of Dawn.*

1990 *AudioFile* Earphones Award for *Listening for the Crack of Dawn.*

1985 ALA Notable Recording for *More Than a Beanstalk.*

Sources

Dixon, Kathy, "Storytelling World Presents Donald Davis," *Storytelling World*, Winter/Spring 1992, 7–10.

"Keepers of the Lore: Storytelling for Adults," *AudioFile Magazine*, August 1994, 1, 12–13.

O'Malley, Judith, "Donald Davis: Every Story Tells a Picture," *Wilson Library Bulletin*, October 1992, 52–53.

Richardson, Peggy Hemlich, "The Texas Storytelling Festival, 1997," http://members.aol.com/storypage/news/97texas.htm.

Shedden, Mary, "Telling Stories in the TV Age," *Long Island, New York, Newsday*, July 18, 1990.

Sobol, Joseph Daniel, "Between Worlds: Donald Davis," *Jack in Two Worlds.* Chapel Hill: University of North Carolina Press, 1994, 204–212.

_____, "Everyman and Jack: The Storytelling of Donald Davis," master's thesis, University of North Carolina, 1987.

_____, "Growing Up with Jack in Haywood County: The Backgrounds and Development of Donald Davis's Storytelling," *North Carolina Folklore Journal*, Summer-Fall 1994, 80ff.

Soltes, Fiona, "Storytime: Yarn Spinners Enthrall Kids with Tales of Cats, Ghosts," *The Tennessean*, October 13, 1991.

Stotter, Ruth, and William Bernard McCarthy, "Tellers and Their Tales: Revivalist Storytelling," *About Story: Writing on Stories and Storytelling 1980–1994.* Stotter Press, 1994; second edition, 1996.

Thrasher, Paula Crouch, "Southern Storytelling Festival the Main Event" *Atlanta Journal-Constitution*, April 29, 1995.

White, Jon, "Spinning Yarns," *Indianapolis Business Journal*, January 1, 1995.

CARMEN DEEDY

Address: c/o Robin DeFoe
384 McGill Place
Atlanta, Georgia 30312
phone 404-521-3579

Focus: reminiscences of childhood in Cuba and the Cuban-American heritage; life in Georgia.

Audience: all ages.

Style: spirited gestures, accents, and characterization.

Instruments/Props: drum by Pedro A. Marrero; guitar ensemble for "Afro-Cuban Lullaby."

The oral biographer of the exiled Agra clan, Carmen Agra Deedy shares with listeners the family's 1963 odyssey from home in Havana, Cuba, to a new life in Decatur, Georgia, following the Cuban Revolution and the rise of dictator Fidel Castro. Her parents, who requested political asylum in the United States, put her on a plane after they grew increasingly disenchanted with the revolution. To questions about what she left behind, Deedy replies, "My heart and my grandmother." The mother of daughters Katie, Erin, and Lauren, Deedy shares stories of her family's past to preserve and pass on Cuban traditions. In memoir and vignette, she recreates Mami, a tough, world-wise mother, who reassures her children that they only need each other. In a melange of reflective stories, Deedy calls up other focal characters — the gentle Papi, Tia Coralia, and El Manicero, the peanut man whose song echoes in Deedy's memory as the essence of her island homeland.

Deedy's two-fold career as storyteller and author has placed her in a number of venues, ranging from PTA meetings, bookstores, museum, and schools to the New Victory Theater on Broadway, Folger Shakespeare Library, Disney Institute in Orlando, Atlanta's 1997 Winter Storytelling Festival and book signings advertising her five picture books. She has appeared at Timpanogos Storytelling festival, the National Storytelling Festival in Jonesborough, Tennessee, and Habitat for Humanity's "Building Homes Story by Story," and was featured teller at the 1997 Tell It in the Mountains and at the Kennedy Center. Her programs include "Growing Up Cuban in Decatur, Georgia," "Scare Me Silly: A Collection of Spinechilling Tales," "Fairy and Folk Tales, Myths, and Legends," "Chaucer's Canterbury Tales," "Lamb's Tales of Shakespeare," and "Heroic and Outrageous Women." She shares reminiscences of Hispanic-American family life on National Public Radio's *Weekend All Things Considered* and *Latino USA* and in her audio collection, *Growing Up Cuban in Decatur, Georgia*, which features a photo of Deedy in early childhood on the cover.

Bibliography

Agatha's Feather Bed: Not Just Another Wild Goose Story (Laura L. Seeley), Peachtree, 1991. The off-beat story of six geese who visit an old woman; for ages 4–8.

The Last Dance (illustrator Debrah Santini), Peachtree, 1996. The story of children who gain wisdom from their grandfather; for ages 8–12.

The Library Dragon (illustrator Michael P. White), Peachtree, 1994. The story of a children's librarian named Miss Lotta Scales; for ages 6–10.

"Mangoes and Magnolias," *Highlights for Children*, December 1996, 23.

"Peanut Man," *Highlights for Children*, September 1995, 30–31.

The Secret of Old Zeb (illustrator Michael P. White), Peachtree 1997. A story about following dreams.

Treeman (illustrator Douglas J. Ponte), Peachtree, 1993. A whimsical story full of inside jokes for ages 4–8.

Audiography

Growing Up Cuban (audiocassette), Peachtree Studios, 1995. Contains "The Trouble with Windows," "Peanut Man," "First Snow," "Chicken Wings," "Bending Steel," "Mother Mouse," "Educating Esther," "The Nature of Bees," "Traffic Court," "Rice Pudding," "You're Gonna Miss Me," and "Mangoes & Magnolias"; also features "Afro-Cuban Lullaby" played by the guitar ensemble of Baldwin High School, Montgomery, Alabama, and drum accompaniment by Pedro A. Marrero.

"Mangoes and Magnolias," on *Rainbow Tales, Vol. 2* (CD), Rounder Records, 1997.

"Trouble with Windows," on *Rainbow Tales, Vol. 1* (CD), Rounder Records, 1997.

Awards

1997 Florida Reading Association Children's Book Award for *The Library Dragon*.

1997 North Dakota Flicker Tale Children's Book Award for *The Library Dragon*.

1997 Washington Children's Choice Picture Book Award nominee for *The Library Dragon*.

1997 Pennsylvania Young Reader's Choice Award nominee for *The Library Dragon*.

1997 Colorado Children's Book Award nominee for *The Library Dragon*.

1996 Parents' Choice Gold Award for *Growing Up Cuban in Decatur, Georgia*.

1995 *Publishers Weekly* Best Audio Book/Adult Storytelling for *Growing Up Cuban in Decatur, Georgia*.

1993 Georgia Author of the Year for Juvenile Literature.

Source

"The Barter Storytellers," *Storytelling Magazine*, July 1997, 5.

Daniel, Alisa, "Book Brag," *Instructor*, April 1996.

Del Negro, Janice, "Review," *Booklist*, January 15, 1996.

Farber, Henry, "There's a Story Behind Annual Habitat Fund-Raiser," *Atlanta Journal/Constitution*, December 5, 1996, JN-12.

Frederick, Lisa, "PTAs' Member Rates Vary: J. H. House Has Most Difficulty Involving Parents," *Atlanta Journal-Constitution*, May 23, 1996.

Kopka, Matt, and John Zinsser, "Listen Up Awards: The Year's Best Audiobooks," *Publishers Weekly*, January 1, 1996.

Marshall, Jane P., "Things to Read Can Make Great Gifts for Kids," *Houston Chronicle*, December 11, 1995.

McLeod, Michael, Angela Peterson, and Tom Raymond, "Once Upon a Time," *Florida Magazine*, November 24, 1996.

Muller, Carol Doup, "Everything Comes from Something," *San Jose Mercury News*, August 13, 1995.

"Original Stories Could Become Kids' Classics," *Houston Chronicle*, July 17, 1992.

"Review," *Booklist*, June 1, 1991.

"Review," *Children's Book Review*, December 1995.

"Review," *Fantastic Flyer*, Summer 1997.

"Review," *Publishers Weekly*, July 25, 1991; November 14, 1994.

Sabulis, Jill, "At Home with Carmen Deedy: Young Readers Rule Roost at Storyteller's House," *Atlanta Journal-Constitution*, October 6, 1995.

JANICE DEL NEGRO

Address: Director, Center for Children's Books
Editor, the *Bulletin of the Center for Children's Books*
University of Illinois
51 E. Armory Avenue
Champaign, Illinois 61820
work phone 217-244-0324
fax 217-333-5603
email delnegro@alexia.lis.uiuc.edu

Focus: ghost stories; feminism; transformation stories; traditional folktales; romantic and eccentric tales; reading motivation through literature and storytelling.

Audience: general.

Style: relaxed.

A multitalented children's librarian, editor of *Bulletin of the Center for Children's Books*, book reviewer for *Booklist*, publishing consultant, educator, and storyteller, Janice Del Negro manages to be where the action is in the storytelling arena. A dynamo of influence

electronic media, her tellings become a personalized form of communication that connects her to each listener.

Currently an adjunct faculty member of the Graduate School of Library and Information Science at Rosary College, Del Negro was featured teller and workshop leader at Illinois Storytelling Festival, Chinquapin Storytelling and Music Festival, Fox Valley Folk Festival, Wild Onion Storytelling Festival, Sake County Storytelling Festival, and Exchange Place at the National Storytelling Festival in Jonesborough, Tennessee. She has conducted workshops on storytelling and reading motivation for librarians, teachers, parents, and educators at the University of Illinois, University of Chicago, Dominican College, and DePaul University. Titles include "StoryCrafting: Retelling Traditional Tales," "Storytelling: The New Tribes," "The Library Oral Tradition," "An Introduction to Storytelling," "Retelling Old Tales," "Multicultural Storytelling," and "Introducing the Folktale." Her performances feature the exploits of women, as in "Live Ghosts and Spirited Women: An Adult Storytelling Concert," which she performed for Sulzer Regional Library.

and enthusiasm, she has written for *Booklist, School Library Journal,* and *Kirkus Reviews,* and has served on National Storytelling Association's library and archives committee and publishing advisory board and as a Newbery and Caldecott committee member. In addition, she is co-founder of Chicago Storyworks and has been an executive board member of Chicago Storyteller's Guild and Northlands Storytelling Network. Despite a lengthy résumé of platform narrative and training, she admits that public speaking comes hard for her. She first combated stage fright in graduate school, where she enrolled in storytelling. As a former consultant for the North Carolina State Library and Chicago Public Library assistant director of systemwide children's services, she began telling traditional folk material and pointing the way to reading. After settling with her husband and two daughters in Chicago, she accepted an invitation to attend the National Storytelling Festival, the impetus for her second career in platform narration. The decline of her terror of public performance parallels the delight her audiences experience by the relaxed narration of plots that they can visualize as they see fit. Unlike

Bibliography

Lucy Dove (illustrator Leonid Gore), DK Ink, 1997.

Audiography

Journeywomen and Ghostly Passages (audiocassette), self-produced, 1991.

Source

"Best of Storytell — Ethics of Storytelling," http://numbers.aol.com/storypage/ethics. htm.

"Folk Tales Are Her Specialty," *Elkhart Truth,* September 5, 1993, 6.

"Janice Del Negro — New Editor of BCCB," http://edfu.lis.uiuc.edu/puboff/ beeb/janice. html.

PLEASANT DeSPAIN

Address: 3400 E. Speedway Boulevard #118-207
Tucson, Arizona 85716

phone 520-577-6672
email PleasantD@aol.com

Focus: historical fiction; animistic trickster lore; the American West; inclusive, nonsexist stories that laud the triumph of good over evil villains, witches, giants, and leprechauns.

Audience: children and adults.

Style: simple, direct using mostly voice and facial expression.

Pleasant DeSpain is a believer in creating only front doors, leaving himself no option but to succeed by the door he entered. He started by passing the hat for stories told in coffeehouses, worked his way up to well paid gigs in auditoriums, and advanced to master raconteur. In preparation for stage narration, he collects all variants of a story before putting his personal stamp on it. For a school audience, he often lets students supply endings and thus acquires hundreds of new possibilities. In one instance he offered young listeners the skeleton of "The Laughing Hat," which they received as a challenge and worked to a number of logical and humorous conclusions. True to his aim to please with stories, he has earned a place as journeyman storyteller from thousands of school appearances in forty states over a 25-year period. He has participated in the Tucson Storytelling Festival, Forest Storytelling Festival, Corn Island Storytelling Festival, and the National Storytelling Festival in Jonesborough, Tennessee. His performances have taken him to the Boeing Corporation and to the Toastmasters International Convention in Reno, Nevada. Health problems drove him to the dry climate of Arizona, where he has earned a new following.

DeSpain is a lifelong storyteller. When visiting school children he shares with them the tales he made up in boyhood. Born in Denver, Colorado, in 1943, to Robert A. and Eleanor J. DeSpain, now Eleanor J. Feazell, he began spinning yarns in third grade with a written version of "The Mystery Artist." His teacher confiscated the page that circulated among eager readers and scolded him for poor spelling. To encourage his joy in yarning, she offered him a notebook in which to record his original plots. The acknowledgment of his talent was a first step to a career. He earned a B.S. in speech and English and an M.S. in oral literature from Southern Illinois University at Carbondale. He completed post-graduate work in oral literature at the University of Colorado at Boulder in 1970, but thanks his stars for stopping short of a doctorate. In his résumé, he recalls the soul-wrenching era: "I decided teaching wasn't for me ... I came within six months of getting my Ph.D. Thank God I didn't. I had a dark night of the soul. I spent five months in Mexico." An instructor in speech and literature at the University of Massachusetts at Amherst from 1966 to 1968, he taught at the University of Washington in Seattle from 1970 to 1972, then painted houses, grilled burgers, and washed dishes for five years while establishing himself as a storyteller.

A full-time platform narrator and author since 1973, DeSpain is recognized as one of the dozen pioneers of professional storytelling in America. He has performed at national and local festivals, schools, and theaters across the United States and has published eight books and 150 stories. From 1977 to 1982, he wrote, produced, and hosted *Pleasant Journeys*, a weekly storytelling series on KING-TV, Seattle, Washington. Simultaneously, he wrote a column by the same title for the *Seattle Times* that appeared in seven other papers. Now established in national circles, he is known for his signature tale, "Old Joe and the Carpenter," which was twice selected by IBM for placement in elementary school libraries across the United States.

Bibliography

The Dancing Turtle, August House, projected spring 1998.

Eleven Nature Tales: A Multicultural Journey (illustrator Joe Shlichta), August House, 1996. Contains "All Things Are Connected," "Sun Catcher," "Cooking with Salt Water," "The Friendship Orchard," "Frog Swallows Ocean," "Rabbit's Tail Tale," "The Savage Skylark," "Cardinal's Red Feathers," "Starfire," "The Grizzly Bear Feast," and "Enough Is Enough," all revealing the interconnections in nature; for young readers.

Eleven Turtle Tales: Adventure Tales from Around the World, August House, 1994. Focusing on the turtle as a symbol of earth and as a trickster and sage.

"The Magic Pot," in *Ready-to-Tell Tales*, August House, 1994.

The Mystery Artist, Willowisp Press, 1996.

"Old Joe and the Carpenter," *Mother Earth News*, January-February 1984.

Strongheart Jack and the Beanstalk (illustrator Joe Shlichta), August House, 1995. A story of action, fun, and justice; for ages 5–8.

Thirty-Three Multicultural Tales to Tell (illustrator Joe Shlichta), August House, 1993. A collection of native American, Brazilian, Chinese, Korean, Russian, African, and Tibetan action stories in retellable form; ages five and up.

Twenty-Two Splendid Tales to Tell from Around the World, Vols. 1 & 2, August House, 1993. An anthology of tales, parables, and myths from North America, Europe, Asia, Africa, and the East Indies focusing on the triumph of pragmatism and good; includes "The Theft of Smell" and "The Wisdom of Solomon."

Audiography

Tales to Tell from Around the World, Vols. 1 & 2 (audiocassette), August House, 1995. An anthology of tales, parable, and myths from North America, Europe, Asia, Africa, and the East Indies focusing on the triumph of

pragmatism and good; includes "The Theft of Smell" and "The Wisdom of Solomon."
Turn Around Turtle's Show and Tell (CD-ROM), Rose Studios, 1995.
Twenty-Two Splendid Tales to Tell, Vols. 1 & 2 (books and audiocassettes), August House, 1994. Accompanied by original guitar and flute music.

Awards

1996 Public Library Association's Adult Lifelong Learning Best New Book for New Readers for *Eleven Nature Tales*.

1995 Parents' Choice Honor Award for *Twenty-Two Splendid Tales to Tell from Around the World*.

1975 proclaimed Seattle's Resident Storyteller.

Source

Come-All-Ye, Winter 1993, 4; Spring 1995, 3.
Corsaro, Julie, "Review," *Booklist*, January 1, 1995, 828.
"Dream Weavers, True to Life Tales of the Storytellers' Trade," *San Jose Mercury News*, August 14, 1984.
"Flights of Imagination, Storytelling and Television," *National Storytelling Journal*, Spring 1984.
"Once Upon a Time, There Was a Storyteller," *Seattle Times*, October 1, 1977.
"Pied Piper of Storytelling Treats Kids Like People," *Seattle Post-Intelligencer*, September 9, 1979.
Regan, Margaret, "Once Upon a Time," *Tucson Weekly*, September 28–October 4, 1995, 36.
"Review," *Kirkus Reviews*, October 15, 1993, 1327.
"Review," *School Library Journal*, August 1994, 16; November 1994, 67.
"Review," *Small Press Reviews*, March 1994, 6.
"Seattle's Master of Storytelling," *Seattle Times*, November 30, 1975.
"Seattle's Resident Storyteller Shares Tales with Fairbanks," Fairbanks, Alaska *Daily News-Miner*, February 7, 1979.
Something About the Author. Vol. 87. Detroit: Gale Research, 1996.

GAY DUCEY

Address: 2808 Hillegass
           Berkeley, California 94705
phone 510-841-6398

Focus: world myths; legends that celebrate cultural connections; true stories.
   Audience: children and adults.
   Style: spunky and animated.

A children's librarian-turned-freelance platform teller, Gay Ducey is a freelance storyteller and storytelling educator. She serves Dominican College, Santa Rosa Junior College, and her alma mater, the University of California at Berkeley Library School, as professor of storytelling. Simultaneous with teaching and performing, she serves as children's librarian at the Rockridge Branch of the Oakland Public Library. A former co-chair of the National Storytelling Association, which serves 7,000 members, and co-founder direc-

tor of the Bay Area Storytelling Festival, she appears on the lists of many raconteurs as an inspiration and mentor.

A descendant of generations of Southern women who treasure independence, spunk, and a sassy mouth, Ducey loves telling stories from the American South as well as tales from a wide range of cultures and traditions, particularly texts that promote tolerance. In 1992 she was a commissioned artist of the Smithsonian Institution's National Museum of American History, where she developed and presented a story on women in the American labor movement. She was featured teller at the Forest Storytelling Festival and the 1995 National Storytelling Festival. In 1996 she appeared on *Mr. Rogers' Neighborhood*. Her workshop topics include "The Tie That Binds," "The Tree of Life," "Spontaneous Combustion," "Sex, Drubs, and Rock 'n' Roll," "Spinning Straw into Gold," "Tell It Together," "George Washington Slept Where," "The Company We Keep: Character Development in Stories," "Two-Part Harmony: Using Song in Stories," "How to Conduct a Really Good Storyhour," "The Enabling Art of Emceeing," and "Using Stories to Celebrate Picture Books."

Bibliography
"Lazy Jack" in *Ready-to-Tell Tales*, August House, 1994.

Awards
1997 National Storytelling Association award for service and leadership.
1997 California Women's Commission Outstanding Woman of Berkeley.

Source
"The Barter Storytellers," *Storytelling Magazine*, July 1997, 5.
"National Storytelling Association's Service and Leadership Awards," *Storytelling Magazine*, July 1997, 42–43.
Timeless Voices: Images of the National Storytelling Festival. Jonesborough, Tenn.: National Storytelling Press, 1997.

DIANE EDGECOMB

Address: : P. O. Box 365422
              Hyde Park, Massachusetts 02136
phone 617-455-1926
fax 617-522-4335
email Wilderwalk@aol.com
web site www.lightlink.com/acstudio/
  wwalk.htm

Focus: nature mythology and nature lore; New England seasonal tales and holiday traditions; participation stories; Arthurian and traditional British legends, seasonal myths and celebrations; pourquoi tales; ecological pieces; original comedic stories; Northern European and Celtic tales; haunting stories; bardic tales with harp accompaniment; traditional songs.

Audience: adults, children, and families.

Style: dynamic, imaginative characterizations, comedy, song, and recitation with lyric intensity.

Instruments/Props: guitar, folk instruments; collaborates with composer Tom

Megan; accompaniment by Celtic harper and vocalist Margot Chamberlain.

A twelve-year veteran of theater, recording studio, and platform narration, Diane Edgecomb is a virtuoso teller. Known for her vivid characterizations, she has played Clothilde, Amanda, George, a shark, a dinosaur-loving monster-child, and a monkey, all with similar grasp of detail. Early on, she demonstrated her transformative abilities when she won a Year's Best Performance award in 1985 for her comedic rendition of Suzannah from the play *Bedroom Farce*. In the end, however, the stage did not hold the fascination for Edgecomb that storytelling did. While performing in story theater, she became deeply aware of the power of image as it related to the spoken word. From the moment she told her first tale, she fell in love with storytelling's endless possibilities. She started on a journey which led her to synthesize diverse interests in story, music, mythology, nature, characterization, comedy, and image-based theater.

Edgecomb's background is thoroughly New England Yankee. Her family on both sides has lived in Maine for centuries. Her father's side settled Saco in the 1640s. While growing up, she heard many Maine yarns and true life tales. She also inherited a love of New England and its changing seasons, which she draws on in performance. With forebears from England, Scotland, Ireland, and Wales, including the Bruce of Scotland and Lord Edgecomb of Cothele Manor House in the England of the 1200s, Edgecomb's ancestry is truly a Celtic knot. She explores these backgrounds through her work with Arthurian legends, Welsh transformation magic, Scottish tales, and Irish stories.

In Edgecomb's family-oriented performances, she often presents thematic tellings such as *Tall Fall Tales, Once Upon a Wintertime, Welcome in the Spring,* and *Summer Escapades,* all celebrating New England's seasons. Also informative and entertaining are *Digging Dinosaurs, Rainforest Legends,* and *Tales for the Earth.* She also presents concerts for adults with long-time collaborators Celtic harper Margot Chamberlain and/or keyboardist Tom Megan. These evenings are a weave of story, song, and music. The harp is often bowed like a cello or used in innovative and unusual ways to create rhythm. Event titles include *A Celtic Evening, Love and Otherwise, Solstice Tales of Greenery and Light,* and *Midsummer Tales.* In these evenings, which often take on the character of seasonal and holiday celebrations, stories alternate between comedic pieces and classic tales. Suitably trained in theater, voice, and dance from Boston Conservatory of Music and experienced in Growtowski-based imagery, experimental stage, and classical drama with the National Shakespeare Company, Edgecomb is well prepared to express enduring lore. Her imaginative comedic pieces stretch from a beat poem entitled "Freddie and the Loon from Maine" to "Pattysaurus," a family fable about a girl with dinosaur mania. Edgecomb adapts stories from native North American, northern European, and Celtic mythology and develops innovative Arthurian lore, including "New Age Gawain and the Green Knight," in which a green bungee jumper visits Arthur's men.

Because of her commitment to the natural world, Edgecomb creates stories that draw on original and folkloric content that celebrates nature and earth-based themes. For young students, she finds entertaining and enlightening ways to link environmental and scientific concepts with folkloric nature stories. She has also created ecological pieces based on true events like "The Boy Who Loved the Swamp," the story of a child who raised community support to stop destructive developers. In addition to classroom and auditorium telling, Edgecomb has performed her stage works for the Old Vienna Kaffeehaus, Me and Thee Coffeehouse, Boston Museum of Science, Maine Audubon Society, Museum Institute for Teaching Science, New England Science Center, National Storytelling Conference, World Trade Center, Three Apples Storytelling Festival, Roger Williams Park Zoo, Harvard University's Arnold Arboretum, Storytellers in Concert, MIT's Biodiversity Conference, Philadelphia's Academy of Natural Science, Appalachian Mountain Club, Bread and Roses Folk Festival, and Loon Festivals from Maine to New Hampshire. She has been featured on WGBH's *Spider's Web Series* and National Public Radio's *Living on Earth*. Her teaching tale, *What Now Cloacina?!!* , an entertaining water conservation story, appears in story collections in North America and England. In 1991, she created original material for the World Trade Center Boston's robotic dinosaur exhibit and she has composed a work for the Centennial Celebration of the Massachusetts Audubon Society.

Articles

"Weaving Whole Cloth: Creating a Winter Solstice Celebration," *Storytelling Magazine*, November 1996, 12–13.

Bibliography

"Baldur and the Mistletoe," *Storytelling Magazine*, November 1996, 14–16.

"What Now, Cloacina?!!," in *Spinning Tales, Weaving Hope*, New Society Press, 1992.

Audiography

New Age Gawain and the Green Knight (harpist Margot Chamberlain) (audiocassette), Wilderwalks Productions, 1995. A comedic adaptation of a classic tale.

Pattysaurus and Other Tales (audiocassette), Wilderwalks Productions 1995. A family tape about a dinosaur-loving monster-child named Patty; includes "The Old Apple Tree," and "Princess Firefly"; for ages 4–8.

Awards

1996 *Storytelling World* Honor Award for *Pattysaurus and Other Tales*.

1985 *Boston Herald* Year's Best Performance Award.

Source

Creasy, Beverly, "Creasy's Choice — Double-Edged Valentine," *Boston Journal*, February 6, 1992.

"A Family-Style Dinosaur Dig," *Boston Globe Northwest Weekly*, August 11, 1996.

"Funny Stuff," Southbridge, Massachusetts *Evening News*, April 30, 1997, 11.

Goslow, Brian, "Upcoming Events," *Worcester Phoenix*, June 21, 1996.

Green, Scott, "A Celtic Evening," *New England Entertainment Digest*, March 1996, 39.

Martin, Suzanne, "Green Grow the Stories," *Storytelling Magazine*, Spring 1992, 18–20.

"Midsummer Magic for Summer Solstice," *Cambridge Chronicle*, June 16, 1994.

"National Storyteller on Stage at the Academy July 11," *Explore*, June/July 1996.

Parente, John R., "Blackstone Summer Readers Captivated by Storyteller's Magic," *Woonsocket Call*, August 20, 1994.

"Review," *Booklist*, January 1, 1997.

"Review," *Publishers Weekly*, July 1996.

"Review," *School Library Journal*, November 1996.

"Storyteller Diane Edgecomb Will Spin Some Yarns This Weekend," *Boston Globe*, August 10, 1991.

Wagner, John Van, "A Celtic Celebration of St. Valentine," *Belmont Citizen-Herald*, February 21, 1991.

DAYTON EDMONDS

Address: P. O. Box 3226
          Omak, Washington 98841
phone 509-826-5549

Focus: ancestral lore, values, and customs; collective tribal memories; stories of present-day struggles; wisdom stories; legends; ghost stories; nature lore; healing stories.

Audience: intergenerational.

Style: oral traditional employing sign and mime; clowning, positive imaging.

Instruments/Props: puppets.

A purist of the old school, native American teller Dayton Edmonds comes from a long line of tribal storytellers and prefers working with live audiences outdoors. A gifted artist, sculptor, and printmaker, he began studying stories with his grandparents, who taught him the trials, wisdom, and humor of the Hasinai of the Caddo nation, once natives of Louisiana, Arkansas, and Texas until they were removed to Oklahoma in the 1830s. His grandfathers were priests of the peyote religion who taught him stories of nature and the power of patient observation; his father was both artist and storyteller. Edmonds helps to

preserve his people's ancient traditions as farmers, moundbuilders, healers, teachers, and storytellers by honoring and relating their stories. At a camp on Puget Sound, Washington, on the Olympic Peninsula, he was initiated into the sacred art of the storykeeper in 1979, when he received the symbolic wing feather of an eagle and the outlines of a story about his experience with nature. He still owns the feather and continues to use camping as a focus of his ministry as a Methodist missionary.

Edmonds travels extensively to tell and to listen to the stories of others. He has applied his skills in numerous venues, including gatherings, audio and videotape, and two films, and publishes annually in *Orientation*, a Methodist magazine for students entering college. Among his memorable performances and lecture sites are John Carroll University, Central State College, Pan-American University, Wenatchee Valley College, University of Puget Sound, University of the Virgin Islands, Washington State University, and Linfield College. He applies artistic forms to storytelling, which he weaves with thought-provoking images to give voice to the voiceless. He explains in his resume, "As an artist, I seek

to give a perspective from a different part of life's circle." Schooled in music education in Jacksonville, Texas, and in business education in San Francisco, he completed his education in theatre in Ashland, Oregon. He performs for churches, schools, fairs and festivals, museums, nursing homes, camps, community groups, and libraries.

Bibliography
The Farmer's Three Sons, Devo'Zine, 1997.
The Gift of Fire, UMC Board of Higher Education and Ministry, 1997.
The Gift of Music, UMC Board of Higher Education and Ministry, 1995.
The Gift of Rabbit, UMC Board of Higher Education and Ministry, 1996.

Audiography
A Storyteller's Story (audiocassette), self-published, 1994. Contains traditional wisdom, humor, and "how things came to be" stories of the native American; a modern coyote tale; and the title story of the teller's initiation into the sacred art of the storykeeper.
Tour Guide, Central Washington Heritage Corridor, Othello to Omak (audiocassette), Washington State Arts Commission, 1995.

Videography
Catch the Spirit, Turtle Clan Story, UMCom Productions, 1989.
Circle of the Heart (film and video), Church World Service, 1983.
Faces on Faith, EcuFilm, 1989. An interview with Dayton Edmonds.
Giving Starts a Chain Reaction (film and video), United Methodist Communications Commission, 1982.

Source
"The Magic of Storytelling," *Columbiana Magazine*, Winter 1988-1989, 14–16.
"Of Eagles, Magic, Music, and the Sacred Art of Storytelling," *Engage Social Action*, January 1987, 20–23.
"Omak Storyteller's World Includes Art, Music, Faith," *Chronicle Scene*, November 22, 1995, 5.

ELLARAINO

Address: P. O. Box 1420
         Studio City, California 91604
         phone 213-654-1922
         fax 213-656-0920

Focus: African and African-American tales; international legends; history of the West; participation stories; trickster lore; ring games and story circles; creation and nature lore; family anecdotes; poetry and chants.

Audience: all ages.

Style: imaginative telling; dramatic solo characterizations; Ellaraino Ensemble with musicians, dancers, and other tellers; performance with her son Bernard Wright and friend Baki.

Instruments/Props: Afro-centric costumes; beads, bracelet, ear cuffs, and ear wings; bright-colored fabrics, traditional African and world musical instruments; artifacts; storyteller's staff and story basket.

A veteran actress and master of the spoken word, Ellaraino brings to her Afro-centric storytelling a broad base of 33 years in film, stage, and television. Playing the part of Biddy Mason, a black woman arriving in San Bernardino with Mormon settlers, Ellaraino voices the character's discontent with servitude, a significant theme in her African-American history vignettes. In addition to platform telling, she has appeared in twenty feature films, including *House Party, Sneakers* and *Fire Down Below*, and has guest-starred or been featured in more than seventy television series, among them *Beverly Hills 90210, One Day at a Time, Ironside, Dan August,* and *Hill Street Blues.* Her stage appearances include the role of Tituba, the Caribbean slave, in Arthur Miller's play, *The Crucible.* She also hosted and starred in *The Fox Cubhouse,* a national television series for preschoolers, and was featured on *Good Day* on FOX-TV and on KCET's *Storytime.* To prepare fledgling tellers for platform narrative, she advises the Compton Unified School District on theater arts and drama and teaches adult and children's storytelling

workshops through the Southwest. She excels at performances for cultural events, holiday observances, celebrations, fairs, Head Start, and storytelling bus tours through southern California. Her workshops and presentations include *Front Porch Tellin', International Legends, Earth, Sea & Sky, Africa!, Critters & Creatures ... Famous and Lesser Known, Eerie ... Scary, The African-American Experience, Holiday Tales, Ring Games & Story Circles,* and *The Black West.*

Born in Kilgore, Texas, Ellaraino was labeled a slow reader in childhood, but overcame her difficulties after high school. Her autobiography, *Another Kind of Treasure,* reveals the drama in her family life. A trip south to attend her great grandmother's 110th birthday brought Ellaraino into the segregated world that troubled her father. Their return reunited him with the good of his past and taught Ellaraino to appreciate the personal reflections of an old lady who remembered the Emancipation Proclamation and the end of slavery. The stories helped shape Ellaraino's skills in platform performance and inspired her to help others tell their family stories. After becoming Los Angeles Metropolitan Business College's first black student body president, she realized personal and family ambitions, crowned by the Triad Award, the school's highest honor. Following a brief stint of clerical work, she initiated a career in acting and performance narrative. In Ellaraino's early acting career, her desire to learn about other peoples took her to Honolulu, Mexico City, Stockholm, Helsinki, Copenhagen, Hamburg, Rome, Madrid, and San Jose, Costa Rica. Where she didn't speak the language, she communicated with laughter, smiles, and song. Since becoming a teller of tales, legends, history, and personal stories, she longs to visit Goree Island, two miles off the coast of Dakar, Senegal, where 85% of African slaves were captured and brought to the Americas. She hopes that such a journey would enhance her repertoire of stories.

Ellaraino's appearances include the Las Vegas Alliance of Black School Educators, Fullerton Museum Center, Los Angeles County Museum of Art, Allensworth State Historic Park, Chinese Moon Festival, Inter-

national Festival of Masks, Cerritos College, Los Angeles African Marketplace, Saturn Street School, The Palms at Palm Springs, and the Higher Education Conference on Black Student Retention for Florida A & M University. In addition, she is a consultant and performance artist for the West Hollywood International House of Blues Foundation and co-created "The Blues Schoolhouse" program, and she is the official storyteller of Allens-worth State Historic Park, California's first African-American town, founded in 1908. She is at work on a second book, *Straight from the Heart*, a collection of folktales, historical and family stories.

Bibliography

Another Kind of Treasure (co-author Bernice Sanders), DreamTime, 1997. The biography of Ellaraino's great grandmother, Silvia Mack, who became literate at age 85 and lived another quarter century to reflect on slavery and old age.

Awards

1996 National Education Association Commendation for *The Fox Cubhouse.*
1995 City of Los Angeles Commendation.
1988 City of Los Angeles Commendation.

Source

"African-American Folktales," *Whittier Daily News*, February 9, 1994.
Aubry, Erin J., "Tightening Bonds by Sharing Stories," *Los Angeles Times*, July 24, 1994.
Casey, G., "Review," *Black Achievers*, June 1997, 12.
Mitchell, Marsha, "*Another Kind of Treasure Is a Jewel to Read*," *Los Angeles Sentinel*, April 10, 1997.
"Mother and Son Together As Storytellers," *Atlanta Daily World*, December 10–11, 1992.
Owchar, Nick, "Up Close," *Whittier Daily News*, February 9, 1994.
"Stories: They Aren't Just for Children," *Los Angeles Times*, October 10–16, 1991.
"Waving Her Staff, Ellaraino Spins Stories," *Los Angeles Times*, July 24, 1994, 1, 2.
Who's Who. Detroit: Gale Research, 1991.

DOUG ELLIOTT

Address: 3831 Painter Gap Road
Union Mills, North Carolina
28167-9749
phone 704-287-2960

Focus: stories and songs celebrating the natural world; native American legends; epic ballads; traditional and historical tales; inspirational stories; hitchhiking and freight-hopping stories and outrageous personal anecdotes; regional songs and original music; maritime ballads; woods lore and recipes.

Audience: children and adults.

Style: regional dialect and humor; some adult material.

Instruments/Props: harmonica and animal sounds; occasional performances with a four-piece backup group playing fiddle, guitar, banjo, bass, bottles, bells, buckets, cans, drums, rattles.

A jongleur skilled at beekeeping, folk medicine, woods lore, fishing, possum hunting, harmonica playing, herbalism, basketry, and writing, Doug Elliott reveres nature as his touchstone as well as the source of stories and anecdotes. A veteran teller at the National Storytelling Festival, he comes well armed to the storyteller's stage. His training derives from lengthy studies through North America in herbal healing and traditional Indian and folk cures. He has conducted back country adventures from Maine to the Florida Everglades. Currently a resident of Rutherford County, North Carolina, he was born to a Northern mother and Southern father who compromised on location and raised their family in the Chesapeake Bay area of Maryland on the Mason-Dixon Line. Elliott holds an art degree from the University of Maryland. To answer his questions about living things, he studied the outdoors and taught himself about plants, mammals, insects, reptiles, and fish. For a number of years he made a living from gathering and selling herbs.

Elliott lives close to nature with his wife, potter Yanna Fishman, and follows his father's penchant for yarning. He has performed at festivals, museums, and schools across the continent and into the Caribbean, and sometimes uses an attention-getter, such as a turtle or snake in his bag or a possum named Blossom on his shoulder. His lecture and storytelling programs for institutions such as the American Museum of Natural History and Royal Ontario Museum cover *Looking for America: A Twentieth Century Hero's Journey, Jungle Adventure: Inside the Rain Forest, Possumology and Groundhogabilia, The Bog as an Environment, Plants and People, Creepy Crawly Critters, Possums, Greens, and Fresh Sardines: Traditional Foodways and Country Cooking from Canada to the Caribbean, Weeds for Your Needs,* and *Fishing, Wishing, and Tales of the Deep Blue Sea: Wrestling Sea Serpents, Tickling Trout, Grabbing Catfish by the Snout!* For twenty years, he has taught at the Omega Institute for Holistic Studies and has lectured on basketry and fiber at the Cleveland Art

Museum, Augusta Heritage Arts Workshops, and the Smithsonian Institution, where he performed "Kids Love Kulintang." In 1997, he was featured teller at Voices for the Earth in Orange Springs, Florida. His stories and articles have appeared in *Wildlife in North Carolina, Shuttle Spindle and Dyepot, Mother Earth News, Co-Evolution Quarterly, Southern World, Well-Being, New Hampshire Profiles, Adirondack Life, Maryland Magazine,* and *The Whole Earth Catalog.*

Bibliography

Crawdads, Doodlebugs & Creasy Greens: Songs, Stories & Lore Celebrating the Natural World, Native Ground, 1995. Collected, retold, and illustrated by Doug Elliott; contains 24 songs as well as stories, nature lore, wild food facts, and recipes.

Roots: An Underground Botany and Forager's Guide, Chatham/Devin-Adair Press, 1976. History, legends, and lore of medicinal and edible herbs.

Wild Roots: A Forager's Guide to the Wild Edible and Medicinal Roots, Tubers, Corms and Rhizomes, Healing Arts Press, 1995. A new edition covering plants for food, shampoo, dye, medicine, and tooth powder; yarns about Captain John Smith, Peter Kalm, and Plato.

Wildwoods Wisdom: Encounters with the Natural World, Paragon House, 1992. Contains adventures in the wild and 100 drawings.

Woodslore and Wildwoods Wisdom, Possum Productions, 1986. Contains "How to Use Road Kills" and information about ramps, rope and basket making, herbs, orchids, bears, ginseng, and millipedes.

Audiography

Bullfrogs on Your Mind (audiocassette or CD), Native Ground, 1997. Contains frog hunting and swamp stories and a creation myth, including "Frogs — Guardians of the Water," "Roosevelt and Ira Lee," "Bake That Chicken Pie," "Who Broke the Lock," "Mole in the Ground," "Bulldog on the Bank," "Muskrat," "Rattlesnaking Papa," "The Snake and the Egg," "Scat Rap," and the title song.

Crawdads, Doodlebugs & Creasy Greens: Songs, Stories & Lore Celebrating the Natural World (audiocassette and CD), Native Ground, 1995. Stories and songs on harmonica, guitar, bass, banjo, fiddle, and acoustics; includes "Ain't No Bugs on Me," "Mosquito Story," "Theron and the Doodlebug," "Doodlebug Song," "Yellowhammers and Domineckers," "Catfish Song," "The Cajuns and the Crawfish," "Crawdad

Hole," "Green Rocky Road," "The Origin of Strawberries," "Strawberry Picking," "Queen Elizabeth and the Frog," "Froggie Went a Courting," "Creasy Greens," "Root Blues," and "Left Hind Leg of a Rabbit."

Raccoon and a Possum (audiocassette and CD), Native Ground, 1989. Stories and songs for ages 4–10, featuring "The Jive Three Bears," "The Story of Aspirin," "Possum, Turtle and the Wolves," "The Fox and the Crow," "Uncle Reuben Run a Coon," "I Had a Dog, His Name Was Blue," and the title song.

Stories, Songs, Jokes & Tales: A Cultural Tour of America's Back Country (audiocassette), Possum Productions, 1986. Contains poems and harmonica songs; covers territory from Maine, the Appalachian Mountains, and Louisiana Cajun country; recorded live in concert with adult audiences and features "The Jive Three Bears," "Ruth Moore's Ballad of Three Green Waves," "Microscopic Orgasm," "Canopy Bed," "Dynamite Fishing," "Beginning Possumology," "Blossom the Possum," "The Possum Growers and Breeders Association," and "The Cajun Rat D'Bois."

Awards

1995 American Library Association Notable Children's Recording Award for *Crawdads, Doodlebugs & Creasy Greens: Songs, Stories & Lore Celebrating the Natural World*.

1989 American Library Association Notable Children's Recording Award for *Raccoon and a Possum*.

1983 Fiddler's Grove Festival Harmonica Champion.

Source

Anderson, Nina L, "The Possumologist," *The State*, March 1990, 20–21.

Martin, Suzanne, "Green Grow the Stories," *Storytelling Magazine*, Spring 1992, 18–20.

"Old-Time Herald," http://www.hidwater. com/OTH/54rev/0.html, 1996.

Saunders, Zane A., "More Interdisciplinary Than Any University," Forest City, North Carolina, *Daily Courier*, December 13, 1989.

Westarp, Elaine, "Blossom's Gone but Her Tales Travel On," Raleigh, North Carolina *News and Observer*, October 18, 1984.

ELIZABETH ELLIS

Address: P. O. Box 720411
Dallas, Texas 75372
phone 214-381-4676
voice mail 800-989-4441 box 200-1205

Focus: folk tales; history and personal experience stories; tales of heroic American women.
Audience: all ages.
Style: occasionally performs with Gayle Ross.

Elizabeth Ellis is the type of storyteller who sparks the abstract and remote to enliven the personal and immediate. A popular teller of history tales, she has evolved a narrative style that suits the challenge level of her material to the audience's capacity to absorb and enjoy. At the lowest level of appreciation is the "Ha Ha" story, the funny tale that requires only a response to comedy. The "Ah Ha" reaction, she says, suits a *"pourquoi* story," such as a ghost tale, which gives an explanation of a phenomenon or anomaly. The "Ah" story, often personal or biblical, requires deeper concentration and moves the audience to a more satisfying response. The last type, the "Amen" story, is the thematic or moralistic tale that brings about a change in behavior. At the end of the "Amen" story, Ellis's hearer is likely to visualize a need for heartfelt commitment to an ideal or ethic. She employs several "Ha Ha" stories and works her way up to a thought-provoking narrative, but drops back to the lower level if the situation lacks intimacy or the audience is unable to focus on an "Ah" or "Amen" sequence. Ellis encourages teachers to tap into her scheme of suiting story to the quality and depth of reception. She believes that stories make ideal attention-getters, focus points, discussion springboards, mood changers, rewards, community builders, and closings. As classroom management techniques, her narratives become powerful modes of pedagogy because children respond to the rudiments of stories better than to bare details, facts, or philosophies. Thus, her stories about Indians are excellent introductions to native American history or culture.

Skilled at assessing human needs, Ellis comes from a background of warm-hearted givers. Born in the story-rich Kentucky hills in 1943, Ellis, who grew up in the Appalachian Mountains of Tennessee and Kentucky, profited from a circle of adults who loved her and cultivated her talents. She preferred imaginative play, whether outdoors exploring or indoors reading. She loved to hear stories read by her mother, Nancy Gabbard Ellis, who encouraged her to memorize passages from the King James Bible. According to Ellis, her aunt Ida Moore contributed "Beauty and the Beast" in a style "to make a rock weep." For parenting, she depended on her grandfather, a circuit-riding minister who replaced her father after his death in World War II. The stories her grandfather gleaned from visits to mountain homes became family entertainment, along with the tales he made up.

Ellis's growth as a storyteller followed a decade of work with children. After she graduated from Milligan College and completed an M.Ed. from East Tennessee State University, she settled in Dallas, Texas, and worked for ten years as children's librarian at the Dallas Public Library, where telling stories was the best part of her job. As an avocation, she collected folk melodies and became a closet song writer. Evenings spent at the Rubaiyat Club

watching folk singers perform became her performance workshop because their technique applied directly to the work of the raconteur. Her friend Gayle Ross agreed that adults have a greater need for stories than children do. In 1978, the two attended the National Storytelling Festival in Jonesborough, Tennessee, and returned committed to becoming tellers themselves. In a daring leap of faith, they resigned their jobs and formed a duo, the Twelve Moons Storytellers. Their mishaps include an evening telling in an outdoor arena between two major highways, where they couldn't hear each other for the roar of traffic. Traveling in a Volkswagen bus dubbed the White Elephant, they spent four years on the road and became featured tellers at the National Storytelling Festival in 1981 and 1982.

After the duo moved into solo performance, Ellis was at first scared of performing alone. She developed a repertory of folktales, history, and personal experience stories before launching a series of tales about heroic American women. Her work has been well received by the Canadian Arts in Religion and Community, Texas Council on Family Relations, Texas Education agency, and Bluebonnet Book Festival. Festival appearances include Corn Island, St. Louis, Michigan, Texas, Michigan, and Prairie Tales in Illinois. She has performed at the Winnepeg, Vancouver, and Kerrville, Texas, folk festivals. Workshops have taken her to the Florida Storytelling Camp, Texas Library Association, Texas Conference on Personal Narrative, Institute of Texan Cultures, and Riverwind Storytelling Weekend in Illinois. Her first taste of honor among her peers came in 1985 with the John Henry Faulk Award for stories from Texas culture. Twelve years later, she advanced to the National Storytelling Association's Circle of Excellence. Humbled by adulation for her natural gift, she claims to be content with her life, rearing grandson Christopher and still playing with her imaginary friends.

Articles

"Contracts and Storytellers: If Only I'd Known," http://members.aol.com/story-page/news/index.htm.

"Researching and Crafting the History Story," *Storytelling World*, Winter/Spring 1997.

Bibliography

"The Birth of Oisin," in *Best Stories from the Texas Storytelling Festival*, August House, 1995.

"Flowers and Freckle Cream," in *Best-Loved Stories Told at the National Storytelling Festival*, August House, 1991.

"Jack and the Haunted House," in *Ready-to-Tell Tales*, August House, 1994.

"Like Meat Loves Salt" and "The Peddler's Dream," in *Homespun: Tales from America's Favorite Storytellers*, Crown, 1988.

Videography

"The Peddler," in *American Storytelling, Vol. 7*, H. W. Wilson, 1986.

Audiography

"Flowers and Freckle Cream," in *Best Loved Stories Told at the National Storytelling Festival* (audiocassette), August House, 1991.

I Will Not Talk in Class (audiocassette), New Moon Productions.

Like Meat Loves Salt and Other Tales (audiocassette), New Moon Productions.

"Obedient Jack," in *Tales of Wit and Humor* (performed with Gayle Ross) (audiocassette), National Association for the Preservation and Perpetuation of Storytelling, 1992.

"The Peddler's Dream," in *Homespun Tales* (contributor) (audiocassette), National Association for the Preservation and Perpetuation of Storytelling, 1986.

Stories ... Imagine That (audiocassette), self-published, 1986. Contains "Maybe It Is, Maybe It Isn't," "Jack and the Mule," "Heaven and Hell," "Hungry Catch the Foolish Boy," "Origin of Strawberries," "Two Old Women Make a Bet," "The Weeping Lass at the Dancing Place," "Zeesha," "The Cowtail Switch," and "The Creator and the Mirror"; music by Karl Anthony.

Tales of Ancient Egypt (audiocassette), New Moon Productions.

Awards

1997 National Storytelling Association Circle of Excellence.

1985 Tejas Storytelling Association's John Henry Faulk Award.

Source

Baltuck, Naomi. *Crazy Gibberish and Other Story Hour Stretches*. Linnet Books, 1993.

Carey, Kim, "McConnell Receives NSA's Lifetime Achievement Award," *Tale Trader*, August 1997, 1, 4.

"Five Storytellers Receive Honors," *Storytelling Magazine*, May 1997, 41.

George, Jerry, Don Stone, and Fay Ward. *On Common Ground*. Canada: Oxford University Press, 1994.

Holt, David, and Bill Mooney. *Ready-to-Tell Tales*. Little Rock, Ark.: August House, 1994.

Mooney, Bill, and David Holt. *The Storyteller's Guide*. Little Rock, Ark.: August House,, 1996.

Smith, Jimmy Neil, ed. *Best Loved Stories Told at the National Storytelling Festival*. Jonesborough, Tenn.: National Storytelling Press 1991.

_____. *Homespun: Tales from America's Favorite Storytellers*. New York: Crown, 1988.

_____, ed. *Why Possum Has No Hair on His Tail and Other Stories from the South*. New York: Avon, 1993.

Stallings, Fran, "Honesty, Respect, Compassion: Strengthening Character Through Stories," *Storytelling Magazine*, January 1997, 24–27.

Stewart, Finley. *Best Stories from the Texas Storytelling Festival*. Little Rock, Ark.: August House, 1995.

See also Gayle Ross.

REX ELLIS

phone 703-437-4013
fax 202-357-5346
email rellis@cms.si.edu

Focus: slave experiences.
Audience: general.

Style: sings gospel songs and spirituals; acts multiple character parts.

Instruments/props: antiques, clothing, and slave possessions from Colonial Williamsburg.

A gifted singer and storyteller, Dr. Rex Ellis treasures history as the source and inspiration for his platform career. Formerly the director of the Department of African-American Interpretation and Presentations at Colonial Williamsburg, he applies his knowledge of the personal side to history in all phases of his career and conducts such workshop as "Using Objects to Tell Stories About Family and Culture." He combines work as director of the Office of Museum Programs at the Smithsonian Institution with intensely dramatic storytelling appearances in which he plays all the parts. Among his notable audiences are the 1997 American Library Association summer conference in San Francisco, the Celebrations of Light V in Midland, Texas, and numerous gatherings in Africa, Puerto Rico, Panama, Canada, the Virgin Islands, and across the United States.

Ellis, a native of Surry County, Virginia, grew up in a museum atmosphere near Williamsburg, a profitable source of employment that constantly reminded him of slavery. He grew up in the early days of television and was a fan of notable black stars Diahann Carroll, Sammy Davis, Jr., and Wilt Chamberlain. In the introduction to *Under the Blazing Sun*, Ellis recalls the period from 1957 to 1964 when he attended Frederick Douglass Elementary, an all-black school in York County, Virginia, and made friends with the janitor. Ellis's best memories are of the librarian, Mrs. Rodgers, who told stories that made him relive fictional episodes as though he were the hero. Despite his father's insistence on a career in medicine or law, he found his niche in poetry recitation and advanced in stage training with the part of Marryin' Sam in a high school stage production of Al Capp's *L'il Abner*. After completing a B.F.A. at Virginia Commonwealth University, M.A. from Wayne State, and Ph.D. from the College of William and Mary, he devoted his life to storytelling to disseminate the contributions of African-Americans to national and world culture. He has published articles in *Colonial Williamsburg Journal, American Visions,* and *History News,* and maintains membership in Screen Actor's Guild, American Federation of Television and Radio Artists, American Association of Museums, American Association for State and Local History, Association of Black Storytellers, and the National Storytelling Association, which he serves as chairman of the board.

Bibliography

African American Folktales: For Young Readers (contributor), August House, 1994.

Beneath the Blazing Sun: Stories from the African-American Journey, August House, 1997. Features 29 stories of African origins, the transatlantic journey, and such signature stories as "Viney's Free Papers," "The Lynching," "Daddy and the Black Barnstormers," and "Going to the Drive-in Movies"; includes additional resources on black history.

"Helping Students Connect with History," in *Tales as Tools: The Power of Story in the Classroom,* National Storytelling Press, 1994, 124–128.

Jump Up and Say; Anthology of African-Amer-ican Storytelling (contributor), Simon & Schuster, 1995.
The Storyteller's Start-Up Book (contributor), August House, 1993.

Audiography
The Ups and Downs of Being Brown (audio-cassette), August House, 1992. A celebra-tion of traditional and contemporary Afri-can-American storytelling.

Source
"Colonial Williamsburg," *American Visions*, August 1990, 14.
Goldstein, Mark, "Storytelling Festival," http://www.seamonkey.ed.asu.edu/swa/dis-cussion/message326.html.
"Rex Ellis," http://www.hometownnet.com/ ellis.html.
"Virginia," *American Visions*, June 1990, 3.

ETH-NOH-TEC

Address: 977 South Van Ness
San Francisco, California 94110
phone 415-282-8705
fax 415-282-8795
email ethnohtec@aol.com

Focus: Asian folktales; myths and legends; journey stories; wisdom tales; trickster tales; stories of heroes and heroines; Asian tales of terror.
Audience: all ages and cultures.
Style: the spoken word woven with Eastern and Western music and movement.
Instruments/Props: white costumes with white face inspired by kabuki theater, Chinese opera, and Asian performing arts; bamboo flutes, Southern Filipino kulintang gongs, Japanese drums, bamboo pole dance, other bamboo instruments.

A San Francisco–based storytelling duo, Robert Kikuchi-Yngojo and Nancy Wang have taken the stage by storm with their innovative act known as Eth-Noh-Tec, a name that weaves (tec) distinct cultural elements of East and West (eth) to create new possibilities (noh).

They are known as cultural advocates, inform-ing and intriguing their multigenerational and multicultural audiences with things Asian. According to performer Yngojo, Eth-Noh-Tec, a non-profit Asian-American perform-ing arts and cultural education organization, is a poetic creation: "Light as a wing her hand gestures the flight of the Bird of Happiness soaring above Himalayas ... a lyrical melody on a bamboo flute dances between lines of an ancient Chinese tale ... then, the thunderous rhythm of Japanese Taiko drums bring the Goddess of the Sun, Amaterasu, out of hiding and light is restored to the World!" The duo tells Asian tales such as "The Long-Haired Girl" from China and "Seven Silly Fellows," a bilingual story from the Philippines, syn-chronizing text with dance, mime, clowning, wrestling, and the sounds of traditional Asian instruments. The effect demonstrates the lure of traditional kabuki drama, Chinese opera, and southern Filipino dance. The blend exag-gerates emotion and action, creating a styl-ized presentation of stories weaving Eastern and Western motifs. By blending non-verbal dialogue, movement, drumming, gestures, and pauses, they create a kinetic sculpture that appeals to maverick listeners, the type of audi-ence that is fast replacing the former white upper- and middle-class cornerstones of American opera, theater, and symphony orga-nizations.

Eth-Noh-Tec spearheads a vital boost to the multicultural market. Since 1978, Yngojo, a third-generation Japanese and second-gener-ation Filipino, has performed Kulintang music, which features a South Filipino bronze gong. He introduced the instrument to the San Francisco Bay Area through children's programs and through directing and per-forming with ensembles for general audi-ences. Supported by grants from the G & G Educational Fund, San Francisco Grants for the Arts, Asian American Arts Foundation, Zellerbach Family Fund, NEA Folk Arts, and the California Arts Council, he displays his talents with Thai, Cambodian, Laotian, Chi-nese, Japanese, and Indonesian instruments as well as synthesizers. He has helped found music groups such as the Noh Buddies, Bam-boo and Yokohama. His musical compositions

undergird two films: Janet Adler's *Still Looking* and Felicia Lowe's *Carved in Silence*, a docudrama on Asian immigration and racism. He also wrote for Wayne Wang's films, *Chan Is Missing* and *Eat a Bowl of Tea*.

After Yngojo's formation of a partnership with dancer/playwright Nancy Wang in 1981, the duo began searching for nonviolent ancient folk tales of courage and triumph. The pair places movement and dialogue in the text and creates the characters they will mime. Wang, who is fifth generation Chinese-American and a psychotherapist, learned modern dance and theatrical satire under Gloria Unti of the San Francisco Performing Arts Workshop. A teacher, dancer, and choreographer, she was involved with the Asian-American Dance Collective and the Asian-American theater when she met Yngojo. His interest in fusion, jazz, folk, and traditional and world music linked with her love of drama and dance. Wedded in talent and point of view, they formed Eth-Noh-Tec in 1985, a departure from the improvisation and loose performance style of traditional storytelling.

After their command of music and dance merged with theater, Eth-Noh-Tec began exploring storytelling at the request of a friend, who asked if they knew any stories to perform for a conference she was putting together. Their first story, "Ten Thousand Treasure Cave," a Chinese folktale, served a dual purpose in opening their performances to narrative and establishing a mission to serve others through storytelling. For Festival 2000, they performed "If We Only Knew," a play of their tightly choreographed repertory. In a collaboration commissioned by the San Jose Taiko drum group, the duo performed "The Legend of Singkil," an award-winning percussion and dance theater piece depicting the origin of the Singkil Bamboo dance from the Filipino island of Mindanao. Their repertoire covers tales from China, Japan, Korea, Tibet, India, and Southeast Asia. In 1994, they were featured tellers at the National Storytelling Festival. They have also been featured tellers at Timpanogos Storytelling Festival, Michigan Storytelling Festival, and Three Apples Storytelling Festival. Annually, they put on 350–400 performances at libraries, festivals, theaters, and schools before more than 350,000 people.

Eth-Noh-Tec's tours carry diversity to a diverse audience with themes of harmony, peace, and acceptance of all cultures. Storytelling, Wang declares, is "a bridge worth building." Yngojo adds that telling inspires his joy and pride in being human and in linking with people of all ages, professions, and backgrounds. The sharing of feeling builds on commonalities and strengthens bonds with others. He expresses a high regard for the "unseen army of volunteers, supporters, presenters, businesses, and organizations that bring together the family of tellers who energize festivals. In 1997, their deft movement in storytelling was a featured act at the Presidential Inauguration Celebration at the Smithsonian Discovery Theater in Washington, D.C., where they performed their duet, "Asian Treasure Bag."

Bibliography
"Tanuki and the Magic Fan," in *We Like Kids*, Good Year Books, 1995.

Videography
"Asian-American Stories," in *Jackie Torrence Presents Stories from Around the World*, National Training Network, 1995.
Asian Treasure Bag of Folktales, Eth-Noh-Tec and Bridge Media, 1994.

Audiography
Tales of Terror, Eth-Noh-Tec, 1995.
Treasure Bag of Asian Tales, Eth-Noh-Tec, 1992.

Awards
1996 Parent's Choice Gold Award for *Asian Treasure Bag of Folktales*.
1996 Emmy for best new children's PBS pilot, "Short Stories, Tall Tales."
1996 Bronze Telly Award for solo videos of Asian-American stories.
1995 Parent's Choice Silver Award for *Asian Treasure Bag of Folktales*.
1991 Izzy Award for sound, score, music, and text of *Legend of Singkil*.
1981–1997 grants from NEA Folk Art, California Arts Council, Zellerbach Family Fund, G & G Education Fund, San Francisco Grants for the Arts, San Francisco Foundation, Haas Fund, Asian American Arts Foundation, New Langton Arts, San Francisco Volunteer Arts Contribution Fund, Cultural Equity Grant, San Francisco Mayor's Office of Children, Youth, and Families.

Source
"Asian Treasure Bag of Folktales," http://www.svemedia.com/asian.html.

"Eth-Noh-Tec," http://www.tcpsf.com/ent.html, May 14, 1997.
Felciano, Rita, "Close to the Edge," *San Francisco Bay Guardian*, October 7, 1992.
"Jackie Torrence Presents ... Stories from Around the World from Curriculum Associates," http://www.curriculumassociates.com//publications/jtorrence.html.
Malitz, Nancy, "Ethnic Voices Call the Tune in the Cities," *New York Times*, February 6, 1994, section 2, pp. 1, 26.
Rodriguez, Johnette, "A Diverse Storytelling Festival," *Providence Phoenix*, September 20, 1994.
"Spinning Yarns," *Indianapolis Business Journal*, September 4, 1995, 16.
Surdut, Beth, "Storytellers Dazzle Children and Adults Alike," *Harvard Spirit*, October 2, 1996.
White, Jon, "Spinning Yarns," *Indianapolis Business Journal*, January 1, 1995.

LINDA FANG
[FAHNG]

Address: P. O. Box 10276
Rockville, Maryland 20849-0276
phone and fax 301-838-9614

Focus: ancient Chinese stories collected from Chinese history, anecdotes, and opera
Audience: all ages.
Style: dynamic gesture and incorporation of the audience into the telling.
Instruments/Props: Chinese costumes, props.

The founder of the Washington Storyteller's Theatre, Linda Fang is at home with fanciful narrative. A native of Summit, New Jersey, she lived two years in the United States before traveling with her parents to their native Shanghai, China, where she spent the rest of her childhood. She recalls evenings after dinner, when her sisters and brother joined her in anticipation of their mother's retelling of a novel she was reading. At age eight, Fang listened to her father read storytelling scripts handed down from the Yüan Dynasty (1271–1368). He

awakened her from a nap and insisted that she join him in reading from *The Outlaws of the Marsh*, which she eventually read alone in an ancient Chinese dialect. In elementary school, a teacher helped her overcome shyness by reading and telling stories. On her own, she learned to love Hsi-ch'ü, or Chinese opera, a cycle of happy and sad tales which date to the T'ang Dynasty (618–907).

Re-established in the United States in 1980, Fang completed graduate study in English at Georgetown University in Washington, D. C. She worked eight years as programmer and community services aid for WRC-TV before moving into full-time storytelling in 1987. Her impetus was a performance of Jon Spelman at which he related "Three Stories Tall." She volunteered to tell before an audience and delighted in their response. Her repertory, illuminated by ethnic props and authentic costume and hairstyle, introduces American audiences to stories gleaned from Chinese history, Peking opera, Ming dynasty novels, and folktales.

A winner of multiple awards from the D.C. Commission on the Arts and Humanities, Fang has performed on WPFW's "Golden Mountain" and National Public Radio's "Crossroads," for the Asia Society and the Arts Club of Washington and at the Kennedy Center, Smithsonian Institution's National The-atre, Wolf Trap, and Round House Theatre. Festivals have taken her to the Clearwater Revival, Corn Island, and House, Texas. Museum and university performances have featured her work at the Southeast Texas Art Museum, Arthur M. Sackler Gallery, Nelson-Atkins Museum, and Johns Hopkins and Maryland universities. She has performed at the Round House Theatre her one-woman show, "Men Li-jun, the Woman Prime Minister," which derives from a Chinese opera. She published *The Ch'i-lin Purse*, a collection of ancient Chinese stories.

Articles
"Chinese Storytelling a Living Tradition," *Tale Trader*, November 1994.

Bibliography
The Ch'i-lin Purse, Farrar, Straus and Giroux, 1995.
"Mr. Yeh's New Year," *Storytelling Magazine*, January 1996, 31–33. A story taken from Yüeh Opera about the custom of settling debts on New Year's Day.

Awards
1996 *Storytelling World* Tellable Tale Award for *The Ch'i-lin Purse*.

Source
"Brushing Up on Chinese Art," *Washington Post*, July 21, 1989.
Burns, Mary W., "Booklist: Folklore," *Horn Book*, May/June 1995, 335–336.
"Chinese Storytelling, a Living Tradition," *Tale Trader*, November 1994.
Devereaux, Elizabeth, and Diane Roback, "Children's Books," *Publishers Weekly*, December 5, 1994, 77.
"Linda Fang Gives American Children a Taste of the Chinese Culture," *World Review*, July 5, 1992.
"The Lost Art of Storytelling," *Northwest Current*, January 13, 1993.
Phelan, Carolyn, "Starred Reviews: Books for Youth," *Booklist*, January 15, 1995, 924.
Philbrook, John, "Book Review: Grades 3–6," *School Library Journal*, May 1995, 202–203.
"Storyteller Captures Young Hearts," *World Journal*, January 29, 1989.
"Storyteller Weaves Oriental Tales," *Beaumont Enterprise*, January 31, 1991.

DIANE FERLATTE

Address: 6531 Chabot Road
          Oakland, California 94518
   phone 510-655-2719

Focus: African-American, Southern, and African folklore; trickster, ghost, and humorous stories; multicultural character stories.

Audience: all ages.

Style: dynamic stage presentation utilizing instrumentation and singing with audience participation.

Instruments/Props: some African costuming, rhythm stick, shakere, Bantu *mbira* or thumb piano, occasionally stage props and accompanying drummer or banjo player.

A gifted, charismatic teller in griot style, Diane Ferlatte was steeped in the oral tradition. She spent her early childhood in Louisiana on her grandparent's porch with the family and neighbors swapping stories, lies, and tales. After moving to California as an adolescent, she made an annual trek back to family in Louisiana, where she recalls fishing in the bayou, wholecake bread, singing, and storytelling. As always, her raconteur father led the way with family news and history. As she grew older, she played the piano and sang in church choirs, performed in various stage productions, and became proficient in American sign language, all of which contributed to a completely unforeseen career in storytelling.

The seed of Ferlatte's career was planted in 1980 after she adopted her second child. Three-year-old Joey had been raised in foster homes in front of a television set. At age four, he knew the names of shows and their characters, but he couldn't recite the alphabet or count. Ferlatte realized that the nightly reading of stories to daughter Cicely was not interesting to Joey. Committed to breaking him from television and increasing his readiness for school, Ferlatte started to read and tell in the style she has made famous—dynamic characterization with animation, expression, and interaction. When her church gave a Christmas party for foster and homeless children, she chaired the program committee. Her career was born after she told some Christmas stories and received requests to tell at parties, schools, and libraries. Eventually, she had to choose between her clerical job of seventeen years and the increasing number of invitations to tell stories. After discussing the move with her husband, she decided that it was worth the risk to make a living at something she loves and finds rewarding.

Currently, Ferlatte is at the forefront of the multicultural renaissance of the oral tradition. She augments inventive stagecraft with an actor's skill at expression, gesture, and intense emotion to create multiple characters for each story. Embracing her role as a traditional transmitter of folk history, culture, and values, she thrives on Southern and African-American lore. A desire to share the morals and ethics that are common to all cultures impels her to include yarns from many cultures in her repertory.

Ferlatte has wowed audiences across the globe from Graz, Austria, to Perth, Australia. She has traveled extensively to Holland, Bermuda, Sweden, Hawaii, and New Zealand, and across the United States to perform at festivals, conferences, symposiums, or tours. Providing workshops for other tellers, ministers, and teachers and serving as keynote speaker/storyteller at professional conferences and conventions makes up a large part of her work. Besides performing at universities, colleges, theaters, museums, churches, rest homes, and youth facilities, she continues to perform at schools and libraries as often as possible to nurture the tradition of storytelling and to teach the lessons in stories. She is featured in McDougal-Littell's textbook and laserdisc, *Language of Literature*, a series for middle school grades.

Among her favorite venues are the "Stories on the Front Porch" project for the Berkeley Arts Festival as well as "Sapelo," the one-woman show she and colleague Beverlee Patton-Miller developed about residents of Hog Hammock. This performance evolved after Ferlatte's month-long immersion in the West African Gullah folk culture of Sapelo Island, one of the Georgia Sea Islands. She has also

African Story Journey: The American South, Filmic Archives, 1997.

African Story Magic, Family Home Entertainment, 1992.

"Interview," *The Twentieth Anniversary of the National Storytelling Festival,* Hometown Entertainment, 1994.

"The Keys to the Kingdom," in *Tell Me a Story, Vol. 2,* Hometown Entertainment, 1995.

"The Witch Woman and the Spinning Wheel," in *A Storytelling Treasury,* Vol. 3, National Storytelling Press, 1993.

Audiography

"Brer Tiger and the Big Wind," on *Sierra Storytelling Festival Best of 1987* (audiocassette), Bennett House, 1987.

Favorite Stories (audiocassette), Olde West, 1991. Contains "Wiley & the Hairy Man," "The Knee High Man," "Horned Animals Party," "Why the Sky Is So High," and "Bubba & the Snake."

"The Knee High Man," on *StorySpinners* (audiocassette), Course Crafters Inc., 1997.

Sapelo: Time is Winding Up (co-author Beverlee Patton-Miller) (audiocassette), self-published, 1992. Contains tales from a Georgia Sea Island

"Why the Sky Is So High," on *Rainbow Tales* (CD), Rounder Records, 1997.

Awards

1996–1998 Selection for the *Touring Artists Directory* of the California Arts Council.

1994 National Endowment for the Arts Grant.

1993 American Library Association Service to Children Notable Recording Award for *Favorite Stories.*

1993 American Library Association Service to Children Notable Recording Award for *Sapelo: Time Is Winding Up.*

1992 Parents' Choice Award for *Favorite Stories.*

1989 Festival 2000 Grant.

made numerous visits to the Appalachians to study the influence that African-Americans have made on mountain music, dance, and folk culture. She received a commendation from the mayor of Oakland, California, for co-directing the Sixth National Festival of Black Storytelling. Her most memorable occasion was meeting and performing for President Bill Clinton at the inaugural "Salute to Children," held at the Kennedy Center in Washington, D.C. Currently, she and husband Tomas and their children are planning to add audio tapes to her collection. In collaboration with other artists, she is working on the *Memory* project for the San Francisco Exploratorium and on *Invisible Wings,* a commemoration of the Underground Railroad with Zaccho Dance Theater.

Bibliography

"The Changer" in *African Americans: Voices of Triumph-Creative Fire,* Time-Life Books, 1994.

"The Cow Tail Switch" (textbook and laserdisc), *The Language of Literature,* McDougal-Littell, 1997, 632–635.

"The Horned Animals' Party" in *Ready-to-Tell Tales,* August House, 1994.

Videography

African Story Journey: Across Time and Place, Filmic Archives, 1997.

Source

"A Brief Look at This Year's Storytellers," *Herald & Tribune,* September 30, 1992, 4C–8C.

Gere, David, "Scarred Spirits Surface in Two Moving Tales," *Oakland Tribune,* October 11, 1990, B5.

Mooney, Bill, and David Holt. *The Storyteller's*

Guide. Little Rock, Arkansas: August House, 1996.

Scott, Nancy, "Stories Her Ticket to the Inaugural," *San Francisco Examiner*, January 13, 1993.

Tucker, Marilyn, "Two Big Pluses at Festival 2000," *San Francisco Chronicle*, October 11, 1990, E2.

Young, Susan, "Storyteller's Own Story Has an Inaugural Ending," San Francisco *Daily Review,* January 9, 1993, D1–D6.

HEATHER FOREST

Address: Story Arts
              P. O. Box 354
              Huntington, New York 11743
phone 516-241-2511
fax 516-271-2046
email hforest@pb.net
web site www.storyarts.org

Focus: feminist and world folktales; beast fables; European fairy lore; group participation stories; the common strands of human experience.

Audience: children, adults, mixed ages.

Style: a blend of prose, verse, original guitar and vocal music, vocal sound effects, dance, and narration; interpretation by signers for the deaf.

Instruments/Props: folk guitar, recorder, wooden box drum and hand drum, sticks.

A rare minstrel who combines original melodies with folk guitar, verse, singing, miming, and prose narrative, Heather Forest is an award-winning spinner of yarns, one of the world's oldest hearthside pastimes. She terms the art of narrative a "human tapestry" and a "mirror for the soul," which allows the audience to transcend the moment as their imaginations take them to secret and wonderful climes. Her work, which tends toward traditional lore rather than personal experience,

displays the kernel of universal wisdom that undergirds a classic fable. To interviewer Dan Keding, a fellow teller and columnist for *Sing Out*, she confided:

> When I'm telling an old story I get a chill up my spine thinking that I'm touching tongue with the same story that someone might have told a thousand years ago. I feel that it's a message that someone long ago felt that this was important enough to save.

Her fresh, original retellings are frequently anthologized, including stories in *Joining In: Audience Participation Stories*; *Spinning Tales-Weaving Hope: Tales of Peace, Justice, and the Environment*; *Best Loved Stories Told at the National Storytelling Festival, Vol. II*; *The Ghost and I*; *Ready to Tell Tales*; and *Chosen Tales*. Thriving in the artistic community of Huntington, New York, she directs Story Arts, which offers workshops, arts-in-education programs, and storytelling concerts. Her children's books grow out of a collaboration with artist Susan Gaber, who illustrated *The Baker's Dozen: A Colonial American Tale*, a holiday book drawn from the legend of Van Amsterdam, a Dutch baker who worked in Albany, New York, in 1655. Gaber attended to important details, such as the use of sackcloth for packaging in an era before the invention of paper and plastic shopping bags. Forest was pleased that the final text reads well aloud, a requisite of storybooks meant to be read by teachers, librarians, recreation leaders, and parents. Her second storybook with Gaber, *The Woman Who Flummoxed the Fairies*, is an old Scottish tale about a strong woman balancing the responsibilities of home and career.

Coming of age during the American folk music renaissance, Forest discovered the guitar at age fourteen and worked at a summer job to buy her first instrument, a Harmony folk guitar. Without formal lessons, she learned popular songs as well as children's ballads. At age twenty, she returned to her favorite reading in folktales, which she had discovered in childhood in the local library's 398.2 section. Realizing that stories lie at the heart of the arts, she tapped into the magic of theater, musical composition, and narrative dance for narrative's unique communication with an audience. To prepare a version for presentation, she practiced by ear, working out the interplay of pause and cadence to suit the mood and themes, interjecting verse, song, and guitar accompaniment as enhancements to the story's dynamics. She chose stories that ancient tellers had pared down over time until they reached the bedrock of meaning. By 1974 she was winning audiences with a grace derived from self-confidence, practice, and studies in mime, modern dance, and ballet. In 1979 she declared herself a professional storyteller and has since become a respected spokesperson for the art, its canon, and its followers.

Forest is a natural at channeling energy and nuance and tailoring gestures, acoustic sound effects, and facial expressions to the needs of the text, which unfolds as she and the audience imagine together the scenic word pictures. Using her flexible, multifaceted voice as a prime instrument, she sets her tales among castles and hearthsides, maidens, talking animals, and supernatural beings. To express these far-flung images, she selects words for her repertoire that convey a metaphorical glimpse of human nature. The founder and executive director of Story Arts, she anchors her work at Fox Hollow Tree Farm in Long Island, New York, where she lives with husband Larry Foglia and their children, Laurel and Lucas.

Underwritten with funds from the New York State Council on the Arts and the Suffolk County Department of Cultural Affairs, Forest travels to local schools and community gatherings and performs for over 40,000 children annually. A favorite troubadour at a variety of gatherings, she was a keynoter at the National Storytelling Congress and has performed at the Smithsonian Institution, Museum of Modern Art in New York City, Edinburgh Festival Fringe, World Festival of Fairytales in Austria, Jakarta International Storytelling Festival, Omega Institute, Timpanogos and Toronto storytelling festivals, Tell It in the Mountains, Clearwater Folk Festival, and National Storytelling Festival in Jonesborough, Tennessee. Performances for educational institutions have taken her to Queens College, University of San Diego, and

North Texas University as well as language and library conferences in Indiana, Colorado, Virginia, California, New York, Massachusetts, Florida, New Jersey, Maryland, Maine, Michigan, Louisiana, Tennessee, and Kansas.

Articles

"Storytellers' Views on Blending Narrative and Song," *Storytelling Magazine*, May 1997, 16–20.

"Storytelling: The Magic of Words," *The Whole Idea*, Summer 1993, 6–7.

Bibliography

The Baker's Dozen ... A Colonial American Tale, Harcourt Brace Jovanovich, 1989. The legend behind the custom of giving thirteen in a baker's dozen.

A Big Quiet House: A Yiddish Folktale from Eastern Europe (illustrator Susan Greenstein), August House, 1996. A Jewish folktale about a wise adviser.

"The Ghost's Gold," *in Scary Stories for Participatory Telling*, Yellow Moon Press, 1992. Features 20 funny and scary stories and songs for ages 5–14.

"King Solomon and the Otter," in *Spinning Tales, Weaving Hope: Stories of Peace, Justice, and the Environment*, New Society, 1992.

"The Lion and the Rabbit," in *Joining In — An Anthology of Audience Participation Stories and How to Tell Them*, Yellow Moon, 1988. Eighteen participation stories for all ages.

Stone Soup, August House, 1997. A traditional European tale about sharing.

"The Tale of Dame Ragnel," in *More Best-Loved Stories Told at the National Storytelling Festival*, August House, 1992.

"The Talking Skull," in *Ready-to-Tell Tales*, August House, 1994.

Wisdom Tales from Around the World, August House, 1996. A compendium of fifty stories taken from the Sufi, Zen, Taoist, Christian, Jewish, Buddhist, African, and native American traditions.

The Woman Who Flummoxed the Fairies ... An Old Tale from Scotland, Harcourt Brace Jovanovich, 1990. A Scottish tale of magic, fun, and good sense.

Wonder Tales from Around the World, August House, 1995. A collection of 27 multicultural folktales complemented by full-page illustration.

Videography

"Arachne," in *American Storytelling Series, Vol. 3*, H. W. Wilson, 1987.

By Word of Mouth, National Storytelling Festival.

"A King Solomon Tale," in *Tell Me a Story, Vol. 3*, Hometown Entertainment, 1995.

Audiography

The Animals Could Talk (audiocassette), August House, 1994. A musical collection of nineteen Aesop's fables, accompanied by an illustrated read-along libretto; original guitar music.

"The Beggar King," in *The Treasury* (audiocassette), National Storytelling Festival, 1993.

The Eye of the Beholder (audiocassette), Yellow Moon Press, 1993. Contains "The Nightingale," the Arthurian legend of Dame Ragnel, and a unique musical version of "Beauty and the Beast."

Sing Me a Story (audiocassette), A Gentle Wind, 1986. A collection of musical tales on cooperation and sharing, including "Three Billy Goats Gruff," "The Little Red Hen," "The Tortoise and the Hare," "Stone Soup," "The Acorn Song," and "Too Much Noise."

Songspinner: Folktales and Fables Sung and Told (audiocassette), Weston Woods 1982. Musical and verse wisdom tales from around the world, this includes "The Garden," an African creation myth; "The Stonecutter," a Japanese circle story that grows out of illusion; "King Solomon and the Otter," a Hebrew fable about peace and interconnectedness; "Bear's Picture," which details the sacredness of vision and freedom of expression; "The Useless Tree," a 2,000-year-old Chinese tale; "The Smuggler," a Sufi story; "Aesop's The Sun and the Wind," and "The Baker's Smell."

"The Squire's Bride," in *Tales of Fools and Wise Folk* (audiocassette), National Association for the Preservation and Perpetuation of Storytelling, 1991.

Tales Around the Hearth (audiocassette), Gentle Wind, 1989. A compendium of world folktales that includes Aesop's fables, "The Turnip," "Try, Try Again," "Rabbit's Hole," and "The Grandfather Clock," a morality tale about a clock overwhelmed by overwork.

Tales of Womenfolk (audiocassette), Weston Woods, 1985. World folktales featuring such courageous and resourceful heroines as Janet, who saves her lover in *Janet and Tamlin*, and three generations of Japanese women who instruct a Sumo wrestler about strength in "Three Strong Women."

Wonder Tales from Around the World (audio book), August House, 1996. Six tales with rhyming refrains; accompanied by original music.

Awards

1997 National Storytelling Association Circle of Excellence Award.

1997 *Storytelling World* Anthology Award for *Wisdom Tales from Around the World*.

1996 American Booksellers Association Pick of the List for *A Big Quiet House*.

1996 *Storytelling World* Honor Tape for *Wonder Tales from Around the World*.

1996 *Storytelling World* Anthology Award for *Wonder Tales from Around the World*.

1995 *Storytelling World* Honor Tape Award for *The Eye of the Beholder*.

1994 Parents' Choice Gold Award for *The Animals Could Talk*.

1993 Parents' Choice Gold Classic Award for *The Eye of the Beholder*.

1990 American Booksellers Association Pick of the List for *The Woman Who Flummoxed the Fairies ... An Old Tale from Scotland*.

1990 Junior Library Guild Selection for *The Woman Who Flummoxed the Fairies ... An Old Tale from Scotland*.

1989 Children's Literature Center of the Library of Congress selection of *The Baker's Dozen ... A Colonial American Tale*.

1989 American Institute for Graphic Arts Award for *The Baker's Dozen ... A Colonial American Tale*.

1982 American Library Association Notable Record award for *Songspinner: Folktales and Fables Sung and Told*.

Source

Carey, Kim, "McConnell Receives NSA's Life-time Achievement Award," *Tale Trader*, August 1997, 1, 4.

Delatiner, Barbara, "Artist, Reciter Try a Collaboration, *New York Times*, December 4, 1988.

_____, "Stories to Pique a Listener's Imagination, *New York Times*, July 11, 1982.

"Five Storytellers Receive Honors," *Storytelling Magazine*, May 1997, 41.

"From Page to Stage," *Storytelling World*, Winter/Spring 1997, 16–17.

Geisler, Harlynne, and Flora Joy, "The Eye of the Beholder" (review), *Yarnspinner*, December 1991.

"Heather Forest," http://www.hometoonet.com/forest.html.

"Heather Forest at Flower Hill," *Huntington, New York, Long-Islander*, March 31, 1988.

"Heather Forest: Tales Around the Hearth," *Creations Magazine*, Winter 1989/1990.

Hornsby, Melanie, "Touching a Full Range of Emotions," *Herald & Tribune*, September 29, 1993, 4-C.

"Images of Transformation," *Arkansas Democrat & Gazette*, April 7, 1995.

Keding, Dan, "The Endless Tale: Heather Forest," *Sing Out*, May/June/July 1995.

Lipschultz, Geri, "Women in the Arts, the Never-Ending Story of Heather Forest," *North Shore Woman's Newspaper*, March 1995.

"Lively Tales from Heather Forest," *London Daily Telegraph*, August 22, 1980.

Maples, Tina, "Her Words Are Worth a Thousand Pictures," *Milwaukee Journal*, August 22, 1985.

Matyascik, Jessica, "Listen Up: Heather Forest Would Rather Entertain Ears, Not Eyes," Penn State *Collegian Magazine*, July 7, 1993.

Miner, Mary-Jean, "The Eighth Festival of Storytelling," *Martha's Vineyard Times*, June 29, 1995.

"Modern Minstrel Heather Forest Enchants the Children," *Rockeville Centre Herald*, July 11–17, 1991.

Mooney, Bill, and David Hold. *The Storyteller's Guide*. Little Rock, Ark.: August House, 1996.

Pantoga, Elfrieda, "Storyteller Taps Imagination," *Milwaukee Sentinel*, August 3, 1984.

Shedden, Mary, "Telling Stories in the TV Age," *Suffolk, Long Island, Newsday,* July 18, 1990.

Smith, Kay, "Storyteller," Edinburgh, Scotland, *Festival Times,* August 21, 1980.

Timeless Voices: Images of the National Storytelling Festival. Jonesborough, Tenn.: National Storytelling Press, 1997.

BARBARA FREEMAN

Address: God's Funny Valentine
Grace Station, Box 18737
Asheville, North Carolina 28814
phone 704-258-0340

Focus: traditional and comic Appalachian tales; ghost stories; Western European tradition; devil tales; lives of Christian saints and martyrs.

Audience: families, children's groups.

Style: concerts meshing intense, dynamic, funny, mild, and tender stories; has performed solo as well as in tandem with Connie Regan-Blake.

Instruments/Props: puppets, stuffed animals, crocheted boa, quilts, limberjacks, overalls, banjo.

Recognized as one of storytelling's pathfinders, Barbara Freeman has been lauded at major North American festivals and in Japan, Korea, and the Philippines as the cream of Appalachian raconteurs. In 1975, at the beginning of the storytelling renaissance, a resurgence of folk culture, she joined her first cousin, Connie Regan-Blake, in a duo called the Folktellers, an innovative traveling act. With only $2,000 to invest, they drove their yellow Datsun truck and camper D'Put to bookings. At the Fox Hollow Folk Festival in Petersburg, New York, a flood forced them to park their truck near the performer's area, where they met other pioneers in the yarning business. From a parking lot experience in Hartford, Connecticut, they improvised their ping-pong-style tandem tellings of "Three Billy Goats Gruff" and Maurice Sendak's *Where the Wild Things Are,* a favorite story-book requested by a child in the audience. A ransacking of their truck robbed them of clothes, money, keepsakes, and tapes, leaving them entirely dependent on their art. A stage triumph preceded requests for their bibliography and offers to teach workshops and credit courses.

Freeman has been recognized on *Good Morning America* and by *Laugh Makers Magazine* and *School Library Journal.* She has performed for UNICEF, Rocky Mountain Healing Arts Festival, National Bicentennial Folk Festival in Washington, D.C., military bases in Okinawa, Philippines, Korea, and Japan, Lincoln Center for the Performing Arts, World's Fair, Old Faithful in Yellowstone National Park, Physician's Weekend at the Grove Park Inn, Belle Cher Celebration, Healing Arts Festival, and Washington D.C. Ethical Society, and to festivals in San Diego, Chicago, Vancouver, Winnipeg, Ithaca, Michigan, Knoxville, Alaska, Long Island, St. Louis, Charlotte, Philadelphia, Maine, Connecticut, Lincoln, England, and Monterey, California.

With promoter Jimmy Neil Smith, the duo helped establish the National Association for the Preservation and Perpetuation of Storytelling (NAPPS) and, for ten years, served as directors and designers of annual festivals and narrative resources. Along the way, they nurtured new talent and earned from Ed Stivender perpetual thanks for being missionaries of storytelling and his personal fairy godmothers. For their two-act play, *Mountain Sweet Talk,* they joined writer-storyteller John Basinger and his daughter Savannah Basinger to create two tough mountain characters, Sarah and Jenny Rose, both outgrowths of Regan-Blake's family stories. Playing at the Folk Art Center near Asheville with technical support from the duo's husbands, Phil Blake and Mike Vaniman, the play ran from 1980 to 1988 and earned strong support from reviewers for *Southern Living, Good Housekeeping,* and *Good Morning America.* Since separating into a solo act, Freeman has introduced a Christian element into her telling. Her material has grown to include biographies of Christian saints and martyrs. She continues to perform with Regan-Blake for reunion festivals.

Bibliography

"No News," in *Best-Loved Stories Told at the National Storytelling Festival*, August House, 1991.

"No News," in *Homespun: Tales from America's Favorite Storytellers*, Crown, 1988.

"Old Drye Frye," in *Homespun: Tales from America's Favorite Storytellers*, Crown, 1988.

Stories for the Telling (bibliography), 1977.

"Two White Horses," in *Homespun: Tales from America's Favorite Storytellers*, Crown, 1988.

Videography

"No News," in *American Storytelling Series, Vol. 5*, H. W. Wilson, 1987.

Pennies, Pets & Peanut Butter: Stories for Children, The Storytellers, 1994. Contains "The Judge," "A Penny a Look," "Peanut Butter," "Crictor," "The Jazzy Three Bears," and "I Know an Old Lady"; for children.

Storytelling: Tales and Techniques, The Folktellers. 1994. Advice to novice tellers concerning sound effects, gestures, music, and selection of material for children; for teachers, librarians, and parents.

Audiography

Chillers (co-producer Barbara Freeman) (audiocassette), Mama-T Artists, 1983. Scary stories blended with humor for teenagers through adults.

Christmas at the Homeplace (audiocassette), The Folktellers, 1992. Old-time stories and songs for the holiday.

"The Foolish Bet," on *Homespun Tales* (audiocassette), NAPPS, 1986.

"The Ghoul," on *Graveyard Tales* (audiocassette), National Association for the Preservation and Perpetuation of Storytelling, 1989.

"Introducing Old Drye Frye," on *Tales of Fools and Wise Folk* (audiocassette), National Association for the Preservation and Perpetuation of Storytelling.

Mountain Sweet Talk (double audiocassette; co-producer Barbara Freeman), self-published, 1988. Contains "Chubbies," "Fishing Lantern," "Time Has Made a Change," "Mary Culhane and the Dead Man," "The Drunkard," "The Mountain Whippoorwill," "No News," "Drye Frye's Teeth," "Two White Horses," "Oliver Hyde's Dishcloth Concert," and "The Bet," along with vocals—"Sweet Sunny South," "Great Aunt Jenny's Theme," "Precious Memories," and "Oliver Hyde"—and accompaniment on fiddle, guitar, and banjo.

Stories for the Road (audiocassette), Mama-T Artists, 1992. Family stories for car travel and rainy afternoons, including "Peanut Butter," "The Sneakout Mountain Diary," "Yellow Ribbon," "Jazzy Three Bears," "The Dancing Man," and "Come Again in the Spring"; for all ages.

Tales to Grow On (co-produced with Barbara Freeman) (audiocassette), Weston Woods, 1983. Mountain tales and participation stories, including "Wicked John and the Devil"; for kindergarten through sixth grade.

White Horses and Whippoorwills (co-producer Barbara Freeman) (audiocassette), Folk Legacy 1983. Powerful and moving mountain tales, including "The Three Bears" and "Two White Horses"; for fifth grade through adult.

Awards

1996 National Storytelling Association Circle of Excellence.

1994 Parents' Choice Silver Honor Award for *Pennies, Pets & Peanut Butter: Stories for Children*.

1994 *Storytelling World* Award for *Pennies, Pets & Peanut Butter: Stories for Children.*

1993 American Library Association Notable Record Award for *Tales to Grow On.*

1992 American Library Association Notable Record Award for *Stories for the Road.*

1992 Parents' Choice Award for *Christmas at the Homeplace.*

1983 American Library Association Notable Record Award for *Chillers.*

Source

Brown, Tony, "Two Tell Tall Tales: Storytelling Cousins Blend Differing Perspective of Their Appalachian Heritage As They Spread Joy from Asheville to Asia," *Charlotte Observer*, March 1, 1989, 1D.

Gibbons, Cathy, "The Folktellers," *Laugh Makers Variety Arts Magazine*, Vol. 12, 1994, 272–274.

LaPrise, Ann West, "Review," *School Library Journal*, July 1993.

Mandell, Phyllis Levy, "1995 Award-Winning Films and Videos: Language Arts," *School Library Journal*, April 1996, 54.

Mitnick, Fritz, "Audiovisual Review: Recordings," *School Library Journal*, July 1993, 52.

Mooney, Bill, and David Holt. *The Storyteller's Guide.* Little Rock, Ark.: August House, 1996.

"Review," *Booklist*, March 15, 1993.

"Review," *National Storytelling Journal*, Winter 1987.

Sanborn, LaVonne, "Review,'" *School Library Journal*, April 1995.

Sellen, Betty-Carol. *What Else You Can Do with a College Degree.* Gaylord, 1980.

Stein, Rachel, "Review," *The Arts Journal*, October 1985.

Stewart, Barbara Home, "The Folktellers: Scheherazades in Denim," *School Library Journal*, November 1978, 17–21.

_____, "The Mountain Sweet Sound of Success: Folktellers '89," *School Library Journal*, November 1989, 17.

Thomas, Dr. James L., Carol Lawrence, and Jennabeth Hutcherson. *Storytelling for Teachers and Media Specialists.* Minneapolis: T. S. Denison & Co., 1980.

Timeless Voices: Images of the National Storytelling Festival. Jonesborough, Tenn.: National Storytelling Press, 1997.

Weyler, Rex, "On the Road with the Folktellers," *New Age*, July 1980, 26–33, 62–63.

White, Barb, "Review of 'Storytelling: Tales & Techniques,'" *School Library Journal*, April 1995.

See also John Basinger; Connie Regan-Blake.

MARA FREEMAN

Address: P. O. Box 3839
Carmel, California 93921
phone 408-622-0330
fax 408-625-2020
email chalice@redshift.com
website www.redshift.com/~celtic/

Focus: Celtic myths and legends; animal tales; wisdom and goddess lore; ballads.
Audience: general.
Style: melodious, poetic; lyric performance.
Instruments/Props: zither, hammered dul-

cimer; with musician Gerry Smida: bagpipe, Celtic harp, whistle, drum.

Bardic storyteller and author Mara Freeman weaves the wisdom and lore of the Celtic tradition. Influenced by Irish storyteller Ella Young, a companion of poet W. B. Yeats, who lived in Carmel, California, in the 1920s, Freeman has revived American interest in the romance and wonder of Celtic lore. She has also been inspired by Robin Williamson, a Scottish musician and storyteller. Freeman, who lives with her English husband and two cats, Prudence and Pandora, is at home in California. She comments, "It's not unlike the Celtic countries when the mist comes in... It has magical sense of place" (Nichols, 1996, 5D). She balances dual careers as mythographer and licensed psychotherapist in private practice. Freeman sets out to recreate the bardic atmosphere of Celtic storytelling with a poetic delivery set to the hypnotic sound of stringed instruments tuned to ancient Celtic scales. She embroiders sea voyages, love stories, shamanic journeys, and animal tales with rhyme and incantatory passages known in Gaelic as *ranns*. Her aim is to take listeners into the Celtic dreamtime as an antidote to the profane modern world.

Born and raised in the British Isles, Freeman has the bard's gift for another time and place. She absorbed the traditions of the Celtic countries and was fascinated by the magic of song and story as gateway to the otherworld. Her first experience with Celtic music came from a film in an elementary school geography class. The experience inspired her to dress in plaid, gather Scottish dialect from storybooks, and change her name to Heather. In her teens, during time she should have devoted to lessons, she spent hours in the library reading Celtic legends and songs and studying a map of Scotland. Educated at Bristol and London universities in England, she achieved honors while earning degrees in literature, language, and education; upon resettling in the United States, she obtained an M.S. in psychology from Chapman University. During her college years she produced story dramas, rituals, dances and songs on themes from Celtic mythology, including a Mayday dance

and verse play entitled "The Three Faces of the Moon Goddess." She took inspiration from such sacred sites as Avebury, Stonehenge, and Glastonbury, the traditional burial spot for King Arthur and Queen Guinevere and traced the source of the bluestones at Stonehenge to the boggy moorland of the Presceli Mountains in Wales. While teaching English and drama at the secondary and junior college levels in London, she inspired students through poetry and imagination.

Freeman came to the central coast of California in 1979, returning to Britain for three months in 1985 to visit sacred places and create a multimedia show from her experiences. On her return to the United States, she performed extensively the show, *Between the Earth and Sky ... an Initiation*, and began presenting workshops and leading ceremonies on Celtic sacred traditions. In 1991, a well-known author asked Freeman to tell stories at a book-signing, an event that launched her solo storytelling career. Currently, she adapts and reworks stories for performance on public radio and at weddings, libraries, bookshops, retirement homes, and children's gatherings. She has taught such workshops as "A Journey to the Celtic Otherworld," on earth-based story, poetry, myths, and legends, which she presented at the Monterey Creative Arts Retreat. She has performed for colleges and universities, conferences, and retreats, and publishes articles and stories in the United States, Canada, and Europe. Festival performances have taken her to the Monterey World One Festival, Festival of the Arts, Thunderbird Books, Shenoa Retreat Elderhostel, University of California at Santa Cruz, First Night, and Bay Books, and on sacred tours in England. She is completing a book, "The Sunwise Path: Teachings and Stories from the Celtic Wheel of Life."

Articles
"The Cauldron of the Goddess and the Western Mystery Tradition," *Gnosis*, Fall 1995.
"Eating the Salmon of Wisdom," *Parabola*, Winter 1996.
"The Enchanted Forest," *Talking Leaves*, Summer 1995.
"Magical Trees of the British Isles" (series of twelve articles) *Keltria*, 1996–1997.

"My Druid Is Christ: Miracles of the Celtic Saints," *Parabola*, Fall 1997.

"Of Stars and Stones," *Home Edition*, Summer 1997.

"Queen of Air and Darkness," *Parabola*, Spring 1997.

"Sacred Waters, Holy Wells," *Parabola*, Spring 1995, 52–57. Details miraculous bodies of water in Great Britain, including the Holy Well of St. Madron; describes pagan temples that became Christian shrines and the desecration of those holy sites.

"Stories from the Otherworld," *Storytelling Magazine*, Winter 1996.

"Sunwise Blessing," *Parabola*, Winter 1996, 34–38. Focuses on human relationships with the divine; includes daily and seasonal prayers, rites, and ceremonies and their origins.

"Touched by the Flame: The Celtic Arts of Seership," *Touchstone Millennium Edition*, Spring 1997.

"Word of Skill: The Celtic Storytellers," *Parabola*, September 1, 1995, 63–67. Details the style of Irish storytellers; uses Sean O'Conaill as a model.

Bibliography

"The Children of Lir," *Storytelling Magazine*, Winter 1996.

"The Connecting Thread," in *Druid Renaissance: The Voice of Druidry Today*, HarperCollins, 1996.

"Druid Blessing of the Sacred Grove," in *Prayers of Love*, Doubleday, projected for 1998.

"The Prince, the Fox and the Sword of Light," *Dalriada*, 1996–1997.

"The Selkie," *Dalriada*, 1996–1997.

Audiography

Between the Earth and Sky ... An Initiation (audio slides, audiocassette), Chalice Productions, 1985. Features original script and music drawn from ancient text and photographs of sacred sites and festivals.

Celtic Tales of Birds and Beasts (two audiocassettes), Chalice Productions, 1996. Features five stories of animals, shapeshifters, and Old Ones, including "The Prince, the Fox, and the Sword of Light," "The Selkie," "The Legend of the Oldest Animals," "The Black Wolf," "Tam Lin," "The Story of Deirdre," "The Wooing of Etain," "The Mother of Oisin," and "The Children of Lir"; accompanied by Gerry Smida on harp, pipe, and whistles.

Tales of Love and Transformation (audiocassette), Chalice Productions, 1996. Classic love stories of passion and beauty that cross the boundary between humankind and the fairy world, including "Tam Lin," "The Story of Deirdre," "Etain and Midir," and "Oisin's Mother"; accompanied by harp, pipe, and whistle.

Source

Mann, Saphire, "Reviews," *Keltria: Journal of Druidism and Celtic Magick*, Spring 1997, 26.

McClear, Mary-Eileen, "Review," *Second Story Review*, Winter 1996.

Nichols, Kathryn McKenzie, "Celtic Workshop Begins Today," *Monterey County Herald*, March 16, 1996, 5D.

"Review: A Book and Two Tapes Bring Ancient Folklore to Life," *Storyline*, November 1996.

"Review," *Booklist*, May 15, 1997, 1594.

"Review," *Celtic Connection*, Dorset, England, Winter 1996.

"Review," *Patchwork Newsletter*, July–August 1997, 10–11.

JUDY GAIL

Address: 13411 S. W. 112th Lane
           Miami, Florida 33186
phone 305-387-3683
fax 305-383-3959
email 102770.3146@compuserve.com

Focus: international tales and tunes; tales with ancient answers to scientific questions; the history of work and labor through story and song; women who have shaped history; the history of America through stories and songs; holiday tales and tunes; tales and ballads of love and marriage.

Audience: children and adults.

Style: blend of stories and songs.

Instruments/Props: accompaniment on guitar, dulcimer, percussion, keyboard, and assorted collected instruments; costume highlights; hand puppets; fossils and artifacts

A vivacious storyteller/balladeer, Judy Gail manages a prodigious performance schedule. She has served as host, teller, and co-author of *Wonder with Me*, a PBS series over WLRN-TV and at the Miami Museum of Science; singer, songwriter, and teller for the WRLN series, *Once Upon a Time, Time;* composer and producer for an NBC-TV special, "Hurricane at the Zoo"; writer, producer and narrator for the WLRN/Dade County four-part documentary, *AIDS — The Plague of Our Times;* writer, producer, and actress for the television pilot, *Madame Pandora's Hodge-Podge Shop;* and director of live science at the Miami Museum of Science, where she performed original entertaining educational programs about science. Her performances include guest spots on *Mr. Rogers Neighborhood* and a WOR-TV special, *Performing for the Handicapped*, and at the Coral Gables International Festival of the Arts, Earth Day, Book Mania, Miami International Book Fair,

Herstory, Jewish Museum of Florida, Boca Raton Historical Museum, Tampa Historical Museum, Children's Culture and Arts Fair, Dade County Center for the Fine Arts, Florida Humanities Council Speakers Bureau, Wolfson Museum, Biltmore Hotel Ghost Stories, and schools, colleges, libraries, parties, camps, cafes, bookstores, labor conferences, and business meetings. She offers workshops which have been presented at the annual FAME conferences, Florida Reading Association, Tropical Storytelling Festival, National Storytelling Conference 1997, American Business Women's Association, and Southern Regional Conference of the AFL-CIO, 1997. Workshop offerings include "The Joy of Creating Stories, Songs, and Programs on Any Topic," "The History of Work and Labor in Story and Song," "Perseverance and the How-to-Path Toward Publication and Recording," "Stories Alive!— Characters, Movement, Puppets, and Music," and "The Big Bad Wolf Versus They Who Called Him Brother: Contrasting Portraits of the Wolf in Folklore." Judy Gail's portrayal of feisty pioneer, environmentalist, activist, and community leader Mary Barr Munroe in "Eight Pioneer Women of Florida," and her one-woman performance in "Women Who Have Shaped History" have engaged audiences with her grasp of history in story form. In "The History of Work and Labor in Story and Song," her plea to audiences to confront the issues of downsizing, global competition, sweat shops, child labor, and the end of work as we have known it, further displays her versatility and talent to utilize storytelling and balladry as a means of educating and inspiring listeners to participate in shaping a livable, humanitarian future. In addition, she owns and operates Poppykettle Enterprises, a recording and producing service for speakers, folksingers, and storytellers.

Judy Gail's background in narration began with her parents, both musicians: her father was a songwriter and record producer, and her mother had a gift for exaggeration. Their work in composing and record production placed her among actors and singers in major recording studios, where she got a start as a child actress and singer. She recalls a record, "Songs of the Auvergne," with harpist/folksinger

Susan Reed, given to Gail by her sister. The songs "Molly Malone" and "Sweet Betsy from Pike" captured her imagination, and she decided that the life for her was that of a balladeer. International balladeers Joseph Marais and Miranda often visited her home and sang their songs and told their stories, reinforcing Judy's desire to sing, and tell stories related to her songs. Already a gifted minstrel at age eight, she took Pete Seeger and the Weavers as additional mentors, learning from them the art of community song leading and how to incorporate historically relevant material into her act while performing at orphanages, homes for the blind and elderly, community centers, and schools and on the popular CBS-TV program "Let's Take a Trip." The Florida and Miami Storytellers Guilds gave her a push toward platform narration, as did the examples of David Novak, Dan Keding, Donald Davis, Nancy Kavanaugh, J. J. Reneaux, Susan Klein, and Johnny Moses. Studies in theater arts and education at Sarah Lawrence College preceded seven years as musical director of the Shadow Box Theatre in Manhattan, where she scripted, composed scores, and created vocal characters for shadow puppets, entertaining 40,000 children annually. She has performed at the Miami Museum of Science for over 400,000 children, parents, teachers, and the public. In summer 1995 she brought her stories and songs to all 29 branches of the Broward County Library as the musical storyteller for their summer reading program, and in 1996, engaged audiences with her fossils and artifacts as the Lee County Library System's science storyteller for "Science Summer." In 1996-1997, through a Broward County Student Enrichment Grant, she gave 20 performances for a total of 8,000 students based on her award-winning book, *Day of the Moon Shadow*. From her research and collaboration with Miami MetroZoo, she has written a healing tale, "Mamma Wind's Answer," and has recorded an album of entertaining educational animal songs and stories.

Bibliography

Day of the Moon Shadow — Tales with Ancient Answers to Scientific Questions (co-author Linda A. Houlding), Libraries Unlimited, 1995. Brief explanations to questions about natural phenomena followed by information about 14 cultures, including the Vikings, ancient Mayas, and Drum People of West Africa; concludes with dramatic stories with songs based on ritual, customs, folktales, and mythology.

Work and Labor: A History in Story and Song — From Stone Age to the Information Age, Libraries Unlimited, projected 1998. Contains a history of work and labor told in stories and songs from the hunter-gatherers, Agricultural and Industrial Revolutions with tales of heroes and heroines, such as John Henry, Mother Jones, Joe Hill, union organizers, miners, child laborers, mill workers, farriers, farmers, immigrants, robber barons, CEOs, and people victimized by today's era of downsizing.

Audiography

Day of the Moon Shadow — Tales with Ancient Answers to Scientific Questions, Sampler (audiocassette), Libraries Unlimited, 1996. Contains the title story from the ancient Maya plus "Monsters of the Sky Land" (Australian Aborigine), "Kiku's Reflection" (Japan), "Helga the Howler" (Viking), and assorted songs from other stories in the book.

Day of the Moon Shadow — Tales with Ancient Answers to Scientific Questions (audiocassette), Vols. 1–3, Poppykettle Enterprises, 1996. Volume 1 contains "The Sun's Consent" (Blackfeet Native American), "In Search of the Ayaymama Bird" (Peru), "The Thunder Drum" (West Africa), "The Magic of Shamus O'Toole" (Ireland); Volume 2 contains "The Khevsouri and the Cure" (Russia), "The Blind Man and the Deaf Man" (India), "They Called Him Brother" (Naskapi Native American), "John Henry and the Steam Drill" (America); Volume 3 contains "Pele's Revenge" (Hawaii) and "Spirits of the Dancing Dead" (Inuit).

Hello Around the World (audiocassette), Poppykettle Enterprises, 1995. Contains "Hello Song" (original), "I Had a Rooster" (traditional), "The Boy Who Couldn't Sleep" (adapted folktale), "How the Lion Got His

Roar," (original song based on West African folktale), "Snake Baked a Hoe Cake," (traditional), "Why Ants Live Everywhere" (original rendition of a Burmese folktale), "Chant of the Spirits," (chant from the book *Day of the Moon Shadow)*, "Aram Sam Sam" (Algerian traditional round), "The Great Florida Alligator Conjure Man" (original rendition of traditional folktale), and "The Day Night Began" (original story).

The History of Work and Labor in Story and Song (audiocassette), Poppykettle Enterprises, 1996. Contains historical stories, songs, and narration spanning the Stone Age through the information age, about mill workers, miners, farriers, farmers, immigrants, child labor, unions, and heroes and heroines such as John Henry and Mother Jones.

Awards

1996 Broward County Student Enrichment Grant.

1995 *Storytelling World* Award for *Day of the Moon Shadow — Tales with Ancient Answers to Scientific Questions.*

1995 Curriculum Administrator Top 100 Districts' Choice Award for 1995-1996 school year.

1994 American Business Women's Association's Citation of Appreciation (Kendall and Biscayne Charter Chapters).

1988 *Miami Herald's* Best Bets for *AIDS — The Plague of Our Times.*

Source

Bethel, Alison, "Youths Travel Around World on TV Show," *Miami Herald*, June 18, 1987.

Grime, Dave, "Miami Elks Celebrate Youth Activity Week," *Kendall News-Gazette*, May 20–22, 1996, 1

"Judy Gail — Ready, Set, Sail!," *Broward Folk Club News*, October 1996, 6.

Muhs, Angie, "Kids Turn Tears into Tunes to Help Zoo," *Miami Herald*, December 3, 1992.

Nash, Jenny, "Telling Tales about Science and Math," *Storytelling Magazine*, Winter 1993, 9.

"Review," *Children's Bookwatch*, January 1996.

"Review," *Library Lane*, August 1996, 2.

"Storytelling World Awards," *Storytelling World*, Summer/Fall 1996.

HARLYNNE GEISLER
[Gy' • sluhr]

Address: 5361 Javier Street
San Diego, California 92117-3215
phone 619-569-9399
fax 619-569-0205
email ilovestories@juno.com
website www.swiftsite.com/storyteller

Focus: participation and improvisation stories, fairy tales; ghost stories; holiday lore; world folktales; teaching tales from world religion; urban legends; feminist stories; *pourquoi* folktales.

Audience: all ages, particularly elementary school students.

Style: humor; kinetic characterization; sign language; hand games.

Instruments/Props: none.

A spirited, genial platform raconteur, Harlynne Geisler brings to storytelling a background in books and language and contends that telling tales in the classroom encourages reading. Listeners to Harlynne Geisler's "The Vanishing Hitchhiker" can attest to her skill with diction, cadence, and nuance. Her contributions to the profession include performance, contemplative analysis of the value of narration, and language theory. A skilled writer and editor, she has produced regular columns for *California Traditional Music Society Journal* and *Laugh Makers Magazine* and articles for forty journals across the United States, including *Alaskan Folklorian, California Reader, Detroit Folklore, Entertainer, Essentially You, Folk Notes, Gateway Grapevine, Golden Ball, Great Lakes Storytellers Gazette, Holistic Living News, Jade Dragon, Jewish Storytelling Newsletter, Joyful Child Journal, Once Upon a Time, Patchwork, Phoenix Rising, San Diego Family, Story Art, Storytelling Magazine, Susquehanna Tellers' News, Tale Trader, Tamiami Tale Tellers, Tennessee Storytelling Journal, Territorial Tattler, Texas Teller, White*

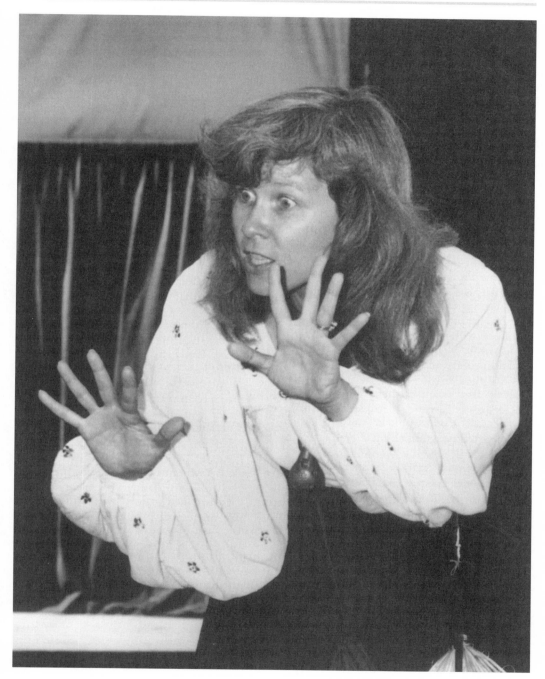

Cockade, Wrapp Up, and two Australian journals, *Story Times* and *Telling Tales.* In addition, she publishes *The Story Bag: A National Storytelling Newsletter,* a bi-monthly publication with practical tips, bibliographies, news, and reviews.

Like many platform tellers, Geisler dates her interest in tales to early childhood. Her neighbors warned that she was going to be run over in traffic if she didn't stop reading and watch her step. She played the part of Rachel at a temple play and, in sixth grade, took the role of a vampish Cleopatra. She holds a B.S. in English and an M.S. in library science from the University of Illinois and has served both public and private school and community libraries. The tedium of meetings and constraints of public education crimped her creative style, sending her to a drama coach as an outlet and to coursework in storytelling at the University of California.

Upon hearing Carol Birch's performance at a state library conference in the late 1970s, Geisler changed her profession from librarian to teller, but didn't issue an official business card until 1980. Her motto, alongside a dragon, read: "Old Stories for a New Age." Assured of her place in a second career, she borrowed $5,000 in retirement funds, took a part-time library job, and began building a client list. Her offbeat humor found a home in such imaginative presentations as "Woof! Dog Tales from Around the World," "Encounters with Truth: Stories for Adults," "Noise in the Night," "Highland Hauntings," "Speaking of the Green," "The Light Within," and "Meeting Elijah." Her enthusiasm spread to local tellers, whom she helped organize into Storytellers of San Diego. Still an educator at heart, she is a consultant to the San Diego school gifted program and has performed at Boy Scout leadership conferences, Brite Divinity School, SMILE Teachers' Conference, Summer Solstice Dulcimer and Traditional Music festival in Beverly Hills, Temple B'Nai Abraham, Drowsy Maggie's Coffeehouse, American Association of Retired Persons, on San Diego TV, as well as at schools, camps, rest homes, and libraries. She was a featured teller at the Forest Storytelling Festival, Magical Art of Storytelling Conference, Oral and Moral Storytelling Festival and Conference, Prairie Tales New Salem Storytelling Festival, Sierra Storytelling Festival, and Storyfiesta. Across the United States and Canada, she has taught narrative skills to clowns, magicians, teachers, children, college students, parents, puppeteers, librarians, ministers, and storytellers. She leads workshops in storytelling in the classroom or library, religious storytelling, becoming a professional teller, improvisation, "The How and Why of Pourquoi Folk Tales," "Getting Kids Involved:

Participation Stories for Children," and "See! Hear! Do!," a workshop explaining eleven methods of learning a story for performance.

Articles
"Bilingual Storytelling," *Phoenix Rising*, 1994.
"Folk Tales," *California Traditional Music Society Journal*, January–August 1986.
"The Gift of a Love Story," *Entertainer*, February 8–21, 1996.
"Got a Minute? Tell a Story," *Tale Trader*, May 1991.
"Holiday Stories: Be an Efficiency Engineer," *Once-Upon-a-Times*, Spring 1993.
"How Much Should Folk Tales Be Tampered With?," *Alaskan Folklorian*, July 1990.
"Male and Female Roles in Your Stories," *Alaskan Folklorian*, May 1987.
"Religious Storytelling," *Phoenix Rising*, January/February 1996.
"Screamers and Critturs: Tall Tales," *California Traditional Music Society Journal*, September–December 1993.
"Sharing Family History with Your Children," *California Traditional Music Society Journal*, September–December 1993.
"Starting a Storyteller's Group," *California Traditional Music Society Journal*, September–December 1991.
"Storytellers and Costumes," *Once-Upon-a-Times*, Fall 1992.
"Teller's Techniques — Storytelling Etiquette," *Phoenix Rising*, January/ February 1996.
"A Treasure of a Dream," *Storytelling Magazine*, September 1996, 28–29.
"Why Have Storytelling in the Schools?," *Alaskan Folklorian*, December 1990.

Bibliography
Storytelling Professionally: The Nuts and Bolts of a Working Performer, Libraries Unlimited, 1997. Practical advice on how to be a freelance storyteller.

Awards
1988 General Mills Storytelling Contest Finalist.

Source
Frankel, Kate, "Review," *Storyline*, Summer 1997.
Jones, Lauralee, "A Ghost of a Tale," *Desert Sun*, June 28, 1995, B1.

"Lessons in Living When Storytelling Goes Worldwide," *Los Angeles Times*, January 9, 1997.

Mitchell, Lisa, "Scary Stories," *San Diego Union Tribune*, August 1993.

"Storyteller Revitalizes Lost Art of Spinning Tales," *Santa Clarita Valley Daily News*, October 22, 1994.

JEFF GERE

Address: P. O. Box 37495
Honolulu, Hawaii 96837
phone 808-592-7029
fax 808-596-7046
email josan777@aol.com

Focus: Hawaiian myths about Pele; Italian, English, and Japanese tales; spooky stories; original tales; personal anecdotes; oral history; ballads; adults-only entertainment; unconventional humor.

Audience: children and adults.

Style: kinetic, dramatic characterizations of ethnic groups, pidgin English.

Instruments/Props: shadow puppets and overhead transparencies of block prints from kabuki drama; goat horns; bells; stilts; accompaniment by two musicians named HearSay, who tell, sing, and play guitar, mandolin, and violin.

Jeff Gere considers stories more than entertainment. In his words, they are the "coin of the realm of human experience" (Chang, A-2). By a meandering route through a degree in painting from the University of California at Davis and exhibits in Florence, Italy, New York City, San Francisco, and Sacramento, he established a thirteen-year career in solo platform narrative, which has taken him to literally every museum, park, community and art center, prison, and homeless center in Hawaii as well as most public and private schools. He has performed at the Los Angeles County Museum of Art, Armand Hammer Museum, 1992 World Expo, Marina Del Rey July 4th Festival, and Boise River Festival and on radio and television broadcasts. Early in his art career, he despaired of the public's poor response to the plastic arts and introduced masks, light, and music to his painter's visions. Readings in Karl Jung, Tarot, astrology, and religion led Gere to myth, folklore, and fairytales, which paralleled the power of his own dreams. He channeled his desire to paint memorable symbols into the systematic images in stories. After completing an M.A. in interrelated arts from San Francisco University, he returned to create Dream Theatre, a non-verbal merger of masks, mime, gesture, lights, and music. His troupe of seven players toured Italy and Germany extensively as he took care of a 600-year-old villa.

To be closer to his parents in California and study Asian mask theater, Gere settled his wife Mary, a tax accountant, and two children, Briah and Mecca, at Waialua on Hawaii's north shore. For the past decade he has worked for Honolulu's Department of Parks and Recreation as city drama specialist. More numerous than audiences for experimental theater, his storytelling fans enjoy his use of kinetics and innovative stage action and have dubbed him "the man with a thousand voices." He has overcome suspicions of the outsider by mastering Hawaiian myths of all kinds, including the ogres of Niihau, bird boy, the seven star sisters, and Pele, a Polynesian fire deity who dates to the first inhabitation of the islands, and true supernatural tales that senior citizens have told him. From his experiences in Italy, he created *Italia: Favorite Tales*, which reset the writings of Italo Calvino and Giovanni Boccaccio. Gere varies his repertory with a Mexican Everyman story, the native American legend of Siyotanka and the first love flute, and assorted tales for children. His signature programs include *Silly 'n' Spooky*, *Treasures from the Tomb of a Storyteller*, *Uncle Benjie's Halloween Stew*, and *Art Off the Wall*, a performance art series interpreting visual art at the contemporary museum. Recently, with his story band HearSay, a blend of violin and guitar with ballads and tales, he performed *Sweet 'N Sour: Love Stories*, which features shadow puppet accompaniment to the English ghost story, "Wind & Rain," and a Japanese ghost story, "The Obi Tale." His diverse career includes puppetry on television, language art curriculum for kindergarten and primary students, Talk Story Island Tours, and the creation and direction of the Bankoh Talk Story Festival, Hawaii's largest celebration of storytelling and oral tradition. At annual gatherings of over 3,500, he coordinates four stages and forty tellers, among them major talent from the mainland. His most memorable tours have covered auditoriums in Guam, Saipan, Samoa, and Seville, Spain, for Universal Expo '92.

Gere doubles as educator and artist. He offers a workshop for students and teachers, "Tell Well: A Nuts-and-Bolts System," and teaches two levels of storytelling, puppetry, creative drama, improvisation, choral reading, mask and mime, and lighting and staging. He has lectured for the Pacific Basin Educators Conference, National Storytelling Conference, and American Theatre in Higher Education Conference. He taught Humanities 100 at Hawaii Loa College and was on the staff of Our Lady of Sorrows School in Wahiawa, where he taught elementary school for two years. He performed through the Getting Dramatic program and Artists in the Schools. He has taught conversational English and elementary art classes in Montaione, Italy, and emotionally disturbed children in San Francisco's Avenues Elementary School. He has served as Hawaiian liaison to the National Storytelling Association and the Governor's Council on Learning, as an officer in the Hawaii Puppet Guild since 1988, and presided over the Storytelling Association of Hawaii from 1988 to 1991.

Articles

"Facing Up to Cultural Stereotypes: Haole in Hawaii," *West Coast Storytelling Journal*, Spring 1995.

"First Night," *West Coast Storytelling Journal*, Spring 1992.

"Superstitions," *Aloha Magazine*, November 1992.

"Talk Story Festival," *West Coast Storytelling Journal*, Fall 1993.

Videography

Apoha, Hawaii Department of Health, 1994. Fish puppet show.

Frank de Lima Too, Pachola Productions, 1992. Comedy featuring a frog puppet.

Huawahine's Dream Story, Kawainui Marsh Heritage Foundation, 1986. Five puppets telling the lore of Kawainui Marsh.

Keiki Calabash, Icon and Malia Productions, 1993. Seven-puppet commercial video for children.

Ohia Projects, Moanalua Gardens Foundation, 1990. Story of the spirit of native forests; for children.

Olelo Project, Department of Educational TV, 1990. Five puppets teaching basics of Hawaiian language.

Silly 'N Spooky: Tales from Hawaii, Talking Island Productions, 1996. One-hour original stories and puppetry for families, containing "First Day on the North Shore," "Muscles of Imagination," "Dapper Dan," "Big Big Fat Fat Frog," "Get on the Bus!," "Little Smarty," "Boy, Bow & Bird," and "The Secret Weapon."

Stopped by Language, Talking Island Productions, 1991. Six-puppet show for Federal Department of Immigration.

Audiography

Oahu Spookies: Unbelievably True Tales from Hawaii, Vols 1 & 2 (audiocassette), Talking Island Productions, 1992 and 1995. Contemporary folklore, featuring "Shark's Cove," "Two Tutus," and "When Kona Winds Blow."

Tales of Kohala (audiocassette), Talking Island Productions, 1993. Stories by kupuna Marie Solomon, Hawaii's Living Treasure.

Awards

1996 Parents' Choice Award for *Silly 'N Spooky*.

Source

Chang, Carol, "Storyteller Spreads Human Experience," *Central Sun Press*, February 20–26, 1992, A-2.

"Interview," *Aloha Airlines Magazine*, February 1994.

"Jeff Gere," *Santa Clarita Valley Signal*, March 4, 1995.

Kondo, Annette, "Myths of Hawaii Shared," *Santa Clarita Daily News*, November 5, 1993, 1, 2.

Pouesi, Daniel, "I'm Not Brown Enough," *Le Pasefika*, Fall 1995.

Schultz, Gloria, "North Shore's Pied Piper," *North Shore News*, 1989.

"Strange Stew," *Honolulu Weekly*, October 25, 1995.

Viotti, Vicki, "Telling Tales: A Feast of Story-telling for Kids and Grownups," *Honolulu Advertiser*, October 12, 1989.

JACKSON GILLMAN

Address: Huckleberry Lane
HCR 62 Box 36A
Mt. Desert, Maine 04660
phone 207-244-3838

Focus: environment, health, substance abuse; Yiddish, Maine humor; ballads; musical comedy; spirit and hope.

Audience: adults and children.

Style: interactive; mime, movement, dance; sign language.

Instruments/Props: piano, guitar, percussion, voice; puppets.

Jackson Gillman's theatrical career began unexpectedly, taking him far afield from his agricultural pursuits and migratory New England jobs as a maple sugarer, cider maker, and landscaper/arborist. After graduating in 1978 from the College of the Atlantic with a degree in human ecology, he decided to do something completely different for one summer. What started as a lark — spending a summer at the Deck House Cabaret as a singing waiter — grew into a devotion as he discovered the ease and joy he took in performing. In subsequent summers, he returned to the cabaret where he took a leading role in the musical ensemble's choreography and direction, and developed a solo act that became a nightly feature. He went on to study many forms of dance and music, to a workshop with mime mentors Tony Montanaro and Benny Reehl, a tour with a children's theater company, and to establish a solo performance career.

In some ways, Gillman still is a migrant worker, packing up his old kit bag to perform at schools, libraries, conferences, and festivals throughout the country. In the summer he tries to stay put for the most part, and has hosted a summer concert series for the past twelve years on Mt. Desert Island, where he lives most of the time when he is not on the road. His environmental background finds its way into some of his shows, but his repertoire has expanded to over twenty different programs ranging in topics from health and substance abuse awareness to a variety of thematic musical revues. Show titles include *Disorderly Conduct, The Perfect High, A Fool for Love,* and *New Agelessness.* Half of his programs are family oriented and include *Riot in the Garden, BUGS!, Autumn Wonders,* and *The Magic of Rudyard Kipling: Just So.* Generally known for comedy and interaction, his more serious side emerges in programs like *Hard Knocks* and *The Man Who Planted Hope.*

What distinguishes Gillman from other storytellers is his skilled use of movement in his telling. His background in mime and dance is apparent in most of his work, especially *Levity in Motion* and *The Dancing Man.* One of his many workshops, *Storyscaping,* has helped other professional storytellers in effective use of movement, space, and visual composition. Another dimension to his work is four full-length programs he performs with his own sign-language interpretation. Playing the male lead opposite a deaf actress in *Children of a Lesser God* (voted Best Theater in Maine 1986) reinforced his love of signing. He claims that his exposure to that visual language significantly benefits all his telling, whether he is sign-interpreting or not. It has conditioned him to approach his craft with what he feels is the core of good narrative: to assist the creation and transfer of clear images and emotions out of events.

While most of Gillman's work is solo, he regularly welcomes opportunities to collaborate with musicians and his favorite storytelling colleagues. He insists that when he shares the stage with Bill Harley, Michael Parent, or Judith Black, the audience gets more than the sum of the parts. Even when performing solo, Gillman peoples the stage with surprise guests. His altered egos find outlet in an assortment of eccentric stage personae, earning him the fitting appellation of the "Stand-Up Chameleon." In contrast, offstage

he is remarkably soft-spoken and sane. A fifteen-year veteran of the Maine Touring Artists Program, he has also served on the theater advisory panel for the Maine Arts Commission. He has been a keynote presenter at many conferences and festivals, and was featured at the National Storytelling Festival in 1985, 1992, and 1996.

Bibliography
"The Carrot's Tale and the Garden Lullaby," *Storytelling World*, Winter/Spring 1994, 7–9.
"The Garden Lullaby," *Children's Music Network*, 1995.

Videography
"How the Whale Got His Throat," in *American Storytelling Series, Vol. 1*, H. W. Wilson, 1987.
"I Was Right, I Was Wrong," in *Tell Me a Story, Vol. 1*, National Storytelling Association, 1995.
Just So Stories, Chip Taylor Communications, 1996. Faithful adaptations of Rudyard Kipling's classic tales, containing "The Elephant's Child," "How the Rhinoceros Got His Skin," "How the Whale Got His Throat," and "How the Camel Got His Hump."
"Just What I Always Dreamed Of," in *The Three Apples Storytelling 10th Anniversary Festival, Vol. 1*, Yellow Moon Press, 1995.
"Lobster Trap Rap," in *Comedy Downeast Style*, Video Services Unlimited, 1994.

Audiography
Downeast Ballads (audiocassette), Maine Squeeze Productions, 1987. Contains "The

Ballad of the Night Charley Tended Weir," "The Ballad of the Three Green Waves," "The Ballad of Tryphosa's Husband," "The Ballad of Willy," "The Hard Luck of Old Randall," "Sam," "Finley and the Funny-Cloud," "The Gray Engineer," "Aunt Shaw's Pet Jug," "Harry Herman and Mary Muggins," "The Dunkin' of Drunken Duncan," and "The Romance"; adult material.
A Medley of Tellers and Tales (contributor) (audiocassette), Yellow Moon, 1982.
The Slob Zone (CD-ROM), Deep River, 1995. Demonstrates voices for animation
Top 40 Answering Machine Messages, Vols. 1–2 (audiocassette), Maine Squeeze Productions, 1994. Includes "The Number You Have Dialed," "Squeeze," "A Paris," "Oh Susannah," "Home on the Range," "Teach Your Children," "When the Saints," "Sundown," "I've Been Working on the Railroad," "So in Love," "Shakespoof," "Wolfman Jackson," "Swami," "Fowl Play," "Nobody's Home," "Game Show," "Mission Impossible," "Soap Opera," "Dark and Stormy Night," "Dragnet," "Beverly Hillbillies," and "Test Signal."

Awards
1996 Maine Organic Farmers and Gardners Common Ground Fair's Most Educational for *Riot in the Garden*.
1989 Maine Arts Commission's Independent Artist Fellowship.

Source
Frame, Selby, "Jackson Gillman Thrives in Innovative Genre," *Kennebec Journal*, January 5–8, 1991.
"Jonesborough's National Storytelling Festival Attracts Thousands to Annual Three-Day Event," *The Loafer*, October 1, 1996, 19, 21.
Mooney, Bill, and David Holt. *The Storyteller's Guide*. Little Rock, Ark.: August House, 1996.
"Storytellers to Weave Their Special Magic During the First Week of October," Jonesborough, Tennessee, *Herald & Tribune*, October 2, 1996, 3C–5C.
"Storytelling Focus: of Curriculum at Fayerweather," *Storytelling Magazine*, May 1997, 8.

Webster, Susan, "A Walking, Talking Story-book," *Maine Sunday Telegram*, July 1, 1984.

DAVID GONZALEZ

Address   Rainart Productions
11 Menocker Road
Monsey, New York 10952
phone 914-352-9031
email rainart@earthlink.net

Focus: traditional lore by Grimm and others; creation stories; Latino folklore from North and South America and the Caribbean; revamped myths from Ovid's *Metamorphosis* and other classic literature; original pieces with a moral.

Audience: teens and general audiences.

Style: bi-lingual solo theater infused with song, dance, comic energy, and imagination; splashy costumes in day-glo colors; teams with keyboard artist Larry Harlow and the Latin Legends Band for a blend of myth and music.

Dr. David Rafael Gonzales, a bicultural *cuentista*/storyteller, has been performing one-man versions of classic literature for fifteen years. His goal is education through parable to teach listeners about trust, courage, hard work, and faith. He has appeared at the Royal National Theater of London, St. Louis Art Museum, International Festival of Ideas, Rockland County Storytelling Festival, International Congress of Music Therapy, American Education Research Association Conference, New Victory Theater, Brooklyn College, Theatreworks, and Tampa Bay Performing Arts Center. "Sofrito!," his sizzling, joyous revue of Latin/Caribbean culture, mixes salsa, mambo, jazz, flamenco, and audience participation with six simple tales from Cuba, Puerto Rico, the Caribbean, Mexico, the Dominican Republic, and the Bronx. Strung together by musical interludes are a Yoruba creation story, a Puerto Rican fairy tale about Malimaki the healer and the royal palm, a personal account called "The Man Who Could Make Trees Sing," about the gift of a guitar from Gonzalez's uncle, "The Beat of My Heart," "Chango and the Power of the Drum," and "The King of My Heart/El Rey del Agua," the story of a little girl and an enchanted goldfish. Gonzalez's offerings for high school audiences include "Jazz Orpheus," a Greek myth spiffed up with music by Charlie Parker, Dizzy Gillespie, and J. S. Bach; "Up in Smoke," a Russian folk story on the theme of compassion; "The Handless Maiden," one of the Brothers Grimm coming-of-age sagas; "Cuentos: Tales from the Latino World"; "Frog Skins and Silver Hands: Stories of Initiation"; and "Spellbound," a family concert. His personal stories energize *Run It Down: The Stories, Music and Poetry of David Gonzalez*, a two-hour stage tapestry outlining the theme of longing with "Jazz Orpheus," "Hickman Device," and "Slash the Boats," a father-son story about family loyalty and the CIA involvement in Chile. For the Brooklyn Academy of Music and Smithsonian Institution, he created "Double Crossed: The Saga of the St. Louis," a multimedia blend of klezmer-mambo storytelling about an ill-fated German refugee ship carrying 937 Jews to Havana in 1938. The program coordinated research from the United States Holocaust Memorial Museum, including readings, archival photos, personal accounts, fictionalized film, and historical footage. The crux of the tragedy is collusion between Cuban immigration officials and Nazis.

An at-risk kid coming of age in the Bronx, Gonzalez was born to a New York–born Puerto Rican mother and an exiled Cuban father who worked for the Central Intelligence Agency and later in shrimping. After his father left the family to settle on the Brazilian frontier with his fourth wife, Gonzalez grew up fatherless in the 1960s among Jews, blacks, Irish, Italians, and other lower middle-class ethnic groups. He credits his mother for providing a safe, stable home and for establishing his character and outlook at a noisy, story-filled table, where banter, fairy tales, and myths, grandma's Juan Bobo episodes, and daily exchanges overruled strict manners.

Influenced by the Beatles, Jimi Hendrix, and John Coltrane, Gonzalez played guitar in

his youth and yearned for a career in rock music. His introduction to the academic musical realm was inauspicious. After one day at Boston's Berklee College of Music, he fled the commercial atmosphere and hurried back to New York. To achieve his goal of aiding disabled youngsters, he volunteered at Willowbrook Mental Hospital. Following a classical education in music with a specialty in mythopoeic music therapy, he completed a doctorate from the New York University School of Education, where he was influenced by the writings of Karl Jung, Robert Johnson, and Joseph Campbell. For twenty years, he has taught music therapy to emotionally impaired children at the Herbert G. Birch School for Exceptional Children in Flushing, New York. With Florence Barrau, he co-hosts a Sunday children's show, "New York Kids," over WNYC-FM, New York public radio.

After marrying jazz singer Lisa Sokolov, Gonzalez decided that he, too, wanted to perform and began working with Learning Expansion Through Arts Programs as a storyteller and took a similar job with Theatreworks/ USA. Tapping research on the depth of meaning in myth, he entered storytelling by the back door in 1981 while working with an autistic boy at the Northside Center for Child Development. The function of narrative in the boy's treatment introduced Gonzalez to story-as-healing. He began performing "Orpheus and Eurydice" and "Delgadina," a Chilean folktale about the price of power. His evolution of 45 myths retailored for a modern repertory has opened venues at theaters, schools, libraries, and museums, where his kinetic style registers positively with a broad cross-section of audiences. A performer for the esthetic education institute at Lincoln Center, Gonzalez is currently working on a program to be performed at the Smithsonian Institution and the Brooklyn Academy of Music in March 1998.

Source

Dominguez, Robert, "Six Stories with a Musical Accent," *Daily News*, March 21, 1997.

Henry, Mallika, "Ageless Wonder," *Inside Arts*, September 1996, 30ff.

Mendez, Juan M, "'Sofrito': Un Delicioso Sofrito de Cuentos," *La Prensa*, March 27, 1997.

"Rainart Productions," http://www.earthlink.net/~rainart.

Serviss, Naomi Freedman, "Helping Kids Be Happier Ever After," *Newsday*, April 14, 1995.

_____, "Magical Storytelling to a Mambo Beat," *Newsday*, March 23, 1997.

_____, "'N.Y. Kids' Gets Good Reception," *Daily News*, January, 30, 1994.

Van Gelder, Lawrence, "Island Fairy Tales with Spicy Rhythms," *New York Times*, March 26, 1997.

LINDA GOODMAN

Address 30 Marlboro Street
Hudson, Massachusetts 01749
phone 978-562-9575
email happytales@aol.com

Focus: Southern Appalachian oral tradition; ghost stories; Jack tales; myths and legends; Bible stories; reminiscences; plays and one-woman shows; personal and family stories drawn from Appalachian heritage.
Audience: adults and children.
Style: traditional; varied voicing and characterization; dialect and colloquial speech.
Instruments/Props: rocking chair for "Daughters of the Appalachians".

Storyteller, author, and playwright Linda Goodman, a product of the poverty of the Virginia Appalachians, has turned the oral traditions of the hill country into a life's work. A sickly child who battled allergies and longed to escape from her bed, she learned narrative skills from her father, Theodore Alexander Wright, a coal miner and master yarnspinner. She began writing stories in elementary school after her family moved from a home without electricity and running water into a ghetto in Portsmouth, Virginia. One of her primary goals in the new setting was to rid herself of the stigma of ignorance that derived from her mountain twang. At Old Dominion University, she studied English, then married and, in 1983, moved to Enfield, Connecticut, where she earned a degree in accounting. Her acting credits cover a broad span of stage demands in plays by Neil Simon, Thornton Wilder, and Tennessee Williams.

The decision to become a professional teller occurred in November 1988, shortly after Goodman's father's death, when she attended the first annual Tellabration. When her mother died the next year, Goodman sought help from a Christian counselor specializing

in grief therapy, who suggested storytelling as a means of dealing with guilt and loss. The suggestion worked after Goodman began using stories as a celebration of the good times. Her first story, "The Radio," captured the value of Christmas riches in human terms rather than costly gifts. The second, "The Punishment," describes a mother's compassion toward her child after a fake whipping. The third story, "The Bobby Pins," brought an end to Goodman's guilt by reassuring her that her mother recognized love despite the fact that they had quarreled only hours before the mother's death. In Goodman's estimation, therapeutic storytelling illuminated positive aspects of her life that she had never properly evaluated.

Since leaving columns of figures — and guilt — to make a career of platform narrative, Goodman has dedicated her material to the perpetuation of Appalachian natives and sees herself as a culture ambassador defending mountain integrity and intelligence. Well known along the East Coast, she regrets that her mentors — her mother and father — never saw her perform. She has appeared at libraries, churches, and conferences, including the Con-

necticut Storytelling Festival, Three Apples Storytelling Festival, Storyfest, Johnnycake Storytelling Festival, Bread and Roses Heritage Festival, Sharing the Fire, New England Modern Storytelling Festival, New England Consortium of Family and Youth, Puppet Showplace Theater, First Night Worcester, and Joseph Campbell Festival of Myth, Folklore, and Story. She also holds a charter membership in the Barter Storytellers of Abingdon, Virginia.

A resident of Hudson, Massachusetts, Goodman is listed in the state Cultural Council directory. For a busy schedule of performances, she has developed a series of innovative stories and monologues: "Anna Wiggins, Mill Girl," "A Little Bit of Kindness Goes a Long, Long Way," "Ordinary Heroes," "Why, Where, Who, and How: Nature's Mysteries," "Melting Pot: Tales from Around the World," and "Shivers and Shrieks." For older audiences, she performs "Daughters of the Appalachians," "Scenes from the Dim, Smoky Past," and "Separate But Not Equal." Her workshops cover techniques for young tellers, making stories from fragments, family and business settings, cultural integrity, and adapting traditional tales. National Public Radio in Johnson City, Tennessee, has aired her audiocassette, *Jessie and Other Stories*. Goodman teaches storytelling at Assabet Center for Continuing Education in Marlboro, Massachusetts, and publishes in *The Museletter, Storytelling World, Tale Trader,* and *The Loom*.

Articles

"History, Herstory, Our Story, Your Story: The Three Apples Storytelling Festival," *The Museletter*, September 1996, 3.

"Points of Light in the Darkness," *The Museletter*, September 1994, 11.

"Sharing the Fire 1995: Time to Rekindle the Flame," *The Museletter*, February 1995, 1.

"16th Sharing the Fire: Listening, Learning, Telling ... Spreading the Sparks," *Tale Trader*, February 1997, 1, 5.

"Telling Tales to the Taxman," *The Museletter*, November 1994, 12–13.

"Three Apples Storytelling Festival Enters Second Decade," *The Museletter*, September 1995, 1.

"What Storytelling Means to Me," *Tale Trader*, November 1995, 9.

"Your Story — Pass It Along," *The Loom*, January 1997, 3.

Bibliography

"The Bobby Pins," *Chicken Soup for the Mother's Soul*, Health Communications 1997.

Daughters of the Appalachians, self-published, 1997. Six original monologues about strong, intelligent and unique mountain women, each of whom shares a piece of a way of life that is fast disappearing.

Empty Wells, self-published, 1992. An autobiographical one-act play about a brother and sister attempting to make peace with each other as their mother lies dying; performed by the Somers Village Players and the Mark Twain Masquers.

"The Girl with the Green Face," *Storytelling Youth Olympics 1997 Guidebook*, Eastern Tennessee State University, 1997.

"Pearl," *Storytelling World*, Summer/Fall 1995, 16–17. A biographical monologue about inner beauty.

Serendipities, self-published, 1997. A one-act play about a young girl who must let go of the past and the stepfather who helps her.

"Thanksgiving," in *A Taste of Storytelling*, League for the Advancement of New England Storytelling, 1997.

Videography

Learning the LRC, Asnuntuck Community College Library, 1989.

Audiography

Jessie and Other Stories (audiocassette), self-published, 1993. Contains "The Punishment" and "The Radio," both autobiographical stories set in Portsmouth, Virginia.

Awards

1995 Storytelling Institute Excellence in Storytelling Award.

1993 certification as a United Methodist Church lay speaker.

1993, 1992 ActConn Best Costume Design, Best Set Design.

1992 Omnibus One-Act Playwriting Competition judge.

1992 Dramatists' Guild membership.

1992 Omnibus One-Act Playwriting Competition finalist for *Empty Wells*.

Source

Anderson, Leslie," A Day for Swapping Stories," *Boston Globe*, May 1, 1994.

"The Barter Storytellers," *Storytelling Magazine*, July 1997, 5.

Garber, Susan L., "Playwrights Find Forum for New Works," *Windsor Locks Journal*, January 24, 1992, 19.

"Goodman Tells Winning Stories," *Hudson Enterprise Sun*, July 24, 1995, 5.

Harris, Craig, "Tales of the Appalachians Celebrate People, Culture," *Boston Globe*, May 7, 1995.

Machado, Helen, "Storyteller Tells Tale with Moral," *Hartford Courant*, February 19, 1993, 3.

"Maynard Students to Hear Area Storyteller," *Maynard Beacon*, November 11, 1993.

Nugent, Karen, "Hudson Storyteller Sees Baaar Market for Tall Tales," *Telegram & Gazette*, March 28, 1994.

Stallings, Fran, "Review," *Yarnspinner*, August 1993.

Steeves, George, "Teaching Through Tales," *Hudson Sun*, January 11, 1996.

Surdut, Beth, "Storytellers Dazzle Children and Adults Alike," *Harvard Spirit*, October 2, 1996.

Taylor, Lucy, "Storyteller Shares Childhood Memories," *Journal Register*, May 8, 1997.

Traub, David, "Storyteller Captivates Her Audiences," *Middlesex News*, December 12, 1995, 1B, 2B.

BILL GORDH
[Gord]

Address Lingonberry Music
1695 Lenox Hill Station
New York, New York 10021
phone 1-888-FUN-SONG or 212-533-2149
fax 212-353-3768
email billgordh@aol.com

Focus: Southern and Western American, Norwegian, Russian, English, and African

folktales; fables and trickster lore; family narratives and original stories; feminist themes; *pourquoi* stories.

Audience: primarily children.

Style: banjo accompanies stories with original songs; fingerplays.

Instruments/Props: banjo, guitar, limberjack, wasp buzz.

Storyteller Bill Gordh, a multitalented performer, author, songwriter, and teacher, was reared in Virginia and nurtured in oral tradition. He began performing in childhood with his two brothers. His maternal grandfather brightened Christmases in south Georgia with original Br'er Rabbit stories. Gordh's father, a chaplain and professor of philosophy and religion at Hollins College, used stories in his sermons. Gordh's mother continues the tradition of family stories with tales for her grandchildren. His education began with a B.A. from Duke University and M.F.A. in theater and directing from New York University School of the Arts.

Gordh comes to improvisation and platform storytelling with a background as performance and exhibitions co-ordinator at the Franklin Furnace Archives and Director of Expressive Arts at the Episcopal School in Manhattan, for which he created a storytelling curriculum for preschoolers. He has published extensively: for Scholastic Inc., "Fifteen Easy Folktale Fingerplays," "Early Childhood Workshop Storytelling Cassettes," "My First Magazine," "Let's Find Out," "Early Childhood Today," and "Multicultural Big Book Series"; "Sunbuddy Math Playhouse" for Sunburst Communications; and "Sesame Street Parents" and "Creative Classroom" for Children's Television Workshop. His family friendly radio broadcasts, stage performances, and tapes appeal to childhood educators, for whom he leads workshops on storytelling, including "Songs and Stories from Africa," "Norwegian Tales," "Spin the Globe," "Around the World for Girls," "Out West," "Coyote Tales," and "Father's Day." He has performed for general audiences at The Kitchen, The Knitting Factory, Danspace, Midway Galleries, Vanguard Gallery, San Francisco Museum of Modern Art, Kidfest, Celebrate Brooklyn Festival, and Feminist Art Collective, and is the recipient of grants from the National Endowment for the Arts, New York State Council on the Arts, New York Arts Foundation, and the Keep America Beautiful Fund. He has interwoven stories with a number of art displays at the Museum of American Folk Art. Other museum performances include American Museum of Natural History and Children's Museum of Manhattan

Bibliography

Fifteen Easy Folktale Fingerplays, Scholastic, 1997.

"The Sand Shark's in the Corner (Now Who Wants to be a Flying Head?)," *High Performance*, Fall 1993, 25.

"Storytelling in the Classroom," *Early Childhood Today*, January 1994, 42–49.

The Sunbuddy Math Playhouse (teacher's guide to accompany CD-ROM), Sunburst Communication, 1997.

Audiography

African Folktales (audiocassette), Scholastic, 1994. Audiocassette accompanies book.

Bill Gordh's Watermelon Patch (audiocassette),

Lingonberry Music, 1996. Contains "Looking for That Big Watermelon," "Heron and Crane," "I Wonder What My Dog Would Do," "Rachel in the Stars," "Buzzard in the Box," "The Beltless Man," and "Sing to the Egg"; features steel guitar, vocals, and a vocal trio.

China Culture Kit (audiocassette and book), Scholastic, 1996.

Early Childhood Workshops (audiocassette), Scholastic, 1995. Storytelling for pre-kindergarten and kindergarten.

Fifteen Easy Folktale Fingerplays (audiocassette), Scholastic, 1997.

Mexico Culture Kit (audiocassette), Scholastic, 1995.

Morning, Noon & Nighttime Tales (audiocassette), Lingonberry Music, 1993. Features "Cody's Car," "Turtle and the Thunder God," "Eye-Yi-Yi-Yi-Yi-Yi-Yi," "The Fat Cat," "The King Who Hated Haircuts," "Jumping Molly," and "The Seven Fathers."

Sunday Morning Songs (co-producer Brook Hedick) (audiocassette), Lingonberry Music, 1991. For pre-schoolers.

Under a Western Sky (co-producer Brook Hedick) (audiocassette), Lingonberry Music, 1992. Folklore of the American West.

Awards

1997 Tribune Media Services Award of Excellence for *Morning, Noon & Nighttime Tales*.

1993 American Library Association Notable Children's Recording for *Morning, Noon & Nighttime Tales*.

Source

McCormick, Moira, "'Bananas' Sprouts 'Singing' Spinoff on Capitol; New Albums from Graf, Gordh," *Billboard*, February 1, 1997.

_____, "Kid Biz Grew Up as Majors Stood Up and Took Notice," *Billboard*, December 26, 1992.

"Review," *Big Apple Parents*, December 1996.

"Review," *Family Fun*, August 1997.

SHOSHA GOREN
[Shoh'•shuhn goh'•rihn]

Address   22 Mappu Street
Tel Aviv, Israel 63434
phone and fax 972-3-5237022

Focus: personal experiences from her life in Baghdad and Tel Aviv; feminist stories and multicultural themes; realistic tales from Eastern Jewry.

Audience: all ages.

Style: dramatic scenarios of life on the Eastern Mediterranean and in New York City growing out of gesture, simple word pictures, and exaggerated facial expression; humor.

Instruments/Props: small items, including a telephone, handbag, and scarves that identify different ethnicities; colorful clothing.

A stage and television actress, writer, producer, comedian, and raconteur, Shosha Goren, a native of Baghdad, Iraq, has delighted thousands of audiences in England, Austria, and Israel. Acclaimed by *Ma'ariv, Yediot Acharonot, Bamachane, Ha'aretz,* and *Ha'ir,* a Tel Aviv weekly, she has established a reputation for purity of presentation. She draws on oriental lore for her original stories and relives the adventures of her grandmother, Tova Mualem-Nissim, a widow and midwife who reared five children alone and who inspired love and creativity. For Goren, the example of a strong survivor became the source of personal strength and of tellable stories, such as the time a battered wife begged for assistance and Tova took off her wooden clog and beat the brutal husband when he rushed through the door. Born in 1943, Goren learned the rudiments of oral technique from her mother, Marcelle Smooha, a government worker and natural raconteur. In 1951, when Goren's father left a clerk's position with the British Army to work in the oil refineries of Haifa, her family migrated to Israel.

Goren's education demonstrates her diligence in finding appropriate outlets for her interests and talents. She earned a B.A. degree from the Jerusalem University and College of

Education. In 1978, she quit her job after seventeen years as a teacher of Hebrew literature and language to immigrate to the United States. She completed the acting coursework for an M.F.A. in drama at Brooklyn College. Along with college classes, she studied ballet and took private acting classes at the studio of actress Uta Hagen. After returning to Israel with her husband, writer-director Yitzhak Gormezano-Goren, and their sons Yoav and Roey and daughter Bat-Shahar, Goren studied psychodrama with Einya Artzi and took enrichment classes with Ruth Dayches, Amir

Orian, and Rina Yerushalmi. Goren, her husband, and playwright Raphael Aharon founded the *Bimat Kedem* [Eastern Stage] as a new venue for Israeli theatrics and an outlet for social issues. The project was meant to orient audiences to Eastern Judaism and the culture of surrounding Arab states.

Goren's experiences as an actress of stage and television and her composition of a one-woman show precipitated an interest in storytelling, a career enhancement encouraged by her husband. Because she enjoyed the immediacy and direct contact with listeners, she began thinking of herself as a master chef and her stories as a good meal. The mental and spiritual nutrition she offered provoked immediate feedback as listeners responded with their enjoyment and thanks. Because she lives in a dynamic, eventful seaside milieu in Tel-Aviv, she takes comfort in drawing her fellow Israelis into narrative that can supplant harsh realities with the optimism of a fantasy world. The immediacy of womanist lore has earned her repeat invitations to Folke Tegetthoff's "Lange Nacht of Storytelling" at the Graz Erzählt Festival in Austria, where she performed in May 1997 along with Susan Klein, Laura Simms, Dan Yashinsky, Michael Parent, Milbre Burch, and John Basinger. She has also appeared at a European storytelling festival organized by Maria Qrevaz in Hall, Austria.

Goren's projects include a show of women storytellers, which she emcees and joins as a participant. A local celebrity, she has been interviewed on Israeli radio and on three televised programs—*Ze Hazman [This Is the Time]*, *Erev Chadash [A New Evening]*, and *Mabat Nashi [A Feminine Point of View]*. She participates regularly with the Yossi Alfie Storyteller's Festival, which is set annually in varying parts of Israel. Her one-woman show, "Nashim Shel Mamash" [Those Real Women], presents seven personae who overcame the social handicaps common to eastern Judaism. From her experience in the United States, she performs "Mi-dmut le-dmut" [From Image to Image], a recreation of her New York experiences as an Israeli outsider. A popular show piece, it has pleased more than 800 audiences all over Israel. Her television drama "Test Ride" tells of a fifty-year-old woman's self-liberation from social strictures. Another feminist role is her part in the television series *Bat-Yam-New-York*, which is currently broadcast on Israel's Channel 2.

Bibliography

"Beyond the Wall," *Moznayim*, Israel, October 1996.

Awards

Israeli Academy Award for *Bat-Yam-New-York*.

LINDA MCNEAR GOSS

Address 6653 Sprague Street
Philadelphia, Pennsylvania 19119
P. O. Box 27456
Philadelphia, Pennsylvania 19118
phone 215-844-5017
fax 610-458-8688, c/o Upattina's

Focus: world beast fables and myths, how and why tales, and trickster stories from the Anansi-the-spider tradition and Uncle Remus's lore; African-American lore; ghost stories; audience participation stories.

Audience: children.

Style: gestures, vocal sound effects, and a soul-healing uplift meant to connect people and to inspire a response to life; teamed with Trinidad storyteller Paul Keens-Douglas for "Journey Through the Black Diaspora."

Instruments/Props: festive African robes, beaded braids, African shell jewelry; animal print cloth; brass cowbells to announce storytime; band.

Although storytelling was often devalued as mere entertainment in the early 1970s, Goss, a generous people lover who claims the Great Smoky Mountains as her home, treasured stories as a medicine for the spirit and healing for the soul. Diminutive and shy, she chose platform narrative as a life's work for the goodness it bears to the teller and the listener. Born in the 1940s in Alcoa, Tennessee, she remembers home as a company town named for the Aluminum Company of America [ALCOA]. The town served an aluminum plant where metalworkers dirtied themselves in the "pot room," where molten metal was formed into cooking vessels. Similarly shaped and formed by home folks, she credits a family of storytellers for whom she was a dedicated listener and observer of animal fables and Bible stories. She recalls, "I would watch Momma, Daddy, Grand-daddy, my aunts, uncles, and cousins gather around and laugh, debate, tell whoppers, jokes and a few fables." From her mother, an inspirational speaker at the St. Paul A.M.E. Church, she gained dramatic flair, style, and grace. Her father, a whistler and jitterbugger who told fractured versions of Cinderella, bequeathed her rhythm and soul; and her grandfather Murphy, a stone-faced janitor, told her stories about his grandfather, who had escaped from slavery in Alabama and hid in a cave until the Emancipation Proclamation set all slaves free. Murphy, a believer in "passing on the wisdom," called his "young'un" to him to relate Joel Chandler Harris's Br'er Rabbit stories. It was Murphy who related her trademark story, about a frog who wants to be a singer.

From grade school, Goss knew that talking was her element. Her teachers wrote "talks too much" on her school report. In time, she matured and learned to profit from her talents. She majored in drama at Howard University, where dorm mates joked about her Tennessee twang. She acted in a play opposite veteran film stars Ruby Dee and Ossie Davis, told stories evolved from her childhood in Alcoa as her senior project, and participated in Theater Black, an experimental troupe that performed the works of Leroi Jones and Norman Jordan. In 1969 during her senior year, she married playwright Clay Goss, a teacher at Howard University, and completed a master's degree in elementary education from Antioch College in Ohio.

A professional performer since a stage performance in Washington, D.C., in 1973, Goss joined Paul Ofori Ansah in an itinerant program that carried stories to inner-city school children. She gave up a job as classroom teacher at Center City's Philadelphia School to become a "gatekeeper of history." In this spiritual, affirmative vocation, she tells to workshops, churches, and school gatherings. A group called the Friends of Linda Goss supported the new career by attending her performance at a library in Germantown, a suburb of Philadelphia. From that moment on, she has not stopped thinking up stories and traveling to places where audiences look forward to her style. Goss excels at Anansi-the-Spider fables, which derive from the Caribbean and Ghana in West Africa. She claims top performers as mentors — Brother Blue, Ella Jenkins, Jackie Torrence, and Mary Carter Smith — and reveres the energetic jazz

of John Coltrane and the literary achievements of Zora Neale Hurston and Langston Hughes, classic authors of the Harlem Renaissance.

A regular at storytelling festivals across the United States, Canada, Africa, and Trinidad, Goss wages a one-woman war against the dehumanization of the technological age. She has performed in a life-size sand castle in California, in riverboats and graveyards, on parade floats, among griots at Calypsocity in Richmond Hills, New York, and in the President's Park behind the White House. She thrives in Philadelphia as the city's official storyteller and storyteller-in-residence at the Please Touch Museum. She lives in the Mount Airy section of town with her husband, who co-produced *The Baby Leopard*, and their three children, daughters Aisha and Uhuru and son Jamaal. Massachusetts-based artist Cynthia Jabar, who trained as a biologist and drew on the example of choreographer Alvin Ailey and quilter Harriet Powers, provided scratchboard illustrations for *The Frog Who Wanted to Be a Singer*, the story of a small creature who invented rhythm and blues. Goss pictures the deeply engrossed frog fingering his imaginary bass fiddle and burbling, "Dooba! Dooba! Doop-Dee-Doop! ... Blurrrrrrp!" (Goss, 1989). Goss also co-authored two more works: *Jump Up and Say!* and *It's Kwanzaa Time,* and edited *Talk That Talk*, a valuable compendium of ninety African-American stories, games, tales, rap, and sermons interspersed with commentary on tricksters, animal lore, the role of the griot, preachers, hauntings, and comic folktales. The work is rich with wisdom, black idiom, and high spirits, and features writings of William Faulkner, Maya Angelou, Sterling Brown, Brother Blue, Langston Hughes, Paul Keens-Douglas, Sonia Sanchez, Martin Luther King, Jr., Winnie Mandela, Alice McGill, Chinua Achebe, Frankie and Doug Quimby, Pearl Primus, and Nikki Giovanni.

A pioneer in the contemporary storytelling mode, Goss wearied of the overly white storytelling circuit, which had too much salt and not enough pepper. To correct the imbalance, she and colleague Mary Carter-Smith founded two African-American outlets: In the

Tradition: National Festival of Black Storytelling and the National Association of Black
Storytellers (NABS), which elected Goss as its
first president. She also founded the Delaware
Valley Storytellers Guild and the Hola Kumba

Ya Cultural Arts Organization in Philadelphia,
and serves the Philadelphia Drama Guild's
Zora Neale Hurston Storytelling Competition
as consultant.

Popular in the Delaware Valley and across

the United States and Canada, Goss draws people from the one-dimensional medium of television to live interaction with a teller. A call and response as old as Southern gospel revivalism pulls them into action:

> caller: Gather 'round, my people
> response: *Well, well.*
> caller: Gonna tell you a story.
> response: *Well, well.*
> caller: Listen now, my children.
> response: *Well, well.*
> all: *Well, well, well, well.*

She performs for the Smithsonian Institution's Folkways Recordings; "The Traveling Storyteller" is featured in a third-grade reader, *On the Horizon*, from Ginn-Silver Burdett. Her signature story, "The Frog Who Wanted to Be a Singer," appears in an eighth-grade reader, *Elements of Literature*, from Holt, Rinehart and Winston, and in *Treasures of Literature* from Harcourt Brace. In addition, original creations of *Unknown Ancestors* and *River Mama* display her talents in direction and production. The first is a pan–African ritual focusing on family unity and heritage; the second is a compendium of folktales blended with instrumental music, song, and dance. She has performed at Lincoln Center, the Kennedy Center, Martin Luther King, Jr., Library, Philadelphia Museum of Art, Smithsonian Institution's Discovery Theater, Walt Whitman Cultural Art Center, Women's Program for the Luther Settlement House in Philadelphia, Newark Art Museum, and the National Storytelling Festival in Jonesborough, Tennessee. She was a guest on *The Today Show* and has been interviewed for the *New York Times, Washington Post, Philadelphia Inquirer, Essence Magazine, Learning Magazine,* and *American Visions.* Two cities — Alcoa, Tennessee, and Washington, D.C. — have celebrated Linda Goss Day.

Bibliography

"Anansi and the Wisdom Tree," *World & I,* February 1995, 272–273.

The Baby Leopard (co-author Clay Goss), Bantam, 1989. An obedience parable about a foolish baby animal that plays with fire.

The Frog Who Wanted to Be a Singer, Orchard Books, 1996. An empowering *pourquoi* tale

that explains the origins of boogie-woogie and rhythm and blues.

"The Ghost Hunt," in *The Ghost and I,* Yellow Moon Press, 1992.

It's Kwanzaa Time (co-author Clay Goss), Putnam, 1995.

Jump Up and Say; Anthology of African-American Storytelling (co-author Clay Goss), Simon & Schuster, 1995.

"Rabbit at the Waterhole," in *Joining In,* Yellow Moon Press, 1988.

Talk That Talk (co-author Marian E. Barnes), Simon & Schuster, 1989. An anthology of multicultural storytelling plus commentary, featuring Goss's "The Frog Who Wanted to Be a Singer," "Song for My Mother, Prayer for My Father," "Spread the Word: A Storyteller's Rap," and "I Cannot Tell a Lie Peach Cobbler Pie."

"The Tree of Love," in *I Hear a Symphony,* Anchor/Doubleday, 1994.

"The Tree of Love," *World & I,* February 1, 1995.

Audiography

Afro-American Tales and Games (LP), Folkways Records, 1981. A collection of Afro-American games, songs, and stories, including "Do You Want to Hear a Story?," "Rabbit at the Waterhole," and "Anansi Went Down to the Water."

The Baby Leopard (book and audiocassette), co-author Clay Goss, Bantam, 1989.

It's Story Time (audiocassette), Folkways Records, 1983.

"Storytelling Rap," in the *Twentieth Anniversary Storytelling Treasury* (audiocassette), National Storytelling Press, 1993.

Awards

1995 Literary Guild Selection for *Jump Up and Say.*

1990 Book-of-the-Month-Club's Quality Paperback selection for *Talk That Talk.*

Source

"A Brief Look at This Year's Storytellers," Jonesborough, Tennessee, *Herald & Tribune,* September 30, 1992, 4C–8C.

Iverem, Esther, "Storytelling Art Mixes Fantasy and Wit," *New York Times,* October 30, 1986.

Penrice, Rona Racha, "Review," *Quarterly Black Review of Books*, December 31, 1995.

"Review," *New York Times Book Review*, December 17, 1995, 28.

Tapley, Mel, "Storytelling Time by Griots of the Diaspora," *New York Amsterdam News*, October 22, 1994.

BONNIE GREENBERG

Address   63 Gould Road
       Newton, Massachusetts 02168
phone 617-969-1665
fax 617-455-6597
email BBonnieG@AOL.com
website www.jamcorp.com/bonnie.htm

Focus: multicultural participation stories from Mexico, Japan, Israel, Ireland, Ghana, and elsewhere; historical, survival, and heroic themes including immigration to America, Holocaust resistance, and righteous gentiles; curriculum-related stories for math, science, and literacy; secular and religious holiday tales.

Audience: children, adults, and families.

Style: humanistic stories, dramatization, and songs from Appalachia, Israel, and Eastern Europe.

Instruments/Props: guitar.

An evocative teller, Bonnie Greenberg stimulates the imagination as she instills the importance of language. Her humanistic approach to varied cultures and special people and events makes her a welcome visitor to parks, churches, synagogues, libraries, museums, and cultural gatherings. A native of Appalachia, she reveals family background in favorite stories such as "If My Candlesticks Could Talk," a tale of family immigration, and "Zusha, the Youngest Partisan," a stirring remembrance of a nine-year-old cousin whom Polish peasants concealed from the Nazis during World War II. Greenberg concentrates on survivors in history, particularly Jews who thrive in spite of unrelenting oppression. She also performs programs with a partner on survival tales of the African-American and Jew-ish people. On stage, she relives the biographies of Marion Pritchard, an Episcopalian who rescued many Jewish children in Holland during the German occupation, and of Hannah Senesh, a young Jewish woman who parachuted behind enemy lines in Hungary to save Jews during World War II.

A native of Princeton, West Virginia, Greenberg grew up among amateur storytellers. Her grandfather, whom she called Zaide, was a Russian émigré in flight from the Cossack pogroms of the early 1900s. He used an effective instructional technique on his granddaughter: he told her stories and asked her to repeat them. In answer to her questions, he told parables and wisdom tales. In the back seat of the family car on Friday evenings when the family traveled forty miles round trip to attend temple in Bluefield, sisters and brothers listened as Zaide shared Bible stories and reflected on the shtetl (village) where he studied Jewish law as a young man. Her father told humorous stories and specialized in surprise endings. By the time she attended her first professional conference in 1990, Greenberg was ripe for an additional career that suited her tastes, talents, and background in shared

narrative. Subsequently, she studied with such master storytellers as Susan Klein and Jay O'Callahan, highly esteemed mentors who aided her development.

Like many colleagues, Greenberg comes to storytelling from education. As a speech-language pathologist, she has served in public schools for over two decades. She holds an M.S. in speech-language pathology from the University of Wisconsin. In addition, she has had coaching in voice, diction, and performance. She performs and teaches all ages. For educators and speakers, she conducts workshops entitled "A Speech-Language Pathologist's Perspective on Preserving Your Voice" and "Go Tell It in the Classroom!" Other examples of her educational outreach include "Preserving the Family History," "Antidote to Television" for parents and families, and "I Can Do It, Too!" for children. Her original programs have entertained listeners over WERS-radio and television, and she's performed at Elderhostel, Hillel at Boston College and Brandeis University, Boston Museum of Science, Danforth Art Museum, the World of Wellesley Festival, Lesley College, Harvard College, Three Apples Festival, Connecticut Storytelling Festival, Sharing the Fire, A Day for Sam, the Boston Esplanade, American Speech, Language, and Hearing Association, and Conference on Alternatives in Jewish Education in Jerusalem, Israel.

Bibliography

"Truly, Truly Me: How My Jewish Heritage Influences My Storytelling," *The Museletter*, September 1995, 1.

Audiography

From the Hearts of the People, Vol. 1 (audiocassette), Hargreen Studios, 1996. Family stories and historic events reflecting universal values, including "If My Candlesticks Could Talk" and "Zusha, the Youngest Partisan"; accompanied by violinist Ken Richmond; for grade 5 and up.

Awards

1997 *Storytelling World* Winner's Award.

1996 Parents' Choice Silver Honor Award for *From the Hearts of the People, Vol. 1.*

Source

"Celebrating Diverse Cultures, Traditions," *The Wellesley (Massachusetts) Townsman*, October 17, 1996, 31.

Glantz, Shelley, "Review: From the Hearts of the People," *School Library Journal*, September 27, 1996.

Taylor, Deborah, "Worcester Celebrates Jerusalem's 3000th Birthday," *Israel Supplement*, May 16, 1996, 1.

ELLIN GREENE

Address   113 Chatham Lane
Point Pleasant, New Jersey 08742
phone 908-899-2270

Focus: folktales from around the world; English folk and fairy tales; literary fairy tales; poetry.

Audience: children.

Style: traditional style and natural delivery.

Ellin Peterson Greene is a blend of scholar, teller, and mentor and has advised a generation of teachers, librarians, and storytellers on using stories as an adjunct to children's literature. Educated at Douglass College with a degree in economics and sociology, she holds an M.L.S. with a concentration in library service to children and an Ed.D. in creative arts education. From 1959 to 1968, she served on the staff of the New York Public Library as storytelling and group work specialist and assistant coordinator of children's services, returning in 1986 as director for the library's early childhood project, funded by a three-year grant from the Carnegie Corporation. In that capacity, she coordinated a national conference entitled "Books, Babies, and Libraries." She has served on several committees of the Association for Library Service to Children for the American Library Association and chaired the Caldecott Award Committee in 1984.

Greene was guest speaker at South Africa's first Children's Book Symposium, held in Cape Town in 1987. In 1989, she returned to South Africa to serve as academic specialist, participating in a community-based education program under the READ (Read, Educate, and Develop) Organization funded by a grant from the United States Information Agency Bureau of Educational and Cultural Affairs. In 1997, she went to Japan to talk about storytelling and American children's picture books in connection with a traveling exhibition of the work of four Caldecott medalists: Marcia Brown, Barbara Cooney, Robert McCloskey, and Marc Simont.

Greene's teaching career has taken her to numerous significant posts affecting childhood literacy. From 1969 to 1997, she served as adjunct professor at the School of Communication, Information and Library Studies, Rutgers, and chaired the committee for the Rutgers Award for Distinguished Contribution to Children's Literature in 1973 and 1978. She was associate professor at the University of Chicago Graduate Library School from 1980 to 1985, serving as dean of students from 1980 to 1982. As recipient of a grant from the National Endowment for the Humanities in 1984, she organized and directed "The Illustrator as Storyteller" project and conference in Chicago. Greene has lectured at numerous universities, among them Columbia University, University of Pennsylvania, University of Illinois, University of Iowa, Louisiana State University, University of South Carolina, and New York University. She has co-directed storytelling residencies with tellers Laura Simms and Susan Danoff. As a professor of narrative, Greene takes pride in her students, among them Carol Birch and Beth Horner, both nationally known raconteurs. Greene has served on the board of the National Storytelling Association, presented at the National Congress, and twice performed at the National Storytelling Festival. She has taught docents at the Field Museum of Natural History and child tellers at the Ocean County Public Library in Toms River, New Jersey.

A native of New Jersey, Greene was born on September 18, 1927, the daughter of Charles M. and Dorothea Hooton Peterson. She credits her mother, who read aloud to her in early childhood, for instilling a love of books and reading. Over tea, her maternal British grandmother shared the rich folklore of England and Wales. Folk and fairy tales were Greene's favorite reading in childhood. Her mentor was Augusta Baker, who co-authored the first two editions of *Storytelling: Art and Technique*. Another influence was Pura Belpre White, Spanish children's specialist at the New York Public Library and reteller of tales from Puerto Rico.

An expert on the method and educational goals and objectives of storytelling, Greene approaches the subject from a librarian's point of view. She believes that narrative is the best way to introduce children to the pleasures of literature and to their literary heritage. In her opinion, listening to stories cultivates in children a sense of wonder. Children respond to the sounds and rhythms of languages, images, and mood. She advocates wise selection of stories, letting the story speak for itself, always keeping the story itself at the forefront rather than the teller. She encourages teachers to value stories for the joy they bring rather than for didactic reasons and would like to see more teachers and media specialists offer in-service workshops on storytelling to adult staff and to the children themselves. Traveling to Europe, South Africa, and Japan, and across the United States, she has shared her expertise for over forty years. Now retired from her academic posts, she continues to serve as consultant, to offer storytelling workshops, to speak at conferences, and to write.

Articles

"Books, Babies, and Libraries: The Librarian's Role in Literacy Development" (co-authors Bernice E. Cullinan and Angela M. Jaggar), *Language Arts*, November 1990, 750–755.

"Early Childhood Centers: Three Models," *School Library Journal*, February 1984, 21–27.

"Eleanor Farjeon: The Shaping of a Literary Imagination," University of Florida, March 1982, 61–69.

"Focus on Research" (columnist and contributing editor), *Journal of Youth Services*, 1983-1984.

"A Multicultural Celebration Through Literature," *Parent and Preschooler Newsletter*, June 1994.

"Nursery Rhymes," *World Book Encyclopedia*

"Once Upon a Time ... The Importance of

Fairy Tales in Children's Lives," *Parent and Preschooler Newsletter*, February 1992.

"A Peculiar Understanding: Re-creating the Literary Fairy Tale," *Horn Book*, June 1983.

"A Peculiar Understanding: Re-creating the Literary Fairy Tale," *The National Storytelling Journal*, Summer 1985.

"Poetry for Young Children," *Parent and Preschooler Newsletter*, June 1993.

"Sharing Literature: A Love Gift," *Parent and Preschooler Newsletter*, November 1986.

"There Are No Talent Scouts in the Audience of Children," *School Library Journal*, November 1982, 25–27.

Bibliography

Best-Loved Stories Told at the National Storytelling Festival, August House, 1992.

Billy Beg and His Bull, Holiday House, 1994.

Books, Babies and Libraries: Serving Infants, Toddlers, Their Parents and Caregivers, American Library Association, 1991.

Clever Cooks: A Concoction of Stories, Charms, Recipes, and Riddles, Lothrop, 1973, 1977.

Films for Children: A Selected List, New York Library Association, 1966.

Growing to Love Books, Lothrop, 1989.

The Illustrator as Storyteller: Caldecott Medal and Honor Books 1938–1984, University of Minnesota, 1984.

The Legend of the Christmas Rose, Holiday House, 1990.

The Legend of the Cranberry, Simon & Schuster, 1993.

Ling Li and the Phoenix Fairy: A Chinese Folktale, Clarion, 1996.

Midsummer Magic: A Garland of Stories, Charms, and Recipes (editor), Lothrop, 1977.

A Multimedia Approach to Children's Literature: A Selective List of Films, Filmstrips, and Recordings Based on Children's Books (coauthor Madalynne Schoenfield), American Library Association, 1972, 1977, 1983.

Princess Rosetta and the Popcorn Man, Lothrop, 1971.

The Pumpkin Giant, Lothrop, 1970.

The Rat-Catcher's Daughter, Atheneum, 1974.

Read Me a Story: Books and Techniques for Reading Aloud and Storytelling, Preschool Publications, 1992.

Recordings for Children: A Selected List, New York Public Library, 1964.

Roger Duvoisin: The Art of Children's Books, Zimmerli Art Museum, Rutgers University, 1989.

Stories: A List of Stories to Tell and Read Aloud, New York Public Library, 1965.

Storytelling: Art and Technique, Third Edition, Bowker, 1996. Features techniques, bibliography, background reading, advice on creating and publicizing programs, storytelling in museums, and the thirteen most tellable tales.

Storytelling: A Selected Annotated Bibliography (coauthor George Shannon), Garland, 1986.

Audiography

Elsie Piddock Skips in Her Sleep (audiocassette), A Gentle Wind.

Awards

1989 Academic Specialist Grant from the U.S. Information Agency Bureau of Educational and Cultural Affairs.

1989 Ezra Jack Keats lecturer at the University of Southern Mississippi.

1987 presenter at the Children's Book Symposium in Capetown, South Africa.

1981 elected to the Douglass Society, composed of distinguished alumnae of Douglass College.

1979 Hans Christian Andersen lecturer at the University of Minnesota.

Source

Horn Book, October 1973; April 1978; June 1978.

Mooney, Bill, and David Holt. *The Storyteller's Guide*. Little Rock, Ark.: August House, 1996.

Something About the Author. Vol. 23. Detroit: Gale Research, 1981.

GRACE HALLWORTH

Address   Tranquillity
    36 Lighthouse Road
    Bacolet Point, Scarborough
    Tobago, West Indies
  phone 809-639-1446

Focus: traditional, world folklore, particularly the Caribbean and Scotland; Anansi trickster lore; counting and game rhymes; beast fables; supernatural; participation stories; urban anecdotes and legends; dilemma stories; riddles and jokes; tall tales and fantasy; audience participation stories.

Audience: children.

Style: sharing, audience participation.

Former librarian, lecturer, and performer Grace Hallworth deserves credit for reviving the old art of yarning in England. Skilled at articulation and timing, she was a storyteller in childhood during the 1930s, drawing on the vibrant lore of Trinidad and relating her narratives at age five to a polite crowd of dolls.

Growing up in a house with teachers, she learned early about involvement in the community, particularly concerts, musicales, and the library. A career staff member at the children's service of the Central Library of Trinidad and Tobago, from 1951 she participated in the expansion of storytelling in the two islands. In the mid–1950s, she served an internship at the Boys and Girls House of the Toronto Library Service to develop a critical understanding of children's literature. The experience prefaced a move to England, where she undertook the position of children's librarian at the Hertfordshire County Library.

Hallworth acquired polish from Eileen Colwell, a doyenne storyteller known throughout the United Kingdom. With Colwell's assistance, Hallworth gained entrée into performances and shared the platform with experienced professionals. At new town Hemel Hempstead, she organized a tour of primary and secondary schools to introduce library services and storytelling to young audiences, the first such program in England. At the Institute of Education at London University in the mid–1970s, she arranged a sabbatical to complete a degree in language education. The experience enabled her to evolve a sharing mode to encourage listeners to become tellers. She has appeared at hospitals, taverns, school auditoriums, in-service training sessions, community centers, clubs, theater and art centers, and bookshops.

A patron of the 250-member Society for Storytelling in Birmingham, England, Hallworth supports all aspects of oral tradition. She has served on four award panels — the Other Award for books highlighting social concerns, Young Observer Award for outstanding young adult books, International Reading Association's literary competition, and the National Book League's Book Week. Early retirement in 1984 gave her more time for telling. She appeared at the Kumba Summer Project for Black and Asian Children, Multicultural Book Fair in Edinburgh, Stories in the Community in Clwyd, Wales, Storytelling for Storyboat Project in Lincolnshire, Common Ground Project in Brixton, National Oracy Project and Health and Storytelling in Birmingham, and the second Danish Storytelling Festival, held at the Karen Blixen Museum in 1997. Residencies and festivals have taken her to Albany, Binghamton, and Buffalo, New York, to the American School at Ruislip, England, and to Wales, Scotland, Ireland, Australia, Spain, Israel, Holland, and Denmark. Media appearances have showcased her on *You and Me, Listen with Mother, Playschool, The Long, the Short, and the Tall, Everybody Here, Listening and Reading, Treasure Islands, Kaleidoscope,* and *Many Voices, One World*, produced by Dutch television for UNESCO.

Bibliography

A. J. Walford's Guide to Reviews and Reviewing (contributor), Mansell, 1986.
Anansi at the Pool, Longman, 1994.
Anansi's Secret, Granada TV, 1985.
Buy a Penny Ginger and Other Rhymes, Longman, 1994.
Carnival Kite, Methuen, 1980.
Cric Crac, Heinemann, 1990.
Dancing to the River, Cambridge University Press, 1996.
Down by the River: Rhymes, Games and Songs, Heinemann, 1996.
Festivals (contributor), Scholastic, 1994. Contains "Play Mas Hannah."
Going to School, Cambridge University Press, 1996.
Gracie's Cat, Cambridge University Press, 1996.
Listen to This Story, Methuen, 1977.
Mouth Open Story Jump Out, Methuen, 1984.
Our Favourite Stories From Around the World (contributor), Longman, 1994. Contains "Anansi at the Pool."
Poor-Me-One, Longman, 1995. Focuses on a Trinidad legend about how a bird got its name.
Rhythm and Rhyme: Songs, Rhymes and Games, Longman, 1995.
Sleep Tight, Cambridge University Press 1996
A Web of Stories, Methuen, 1990.

Video

Buy a Penny Ginger and Other Rhymes, Longman, 1994.

Audiography

"Anansi at the Pool" on *Our Favourite Stories From Around the World* (audiocassette), Longman, 1994.
Anansi's Secret (audiocassette), Granada TV, 1985.
Ball of Fire and Other Stories (audiocassette), Culture Waves, 1990.
Buy a Penny Ginger and Other Rhymes (audiocassette), Longman, 1994.
The Devil's Mare and Other Stories (audiocassette), Culture Waves, 1990.
Rhythm and Rhyme (audiocassette), Longman, 1995.

Awards

1996 Kate Greenaway Award runner-up for *Down by the River: Rhymes, Games and Songs*
1991 Woodfield Lecturer at the Loughbor-

ough University Storytelling in an International World.

Source

McFerran, Ann, "Raw Imagination: Ann Mc-Ferran Talks to Grace Hallworth About Telling Stories," *Times Educational Supplement*.

"Six Tellers at Wailing Wall in Jerusalem," *Tale Trader*, February 1997, 9.

"Storied Trip to Dublin," West Cork, Ireland, *News*, May 13, 1994, 6.

MARY HAMILTON

Address   65 Springhill Road
            Frankfort, Kentucky 40601
    phone 800-438-4390

Focus: native Kentucky lore; world folktales; spooky stories; family anecdotes; tall tales.

Audience: children and adults, especially school groups; conferences.

Style: gesture, vocal characterization, and facial expression.

Mary June Hamilton is a trouper performer, tailoring her programs for the tastes and interests of varied audiences from young children to adults. Born August 3, 1952, to nurse Martha Jane Hager Hamilton and farmer Robert F. Hamilton, Jr., she recalls that her father was a natural storyteller who told her family anecdotes from infancy. Hamilton grew up on a family farm just a few miles from grandparents and great-grandparents. A rural child, she was accustomed to hoeing beans and tobacco, tending pigs and cattle, and chopping out thistles. At St. Martin of Tours Catholic Church and Flaherty Elementary School, she learned to tell stretchers and to treasure fairy tales and folktales, a dual focus that has enhanced her three careers as high school English teacher, children's librarian, and storyteller. She finished eleventh grade at Flaherty High with a class of 40 students, graduated the next year from Meade County High School, and entered the University of Kentucky, where she completed a B.A. in secondary education and an M.S. in library science. During this period she taught at Meade County High School in Brandenburg, Kentucky. While working as children's librarian at the Grand Rapids Public Library in Grand Rapids, Michigan, she told stories as part of the job.

Inspired by the expertise of The Folktellers, Connie Regan-Blake and Barbara Freeman, who presented at the Michigan Children's Librarian's Conference in the early 1980s, Hamilton determined to refine her skills by reading up on the art in Marie Shedlock's *The Art of the Storyteller*. Hamilton also learned by watching and hearing the storytellers who passed through Michigan in the early 1980s, including Donald Davis, Jackie Torrence, Ed Stivender, Gamble Rogers, Heather Forest, Chuck Larkin, Carol Birch, Doc McConnell, and Kathryn Windham. From 1983 to 1987, Hamilton studied voice with Gordon Van Ry and, in the mid–1980s, learned the "heart of the art of retelling a tale" in several storytelling residencies with veteran teller Laura Simms.

Beginning in 1983, Hamilton has performed full-time — more by default than plan. She had intended to resign as soon as she had saved up a cushion of money to finance her career change, but the job ended during budget cuts. Since that unceremonious thump to earth, she has developed a repertoire of over 200 stories. Her motto is "Telling stories ... creating worlds." Her résumé speaks congenially of her style:

> I surround myself with story; then trust that tales I must retell will make themselves known. When a tale inhabits my dreams and imaginings, I know it is claiming space in my repertoire. Without scripting or memorizing, I learn the tale so each telling with an audience resembles fine conversation with an old friend — well-known, yet not fully predictable, both fresh and refreshing.

Hamilton moved back to Kentucky in 1987 to live near her family. In 1990, she and colleague Cynthia Changaris founded Scheherazade's Legacy, a storytelling partnership that produced Louisville's Tellabration! The Night of Storytelling from 1991 to 1996. Currently, they

produce "Telling Tales in School" workshops for educators and "Family Story, Family Celebration" events. On her own, Hamilton performs "Kentucky Tales" and "A World of Folktales," leads workshops entitled "Learn a Folktale Today" and "Explore-a-Story," and opens conferences with "Sailing the Flying Ship."

Hamilton married state civil service worker Charles Wright in 1994 and moved to Frankfort. Currently, she is a regular at the Corn Island Storytelling Festival, Winter Tales, Crosswell Opera House, Cherokee Rose Storytelling Festival, Almost Bugaboo Springs Festival, Florida Storytelling Camp, and the National Storytelling Festival in Jonesborough, Tennessee. Her keynoting and workshop experiences cover a wide range of audiences from the Kentucky Credit Union League and Marion General Hospital in Marion, Ohio, to the Grand Rapids Council of Performing Arts for Children, Kentucky Arts Council, Battle Creek and Springfield Schools, and residencies in Florida, Kentucky, Indiana, Ohio, Michigan, Missouri, and North Carolina. She has taught at Arts Unlimited at Bowling Green State University, Howl-o-Ween at Opryland, Ohio Speakers Forum, and

Kentucky Speakers Association, and led Storyworks Seminars in Grand Rapids, Southfield, and Traverse City, Michigan. She has performed at private gatherings for the Ford Motor Women's Club, St. Meinrad's Seminary, Michigan Dunes Correctional Facility, League of Jewish Women's Organizations of Greater Detroit, Clemson University's Professional Development Conferences for Women, and Kentucky Association of Memorial Dealers. Renewing herself with vegetable and native wildflower gardening and watching deer, squirrels, groundhogs, and birds, she enjoys oneness with nature, broken by get-togethers for contra dancing.

Bibliography

"The Princess and the Dove," in *Best-Loved Stories Told at the National Storytelling Festival*, August House, 1991.

Audiography

Haunting Tales Live from the Culbertson Mansion State Historic Site (audiocassette), Hidden Spring, 1992. Spooky stories set in Victorian days.

One Thousand Ideas and Then Some (audiocassette), Hidden Spring, 1992. Six world folktales.

"The Poor Man and the Rich Man's Purse," in *Tales of Fools and Wise Folk* (audiocassette), August House.

Some Dog and Other Kentucky Wonders (audiocassette), Hidden Spring, 1992. Four Kentucky tales retold by a native Kentuckian, chosen for the Elementary School Library Collection.

Stepping Stones: Stories for ages 4–10 (audiocassette), Hidden Spring, 1992. Five stories for younger children.

The Winter Wife (audiocassette), Hidden Spring, 1988. Four North American tales and two family anecdotes.

Source

Alexander, Constance, "Adult Storyhour Appeals to Child in Us All," *Murray (Kentucky) Ledger & Times*, February 1, 1990, 4.

Allen, John, "Gather 'Round and Hear Her Stories: Mary Hamilton Keeps the Oral

Tradition Alive with Magical Tales," *Grand Rapids Magazine*, May 1985, 87, 89.

Blowers, Diana, "Students Enjoy Tales: Storyteller Visits Beavercreek Elementary Schools, *The Dayton (Ohio) Daily News*, May 17, 1995.

Franklin, Frances, "Vivid Images Spellbound Young Listeners: Ex-librarian Makes Living Telling Tales," *Battle Creek Enquirer*, January 31, 1985.

Gross, Karin, "Storyteller Rekindles Tradition," Adrian, Michigan *Daily Telegram*, November 11, 1993.

McQueen, Tracy L., "Writer, Storyteller Visit Ohio County Schools: Tales Help Expose Students to Folklore," *Owensboro (Kentucky) Messenger-Inquirer*, October 14, 1994, 1B, 6B.

Slater, Paul, "Telling Tales: Of Black Snakes and Ghostly Young Women," Linn, Missouri, *Unterrified Democrat*, March 2, 1988, 1, 9.

Summers, Lisa, "She Tells the Tales: Mary Hamilton Found an Unusual Niche in the Career World, Earning a Living by Spinning Yarns," Frankfort, Kentucky *State Journal*, December 5, 1994.

Thomas, Craig, "New Year's Is Story Time," *Kalamazoo Gazette*, December 1991.

Yost, Carolyn, "Storyteller Brings Books to Life at Jenison School," *The Grand Rapids Press*, April 1987.

BILL HARLEY

Address   301 Jacob Street
            Seekonk, MA 02771
        phone 508-336-9703
        fax 508-336-2254
        website www.billharley.com

Focus: the lifestyle and dilemmas of contemporary childhood; personal stories told in the confessional mode; adult theater.

Audience children and parents.

Style: hilariously direct and honest; nonsense songs and silly lyrics; high-pitched voice and mobile facial expressions; has performed in tandem with veteran platform performer Len Cabral; solo performances and collaboration with the Troublemakers, a three-piece band.

Instruments/Props: guitar; recordings backed up by a children's chorus and an adult chorus.

Bill Harley is a teller with a mission: he believes that people need stories more than ever to make sense out of their lives. Labeled the Mark Twain of contemporary kids' music, he is a witty, engaging child advocate who entertains with funny, quirky, uninhibited songs and stories, either solo or in concert with his three-piece band, the Troublemakers. In Bill Mooney and David Holt's *The Storyteller's Guide*, Harley explains that telling demands heavy research into the background and "bones" of a story. He makes notes on his version, which he visualizes during rehearsal, and performs trial runs before friends. He depends on idiosyncratic characters and a personalized style of pacing and delivery to make each tale stand out as authentic and memorable.

Harley's instinctive feel for communicating with others springs from a Midwestern background and from his mother, children's author Ruth Wolfe Harley. He grew up in Ohio and Indiana, completed high school in Connecticut, and graduated from Hamilton College in Clinton, New York, with a B.A. in religion. His humanistic point of view evolved from social services consulting in the late 1970s, when he directed a project on conflict resolution for parents, teachers, and children, and from experience on the staff of the Learning Connection in Providence, Rhode Island. Using Debbie Block, his wife and business manager, and their sons, Noah and Dylan, as source material, he currently writes, sings, and tells about normal home frustrations, such as Dylan's first attempt at reading *Hop on Pop* and *Fox in Sox*. His story "Zanzibar" details the childhood trauma of geography homework. In 1991, Harley advanced in professional outreach after he signed a contract with A & M Records and attended Robert Redford's Sundance Institute in Utah, where he developed "Growing Up Is a Full-Time Job: An Adult Competency Exam." Listeners enjoy his sixteen award-winning tapes, accompanied by

rock, reggae, folk, and samba, in the grade school classroom, car, or children's room.

Despite his zaniness, Harley takes childhood seriously. His stories connect with parents and children, both of whom profit from a genial, forgiving look at human foibles and shortcomings. He is a regular on National Public Radio's *All Things Considered*. Working at a fervid pace, he has entertained junior high school student bodies and performed at the Alabama Association for Young Children, Mansfield University's Storytelling '96, Kingston Free Library, Celebrations of Light V in Midland, Texas, Stone Soup Coffeehouse, Van Wezel Performing Arts Hall, Ravinia Festival, Mayo Civic Center, National Storytelling Festival, and the International Children's Festival in Ottawa.

Bibliography

"The Art of the Crab Walk," *Horn Book*, 1993.

"Carna and the Boots of Seven Strides," in *Best-Loved Stories Told at the National Storytelling Festival*, August House, 1991.

Carna and the Boots of Seven Strides, Riverbank Press, 1994.

"Fox's Sack," in *Ready to Tell Tales* , August House, 1994.

"Guys Who Lunch, " *Rhode Island Monthly*, January 1996.

"Happy Birthday, Mrs. Nottingham," *Storytelling World*, Summer-Fall 1993, 27–30.

Joining In — An Anthology of Audience Participation Stories and How to Tell Them (contributor), Yellow Moon, 1988. Eighteen participation stories for all ages.

"Looking for a Hill," *Rhode Island Month's Holiday Guide*, December 1995.

Nothing Happened (illustrator Ann Miya), Tricycle Press, 1995. A story about a boy who stays up late to search for a secret party at his house.

Open Ears: Musical Adventures for a New Generation, Ellipsis Kids, 1995.

Sarah's Story (illustrator Eve Aldridge), Tricycle Press, 1996. A story about a girl who must tell a story in class.

Sitting Down to Eat (illustrator Kitty Harvill), August House, 1996. A story about animals that interrupt a young boy's snacktime; for elementary readers.

"That Hunger Within," *Michigan Reading Journal*, Summer 1994.

Who Says? Essays on Pivotal Issues in Storytelling (contributor), August House, 1996. Contains essays by Rafe Martin, Peninnah Schran, Joseph Bruchac, and six others.

You're in Trouble, August House, projected for 1999.

Video

Who Made This Mess?, A & M Records, 1992.

Audiography

Already Someplace Warm (audiocassette), Round River Records, 1994.

Big, Big World (audiocassette), A & M, 1993. Children's songs, including "Pizza Shake," "Who Made This Mess?," "I Don't Wanna Wait," and "Tommy Says," a child's view of divorce.

Come on Out and Play (audiocassette), Round River Records, 1990. Covers similar domestic situations in "Staying Up," "I'm Busy," and "Sitting Down to Eat."

Cool in School: Tales from 6th Grade (audiocassette), Round River Records, 1987.

Coyote (audiocassette), Round River Records, 1987.

Dinosaurs Never Say Please (audiocassette), Round River Records, 1987. Contains the title story plus "I'm Busy," "Bojabi," and "Master of All Masters"; for grades K–3.

Fifty Ways to Fool Your Mother (audiocassette), Round River Records, 1986. Contains "I'm on My Way," "There Goes My Brother Again," "Havin' a Party," "My Dog Sam," "When I First Came to This Land," "Under One Sky," "Mr. Spaceman," "Nobody Knew," "Somos el Barco [We Are the Boat]," and the title story.

From the Back of the Bus: Complete True Stories by Bill Harley (audiocassette), Round River Records, 1995. One song and two long stories — "Mr. Anderson" and "Bottlecaps" — about Harley's elementary school days; for ages 8 to adult.

Grownups Are Strange (audiocassette), Round River Records, 1990.

I'm Gonna Let It Shine: A Gathering of Voices for Freedom (audiocassette), Round River, Records 1990.

Lunchroom Tales (audiocassette), Round

River Records, 1996. Contains a shorter version of "Mr. Anderson" and "The Back of the Bus" song.

Monsters in the Bathroom (audiocassette), Round River Records, 1984.

Nho Lobo and Other Stories (contributor) (audiocassette), Story Sound Productions, 1984.

Peter Alsop & Bill Harley: In the Hospital (co-author Peter Alsop) (audiocassette), Moose School Records, 1989.

Sitting on My Hands: A Collection of Commentaries As Aired on National Public Radio's All Things Considered (audiocassette), Round River Records, 1995. Eleven pieces for all ages.

Tales of Fools and Wise Folk (contributor) (audiocassette), National Association for the Preservation and Perpetuation of Storytelling. Features "Monsters in the Bathroom."

There's a Pea on My Plate (audiocassette), Round River Records, 1997. Contains children's songs.

Wacka Wacka Woo & Other Stuff (audiocassette), August House, 1995. Contains "Soap, Soap," "Aunt Edith Meets Tricky," "Tara and the Magic Sack," "Aiken Drum," the title song and other nonsense songs; for ages 4–8.

Who Made This Mess?, A & M Records, 1992.

You're in Trouble, A & M Records, 1992.

Awards

1996 *Storytelling World's* Honor Award for *Wacka Wacka Woo and Other Stuff.*

1996 *Newsweek's* Best Kids Books of the Year for *Sitting Down to Eat.*

1996 American Bookseller Association Pick of the List for *Sitting Down to Eat.*

1996 Notable Children's Trade Book for *Sitting Down to Eat.*

1996 *Storytelling World* Honor Award for Best Audio Recording for *From the Back of the Bus.*

1996 Parents' Choice Silver Honors for *Wacka Wacka Woo and Other Stuff.*

1995 NAIRD finalist for *From the Back of the Bus.*

1992 Parents' Choice Gold Award for *Who Made This Mess?.*

1992 *Storytelling World's* Honor Award for *Who Made This Mess?*

1990 Parents' Choice Silver Honors for *Come on Out and Play.*

1990 Parents' Choice Gold Award for *I'm Gonna Let It Shine.*

1990 NAIRD award for *Come on Out and Play.*

1990 ALA Notable Recording for *I'm Gonna Let It Shine.*

1989 Parents' Choice Gold Award for *Peter Alsop & Bill Harley: In the Hospital.*

1988 Parents' Choice Gold Award for *You're in Trouble.*

1987 Parents' Choice Silver Award for *Cool in School: Tales from 6th Grade.*

1987 NAIRD's Indie Award for *Dinosaurs Never Say Please.*

1986 Parents' Choice Gold Award for *Fifty Ways to Fool Your Mother.*

1984 NAIRD's honorable mention for *Monsters in the Bathroom.*

Source

Band, Carol, and Phyllis Lindsay, "Bill Harley: Understanding How Kids Feel," *Boston Parents' Paper*, March 1996.

Beavin, Kristi, "Review of 'From the Back of the Bus' and 'Wacka Wacka Woo,'" *Booklist*, November 1, 1995.

Burke, Lynne T., "Audio Books for Summer Car Trips," *Mahoning Valley Parent*, June 1996, 9.

Campbell, Karen, "Bill Harley's Engaging Tales of Everyday Life," *Boston Parent's Paper*, September 1994.

Cella, Cathering, "Talent 4 Children," *Billboard*, February 22, 1992.

Flocken, Corinne, "A Storied Event? Do Tell!," *Los Angeles Times*, October 10, 1996.

"Greenwood Friends School, Millville, Pennsylvania, Newsletter," http://www.greenwood-friends.org/newsltr_sep.html, August 18, 1996.

Kohn, Paula Noonan, "Review of 'Open Ears: Musical Adventures for a New Generation,'" *Family Fun*, December 1995.

MacDonald, Sandy, "What's Cool … What's Not So Cool," *Parents' Choice*, Summer 1996, 6.

McCormick, Moira, "Review of 'Wacka

Wacka Woo & Other Stuff,'" *Family Fun*, November 1995.

McKeever, Jim, "Harley Seeks to Make Children, Adults Part of Something Special," Syracuse, New York *Post-Standard*, May 5, 1994.

Miller, Alexis Magner, "A Class Clown with a Message Youngsters Can Understand," *Providence Sunday Journal*, April 14, 1991, H1–2.

Mooney, Bill, and David Holt. *The Storyteller's Guide*. Little Rock, Arkansas: August House, 1996.

O'Donnell, Frank, "Grown-ups Tune in to Story Time," *The Times*, March 7, 1994, 19.

"Review of 'Big, Big World,'" *Patriot Ledger*, December 9, 1993.

"Review of 'Lunchroom Tales' and 'From the Back of the Bus,'" *Choice Music For Kids*, September 1996, 2.

"Review of 'Wacka Wacka Woo & Other Stuff," *Parent Council*, October 1995.

Rodriguez, Bill, "Almost Grown: Bill Harley's Adult Education," Providence, Rhode Island *Phoenix*, April 8, 1994.

Something About the Author, Vol. 87. Detroit: Gale Research, 1996.

Timeless Voices: Images of the National Storytelling Festival. Jonesborough, Tenn.: National Storytelling Press, 1997.

Vessell, Nancy, "Bill Harley," Jefferson City, Missouri *News Tribune*, February 27, 1994, 1B.

Vieira, Michael J, "Silliness Is Serious Business for Singer of Children's Songs," *Providence Journal*, December 27, 1990.

Yonke, David, "Tales That Touch the Entire Family," *Toledo Blade*, February 26, 1993.

JANICE N. HARRINGTON

Address   414 Hessel Boulevard
            Champaign, Illinois 61820
   phone 217-355-1679

Focus: traditional folktales from many cultures; participation stories; African-American folktales; stories that speak to current issues
   Audience: all ages.

Style: lively, dramatic performance with audience involvement.

The South has given Janice Harrington not only sense memory but also remarkable family stories about pioneering, courage, and bridge-building, which she learned from her mother and has cultivated in her platform career. The storyteller who influenced Harrington most was her mother. The first — and best — audience was her "Big Mama," Lillian. Growing up in rural Alabama, Harrington lived in the world of Br'er Rabbit, red dirt roads, cotton fields, smoldering hot sun, and rusting roofs, all of which she incorporated into her storytelling.

Harrington's family, a part of the black migration, resettled in Lincoln, Nebraska, in the 1960s. Considering herself bi-regional, she grew on the Midwestern plains among white frame houses, the mythology of the plains pioneer, and wild "tag-you're-it" games. In 1978, she earned a B.S. in education from the University of Nebraska, followed by an M.A. in library science from the University of Iowa in 1981. After completing her education, she embarked on several years of travel and career change, moving from seventh-grade teacher,

school librarian, and university professor to reference librarian and reviewer for the *Bulletin for the Center of Children's Books*.

As a freelance storyteller since 1982, Harrington has drawn on a strong local guild of storytelling advocates. Mentored by Beth Horner, she developed a repertoire that includes "Mr. Roach and Mrs. Chicken" and her original ghost story, "The Devil's Dulcimer." Her evolving roster of programs includes "From Heart and History," "A Questions of Leaders," "Scared Skinless," "Everybody Join In," "Audience Participation for Families," and "Finding Your Strength." For a 1989 Louisiana State Library grant, she promoted the Summer Reading Club and presented over forty storytelling performances in public libraries across the state. She conducts workshops for professional groups on storytelling, writing family stories, children's literature, poetry, and youth programming. Her storytelling experiences include the 1993 Eleventh Annual National Festival of Black Storytelling, Hoosier Storytelling Festival, 1995 American Library Association Conference, Stories from the Heartland, and the 1995 National Storytelling Festival in Jonesborough, Tennessee.

Bibliography

"The Devil's Dulcimer," in *Talk That Talk: An Anthology of African-American Storytelling*, Simon & Schuster, 1989.

"The Need for Cultural Diversity in Preschool Services," *Journal of Youth Services in Libraries*, Winter 1993, 175–180.

"The Risks of Storytelling," *Illinois Libraries*, January 1985, 57–60.

"Storytelling in the Media Center," *Indiana Media Journal*, Spring 1989, 3–10.

Audiography

Janice N. Harrington, Storyteller (audiocassette), Pogo Studio, 1996. Contains "Mr. Roach and Mrs. Chicken," "Tiger's Minister of State," "The Girl with Large Eyes," "Talk," "Sister Wind's Children," and "Uncle Rabbit and Uncle Buzzard."

Awards

1995 American Library Association featured teller for Storytelling Showcase.

1989 Louisiana State Library grant.

Source

Lacy, Mike, "Professional Storyteller Brings to Life a Different Kind of World for Children," *Sun Herald*, January 28, 1989.

Mabry, Becky, "Champaign Librarian Has Head for Tales," *Champaign-Urbana News-Gazette*, November 12, 1995, E3.

Oglesby, Christy, and Jonathan Harris, "Encouraging Children to Read," *Atlanta Journal-Constitution*, October 31, 1996.

Rainwater, Roberta, "Librarian Pulls Out Stops for Storytelling Magic," *River Parishes Picayune*, January 4, 1990, 1I.

White, Jon, "Spinning Yarns," *Indianapolis Business Journal*, January 1, 1995.

KENDALL HAVEN

Address　1155 Hart Lane
Fulton, California 95439
phone 707-577-0259

Focus: realistic stories from science and history; stories that meet the needs of people in crisis.

Audience: children and adults.

Style: realistic, engaging.

The only West Pointer to choose storytelling for a career, Kendall Haven, dubbed the "best teller in the West" by print and video in fifteen Western cities, brings to the profession an unusual mix — a B.S. in general engineering, M.S. in oceanography, and six years as senior research scientist for the Department of Energy. Born in Asheville, North Carolina, and raised on the West Coast, he recalls loving the ocean and thinking that science was a good subject to study. The influence of his yarn-spinning Uncle Ev lodged in his mind, as did his mother's family stories. Once developing his own skill at expending images, Haven established a career as a platform performer and now works for corporate America to market stories as a positive method of communication for adults. The authenticity of his performance grows out of his belief that telling brings out the humanity in each listener, whether in schools, factories, or offices.

After workshops in 27 states for 15,000 teachers in 900 schools and performances in 40 states before 800,000 adults and over two million children, Haven has established his philosophy that stories provide practical teaching power and belong in the standard kit of pedagogy. A worthy example is "Storytelling in the Classroom: If They Tell It, They Will Learn," presented to the 18th National Storytelling Conference to express methods of teaching oral communications skills through story formation and delivery. As he explained in an article for *The Companion*, children and adults are drawn to narrative because oral delivery is the most engrossing, most enjoyable way to communicate with others. An amalgam of teller and educator, he has taught graduate-level courses for six universities and produced stories for the American Cancer Society, Institute for Mental Health Initiatives, Crisis Centers, Children's Television Resource and Education Center, and the Child Abuse Prevention Training Center of California. In 1992, his work aired on *National Public Radio Playhouse*. As of 1997, his résumé reads like a rollcall of festivals, which take him up and down the West Coast and to Hawaii, and east to Florida, South Carolina, and Maryland. His articles on classroom use of storytelling have appeared in *National Storytelling Magazine, National Storytelling Newsletter, GRIT, Texas Storytelling Magazine, California Reader, Teacher in Focus National Magazine, Companion, Sing Out!, Teaching Points*, and *Kid Connection Magazine*.

Haven believes that the generation of tellers who came of age in the 1980s were self-made. The first teller who told stories in the style Haven aspired to was Jay O'Callahan, whom he studied in the late 1980s. Haven's major performances include Frostburg Children's Literature Conference, Flying Leap Storytelling Festival, California State Reading Conference, Mariposa Storytelling Festival, National Women's History Conference, Cambria Storytelling Festival, Kansas State Reading Conference, and the 1986 National Storytelling Festival in Jonesborough, Tennessee. He serves on the board of directors of the National Storytelling Association, as a member of the NSA Educational Advisory Committee, and as founder and chair of the International Whole Language Umbrella Storytelling Interest Group. To support the next generation of tellers, he co-directs the Sonoma Storytelling Festival, chairs the Bay Area Storytelling Festival, and founded festivals in Las Vegas, Nevada, Boise, Idaho, and Mariposa, California.

Articles

"Have Your Cake and Eat It, Too: Tell the Stories You *Create*," *The Companion*, November 1996, 20–21.

"Meat and Potatoes Storytelling: Finally a Storytelling System Designed Around the Needs of Teachers," *The California Reader*, Fall 1994.

"Student Storytellers: If They Tell It, They Will Learn," *The California Reader*, Spring 1995.

"Telling Tales Out of School and In It," *Teacher in Focus Magazine*, January 1994.

"Three Better Rules: Using Oral Storytelling Techniques to Improve Student Creative Writing," *The California Reader*, Summer 1997.

Bibliography

Amazing American Women: Forty Fascinating Five-Minute Reads, Libraries Unlimited, 1995. Stories for third grade and up about little-known accomplishments by women.

Bedtime Stories, StoryStreet USA, 1997.

Bingo and Molly (television scripts), Learning Channel, 1997.

Getting Along, Children Television Resource and Education Center, 1993. Ten stories on social behavior for K–3.

Getting Along — Preschool, Children Television Resource and Education Center, 1993. Five stories on social behavior for ages 3–5.

Great Moments in Science: Readers Theater and Experiments, Libraries Unlimited, 1996. Twelve scripts based on stories in *Marvels in Science* linked to student experiments, such as Galileo's study of falling objects; covers physics, astronomy, chemistry, biology, rocketry, and genetics; for grades 4–9.

The Invisible Game: Stories of Fathers and Sons, Commonwealth, 1998. Seventeen stories about male parents and children.

Many Voices (contributor), National Story-

telling Press, 1995. Story of Robert Goddard's first attempt at rocketry.

Marvels of Science: 50 Fascinating Five-Minute Reads, Libraries Unlimited, 1994. Science stories featuring intrigue, drama, mystery, risk, tragedy, and triumph; for third grade and up.

"A Path to the Promised Land," *The Companion*, November 1996, 18–19.

Stepping Stones to Science, Libraries Unlimited, 1997. Fifteen K–3 stories and activities paralleling the primary science curriculum.

Stories of Celebration: Stories about Forty Worldwide Celebrations, Fulcrum, 1997.

The Wrong Side of a Neighborhood Witch, Commonwealth 1997. Children's fiction.

Audiography

The Adventures of Christina Valentine (audiocassette), Children's Television Resource and Education Center, 1991. Three-hour adventure drama for radio.

The Baby Sitter, Institute of Mental Health Initiatives, 1990.

Bully, Contra Costa Crisis and Suicide Intervention Service, 1986.

Dinosaur Tales, HavenBerg Productions, 1988.

Fathers and Sons, HavenBerg Productions, 1992. Original stories; recommended by ALA *Booklist* and *School Library Journal*.

Frog Pond Blues, American Cancer Society, 1988.

Getting Along, JTG, 1988.

The Killer Brussels Sprouts, JTG, 1990. Book and audiocassette.

Neighborhood Magic, HavenBerg Productions, 1990. Original stories recommended by ALA *Booklist*.

Reluctant Heroes, HavenBerg Productions, 1986.

Awards

1997 *Storytelling World* Award for Best Storytelling Anthology for *Great Moments in Science*.

1996 *Storytelling World* Silver Award for Best Storytelling Anthology for *Amazing American Women*.

1995 *Storytelling World* Silver Award for Best Storytelling Anthology for *Marvels of Science*.

1993 International Festival Association Silver Award for Best Educational Program at a Major National Festival for "Tux & Tales."

1993 American Library Association Notable Recording Artist for *The Adventures of Christina Valentine*.

1993 American Library Association's Best of the Best for Children for *The Adventures of Christina Valentine*.

1992 Corporation for Public Broadcasting Silver Award for Best Children's Public Radio Production for *The Adventures of Christina Valentine*.

1992 New York International Radio Festival honorable mention.

1992 American Library Association Notable Recording Artist for *Fathers and Sons*.

1992 American Library Association's Best of the Best for Children for *Fathers and Sons*.

1991 Award for Excellence in California Education for *Neighborhood Magic*.

1990 American Library Association's Best of the Best for Children for *Neighborhood Magic*.

1989 American Library Association Notable Recording Artist.

1989 California Special Recognition Award for *Frog Pond Blues*.

1988 American Library Association Award

for Best Western Regional Storytelling Competition.

1987 National Storytelling Competition.

1987 California Conference Local Mental Health Directors Award for Excellence for *Voices* and *Bully*.

1986 American Library Association Award for Best Western Regional Teller.

1985 American Library Association Award for Best Western Regional Storytelling Competition.

Source

Keding, Dan, "The Endless Tale," *Sing Out!*, March/April 1997, 118–120.

JOE HAYES

Address P. O. Box 8619
Santa Fe, New Mexico 87504

Focus: Southwestern myths and tales from Pueblo, Navajo, Tohono O'odham, Hopi, Snohomish, and Hispanic sources; bilingual tales; beast fables; trickster stories; ecology and nature lore; *pourquoi* stories; tall tales; holiday lore; tales of strong women.

Audience: primarily school children.

Style: facial contortions and audience participation; non-verbal vocabulary, drama, and kinetics; acting out bilingual stories to demonstrate Hispanic vocabulary.

Instruments/Props: chair.

The Southwest's foremost bilingual platform narrator, Joe Hayes values the mystical link between teller and listener. A regular visitor to schoolrooms, he maintains that storytelling demonstrates acceptance and affection by developing a one-on-one relationship with each member of the audience. To share imaginative personae from folklore, he invites his audience to experience characters both aurally and visually. He pours himself into the recreation of a Hopi story about a drought that threatens a locust and frog, who petition the rain god for relief. To maximize involvement, he emphasizes repetition and calls on the audience for help in telling his stories. When he throws in Hispanic terms such as *gallina* and *unos, dos, tres, cuatro*, he flaps his arms and makes a beak with his mouth and counts off on his fingers the hen's four chicks; to explain *mano* and *metate*, he demonstrates the primitive method of grinding corn by hand under a roller. His illustrative method eases the gap between majority Anglos and minority Hispanics by letting the latter be translators and by elevating the Spanish language in importance.

A Pennsylvanian by birth, Hayes grew up in southern Arizona fifty miles from the Mexican border. He learned Spanish in grade school and absorbed Hispanic culture and lore. A Latino background aided him in finding work in mineral exploration in Mexico and Spain. In 1976, he made his home in Santa Fe, New Mexico. After graduating from the University of Arizona with a B.A. in English literature and teaching high school English for six years, he became a bilingual teller and researched regional folklore. Stirrings of his father's stories initiated tellings to his own children, Kathleen and Adam.

In 1979, Hayes changed careers to full-time professional platform narration, the first in the state of New Mexico. He is the resident teller at the Wheelwright Museum of the American Indian and devotes his career to collecting and telling authentic Southwestern lore in both English and Spanish. He has visited over 1500 schools, performed at Celebrations of Light V in Midland, Texas, and spoken at educational conferences throughout the United States. In 1992, he delivered the commencement address at U.C.L.A.'s Graduate School of Library and Information Science. His courses taught at the University of New Mexico and guest lectures at other colleges and universities nurture and develop the talents of beginning tellers.

Articles

"The Day After It Snowed Tortillas" in *Sitting at the Feet of the Past: Retelling the North American Folktale for Children*, Greenwood Press, 1992.

Bibliography

Antonio's Lucky Day, Scholastic, 1993.
The Butterflies Trick Coyote, Scholastic, 1993.

The Checker Playing Hound Dog: Tall Tales from the Southwest, Mariposa, 1986. Contains "The Gum Chewing Rattler."

Coyote & (illustrator Lucy Jelinek), Mariposa, 1982. Contains "Coyote and the Mice."

The Day It Snowed Tortillas, Mariposa, 1982. Hispanic stories from New Mexico, including "The Cricket"; for children.

"The Day It Snowed Tortillas," in *More Best-Loved Stories Told at the National Storytelling Festival*, August House, 1992.

Everyone Knows Gato Pinto: More Tales from Spanish New Mexico (illustrator Lucy Jelinek), Mariposa, 1992.

A Heart Full of Turquoise, Mariposa, 1988. A compendium of Pueblo animistic lore; contains "Frog and Locust" and "Be Careful with Promises."

Here Comes the Storyteller, Cinco Puntos Press, 1996. Contains "Rain," "The Gum Chewing Rattler," "Valgame Dios!," "One Day, One Night," "Sky Pushing Poles," "Yellow Corn Girl," "The Earth Monster," "Yellow Behind the Ears," and "The Cricket" plus candid photos of Hayes telling participation stories to children.

Mariposa, Mariposa (storybook alone or storybook and audiocassette), Trails West, 1988. A *pourquoi* story about how the butterfly got her yellow dress with black spots.

Monday, Tuesday, Wednesday, Oh!, (storybook alone or storybook and audiocassette), Trails West, 1987. A poor woman helps some elves and receives a pot of gold.

No Way, Jose!/De Ninguna Manera, José! (storybook alone or storybook and audiocassette), Trails West, 1986. A beast fable about how the rooster José gets to his Uncle Perico's wedding.

Soft Child: How Rattlesnake Got Its Fangs (illustrator Kay Sather), Harbinger House, 1993. A Tohono O'Odham tale about how the Sky God gave the rattlesnake its fangs.

A Spoon for Every Bite (illustrator Rebecca Leer), Orchard Books, 1996. Inspired by Hispanic lore, a revenge tale about a rich man who brags about having a spoon for each day of the year until he learns of a man who uses a different spoon for each bite.

The Terrible Tragadabas/El Terrible Tragadabas (storybook alone or storybook and audiocassette), Trails West, 1987. A grandma sends three granddaughters to the store for food.

That's Not Fair! Earth Friendly Tales, Trails

West, 1991. Five stories for children and adults about earth stewardship.

Watch Out for Clever Women/Cuidado con las mujeres astutas (illustrator Vicki Trego Hill), Cinco Puntos, 1994. A bilingual collection of New Mexican folklore celebrating strong Hispanic women, including "The Honest Daughter," "In the Days of King Adobe," "Just Say BAAAA!," "The Day It Snowed Tortillas," and the title story; for age five and up.

The Weeping Woman/La Llorona (storybook alone or storybook and audiocassette), Cinco Puntos, 1987. The best known Hispanic-American folk story about a vain woman who insists on marrying the world's handsomest man.

Where There's a Will, There's a Way/Donde Hay Ganas, Hay Mañas, Trails West, 1995. A shy boy conquers the stigma of being thought a fool.

The Wise Little Burro: Holiday Tales from Near and Far (illustrator Lucy Jelinek), Trails West, 1990. Seven stories of the Winter Solstice from different countries and traditions.

Videography

Stories at Sundown, Cinco Puntos, 1987. Contains "My Pet Rattlesnake," "The Big Toe," "The Earth Monster," "Coyote and Locust," and "Pedro and Diablo."

Audiography

Best Loved Stories Told at the National Storytelling Festival, Vol. 2 (contributor) (audiocassette), August House, 1992. Featuring "One Day, One Night."

The Checker Playing Hound Dog: Tall Tales from the Southwest (audiocassette), Mariposa, 1986. Contains "The Gum Chewing Rattler."

Coyote &: Native American Folk Tales [stet] (audiocassette), Trails West, 1983. Contains "Coyote & the Turkey," "Coyote & the Rabbit," "Coyote & the Mice," "Coyote & the Locust," "Coyote & the Rattlesnake," "Coyote & the Turtle," "Coyote & the Quail," and "Coyote & Horned Toad."

A Heart Full of Turquoise (audiocassette), Mariposa, 1988. A compendium of Pueblo animistic lore; contains "Frog and Locust" and "Be Careful with Promises."

Mariposa, Mariposa (audiocassette and storybook), Trails West, 1988. A *pourquoi* story about how the butterfly got her yellow dress with black spots.

Monday, Tuesday, Wednesday, Oh!, (audiocassette and storybook), Trails West, 1987. A poor woman helps some elves and receives a pot of gold.

No Way, Jose!/De Ninguna Manera, José! (audiocassette and storybook), Trails West, 1986. A beast fable about how the rooster José gets to his Uncle Perico's wedding.

Stories at the Tipi (audiocassette), Cinco Puntos Press, 1996. Accompanies *Here Comes the Storyteller;* recorded live at Wheelwright Museum in Santa Fe.

Tell Me a Cuento/Cuéntame Un Story (audiocassette), Cinco Puntos. Four bilingual stories told in English with Spanish on one side and Spanish with English on the other.

The Terrible Tragadabas/El Terrible Tragadabas (audiocassette and storybook), Trails West. A grandma sends three granddaughters to the store for food.

That's Not Fair! Earth Friendly Tales (audiocassette), Trails West, 1991. Five stories for children and adults about earth stewardship.

Watch Out for Clever Women/Cuidado con las mujeres astutas (audiocassette), Cinco Puntos, 1994. A bilingual collection of New Mexican folklore celebrating strong Hispanic women, including "The Honest Daughter," "In the Days of King Adobe," "Just Say BAAAA!," "The Day It Snowed Tortillas," and the title story; for age five and up.

The Weeping Woman/La Llorona (audiocassette and storybook), Cinco Puntos, 1987. The best known story in Hispanic-American folklore about a vain woman who insists on marrying the world's handsomest man.

The Wise Little Burro: Holiday Tales from Near and Far (illustrator Lucy Jelinek), Trails West, 1990. Seven stories of the Winter Solstice from different countries and traditions.

Awards

1997 Texas Bluebonnet Master List nomination for *Watch Out for Clever Women/Cuidado con las mujeres astutas.*

1995 Southwest Book Award for *Watch Out for Clever Women/Cuidado con las mujeres astutas.*

1995 Texas Bluebonnet Award nomination for *Watch Out for Clever Women/Cuidado con las mujeres astutas.*

1995 New Mexico Governor's Award for Excellence in the Arts.

1993 Arizona Library Association Outstanding Children's Author Award for *Soft Child.*

1993 Arizona Young Readers' Award for *Soft Child.*

1989 New Mexico Commission on Higher Education Eminent Scholar.

1982 *Bloomsbury Review* Best Children's Book for *The Day It Snowed Tortillas.*

1982 Arizona Young Reader's Award nomination for *The Day It Snowed Tortillas.*

Source

"A Brief Look at This Year's Storytellers," Jonesborough, Tennessee *Herald & Tribune*, September 30, 1992, 4C–8C.

Bulletin of the Center for Children's Books, December 1994, 130.

Messier, Gisele, "Review," *New Mexico Magazine*, June 1997, 11.

Powers, Becky, "Storytelling Exercises Children's Imagination," *El Paso Times*, December 4, 1994, 5F.

"Review," *Bulletin of the Center for Children's Books*, December 1994.

"Review," *Houston Post*, September 11, 1994.

Something About the Author, Vol. 88. Detroit: Gale Research, 1996.

RAY HICKS

Address   218 Old Mountain Road
Beech Mountain, North Carolina
28804

Focus: traditional and original Jack Tales; reminiscences; mountain mysteries; witches, ghosts, and other supernatural events.

Audience: all ages.

Style: spontaneous telling in authentic Appalachian dialect with repetition and obsolete diction; performed in tandem with his double first cousin, storyteller Stanley Hicks, who died in 1990.

Instruments/Props: bib overalls, brogans, Army camouflage cap, wooden chair, hand-rolled cigarettes, cuspidor.

A scion of Southern mountain ancestry dating to the seventeenth century, Ray Hicks, an irrepressible folksayer, stands out from most storytellers by his height — a lanky six feet seven inches — and the authenticity of his Anglo-Saxon diction and Southern mountain twang. At home in a tin-roofed frame house at Gold Rock Point outside Banner Elk, North Carolina, on Beech Mountain near the Tennessee line, he lives in the style of his parents, Nathan and Rena Hicks, and paternal grandparents, Benjamin and Julie Hicks. It was his grandfather who built the Hicks family homeplace and gave him a start in spinning adventure yarns by teaching him mountain airs and ballads. Hicks's narratives are so true to English tradition that they have earned the praise of experts, including American folklorist Alan Lomax and storyteller Richard Chase.

Born in an isolated cabin on August 28, 1922, Hicks, the fourth of a family of ten, was a woodcutter, plowman, and ox-teamer with a grade-school education. His mother and grandmother cut and sewed the family's garments and spun wool into thread on a spinning wheel for knitted stockings and gloves. He wore shoes cobbled by his grandfather Samuel and tapped his toes to hand-crafted dulcimers that his cousin Stanley made from local wood and groundhog hides. The Beech Mountain lifestyle he enjoyed harks back to a time when neighborhood cornhuskings and logrollings were the only entertainments available to the mountain poor, who earned a living piecemeal by farming, lumbering, spare labor, and wildcrafting.

Hicks knew cold, hunger, and suffering during the Depression. One vivid remembrance of his father recalls how Nathan set Ray on that family's only mule, took him to Boone, and joined him in performing for passersby until police ordered them to leave. A few listeners ordered dulcimers from Nathan, who was delighted to find customers for his handicraft. The public's largesse was short-lived. Soon returned to hunger and cold, the family endured privations and despair so dismal that their baby son starved to death, Nathan committed suicide, Ray's brother Jack drowned, and their mother became a virtual invalid. Hicks fell behind in school while tending her and left school at age fourteen to support the family. Often without shoes, he chopped timber, plowed the family's stony ridge, and carried his meager crop to market. Themes of suffering and financial hardship dot the Jack tales told by his father and his grandfather's haint and witch tales and ballads, and the Indian lore of his grandmother Julie. After Hicks's brother-in-law, Frank Proffitt, marketed his version of "Tom Dooley," folk collectors discovered Hicks and buoyed him to stardom.

Hicks is a marvel of linguistic preservation. Seemingly without artifice or intent, he retains the pure Scotch-Irish speech of his ancestors, the pioneer herders and tobacco growers who settled southern Appalachia before the arrival of Davy Crockett and Daniel Boone. Hicks's conversation and tellings chime true with such archaisms as bairn for born or infant and holp as the past tense of help. He has worked as a truck driver, self-taught mechanic, hired laborer, and barber, but mostly, he farms. He and his wife, Rosa Harmon Hicks, and five children have cropped potatoes, cabbages, and onions, which they swapped for goods from merchant Howard Mast, Sr., at the Mast General Store in Valle Crucis. Hicks earns no income from media coverage, including profiles in *New Yorker* magazine and on PBS-TV's *Story of English* series. Annually, he journeys to Tell It in the Mountains in Asheville, North Carolina, and the National Storytelling Festival in Jonesborough, Tennessee, which he helped to establish in the early 1970s. Much in demand by aficionados of regional history, genealogy, and pure Appalachian narrative, he is the patriarch of the classic tale and a fixture of local oral tradition. Unlike his contemporaries, he makes no attempt to profit from telling—no agent, no bookings, just a quick removal of his false teeth, a rolled fag from Prince Albert tobacco, and a casual spell of yarning for the delight of fans. The rest of the year, he tends his acreage and woodlot, collects herbs and wild plants, and travels to local schools and colleges for sessions of storytelling. While he tells, Rosa sells cut flower bouquets, dried apple slices, and copies of his only record.

Hicks's repertory of fifty tales, such as "Grinding at the Mill" and "Lucky and Unlucky Jack," derive from the Jack cycle and resemble the familiar fables "Jack and the Beanstalk" and "Jack the Giant Killer," traditional trickster and morality lore in which only the focal character is fully developed. Robert Isbell's biography, *The Last Chivaree: The Hicks Family of Beech Mountain*, which is based on one-on-one interviews with Ray, is a treasury of these enduring stories and anthologizes "Jack and the Three Sillies," "Jack and the Northwest Wind," "Old Man's Cold Hands," "The Good Man and the Bad Man," and a legend of lost gold on Beech Mountain. Hick's style draws on the Celtic bard lore of Ossian, the mythic romanticist of Ireland. Hicks followed the example of Richard Chase in cleansing his repertory of vulgarisms and Rabelaisian elements, none of which he felt belong in performances for general audiences. His unique style won him a Washington audience with then–Vice President George Bush for a telling session at which he recounted "Whickety-Whack," Jack's capture of Death in a magic sack. Hicks was glad to return home and has since rejected other invitations to distant cities. He still welcomes folklorists, camera teams, and recorders of tales and informal harmonica concerts, which he shares for free from his front porch.

Bibliography

"The Day the Cow Ate My Britches," in *Best-Loved Stories Told at the National Storytelling Festival*, August House, 1991.

"Hardy Hard-Ass," in *Jack in Two Worlds*, University of North Carolina Press, 1994, 10–26.

"Interview for Robert McNeil," in *The Story of English*, a nine-part series for PBS-TV, 1986.

"Jack and the Old Bull," *North Carolina Folklore*, 1989, 73–120.

"Jack and the Three Steers," in *More Best-Loved Stories Told at the National Story-telling Festival*, August House, 1992.

"Whickety-Whack, into My Sack," in *Home-spun: Tales from America's Favorite Story-tellers*, Crown, 1988.

Audiography

Jack Alive! (audiocassette and CD) JuneAppal, 1989.

Ray Hicks Tells Four Jack Tales (audiocassette), Folk Legacy Records, 1963.

Awards

1996 National Storytelling Association Circle of Excellence.

1995 National Storytelling Association's Lifetime Achievement Award.

1983 Folk Arts Program of the National Endowment for the Arts Award for Storytelling.

Source

"Award-Winning Tale Tellers Unfazed by Fame," *Charlotte Observer*, January 19, 1986.

"A Brief Look at This Year's Storytellers," Jonesborough, Tennessee *Herald & Tribune*, September 30, 1992, 4C–8C.

DeParle, Jason, "Mountain Voice Shares Ageless, Magic Tales," *New York Times*, June 22, 1992, A1.

Horn, M., "Have We Got a Great Tale for You," *U.S. News and World Report*, November 2, 1987, 65.

Isbell, Robert. *The Last Chivaree: The Hicks Family of Beech Mountain*. Chapel Hill: University of North Carolina Press, 1996.

Kinkead, Gwen, "Profiles: An Overgrown Jack," *New Yorker*, July 18, 1988, 33–41.

McLeod, Michael, Angela Peterson, and Tom Raymond, "Once Upon a Time," *Florida Magazine*, November 24, 1996.

"Mountaineer's a Poor Galax Picker But Great at Grinning," *Charlotte Observer*, July 16, 1989.

"A Mountain Man and His Magic Tales," *Charlotte Observer*, February 12, 1989.

"NSA Recognizes Lifetime Achievers," *Inside Story*, September 1996, 33–34.

Pennington, Lee, "Review," *Tale Trader*, May 1996, 18.

"Ray Hicks Presented NSA's Lifetime Achieve-ment Award," *Tale Trader*, November 1995, 9.

Schimmel, Nancy, "Storyteller's: Live," *Just Enough to Make a Story*, Berkeley, Calif.: Sisters' Choice Press, 1982, 11.

Sobol, Joseph Daniel, "Jack in the Raw: Ray Hicks," *Jack in Two Worlds*. Chapel Hill: University of North Carolina Press, 1994.

Stone, Kay, "Old Stories/New Listeners" in *Who Says? Essays on Pivotal Issues in Storytelling* , August House, 1996, 155–176.

"Storyteller's Yarns Earn Him Wide Acclaim," *Charlotte Observer*, April 14, 1986.

Stotter, Ruth, and William Bernard McCarthy, "Tellers and Their Tales: Revivalist Storytelling," *About Story: Writing on Stories and Storytelling 1980–1994*. Stotter Press, 1994; second edition 1996.

Timeless Voices: Images of the National Story-telling Festival. Jonesborough, Tenn.: National Storytelling Press, 1997.

"Water Witches," *Charlotte Observer*, October 2, 1989.

DAVID HOLT

Address   High Windy Productions
P. O. Box 28
Fairview, North Carolina 28730
phone 704-628-1728
fax 704-628-4435
website www.riverwalk.org/holt

Focus: folktales, ghost stories, ballads, Southern mountains tunes, and real-life experiences; audience participation; clog dancing.

Audience: all ages.

Style: congenial, personable, direct; has performed in tandem with Bill Mooney.

Instruments/Props: banjo, slide guitar, squeeze box, ukulele, fiddle, harmonica, bones, spoons, autoharp, dulcimer, bottle, washboard, jaw harp.

Dubbed a "one-man celebration," Grammy award–winner David Holt combines the talents of musician, historian, emcee, entertainer, and storyteller. He believes that stories convey mantras — ancient lore that communicates relevance, morals, and wisdom to the hearer. He has relied on instinct in the development of a repertoire of adventure, mystery, and character stories that audiences lean forward to hear. One of his wrestlings with story form interjected an account of a ten-year-old survivor into a story about the sinking of the Titanic in 1912. The focus is typical of Holt's style — personal and dynamic. A humorous tale, "The Hogaphone," derives from an anecdote contributed by a real person, Uncle Ike, but the fleshed-out story belongs to the teller, who gave it life and substance.

A Grammy winner and three-time nominee musician-storyteller, Holt has been a professional raconteur since 1981 and has traveled for the U.S. State Department to Africa, Brazil, Venezuela, Nepal, India, Burma, and Thailand as an American musical ambassador. His talents in music, storytelling, history, and entertainment place him in the forefront of the effort to preserve and promote traditional American music and stories. He has appeared on *Hee Haw, Nashville Now* and *Music City Tonight,* and *The Grand Ole Opry* and has hosted the Nashville Network's *Fire on the Mountain, Celebration Express, American Music Stop,* PBS *Folkways Series,* and Public Radio's *Riverwalk: Classic Jazz from the Landing,* broadcast from San Antonio, Texas. His tours with *From Here to Kingdom Come* and *Banjo Reb and the Blue Ghost* have introduced his one-man shows and the music of the Civil War. Festivals have taken him to the National Storytelling Festival in Jonesborough, Tennessee, and the Northern Appalachian Storytelling Festival in Mansfield, Pennsylvania. In 1994 he joined colleague Bill Mooney to compile *Ready-to-Tell Tales: Surefire Stories from America's Favorite Storytellers,* an anthology of the best in storytelling; two years later they produced *The Storyteller's Guide,* a revered handbook of practical information and tips on career planning for professional performers.

Holt is a product of Southern tradition. Born October 15, 1946, he derives from Garland, Texas, and lived in Pacific Palisades, California, from his early teens. His stories began with frontier lore dating to the settlement of Texas, which were a natural part of the local history he learned in childhood. His love of music began with his father's expertise on bones and spoons that were family heirlooms for five generations. Holt developed a flare for rhythm by playing drums. In 1968, while studying harmonica, he learned original cowboy stories from an eyewitness, Carl Sprague, and listened to recordings of Midwestern poet Carl Sandburg, Uncle Dave Macon, and Ralph Stanley.

Holt graduated *magna cum laude* from the University of California at Santa Barbara with degrees in art and biology and completed an advanced degree in education, but his career as an elementary teacher was unsatisfying. When he began collecting mountain stories and music, he used a $2,000 bequest from his grandmother Kate "Nannie" Lowrey to return to his roots for themes for platform performances. With banjo picker Steve Keith, he journeyed to fiddle conventions and front porches where mountaineers joined in jam sessions on traditional homemade instruments. His first attendance at the Asheville, North Carolina, Folk Festival convinced him to settle in hill country among the best of bluegrass musicians and classic tellers Ray Hicks, Richard Chase, and the Harmon family. Holt shared the post of storyteller on WLOS-TV's *Mr. Bill Show* with veteran teller Gwenda LedBetter. His perusal of material from western North Carolina provided folktales and real-life experiences, which became the focus of an Appalachian music program that he founded in 1975 at Warren Wilson College in Swannanoa, North Carolina. He has added to the permanent collection of the Library of Congress and received a grant from the National Endowment for the Arts to study hammered dulcimer player Virgil Craven. He is a three-time winner of the *Frets* magazine readers poll for best old-time banjoist. Settled in Fairview in North Carolina's Great Smokies, he lives with wife Ginny Callaway, who manages his recordings on the High Windy Audio label.

Articles

"Storytellers' Views on Blending Narrative and Song," *Storytelling Magazine,* May 1997, 16–20.

Bibliography

"The Fiddler of Rattlesnake Ridge," in *More Best-Loved Stories Told at the National Storytelling Festival*, August House, 1992.

"The First Motorcycle in Black Mountain," in *Best-Loved Stories Told at the National Storytelling Festival*, August House, 1991.

"The First Motorcycle in Black Mountain, North Carolina," *Storytelling World*, Summer-Fall 1993, 13–14.

Ready-to-Tell Tales: Sure-fire Stories from America's Favorite Storytellers (co-editor Bill Mooney), August House, 1994. Forty-one world tales collected from the nation's best storytellers, including "Trouble! or How the Alligator Got Its Crackling Hide" and "Is It Deep Enough?," and Holt's "The Freedom Bird."

The Storyteller's Guide (co-author Bill Mooney), August House, 1996. A how-to for storytellers.

"Tailybone" in *Homespun: Tales from America's Favorite Storytellers*, Crown, 1988.

Videography

"Barney McCabe," in *American Storytelling Series, Vol. 5*, H. W. Wilson, 1987.

Fixin' to Tell About Jack, Appalshop, 1974.

Folk Rhythms, Homespun Tapes, 1997.

The Hogaphone and Other Stories, High Windy Audio, 1991. A collection of Southern folktales, featuring the story of a homemade telephone wire strung between groundhog hides.

Old Time Banjo I, II, III, Homespun Tapes. 1997.

Audiography

Grandfather's Greatest Hits (audiocassette and CD), High Windy Audio, 1992. Contains "John Henry," "Fire on the Mountain," "Wabash Cannonball," "Pretty Polly," "Little Log Cabin in the Lane," "Corrina," "Bound to Ride," "Cripple Creek," "Old-time Medley" ("Soldier's Joy," "Mississippi Sawyer," "Arkansas Traveler"), "Wreck of the Old 97," "Wildwood Flower," and "Dixie."

The Hairyman and Other Wild Tales (audiocassette), High Windy Audio, 1981. Southern folktales, including "Groundhog," "The Hogaphone," "The First Motorcycle in Black Mountain, North Carolina," "Barney McCabe," "The Magic Fiddle," "The Apple Tree," and the title story; for ages four and up.

"The Hogaphone," in *Tales of Wit and Humor* (contributor) (audiocassette), National Association for the Preservation and Perpetuation of Storytelling, 1992.

I Got a Bullfrog: Folksongs for the Fun of It (audiocassette and CD), High Windy Audio, 1994. Contains "Doodle Daddle Day," "The Cat Came Back," "Blackeyed Susie," "Ain't No Bugs on Me," "C-H-I-C-K-E-N," "Mole in the Ground," "Who Broke the Lock?," "Cindy," "The Glendy Burke," "Long John," "Keep on the Sunnyside," "Sail Away Ladies," "Yes, Papa," "When the Train Comes Along," and "This Little Light of Mine."

It Just Suits Me (audiocassette), June Appal Records, 1981. Contains "Morning Blues," "Dinah," "Lost John," "Ragtime Annie," "Little Stream of Whiskey," "Too Late to Pray," "The Old John Hardy," "Cotton-Eyed Joe," "Jerusalem Mourn," "Leather Britches," "Hambone," "Roustabout,"

"Paddy on the Turnpike," "Hop-light Ladies," and the title song.

Mostly Ghostly Stories (audiocassette), High Windy Audio, 1995. Contains "The Jealous Bones of Aaron Kelly" from South Carolina, "Fancy," the story of a flood that dislodges coffins, "Scalped Alive," "The Blood-Drawing Ghost," "The Titanic," and "The Magic Lake"; for ages seven and up.

Play the Jaw Harp Now (audiocassette), High Windy Audio, 1988. How-to tape comes with free jaw harp and instruction from beginning to advanced.

Reel and Rock (audiocassette), High Windy Audio, 1985. Features "Free Little Bird," "Dixie Darlin'," "The Coo Coo," "Texas Bound," "Preacher and the Bear," "I've Got You," "Sail Away," "Raincrow Bill Goes Up Cripple Creek," "Forked Deer," "Meeting Is Over," "Goodbye, Goodbye," and the title song plus music by Doc and Merle Watson.

Spiders in the Hairdo: Based on Contemporary Urban Legends (co-producer Bill Mooney) (audiocassette), High Windy Audio, 1997. Urban legends, including "The Hook," "The Choking Doberman," "The Vanishing Hitchhiker," "The Cement-Filled Cadillac," and the title story; for teens and adults.

Stellaluna (audiocassette and CD), High Windy Audio, 1996. Stories and facts about bats from Janell Cannon's best-selling book.

Tailybone (audiocassette), High Windy Audio, 1985. Contains the title story plus "Ross and Anna," "Spearfinger," "Ducks on the Pond," "Last Chance," "The Hairywoman," "Sioux Indians," and "The Fiddler of Rattlesnake Ridge."

Verdi (audiocassette and CD), High Windy Audio, 1997. Reading of Janell Cannon's story of a yellow striped snake who turns green.

Why the Dog Chases the Cat: Great Animal Stories (co-performer Bill Mooney) (audiocassette), High Windy Audio, 1994. Contains "Why You Never Hear Rabbit Play Banjo," "Trouble or How the Alligator Got Its Hide," "Is It Deep Enough?," "Why the Cat Washes Its Paws Before It Eats," "The Whirlwind," and the title story; for ages four and up.

"Wiley and the Hairy Man," in *Homespun Tales* (audiocassette), National Association for the Preservation and Perpetuation of Storytelling, 1986.

Awards

1996 National Storytelling Association's Circle of Excellence.

1996 Parents' Choice Award for *Stellaluna*.

1996 Grammy Award for *Stellaluna*.

1996 American Booksellers Association Pick of the List for *Stellaluna*.

1996 American Library Association's Notable Recording for *Stellaluna*.

1996 Grammy nominee for *Why the Dog Chases the Cat: Great Animal Stories*.

1996 *Storytelling World* Honor Award for Best Audio Recording for *Mostly Ghostly Stories*.

1995 Parents' Choice Gold Award for *Why the Dog Chases the Cat: Great Animal Stories*.

1995 NAIRD Indie Award for *Mostly Ghostly Stories*.

1995 American Library Association Notable Recording for *Why the Dog Chases the Cat: Great Animal Stories*.

1995 NAIRD Indie Award for *Why the Dog Chases the Cat: Great Animal Stories*.

1994 *Storytelling World* winner for *Ready-to-Tell Tales*.

1994 Pennsylvania School Library Association Young Adult Best of the Best Pick for *Ready-to-Tell Tales*.

1994 American Library Association Notable Recording for *I Got a Bullfrog: Folksongs for the Fun of It*.

1994 NAIRD Indie Award for *I Got a Bullfrog: Folksongs for the Fun of It*.

1994 Parents' Choice Award for *I Got a Bullfrog: Folksongs for the Fun of It*.

1993 University of North Carolina Razor Walker Award.

1992 Parents' Magazine's Very Best for the Very Young for *Grandfather's Greatest Hits*.

1992 Grammy Award nomination for Best Traditional Folk Recording for *Grandfather's Greatest Hits*.

1989, 1988, 1986 Frets Magazine Best Old-time Banjoist.

1985 NAIRD Indie Award for *Reel and Rock*.

1985 American Library Association Notable Recording for *Tailybone*.

1986 NAIRD Indie Award for *Tailybone*.

1984 *Esquire* Magazine Annual Register of Men and Women Who Are Changing America.

1981 American Library Association Notable Recording for *The Hairyman*.

Source

Cote, Maria, "Musician a Delight from Head to Toe," *Miami Herald*, January 27, 1992.

Hatfield, Jack, "David Holt Interview," *Banjo Newsletter*, October 1991, 6–8.

"High Windy Artist: David Holt," http://www.megnet.com/hi-windy/holt.html, October 11, 1996.

Hill, Jennifer, "Storytellers Recall Festival's First Years in Jonesborough," Jonesborough, Tennessee, *Herald and Tribune*, September 30, 1992, 2C, 4C.

"Holt Wins Grammy," *Tale Trader*, August 1997, 10.

"Jonesborough's National Storytelling Festival Attracts Thousands to Annual Three-Day Event," *The Loafer*, October 1, 1996, 19, 21.

Keding, Dan, "David Holt: Holding on to Treasures," *Sing Out!*, May–July 1996, 35–42.

Smith, "Third Time's the Charm for Grammy-Winning David Holt," *Times-News*, March 1, 1997.

"Storytellers Receive Grammy Nominations," *Storytelling Magazine*, May 1996, 7.

White, Jon, "Spinning Yarns," *Indianapolis Business Journal*, January 1, 1995.

Woodard, Josef, "Stories and Songs from a Bygone Era," *Los Angeles Times*, September 19, 1996.

Zoppa, Linda, "Review," *School Library Journal*, July 1995, 28.

BETH HORNER

Address   P. O. Box 540
              Wilmette, Illinois 60091-0540
       phone 847-864-9588

P. O. Box 836
Columbia, Missouri 65205-0836
phone 573-443-3816

Focus: American lifestyle; women's stories; farm tales; musical stories; contemporary humor; personal and family escapades; traditional worldwide tales; ghost stories.

Audience: children and adults.

Style: vivacious, traditional style enhanced with music, evoking raucous laughter and insightful reflection.

Instruments/Props: bones, autoharp.

A former children's librarian and creative theater teacher, Beth Horner has been a touring storytelling and recording artist since 1984 and has spent much of her adult professional life in Chicago. Born and raised in Boone County, Missouri, she was fascinated by storytelling at an early age, inspired by her St. Louis grandmother, who memorized folk and fairy tales from library books and recounted them to her grandchildren. These tales created a foundation and particular interest in traditional tales. In addition, both of Horner's parents contributed to her love of character and narrative. Her father, a farmer and meteorologist, filled her early years with stories of notable ancestors, of both lofty and questionable repute. Her mother, who later became an English professor, read poetry and novels aloud to her children. Two of Beth's most popular original stories were inspired by these early years: "Winifred's Journey: Party Girl … Farmer … Scholar … Mom," the near epic tale of her mother's transition from a St. Louis party girl to a globe-trotting scholar at age 70; and "What's in a ?," the humorous and touching story of Beth's search for her own middle name via childhood research into characters who made up her ancestry.

With an undergraduate degree in library science/child development/theater and a master's degree in library science, Horner became a children's librarian in order to tell stories. In 1983, at the age of 30, however, she embarked on a full-time career as a storyteller and has been a nationally touring performer and recording artist since then. "Encounter with a Romance Novel," her most frequently requested story for adults, is a raucously humorous spoof on a particular genre of literature from a librarian's perspective.

Horner's repertoire is a rich mix of both traditional and original stories. Accompanying herself on autoharp and bones, she has created programs for adults, including "Love Lost, Found, and Fumbled," "Strong Women: Stories of Laughter and Light," "The Haunting and the Humorous," "The Environmental Illness Talking Blues," "The Water Oaks Trilogy," and "Missouri Memories." For children, she performs "Cindermaids and Wonder Boys," "Spine Chillers and Funnybone Ticklers," "Stories of the Stars and Sky," "Heroines and Heroes Across the World," "The Story of the Civil War," "American Folk Tales and Folk Songs," and "The Christmas China Doll." Horner brings her varied and long experience to a keynote speech, "Storytelling: Education, Entertainment, Empowerment," and to her workshops, which focus on incorporating music into storytelling, how to tell stories to teenagers, structuring personal and family tales, and enriching practice and performance.

Horner has been featured on *PM Magazine* and WGN-radio's *Roy Leonard Show*. She has produced a six-part storytelling series for radio and has performed at the National Storytelling Festival, National Council of Teachers of English, American Library Association, National Conference on Storytelling, Missouri Folklore Society, Texas Storytelling Festival, Festival of Stories on Martha's Vineyard, Pacific Storytelling Festival, Busch Gardens, Women in Management, and other major storytelling festivals across the United States. She is also an active local performer in Illinois and Missouri, many of her performances being funded by the Illinois Arts Council's ARTS-TOUR program and the Missouri Arts Council's Touring program.

In addition to solo performance, Horner is known for artistic collaborations. She often tours with fellow performers Nancy Donoval and Susan O'Halloran in their program "Mothers and Other Wild Women." Her four-year, 40-plus performance collaboration with the Oriana Singers, a madrigal singing group, took Horner to Chicago's prestigious Ravinia

Festival. She and Missouri songwriter Bob Dyer present "Story into Song," exploring the subject's practical, artistic, and historical elements within the context of Missouri lore. She is active in the current storytelling renaissance and served from 1985 to 1991 on the board of directors of the National Association for the Preservation and Perpetuation of Storytelling.

Articles

"A Foot in Each World: Maintaining a Full-Time Library Position While Developing a Free-Lance Business," *Library Trends*, Winter 1984, 283–290.

"Storytelling Is Not the Handing Out of Morals," *Chicago Tribune*, May 8, 1988, Section 10, p. 31.

"To Tell or Not to Tell: Storytelling for Young Adults," *Illinois Libraries*, September 1983, 458–464.

Bibliography

"The Mischievous Girl & the Hideous Creature," in *Ready-to-Tell Tales*, August House, 1994.

Videography

We Hear Ya Talkin', Library Cable Network, 1989. Features "The Mousedeer and the Buffalo Chip," an Indonesian folktale, and

"Elsie and Mr. Fox," a retelling of an Ozark folktale with autoharp accompaniment.

Audiography

Encounter with a Romance Novel: Heroines in Everyday Life (audiocassette), self-produced, 1993. A spoof on the stereotypical romance novel, featuring "The Witch Song," "My Childhood Life Jacket," "Generations," "The Young Woman of Vietnam," "The Skull," and the title story; for older children, families, and adults.

An Evening at Cedar Creek (audiocassette), Wellspring Music, 1987. Seven traditional tales with music, including three Missouri tales: "The Phantom Black Carriage," "Elsie and Mr. Fox," and "Hootie Jones"; also includes "My Dog," "Nasrudin's Coat," "Abiyoyo," "The Mousedeer and the Buffalo Chip," and "Li Chi Slays the Serpent"; accompaniment on autoharp, fiddle, mandolin, guitar, and accordion; for children, families, and adults.

Mothers and Other Wild Women, Vol. I, Mostly Wild (co-performers Nancy Donoval and Susan "Supe" O'Halloran) (audiocassette), Wild Women Collective, 1993. Contains "Be Nice," "Wild in Milwaukee," "Good Mom/Bad Mom," and "Encounter with a Romance Novel"; for teens and adults; recorded in live performance at St. Scholastica High School in Chicago.

Source

Greene, Ellin, ed. *Storytelling Art and Technique.* 3rd Edition. Bronx, N. Y.: Bowker, 1996.

"Heroic Tales and Other Stories," *Chicago Tribune*, April 14, 1996.

"Jonesborough's National Storytelling Festival Attracts Thousands to Annual Three-Day Event," *The Loafer*, October 1, 1996, 19, 21.

Mooney, Bill, and David Holt. *The Storyteller's Guide.* Little Rock, Arkansas: August House, 1996.

Smithson, Shelley, "Mothers and Other Wild Women," *San Juan Sun*, May 7, 1997, 13.

"Storytelling Is Not the Handing Out of Morals," *Chicago Tribune*, May 8, 1988, Section 10, p. 31.

BOB JENKINS

Address   15881 Longwood Drive
             Los Gatos, California 95032
email drbobj@pacbell.net

Focus: imaginative, original stories; mystery lore; folktales.
Audience: all ages.
Style: dramatic, humorous.

Raconteur Bob Jenkins got his start in telling from a grandmother who read aloud from Henry Wadsworth Longfellow's *Song of Hiawatha*. Jenkins shaped and developed his interest in literature through theater and siddha yoga. Trained by Stan DeHart, his high school drama coach, and by Gil Lazier, the dean of the school of theater at Florida State, Jenkins augmented stage experience with yoga from Baba Muktananda and Gurumayi Chidvalasananda. The urge to tell came in the 1960s in Chu Lai, Vietnam, where he was a Marine enlistee teaching dental hygiene to children as part of a MEDCAP team. To express the importance of sound teeth, he told "Tommy Tooth and Dirty Dan Decay."

Returning to college at Florida State University in 1969, Jenkins honed skills in child education and theater. Creative dramatics prepared him for children's theater groups, where he specialized in oral interpretation for children. His first platform narration was "Waitin' for Martin," a folktale he used on school tours. After several years of tours, acting and directing, graduate school in Tallahassee, and a doctorate, he was ready for real work at the theatre arts department of San Jose State University in 1975 as children's theater director. While teaching storytelling, he drew on the Vietnam experience and his background as a native of North Carolina, an area that appreciates oral tradition. In his résumé, he claims to have "thrashed around for a couple of years, hopefully not hurting any of my students too badly, teaching Godknowswhat, voice and diction, characterization, probably" before attending a festival in Santa Cruz in the late 1970s. The experience introduced him to the

professional artistry of serious, capable performers.

From the start, Jenkins was a celebrity. He claims as mentors a list of respected platform professionals: Kathryn Windham, Mary Carter Smith, Steve Sanfield, Katy Rydell, Bill Harley, Ed Stivender, Gay Ducey, Olga Loya, Martha Holloway, Johnny Moses, and Milbre Burch. His favorite festivals include the National Storytelling Festival in Jonesborough, Tennessee, Mariposa Festival, Tellabration! in Los Altos, California, and the Sierra Storytelling Festival, where he is a twelve-year veteran. After teaching a hundred classes in storytelling, he has heard approximately 12,000 stories. An organizer and promoter of storytelling, he helped establish the First Pacific Storytelling Congress.

Bibliography

"Huntin' Werewolf for Papa Keel," in *More Best-Loved Stories Told at the National Storytelling Festival*, August House, 1992.

"The Man Who Wanted Incredible Things," in *Tell Me a Story, Vol. 1*, Hometown Entertainment, 1995.

Audiography

Dangerous Nights (audiocassette)

The Man Who Wanted Incredible Things (audiocassette), Strange and Jenkins, 1989.

Contains the title story plus "No Story?," "The Sassy Daughter," and "Fickle Finger of Fate."

Tell Me a Story, Vol. I (audiocassette), National Storytelling Association, 1995.

Videography

Ghost Stories.

Source

"A Brief Look at This Year's Storytellers," Jonesborough, Tennessee, *Herald & Tribune*, September 30, 1992, 4C–8C.

Timeless Voices: Images of the National Storytelling Festival. Jonesborough, Tenn.: National Storytelling Press, 1997.

LARRY JOHNSON

Address   Key of See Storytellers
Box 27314
Minneapolis, Minnesota 55427-0314
phone (home) 612-546-1074
phone (work) 612-627-2673

Focus: stories of humor and healing for earth and everyone; therapeutic storytelling; gardening imagery and ecology stories.
Audience: all ages.
Style: joint workshops and presentations with Elaine Wynne, a storytelling therapist.
Instruments/Props: puppet, unusual musical instruments made from garden hose and other discarded junk that won't compost.

Larry D. Johnson, a Swedish-American gardener/storyteller, believes that stories are a living, personal function that is integral to human emotions. Like other tellers of the electronic generation, he declares that telling should hold primacy over mechanical entertainments. A proponent of mental health, he maintains that telling fosters healing at home and in the workplace. Like many storytellers, he blends his talents into a workable mix. Coordinating interests in education, gardening, wellness, video, and storytelling, he has turned to practical use his numerous talents and avocations, which have taken him to

Ecuador, Japan, England, Scandinavia, and across the United States. A master gardener and storyteller and video teacher for fifteen years in a university setting, he influences educators and future tellers. He has taught storytelling and video at the Longfellow International Fine Arts School in Minneapolis and told stories through Tyler, his puppet persona, over a closed circuit television channel at the Minneapolis Children's Medical Center. In addition, he was a featured teller at the NEA conference at the Kennedy Center for the Performing Arts in Washington, D.C.

Johnson credits his grandparents with introducing him to the importance of gardening and storytelling walks, when he searched for popsicle sticks to support the stems and leaves of his grandmother's African violets. In the late 1960s in his own garden in Bloomington, Minnesota, and in the asparagus fields outside of town, he harvested vegetables and sold them to pay his way through broadcast school. Tinkering with portable video equipment, he adapted the mechanisms to storytelling to help troubled kids tell their own stories. He began to cultivate the analogy of telling and gardening: planting a story and cultivating it in the mind required the attention that seedlings demand. Harvesting occurred at the moment when the teller passed the story to a real listener. The story bore fruit in the form of audience response. In 1970, he lived in New Ulm, Germany, while researching the tales of Baron Karl Friedrich von Munchausen. Resettled in Austin, Minnesota, in 1972, he produced and hosted *Kids for Ecology*, an environmental show for children's television and encouraged children to write their own gardening and composting stories. The job segued into a camp residency in Mound, Minnesota, where he developed a child-produced television laboratory. In 1977, he created Tyler the Angleworm, a puppet who planted a roof garden, and emceed "Electronic Get Well Card," a live, participatory television channel in Minneapolis Children's Hospital. It was during this pro-green period that Johnson ran for the United States presidency as candidate of the Old Garden Party. His blend of gardening, telling, and video grew into letter exchanges between pen pals around the world who had stories to tell about their gardens.

A lifetime member of the National Story League, Johnson and his wife, psychologist Elaine Wynne, have been hearty tellers since the late 1960s. In 1982, they helped found the Northlands Storytelling Network, and, in 1991, helped establish the Cultural Environment Movement (CEM), a coalition that makes story distribution fair and equitable. Together, they opened the 1996 CEM convention by demonstrating "The Legend of Sadako," a healing story about a real Japanese girl who contracts leukemia in 1945 from the atomic fallout at Hiroshima. To foster hope and world peace, Johnson and Wynne have told the story annually since 1982 at the Hiroshima/Nagasaki Remembrance and throughout the United States, and in England, Ecuador, and Scandinavia. In addition to public appearances, Johnson writes a children's garden column that centers on outdoors activity and storytelling. His main outreach is through media literacy, gardening, videomaking, and narrative, which he performs for local schools. A popular feature of Johnson's telling is a call-in television special, "Finish That Story," which invites children to complete an unfinished plot.

Bibliography

"Digging Deeper Through Video Exchange," *Creating Context*, Zephyr Press, 1996.

"The Giant's Junkyard," *Not Like Any Other Children's Book*, Smith Publishers, 1982.

"The Legend of Sadako," *Storytelling Magazine*, July 1997, 28–29.

"Let Me Die Laughing," *National Storytelling Journal*, Winter 1984.

"Making TV Behave Like a Storyteller in the Garden," *Plant Allies*, Spring 1996, 17–19.

Minnesota Horticulturist, monthly columns since 1995.

"Storytelling: A Focus: at Cultural Environment Movement Founding Convention," *Tale Trader*, February 1997, 1, 7.

"Storytelling on Video Is Not Storytelling," *Storytelling Magazine*, Spring/Summer 1988.

"Take Action on CEM Storytelling Action Statements," *Grapevine*, October 1996.

"A Tale of Two Touching Trees," *Solstice Evergreen*, Aslan Publishing, 1997.

"Telling Stories in an Age of Television," *Creating Context*, Zephyr Press, 1996.

"Video Letter Exchange," *Linking Through Diversity*, (contributor) Zephyr Press, 1993.

Awards

1986 Tokyo Video Festival grand prize (with Elaine Wynne) for child-created international video exchange.

1982, 1980 Action for Children's TV National Achievement Award.

Source

"Cultural Environment Movement Holds Convention," *Storytelling Magazine*, July 1996, 6.

"Key of See: Tellers, Teachers, Activists," *Storytelling Magazine*, July 1997, 29.

Mizui, Yoko, "A Touching Tale of Kids Wows Video Fest Judges," Tokyo *Daily Yomiuri*, November 21, 1986.

"What Other Kids Are Doing," *Junior Storyteller*, Spring 1995, 4–5.

See also Elaine Wynne.

MATT JONES

Address   2710 Cable Avenue
              Lincoln, Nebraska 68502
phone 402-472-3522
fax 402-472-8675
email mlj@unlinfo.unl.edu

Focus: Kiowa/Otoe-Missouri tales; beast fables; creation stories; personal anecdotes; tales of cultural identity.

Audience: general.

Style: kinetic, humorous retellings of traditional Indian lore; animal characterizations.

Instruments/Props: drum; Kiowa ceremonial dress and jewelry.

Matthew L. "Sitting Bear" Jones is a burly, jovial storyteller capable of turning himself into a possum or coyote or Indian drummer for the delight of listeners. Skilled at a host of episodes of Midwestern nature and animal lore, he enacts all the parts, throwing his voice to duplicate the personae of anguished, joyful, bemused, and wily creatures involved in convoluted plots to thwart or humiliate each other. Equally adept as a stage raconteur, Jones tells of his life as a student within the Bureau of Indian Affairs education system. His didactic purpose is to demonstrate how white government officials and bureaucrats have imposed the Anglo point of view on native Americans, to the detriment of the Indian's achievement and self-esteem.

Jones's career belongs on the plains. He was born in Wichita, Kansas, where his father worked in aviation; his mother was a housewife. From both parents, grandparents, and uncles and aunts he learned the lore that became his oral material. Currently a sales and acquisitions specialist for Native American Public Telecommunications in Lincoln, Nebraska, Jones derives his platform skills from a varied background. He obtained an A.A. degree in theater from Haskell Indian Junior College and a B.G.S. in mass communications from Wichita State University. He has appeared in eleven theater performances, including *Sitting Bear, Annie Get Your Gun, Barefoot in the Park, The Skin of Our Teeth, Come Blow Your Horn*, and *One Flew Over the Cuckoo's Nest*, in which he co-starred as Chief Bromden. Jones co-hosted a *Sunday Magazine* over KAKE-TV. A veteran of numerous television productions, he was featured in *Storytellers Theater* by Americana Television Network in Branson, Missouri, and in *America's Special Days: Native American Day* in Lincoln, Nebraska, and has played in seven movies, notably as a war chief named Red Coat and a British colonial soldier in *The American Phoenix*, produced by Centron in Lawrence, Kansas.

Jones's storytelling experiences have taken him throughout the United States. In June 1993, he appeared in fringed buckskins, moccasins, and headdress to tell animal fables at the American Library Association convention in New Orleans. His other telling engagements span the map from Daphine, Canada, to Mexico City, from Baltimore to San Francisco, and have put him before audiences of the Missouri Association of School Librarians, Nebraska

Public Radio Network, Iowa Library Association, Saint Mary's College, Kansas State University, Haskell Indian Nations University, Nebraska Library Association, Americana Cable Television Network, and International Society of School Librarians.

Bibliography

Native America in the Twentieth Century: An Encyclopedia (contributor), Garland Publishing, 1994.

Videography

America's Special Days — Native American Day, Great Plains National, 1994. A program highlighting Native American contributions to the United States and the world.

Distant Voices ... Thunder Words, Vision Maker Video, 1990. Describes how Native American oral tradition influence Native American writers.

In the White Man's Image, PBS-TV, 1992. A look at the impact of the United States boarding school system on generations of American Indians.

The Runaway, Vision Maker Video. 1987. A training program for counselors in the urban Indian community.

Speaking with Confidence, NETCHE, 1997. An educational program on public speaking.

Storyteller Series, Americana Television Network, 1994. A series of programs highlighting Native American storytellers.

You the Juror, Carr Production Group, 1997. A training program for prospective jurors.

Awards

1995 Center for Great Plains Studies Fellow.

1995 Red Earth Film and Video Festival Best Native American Industrial/Promotional Program.

1993 Red Earth Film and Video Festival first place for *In the White Man's Image*.

1993 Ohio Stave Award for *In the White Man's Image*.

1993 National Education Film & Video Festival Silver Apple for *In the White Man's Image*.

1993 Gabriel Award for *In the White Man's Image*.

1993 Great Plains Film Festival Best Native American Production for *In the White Man's Image*.

1993 Erik Barnous Award for *In the White Man's Image*.

1993 Great Plain Storytelling Festival First Place.

1992 CINE Golden Eagle Award for *In the White Man's Image*.

Source

"Acclaimed Native American Storyteller to Visit Dec. 3," University of Nebraska *Scarlet*, December 1, 1995.

"Distant Voices ... Thunder Word," (video), Vision Maker Video.

"It's Storytime in Gibbon," *Kearney* (Nebraska) *Hub*, June 17, 1994.

"Kiowa Indian Legends Told in Belvidere," *Hebron* (Nebraska) *Journal Register*, April 13, 1994.

"Learning By Listening," *Norfolk* (Nebraska) *Daily News*, November 19, 1991.

"Matthew Sitting Bear Jones Entertains All Tuesday," *Sidney* (Nebraska) *Telegraph*, July 12, 1989.

"Native American Storyteller Entertains at Ceresco, Valparaiso," *The* (Waverly, Nebraska) *News*, January 25, 1996.

"Nebraska Story Fest Held Here," *Hastings* (Nebraska) *Tribune*, June 3, 1991.

"'Sitting Bear' Jones to Be at Indian Summer Rendezvous," *Keith County* (Ogallala, Nebraska) *News*, September 7, 1992.

Storytellers Series (video), American Television Network, Branson, Missouri.

"Story Time," *Wahoo* (Nebraska) *Newspaper*, May 15, 1997.

"Students Discover 'Small World,'" Columbus, Nebraska *Telegram*, April 18, 1991.

"Students on Edge of Seats As Sitting Bear Tells His Stories," *North Platte* (Nebraska) *Telegraph*, November 5, 1994.

"Telling the Past," *Keith County* (Nebraska) *News*, September 16, 1992.

"When This Bear Talks People Listen," *Hastings* (Nebraska) *Tribune*, June 9, 1993.

"Who's Who in America," New Providence, N.J.: Marquis 1996.

RON JONES

Address   1201 Stanyan
             San Francisco, California 94117
      phone 415-566-8470

Focus: real experiences with the handicapped; personal anecdotes about his tour of Nuremburg, Germany.

Audience: general.

Style: relaxed telling; off-beat humor; monologues and on-stage characterization; performs with jazz guitarist Kenny Martha.

An energetic humanist with a strong interest in the Holocaust, Ron Jones has progressed

through the literary arts from novels and plays to platform narrative about the exercise of freedom and the personal choice to counter prejudice and racism. Born to a Jewish mother and gentile father in San Francisco in 1940, he was reared out of the faith, but attended synagogue services for holidays and bar mitzvahs. His most enduring tie with Judaism came from his maternal grandmother, who told stories at the dinner table. After graduating from San Francisco State University in 1969 with a social studies degree and from Stanford with an M.A. in education and international relations and a minor in sports, Jones coached basketball and taught history at Cubberley High School in Palo Alto, California, until he was fired at the end of his tenure year for such innovations as modeling fascism, questioning the U.S. involvement in Vietnam, and arranging student exchanges between all-black and all-white neighborhoods. The abrupt separation ended his eligibility for future public classroom jobs. For thirty years, he compensated by teaching at private facilities and hospitals.

Undaunted by defeat and motivated by his grandmother's spirit, Jones redirected his tal-ents to literary art. He currently maintains a dual career in freelance storytelling and writing, averaging one title annually for 23 years. In addition to publication, in 1972, he originated *Zephyros,* a nonprofit education clearinghouse for creative teaching ideas. He has worked with adults and children at the San Francisco Recreation Center for the Handicapped since 1978 and serves as basketball coach for the Special Olympics. A soft-spoken, unassuming man, he lives in the Haight-Ashbury section of San Francisco with his wife, Deanna, a professional potter who gave him the impetus to write, and their daughter, Hilary. He loves to read letters from readers and receives a quantity of responses from elementary and junior high students, both normal and handicapped.

Jones first won acclaim as a writer of young adult literature. His most popular books include: *The Acorn People*, the nonfiction account of his tenure as counselor at a camp for seriously ill children; *Say Ray*, the story of the kidnap of a handicapped man; and *B-Ball*, about Special Olympics basketball. His play, *Kids Called Crazy,* taken from teaching experiences in the teen psychiatric ward of San Francisco's Mount Zion Hospital, opened at the New Conservatory Theater in San Francisco in April, 1988. *The Wave*, the true account of a dramatic classroom experiment to demonstrate Fascism at Cubberley High in the late 1960s, catapulted him to fame, particularly in Germany, where the story is required reading for public school students. As a guest of the German government, he toured Hitler's private chamber and formulated a one-man presentation on Eva Moses, survivor of the infamous Dr. Joseph Mengele's inhumane laboratory experiments on twins incarcerated in Nazi death camps. As a consequence of on-site research, he began delivering a monologue about Nazism called "Her Name Was Eva Moses," a tribute to a lone Jewish freedom fighter. In 1986, he attended a conference in Terre Haute, Indiana, that Eva Moses organized to investigate reports of Joseph Mengele's death. His personal commitment to stop future Holocausts takes shape in platform narratives about how easy it is to lose personal freedom.

For enjoyment, Jones took up lighter forms of storytelling while developing Theatre Unlimited, an in-house troupe for his handicapped students. Invited to take a play on tour, he filled in for characters his troupe could not cover. To flesh out their parts, he stood on-stage and told their experiences. As he evolved a unique style, he studied master tellers Marga Gomez and Anne Galjur, both of whom rely on autobiographical material. For ten years, Jones has related to audiences in European and American coffeehouses, jazz clubs, and small theaters through reenactments of personal and work experiences. He frequently conducts workshops and lectures at the Holocaust Center in San Francisco. He has garnered critical acclaim both for innovative, courageous teaching methods and for his delivery of reflections on Nazism, history, and destiny, and has been featured in the *New York Times, Christian Science Monitor, Der Spiegel, People, In These Times, CTA Action, California Living, Readers Digest, Books West,* and *Disabled USA* on *Good Morning, New Dimensions Radio, America, Phil Donahue Show,* and National Public Radio.

Bibliography

The Acorn People, Bantam Doubleday Dell, 1976.

"The Acorn People: What I Learned at Summer Camp," *Psychology Today*, June 1977, 70–81.

Airman, self-published, 1982.

B-Ball, Bantam Doubleday Dell, 1990. A novel about Special Olympics basketball.

The Boy Who Thought He Was Elvis, self-published, 1994.

The Christmas Coat, Island Press, 1979. The story of an aging San Francisco musician who tries to reunite his family.

Die Wirliche, Ravensburger (Germany), 1994.

Finding Community, Freel and Associates, 1971.

Kids Called Crazy, Bantam Doubleday Dell, 1982. A play taken from the author's experiences as a teacher in the teen-age psychiatric ward of San Francisco's Mount Zion Hospital.

No Substitute for Madness, Island Press, 1981.

Say Ray, Bantam Doubleday Dell, 1984. *An* adventure novel about a handicapped man who comes into money, is kidnapped, and must struggle to survive.

Shared Victory, self-published, 1980.

"Taken As Directed," *Whole Earth Review*, Spring 1976.

The Team That Never Lost a Game, Kaleidoscope (Denmark), 1996.

The Vacant Lot, self-published, 1994.

VWR, self-published, 1991.

"The Wave," *Whole Earth Review*, 1981.

Your City Has Been Kidnapped, Addison Wesley, 1972.

Zephyros #1-16, self-published, 1971–1983.

Videography

The Acorn People, Joffee, CBS, 1985.

B-Ball, NBC-TV, 1992.

Mint Jammin', Dirksen-Malloy Productions, 1997. Eight original stories, featuring the special gift of Jones's father to his son, a story about skinny dipping in a pond, the mysterious death of insect lady, and the sexual prowess of mint jam.

One Special Victory, Laroquette, NBC, 1994.

The Team That Never Lost a Game, Dirksen-Malloy Productions, 1997. A true story of a Special Olympic basketball team on a winning streak.

The Wave, Dirksen-Malloy Productions, 1996. Jones talks about an exorcism, his haunting vision of fascism, and what really happened in his high school classroom experiment.

The Wave, Lear, ABC-TV, 1997. A personal account of a classroom experiment to teach students about Fascist oppression.

Awards

1996 San Francisco Video Poetry Film Festival Grand Prize Winner for *Mint Jammin'*.

1994 German Play of the Year for *The Wave*.

1992 Outstanding Achievement in the San Francisco Special Olympics.

1987 Kohl Foundation's International Outstanding Teacher Award.

1984 Columbia Foundation's American Book of the Year for *Say Ray*.

1982 Pulitzer Prize nomination for *Kids Called Crazy*.

1981 Peabody Award for *The Wave*.

1981 Golden Globe Award for *The Wave*.
1981 Emmy for Outstanding Television Program for Children for *The Wave*.
1976 Christian Book of the Year Award for *The Acorn People*.
Motion Picture Council's Golden Halo Award.
House International Film Festival Silver Medal.

Source

Psychology Today, June 1977.
Sterling, Greg, "Mengele Survivor Inspires Monologue on Holocaust," *Northern California Jewish Bulletin*, January 28, 1994.
Wilhelm, Maria, "Classroom Innovator Ron Jones Has Made a Career of Grappling with Challenges Others Shirk," *People*, October 5, 1981, 111–112.

DAN KEDING
[Keh' • dihng]

Address Box 1701
    Springfield, Illinois 62705
  phone 217-787-1448

Focus: childhood reminiscences and personal anecdotes about Chicago's ethnic neighborhoods; ghost stories; original tales; participation songs; traditional world folktales, fairy tales, ballads, and stories that tell about another time, another culture, another people.

Audience: all ages.

Style: direct presentation of focal ideas with no accents or silly voices, and minimal details; sings and interprets traditional lore; offers an organic whole that the listener develops along with the teller.

Instruments/Props: banjo, guitar, spoons.

Dan Keding is a believer that stories are precious letters from the past, which he keeps alive in his repertory. A tall, rangy troubadour with an easy way before audiences, he fills narrative with memorable prodigies, dragons, giants, heroes, heroines, ghosts, and goblins from traditional lore. A native of Chicago's South Side, he grew up in a community of ethnic neighbors who lived out the culture of the Old Country. His immigrant Yugoslavian grandmother Noni shared stories from Croatia, which she used as vehicles of moral guidance or solutions to problems. She acquired a repertory from Eastern European coffeehouses where fishermen and their families gathered after work for conversation and stories. He recalls being the only grandchild for a long time and being treasured by Noni, who lived with his family and told him horror tales and witch stories. In personal narratives, he stresses his own coming of age in Chicago's South Side and invites listeners to visualize Noni and others who influenced his life.

Against the backdrop of a predominantly Catholic neighborhood, Keding's youth was permeated by the rituals and mysteries of strict church orthodoxy, as taught by the Dominican sisters at his school. His childhood memories rove from baseball games in vacant lots, climbs to the top of billboards, and grape-stealing from an old Italian man's vineyard, to listening to the stories of Gypsy fruit and vegetable vendors, who arrived each Tuesday in the summer by horse-drawn wagon. On his own, he read Greek and Roman mythology and the Celtic lore of Robin Hood and King Arthur. When television was young, he enjoyed Errol Flynn's performances in *The Sea Hawks, Captain Blood*, and *The Adventures of Robin Hood*. In high school, he participated in recitation and public speaking competitions.

Keding credits the zeitgeist of the late 1970s and its demand for a personal, intimate art form for luring him into serious stage narrative. While attending college in Chicago, he played and sang narrative ballads in area coffeehouses. Lured into the magic of traditional story-songs, he thrilled to themes of cunning, loyalty, and virtue — the same ingredients he had admired in childhood stories. While honing platform performances, he was drawn to stories from other cultures and studied the technique of singers Martin Carthy, Louis Killen, Jean Redpath, Jean Ritchie, and Art Thieme. After a one-year stint as a high school English teacher, Keding turned pro, touring with a trio and duet until 1982, when he went solo. Although he had been using traditional folktales in performance for some time, he began to concentrate on storytelling, specializing at first in Celtic and Croatian motifs and lore which reflects his lineage. After moving to Wisconsin in the late 1970s, he worked as an artist in residence with the Wisconsin Arts Council and met storyteller Mark Wagler, who became a valued colleague and sounding board. While performing at the Great River Festival in the late 1970s, he met Elizabeth Ellis and Gayle Ross, who encouraged and supported his decision to specialize in more serious material. Keding returned to his home state in 1983, where he began to work for the Illinois Arts Council as an artist in residence and performer at schools, libraries, concerts, and festivals throughout the country. Since moving to Springfield, he directed the Clayville Music and Storytelling Festival from 1986 to 1989, served as president and board member of Directors of the Prairie Grapevine Folklore Society for five years, and is currently artistic director of the Bluestem Storyfest.

While performing and conducting workshops and residencies, Keding has expanded his repertoire of stories by collecting folktales, ballads, fairy tales, and folklore and acquiring a library of over 2,000 volumes on these subjects. He also attended the University of Illinois at Springfield and received an M.A. in the history and performance of traditional ballads and folktales. With such a background in collecting and research, he often resets action and updates European folktales such as the Pied Piper into "The Banjo Player of Franceville," a story of hard justice about a musician in West Virginia who lures children away from a town that refused to pay him for ridding it of snakes. These original pieces based on old folktales or ballads keep alive the intent of the story and introduce it to new generations. To link his imagination with the listener he leaves some details vague so that the audience can set their own limits and use their own imagination. For example, in "The Tear," an original story about the last dragon, he purposely is vague about the dragon's size and the physical looks of the human characters so that the audience can participate and become part of the artistic process. He strongly believes that storytelling is a two-way street with teller and listener creating the story together.

In 1987, Keding married Tandy Lacy, a curator of education at the Illinois State Museum. They live in Springfield with their two dogs, Jack and Dido. For a quarter century, Keding has performed through the United States and Great Britain. He has been featured at the National Storytelling Festival, Northern Appalachian Storytelling Festival, Illinois Storytelling Festival, St. Louis Storytelling Festival, Wild Onion Storytelling Festival, Michigan Storytelling Festival, Disney Institute, Festival of Storytelling on Martha's Vineyard, Detroit Story League Festival, and National Storytelling Concert. In England, he performed at the Festival at the Edge in Shropshire, Sidmouth International Folk Arts Festival, Whitby Festival, and Towersey Village Festival. He has been a workshop/seminar leader at the 1992, 1994, and 1996 National Storytelling conferences, the Once Upon a Time Storytelling Conference at Kent State, 1995 International Storytelling Institute at East Tennessee State University, and Florida Storytelling Camp. Since 1994, he has hosted a cable show, *Grapevine Harvest*, which showcases storytelling and folk music and which won Best of the Best in the *Illinois Times Reader Poll.* Since 1989, he has written a storytelling column, "The Endless Tale," in *Sing Out! The Folk Song Magazine,* a quarterly journal in which he interviews storytellers and discusses issues in the storytelling world. In 1996, he was elected to the board of the National Storytelling Association.

In summing up his career, Keding says, "I didn't find storytelling, nor did it find me. It was always there throughout my life, moving me in the direction that I now willingly and joyfully follow. I feel most alive when I am on stage telling stories. I feel that is why I am here. It is my purpose — it's what I do best."

Bibliography

"Storytellers' Views on Blending Narrative and Song," *Storytelling Magazine,* May 1997, 16–20.
"The Transformation of a Ballad," *Storytelling Magazine,* May 1997, 22–23.

Video

The Large Mouth Frog, 1993. Traditional children's stories and songs including directions for making a frog with your hands and for playing the spoons.

Audiography

Beyond the Hero (author Allan B. Chinen) (audiocassette), August House, 1997. Myths and ancient stories of the solitary modern hero and healer.
Giants, Dragons, and the Devil's Hide (audiocassette), Turtle Creek Recordings, 1992. World wonder tales, featuring "Errki and the Devil's Hide" and "The Wizard & the Golden Thread."
Homework: Songs and Stories for Kids (audiocassette), Turtle Creek Recordings, 1989. Includes "The Large Mouth Frog."
MacPherson's Lament and Other Ballads (audiocassette), Turtle Creek Recordings, 1991. Traditional ballads from England, Ireland, Scotland, and the United States, including "Clayton Boone," "Lady of Carlile," "The Lady and the Glove," "Rigs of Time," "Johnny I Hardly Knew You," accompanied by Bill Rintz on fiddle, Julie Luther on banjo, and Dave Williams on guitar, mandola, and requinta.

A Man of Simple Pleasures (audiocassette), Turtle Creek Recordings, 1987. Original tunes and traditional sea songs from America and the British Isles, featuring "Bold Daniels," "We'll Rant and We'll Roar, " "Now We Steer Our Course for Home, "A Captain's Dream," "The Two Sisters," "Bonnie Light Horseman," "The Butcher Boy," and "The Field Behind the Plow," accompanied on mandolin, banjo, bass, concertina, and fiddle.
Once Upon a Midlife (author Allan B. Chinen) (audiocassette), August House, 1997. A joint telling with Janice Del Negro of old stories about middle-aged men and women facing responsibility, failed ideals, gender differences, crises, aging, mortality, and the yen for renewal.
Promises Kept, Promises Broken (audiocassette), Turtle Creek Recordings, 1995. Traditional and original stories about promises, including "Willy's Lady," "The Tear," "The Banjo Player of Franceville," "The Golden Vanity," "The Pinery Boy," and "The Letter," a macabre story from the American Civil war, followed by "Johnny I Hardly Knew You," a plaintive Celtic version of "When Johnny Comes Marching Home."
Rudy and the Roller Skates (audiocassette), Turtle Creek Recordings, 1996. Traditional and original stories for children, including "The Hero."
South Side Stories (audiocassette), Turtle Creek Recordings, 1993. Personal stories from a Chicago boyhood, including "I Never Sang for My Grandmother" and "The Gypsy Wagon."
Stories from the Other Side (audiocassette), Turtle Creek Recordings, 1990. Traditional ghost tales for mature children and adults from France, Great Britain, and America, including "Mr. Fox," "Marie Yvonne and Her Shroud," "Martin and the Snakes," "The Dancing Fiddle," "The Great Silkie," "The House Carpenter," and "Tieg O'Kane and the Corpse," accompanied by fiddler Bill Rintz.
Strawberries in Winter (audiocassette),Turtle Creek Recordings, 1997. Traditional folktales for younger listeners, including "Fill-

ing Up the House," "Nail Soup," and the title story.

Awards

1997 *Illinois Times* Best of the Best readers' poll for local cable-access show host.

1995 *Illinois Times* Best of the Best readers' poll for storyteller.

1995, 1994 Springfield Area Arts Council Artist Advancement Award.

1993 Sun Foundation for the Arts & Environmental Sciences Distinguished Service Award.

1990 American Library Association Best of the Best for Children for *Stories from the Other Side*.

1989 Special Recognition Award from the Illinois Alliance for Arts Education.

Source

Bettendorf, Elizabeth, "Dan Keding — Folk Music's Meandering Muse," Springfield, Illinois, *State Journal-Register*, September 21, 1988, 45–46.

"Dan Keding," *Facts & Fiction*, December 1995, 6–9.

Furry, Bill, "The Ballad of Folkie," *Illinois Times*, August 3, 1989.

Naber, Cyndi, "Singer Teaches with Folk Music," *Northwest Herald*, October 20, 1992, 1D.

"Review," *Common Times,* Summer 1992.

"Review," *Dirty Linen*, February/March 1992.

"Three Elected, Two Appointed to NSA Board," *Storytelling Magazine*, May 1996, 33.

Walker, Richard, "Review of 'Promises Kept, Promises Broken,'" *Facts and Fiction*, December 1995, 3.

Welch, Wendy, "How Dan Keding Creates Stories," *Storytelling World*, Winter/Spring 1997, 9–11.

Winick, Steve, "Review of 'A Man of Simple Pleasures' and 'Stories from the Other Side,'" *Dirty Linen*, November 1990.

PAUL KEENS-DOUGLAS

Address   21 Old Paddock Road
Blue Range

Diego Martin, Trinidad, West Indies
phone and fax 868-632-1647

Focus: myth and folklore; spirit lore, jumbie stories; vernacular verse; monologues; short stories in standard English and vernacular; affirmation of the black experience; social commentary reflecting Caribbean lifestyles.

Audience: all ages.

Style: wholesome, family-oriented presentations in relaxed dialect/standard English narration; Caribbean-style humor; verse recitation; stand-up comedy.

Instruments/Props: tall stool, lectern; musical accompaniment either live or on tape

Known as Mr. Tim Tim in the storytelling world, Paul Keens-Douglas is one of the most eloquent and best known tellers in the Caribbean region. Distinct in his writing is a belief in storytelling as an educative force in non-literate societies, a philosophy he expounds in the introduction to *Tell Me Again*. He credits tales with providing collective group wisdom, comprised of morals, proverbs, riddles, religious ritual, celebrations of love and life, and acknowledgments of loss and infidelity. He notes that the true human

experiences are found in stories, rhythmic work songs, word games, riddles, speeches, narrative, and teasing. Because of the authenticity and life affirmation in stories, he keeps oral traditions alive to transmit to future generations their background and beliefs.

One of a family of seven and the father of Johann and Tara, Keens-Douglas and his wife Marilyn relish a spiritual life, rich in Catholic background, strong family ties, and earth-based values. Born in Trinidad, he grew up in the Spice Isles of Grenada, where he and younger brother Richardo were eager listeners to the stories of their father Templeman, one of which told of his stowing away on a boat to South America so he could earn better wages in the oilfields of Maracaibo. To sustain him on the voyage, he carried only twelve apples, one for each Apostle.

After attending Presentation Boys College and obtaining diplomas in commercial broadcasting and radio and television production from Announcer Training Studios and RCA Institutes in New York City, Keens-Douglas earned an honors degree in sociology from Sir George Williams University in Montreal, and completed post-graduate work at the University of the West Indies, Mona, Jamaica. During his formative years he obtained a varied background in theater, which became his springboard to platform narrative. He began writing in the local vernacular and reading his original stories and poems on Radio Trinidad for the "Tim Tim" and "Is Town Say So" series. His television appearances include "Three Tales Tall" on NBC-TV in Washington and CBC-TV Canada, "Black on Black/Ebony/Omnibus" on the BBC in London, "Poetry in Motion for Design Media" for Nickelodeon, UNESCO Storytelling Series in Holland, and National Geographic Explorer's "Vampires, Devil-Birds, and Spirits of the Twin Isles." From this varied initiation into media, he developed into a platform performer, taking as mentor Jamaican folklorist and performer Louise Bennett, and the spirit of black poets and their oral renditions of the 1970s, including Alice McGill, Linda Goss, Rita Cox, Oscar Browne, Jr., Alfred Pragnell, Thelma Phillips, Dem Two, Miguel Browne, Fish Alphonse, and Keens-Douglas's brother

Richardo. Keens-Douglas's theatrical performances have placed him in BeeWee Ballet in Grenada; *Hail Columbus, Man Better Man, No Rain No Play, The Wall,* and *Macbeth* in Jamaica; *Chant of the Blacks* in Canada, *Mas in yuh Mas, Ah Pan for Christmas,* and *J'Ouvert* in Trinidad; and *Africa in the Caribbean* in Montreal.

By 1979, Keens-Douglas was a full-time writer, performer, and storyteller, a career that has taken him about the Caribbean, Great Britain, Canada, and the United States. He has promoted the Family Planning Affiliation, Caribbean Association of Teachers, Rotary International Conference, Foundation for International Training, BWIA Funventure, Insurance Association of the Caribbean, and UNESCO/WHO Communications' "Making Measles History." His most memorable performances include the Caribbean Festival of Arts Jamaica/Barbados, Caribbean Focus: at Westminster Abbey and the Royal Albert Hall in London, National Storytellers Festival in Jonesborough, Tennessee, and the 1996 West Indies Cricket Board Banquet honoring Jamaican cricket players.

Keens-Douglas produces and directs two annual productions in which he highlights the vernacular. In 1976, he first produced "Tim Tim Show ... A Festival of Stories," at which he launched his story "Tanti at de Oval." The story brought him acclaim. In 1983, he initiated "Carnival Talk Tent," a platform for various styles within the oral traditions in Jamaica. In nine volumes of stories, thirteen albums, and three videos, he has created a cast of personae — Tanti Merle, Vibert, Slim, Sugar George, Timultaneous, Tall Boy, and Dr. Ah-Ah, who come to life in such poems and stories as "Carnival Is Marse," "Pan Rap — The Story of Pan," "Tanti Merle Drapes," "Boopsy an' de Beauty Contest," "Vibert Reach Home," "Jumbie, Duppy an' Spirits," and "Party Nice." One Story, "Dark Nite People," features a typical overbearing matriarch, a folkteller and tanti (aunt) whose lore, beliefs, and myths are representative of island culture. She warns of numerous spirits — La Diablesse, the woman-spirit with one cloven hoof; Mama Maladé, who dies in childbirth; Loupgarou, a flying bloodsucker; Socouyant, Loupgarou's female counterpart; Baccoo-man, a Buyanese genie; Steel Donkey, a Barbadian folk spirit; and Rolling Calf, its Jamaican counterpart.

A popular Caribbean personality, Keens-Douglas broadcasts his distinctive voice and style on radio and television throughout the region. His radio credits include "Start the Week for Radio London," "Calling the Caribbean" for CBC Canada, and WLIB in New York. In addition to freelance work in advertising and publication in Heinemann's *Facing the Sea* and *New English for the Caribbean*, Keens-Douglas tours, lectures, performs, and conducts workshops and makes after-dinner and motivational presentations. His lectures cover three main topics: "When Moon Shine," on the art of storytelling; "Writing with a Purpose," on the use of Eastern Caribbean vernacular in commercial messages and the media; and "What's Your Story?," which uses humor and narrative to examine and demonstrate interpersonal and cross-cultural communication for management, staff-training, customer relations, and tourism and hospitality. His one-man shows accommodate schools, libraries, and home and business groups.

Bibliography

"De Wedding" in *Talk That Talk*, Simon & Schuster, 1989.

Is Town Say So, College Press, 1981.

"Jumpie, Duppy, an' Spirit," in *Talk That Talk*, Simon & Schuster, 1989.

Lal Shop, Keensdee Productions, 1984.

Roll Call: Poetry and Short Stories by Paul Keens-Douglas, Keensdee, 1997.

Savannah Ghost: Selected Works of Paul Keens-Douglas, Keensdee, 1996.

Tanti at de Oval: Selected Works of Paul Keens-Douglas, Keensdee, 1992. Reprises some of his best stories, including "When Moon Shine," "Sugar George," "Ah Fire de Wuk," and "De Beauty Contest."

Tell Me Again, College Press, 1979. Contains stories, poems, dramatizations, and monologues.

Tim Tim: The Dialect Poetry of Paul Keens-Douglas, College Press, 1976. Verse lyrics and monologues.

Twice Upon a Time, Selected Works of Paul Keens-Douglas, Keensdee Productions, 1989. Contains stories, poems, dramatizations, and monologues.

"Vibert Reach Home," *Caribbean Beat*, January/February 1997, 62.

When Moon Shine, College Press, 1975.

Videography

Mr. Tim Tim, Keensdee, 1993.

Paul Keens-Douglas Live, Keensdee, 1997.

Two of a Kind, Keensdie, 1996.

Audiography

Anancy Beatin' Pan (audiocassette), Keensdee Productions, 1992. Contains "De Small Island," "That Something," "A Woman," "We Kind of People," "Real Estate," "I and I and You," and "Pot Holes" in addition to the title story.

Bobots (audiocassette), Keensdie Productions, 1983. Contains "Dis Bajan Girl," "Last Lick," "Peltin'," "De Sugar Problem," "Tanti an' de Fire," "Windjammer," and "De Dry Bones."

Carnival Is Marse (audiocassette), Rainbow Wirl, 1989. Contains "De Wedding," "Coucou Village," "This & Dat," "Tanti Merle at Panorama," "Vibert Dog," and "Foolish People" in addition to the title story.

Fedon's Flute (audiocassette), self-produced, 1980. Contains "Passport," "Banza," "All Fall Down," "Breakword," "One to One/Maybe," "Ah Pan for Christmas," "Sugar Apple People," and the title story.

Fete Match (audiocassette), Keensdie Productions, 1984. Contains "My Trinidad," "My Daddy," "Mancrab," "Choir Practice," "Gas Crisis," "De Great Race," "De Master Batsman," and the title story.

Is Town Say So (audiocassette), self-produced, 1982. Contains "Pan Rap I," "Pan Rap II," "De Christenin'," "Slim Teet (Dr. Ah Ah)," "Jumbies, Duppys & Spirits," and "Bogoville."

Live a Little, Laugh a Lot (audiocassette), Keensdee Productions, 1990. Contains "Tanti an' de Coup," "I Bat," "England Rain," "Ah Don't Want to Know," "Ma Kokline," "Tanti an' de World Cup," "Anancy an' de Cow," excerpts from "Choir Practice," "Lal Shop," "Jogging," and the title story.

More of Me (audiocassette), Keensdee Productions, 1987. Contains "It's Not easy," "Highway Code," "De Pamper Crowd," "Boopsy an' de Beauty Contest," "If Yu Red Yu Red," and "Bottle Business."

One to One (audiocassette), self-produced, 1978. Contains "Between de Breakin'," "Blackman Look for Yu God," "Tell Me Again," "In de Square," "I Ball," "Coconut," "Good Mornin' Mister Freedom," "Ah Bitter Frustration," "Jus' Like Dat," "Tanti Merle Drapes," and "Pan Down de Hill/Percy."

Savannah Ghost (audiocassette), Keensdee Productions, 1996. Features "Ah Fire de Wuk," "Vibert Reach Home," "Ent Dat Nice?," "De Band Passin'," "Party Nice," and the title story.

Selected Works of Paul Keens-Douglas (audiocassette), Keensdee Productions, 1990. Contains "Ah Fire de Work," "Vibert Reach Home," "Party Nice," "Banza," "Tell Me Again," "Sugar Apple People," "Passport," "Fedon's Flute," "Tanti Merle Drapes," and "I Ball."

Stress an' Strain (audiocassette), Keensee Productions, 1995. Includes "The Dragon," "Stress," "Strange Conversations," "Ah Want to Be Dey," "Medal," "Strain," "Cobweb," "Simple Camera," "Written Excuse," "Christ Is," and "De Sponsor."

Tim Tim (audiocassette), self-produced, 1976. Features "When Moon Shine," "Dark Nite People," "Storm Comin'," "Tanti at de Oval," "Fish," "Wukhand," "String Bank," "Sugar George," and "Papa God."

Awards

1997 Rotary International Meritorious Service Award.

1997 *Everybody's Magazine* Commemorative Award.

1996 Pan-African Community and Family Griots Planning Committee Award.

1994 National Hummingbird Silver Award for Culture.

1994 Bank of Antigua Appreciation Award.

1994 Wildlife Film Best Narration Award for *National Geographic: Explorer*.

1993 Bermuda Ministry of Education Award.

1992 WPFW Community Service Award.

1991 University of the Virgin Islands Community Services Award.

1987 Beryl McBurnie Foundation for the Arts Award.

1987 Trinidad & Tobago Society of Winnipeg, Inc. Award.

1985 Association of Black Storytellers of America's Zora Neale Hurston Award.

1984 Caribbean American Intercultural Organisation Award.

1979 New Voices Literary Award.

Source

Coleman, L. G., "Black Comic Performance in the African Diaspora," *Journal of Black Studies*, September 1984, 67–78.

Maxwell, Marina Ama Omowale, "Paul Keens-Douglas," *Caribbean Voice Magazine*, http: //lg.wing.net/~cvoice/is'l.htm, May 21, 1997.

Tapley, Mel, "Storytelling Time by Griots of the Diaspora," *New York Amsterdam News*, October 22, 1994.

Thomas, Novel, "Two Great Performers," *Montreal Community Contact*, October 31, 1994.

"Your Audio Entertainment," *Caribbean Beat*, January/February 1997, 86.

SUSAN KLEIN

Address   P. O. Box 214
Oak Bluffs, Massachusetts 02557
email RubyWindow@aol.com
website www.GeoCities.com/SoHo/studios/1794

Focus: world folklore, fables, and myth; Grimm brothers tales; audience participation stories; rites of passage; adult love stories; material that transcends cultural barriers.

Audience: adults, children, special interest groups.

Style: dynamic one-woman shows; playful, tender, wise, and funny.

Susan Klein was jolted into the storytelling profession by a friend who forced her to attend a session for adults. While absorbing Jay O'Callahan's "Magellan," Klein saw a promising way to merge education, her college major, with theater. On the spot, she made a mental career change, signing on for life as a platform performer. Immediately, she found herself intuitively drawn to usable stage material. She selects stories that follow the dramatic paradigm of characters, action, conflict and resolution. By rereading the written narrative, she lets her subconscious take charge of style and presentation and depends on an inner editor to weed out the chaff. In the early 1980s, her first foray took her by a well-used Chevette to every festival between Massachusetts and Georgia. The tour brought an offer of two months' work in Alaska, where she served Yup'ik Eskimo villages in the Lower Kuskokwim River Delta as itinerant storyteller. On the return to the East Coast, she settled in her hometown and launched fifteen years of storytelling, some of which glimpse her past. One of her original stories of Massachusetts life is "Beach Party," from *Through a Ruby Window*, a blend of her strengths — passion, poignance, wit, and charm.

A native of Martha's Vineyard, Massachusetts, Klein grew up in the 1950s and relished easy days at the beach, where summer was the most distinct part of the year. On the strand, her family cooked out and treated her to rides on the merry-go-round. A treasured memory is of annual beach plum hunting and jelly making. She taught school in the 1970s before becoming a professional platform teller. She came to value the best of her peers — Patrick Ball, Carol Birch, Milbre Burch, Len Cabral, Donald Davis, Gay Ducey, Elizabeth Ellis, Don Doyle, Rex Ellis, Diane Ferlatte, Heather Forest, David Holt, Dan Keding, Jamal Koram, Barbara Lipke, Jim May, Chuna McIntyre, Jeannine Pasini Beekman, Connie Regan-Blake, August Rubrecht, Sparky Rucker, Steve Sanfield, Jon Spelman, and Kathryn Windham. Klein is noted for keynoting and inspirational speeches, autobiography, and her work with teaching adolescents about storytelling.

In 1988, Klein founded the Festival of Storytelling on Martha's Vineyard. A performer and emcee, she has presented at 45 storytelling festivals and is a popular choice for kicking off new-born festivals. She takes her one-woman show to schools, theaters, coffeehouses, libraries, universities, institutes, and conferences. Her festival experience has covered the Tejas Storytelling Festival, National Storytelling Concert, Word-of-Mouth Storytelling Series, Sierra Storytelling Festival, the Neighborhood Convention, and, three times, the National Storytelling Festival in Jonesborough, Tennessee. She has been featured on "The Storytellers" on ABC-TV *News Nightline* in 1993, hosted and told for Womens' History Month at Middle Tennessee University at Murfreesboro, performed on Minnesota Public Radio's *Good Evening* in 1987 and 1988, and toured the United States and Europe with inspirational storytelling workshops and in-service training sessions for educators entitled "Storytelling from the Inside Out" and "When the Heart Is Full, It Moves to Speak." In May 1997, she was featured at Folke Tegetthoff's "Lange Nacht of Storytelling" at the Graz Erzählt Festival in Austria, where she appeared along with Shosha Goren, Laura Simms, Dan Yashinsky, Michael Parent, Milbre Burch, John Basinger, and Dianne Ferlatte.

Bibliography

Through a Ruby Window, August House, 1995.
Twenty stories about growing up in

Martha's Vineyard, including the title story, "Beach Party," "A Scent of Oils," "The Flying Horse," and "Ruby Window II."

"Willie the Bug-Man," in *Best-Loved Stories Told at the National Storytelling Festival*, August House, 1991.

"The Wise Judge," in *Ready-to-Tell Tales*, August House, 1994.

Audiography

Aphrodite's Nosegay (audiocassette), self-published, 1992. Five love stories, including "The Salon of Dubious Decorum," "Edith & Bessie," "Rapunzel," "The 13th," and "A Brittle Enchantment," a retelling of "Lady Ragnall and Sir Gawain."

Old Standbys (audiocassette), self-published, 1994. Updated children's stories — "The Little Reds" (hen and riding hood) and the "3's" (pigs and bears), plus "Rumpelstiltskin," "Hansel & Gretel," "Two Little Monkeys," "Diddle Diddle Dumpling," "Fox and Crow," "This Little Piggy," "Pease Porridge," and "Hey Diddle Diddle."

Spirit of the River (audiocassette), self-published, 1986. Describes Klein's first week in an eight-week storytelling residency with the Yup'ik Eskimos in the Kuskokwim River Delta of Alaska.

Through a Ruby Window (audiocassette), self-published, 1993. A double cassette of stories about growing up on Martha's Vineyard in the 1950s and 1960s, including "Aunt Fanny," "Flying Horses," "Beach Party," "Packages Home," "On the Wing," "Harry," and the title story; recorded live at the Wintertide Coffeehouse for ages seven and up.

Willie the Bug Man and the Stories He Loves (audiocassette), self-published, 1987. Contains the title story plus "Brer Rabbit & Brer Raccoon," "The Magic Orange Tree," "The Gunniwolf," and "Frog and Centipede."

Wisdom's Tribute (audiocassette), Ruby Window Productions, 1997. Contains rites of passage stories for young adults, including "The Wood-Ash Stars" from South Africa, "Bong Nam and the Pheasants" from Korea, "A Chinese Fairy Tale" by Laurens Hausman, and "Thanksgiving," a bio-graphical tale by American cowboy poet Ray Lashley.

Awards

1995 *Publishers Weekly* Listen Up Award for best recording, *Through a Ruby Window*.

Source

Bovey, Julia Hodges, "Morning of Laughter, Tears," *Martha's Vineyard Times*, June 29, 1989.

Brophy, Wendy Arnell, "The Wisdom of the Storyteller," *Martha's Vineyard Times*, April 17, 1997.

Dunn, Gary A., "Review," *Entomologists Society*, August 1993.

Ellis, Jib, "Who's Who — Susan Klein," Vineyard Haven, Massachusetts *Planet Vineyard*, Winter 1996.

"Former Teacher Sees Renaissance of Storytelling Across America," Brockton, Massachusetts *Enterprise*, October 24, 1986.

Hancock, Dr. Joyce A., "Review," *Tale Trader*, May 1994.

Hudson, Berkley, "Look Who's Talking," *Los Angeles Times Magazine*, July 27, 1997.

_____, "Travel News," *United Airlines Hemispheres Magazine*, September 1997.

Keding, Dan, "The Endless Tale," *Sing Out! The Folk Song Magazine*, Fall 1995.

_____, "Review," *Sing Out! The Folk Song Magazine*, Fall 1997.

"Kids Being Kids," Holbrook, Massachusetts *Patriot Ledger*, July 24, 1986.

MacCarry, Bert, "Review," *Tamiami Tales Newsletter*, January 1996.

McLeod, Michael, "Once Upon a Time," *Reader's Digest*, May 1997.

_____, Angela Peterson, and Tom Raymond, "Once Upon a Time," *Florida Magazine*, November 24, 1996.

Mooney, Bill, and David Holt. *The Storyteller's Guide*. Little Rock, Ark.: August House, 1996.

"Sippican Students Enjoy Susan Klein's Storytelling," Wareham, Massachusetts *Sunday News*, September 25, 1988.

Stallings, Fran, "Review," *National Storytelling Journal*, Summer 1987.

"Storyteller Loves Magic of Metaphors," Idabel, Oklahoma *McCurtain Daily Gazette*, March 31, 1993.

"Storyteller Spins Yarns for Crescent Students," Griffin, Georgia *Daily News*, May 20, 1995.

"Storyteller Stimulates Pupils' Imaginations," Assawompset, Massachusetts *Gazette*, October 1984.

"Susan Klein Comes Home to Roost," *Martha's Vineyard Times*, November 18, 1993.

"Susan Klein, Storyteller," *Martha's Vineyard Magazine*, Spring 1986.

"Tall Tales Fill a Tall Order; Storyteller Lends Talents to Area Schools," Palmer, Massachusetts *Journal Register*, May 11–17, 1989.

"Tell Me a Story," Holden, Massachusetts *Landmark*, May 14, 1987.

"Vineyard Childhood Inspires Storyteller at Three Apples," *Worcester* (Massachusetts) *Telegram & Gazette*, September 28, 1995.

CHUCK LARKIN

Address Bluegrass Storyteller
P. O. Box 54573
Atlanta, Georgia 30308-0573
phone and fax 404-873-3868
phone 800-952-7552
email mythteller@aol.com

Focus: Appalachian tall tales and Jack tales; haint and ghost lore; beast fables; rural lore; Celtic sagas.

Audience: general.

Style: traditional bluegrass Appalachian and *seanachie* humor.

Instruments/Props: musical saw, fiddle bow, jaw harp, bones, spoons, nose whistle, straws.

A farm boy turned folksayer and joker, Chuck Larkin taps a wealth of rural memories and Irish blue collar and white collar blarney for his outrageous yarning. The grandson of one of the world's first ophthalmologists, Larkin was born in 1931 in a Salvation Army hospital in New York's Bowery. His mother, a radical fleeing old boyfriends, chose the out-of-the-way maternity ward for its privacy. Because Larkin's father was a sailor in the U.S. Navy, the family lived at various locations on the Eastern seaboard, including a farm above Cape Charles in Pocomoke, Maryland, and St. Petersburg, Florida, where he attended high school. Larkin followed his father's example and served as a sailor and hospital corpsman during the Korean War. He was educated in sociology and psychology at the University of Florida, where he earned an M.A. in rehabilitation counseling in 1960. For 35 years throughout Florida and the Southeast, he offered holistic training and employment services to people with job handicaps. For 28 of those years, he was a trainer and employment program specialist for the U.S. Department of Labor.

Larkin got his start in emceeing and storytelling during ten years with Toastmasters' speaking contests. Still looking for venues for oral presentation, he researched tall tales in East Tennessee, such as "Split Dog" and "Mr. Bass," the story of a fish that drowned, which he began retelling in 1970. His material includes "Aunt Irene," "Fergus O'LorCain, the Irish Lad Who Had No Story," "The Marriage of Sir Gawain and Dame Ragnell," and stories about Jack, Sister Rabbit, Brother Possum, haints, Old Dryfry, and Celtic sagas. A four-

time featured teller at the National Story-telling Festival in Jonesborough, Tennessee, he is a regular at banquets, on radio, and on the platform narrative circuit and, in 1995, hosted the Gwinnett Historical Museum's second annual Folk Music Festival. He has told in fourteen states at 45 festivals around the country, but primarily in the South, Southwest, and along the East Coast, including the Cherokee Rose Storytelling Festival, Albuquerque Storyfiesta, Atlanta Storytelling Festival, Stoval House, Atlanta Celtic Festival, Folk Life Center of the Smokies, Okefenokee Swamp Storytelling Festival, Bayside Yarnspinner Festival, and Olde Christmas Storytelling Festival. He has broadcast on *Tell Me a Story* over KVC-radio in Indianapolis and hosted a PBS-TV series, *A Night at Ferlinghetti's*, for WPBA/WABE in Atlanta. His workshops for beginning and advanced storytellers elucidate methods of joke telling, finding and remembering material, collecting family stories, structuring personal anecdotes, intonation, and spoken word. He models and discusses energy, vocal stress, pause, gesture, movement, rhythm, pitch, and volume and explains how to use a microphone, diversify style, improve creative imagery, and vary material.

Bibliography

"Battle of the White Strand," http://luna.cas. usf.edu/~miller/ lore/white.html, June 5, 1997.

"The Electricity Elixir," in *Ready-to-Tell Tales*, August House, 1994.

Old Christmas Stories, http://www.tiac.net/ users/papajoe/chuck01.htm, June 5, 1997. Contains "And It Came to Pass," "The First Christmas Gift," "Animals from the Wild Visit and Ms. Cat Stays," "Ms. Horse, Ms. Mule and Ms. Cow," "The Baby Speaks," "The Holly Tree," "The First Christmas Tree," "Candles in the Window and Mistletoe," "Fergus O'Lorcain, the Irish Lad Who Had No Story," "The Birthday Story," "Hanukkah and a Story," "About Old Christmas vs. Epiphany and the Birth of Santa Claus."

Tall Tales, http://www.tiac.net/users/papajoe/chuck00.htm, June 5, 1997. Contains thirty stories on fishing, hunting, and other personal experiences, featuring "My First Job," "Dogs: Frosty, BJ and Spot," "My Mother's Brother Ike's Family, " "Aunt Irene," "Mr. Bass," "Mississippi River Fishing," "Fishing with Little Green Frogs," Ringtail, the Hobo Fish," "Joan Shilling's Catfish Farm," "Lee Shilling's Circus Catfish," "Fishing," "Pop Corn, on Being Poor and Fog," "The Fence Posts," "Aloysius (Rocky) the Rooster," "The Georgia Peach," "The Electricity Elixir," "The Trained Squirrels," "My Father's Brother's Family," "Rutledge," "Road Building," "Nassawango Creek Rip Tail Roarer," "Hot, Dry, Cold and Windy," "Rain and Mud," "Dynamite," "Will the Tornado," "Donald and the Wild Tornado," "The Lightning Bolts," "My Vita," "I Don't Tell Lies," and "Read My Lips."

"What Is Storytelling?," http://kirov.seanet. com/!eldrbarry/roos/art.htm, June 5, 1997.

Videography

"Mr. Bass," in *American Storytelling Series, Vol. 4* , H. W. Wilson, 1986.

A Night at Ferlinghetti's (host), PBS-TV, 1986-1987.

Tell Me a Story (contributor), KVC, 1987. Contains "It Was So Cold," "Frozen Snakes as Fence Posts," "The Musical Saw," "It Was So Hot," and "Brother Possum, Brother Snake, and Sister Rabbit."

To Tell a Story, KVS, 1986.

Audiography

Tall Tales I and II (audiocassette), self-published, 1986.

Source

"A Brief Look at This Year's Storytellers," Jonesborough, Tennessee *Herald & Tribune*, September 30, 1992, 4C–8C.

Newcom, Josh, "Folk Music Festival Performers Will 'Keep Old Traditions Alive,'" *Atlanta Journal-Constitution*, August 10, 1995.

Rhoden, David, "Telling Artful Lies," *Storytelling Magazine*, Spring 1992, 34–35.

Thrasher, Paula Crouch, "Southern Storytelling Festival the Main Event," *Atlanta Journal-Constitution*, April 29, 1995.

GWENDA LEDBETTER

Address   55 Beaverbrook Road
            Asheville, North Carolina 28804
    phone 704-254-3133

Focus: English and Celtic lore; traditional fairy stories; Jack tales; native American creation stories and animal lore; tall tales; pioneer adventures; ghost stories; personal anecdotes; women's stories.
  Audience: general.
  Style: traditional.

A Southerner from birth in Onancock, Virginia, Gwenda LedBetter has been telling stories professionally since 1964. She knew storytelling as a part of the farming, fishing, and small town easy talk on the eastern shore of Virginia. She fell in love with the magic of words from seeing Jack Sprat and Jack Be Nimble, two figures that decorated the walls of her mother's kindergarten. LedBetter's mother taught her to value stories in books and, during the era of Shirley Temple worship, encouraged her singing, dancing, and acting from age three. In adulthood LedBet-

ter opted for her mother's profession. She majored in education and voice at Queens College in Charlotte, North Carolina, and taught elementary school. After she and her husband John, a physician, and their three children settled in Asheville, North Carolina, in 1959, she came under the influence of classic teller Richard Chase, who told "Sody Saleratus" and Jack tales. The chemistry was right and LedBetter changed her career from classroom teaching to storytelling.

While working as a storyteller at Pack Memorial Library, LedBetter attended Jay O'Callahan's first workshop and refined her technique by studying Ruth Sawyer's *The Way of the Storyteller* and listening to mountain teller Mrs. Grover Long, fairy tale artist Gioia Timpanelli, and folklore specialist Diane Wolkstein. This sturdy background helped boost her to the job of "Storylady" and a spot on the *Mr. Bill Show* over WLOS-TV in Asheville, a post she later shared with David Holt. Advancing from library teller to freelancer in 1978, LedBetter has profited from the influence of Jackie Torrence, Jay O'Callahan, Connie Regan-Blake, and Barbara Freeman and made the first of several appearances at the National Storytelling Festival with "Sweet Harmony Chapel." She has told stories in schools, libraries, and churches. Her reward comes from delighted listeners, particularly the small, round-faced woman who beamed up at her at a recent telling at a wellness center, "Your stories would make me feel good even if I were upside down."

For four summers, LedBetter has conducted workshops for the National Storytelling Association and has served on the *National Storytelling Journal* review committee. She treasures tellings of Jack tales, "The Nightingale," "The Marriage of Dame Ragnell and Sir Gawain," "Sam's Wife," and "The Ragman." Since 1994, LedBetter's travels with her husband have produced additional material from varied settings. In a summation of the storytelling renaissance, she comments, "In this age of overcommunication, this heart language recreates, transforms, and makes new life for anyone wise enough to listen."

Articles

"Creating Simple Stories," in *Tales as Tools: The Power of Story in the Classroom*, National Storytelling Press, 1994, 10.

"Permission to Tell the Stories of Others," *Storytelling World*, Fall 1996, 13.

Bibliography

"The Bee, the Harp, the Mouse, and the Bumclock," in *Best-Loved Stories Told at the National Storytelling Festival*, August House, 1991.

"Goodbye to Eden," in *More Best-Loved Stories Told at the National Storytelling Festival*, August House, 1992.

"The Sprightly Tailor," in *The Ghost and I*, 1992.

"Sweet Harmony Chapel," in *Ready-to-Tell Tales*, August House, 1994.

Audiography

The Bee, the Harp, the Mouse, and the Bumclock and Other Tales (audiocassette), Butterside Music, 1986. Contains "Tom Tit Tot," "Molly Whuppie," "In the Beginning," and the title story.

In Sound and Sight of the Sea (audiocassette), Butterside Music, 1990. Stories of growing up on Virginia's eastern shore.

Awards

1986 American Library Association Notable Award for *The Bee, the Harp, the Mouse, and the Bumclock and Other Tales*.

Source

"A Brief Look at This Year's Storytellers," *Herald & Tribune*, September 30, 1992, 4C–8C.

Chandler, June, "Tall Tales," *Knoxville Journal*, October 5, 1989.

Marlowe, Nancy, "Tall Tales," *Asheville Citizen-Times*, August 4, 1991.

"Storytelling North Carolina Style," *Mountaineer Times*, Summer 1988.

SYD LIEBERMAN
[lee'•buhr•muhn]

Address   2522 Ashland
Evanston, Illinois 60201
phone 847-328-6281

Focus: traditional Judaic lore and Hasidic tales; Bible stories; stories of Israel; color pieces and anecdotes of immigrant and Jewish-American urban and suburban experience; holiday lore; Yiddish folktales; reminiscences in childhood slang and Chicago dialect.
Audience: adults and children.
Style: traditional humor and narrative.

An internationally acclaimed humorist, lecturer, and storyteller, Syd Lieberman has appeared on television, on American Public Radio's *Good Evening* as teller and host, and at major gatherings, including five appearances at the National Storytelling Festival in Jonesborough, Tennessee. His fine-tuned voice has recorded the story of the 1889 flood in Johnstown, Pennsylvania and an autobiographical memoir, *Street and Alleys: Stories with a Chicago Accent*. As a featured performer at the Smithsonian Institution in 1991, he performed "Word of Mouth," a program for educators. In 1992 and 1993, he made repeat visits with "The Renaissance in Storytelling: America's Master Storytellers Come to the Smithsonian" and "The Intrepid Birdmen," a piece commissioned for the National Air and Space Museum. The Philadelphia Art Museum featured him as part of an exhibit, "A Visual Testimony: The Vatican's Collection of Judaica." In 1996, he starred in Chicago with

Peter Yarrow of folksinging trio Peter, Paul and Mary in "Do it Yourself Chanukah." In May 1997, he was featured teller at the Ohio Order for the Preservation of Storytelling.

One of the distinguished American tellers of Jewish lore and one of Jay O'Callahan's many protégés, Lieberman is a native of Chicago and father of two children, Zach and Sarah. Influenced by grandparents who immigrated from Eastern Europe, he steeps stories in memories of childhood and membership in a close family circle. He comes to the narrative platform with an A.B. from Harvard and an M.A.T. from Harvard Graduate School of Education. Before leaving education, he taught in Sierra Leone for the Peace Corps and in surburban Chicago high schools for twenty years, and freelanced local color and character portraits for local papers. Classroom experience helped him select material that aided children in identifying the important values in their lives and the experiences of others. To provide grist for his telling experiences, he reads widely, selects events that suit his colloquial rhythms, and demands that the material keep audiences alert and interested. He deems such original oral presentations as "The Italian T-Shirt" as composition and performs them as literature.

Since changing careers, Lieberman has worked in a number of venues, including performing and teaching in schools and serving as storyteller-in-residence at colleges. Appearances have taken him to the B'nai B'rith National Convention, Corn Island Storytelling Festival, New Zealand's Glistening Waters Storytelling Festival, Hoosier Storytelling Festival, Jewish Storytelling Conference, Timpanogos Storytelling Festival, Winter Tales, Wild Onion Storytelling Festival, and gatherings in Illinois, Michigan, St. Louis, Nebraska, and the Sierras. In 1985, he taught a professional development program for teachers at the Kennedy Center. His works have inspired doctors, hospice workers, clergy, and attorneys and have won repeated honors for immediacy and skillful performance. *Good Housekeeping* magazine lauded *Joseph the Tailor*, which the company sent to every United States elementary school as part of its "Tell Me a Tale Celebration."

Bibliography

"Brainstorming for Self-Discovery," in *Tales as Tools: The Power of Story in the Classroom*, National Storytelling Press, 1994, 81–82.

"The Debate in Sign Language," in *More Best-Loved Stories Told at the National Storytelling Festival*, August House, 1992.

"The Italian T-Shirt," in *Who Says? Essays on Pivotal Issues in Storytelling*, August House, 1996, 215–216.

Streets and Alleys: Stories with a Chicago Accent, August House, 1995. Stories of four generations of an urban Jewish-American family.

"The Wise Shoemaker of Studena," in *Best-Loved Stories Told at the National Storytelling Festival*, August House, 1991.

The Wise Shoemaker of Studena, Jewish Publication Society, 1994.

Videography

"The Debate in Sign Language," in *Tell Me a Story, Vol. 3*, Hometown Entertainment, 1995.

"Interview," *The Twentieth Anniversary of the National Storytelling Festival*, Hometown Entertainment, 1994.

"The Wise Shoemaker of Studena," in *Tell Me a Story, Vol. 2*, Hometown Entertainment, 1995.

Audiography

The Intrepid Birdmen: The Fighter Pilots of World War I (audiocassette), self-published, 1993.

The Johnstown Flood of 1889 (audiocassette), self-published, 1989.

Joseph the Tailor and Other Jewish Tales (audiocassette), August House, 1995. Twelve stories of Jewish wit, wisdom, and tradition plus folk music for ages 5–adult.

The Old Man and Other Stories (audiocassette), Metro Mobile, 1985. Contains "Saved by a Sale," "The Whole Megillah," "Challahs in the Ark," "The Italian T-Shirt," "Marriage: A Fable," "The Dawning of a New Day," "Zachary," and the title story.

The Tell-Tale Heart and Other Terrifying Tales (audiocassette), August House, 1995. Classic horror stories from Edgar Allan Poe,

Geoffrey Chaucer, and Ambrose Bierce; for ages 10–adult.

A Winner and Other Stories (audiocassette), self-published, 1986.

"The Wooden Sword" on *Rainbow Tales, Vol. 1* (CD), Rounder Records, 1997.

Awards

1997 Great Lakes Writers Award finalist for *Streets and Alleys: Stories with a Chicago Accent.*

1996 *Storytelling World* Honor Award for Best Audio Recording for *Joseph the Tailor and Other Jewish Tales.*

1996 American Library Association Notable Children's Recording for *The Tell-Tale Heart.*

1995 IBM Award for *Joseph the Tailor.*

1995 American Library Association Notable Children's Recording for *Joseph the Tailor and Other Jewish Tales.*

1995 *Storytelling World* Honor Book for *Joseph the Tailor and Other Jewish Tales.*

1994 American Library Award for *The Intrepid Birdmen.*

1994 Parents' Choice Award for *The Intrepid Birdmen.*

1989 American Library Association Award for *The Johnstown Flood of 1889.*

1986 Parents' Choice Award for *A Winner.* Foundation for Excellence in Teaching's Golden Apple Award.

Source

"A Brief Look at This Year's Storytellers," Jonesborough, Tennessee *Herald & Tribune*, September 30, 1992, 4C–8C.

Kapnek, Shelley, "Making Book on Success: Communitywide Festival to Focus on the Richness of Jewish Literature," *Jewish Exponent*, November 18, 1994.

"Keepers of the Lore: Storytelling for Adults," *AudioFile Magazine*, August 1994, 1, 12–13.

Mooney, Bill, and David Holt. *The Storyteller's Guide.* Little Rock, Ark.: August House, 1996.

Sobol, Joseph, "Innervision and Innertext: Oral and Interpretive Modes of Storytelling Performance," in *Who Says? Essays on Pivotal Issues in Storytelling* , August House, 1996, 208–219.

Timeless Voices: Images of the National Storytelling Festival. Jonesborough, Tenn.: National Storytelling Press, 1997.

DOUG LIPMAN

Address   P. O. Box 441195
West Somerville, Massachusetts 02144
phone or fax 617-391-3672
email DougLipman@Story.lover.org or doug@storypower.com
website http://world.std.com/~loistalk

Focus: Jewish mystical tales; personal anecdotes; Southern Appalachian folktales; world folklore; participation stories; gender issues.

Audience: all ages.

Style: traditional storyteller-songster; one-man shows.

Instruments/Props: banjo, guitar, dulcimer, flute, button accordion.

A teacher, prolific recording artist, and performer, Doug Lipman believes that his job is to become invisible — to push the story ahead of the teller. Reverence for narrative is at the heart of his wish for the same respect for tellers that other artists receive. Like fellow performers who came of age during the storytelling renaissance of the 1970s, he began in folk music and adapted his act to platform narration in 1976, when the market for folksingers was waning. To make the most of oral language, he has perfected tone, posture, gesture, eye contact, timing, rhythm, and intonation. Since 1977, he has performed among the best at Pete Seeger's Hudson River Revival, Smithsonian Institution's Museum of American History, and at festivals, community centers, coffeehouses, temples, schools, radio stations, and workshops. His one-man shows have inspired audiences at Brandeis University, Boston University, Lesley College, and Storytellers in Concert, of which he is a founding member. He was featured performer at the 1996 Missouri River Storytelling Festival. His repertory includes workshops featuring "Making Fairy Tales from Personal Stories," "Storytelling Coaching," "Spiritual Stories," and "Long Stories Coaching."

Whether Lipman's appearances take him to Auckland or Seattle, Quebec or Abilene,

Atlanta or Washington, D.C., his style evolves from who he is and where he came from. Born in assimilated Jewry in Chicago, he recalls hearing his father pass on Jewish traditions, history, and legends in story form, which are easy for children to understand. Lipman earned a degree in math from Johns Hopkins University, an M.A. in English writing from Hollins College, and completed doctoral course work in English literature from Washington University and in music performance at the Kodály Musical Training Institute. Since 1969, he has taught music and story to preschool and handicapped children in Cambridge, Massachusetts, and served as a child-care worker at the Massachusetts Mental Health Center. He has presented over 100 courses in storytelling to teachers, parents, librarians, and professional performers and has spoken to National Council of Teachers of English, National Storytelling Institute, National Storytelling Conference, New England Kindergarten Conference, Springboards Reading Conference, and Sharing the Fire. He characterizes his type of Judaica as stories influenced by the Jewishness of the teller. Jewish themes, he emphasizes, are non-violent triumphs of wisdom and cleverness over a

seemingly insurmountable adversary, as demonstrated by his favorite stories: "The Clever Wife of Vietnam," a comeuppance parable, "The Forgotten Story: Tales About Wise Jewish Men," and "The Soul of Hope: An Epic Tale of the Baal Shem Tov," a classic Hasidic story about the gain and loss of wisdom. He emphasizes the importance of expressing his culture in any venue, even when he is the only Jewish teller on the program.

Articles

"After the Tale," *The Yarnspinner*, September 1989.

"Discovering the One and Only You," *Storytelling*, Winter 1992.

"Don't Bet on Didactic Writers," *Phoenix Rising*, April 1990.

"Finding the Most Important Thing," *Storytelling*, May 1994.

"Friendly Persuasion," *Storytelling*, Winter 1991.

"In Quest of the Folktale," *Yarnspinner*, June 1990.

"Making Fairy Tales from Personal stories, Parts 1 and 2," *National Storytelling Journal*, Fall 1988-Winter 1989.

"Max Lüthi," *National Storytelling Journal*, Spring 1987.

"Mayn Yingele," *Changing Men*, Spring 1987.

"More Cultural Than Thou?" in *Tales as Tools: The Power of Story in the Classroom*, National Storytelling Press, 1994, 165–166.

"New Tales from Old," *National Storytelling Journal*, Summer 1987.

"Remembering Reuven Gold," *Jewish Storytelling Newsletter*, Winter 1989.

"Resources," in *Making Musical Things*, Charles Scribner's Sons, 1979.

"Romping," *National Storytelling Journal*, Fall 1985.

"Story Games, Parts 1 and 2," *National Storytelling Journal*, Fall 1986, Winter 1987.

"Storytelling Ethics" (co-author Lee Ellen Marvin), *National Storytelling Journal*, Summer 1986.

"Superhero Play and Preschoolers," *Wingspan*, Autumn 1987.

"Tips from the Storytelling Coach: Doug Lipman," *Storytelling World*, Summer-Fall 1993, 5.

"Touch Magic," *National Storytelling Journal*, Winter 1985.

Bibliography

"Chew Your Rock Candy," in *Spinning Tales, Weaving Hope: Stories of Peace, Justice, and the Environment*, New Society, 1992.

"The Clever Wife of Vietnam," in *More Best Loved Tales Told at the National Storytelling Festival*, August House, 1992.

"Growing up. Jewish?" in *Jewish Storytelling Newsletter*, Winter 1990.

"How I Learned to Study Torah," in *Chosen Tales: Stories Told by Jewish Storytellers*, Jason Aronson, 1995.

"La Muerta: Godmother Death," in *Ready-to-Tell Tales*, August House, 1994.

"Riddle Story: In Summer I Die," in *Joining In: Audience: Participation Stories and How to Tell Them*, Yellow Moon Press, 1988.

"The Shammes Candle: A Participation Story for Hanukkah," *Storytelling Magazine*, November 1995.

The Storytelling Coach: How to Listen, Praise, and Bring Out People's Best (introduction by Jay O'Callahan), August House, 1995. For use in teaching oral communication.

Storytelling Games: Creative Activities for Language, Communication, and Composition Across the Curriculum, Oryx, 1996.

"Such Things to Write About," in *Many Voices: Tales from America's Past*, National Storytelling Press, 1995. A story derived from Lipman's father's letters home during World War II.

"The Sword of Wood," in *A Call to Character*, HarperCollins, 1996.

"The Tailor: A Jewish Folktale," in *Teacher's Read Aloud Anthology*, Macmillan/McGraw-Hill, 1993.

"Tell Me More, Daddy," in *Jewish Storytelling Newsletter*, Fall 1989.

"There's No Such Thing," in *The Ghost and I*, Yellow Moon Press, 1992.

We All Go Together: Creative Activities for Children to Use with Multicultural Folksongs, Oryx, 1994. Thirty multicultural folk songs and 140 games and curriculum for children.

Videography

Coaching Storytellers: A Demonstration Workshop for All Who Use Oral Communication, Enchanters Press, 1993.

Audiography

The Amazing Teddy Bear (audiocassette), Enchanters Press, 1991. Original stories and songs for parents and children; focuses on real issues children face.

Folktales of Strong Women (audiocassette), Yellow Moon Press, 1984. Contains "The One with the Star on Her Forehead," "La Muerta," "The Chicken Woman," and "The Woman Who saved the City"; for ages 10 through adult.

The Forgotten Story: Tales of Wise Jewish Men (audiocassette), Yellow Moon Press, 1988. Folktales, historical anecdotes, and Hasidic tales; accompanied by twelve-string guitar.

Grass Roots and Mountain Peaks: Taking Charge of Our Future (audiocassette), Enchanters Press, 1993. Visions for the storytelling movement.

Hopping Freights: A Wild 60s Adventure (audiocassette), Yellow Moon Press, 1990. A mythic journey to a bizarre barbecue, guitar concert at gunpoint, and the draft board; includes "Papa Mario" and other coming-of-age anecdotes; guitar accompaniment.

Keep on Shaking: Participation Stories and Songs (audiocassette), A Gentle Wind, 1984. Participation stories and songs, featuring "Stop That Shaking!," "Good Night, Sleep Tight," "The Old Woman and Her Pig," "The Three Sillies," and "Rabbit and the Mosquitoes"; for children 3–10.

A Medley of Tellers & Tales (contributor) (audiocassette), Yellow Moon Press, 1982. Seven stories by master tellers.

Milk from the Bull's Horn: Tales of Nurturing Men (audiocassette), Yellow Moon Press, 1986. Six folktales about nurturing men from Israel, Ireland, Japan, and the Appalachians; includes "The Man Who Had No Story" and "Jack and the Bull"; for ages 10–adult.

Now We Are Free: Stories and Songs of Freedom for Passover and Anytime (audiocassette), Enchanters Press, 1992. For children 3–10.

One Little Candle: Participation Stories and Songs for Hanukkah (audiocassette), Enchanters Press, 1990. For children 3–10.

Story Stone 5 (contributor) (audiocassette), Story Stone, 1988.

A Storytelling Treasury: Live from the 20th National Storytelling Festival (contributor) (audiocassette), National Storytelling Press, 1993.

Tell It with Me: More Participation Stories & Songs (audiocassette), A Gentle Wind, 1986. Participation stories and songs for children 3–10.

"The Woman Who Saved the City" on *Rainbow Tales* (CD), Rounder Records, 1997.

Awards

1996 *Storytelling World* Honor Resource for *Storytelling Games: Creative Activities for Language, Communication, and Composition Across the Curriculum*.

1996 *Storytelling World* Award for *The Storytelling Coach: How to Listen, Praise, and Bring Out People's Best*.

1986 Parents' Choice Gold Award for *Tell It with Me*.

1985 Somerville, Massachusetts Arts Council grant.

1978, 1976 Kodály Musical Training Institute Fellowship.

1968 Schubert Foundation Fellowship in Playwriting.

1964 Johns Hopkins University scholarship.

1964 National Merit Scholar.

Source

Beck, Linda, "Let's Play a Game," *School Library Journal*, October 1995, 52.

Denger, Laurie, "Stories Staging Revival, Storyteller Says," *Dayton Daily News*, February 22, 1988.

Doiron, Ray, "Professional Reading," *Emergency Librarian*, November/December 1995, 40–41.

Fanning, Ellen, "Lipman Likes Telling Stories," *Winchester Star*, October 18, 1990, 1A, 9A.

Gelbwasser, Michael, "Lipman Works to Tell the Story," *Jewish Advocate*, November 2, 1995.

"Hasidic Stories Home Page," http://www.hasidic.storypower.com.

"Lipman's Stories of Differences Tell Students about Other Cultures," *Winchester Star*, March 12, 1987.

McCray, Nancy, "Video," *Booklist*, August 1993, 2074.

"New Faces Shine on NSA Board," *Storytelling Magazine*, May 1997, 40–41.

Osborne, Linda, "The Wisdom of Nations," *World & I*, May 1993.

Salvayon, Leon, "Video Reviews," *Library Journal*, December 1993, 190.

"Storytelling World Awards," *Storytelling World*, Summer/Fall 1996.

"Two Local Performances Planned by Storyteller Doug Lipman," *Marlboro Enterprise/Hudson Daily Sun*, April 12, 1991, 13.

Ulmer, Gloria, "Young Performer Practices the Ancient Art of Storytelling," *Cleveland Jewish News*, March 17, 1989.

"Web Sites for Tellers," *Storytelling Magazine*, July 1997, 8.

NORMA LIVO

[lee'• voh]

Address 11960 West 22nd Place
Lakewood, Colorado 80215
phone 303-237-7107

Focus: folktales of the Hmong; fairy stories; family and bedtime stories; parent-child participation stories; family history; stories of nature and music.

Audience: general.

Style: traditional.

An expert on mythology and folklore, Dr. Norma Livo, professor emeritus from the University of Colorado at Denver, is a blend of scholar and pragmatist. A learned spokesperson for storytelling, she has published handbooks and texts on oral tradition and presented stories at libraries, schools, churches, parks, and nursing homes. In her own community in Denver she has helped preserve the folk tradition of Hmong emigrants from the Laotian Hills, whom she first discovered while purchasing a hand-embroidered storycloth. Although she was carrying no money at the time, she waylaid a local man, borrowed $200, and bought her treasure, a piece of Hmong appliqué and cross-stitching worked on layered cloth in the *pa ndau* or "flower cloth" style, incorporating history, animism, creation myths, and folk traditions. From the purchase of the prized cloth, detailed with houses on stilts, shamanistic rites, courtship games,

farming, and other village activities, in the early 1990s Livo advanced to research and the publication of two books on Hmong textiles and folk stories, *Hmong Folkstories* and *Hmong Textile Designs*. Three years later, her knowledge of storytelling's power over the human spirit also led to *Who's Afraid ... ? Facing Children's Fears with Folktales*, a book on childish fears and conflict resolution.

Livo prepared well for her life's work of preserving and telling folktales. Born July 31, 1929, in Tarentum, Pennsylvania, she grew up in an oral blend of Pennsylvania Dutch stories from her mother and Scotch-Irish blarney from her father. Both parents joined for piano, mandolin, and fiddle playing and story concerts, which influenced Livo's childhood. The family story tradition continues with her four children, one of whom had difficulty learning to read. To assist him, she listened to his stories, wrote them in book form, and produced them for him to enjoy. The method restored his self-esteem and helped him learn to read.

In the academic realm, Livo earned a B.S., M.Ed., and Ed.D. from the University of Pittsburgh and completed post-graduate studies at the universities of Utah and Colorado. Her experience as a geophysical assistant at Gulf Research Laboratory contrasts more scholarly work as professor at the University of Colorado, where she launched an innovative course in oral tradition. In addition to storytelling appearances, at the Faith and Family Conference, Livo led a workshop entitled "Building Strong Families Through Stories." She has served as a director of the National Storytelling Association, presided over the Colorado IRA, organized and directed the Rocky Mountain Storytelling Conference, and written articles for *Media and Methods, Colorado Outdoors, Rocky Mountain News, ALAN Review, Reading Teacher, English Journal, Storytelling Magazine,* and *The National Storytelling Journal.*

Bibliography

Folklore and Folkstories of Finland (co-author George O. Livo), Libraries Unlimited, 1998.

Folk Stories of the Hmong: Peoples of Laos, Thailand, and Vietnam (co-author Dia

Cha), Libraries Unlimited, 1991. The first published collection of Hmong tales in English, featuring 27 tales on beginnings, how and why stories, and love, magic, and fun; 16 pages of color photos of native dress and needlework.

Free Rein, Allyn & Bacon, 1978.

Hmong Textile Designs, Stemmer House, 1990. Highlights traditions from Viet Nam, Burma, Laos, and Thailand.

Joining In — An Anthology of Audience Participation Stories and How to Tell Them (editor), Yellow Moon, 1988. Eighteen participation stories for all ages, featuring "Freedom Bird."

Of Bugs and Beasts: Fact, Folklore, and Activities (co-author Lauren J. Livo and Glenn McGlathery), Teacher Ideas Press, 1995.

Stories with Sustenance, Fulcrum, 1998.

Storytelling Activities (co-author Sandra Rietz), Libraries Unlimited, 1987. Activities to expand storytelling by combining songs, dances, games, ballads, nonsense, and play with art and research projects to teach language arts skills; checklist of Bloom's taxonomy.

Storytelling Folklore Sourcebook (co-author Sandra A. Rietz), Libraries Unlimited, 1991. Sources of costumes, customs, dances, drama, food, games, and legends plus oral literature, music, proverbs, rhymes, riddles, tales, beliefs, and superstitions for upper elementary and secondary students.

"Storytelling Pairs Learn Together" (co-author Sandra Rietz), in *Tales as Tools: The Power of Story in the Classroom*, National Storytelling Press, 1994, 48.

Storytelling: Process and Practice (co-author Sandra Rietz), Libraries Unlimited, 1986. Techniques for finding material, analyzing structure, and developing, shaping and delivering a story; for scholars, folklorists and storytellers.

Troubadour's Storybag, Fulcrum, 1996. A collection of 38 world stories that celebrate the language of music, including "One-String Fiddle," "The Singing Bones," "The Talking Bird and the Singing Tree," and "The Young Chief Who Played the Flute"; organized thematically with activities and extensions.

Who's Afraid … ? Facing Children's Fears with Folktales, Libraries Unlimited, 1994. Stories about losing a parent, getting lost, and other common fears; suggested discussion topics, activities, and bibliography.

Who's Endangered on Noah's Ark (co-author Glenn McGlathery), Libraries Unlimited 1992. Traditional folktales, original stories, readers theater, and a study of the animals in folklore; features wolves, bears, elephants, tigers, leopards, California condors, northern spotted owls, bald eagles, whooping cranes, and alligators; contains bibliography for each section.

Videography

Hmong at Peace and War, Colorado Endowment for the Humanities, 1989.

Hmong Folkstories, Colorado Endowment for the Humanities, 1989.

Mining Stories of Colorado, University of Colorado, 1988.

Awards

1996 *Storytelling World* Honor Resource for *Of Bugs and Beasts: Fact, Folklore, and Activities.*

1996 National Storytelling Association Service and Leadership Award.

1995 Colorado Governor's Award for Excellence in the Arts.

1995 *Storytelling World* Award for *Storytelling Folklore Sourcebook.*

1995 *Storytelling World* Award for *Who's Afraid … ? Facing Children's Fears with Folktales.*

1990 American Newspapers Publishers Association Outstanding Achievement Award for Newspapers in Education.

1987 University of Colorado Award for Excellence in Research and Creative Endeavor.

1985 Colorado Division of Wildlife Outstanding Service Award for "Project Wild."

1981 University of Pittsburgh Meritorious Professional Achievement.

Source

"Folk Tales or Family History, Children Love to Hear Stories," *Houston Post*, March 10, 1991, E11.

Foulkes, A., "Reviews: Nonfiction," *Book Report*, May 1992, 58.

Freeman, Judy, "Saving Lives," *Instructor*, April 1994, 66.

Gardner, Carrie, and Elizabeth T. Joseph, "Reviews and News," *School Library Media Quarterly*, Fall 1994, 68.

Hinkemeyer, Joan, "Folk Tale Collection Features Fiddles, Flutes, Favorite Fables," *Rocky Mountain News*, December 15, 1996, 30D.

"Hmong Textile Designs," http://literary.com/ stemmer/pages/1130/ index.html, June 24, 1997.

"Joining In," http://www.wolfe.net/~uujim/ joining_in.html, June 24, 1997.

Lodge, Herbert R., "Fulcrum Aims for New Niche in Teacher Market," *Publishers Weekly*, November 11, 1996, 32.

Mason, M. S., "Teaching Tale-Tellers to Tell Tales," *Christian Science Monitor*, December 24, 1990, 14.

Mason, Marilynne S., "Telling Stories Isn't Just Kid Stuff," *Christian Science Monitor*, December 23, 1993, 12.

"Norma Livo: Veteran Teller, Ceaseless Advocate," *Storytelling Magazine*, May 1997, 34.

Price, S., "Professional Reading," *School Library Journal*, August 1991, 102.

"Review," *Faces*, October 1994, 38–39.

"Review," *Publishers Weekly*, October 21, 1996, 85.

"Review," *Teaching*, April 1997.

Rodriguez, Robert, "Music and Narrative," *Come-All-Ye Books*, May 1997.

Something About the Author, Vol. 76. Detroit: Gale Research, 1993.

OLGA LOYA

Address   P. O. Box 6482
San Jose, California 95150
phone & fax 408-297-3550
email olgaloya@aol.com

Focus: myths, legends, and folktales from Latin America; personal and family stories; Day of the Dead and Halloween stories; love and ghost tales, trickster lore; s/hero tales; participation stories; healing stories.

Audience: English and Spanish-speaking audiences; all ages.

Style: combination of voice, body, and imagination; bilingual telling; theatrical one-woman shows.

Instruments/Props: drums and rhythm instruments.

Olga Loya, a descendant of Mexican immigrants, is a teller of traditional tales from Latin America and around the world, including stories from her varied and colorful life. She speaks fluent English and Spanish, often telling stories in a creative and dramatic mix of the two languages. Her stories are filled with humor and emotion. They are poignant and true to her life and to memories of family and growing up in East Los Angeles. She recalls her grandma Loya and father Sandy Loya telling stories to her and her cousins. For eleven years she used storytelling skills in teaching. Wanting to explore more of the world, she left the classroom and lived in Mexico, Ireland, and New Mexico. She worked as a cocktail waitress, daffodil picker, carpenter, and solar technician. She was also part of "the same old people," a group in Humboldt County, California, who coordinate commu-

nity events, one of which is a storytelling festival. As a result of the festival, she developed a correspondence with teller Ruthmarie Arguello Sheenhan, who invited Loya to her first storytelling conference in November 1980. In Loya's words, "It was like a thunderbolt to my heart. I knew I had found my new passion — storytelling — and I have never looked back."

Loya's interests in telling cover a wide span of venues. She enjoys sharing customs and rituals such as "El Día de Los Muertos/The Day of the Dead," a Mexican holiday celebrated on November 1, and tells an original story, "La Cucarachita/The Little Cockroach." She uses teaching skills to train parents and teachers in the art of storytelling. As an adjunct to educators, she encourages teachers to apply stories in the classroom and helps parents relate their personal stories to their children and teaches games that families can play.

Loya received a California Arts Council Grant to develop a storytelling troupe and worked with children from kindergarten through eighth grade as well as teachers and parents. With a California Arts Council Touring Grant, she performs for schools, museums, universities, theaters, libraries, and festivals in the United States and Mexico. She has performed at the Chicano Voices Festival, Oregon Multicultural Storytelling Festival, San Jose Museum, Nebraska Storytelling Festival, San Francisco Mexican Museum, 21st National Storytelling Festival, Las Vegas Storytelling Festival, and Illinois Story Festival, where she shared top billing with Donald Davis, Shanta, and Duncan Williamson. Loya has produced and performed a four-part television series on KEET in Eureka, California, and a weekly storytelling program for KHSU-radio in Arcata.

Loya tours with a one-woman show, "Dancing Through La Vida," a combination of s/heroes and love and ghost stories from south of the border. The program features "La Diosa Hambrienta/The Hungry Goddess," an Aztec myth, and "La Llorona/The Weeping Woman," a traditional Latino legend. Loya has enjoyed performances at the San Francisco Art Museum, Willamette University, National Festival of Women's Theater, Amherst College Festival, Chicago's Mexican Museum of Fine Arts, and the First Latin American Storytelling Festival in Guadalajara, Mexico. In 1997 she presented "Storytelling of the Americas: Tales from Native American, Mexican, and South American Cultures" at the Children's Museum at La Habra in Los Angeles. She also conducts workshops on beginning storytelling, tapping the files of the mind, games storytellers play, unfolding self through stories, and parents as storytellers. Her topics include "Gods, Virgins, and Death — Latin American Folklore," "Our Culture Ourselves," and "Zeroing in on the Story." She is completing a play, "Sor Juana Inés de la Cruz," the biography of a seventeenth-century feminist nun and poet. She is also researching another show, "Juana Briones, a Mexican Settler in San Francisco," commissioned by the California Council for the Humanities.

Articles

"Telling a Tale Bilingually," http://members.aol.com/storypage/ news.blingolg.htm.
"Telling Tales Bilingually," *Texas Teller*, April 1994, 1–2.

Bibliography

Momentos Mágicos/Magic Moments, August House, 1997. Fifteen Latin American folktales, legends, and myths in English and Spanish from Mexico, Cuba, Guatemala, Yucatan, Nicaragua, Colombia, and Puerto Rico, including "How Monkey Tricked Crocodile," "Blanca Flor/White Flower," "The Flying Skeleton," and "How People Came to Be," from the Mayan Popol Vuh.

Videography

Stories from Around the World (three English videos and three Spanish videos), National Training Association, 1992. A dual set in English and Spanish for pre-school, primary, and intermediate grades.
Storytellers (four cassettes and four videos), Atlas Video, 1992. Contains stories by Joseph Bruchac, Jon Spelman, and Alice McGill. Cassettes are labeled "Tall Tales, Yarns, and Whoppers," "Animal Stories," "Magic Tales," and "Scary Stories."

Audiography

"The Hungry Goddess," on *Rainbow Tales,*

Too (CD), Rounder Records, 1997. An Aztec creation myth.

Latin American Stories: The Tricks of Life and Death/Las Astucias de la Vida Y de la Muerte (audiocassette), 1989.

Awards

1997 California Arts Council Tour.

1997 California Council for the Humanities for California Sesquicentennial commission to perform the character of Juana Briones.

1995 Commission to research the life of Sor Juana Inés de la Cruz.

1990 American Library Association Notable Award for *Latin American Stories: The Tricks of Life and Death/Las Astucias de la Vida Y de la Muerte.*

1989 California Arts Council storytelling model program.

1985–1990 Humboldt County Art grant.

Source

Conrad, Katherine, "Day of Dead Skeletons Intrigue Kids," *San Jose Mercury News,* October 13, 1993.

"Featured Storytellers ... Olga Loya," Jonesborough, Tennessee *Herald & Tribune,* September 29, 1993, 1C.

Flocken, Corinne, "Playing Mind Games: Dozens of Events at the Imagination Celebration," *Los Angeles Times,* April 24, 1997.

"Jackie Torrence Presents ... Stories from Around the World from Curriculum Associates," http://www.curriculumassociates. com// publications/jtorrence.html.

Vallongo, Sally, "A Teller of Tales: Bilingual Storyteller Gives Migrants Food for Thought," Toledo, Ohio *Blade,* August 2, 1991, 29.

Zad, Martie, "'Storytellers' Captives Kids of All Ages," *Washington Post,* October 20–26, 1991.

MARGARET MACDONALD

Address   11507 NE 104th Street
        Kirkland, Washington 98033
phone and fax 425-827-6430
margmacd@rain.kcls.org

Focus: world folklore; scholarly research.
Audience: children; educators.
Style: traditional.

Margaret Read MacDonald, born January 21, 1940, grew up in Southern Indiana. The speech cadences of that region and her mother's readings of James Whitcomb Riley's poetry had a lasting influence on her own use of language. As an anthropology undergraduate at Indiana University she dreamed of one day completing a study of her home community. She studied for a master's degree in library science at the University of Washington, intending to work in an academic library. However, in the last semester, she enrolled in a storytelling class taught by Bob Polishuk, Coordinator of Children's Services at the King County Library System. Polishuk made the role of children's librarian sound so intriguing that MacDonald switched career paths and went to work for him with the King County Library System in 1964.

A year later, MacDonald married federal auditor James Bruce MacDonald and began a series of moves—first to the San Francisco Public Library, then to the Oahu Bookmobiles, to the Singapore American school as children's consultant for the Mountain-Valley Library System in Sacramento, and to the Montgomery County Library System in Maryland. In 1972 she gave birth to Jennifer Skye MacDonald and moved to Buenos Aires, where her husband was working. Having honed her storytelling skills on many jobs and among various audiences, MacDonald set out to create an index to folktale collections, to provide easier access to the library's many collections. Dr. Richard Dorson of the Indiana University Folklore Institute concurred on the importance of the project, which MacDonald began while living in Argentina. In August 1974, she returned to Indiana University to work toward an advanced degree. Her second child, Julie Liana, was born in September 1974. Five years later, MacDonald completed her Ph.D. and, in 1982, published *The Storyteller's Sourcebook: A Subject, Title, and Motif-Index.*

After the family resettled in Seattle, MacDonald taught as adjunct faculty member at the University of Washington School of

Librarianship. Needing easy texts for story-telling students, she prepared *Twenty Tellable Tales*, which readers admired for their simple texts and for her methods of honing stories through repeated telling. To bring stories to life, she researched tales which had teller potential to add to tale collections and located texts for beginning tellers. She defended the right of the tale to seek an audience in a different time and culture among new listeners.

Returning to American culture, MacDonald employed participant observation techniques to produce over 200 hours of taped conversation among old friends in Scipio, Indiana, her mother's hometown. From this project came her community history, *Scipio, Indiana: Threads from the Past,* and a folkloric study of Scipio telling styles, *Scipio Storytelling: Talk in a Southern Indiana Community.* Since 1977, she has worked as children's librarian at the Bothell Library, a branch of the King County Library System. From her work grew programming sourcebooks such as *Booksharing,* useful collections such as *The Skit Book,* and heavy-duty reference titles such as *The Folklore of World Holidays.*

MacDonald served on the board and co-chaired the National Storytelling Association and presided over the children's section of the American Folklore Society. She was a founding member and president of the Washington State Folklife Society and president of Youth Theatre Northwest. For years, she was a board member of the Seattle Storytellers Guild. In 1993, she teamed with fellow librarian Su Vathanaprida to produce *Thai Tales: Folktales of Thailand.* In 1995, MacDonald traveled to the University of Mahasarakham in Thailand as a Fulbright scholar and trained university students in storytelling. In 1996, she returned to tour with her students and Dr. Wajuppa Tossa through nineteen provinces of Isaan. Connections begun through this tour encouraged MacDonald to offer storytelling workshops in Bangkok, Chiang Mai, Songhkla, Jakarta, Kuala Lumpur, Penang, Ipoh, and Sabah and Sarawak.

Still employed at the Bothell Library, Mac-Donald tours extensively on weekends and during vacations, telling at the National Storytelling Festival of Japan, Australian National Storytelling Festival, Glistening Waters Storytelling Festival in New Zealand, and throughout the United States and Canada. She is known for her "Playing with Story" workshops, which teach several short stories in one brief, intensive session. *The Old Woman Who Lived in a Vinegar Bottle, Tuck-Me-In Tales, Slop!,* and other picture book folktale retellings have widened her audience among teachers, librarians, and parents.

Articles

"All Pigs Are Equal But...," *School Library Media Activities Monthly*, September 1989.

"Finding Folklore," *Once Upon a Folktale: Capturing the Folklore Process with Children*, Teachers College Press, 1993.

"From 'Told Tale' to Picture Book: One Path," *Storytelling World*, Winter/Spring 1997, 14–15.

"The Imagination Machine," *Children's Book Review Magazine*, Holiday/Winter 1995, 9–10.

"'It Don't Take Long to Look at a Horseshoe': The Humorous Anecdote Catch-Phrase as Proverbial Saying," *Indiana Folklore and Oral History*, Vol. 15, No. 2, 1986, 95–120.

"Making Time for Stories," in *Tales as Tools: The Power of Story in the Classroom,* National Storytelling Press, 1994, 9–10.

"Not Our Problem," in *Tales as Tools: The Power of Story in the Classroom,* National Storytelling Press, 1994, 109.

"The Preschool Storytime as Parent Education," *Nebraska Library Association Quarterly*, Spring 1989, 19–23.

"Put Your Book on the Publishing Path," *Yarnspinner*, September 1991.

"Reading Your Way Around the World," *Children's Book Review Magazine*, Spring 1996, 9–10.

"Sources: About Stories and the Folks Who Tell Them," *In the Wind*, a column running from 1987 to the present.

"Strength," *Ready-to-Tell Tales*, August House, 1994.

"Take Time to Tell," *School Library Media Activities Monthly*, May 1989, 30–31.

"The Theme of Peace in Folk Tales" in *Tales as Tools: The Power of Story in the Classroom,* National Storytelling Press, 1994, 107–108.

"Turning Teachers into Tellers," *National Storytelling Journal*, Spring 1988.

"You, Yes, You, Telling Stories from Many Cultures," *Childcare Information Exchange*, July/August 1994, 35–38.

Bibliography

Bookplay: 101 Creative Themes to Share with Young Children, Libraries Professional Publications, 1994. Varied children's activities in the whole language mode.

Booksharing: 101 Programs to Use with Preschoolers, Libraries Professional Publications, 1988.

Celebrate the World: Twenty Multicultural Folktales, H. W. Wilson, 1994. Holiday stories featuring Chinese New Year, Hina Matsuri, Charro Days, Id Al Fitr, Midsummer Eve, Diwali, and Kwanzaa; suggestions for crafts, music, food, books, and games.

The Folklore of World Holidays, Gale, 1991.

Ghost Stories from the Pacific Northwest, August House, 1995 Humorous and serious stories of hauntings in British Columbia, Washington, and Oregon.

The Girl Who Wore Too Much: A Folktale from Thailand (illustrated by Yvonne LeBrun Davis), August House, 1997.

Look Back and See: Lively Tales for Gentle Tellers, H. W. Wilson, 1991. Contains 20 singing tales, audience participation, teaching tales, tales for quiet moments, and tales with improvisational slots.

The Old Woman Who Lived in a Vinegar Bottle (illustrated by Nancy Dunaway Fowlkes), August House, 1995. A rhythmic, comic fairy tale about greed.

The Parent's Guide to Storytelling: How to Make Up New Stories and Retell Old Favorites, HarperCollins, 1995.

Peace Tales: World Folktales to Talk About, Linnet Books, 1992.

Pickin' Peas (illustrated by Pat Cummings), HarperCollins, 1998.

The Round Book (co-author Winifred Jaeger), Linnet Books, 1998.

Scipio, Indiana: Threads from the Past, Ye Galleon Press, 1988.

Scipio Storytelling: Talk in a Southern Indiana Community, University Press of America, 1996.

The Skit Book: 101 Skits from Kids, Linnet Books, 1990.

Slop! (illustrated by Yvonne LeBrun Davis), Fulcrum, 1997.

The Storyteller's Sourcebook: A Subject, Title, and Motif-Index to Folklore Collections for Children, Gale, 1982. An index of folk and fairy tales by title, subject, author, and theme.

The Storyteller's Start-Up Book, August House, 1993. An introduction to storytelling with tips on finding, learning, performing, and using folktales.

Tom Thumb, Oryx, 1993.

Tuck-Me-in-Tales: Bedtime Stories from Around the World (illustrator Yvonne Le Brun Davis), August House, 1996. Featuring "Snow Bunting's Lullaby" from Siberia, "Chin Chin Kobokama" from Japan, and tales from South America, Liberia, and the British Isles.

Twenty Tellable Tales: Audience Participation Folktales for the Beginning Storyteller, H. W. Wilson, 1986. Contains "A Whale of a Tale," "Coyote's Crying Song," "The Gunny Wolf," "How to Break a Bad Habit," "Mr. Fox," and 15 other world tales.

When the Lights Go Out: 20 Scary Tales to Tell, H. W. Wilson, 1988. Contains 20 jump tales, tales to act out, scary stories, and supernatural and ghost lore.

Videography

Folktales of Peace (adviser), J. B. Motion Graphics, 1996.

Visual Tales (scriptwriter), Sign-A-Vision, 1986, 1987.

Audiography

"The Gunny Wolf," in *Teachers Read Aloud Anthology, Grade 3* (audiocassette), Macmillan/McGraw-Hill, 1993.

"Kanji-Jo the Nestlings," in *Teacher's Read Aloud Anthology, Grade 1* (audiocassette), Macmillan/McGraw-Hill, 1993.

Tuck-Me-in-Tales (co-produced with musician Richard Sholtz) (audiocassette), August House, 1997. Lesser-known tales from many cultures featuring "Snow Bunting's Lullaby" from Siberia, "Chin Chin Kobokama" from Japan, and other tales, rhymes, and repetition from South America, Liberia, and the British Isles and music on dulcimer and autoharp.

Awards

1997 Children's Catalog recommendation for *The Storyteller's Start-Up Book*.

1996 *Storytelling World* Award for *The Parent's Guide to Storytelling*.

1996 *Storytelling World* Award for *The Old Woman Who Lived in a Vinegar Bottle*.

1996 Southern Books Competition honorable mention for *The Old Woman Who Lived in a Vinegar Bottle*.

1996 Elementary School Library Collection recommendation for *The Old Woman Who Lived in a Vinegar Bottle*.

1996 *Storytelling World* Award for "Little Snot Nose Boy."

1996 *Storytelling World* Award for *Peace Tales*.

1995 Fulbright Scholar, Mahasarakham University, Thailand.

1994 *Storytelling World* Award for *The Storyteller's Start-Up Book*.

Source

Contemporary Authors, Vol. 110. Detroit: Gale Research, 1984.

Contemporary Authors New Revision Series, Vol. 27. Detroit: Gale Research, 1989.

Mooney, Bill, and David Holt. *The Storyteller's Guide*. Little Rock, Ark.: August House, 1996.

Something About the Author, Vol. 93. Detroit: Gale Research, 1996.

"Storytelling World Awards," *Storytelling World*, Summer/Fall 1996.

RAFE MARTIN

Address   (home) 56 Brighton Street
Rochester, New York 14607
phone 716-442-2826

(office) 62 Cornell Street
Rochester, New York 14607
phone 716-271-2401

Focus: sharing tales that relate personal, cultural, and universal experience; world myth and folk stories; animal and child interaction.

Audience: all ages.

Style: narrative.

Instruments/Props: microphone.

Author and storyteller Rafe Martin describes his stories, books, and tapes as an antidote to the negative effect of overly visual technologies and an encouragement of reading and language. One conference director found his influence so valuable to readers and storytellers that she declared him a national treasure. He is in growing demand; his résumé reads like an airline schedule — from his home in Rochester, New York, to Japan, Honolulu, Detroit, Pennsylvania, Ohio, California, Texas, Alaska, and points in between. At libraries, schools, children's literature and whole language conferences, and festivals, he gathers audiences for joyful, powerful, and dramatic tellings. He has created four audio collections and appears on several others, including the National Storytelling Festival's Twentieth Anniversary audio collection. He has written articles for *Parabola, Enquiring Mind, Zen Bow, The Sun,* and *Animals' Voice.* His works are available in French, Spanish, Xhosan, Zulu, Afrikaans, Japanese, and Swedish.

Martin, born January 22, 1946, in Queens, New York, collected an array of material in childhood from his mother's sharing of fairy tales and family stories and his father's stories of growing up on New York City's lower east side and, later, of flying intelligence and rescue missions over the Himalayas, and traveling in India during World War II. His grandmothers added to the mix with stories of the Russian Revolution of 1917, and of their own childhoods and migrations to the United States as young women. On his own, Martin read Arthurian lore, Robin Hood stories, and Rudyard Kipling's *The Jungle Book.* Graduating with highest honors in English literature, Martin wrote a thesis on Herman Melville's *Moby Dick* and prepared for his career with a B.A. from Harpur College and an M.A. in English literature and literary criticism from the University of Toronto, where he studied with noted critics Northrop Frye and Marshall McLuhan.

With his wife Rose, Martin created the Ox Cart Bookshop in Rochester in 1969, where he also initiated his storytelling career. He worked as artist-in-residence in the city school and as a master performer in the Lincoln Center extension program. In 1983, he received the first Pannell award from the Women's National Book Association as "the bookseller in the United States and Canada who has been most creative in bringing children and books together." Martin has been the featured speaker at a variety of significant events: Ganandagan, the New York State Historic and Sacred Native American Site, American Museum of Natural History, New York City Storytelling Center, George Eastman House International Museum of Photography, Zuñi Pueblo, Buddhist Peace Fellowship, Cherokee Rose Storytelling Festival, and Joseph Campbell Foundation Festival of Myth, Folklore, and Story. A two-time presenter at the National Storytelling Festival, he has also performed for the American Booksellers Association National Institute, International Reading Association International Convention, National Council of Teachers of English, National Whole Language Conference, Vassar College Institute on Children's Literature, Chautauqua Institute, and International Storytelling Institute. An award-winning author of fourteen books, Martin has produced classic bestsellers, notably, *The Rough-Face Girl, Will's Mammoth*, and *Foolish Rabbit's Big Mistake*. Martin has received three Parents' Choice Gold awards, two ALA Notables, an IRA Teacher's Choice, several ABA Pick of the Lists, and the Anne Izard Storyteller's Choice, Golden Sower, and Georgia Picture Book Award.

Articles

"Between Teller and Listener: The Reciprocity of Storytelling" in *Who Says: Essays on Pivotal Issues in Contemporary Storytelling*, August House, 1996.

"Fur," *The Sun*, October 1997.

"Once Upon a Time…, " *Turning Wheel*, Spring 1997.

"Zen Failure," *The Sun*, July 1995.

Bibliography

"Among the Animals," *Storytelling World*, Winter/Spring 1992, 20.

"The Banyan Deer," "The Brave Little Parrot," "Great Joy the Ox," and "King Sivi" in *Stories of the Spirit, Stories of the Heart*, HarperCollins, 1991.

"The Black Hound," in *Peace Tales*, Linnet Books, 1992.

The Boy Who Lived with the Seals (illustrator David Shannon), G. P. Putnam's Sons, 1993. A Chinook coming-of-age tale; for second grade and up.

The Boy Who Loved Mammoths (illustrator Richard Wehrman), Yellow Moon Press, 1996. An original story; for third grade and up.

"The Brave Little Parrot," in *More Best-Loved Stories Told at the National Storytelling Festival*, August House, 1992.

Dear As Salt (illustrator Vladyana Krykorka), Scholastic Canada, 1993. A traditional Italian Cinderella story; for first grade and up.

"The Dove's Tale," in *Reading Between the Lines: A Collection of Modern Midrash*, Jason Aaronson, 1996.

The Eagle's Gift, G. P. Putnam's Sons, 1997. An Alaskan Eskimo tale about the Eagle Mother; illustrated with oil paintings by Tatsuro Kiuchi; for all ages.

Foolish Rabbit's Big Mistake (illustrator Ed Young), G. P. Putnam's Sons, 1985. A jataka tale; for pre-kindergarten and up.

The Ghost and I: Scary Stories for Participatory Telling (contributor), Yellow Moon Press, 1992. Features 20 funny and scary stories and songs for ages 5–14.

The Hungry Tigress (illustrator Richard Wehrman), Yellow Moon Press, 1997. Forty-one Buddhist stories about wisdom and compassion; for fourth grade and up.

The Monkey Bridge (illustrated in Persian miniature style by Fahimeh Amiri), Knopf, 1997. A 2,500-year-old tale from India about a monkey king that teaches a human king to rule with compassion; for kindergarten and primary readers.

Mysterious Tales of Japan (co-author and illustrator Tatsuro Kiuchi), G. P. Putnam's Sons, 1996. Traditional Japanese mystery tales; for third grade and up.

One Hand Clapping — Zen Stories for All Ages (co-author Manuela Scares; illustrator Junko Morimoto), Rizzoli International, 1996. Tales by Buddha and Zen masters from China and Japan; for third grade and up.

The Rough-Face Girl (illustrator David Shannon), G. P. Putnam's Sons, 1992. A multi-award-winning Algonquin Cinderella story; for second grade and up.

A Storyteller's Story (photographer Jill Krementz), Richard C. Owen Publishers. 1992. An autobiographical account of Martin's work, travels, and writing; for first grade and up.

"Urashima Taro," in *Ready-to-Tell Tales*, August House, 1994.

Will's Mammoth (illustrator Stephen Gammell), G. P. Putnam's Sons, 1989. An imaginative, creative animal story; for pre-kindergarten and up.

Videography

Big Long Man and Mountain Lion and *Bird Man*, Film Ideas, 1993. A creation legend about humans and animals; a tale of a man who yearned to fly.

The Boy Who Drew Cats, Film Ideas, 1993. A Japanese family folk story

The Boy Who Went to Live with the Seals, Film Ideas, 1993. A Chinook story of how a six-year-old boy discovers his true identity.

Dear As Salt, Film Ideas, 1993. A poignant Italian "King Lear" tale about a banished princess with a happy ending.

Foolish Rabbit, Film Ideas, 1993. A jataka adaptation of "Chicken Little."

Great Joy, Film Ideas, 1993. A jataka legend about a bet.

Ho Ichi, Film Ideas, 1993. A Japanese ghost tale about a ruling family and a blind storyteller.

Kogi, Film Ideas, 1993. An original story about a man who becomes a whale.

The Lost Princess, Film Ideas, 1993. An original fairy tale about a prince's betrothal to a beautiful bride.

Prince Five Weapons, Film Ideas, 1993. A Buddhist legend from ancient India.

The Rough-Face Girl, Film Ideas, 1993. A Native American Cinderella story set on Lake Ontario four hundred years ago.

Snow Woman, Film Ideas, 1993. A Japanese ghost tale about a woodcutter.

The Treasure, Film Ideas, 1993. A folk tale about a poor man's search for treasure

Will's Mammoth, Film Ideas, 1993. An original story about a boy who loved mammoths.

Audiography

Animal Dreaming: Encounters in the Natural World (audiocassette), Yellow Moon Press, 1992. Mythic tales of earth and animals for older children and adults.

The Boy Who Loved Mammoths and Other Tales (illustrator Richard Wehrman) (audiocassette), Weston Woods, 1996. An original story for ages eight and up.

Ghostly Tales of Japan (audiocassette), Yellow Moon Press, 1990. Mysterious stories from Japan for older children and adults, including "The Boy Who Drew Cats," "Urashima Taro," "Kogi," and "Ho-Ichi the Earless."

Rafe Martin Tells His Children's Books (audiocassette), Yellow Moon Press, 1995. Oral versions of *The Rough-Face Girl, Foolish Rabbit's Big Mistake, Will's Mammoth,* and *The Boy Who Lived with the Seals.*

"The Snow Woman," on *The National Storytelling Festival Twentieth Anniversary Collection* (audiocassette), 1992.

Awards

1996 *Storytelling World's* Anthologies Award for *One Hand Clapping — Zen Stories for All Ages.*

1996 Parents' Choice Gold Award for *The Boy Who Loved Mammoths.*

1996 American Bookseller Association's Spring Children's Pick of the List for *The Boy Who Loved Mammoths.*

1996 American Library Association Book Award for *Mysterious Tales of Japan.*

1996 American Folklore Society's Aesop's Accolade for *Mysterious Tales of Japan.*

1994 Parents' Choice Gold Award for *Rafe Martin Tells His Children's Books.*

1994 Pennsylvania School Library Association Master List for *The Rough-Face Girl.*

1994 Texas Bluebonnet Honor Book Award for *The Rough-Face Girl.*

1994 Georgia Children's Picture Storybook Award for *The Rough-Face Girl.*

1994 Golden Sower Award for *The Rough-Face Girl*.

1994 North Carolina Children's Book Award for *The Rough-Face Girl*.

1994 Kansas State Reading Circle Master List for *The Boy Who Lived with the Seals*.

1994 CBC and NCSS Notable Children's Book in Social studies for *The Boy Who Lived with the Seals*.

1993 Child Study Children's Book Committee Book of the Year for *The Rough-Face Girl*.

1993 *Newsweek* Best Children's Books for *The Boy Who Lived with theSeals*.

1993 *Booklist* Editor's Choice for *The Boy Who Lived with the Seals*.

1992 American Bookseller Pick of the Lists for *The Rough-Face Girl*.

1992 IRA Teacher's Choice Award for *The Rough-Face Girl*.

1992 Anne Izard Storyteller's Choice Award for *The Hungry Tigress*.

1992 *USA Today* Best Children's Books for *The Rough-Face Girl*.

1992 *Newsweek* Best Children's Books for *The Rough-Face Girl*.

1990 Parents' Choice Gold Award for *Ghostly Tales of Japan*.

1989 *Time* Magazine's Best Children's Books for *Will's Mammoth*.

1989 American Library Association Notable Children's Book for *Will's Mammoth*.

1989 *School Library Journal* Best Book of the Year for *Will's Mammoth*.

1989 Horn Book Fanfare Book for *Will's Mammoth*.

1989 Child Study Association Book of the Year for *Will's Mammoth*.

1987 Women's National Book Association Lucille Micheels Pannell Award.

1985 American Library Association Notable Book for *Foolish Rabbit's Big Mistake*.

1985 American Bookseller Pick of the List for *Foolish Rabbit's Big Mistake*.

1985 Horn Book Fanfare Book for *Foolish Rabbit's Big Mistake*.

1985 New York Public Library's 100 Titles for Reading and Sharing for *Foolish Rabbit's Big Mistake*.

1985 Booklist Children's Editors' Choice for *Foolish Rabbit's Big Mistake*.

Source

"ALA Recognition," *Storytelling Magazine*, July 1997, 7.

"Children's Audio/Video Reviews," *Publishers Weekly*, April 15, 1996, 35.

Larson, Jeanette, "Audiovisual Media; Audio," *Booklist*, April 15, 1996, 1455.

"Mysterious Tales of Japan," http://www.uni-vstudios.com/putnam/books/tales_japan/book.html, May 27, 1997.

Olson, Renee, and Randy Meyer, "Awards," *School Library Journal*, September 1995, 116.

"Parents' Choice Audio," http://family.star-wave.com/reviews/pchoice/9511/audio_products/ 0612.html, May 27, 1997.

"Rafe Martin," http://www.mca.com/putnam/authors/rafe_martin/author.html, June 4, 1997.

"The Rough-Face Girl," http://www.2.pbs.org/kcet/storytime/books/14.6.htm, June 4, 1997.

Sanborn, LaVonne, "Audiovisual Review: Recordings," *School Library Journal*, August 1993, 125–126.

DAVID MASSENGILL

Address   179 East Third Street #20
New York, New York 10009
phone 212-533-6297
fax 212-366-0465

Focus: gentle, humorous stories.
Audience: general.
Style: relaxed, folksy songs and tellings.
Instruments/Props: Appalachian dulcimer.

In his résumé, singer/composer/raconteur David Massengill claims to tell true stories about friends and family, but adds, "*Basically true … or stories I made up about friends and family.*" Storytelling evolved naturally from a career that began with singing and songwriting. A native of Bristol, Tennessee, born in 1954, he taught himself to play mountain music while studying English at the University of North Carolina at Chapel Hill. His motivation was a dual loss — the departure of a girl friend and George McGovern's unsuccessful

bid for the presidency. Influenced by *Bound for Glory*, the biography of Woody Guthrie, and by the career of Bob Dylan, Massengill honed his writing into art while residing in Greenwich Village, combining gentle wit and a literate sensibility to create story-songs that stand out in the fertile folk renaissance of the late 1970s and early 1980s. He began fitting stories to the two-fingered pluck and strum of his Edsel Martin dulcimer, a high quality lap instrument made by—and named for—an expert craftsman in Old Fort, east of Asheville, North Carolina. Massengill recalls that his mother special-ordered the dulcimer for her children and demanded the best, but the instrument had lain unused under the bed at home until he was inspired to play.

Massengill joined the Songwriters Exchange, an informal association of emerging folk musicians, and placed two titles on the 1980 Stash Records album *Cornelia Street*, which was reissued on CD in 1990 with four added songs. Fifty-five years after the exchange evolved into Fast Folk, he continues publishing original music on its discs. "On the Road to Fairfax County," performed by the Roches and folksinger Joan Baez, contains the eighteenth-century motif of a highwayman and his lover, a libretto that parallels traditional English ballads. He is best known for "My Name Joe" on *Legacy*, the story of Joe, a Thai cook and illegal immigrant in an alien culture, "Jesus, the Fugitive Prince" on *The Return*, about an escape from an asylum on Christmas Eve, "The Great American Dream," unofficial anthem and portrait series of the New York folk scene of the early 1980s, and "Number One in America," a ballad reflecting on the 1986 Ku Klux Klan march in Bristol, Tennessee.

New on the platform narrative circuit, Massengill makes use of a rural Southern upbringing, which surfaces in his original tellings. He continues developing his narrative flair with the half-hour saga "Jack and the Beanstalk," written in sonnet form and subtitled, "What Once Was Just a Bean." Massengill's music was featured on *Folk City's Twenty-Fifth Anniversary Concert*, a special on PBS-TV and BBC-TV in Europe, and was featured teller at the National Storytelling Festival in 1994. In addition to a tour of Europe, he has performed at the Newport Folk Festival, Carnegie Hall, Philadelphia Folk Festival, Mountain Stage, San Francisco Storytelling Festival, Old Town School of Music, Vancouver Folk Festival, The Bottom Line, Nebraska Storytelling Festival, and the Kennedy Center in Washington, D.C. A bit of family heritage from his album *The Return* surfaces in "A Girl's Daring Escape." The story relates the late-night elopement of Bessie Slaughter to marry Alexander Massengill, as reported in a 1910 edition of *The Comet*. With accomplices James Bettner and Creed Reagan, the couple flees by closed carriage pulled by dappled grays to Jonesborough, Tennessee, where a county clerk issues a license. Reverend G. W. Lee weds the couple, who depart by Number Two for Bristol. In a pensive reflection over his music and storytelling career, Massengill concludes, "I have just decided that whatever gives me joy is the right thing to do, and this has given me a great deal of joy."

Bibliography

"Rider on an Orphan Train," in *Many Voices: True Tales from America's Past*, National Storytelling Association, 1995.

Audiography

Coming Up for Air, (audiocassette and CD), Flying Fish, 1992. Contains "My Name Joe," "Number One in America," "Don Quixote's Lullaby," "It's a Beautiful World," and "The Road to Fairfax County."

The Great American Bootleg Tape (audiocassette), self-published, 1986.

The Kitchen Tape (audiocassette), self-published, 1987.

The Legacy (contributor) (audiocassette), Windom Hill, 1990. Contains Massengill's "My Name Joe," "I Saw a Stranger with Your Hair," "Insanity Street," and the title song.

The Return (audiocassette and CD), Plump Records, 1995. Contains "The Great American Dream," "Jesus, the Fugitive Prince," "Blind Man/Black Swan," "Sightseer," "A Girl's Daring Escape," "The Great American Dream," and "Rider on an Orphan Train," the story of brothers who are separated after being sent west to be adopted; vocals by Maggie and Terre Roche.

Videography

Folk City's Twenty-Fifth Anniversary Concert, Rhino, 1990.

Awards

1996 NAIRD Indie Award finalist for *The Return*.

1992 New York Music Awards Best Album Award for *Coming Up for Air*.

1992 NAIRD Indie Award finalist for *Coming Up for Air*.

1989 New York Music Awards Best Folk Act nomination.

1989 Kerrville Folk Festival New Folk Award.

1988 New York Music Awards Best Folk Act nomination.

1987 New York Music Awards Best Folk Act nomination.

Source

Adams, Noah, "David Massengill Shares Dulcimer Folk Songs," *All Things Considered (NPR)*, December 13, 1995.

Boehm, Mike, "Folk Festival Concludes with Calls for '86 Encore," *Providence Journal*, August 5, 1985.

_____, "Singer, Yarn Spinner and American Dreamer," *Providence Journal-Bulletin*, February 7, 1986.

"David Massengill," http://www.plump.com, April 16, 1997.

Fricke, David, "On the Edge," *Rolling Stone*, December 10–24, 1992.

Gewertz, Daniel, "An Evening of Folk Fun," *Boston Herald*, June 6, 1987.

Hinckley, David, "The Uncommon Pursuit," *New York Daily News*, April 24, 1987.

Ide, Stephen A., "Take a Breather to the Sounds of 'Air,'" *Patriot Ledger*, August 1–2, 1992.

Johnson, Kenneth, "Into the Night," *Charlotte Observer*, December 31, 1993.

Joyce, Mike, "Whimsical Massengill," *Washington Post*, October 4, 1996.

Matre, Lynn Van, "Success Begins at 40," *Chicago Tribune*, April 10, 1994.

McLaughlin, Jeff, "Trying to Make a Go of It," *Boston Globe*, March 3, 1985.

Ochs, Sonny, "Review of 'The Return,'" http://www.acousticmusic.com/fame/p00171.htm, June 23, 1997.

Rowe, Jonathan, "Urban Folk Music Takes a Political Swing," *Christian Science Monitor*, February 5, 1990.

Ruhlmann, William, "For Massengill, Every Song Tells a Story," *New York City Tribune*, February 28, 1985.

Wald, Elijah, "Strong, Simple and Earthy," *Boston Globe*, January 23, 1987.

"What's Hot," *New York Times*, November 7, 1985.

Wilson, Susan, "Fast Folk Had Its Moments," *Boston Globe*, April 6, 1987.

Woliver, Robbie, "David Massengill," Long Island, New York *Newsday*, Tuesday 27, 1996.

CHARLES "UNCLE CHARLIE" KAULUWEHI MAXWELL, SR.

Address   157 Alea Place
            Maui, Hawaii 96768
phone 808-572-8038
fax 808-572-0602
email kale@maui.net

Focus: Hawaiian chants, dance, songs, history, genealogy, sacred sites, and lore; native fairy tales; defense of island sovereignty and of native plants and animals.
   Audience: Hawaiians.
   Style: traditional.
   Instruments/Props: native dress; leis.

Storyteller and children's author Charles Kauluwehi Maxwell, Sr., better known as Uncle Charlie, has made a name for himself as an advocate for the affairs of Kanaka Maoli or native Hawaiians. He believes that islanders must retain their indigenous culture if they are to safeguard the area's well being. He maintains that Kanaka and Western values are incompatible, particularly in strengthening the ecology, which local islanders revere and protect, and in fostering the "Aloha" spirit of tourism, which Westerners promote with faulty theatrics. Through didactic storytelling, he instructs Hawaiians about historic sites, burial, language, art, dance, and canoe migration as a means of nurturing and preserving island lore and passing on Pacific traditions to future generations. His explanation of ancestral blood expresses the mythic oneness of Hawaiian people with the earth and sky, the natural elements that created life in the Pacific.

Music is a significant part of Maxwell's life. He was born a mile from the ritual Polynesian burial site at Napili, Maui, and treasures the old koa guitar of his father, a small string instrument carved from the red wood of an acacia tree, which he describes in a nostalgic tale. He recalls his childhood in Pulehu on the slopes of Haleakala in the days prior to the bombing of Pearl Harbor. Daily, he welcomed his father, William Kupahu Maxwell, home from work and listened to his mother play the guitar and piano for the family. Neighbors visiting on the front porch sang familiar island melodies as well as "You Are My Sunshine," "Irene, Good Night," "Tennessee Waltz," "Mares Eat Oats," and "Pistol-Packing Mama." From childhood, Maxwell was a skilled performer and enjoyed singalongs with musicians hired to serenade at local political rallies. Among guests at informal gatherings, he shared meals of laulau, Kalua pig, Portuguese soup, fresh bread, butter, and milk. In adulthood, he married a musician, hula master Nina Boyd, and, in 1989, wrote the hit song "Honokahua Nani E."Retired from police work because of physical disability, Maxwell has developed a specialty in Hawaiian culture and devotes his time to serving island interests in negotiations with Rockwell Power Systems and the U.S. Civil Rights Commission. In 1975, he helped initiate the Kahoolawe movement to return the island of Maui to Hawaiian nationals. He is a consultant to Bio-Genesis Pacific Inc., the contractor testing unexploded ordnance. Maxwell also teaches at schools, colleges, and universities in the islands and Alaska, and has appeared on "Harry Kojima's Cooking Show," "ABC Home Show," and the Discovery Channel.

Bibliography

"The Kohola in Hawaii," http://www.hookele.com/storyteller/kohola.html, 1997.

"Mana'O I'O," http://hookele.com/storyteller.html, May 5, 1997.

"Papa's Old Koa Guitar," http://www.hookele.com/storyteller/guitar.html, 1997.

"The Three Menehune of Ainahou," http://www.hookele.com/storyteller/menehune.html, 1997.

Uncle Charlie's Bedtime Stories.
The Warrior Within.

Awards

1996 One of Hawaii's "People Who Made a Difference."

1990 Na Hoku Hanohano Album of the Year for "Honokahua Nani E."

Source

"Hawaiian Culture," http://hawaiianculture.miningco.com/library/weekly/mcurrent.html, 1997.

"Interview," *Pacific Connections*, September/October 1996.

"One Heart Journal," http://www.hookele.com/oneheart/journal.html, August 4, 1996.

JIM MAY

Address   Box 1012
Woodstock, Illinois 60098
phone 815-648-2039

Focus: rural Midwestern lore; memoirs and original tales; folktales, legends, ghost stories; participation songs.
Audience: general.
Style: conversational delivery with an emphasis on humor and variety to suit the mood and interests of his audience.

An expert on horse swapping, dairy farming, general stores, and rural affairs of McHenry County, Illinois, Jim May follows Southern novelist William Faulkner's advice and returns to his hometown for such personal memoirs as "Most Valuable Altar Boy" and "Horse-Snot, or Everything You Always Wanted to Know About Sex Education at St. Peter's." May's background in Spring Grove is essential to his relaxed, unself-conscious style. Of German Catholic background, he grew up on family acreage that had passed four times to the succeeding generation. The dimensions and rhythms of the dairying community resonate through his small-town stories. Although he earned a degree in Russian history and urban planning at the University of Illinois, his return to modest roots has strengthened a substantial skill in storytelling, influenced by Carolina classic traditionalists Ray Hicks and Jackie Torrence. The profound discovery of a life built around stories prompted May to follow their lead by tossing out lesson plans for his history class and relating "Soldier Jack," a story already worn smooth by both Hicks and Torrence.

Pragmatic and intuitive about the interests and tastes of his audience, May specializes in straightforward stories of community building and self-understanding, but maintains a varied program to spark interest and keep his tellings fresh. He advocates keeping an open mind about stories and expects to inject a little something extra when memory of the main details fails him. One of his successes is an "Amazing Grace Trilogy," a tripartite story about how slaver John Newton fled the human flesh trade to become a minister and wrote his classic hymn in 1779, how Danes resisted Nazi oppression by joining Jewish refugees in wearing the required armband displaying a yellow star, and how the Catholic community of Spring Grove honored former slave John Henry Higler.

May thrives in both intimate settings and large group gatherings by stressing humor and intimacy. For visits with children, he prefers arranging them in a semicircle at his feet to personalize his encounter with each listener. A proponent of storytelling as a vehicle of culture, he co-founded and directs the Illinois Storytelling Festival. He was featured at the Southern Illinois Storytelling Festival, Jackson Storyfest, Montana Storytelling Retreat, National Storytelling Festival, and Storytelling '97 at Mansfield University, and leads workshops for storytellers, educators, and human service workers on improving technique, personal and family narrative, living the myth, and cultural pride and perspective. In summer 1997 he joined Virginia Korus for the Montana Storytelling Retreat to foster writing, creating, group interaction, critiquing, and presentation. A September appearance at the Corn Island Storytelling Festival joined his talents with those of tellers Jackie Torrence and Milbre Burch. A standout workshop at the 18th National Storytelling Conference, "Cultural Pride and Perspective and Its Relationship to Personal Narrative," expressed May's belief that individuals have unique cultural heritage and that stories convey cultural influence on personal, social, and moral development.

Bibliography

Boo Baby Meets the Ghost of Mable's Gable (say-along), 1996.
"The Dead Mule," in *Ready-to-Tell Tales*, August House, 1994.
The Farm on Nippersink Creek, August House, 1994. Stories of rural life in Spring Grove, Illinois.
"Most Valuable Altar Boy," in *Who Says? Essays on Pivotal Issues in Storytelling*, August House, 1996, 214–215.

Audiography

"A Bell for Shorty," in *Best Loved Stories Told at the National Storytelling Festival, Vol. 2* (audiocassette), August House, 1992.

The Farm on Nippersink Creek (audiocassette), August House, 1994. Stories of rural life in Spring Grove, Illinois.

Horse Sense (audiocassette).

Purple Boogies and Other Ghost Tales (audiocassette), self-published, 1986.

"The Specialist," in *Tales of Fools and Wise Folk* (audiocassette), National Association for the Preservation and Perpetuation of Storytelling.

Awards

1997 Great Lakes Book Award for *The Farm on Nippersink Creek.*

1994 Public Library Association's Adult Lifelong Learning Best Book for New Readers for *The Farm on Nippersink Creek.*

1989 Chicago Emmy for a WTTW-TV performance of "A Bell for Shorty."

Source

"A Brief Look at This Year's Storytellers," *Herald & Tribune*, 4C–8C.

Hanson, Trudy Lewis, "United in Story and Song: The Power of Music in Storytelling," *Storytelling Magazine*, May 1997, 14–15.

Mills, Marja, "Many a Yarn to Be Spun at Festival," *Chicago Tribune*, July 24, 1989, 2.

_____, "Storytellers Bring Their Tales to Life," *Chicago Tribune*, July 31, 1989, 1.

Mooney, Bill, and David Holt. *The Storyteller's Guide*. Little Rock, Ark.: August House, 1996.

Sobol, Joseph, "Innervision and Innertext: Oral and Interpretive Modes of Storytelling Performance," in *Who Says? Essays on Pivotal Issues in Storytelling*, August House, 1996, 208–219.

Stotter, Ruth, and William Bernard McCarthy, "Tellers and Their Tales: Revivalist Storytelling," *About Story: Writing on Stories and Storytelling 1980–1994*. Stotter Press, 1994; second edition, 1996.

_____, "The Tellers and the Tales: Revivalist Storytelling," *Jack in Two Worlds*, University of North Carolina Press 1994, 164–165.

BARBARA MCBRIDE-SMITH

Address   Rt. 2, Box 132
          Stillwater, Oklahoma 74075
          phone 405-624-1155 or 405-743-6393
          fax 405-624-0830
          email BMcBrideS@aol.com

Focus: Bible stories; Greek mythology; children's stories; family anecdotes; ghost tales; tall tales.

Audience: educators and professional workers; clergy; general audiences.

Style: traditional narration with a Texas drawl; presents reformatted Greek myths and biblical stories with a feminist slant; teams with her husband, Dr. Dennis E. Smith, for workshops.

One of storytelling's most influential mentors, Barbara McBride-Smith, known for intuitive tellings of classic mythology, is generous in sharing her triumphs. She values coursework preceding her B.S.Ed. degree in elementary education and speech and communications at Abilene Christian University and an M.Ed. in library science and educational technology from Boston University and has pursued post-graduate coursework in literature, drama, and education. She credits her mother, Carrie McBride, with taking her to church every Sunday and her husband, Dr. Dennis Smith, a professor/theologian who taught her the humor and humanity in scripture and ancient mythology. Professional training and experience also account for her command of platform performance.

In reflections on an early interest in spoken lore, McBride-Smith recalls growing up a citizen of Waco and a true Texan in the 1950s, although she has also lived in New Jersey, Massachusetts, and Oklahoma. Her parents, grandparents, and aunts and uncles were all active tellers. Her father, George McBride, recreated for his young children the drama of the bread lines and hardships of the Great Depression. Because her two older sisters are deaf, she learned how to interpret with sign language. By age eight, she was writing, producing, and starring in original plays and enjoyed debate, drama, and oral interpretation in junior high and high school. In 1974 and 1976, summer archeological digs in Greece and Italy introduced her to the true bases of classical mythology. Four years later, she was surprised to learn that her students in New Jersey, where she was employed as school librarian, were unaware of their own Jewish lore. By helping them discover their heritage of stories, she discovered her own. She turned her experiences and gathered lore into myths and stories for elementary and middle school students, threading plot with wit, clever repartee, and a Southwestern twang.

After moving to Oklahoma, McBride-Smith joined psychiatrist Dale Maxwell and her husband, a professor of Greek and New Testament, in updating the Orpheus cycle. The trio restated a series of Greek myths, including stories of Perseus, Medusa, brothers Prometheus and Epimetheus, and Pandora, mythic bringer of evils into the world. In 1986, McBride-Smith attended the First Annual Texas Storytelling Festival, where she told her first updated myth. Delighted with performing for large audiences, she helped establish Oklahoma's state storytelling association, Territory Tellers, and chaired the group for two years. She also served the Tejas Storytelling Association and the National Storytelling Association as board member. She has been keynote speaker at International Reading Association, Storytelling in Education Conference, and Network of Biblical Storytellers, and has chaired the Sequoyah Children's Book Award Committee. Her travels have taken her to the St. Louis Storytelling Festival, Corn Island Festival, Illinois Storytelling Festival, Bay Area Festival, and the National Storytelling Festival in Jonesborough, Tennessee. A writer and editor as well as teller, she has published in *The Storyteller's Companion to the Bible*. Although she still serves as seminary instructor at Phillips Theological Seminary in Enid and Tulsa, Oklahoma, and library information specialist for the Stillwater public schools, her interest in narrative keeps her active at festivals and gatherings where scholarship and storytelling predominate.

Articles

"Greek Mythology: It's the Truth!," *Texas Teller*, Summer 1991, 1, 3.

"Oral Language to Printed Language — Bridging the Gap with Storytelling," *The Yarnspinner*, May 1991.

Bibliography

"Medusa," in *More Best-Loved Stories Told at the National Storytelling Festival*, August House, 1992.

"Pandora," in *Best Stories from the Texas Storytelling Festival*, August House, 1995.

The Storyteller's Companion to the Bible: New Testament Women (contributor), Abingdon Press, 1998.

"The Twelve Labors of Hercules," in *Ready-to-Tell Tales*, August House, 1994.

"The Wedding Feast at Cana" and "The Samaritan Woman," in *The Storyteller's Companion to the Bible, Vol. 10*, Abingdon Press, 1996.

Audiography

Amazing Bible Stories (audiocassette), Pandora Productions, 1995. Contains "Samson & Delilah," "The Birth of John the Baptist," "Mary & Gabriel," "Water Into Wine," "The Prodigal Son," and "Do I Know the Bible?"

Beauties & Beasties: Multicultural Stories for

Kids (audiocassette), Pandora Productions 1993.

Greek or Whut?: Down Home and Irreverent Myths for Adults and Teens(audiocassette), Pandora Productions, 1989. Recorded live in Atlanta, Georgia; contains "Pandora", "Orpheus," and "Medea."

Medusa and Other Good Ol' Greeks (audiocassette), Pandora Productions, 1990. Contains vernacular stories of Medusa, Demeter, and the Trojan War.

Toga Tales n' Tunes (audiocassette), Pandora Productions, 1991.

Source

"A Brief Look at This Year's Storytellers," Jonesborough, Tennessee *Herald & Tribune*, September 30, 1992, 4C–8C.

Goff, Kevan, "Let Us Tell You a Story," *Daily Oklahoman*, January 25, 1991.

Martin, Susan, "Myth Adventures," *Storytelling Magazine*, Fall 1993, 8–11.

Pike, Larry, "Profiles: Teller of Mythical Proportions," *Storytelling Magazine*, Winter 1991, 22–23.

Richardson, Peggy Hemlich, "The Texas Storytelling Festival, 1997," http://members.aol.com/storypage/news/97texas.htm.

Timeless Voices: Images of the National Storytelling Festival. Jonesborough, Tenn.: National Storytelling Press, 1997.

Wenzel, Lynn, "New Myths," *New Directions for Women*, January/February 1991.

DOC MCCONNELL

Address   403 Gray Street
            Rogersville, Tennessee 37857
   phone 423-272-8549

Focus: tall tales and yarns; stretchers about Tucker's Knob, his home town in Tennessee.
Audience: all ages.
Style: historically accurate medicine showmanship; rollicking humor, tasteful family fun.
Instruments/Props: straw hat and corncob pipe; bowler, string tie, and vest; banjo, guitar, and other musical instruments; medicines, herbs, roots, barks; medicine wagon; trained fleas.

A pictorial narrator, revivalist, liar, teller of tall tales, and medicine showman, Doc McConnell has created a colorful niche among storytellers. His travels with "Doc McConnell's Old Medicine Show" take him across the eastern United States, to Minnesota, and about the Midwest. Unlike those who consider storytelling literature or folk art, he values stories because they create mental images that are open to individual interpretation, whether literary, artistic, or personal. Aboard a gaily painted medicine wagon, he and his daughter, Hannah Gillenwater, combine antics with novelty performances, humor, magic tricks, trained fleas, and music for tasteful family fun. At the heart of the entourage is Doc himself, the irrepressible barker chanting the efficacy of his roots, barks, brews, and "yarbs."

A lifelong Tennessean currently residing in Rogersville, Doc was born in 1929 in a hand-hewn cabin in Hawkins County, which borders on western Virginia. In classic McConnell satire, he describes the area as pretty, with the moon coming over the rise in half-gallon fruit jars. His mother sang ballads and hymns while she worked; both his parents told stories about family. For reading material he had a copy of the Bible and occasional out-of-date copies of the *Knoxville Journal* he retrieved from the general store. One of his yarns claims that, in 1937, the temperature in Tucker's Knob fell to –165 degrees. When words froze in the air, he relieved the silence by gathering up handfuls, thawing them by the fire, and listening to what people had said. In one of his concocted episodes he declares that he lives in the middle of the world and can travel to any spot on earth from his home town, and adds that most local folk have already gone.

After growing up in a family that told tales, McConnell became a teller of his trove of yarns. He began passing on anecdotes that he heard in boyhood by the pot-bellied stoves at John Mauk's country store, at the depot, and on his own front porch. From local yarners, he learned to gamble, philosophize, farm, procreate, and worship, and first considered

a career in telling in 1973 at the National Storytelling Festival. For nearly four decades, he has introduced audiences to old-time lore, especially the antics of the medicine hawker. He developed his style and spiel among fellow hospital workers. He first performed his medicine show act at the second National Storytelling Festival in 1974. His signature line promises the purchaser ten dollars toward funeral expenses if the elixir fails to cure the ailment. In 1975, he helped establish the National Association for the Preservation and Perpetuation of Storytelling and, for many years, served as a director. He passed along the tradition to his daughter Hannah, who paid college tuition out of her earnings as an associate medicine show barker.

McConnell believes in the permanence of stories. He describes them as old as language and fresh as the morning newspaper. A vital art, stories record and express the experiences of all people and cover the gamut of joyful, painful, and challenging times. Like many tellers, he believes that America's oral tradition has fallen quiet, but that the tumult of contemporary life has forced individuals to seek stories as a more personal way to communicate. Stories, he concludes, offer people new ways to preserve and celebrate their humanity. With stories, people can laugh, weep, reminisce, dream, imagine, desire, and make decisions. Because storytelling is indigenous at all levels of civilization, it serves as a useful link between sophisticated and primitive peoples. At libraries, schools, stadiums, colleges, workshops, festivals, conferences, and conventions, he applies the benefits of homespun narrative to business, education, and friends by enhancing emotional well being and encouraging individual talents. He has entertained at the Johnny Appleseed Festival, Corn Island Festival, Alabama Tale Telling, and Florida Festival. His philosophy and practice of storytelling ethics have earned him interviews for newspapers and journals, appearances at the 1982 World's Fair, and on the *Prairie Home Companion, Hee Haw,* National Public Radio's *Folkways USA, PM Magazine, American Trails, Today Show,* and *CBS Morning News.*

Bibliography

"The Mule Egg" and "The Snake-Bit Hoe Handle," in *Homespun: Tales from America's Favorite Storytellers*, Crown, 1988.

"The Snake-Bit Hoe Handle," *Laughter in the Mountains*, http:mcweeb.martin.KIZ.ky.us/schs/faculty/hillsweb/laugh7.htm, May 21, 1997.

"The Storekeeper," in *Ready-to-Tell Tales*, August House, 1994.

Storytelling Treasures (contributor), National Storytelling Press, 1993.

"Tucker's Knob and the Weather," *Laughter in the Mountains*, http:mcweeb.martin. KIZ.ky.us/schs/faculty/hillsweb/laugh7.htm, May 21, 1997.

"The Walkin' Catfish," in *Best-Loved Stories Told at the National Storytelling Festival*, August House, 1991.

Audiography

"The Snake and the Frog," in *Homespun Tales* (audiocassette), National Association for the Preservation and Perpetuation of Storytelling, 1986.

Spinning More Magic (audiocassette), Sound True, 1987.

Storytelling Sampler (contributor) (audiocassette), National Association for the Preservation and Perpetuation of Storytelling, 1982.

"The Walkin' Catfish," in *Tales of Wit and Humor* (contributor) (audiocassette), National Association for the Preservation and Perpetuation of Storytelling, 1992.

Where's Tucker's Knob (audiocassette), Sound True, 1987.

Awards

1997 National Storytelling Association Lifetime Achievement Award.

1996 National Storytelling Association Circle of Excellence.

Source

Allen, Geneva, "Storyteller Brings Liars Club Home to Hills of Tennessee," *Daily Beacon*, July 2, 1985.

"The Barter Storytellers," *Storytelling Magazine*, July 1997, 5.

"A Brief Look at This Year's Storytellers," Jonesborough, Tennessee *Herald & Tribune*, September 30, 1992, 4C–8C.

Carey, Kim, "McConnell Receives NSA's Lifetime Achievement Award," *Tale Trader*, August 1997, 1, 4.

"Five Storytellers Receive Honors," *Storytelling Magazine*, May 1997, 41.

Hill, Jennifer, "Storytellers Recall Festival's First Years in Jonesborough," *Herald and Tribune*, September 30, 1992, 2C, 4C.

"The McConnells' 'Ole Medicine Show,'" Jonesborough, Tennessee *Herald & Tribune*, September 29, 1993.

Menagh, Melanie, "Once Upon a Time: Keeping Alive the Power of Imagination, " *Omni*, September 1992, 27.

Timeless Voices: Images of the National Story-telling Festival. Jonesborough, Tenn.: National Storytelling Press, 1997.

ALICE MCGILL

Address P. O. Box 1607
Columbia, Maryland 21044
phone 410-799-0627
fax 410-799-8058

Focus: African and African-American lore; West Indian folklore; one-woman show on Sojourner Truth; "Nothin' But Da Blues"; themes of courage, life experiences, self-love, hope, humanitarian pursuits, women's rights.
Audience: all ages.
Style: dynamic monologues in Dutch/African accent; storytelling featuring oral tradition with music, standard English, dialects.
Instruments/Props: podium, chair, authentic costumes, sage broom; two blues guitars, harmonica; two musicians for "Blues" performance.

Alice McGill, a veteran of over 3,000 performances, may be the only storyteller honored by the Post Office. For her recreations of the life and oratory of Sojourner Truth, McGill was recognized at the introduction of a commemorative stamp featuring the famed eighteenth-century American feminist and freedom fighter. Born around 1797, Sojourner Truth's courage, self-love, and love for humankind are the focus when McGill portrays the historic 83-year-old ex-slave. A native of Scotland Neck, North Carolina, McGill and her nine siblings were the children of share-croppers and grew up in the community of Mary's Chapel. The town is small enough for people to park cars in the middle of the street. She recalls the childhood privations of World War II, when her parents bought gas, butter, and shoes with ration coupons. The leftover books of stamps now reside along with her great-grandmother's purse and amethyst pin and a trove of village stories, all reminders of her past.

Following graduation from Brawley High

School in 1955 with awards in oratory and acting, she received a scholarship to cover most of the tuition at Elizabeth City State Teachers College; her mother made up the $125 difference by selling a beloved cow. McGill earned a B.S. in education and an M.Ed. from Towson State University. She taught in Scotland Neck and Baltimore, where she displayed storytelling talents for pupils in Thursday afternoon narrative sessions.

McGill treasures the stories about Br'er Rabbit, Sis Possum, the High Sheriff, the preacher, a headless mule, and the wedding day of the town's prettiest girl, all creations she heard in the front yard or around the wood stove when her father entertained the family. Sometimes his stories were so believable she and her younger siblings would search under the bed for Br'er Rabbit. At her father's knee, McGill learned the oral tradition and could paint picturesque stories with words and music. She has a repertoire of 200 stories that include tales of travel, historical characters, personal stories, as well as the many stories that were passed down in her family. During her research for new material, she traveled throughout the rural South and urban areas to reunite with the narratives behind country blues music. She successfully debuted her newest show, "Nothin' but Da Blues," at the Washington Storytellers Theater in 1995.

McGill launched a career in platform narrative in 1983 and began to travel internationally when her husband, Marion, retired from the auto industry. She chose wisely the mentors that shaped her style — her father, Sam Pope, Jackie Torrence, and Linda Goss. Later, she added Donald Davis, Rex Ellis, and Paul Keens-Douglas to her list of inspirational tellers. Performances have taken McGill to Europe, Africa, Canada, and the West Indies, and across the United States with her trademark stories and one-woman show — *Sojourner Truth Speaks, Life Stories, Nothin' But Da Blues,* and *Songs and Tales/African-American Folklore.* She offers two workshops, "Tell It Out of Your Mouth" and "What's in a Folk Tale?"

In 1994, McGill received an invitation to represent Arts America (USIA) by performing for three weeks in Swaziland, Southern Africa.

She appeared at the University of Swaziland and at theaters. Along the way she explored the countryside, looking for stories that she could weave from the "Go-Go" women (grandmothers) and English-speaking dairy farmers and taxi drivers.

McGill has been a featured teller at the National Storytelling Festival, Hudson River Festival, Tim-Tim Festival in Trinidad, and the Anacostia Museum. Her long list of performances also includes the National Museum of American History, Children's Literature Festival, Apollo Theater in Harlem, Smithsonian Institution, Indiana State University, Kumbaya Festival in Toronto, Washington Storytellers Theater, University of Massachusetts, University of Maryland, Atlantic Union College, and the Stone Soup Storytelling Festival. McGill appeared in the movies *Protocol* and *St. Elmo's Fire* and on television in "The Adventures of Superboy," "A Man Called Hawk," "Pudd'nhead Wilson," "Jacqueline Bouvier Kennedy," and "One Life to Live." She has been featured on WGBH radio in Boston and National Public Radio's *Weekend All Things Considered*.

Bibliography

Banaky, Houghton Mifflin, projected 1998.

Best Loved Stories (contributor), August House, 1996.

The Griot's Cookbook: Rare and Well-Done (co-authors Mary Carter Smith and Elmira M. Washington), C. H. Fairfax, 1985.

In the Hollow of Your Hand, Houghton Mifflin, projected 1998–1999.

Jump Up and Say (contributor), Simon & Schuster, 1995.

"The Lion and Elephant," in *More Best-Loved Stories Told at the National Storytelling Festival*, August House, 1992.

Talk That Talk (contributor), Simon & Schuster, 1989.

"The Two Sons," in *Best-Loved Stories Told at the National Storytelling Festival*, August House, 1991.

Videography

National Geographic Presents: Storytelling Live (contributor), National Geographic Society, 1994.

Sojourner Truth Speaks, self-published

Storytellers (four cassettes), Atlas Video, 1991. Contains stories by Alice McGill, Jon Spelman, and Olga Loya. Cassettes are labeled "Tall Tales, Yarns, and Whoppers," "Animal Stories," "Magic Tales," and "Scary Stories."

Audiography

Flying Africans (audiocassette), Earwig Music Co., 1988. Features "I Smell My Mama's Biscuits Burning," "Ole Man Bucket," and "Go to Sleepy" as well as the title story.

Green Pines (audiocassette), Seagull, 1978. Anecdotes, music, and folk poetry about McGill's father.

A National Treasure (contributor) (audiocassette), National Storytelling Press, 1996.

Filmstrip

Storytelling in North America (contributor), National Geographic Society, 1992. Features "Flying Africans" and "The Monkey Takes a Ride."

Awards

1997 Maryland State Arts Council Artist-in-Residence.

1997 W. K. Kellogg Grant as Expert-in-Residence.

1990–1997 Artist-in-Education Grant.

1995 U. S. Postal Service Award for Perpetuating American/African-American Culture and History.

1991 National Association for Equal Opportunity in Higher Education Citation for Excellence.

1989 American Library Association Notable Award for *Flying Africans*.

1989 Towson State University Notable Award for *Flying Africans*.

1985 First Day of Issue Award for portrayal of Sojourner Truth.

Source

Arnold, Everett, "Storyteller's Authenticity Grew from Life," *Battle Creek Gazette*, April 1997.

Frye, Barbara, "From African Fables to the Tale of Sojourner Truth," *The Laurel Leader*, March 2, 1989, B3.

Heyward, R., "Alice McGill Awarded Library Assn. Honor," *Jet*, February 27, 1989, 9.

Lefiles, Diane, "Schools Visited by 'Truth,'" Edgecombe County, North Carolina, *Daily Southerner*, November 10, 1993 1.

Richardson, Donna, "Storytelling Pied Piper," *Fairfax County Journal*, 1996.

Scriber, Clarice, "Alice McGill: Actress and Storyteller Stages One-Woman Shows," *The Evening Sun*, August 11, 1987, 3.

"Up from Slavery," *Washington Post*, February 22, 1986, G3.

Wyatt, Liz, "Truth Brought to Life," *Battle Creek Inquirer*, April 1997.

Zad, Martie, "'Storytellers' Captives Kids of All Ages," *Washington Post*, October 20–26, 1991.

BILL MOONEY

Address   Half Horse Productions
        P. O. Box 802
        East Brunswick, New Jersey 08816
    phone 732-257-7707
    fax 732-254-1828
    email BMooney303@aol.com

Focus: New Jersey hero stories; world Christmas stories; ghost and devil stories; beast fables; poetry recitations; participation stories; tall tales and classic American lore.

Audience: all ages.

Style: one-man shows; tandem performance with David Holt.

Instruments/Props: empty dog harness; bones.

Bill Mooney has mastered a panoply of creative arts, from scriptwriting and acting in soaps and Citibank commercials and on Broadway to stints with the Negro Ensemble, Plays in the Park, and Punch Line One-Act Play Festival. He is best known for one-man shows, recitations of Lenape tales, and platform narrative of such classic American tales as "The New Jersey Devil," "Old One Eye," and "The Tailypo." His credits include stage plays, *A Man for All Seasons, A Place for Polly, Lolita, We,* and *The Brownsville Raid*; movies, *Network, C. A. T. Squad, Second Sight, The Next Man, Beer,* and *A Flash of Green*; and television series, *Loving, The Guiding Light, One Life to Live,* and *All My Children,* the ABC-TV daytime series for which he twice won an Emmy in the role of Paul Martin. Often identified as a New Jersey native, Mooney was born in Missouri and grew up in Arkansas and Colorado, where he valued the whoppers and native lore that served as entertainment in the pre–TV era. He began telling stories in the late 1950s, long before the art resurged in American culture. In his résumé, he declares his admiration for the storytelling circuit's classic performers — Laura Simms, Kathryn Windham, Donald Davis, David Novak, Jim May, Barbara McBride-Smith, Connie Regan-Blake, Jay O'Callahan, Susan Klein, and his long-time colleague, David Holt, with whom he wrote *The Storyteller's Guide* and *Ready-to-Tell Tales.* Mooney's one-man show, *Half Horse, Half Alligator,* premiered in 1964 at the Palais Erzherzog Karl in Vienna, Austria, simultaneously with a performance by his wife, lyric soprano Valorie Goodall, at the Graz Opera House. Mooney's successful performance of frontier wit draws on the late nineteenth-century Mississippi riverboat lore of Mark Twain plus humor derived from Will Rogers, Chic Sale, and George Washington Harris, one of the South's

ribald tellers of tall tales. Mooney's show was recorded by RCA Victor, filmed by CBS-TV, and taken on an American tour. Another one-man show, *Damn Everything but the Circus*, was based on the writings of poet e. e. cummings.

In 1996, Mooney scripted *With a Dog's Eyes: Capturing the Life of Morris Frank*, the 65th anniversary celebration of the seeing eye dog. Composing from taped interviews with Frank and from on-the-scene research in Switzerland, Mooney participated in training sessions, complete with blindfold and guide dog. In a forty-minute monologue, Mooney depicts Frank as a spirited storyteller spinning yarns about traveling with Buddy to prove that the blind can manage without assistance. The program lauds the creation of North America's first guide dog school, headquartered in Morristown, New Jersey.

As a storyteller, Mooney has appeared at the Alabama Tale-Tellin' Festival, Stone Soup Festival, New Jersey Book Fair, and New Jersey Folk Festival, and at the 1995 National Storytelling Festival in Jonesborough, Tennessee, as well as aboard various Holland America Line ships as a featured storyteller. He and Holt wrote and performed *Banjo Reb and the Blue Ghost*, a touring Civil War play; alone, Mooney has performed *Sir Gawain and the Green Knight*, an English classic poem in the Arthurian tradition composed anonymously in the late fourteenth century. One of Mooney's most memorable endeavors was a 1995 research project among the Navaho in Gallup, New Mexico, from whom he learned the stories of Native American Marines who served in World War II as code talkers, baffling the enemy with such Navaho terms as chicken hawk and shark to indicate dive bomber and submarine. In the works is research on the smokejumpers, whom he intends to immortalize with a dramatization. In the introduction to *The Storyteller's Guide*, Mooney justifies the effort of learning and telling these stories: "They help us to understand why people act the way they do. If we know the story behind an action, we are better able to understand and forgive it."

Bibliography

ASAP — The Fastest Way to Create a Memorable Speech (co-author), Barrons, 1993.

Ready-to-Tell Tales (co-author David Holt), August House, 1995. Contains "The Wreck of the Sea Rover."

The Storyteller's Guide (co-author David Holt), August House, 1996.

Video

With a Dog's Eyes: Capturing the Life of Morris Frank, 1997.

Audiography

Half Horse, Half Alligator: The Roots of American Humor (audiocassette), August House, 1995. Contains "Jack Downing's First Visit to Portland," "The Tennessee Frolic," "The Eraser Soap Man," "The Dog Who Paid Cash," "Remarkable Bugs," "A Message to the Pope," "They Shall Gnaw a File," "The Pious Commodore," "A Sage Conversation," and "The Specialist."

Spiders in the Hairdo: Modern Urban Legends (co-producer David Holt) (audiocassette), High Windy Audio, 1997. Urban legends, including "The Hook," "The Choking Doberman," "The Vanishing Hitchhiker," "The Cement-Filled Cadillac," and the title story; for teens and adults.

Why the Dog Chases the Cat: Great Animal Stories (co-performer David Holt) (audiocassette), High Windy Audio, 1994. Contains "Why You Never Hear Rabbit Play Banjo," "Trouble or How the Alligator Got Its Hide," "Is It Deep Enough?," "Why the Cat Washes Its Paws Before It Eats," "The Whirlwind," and the title story.

Awards

1996 Grammy nominee for *Why the Dog Chases the Cat: Great Animal Stories*.

1995 Parents' Choice Gold Award for *Why the Dog Chases the Cat: Great Animal Stories*.

1995 American Library Association Notable Recording for *Why the Dog Chases the Cat: Great Animal Stories*.

1995 NAIRD Indie Award for *Why the Dog Chases the Cat: Great Animal Stories*.

1995 *Publishers Weekly*'s Listen-Up award for best adult storytelling recording for *Half Horse Half Alligator: The Roots of American Humor*.

Source

Colo, Emily, "Actor Finds His Calling in Telling Scary Stories," *The* (Flemington, New Jersey) *Democrat,* January 28, 1993.

"Echoes of a Storyteller Opening Reception," *The* (Middlesex County, New Jersey) *Signal Fire,* December 1992.

"Everybody Loves a Good Tale," *The Home News & Tribune,* October 18, 1995.

Filichia, Peter, "One-Man Show Tells Story of Morris Frank, Who Brought Seeing Eye Dogs to U.S.," *Star-Ledger,* November 23, 1994.

Hart, Steven, "Actor Tells a Good Story," *News Tribune,* October 22, 1992.

Jaffe, Jonathan, "'Once Upon a Time ...' Vet-

eran Actor Finds Calling as Storyteller,"
Star-Ledger, March 14, 1993.

Kendall, Leslie, "Dream Weavers," *New York Times*, November 10, 1996, Section 13, pp. 1, 10.

Kopka, Matt, and John Zinsser, "Listen Up Awards: The Year's Best Audiobooks," *Publishers Weekly*, February 1, 1996, 37.

Nutt, Bill, "Storyteller Accents State's Richness of Life," *Star-Ledger*, March 21, 1996, CE-6.

Sinkhorn, J. Eric, "Half Horse, Half Alligator," *Tale Trader*, August 1997, 16.

"Storytellers Receive Grammy Nominations," *Storytelling Magazine*, May 1996, 7.

Turner, Patricia C., "Medieval Magic: Actor Takes 600-Year-Old Tale on the Road," *Star-Ledger*, April 18, 1993.

Who's Who in America. Marquis, 1996.

ROBIN MOORE

Address Groundhog Press
Box 181
Springhouse, Pennsylvania 19477
phone 215-646-2150

Focus: traditional Pennsylvania stories; Celtic lore; the supernatural; environmental awareness and living history; participation stories; feminist themes.

Audience: primarily children.

Style: traditional narrative; dramatic characterization.

Instruments/Props: Celtic harp, flute, hunting horn, and other traditional musical instruments; suede vest, fur cape.

A professional platform performer since 1981, Robin Moore has carried his extensive repertoire to over 3,000 audiences with one goal in mind — to restore imagination, the landscape on which dreams take shape. A regular at schools, museums, conferences, and radio and television, he specializes in reviving fantasy and creativity in listeners; in a similar vein, he offers a workshop, *Awakening the Hidden Storyteller: How to Build a Storytelling*

Tradition in Your Family. Native to Boalsburg, the birthplace of the Memorial Day celebration, in central Pennsylvania, Moore expands on two centuries of Scotch-Irish ancestry, which dates to frontier farmers from northern Scotland who settled the area in the late eighteenth century. He began acquiring material in childhood when he heard the tales of relatives. With no thought to a fee, his father, an amateur teller, performed at Boy Scout outings to please children.

A soft-spoken, contemplative man, Moore has the ability to exist in an inner milieu and to shape images that he describes for his listeners. In his late teens he was a soldier serving in reconnaissance and with a line unit in the Vietnam War. He declares himself lucky that he had to find people, but not kill them. The wrenching experience forced him to do some emotional fence mending. To relive the past, he moved into a cabin in the Pennsylvania woods and lived for two and a half years while honing his woodcraft and researching stories for books and performance. Countering the macho atmosphere of a foreign war, he revisited seven generations of Pennsylvania farm women, including his grandmothers, and developed biographical tales of strong women in America's past. After his return from the woods, he earned a journalism degree from Penn State and reported and edited for the press.

This varied background prefaced Moore's career as a full-time writer, raconteur, and publisher with Groundhog Press, his own company. As a storyteller, he varies the texture and length of stories for maximum listener involvement and treasures what he calls "planet time," when the audience departs from the temporal to experience the esthetic. The experience binds listener with teller, a synergy that depends on intimacy and concentration to release his focus, the essence of the story itself. He applied his synergistic method at Storytelling '97 at Mansfield University, where he shared a stage with veteran tellers Jay O'Callahan, Diane Ferlatte, and Susan Klein. Moore's children's books tap a rich lode of Pennsylvaniana, particularly the captivity lore that grew from the diary of Mary Jemison, a prisoner of the Seneca who married twice

within the tribe and chose to remain with her Indian family rather than return to white society. His most recent books include a non-fiction account of Jemison's adventures as well as a science-fiction novel and a retelling of the Greek myths of Hercules.

Bibliography

Area 51, Kingfisher-Larousse, 1997. Science-fiction for young readers

Awakening the Hidden Storyteller: How to Build a Storytelling Tradition in Your Family, Random House, 1991. A workbook for storytellers.

The Bread Sister of Sinking Creek, Harper-Collins, 1984. A survival story set during the Revolutionary War.

The Cherry Tree Buck: Adventures in the Woods with My Grandfather, Random House, 1995. Tall tales set in frontier Pennsylvania, including "The Diamondback Rattler."

Encounter on the Moon, Kingfisher-Larousse, 1996. An inventive story about a secret flight to the moon.

Hercules, Simon & Schuster, 1997. The traditional Greek hero cycle for ages 8–12.

"How the Turtle Cracked His Shell," in *Ready-to-Tell Tales*, August House, 1994.

The Hunchback of Notre Dame, Simon & Schuster, 1996. An adaptation of Victor Hugo's classic novel written for ages 8–14.

Maggie Among the Seneca, HarperCollins, 1987. A captivity story set during the 1770s in a Seneca Indian village.

My Life with the Indians, Franklin Watts, 1998. A nonfiction adaptation of Mary Jemison's diaries in which she describes her residence with the Seneca.

"Sweetnosia," *Storytelling World*, Winter/Spring 1992, 21–22.

Up the Frozen River, HarperCollins, 1993. A survival story that takes the heroine into danger while she searches for a small boy.

When the Moon Is Full: Supernatural Stories from the Old Pennsylvania Mountains, Alfred A. Knopf, 1994. Traditional and scary stories for age 8 and up.

Audiography

All About Me (computer program), HarperCollins, 1994. An interactive construction of family trees and collection of family stories.

Awakening the Hidden Storyteller: How to Build a Storytelling Tradition in Your Family (audiocassette), Shambhala, 1991. Voyages into the imagination to reclaim storytelling skills; accompanied by Celtic harp and acoustic guitar.

Fins, Furs and Feathers: Animal Tales from the Pennsylvania Mountains (audiocassette), Groundhog Press, 1990. Traditional animal lore, including "The Silver Lake Trout," "How Rabbit Stole Fire," "The Eagle and the Chickens," "Groundhog and the Bears," "The Cherry Tree Buck," "Turtle and the Wolves"; for ages eight and below.

What's Wild Is Wild: A Journey into the Wilderness of the Imagination (audiocassette), Groundhog Press, 1990. "Call of the wild" stories, including "The Bear Man," "What's Wild Is Wild," "Hairy-Woman," "Hodadenon," "Caribou Man," "A Dream of Birds"; for ages eight and up.

When the Moon Is Full (audiocassette), Groundhog Press, 1990. Chilling tales accompanied by fiddle and wolf howls; includes "Stuffed Panther," "Skullplayer," "Uncle Bill's Dream," "Spearfinger," "Dark Catrina"; for ages eight and up.

Awards

1996 *Storytelling World* Tellable Tale Award for "The Diamondback Rattler" in *The Cherry Tree Buck and Other Stories*.

1995 Pennsylvania School Librarians Association Author of the Year.

1995 Storytelling World Silver Award for Best Storytelling Anthology for *When the Moon Is Full — Supernatural Stories from the Old Pennsylvania Mountains*.

1991 Parents' Choice Award for *Awakening the Hidden Storyteller: How to Build a Storytelling Tradition in Your Family*.

Source

Gagliardi, Melissa, "Tell Us a Story," *Sunbury Daily Item*, April 4, 1997, C1–C3.

Hararldson, Lynn, "Storyteller Weaves Folklore Tales for Local Students," *Clarion News*, March 13, 1997.

Mooney, Bill, and David Holt. *The Storyteller's Guide*. Little Rock, Ark.: August House, 1996.

JOHNNY MOSES

Address 1582 Reservation Road
LaConner, Washington 98257
phone 206-691-6131
also 206-325-4280

Focus: Sisiwis spiritual and healing medicine from songs, dance, wisdom, stories, ritual; morality tales; nature lore; contemporary stories; epics; participation stories.

Audience: all ages.

Style: ethereal shamanism; sign language; audience involvement through sign language and repeated refrains and songs.

Instruments/Props: authentic costume, braids.

Telling in the Native American tradition of the northwest coast, lecturer, dancer, and raconteur Johnny Moses elucidates Nootka/ Spokane lore with traditional myths and illustrative stories. Both dreamscapes and symbol lace his morality tales, for example, the story of the Saanich boy who suffered from cancer and who dreamed of monsters eating the cancer until it disappeared, both in his dream and in reality. Bearing the traditional name of Whis.tem.men.knee or Walking Medicine Robe, Moses, a native of Ohiat, Vancouver Island, British Columbia, was reared by his grandparents, who taught him native traditions and demanded excellence from him. While fighting cancer of the lungs and stomach, he saw a vision and heard a voice compelling him to encourage others or die. The incident served as a portal to his career. He prepared for a demanding future as tribal ambassador by internalizing wisdom lore, studying tales of ants, bears, and coyotes, and learning eight native languages. A chosen tribesman, Moses earned a B.E. from the University of Victoria at age 18 and became an ordained minister in the Indian Shaker Church. As leader of Sisiwis or sacred breath medicine, he works under the supervision of tribal elders as master storyteller, oral historian, traditional healer, and respected spiritual leader.

In the Puget Sound and Seattle area and across the United States and Canada, Moses has role-played the four seasons and Grandmother Tree and has acted out such character duos as Crow and Octopus Lady and Bear and Ant. He uses storytelling in print and sign language, on the Internet, and in workshops, classes, and lectures to apply his learning to individual needs. He also organized the Red Cedar Dancers, traditional performers at northwestern cultural events. Well respected for his seemingly effortless narration, he appears at libraries, schools, and colleges and introduces groups to Sisiwis spirituality with *Medicine Teachings of the Earth*, an introduction to the power of the Creator. He was a featured teller of multicultural tales at the Bankoh Talk Story Festival in Honolulu; in July 1997 he shared top billing with master tellers Donald Davis, Olga Loya, and Peter Cook at the Fourteenth Illinois Storytelling Festival. He has appeared at Tell It in the Mountains in Asheville, North Carolina, and the National Storytelling Festival in Jonesborough, Tennessee.

Bibliography

"A Dream Time Story," *Storytelling Magazine*, September 1996, 12–13.

Ghostwise, A Book of Midnight Stories (contributor), August House, 1997. Ghost stories and strange and scary lore by 41 authors from Africa, Japan, and Canada.

Videography

Baskets of the Northwest. Styles and techniques of northwest coast basketry; demonstration and commentary by Klickatat crafter Nettie Jackson.

"The Boy Who Wished for a Bicycle," in *Tell Me a Story, Vol. 1*, Hometown Entertainment, 1995.

Johnny Moses, Storyteller, American Indian Voices, 1992. Contains "The Bear and the Ant," "Potlatch Song," "Octopus and Crow Story," "The Boogie Woman Story," "The Missionary Story," "Su-yah-pi: Upside Down Face Story," "Grandma Cedar Tree Story," "The Boy and the Bicycle Story," "The Um and Ugh Story," and "The People Story."

"The Missionary," in *Tell Me a Story, Vol. 3*, Hometown Entertainment, 1995.

Storytelling by Johnny Moses. Favorite stories, including "Crow and Octopus Lady," "The Bear and the Ant," "Grandmother Tree," and others, recorded live.

Traditional Stories of the Northwest Coast, self-published, 1992.

Audiography

American Indian Voices Presents Johnny Moses (audiocassette). Varied stories from the Puget Sound area and Vancouver Island for all ages.

Fall Medicine Songs (audiocassette). Songs of change and transformation that prepare for death, including "Fall Welcome Song" and other melodies of the Frasier River people.

Fire Circle Songs (audiocassette). Varied social and spiritual songs of Puget Sound, Snohomish, Clallam, Nootka, and Vancouver.

Octopus Lady and Crow & Other Animal People Stories of the Northwest Coast (audiocassette), Parabola Storytime Series, 1994.

Spring Medicine Songs (audiocassette). Sixteen seasonal melodies, including "Spring Welcome Song," "Song of Love," "Grandmother Wind," "Waterfall Song," "Traveling Canoe Spring Song."

Summer Medicine Songs (audiocassette). Twenty-six harvest songs, including "Deer Song," "Cedar Root Song," "Fire Song," "Summer Giveaway Song," and "Eating Song."

Winter Medicine Songs (audiocassette). Intensely spiritual teaching songs, including "Northwind Song," "Winter Moon Song," "Thunder Spirit Song," "Spirit Traveling Song," and twenty others along with drumming and instructions for spirit traveling.

Internet

"Johnny Moses," http://www.hometownet. com/moses.html, May 23, 1997. Features "The Boy Who Wished for a Bicycle."

Source

"A Brief Look at This Year's Storytellers," Jonesborough, Tennessee *Herald & Tribune*, September 30, 1992, 4C–8C.

"Jackie Torrence Presents ... Stories from Around the World from Curriculum Associates," http://www.curriculumassociates. com//publications/jtorrence.html.

"Johnny Moses," http://www.oro.net/~bobg/rccjm.html, May 23, 1997.

Mack, Dr. Dorothy Blackcrow, "Teachings from the Sisiwis Tradition," *Storytelling Magazine,* September 1996, 13–15.

McLeod, Michael, Angela Peterson, and Tom Raymond, "Once Upon a Time," *Florida Magazine,* November 24, 1996.

Ruiz, Ben, "Johnny Moses," *Tale Trader,* May 1997, 13.

BOBBY NORFOLK

Address   Folktale Productions
P. O. Box 9182
St. Louis, Missouri 63117
phone 314-968-2606
fax 314-968-4438
email JDolan9928@aol.com

Focus: character education traits including responsibility, respect, honesty, cooperation, self-esteem, humanity; cultural diversity

themes; poetry and prose; folktales from around the world; ghost stories; monsters, dragons, and ogres; Harlem Renaissance; straight talk; Scott Joplin; drums of Africa; nature stories; fairy tales and legends; audience participation; imagination workshops; historical vignettes; family stories.

Audience: children to adults.

Style: high-energy performances, lively animation, period dialect, tandem performances with musicians and naturalists, dancing and strutting, vocal sound effects, surprise and jump stories.

Instruments/Props: African drums, kalimba, period costume.

Applauded in Ireland, Egypt, Ghana, Japan, Vancouver, and throughout the United States, Bobby Norfolk offers concerts, workshops, special theatre presentations and residencies for audiences of all ages. He is an actor, mime, television personality, and story performer. He is known for his oral interpretations of such famous literary giants as Paul Laurence Dunbar, Langston Hughes, Booker T. Washington, James Weldon Johnson, Dudley Randall, W. E. B. Du Bois, and Richard Wright. Norfolk began his career 28 years ago as a stand-up comedian opening local St. Louis shows for Roberta Flack, B. B. King, Peabo Bryson, and Lou Rawls. He received rave reviews as an actor for appearances with the St. Louis Imaginary Children's Theatre Company and the Black Repertory Theatre and for acting roles in *Zooman and the Sign* and *The Brownsville Raid.* Television credits include three Emmy awards for *Gator Tales,* a CBS Saturday morning children's show, and the Emmy-nominated cable show *Children's Theatre at Bobby's House.* He also served as a national role model for a storytelling chapter in the McGraw-Hill textbook, *Writer's Choice,* and was commissioned for a storytelling project with Telecom Japan International.

In grade school, Norfolk stuttered and hid away in books and imaginary worlds. He used theater, poetry, and storytelling to overcome both his shyness and stuttering in high school and college. He learned to relax with meditation and stretched his imagination with radio shows such as *Gangbusters, The Lone Ranger,* and *The Shadow*. An admirer of veteran storytellers Jay O'Callahan, Jackie Torrence, Donald Davis, and the late Gamble Rogers, Norfolk officially began his career in coffeehouses during his years at the University of Missouri, where he majored in history. From 1976 to 1986, he broadened his range during a decade of work for the National Park Service as a park ranger. His move toward professional telling began in 1976, when he began entertaining his son with animated bedtime tales. He appeared as a teller at the St. Louis Storytelling Festival at his worksite at the Gateway Arch. He and fellow ranger Jan Dolan initiated Folktale Productions in 1987. One of Norfolk's earliest stories, "Anansi the Spider and His Six Sons," was well received in festival performance and is a signature piece.

While working as a stand-up comedian, Norfolk discovered his talent had a strong impact on children and began educating them through entertainment. His story performances promote strong moral messages and teach children positive values. Themes include self-esteem, conflict resolution, race awareness, and a "Straight Talk" program that warns of peer pressures and the temptations of alcohol and drugs. Currently, he performs internationally at festivals, schools, museums, libraries, and corporations. Venues include the Smithsonian Institution, Wolf Trap Barn Theatre, Grand Canyon National Park, Anchorage School District, Denver Center Theatre Company, and the National Storytelling Festival in Jonesborough, Tennessee.

Bibliography

"Anansi the Spider and His Six Sons," in *We Like Kids*, Good Year Books, 1995.
"Jack and the Magic Beans," in *Reading to Tell Tales*, August House, 1994.
"Norfolk Tells Tales," *Writer's Choice: Composition and Grammar*, Glencoe, 1993.
"Scott Joplin: Master of Ragtime," in *Many Voices, True Tales from America's Past*, National Storytelling Press, 1995.

Audiography

Norfolk Tales (audiocassette), Earwig Music, 1988. Contains "Wiley and the Hairyman," "How the Spider Got a Bald Head," "Jack and the Three Sillies," "Tilly and the Eight Steps," and "Anansi the Spider and His Six Sons."
Storyteller in a Groove (CD), Earwig Music, 1992. Contains "Morning Train," "The Creation," "True Blues," "Booker T. and W. E. B.," "Feet Live Their Own Life," "Callaloo and the Crab," "A Negro Love Song," "No Images," "Landladies," "Murf on My Turf," and "Teen Rap Crisis."
Why Mosquitoes Buzz in People's Ears (audiocassette), Earwig Music, 1987. Contains the title story plus "Wicked John and the Devil," "The Bremen-Town Musicians," "Kwaku Anansi and the Whipping Cord," and "Jack and the Magic Beans."

Awards

1990 Emmy for *Gator Tales*.
1989 Parents' Choice Gold Awards for *Norfolk Tales*.
1989 Emmy for *Gator Tales*.
1988 Parents' Choice Gold Awards for *Why Mosquitoes Buzz in People's Ears*.
1988 Emmy for *Gator Tales*.
1981–1979 National Park Service Achievement Awards.

Source

"A Brief Look at This Year's Storytellers," Jonesborough, Tennessee *Herald & Tribune*, September 30, 1992, 4C–8C.
Dighton, Daniel, "Storyteller Spins Tales That Teach," *The Pantagraph*, October 11, 1990, A5.
Farber, Henry, "There's a Story Behind Annual Habitat Fund-Raiser," *Atlanta Journal/Constitution*, December 5, 1996, JN-12.
"Gator Aid," *St. Louis Sun TV Week*, October 21–27, 1989.
Mooney, Bill, and David Holt. *The Storyteller's Guide*. Little Rock, Ark.: August House, 1996.

SHERRY NORFOLK

Address 515-A Nelson Ferry Road
Decatur, Georgia 30030
phone 404-371-8206
email shnorfolk@aol.com

Focus: world folklore; ghost tales; legends and romantic stories; universal values themes; participation stories.

Audience: all ages.

Style: traditional plus rap music, rhythm and rhyme activities, songs, and sound effects.

A storyteller since 1982, Sherry Cotter Des Enfants Norfolk has always loved literature and books. She earned a B.A. in elementary education, an M.A. in library science from Indiana University and certification in public management from the University of Georgia. While working as a librarian at the Miami-Dade Public Library she told stories as a means of bringing children and books together and of drawing children to the library. Her reputation spread as she coordinated children's outreach services for the library, making appearances at 540 public schools in the Miami area. She moved to Decatur, Georgia, in 1988 to become the youth services coordinator of the DeKalb County Public Library, and left that position in 1996 to pursue her dream of telling full-time. Supporting her in that dream was her husband, teller Bobby Norfolk, whom she married in 1994.

Traveling to Freeport, Bahamas; Anchorage, Alaska; and Derry, Ireland; and across the United States in personal appearances and radio and television broadcasts, Norfolk currently tells stories from around the world as a means of teaching universal values, and conducts in-service workshops teaching her philosophy of storytelling in the classroom. Her full schedule includes a post as storyteller-in-residence at Callaway Gardens, Georgia, and a place on the rosters of the Georgia Council for the Arts, Alabama Arts-in-Education, Special Audiences of Atlanta, and Kentucky Arts Council. She has co-produced and co-starred on *Cric-Crac* and *Tell Me a Story* for Miami television and served residencies at schools, libraries, and museums through the southeast and Alaska. As an adjunct professor in storytelling and children's literature at Mercer University, she achieves her aim of being a story educator. Festival performances have showcased her at the National Storytelling Festival Exchange Place, Habitat for Humanity "Building Homes Story By Story," Big South

Fork Recreation Area, St. Louis Storytelling Festival, Callenwolde Tales for a Wednesday Evening, Stone Soup Storytelling Festival, Goosebumps!, Bayside Storytelling Festival, Virginia Commonwealth University, Tellabration 94!, Blueberry Jubilee Storytelling Festival, Tallahassee Tale-Tellin' Time, Broward Children's Literature Conference, and Cherokee Rose Storytelling Festival.

Articles

"Grantsmanship," *Youth Services Librarians as Managers: A How-to Guide from Budgeting to Personnel.* Chicago: American Library Association, 1994.

"Project Horizons: A Closer Look," *Journal of Youth Services in Libraries*, Spring 1995.

"Project Horizons: Library Services for Homeless Children," *Journal of Youth Services in Libraries*, Spring 1994.

"Reach Out and Let Them In: Programs in Libraries for Children and Youth with Special Needs," *Interface*, Fall 1995.

Bibliography

"Rabbit's Tail," in *Why the Possum's Tail Is Bare*. New York: Avon, 1993.

Audiography
Haunted Hearts: Tales of Love and Tragedy (audiocassette), self-produced, 1994. Contains "Song of the Shepherdess," "Woman of the Wood," "Tezin," "Revenge," "Very Pretty Lady," and "The Tiger's Whisker."
Tenth Annual Stone Soup Storytelling Festival: Cream of the Soup (contributor) (audiocassette), Stone Soup. 1995.

Awards
1994 Urban Libraries Council Award for Excellence for "Project Horizons" for homeless children.

1994 American Library Association Margaret Alexander Edwards Trust Award for Outstanding Service to Young Adults for "Building Blocks to Literacy" for family literacy initiative.

1994 American Library Association H. W. Wilson Staff Development Award for "Focus on Youth" training program.

1993 National Association of Counties Award for "Building Blocks."

1992 American Library Association ALSC Econo-Clad Children's Literature Program Award for "Project Horizons."

1991 National Association of Counties Award for "Project Horizons."

1987 Florida Library Association Children's Services Award for Children's Outreach Services.

1987 National Association of Counties Award for children's video programming.

Source
Farber, Henry, "There's a Story Behind Annual Habitat Fund-Raiser," *Atlanta Journal/Constitution*, December 5, 1996, JN-12.
"Fourth Annual Haunting in the Hills Storytelling Festival This Saturday," Oneida, Indiana *Independent Herald*, September 12, 1996, 4.
Josephson, Lori, "Storytelling Takes on Many Faces," *South Dade News Leader*, March 27, 1987.
"Local Storytellers Plan to Tell Stories at Festival," *Decatur-DeKalb News/Era*, October 12, 1994, 16A.
"Metro-Dade Public Library Presents New Children's Series," *Signal*, November 1985, 1.

Mooney, Bill, and David Holt. *The Storyteller's Guide*. Little Rock, Ark.: August House, 1996.
"Sherry Cotter Des Enfants," *Woodruff (South Carolina) News*, March 23, 1995.

DAVID NOVAK

Address A Telling Experience
P. O. Box 620327
San Diego, California 92162

1334 Grove Street
San Diego, California 92102
phone 619-232-1019
email NovaTeller@aol.com

Focus: eclectic mix of history, traditional stories, trickster lore, original and personal narrative; participation and rhyming stories.
Audience: all ages.
Style: versatile and animated; dramatic characterization, expressive movement, rich language and voice; intuitive interpretation of traditional and contemporary culture.
Instruments/Props: occasionally employs ordinary objects, such as string, newspaper, cloth, or balloons; simple instruments such as kalimbas or flutes.

A master of literary collage, David Novak has referred to his style of storytelling as "aerobics for the mind" in an age oversaturated with images from electronic media. He comes to platform narration with a background in theater arts, including Shakespeare, mime, clowning, creative dramatics, playwriting, design, and directing. A native of Ft. Lauderdale, Florida, in childhood he eavesdropped on adult conversations while playing the make-believe character Mr. Smith among grownups. He first performed on-stage with the Ft. Lauderdale Children's Theatre (F.L.C.T.) at age seven in *Aladdin's Wonderful Lamp* and continued to study and practice the theatrical art throughout his childhood. While still in high school, he wrote a number of children's plays, which were produced by Broward Com-

munity College and the F.L.C.T., earning him numerous community service awards. At the same time, he organized a pantomime troupe as a part of a self-study program. His company, *The Pantomime Players*, toured throughout Florida for three years, providing performances and education for students from kindergarten through high school.

Novak received a B.F.A. in directing for theater at Southern Methodist University and an M.F.A. in the professional actor training program at the University of California at San Diego. Between the two theater degrees, he worked for acting companies in Milwaukee, Providence, and St. Louis. While artist-in-residence with the Theatre Project Company in St. Louis, he discovered storytelling. In 1978, his future wife, Courtney, suggested that he try solo storytelling and tour area schools to provide programs to serve teacher requests. Shortly after he began his storytelling work, the St. Louis Storytelling Festival was founded. While participating in this festival as a local artist, he was influenced by storytellers Ken Feit, Gamble Rogers, Ed Stivender, Heather Forest, and Jay O'Callahan. At the second St. Louis Storytelling Festival, he ad-libbed his own version of the Japanese folktale "The Stonecutter" for an audience of 300. Novak

recalls, "At the very moment I was telling this simple story of a man who sought to be something other than himself and kept changing and changing until he came back to where he started, I realized I was telling the story of my journey as an artist. Suddenly, I was coming back to myself, understanding for the first time that I was a storyteller and was happy as such."

Novak did not immediately jettison his acting career. After a series of jobs in regional theaters and co-founding the San Diego Actor's Alliance, he abandoned the perpetual search for stage work and welcomed the autonomy of storytelling. He explained in his résumé, "It was a combination of things: the limitations of the acting profession, the desire to create for myself, and the birth of my son all conspired to make me choose storytelling as my full-time pursuit." Experienced with such roles as Hamlet, Troilus, and Scapino, Novak draws on drama as well as myth and folklore for original material. He begins each story with the bare bones of a plot, then fleshes out details from his own milieu. His eclectic method relies on artistry of actor and mime for emotional, kinetic telling and on the poet for a stock of puns, paradox, irony, and alliteration. One story, "Salt Loves Meat," combines the drama of *King Lear* with the folktale "Cap o' Rushes," which predates the Renaissance and may have influenced Shakespeare's tragedy. Another favorite, "Smoke from the Everglades," recounts the home life of a Florida boy named Carl whose family disintegrates and whose father remarries.

Novak is perhaps best known for his epic rendition of the Itsy Bitsy Spider nursery rhyme. Novak describes the spider as "Homer meets Mother Goose," the story of a lone spider facing the great storm takes on deep power and delightful humor as the heroic struggle unfolds. Novak also draws on myths like "Theseus and the Minotaur" and such fairy tales as "Little Red Riding Hood" or "Jack and the Beanstalk," giving each a unique treatment. He creates new stories with the help of old ones, taking the motifs of thumbling stories such as Tom Thumb to create "Little Yellow Jello Fellow," and the Gingerbread Man to create "The Cookie Girl." No less interested in legitimate theater than in his youth, he counts Luigi Pirandello, Bertolt Brecht, and Samuel Beckett among his influences.

A veteran teller at the National Storytelling Festival, Novak has served as consultant for the Disney Company and as master storyteller for the Disney Institute. He has performed at numerous festivals, including the Tejas Festival, Alaska Shorebird Festival, Hawaiian Talking Island Festival, San Juan Capistrano Festival, Northern Appalachian Festival, and Mariposa and Sierra storytelling festivals. He has been a keynote speaker for the Mid-Atlantic Storyteller's Conference, the Greater California Reading Association, and numerous library and educational conferences. Grants from the California Arts Council have supported his company, A Telling Experience, in the form of residencies and touring subsidies since 1990. His esthetic education programs have found audiences across the country — at the Lincoln Center Institute, Los Angeles Music Center on Tour, Aesthetic Education institutes in Rochester and Utica, New York, Delaware Institute for Arts Education, and San Diego Institute for Young Audiences. He has been guest instructor for the University of San Diego International Storytelling Institute, Oklahoma Arts Institute, Walt Disney Imagineering, and McDonald's Hamburger University. He lives in San Diego with his wife and their son Jack.

Articles

"Is the World Telling You Stories?," *Faces Magazine*, Cobblestone, 1991.
"Recipe for Storytelling," *Faces Magazine*, Cobblestone, 1991.
"The Scattered Brain," *Storytelling World*, Winter/Spring, 1998.
"Stories on a Shoestring," *Storytelling World*, Winter/Spring 1994, 11–12.
"String Figure Jack and the Beanstalk," *Storytelling World*, Winter/Spring 1993.
"Word Choices: The Icing on the Cake," *Storytelling World*, 1995.

Bibliography

"Jack and the Beanstalk," *Storytelling World*, Winter/Spring 1993, 9–10.
"Jack and the Beanstalk" http://www.home-

townet.com/volume 1/ novaks1.html, September 26, 1996.
Johnny Appleseed and the Bears, Riverbank Books, 1995.
A Letter from Dad/Mom, Medlicott, 1993.
The Little Ant, Riverbank Books, 1994. An adaptation of a Mexican folktale.
"The Three Dolls" in *Ready-to-Tell Tales*, August House, 1994.

Videography

"Interview," *The Twentieth Anniversary of the National Storytelling Festival*, Hometown Entertainment, 1994.
"The Itsy Bitsy Spider," in *Tell Me a Story, Vol. 1*, Hometown Entertainment, 1995.
"Jack and the Beanstalk," in *Tell Me a Story, Vol. 1*, Hometown Entertainment, 1995.
The Storyteller's Fire, A Telling Experience, 1990.

Audiography

The Cookie Girl & Other Stories (audiocassette), August House, 1995. Original stories and remakes of classics.
The Heroic Climb of the Itsy Bitsy Spider & Other Stories (audiocassette), A Telling Experience, 1991.
Itsy Bitsy Spider's Heroic Climb (audiocassette), August House, 1993. Stories for young children and their parents; recorded live.
Little Yellow Jello Fellow (audiocassette), A Telling Experience, 1993.
More Rhyme Than Reason (audiocassette), A Telling Experience, 1997.
The Pickle Jar (audiocassette), A Telling Experience, 1990.
Sleeping Kingdoms (audiocassette), A Telling Experience, 1990.
Sterling (audiocassette), A Telling Experience, 1997. Recorded live at the 1996 National Storytelling Festival.

Source

"A Brief Look at This Year's Storytellers," Jonesborough, Tennessee *Herald & Tribune*, September 30, 1992, 4C–8C.
Dixon, Kathy, "Storytelling World Presents David Novak," *Storytelling World*, Winter/Spring 1993, 6–8.
"Jonesborough's National Storytelling Festi-

val Attracts Thousands to Annual Three-Day Event," *The Loafer*, October 1, 1996, 19, 21.

Kaufman, Laura, "Storyteller Spins Web That Captures Lessons of Life," *Los Angeles Times*, January 6, 1990, F1, F18.

Keding, Dan, "The Endless Tale," *Sing Out!*, Aug./Sept./Oct. 1996.

Kenyon, Karen, "Inspired by the Bard," *Storytelling Magazine*, Summer 1993.

McLeod, Michael, Angela Peterson, and Tom Raymond, "Once Upon a Time," *Florida Magazine*, November 24, 1996.

Mooney, Bill, and David Holt. *The Storyteller's Guide*. Little Rock, Ark.: August House, 1996.

"Storytellers to Weave Their Special Magic During the First Week of October," Jonesborough, Tennessee *Herald & Tribune*, October 2, 1993, 3C–5C.

"Storytelling World Presents: David Novak," *Storytelling World*, Winter/Spring 1993.

Watson, Bruce, and Tom Raymond, "Before Electricity, There Was Storytelling," *Smithsonian*, March 1997.

Wickers, John, "Original Virtual Reality," *San Diego Union Tribune*, March 26, 1995, D1, D3.

JAY O'CALLAHAN

Address   Box 1054
            Marshfield, Massachusetts 02050
phone 617-837-0962 and 800-626-5356
website www.ocallahan.com

Focus: ethical theme; personal anecdotes and original stories; fantasy; history; traditional lore; repetition and audience litanies.

Audience: general.

Style: kinetic use of voice and body to create characters.

At home at the Yeats International Theatre Festival, The Hague, Boston Symphony Orchestra, Stonehenge, and Lincoln Center, Jay O'Callahan is one of platform narrative's most revered platform artisans, both on stage and behind the scenes. A Cambridge native

born August 15, 1938, he grew up in a rambling house on Pill Hill in Brookline, Massachusetts, where he learned to love stories from hearing the talk, arguments, and discussions of literature and drama by his parents, both educators. Patterning his performance after the adults, he shared stories with a younger brother and sister without considering the skill a life's work. He graduated from Brookline High and Holy Cross College. Following service in the Navy, he taught and served as dean of Wyndham Hill Secretarial and Finishing School, which his parents had established in the 1940s. After five years, he knew that his parents' work would never satisfy him.

In the in-between years, O'Callahan and his wife Linda took up residence near the YWCA in Marshfield, where he served as caretaker and she as director. He began writing fiction, published one short story, and completed two unpublished novels. Storytelling sessions with their children, Ted and Laura, turned his attention to a talent that had gone untapped since childhood. For material, he composed children's stories and selected from the wealth of memories of Pill Hill, using free association to relive scenes from his youth. By the 1980s, he earned a substantial living at oral narrative and enjoyed working with his associate, veteran teller Doug Lipman. For the cyclical "Pill Hill Stories," O'Callahan extracts characterization and impetus from his childhood. By establishing a focal image, he creates stories like "The Bubble," "The Dance," and "Raspberries."

After achieving a reputation for quality platform performance, O'Callahan began accepting commissions, adapted "The Little Dragon" for a chamber ensemble, and wrote "The Birth of the Myth of Billy the Kid" for National Public Radio, "The Bread and Rose Strike" for the city of Lawrence, Massachusetts, and "Háry János" and "Peer Gynt" for the Boston Symphony Orchestra. In 1994, Three Apples Storytelling Festival commissioned O'Callahan to write and perform "Labyrinth of Uncle Mark"; the next year, for the 50th anniversary of the bombing of the aircraft carrier the U.S.S. *Franklin*, the Washington Storytellers Theatre commissioned him to perform "Father Joe," the biography of a courageous Jesuit chaplain. Currently, he is completing a commission to write "The Spirit of the Great Auk," a story funded by the Quebec-Labrador Foundation and Stellwagen Bank National Marine Sanctuary.

Bibliography

"The Bubble," http://www.web.concepts.com/day4sam/jayo1.htm, May 23, 1997.

Call to Character (contributor), Harper-Collins, 1996.

"Connor and the Leprechaun," in *Once Upon a Time*, Nelson-Hall, 1983.

"Connor and the Leprechaun," in *Spinning Tales, Weaving Hope*, New Society, 1992.

"Edna Robinson," in *Homespun: Tales from America's Favorite Storytellers*, Crown, 1988.

Herman & Marguerite: An Earth Story (illustrator Laura O'Callahan), Peachtree, 1996. Picture book about the special friendship between a worm and a caterpillar; also available, three felt finger puppets to accompany the plot; for ages 4–8.

"The Herring Shed," in *Homespun: Tales from America's Favorite Storytellers*, Crown, 1988.

"The Herring Shed," in *More Best-Loved Stories Told at the National Storytelling Festival*, August House, 1992.

"How Jay O'Callahan Created 'The Herring Shed,'" *Storytelling World*, Winter/Spring 1997, 23.

"The Magic Mortar," *Ready-to-Tell Tales*, August House, 1994.

A Medley of Tellers and Tales (contributor), Yellow Moon, 1982.

"Old Man Daniker," in *The Ghost & I: Scary Stories for Participatory Telling*, Yellow Moon Press, 1992.

Orange Cheeks (illustrator Patricia Raine), Peachtree Publishers, 1993. A picture book about four-year-old Willie's visit to his grandmother's house.

"Orange Cheeks," in *Best-Loved Stories Told at the National Storytelling Festival*, August House 1991.

Stories to Read Aloud (contributor), Pembroke, 1992.

"Torrid Torts," Houghton Mifflin, 1975.

Tulips (illustrator Debrah Santini), Peachtree, 1992, 1996. Picture book about Pierre, who plays tricks while visiting the house of his Grandma Mere.

Videography

"Fool's Bells," in *Tell Me a Story, Vol. 2* , Hometown Entertainment, 1995.

"Frogs, Dodge City," in *American Storytelling, Vol. 6* (contributor), H. W. Wilson, 1986.

Herman & Marguerite: An Earth Story, Vineyard Video, 1986. The tale of a worm and a caterpillar.

"Interview," *The Twentieth Anniversary of the National Storytelling Festival*, Hometown Entertainment, 1994.

Jay O'Callahan: A Master Class in Storytelling, Vineyard Video, 1984.

"The Little Dragon," *Storyland Series* (contributor), Family Circle/ Paperback Video, 1988.

Many Voices, One World (contributor), UNESCO, 1988.

Six Stories about Little Heroes, Vineyard Video, 1986. Contains "The Bubble," "Raising," "Don't You Dare," "Woe Is Me Bones," "The Boy Who Loved Frogs," and "The Red Ball."

Audiography

Around the Year with Jay O'Callahan (CD), Artana Productions, 1993. Features "Super Bowl Sunday," "Connor and the Leprechaun," "Tulips," "The Bubble," "Brian," "Nonsense," "Don't You Dare," "Jonathan," "Woe Is Me Bones," "The Red Ball," "Old Man Daniker," "Christmas Candles," and "Mary, New Year's Eve"; all ages.

The Boy Who Loved Frogs (audiocassette), High Windy Audio, 1988. Five rhythmic, humorous stories for children.

Coming Home to Someplace New: Pill Hill Stories (audiocassette), Artana Productions, 1990. For teens to adults; contains "Glasses," "Chickie," and "Politics."

The Dance: A Pill Hill Story (two audiocassettes), Artana Productions, 1992. Contains the inner world of a boy coming to manhood, a sequel to *Coming Home to Someplace New: Pill Hill Stories.*

Earth Stories (audiocassette), Artana Productions, 1984. Contains "Herman & Marguerite," "Brian," "Hyena," "The Boy Who Loved Frogs," and "Frogs, Dodge City"; for young children.

Father Joe: A Hero's Journey (audiocassette), Artana Productions, 1994. Contains the story of the bombing of the U.S.S. *Franklin* on March 18, 1945

The Golden Drum (audiocassette), Artana Productions, 1984. The story of Ororingy, who uses wit and courage to locate a magic drum to save the enchanted land of Artana; for older children.

The Gouda (audiocassette), Artana Productions, 1984. The story of three people who use high technology, a UPS truck and New Orleans jazz to discover the gouda's secret; for older children.

The Herring Shed (audiocassette), Artana Productions, 1983. Contains the title story plus "Home on the Range," "The Iceman," "Háry János," "Connor and the Leprechaun," and "The Cliffs of Culdurragh"; for adults.

The Island (audiocassette), Artana Productions, 1988. A story of enchantment and romance in which good and evil castaways on an island encounter strange creatures; for older children.

Jeremy: A Christmas Story (audiocassette), Artana Productions, 1991. The title story plus "Christmas Candle, A Pill Hill Story"; for all ages.

The Little Dragon and Other Stories (audiocassette), Artana Productions, 1991. Contains the title story plus "Orange Cheeks," "Woe Is Me Bones," and "Tulips"; for young children.

Little Heroes (audiocassette), Artana Productions, 1985. Contains "Michael the Grasshopper," "Raising," "The Bubble," "Don't You Dare," "Nonsense," "Miriam," and "The Red Ball"; for young children.

The Minister of Others' Affairs (audiocassette), Artana Productions, 1984. A funny sketch on the politics of the magical land of Artana; for kids and adults.

Mostly Scary (audiocassette), Artana Productions, 1987. Contains "Vargo," "The Russian Claw," and "Old Man Daniker."

"Orange Cheeks," in *Best Loved Stories Told at the National Storytelling Festival* (audiocassette), Artana Productions, 1991.

Petrukian (audiocassette), Artana Productions, 1986. Contains "Wok," "Petrukian," and "Super Sundae"; for older children.

Raspberries (audiocassette), Artana Productions, 1983. The story of Simon's magical berries that change a farmer's luck; for young children.

The Silver Stream (audiocassette), Artana Productions, 1990. Contains the title story plus "Jack, Jack Dump," "Mary, New Year's Eve," and "The Lost Fiddle"; for young children.

The Strait of Magellan (audiocassette), Artana Productions, 1985. The story of Antonio Pigafetti's journals of Ferdinand Magellan's voyages.

"Super Sundae," on *Rainbow Tales* (CD), Rounder Records, 1997.

Village Heroes (two audiocassettes), Artana Productions, 1986. Contains "Háry János," "The Lighthouse Man," "Fool's Bells," and "Edna Robinson."

Awards

1996 National Storytelling Association Circle of Excellence.

1994 New England Reading Association Special Recognition Award.

1994 Kids First Endorsement.

1994 Coalition for Quality Children's Video for *Six Stories About Little Heroes* and *Herman and Marguerite*.

1993 Parents' Choice Classic Award for *Jeremy: A Christmas Story*.

1992 Ohio State Award for WGBH radio's production of "Arts & Ideas: Coming Home to Someplace New."

1991 National Endowment for the Arts Fellowship.

1989 Parents' Choice Award for *The Island*.

1988 NAIRD Indie Award for *The Boy Who Loved Frogs*.

1988 Parents' Choice Award for *The Boy Who Loved Frogs*.

1988 ALA/Carnegie Award for *Jay O'Callahan: A Master Class in Storytelling*.

1987 Parents' Choice Award for *Earth Stories*.

1987 New England Theatre Conference Award.

1987 Birmingham International Educational Film Festival Award for *Herman & Marguerite*.

1987 Family Channel Seal of Quality for *Herman & Marguerite*.

1987 Boston Parents' Paper Award.

1986 National Educational Film Festival Award for *Six Stories about Little Heroes*.

1985 National Educational Film Festival Award for *Jay O'Callahan: A Master Class in Storytelling*.

1984 Parents' Choice Award for *Raspberries*.

1980 Official Storyteller for the Winter Olympics.

Source

Abbott, Deborah, "Review," *Booklist*, July 1993, 1976.

Baldwin, Robert, "Stories from the Marsh," *Traditional Home*, October 1991.

Corsaro, Julie, "Review," *Booklist*, April, 15, 1992.

Grossman, John, "Homeward Bound," *USAir Magazine*, October 1992.

Koch, Jon, "A Storyteller's Tale," *Boston Sunday Globe*, March 29, 1992, B1, B22.

McLeod, Michael, Angela Peterson, and Tom Raymond, "Once Upon a Time," *Florida Magazine*, November 24, 1996.

Mills, Marja, "Storytellers Bring Their Tales to Life," *Chicago Tribune*, July 31, 1989, 1.

Mooney, Bill, and David Holt. *The Storyteller's Guide*. Little Rock, Ark.: August House, 1996.

Osborne, Linda, "The Wisdom of Nations," *World & I*, May 1993.

Something About the Author, Vol. 88. Detroit: Gale Research, 1996.

Timeless Voices: Images of the National Storytelling Festival. Jonesborough, Tenn.: National Storytelling Press, 1997.

PAPA JOE

Address   Oak & Ivy Cottage
16 Beach Street
Fremont, New Hampshire 03044-3565
phone 800-466-6835, code 7272
email papajoe@tiac.net
websites "The Storyteller's Internet Toolbox," http://www.tiac.net/users/papajoe/toolbox1.htm
"The Storytelling Ring," http://www.tiac.net/users/papajoe/ring.htm.

Focus: interactive folktales; English lore; jump stories, fairy tales; formula story-games; verse; original tales.
Audience: primarily children and families
Style: traditional.
Instruments/Props: tenor recorder.

Joseph Philip Gaudet, who performs under the name Papa Joe, is both teller and mentor to aspiring platform performers. A symbol of his selflessness toward others is his complimentary closing in letters—"Pax and Amicitia," the Latin phrase for peace and friendship. Born of Acadian heritage in Andover, Massachusetts, on March 19, 1958, Papa Joe was aptly named for the feast day of St. Joseph. The seventh of John and Dorothy Gaudet's ten children, he and his siblings learned construction skills from their father and storytelling from their mother, who first told him "Poccamandas." The art of storytelling enabled Papa Joe to entertain his little brother and other children, whom he taught stories and folk games. He regretted entering first grade because school interfered with sessions at the library club, where storytellers seemed more interesting than classroom teachers. In time, he acclimated to school after he was allowed to read as much as he wanted. It is not surprising that his favorite book was Joseph Jacob's *Tales*. Resettled in Fremont, New Hampshire, at age twelve, he mucked out barns, cut grass, raked leaves, shoveled snow, and did odd jobs to earn money. His family was too poor to provide tuition to college, so he joined the Army to gain college credits and travel Europe. After hitchhiking across North America and camping in the forest, he returned to school to complete a degree in psychology because he wanted to be a healer of troubled children, but switched to communication and early childhood education as a way of promoting mental health and self-esteem in young audiences.

Papa Joe's discovery seems like a scene from a fairy tale. While selling handcrafted toys and playing his recorder at a renaissance fair during his college years, he attracted the attention of an agent, who signed him up for an audition and began booking him for professional performances. Influenced by the style of Jay O'Callahan and Len Cabral and by Diane Wolkstein's notes in *The Magic Orange Tree*, Papa Joe moved directly into the storytelling scene and found the community of performers both supportive and sharing. In 1987, he began telling stories at children's parties while he completed college.

Papa Joe's first job teaching communication skills at a children's center gave him an opportunity to weave stories into curriculum for a program he calls "Step into a Story with Papa Joe's Storytelling Show." By the next year, he had hit the road behind license plate PAPAJO in Vardo, his motor home and traveling office, to tell 100 different stories for 400 programs. He became one of only 200 troubadour tellers in the country. His lifestyle was simple, sometimes he was reduced to bathing in ponds and streams, residing in an attic or the back of his truck, and gathering fiddleheads and wild roots for supper so he could afford to be an itinerant storyteller. He excelled at telling "The Old Woman and the Pig," "Jack Frost," "Three Little Pigs and the Ogre," and "Poccamandas." One original story, "The Ghost and the Apple Sauce," he made up on the spot to the specifications of a group of preschoolers in Lee, New Hampshire. Within ten years he had performed 4,000 programs. During this fertile period, he acquired the name Papa Joe from an exuberant audience member who lived in his neighborhood.

Subsequent experiences have groomed Papa Joe into a major performer on the storytelling circuit. A member of the Seacoast Storytelling Circle, he serves on the planning committee of Sharing the Fire and on the steering committee of the League for the Advancement of New England Storytellers, and has directed the storytelling component of the Great Bay Folklife Festival in New Market, New Hampshire. Papa Joe's travels have taken him on tour for Columbus Day in Barcelona, Spain, in 1989, up the west coast of Newfoundland in 1990, and across the United States and six Canadian provinces. In 1995, he and wife Sues opened a publishing cottage, Clap Books. Proceeds from his 1996 tape underwrite an outreach to remote communities that receive few cultural opportunities. His busy itinerary has placed his traveling show and workshops at

Washington University, Sharing the Fire, Corner House Inn, Earthfest, Spokane libraries, Maine Special Olympics, Beverly School for the Deaf, Hudson Valley Garlic Festival, Project for Literacy and Storytelling, First Night, Children's Metamorphosis Museum, Texas Elks Children's Services, Three Apples Storytelling Festival, and Phillip's Exeter Academy. In 1997, he emceed the Michigan Storyteller's Festival and performed for local library summer reading programs. His "Internet Storyteller's Tool Box" serves students, researchers, civic leaders, and would-be tellers as an electronic resource center.

Bibliography

"The Bigga da Redda da Rosa," http://www.tiac.net/users/papajoe.

Chris Mouse and Other Stories, self-published, 1996. Contains "Dark and Stormy," "A Long Long Story," "I Don't Know," "The Shortest Story," and "Chris Mouse Tree."

"Chris Mouse and Other Tales," http://www.tiac.net/users/papajoe.

Four Silly Tales, self-published, 1996. Features "Old Woman and the Pig," "Teeny Tiny," "Master of Masters," and "Me," all adapted from English folktales.

The Ghost and the Apple Sauce, self-published. A new New England folktale about a miser who won't share with a beggar until a ghost scares him.

"Idle Madness," http://www.tiac.net/users/papajoe.

"In the Walnut Forest," http://www.tiac.net/users/papajoe.

Jack Frost, self-published, 1996. The story of Jack Frost's icy hand and a young girl who must be polite to Jack; adapted from a Russian folktale.

"Johnny, I'm on the First Step," http://www.tiac.net/users/papajoe.

"Jump off the Bridge!," http://www.tiac.net/users/papajoe.

Keen-witted Orphan, self-published, 1996. A story of an orphan girl who must stall for time to avoid marrying one of the devil's sons; adapted from an Estonian folktale.

"Master of Masters," http://www.tiac.net/users/papajoe.

"New Pots for Old," in *Spinning Tales, Weaving Hope: Stories of Peace, Justice and the Environment*, New Society Press, 1992. About potters who learn to make things from clay until they use it up.

Poccamandas, self-published, 1996. An adaptation of a Southern folktale about a man who does what he is told.

The Prince Who Wouldn't Shut Up, self-published, 1996. The story of a stutterer who relies on wit; adapted from a Scandinavian folktale.

"Robin Hood in Gotham" in *Joining In, Vol. 2: American Holidays*, 1998.

Robin Hood in Gotham, self-published, 1996. The story of how Robin Hood and villagers fool Prince John on April Fool's Day; adapted from an English folktale.

"Story-Games Threat and the Giant Vegetable," http://www.tiac.net/users/papajoe.

St. Patrick and the Leprechauns, self-published, 1996. A riddle story about the struggle between humans and leprechauns.

Three Hairs, self-published, 1996. The tale of Julien's quest for three of the devil's hairs; adapted from a Haitian folktale.

Too Much Christmas Pudding, self-published, 1996. The tale of how three sisters search for a perfect Christmas tree; in the style of a Celtic folktale.

Unanana and the Elephant, self-published, 1996. The story of children stolen by an elephant; adapted from an African folktale.

"What Storytelling Means to Me," *Tale Trader*, August 1997, 3.

"A Working Storyteller," *LANES Newsletter*, April 1996.

Audiography

For a Wish, self-published, 1996. Contains "The Ghost and the Apple Sauce," "Master of Masters," "Poccamandas," and the title story, which is adapted from a Swedish folktale and tells of a poor boy sprinkling salt on the tail of a princess bird.

Source

Crinite, Tina, "Papa Joe Captures Laughter with Story," Pullman, Washington *Daily News*, June 13, 1996, 1.

"Papa Joe Tickles Kids at the Jesup Library," *Bar Harbor Times*, August 17, 1995.

MICHAEL PARENT

Address   P. O. Box 40
Charlottesville, Virginia 22902
phone 804-971-1829

Focus: world folklore; French-Canadian folk tales and songs; original stories and family anecdotes; participation stories and songs.
Audience: all ages.
Style: dramatic telling combined with occasional juggling and French-Canadian foot-tapping to jaw harp rhythms.
Instruments/Props: six-string ukulele, guitar, jaw harp, spoons, bones.

Since 1977, Michael Parent has become a master storyteller. He flourishes mimicking characters and telling stories in a blend of English and Canadian French. A native of Lewiston, Maine, he grew up in a working-class apartment where winos and hoboes sometimes took shelter on the stairs. He could step out of his bedroom window onto the roof of an adjoining grocery store, where he plugged the drains to make a private ice rink and practice his skating. In humble surroundings, his inheritance amounted to a bilingual family full of French-Canadian singers, talkers, and tale-tellers who took him to family gatherings, where he enlarged his imagination from animated conversation. His father, Gerard Parent, kept a store of song lyrics in his head. On his father's side, grandfather Ferdinand Parent sang; grandmother Adeline Parent was the official story keeper and teller. His grandfather Honoré Fournier, the ancestor who most excites Parent's imagination, earned a reputation as "Pop," the vivid talker and overseer of a textile mill. After graduation from Providence College with a B.A. in English literature and minor in education, Parent taught high school English for seven years in Rhode Island, Connecticut, and Massachusetts. The arrival of Haitian immigrants to Boston's Cathedral High required his fluency in French to introduce the Caribbean teenagers to America. At length, he altered his course to meld singing, juggling, and narration in 1977, which developed into a span of stories in New England's Franco-American tradition. He created a one-man show, *Grandpa's Birthday,* based on the life of his grandfather Honoré Fournier.

Parent has advanced from teller to storytelling mentor for the next generation of performers. In his developing years, he chose Brother Blue as a model because of his ability to transform tough city kids into wide-eyed listeners by energizing stories with movement, voice, fantasy, and story magic. An admirer of Brother Blue and his wife Ruth, Parent declares in his résumé that he values their support as "spirit-anchors." His travels carry him to the Selma Tale-Tellin' Festival, Atlanta Olde Christmas, Martha's Vineyard Festival of Storytelling, Open Borders U.S.–Quebec Cultural Exchange, and the National Storytelling Festival in Jonesborough, Tennessee, and place him alongside colleagues Kathryn Windham, Susan Klein, Gwenda LedBetter, Sam Cannarozzi, and J. J. Reneaux. At the International Colloquium on Storytelling in Paris, France, he translated for Jim May and Jon Spelman and did his own performance in French. In May 1997, he was featured performer at the Winter Storytelling Festival in Atlanta and at Folke Tegetthoff's "Lange Nacht of Storytelling" at the Graz Erzählt Festival in Austria. His workshops for performers and educators cover story activities for children, storycrafting, and performance tips. His theatrical performances have cast him as Jake in Sam Shepard's *Lie of the Mind,* as Mr. Fleet the Hare (on roller blades) in *The Great Cross-Country Race,* as Reverend Eddie in Larson and Lee's *Illuminati,* as William in *Left-Handed Free Throws,* as Jake Tomlinson in Steven Dietz's *More Fun Than Bowling,* and as the storyteller in *Golden Apple Odyssey.* Still performing *Grandpa's Birthday,* he also joins others for two original stage scenarios: with Larry Goldstein for *Flying By the Seat of Their Pants* and Philip Kerl for *Left-Handed Free Throws.*

Bibliography

"The Archduke and the Wizards," *Spinning Tales, Weaving Hope,* New Society Publishers, 1992.

Growing Up Is a Full-Time Job, projected 1998. Five fictional stories for juvenile readers.

Of Kings and Fools: Stories of the French Tradition in North America (co-author Julien Olivier), August House, 1996. Contains 32 Franco-American stories of princesses, witches, dragon slayers, lutins, loups-garous, and the trickster Ti-Jean as well as Pierre and the chainsaw; oral lore from two grandfathers — Honoré Fournier and Alexis Lacasse; includes glossary and notes.

"Olive and Bidou," *Lives in Translation*, Soleil Press, 1991.

"Panther and Rabbit," *Ready-to-Tell Tales*, August House, 1994.

"The Pinch-Hitter" in *Best-Loved Stories Told at the National Storytelling Festival*, August House, 1991.

"The Pinch-Hitter" in *On Common Ground*, Oxford University Press, Canada, 1994.

Videography

American Storytelling: Michael Parent, Second Story Television, 1984.

"Charlie Pinch Hits," *American Storytelling Series, Vol. 7*, H. W. Wilson, 1986.

"The Pope in New York City," in *Tell Me a Story, Vol. 2*, Hometown Entertainment, 1995.

Audiography

Stories and Songs (audiocassette),self-published, 1979. Indian and African tribal lore, featuring a Shoshone story, "Rainbow Snake," and an African tale, "Panther and Rabbit."

"String of Trout," on *Rainbow Tales, Too* (CD), Rounder Records, 1997.

Sundays at Grandma's (audiocassette), Virginia Arts Recording, 1990. Family tales in English interspersed with easily translated French.

Tails and Childhood (audiocassette), Weston Woods, 1986. Two beast fables plus "The Kite Story" and "Angela and the Mud Girl"; for all ages.

Awards

1989 Parents' Choice Gold Award for *Sundays at Grandma's*.

1986 American Library Association Notable Record for *Tails and Childhood*.

1984 Cine Golden Eagle Award for *American Storytelling: Michael Parent*.

Source

"A Brief Look at This Year's Storytellers," Jonesborough, Tennessee *Herald & Tribune*, September 30, 1992, 4C–8C.

Delatiner, Barbara, "Stories to Pique a Listener's Imagination," *New York Times*, July 11, 1982.

"Michael Parent," http://www.hometownet.com/parent.html, May 28, 1997.

"Review: 'Of Kings and Fools,'" *Second Story Review*, September 1996.

"Room for Imagination," *Storytelling Series*, WVPT-TV, Harrisonburg, Va., 1979.

MAC PARKER

Address   Rd. 2, Box 2349
Vergennes, Vermont 05491
phone 802-877-6834

Focus: rural-based inspirational, introspective, and non-violent themes that educate and entertain.

Audience: mature audiences.
Style: humor, some adult language.

Known as the Voice of Vermont, Mac Parker cares about animals, children, and adults who lack a political voice. For their sakes, he writes verse and tells contemporary, original stories of American farm and rural life in a wry, witty spiel. At a restaurant, an unidentified admirer left a thank-you note on a paper napkin for the stories that Parker tells about farmers and for the respect and dignity he awards to a way of life that society tends to devalue. Born Malcolm H. Parker on a dairy farm in North Danville, Vermont, in 1957, he is the youngest of the five children of Scudder Parker, Sr., a newspaper publisher and gentleman farmer. After the family farm burned when Parker was an infant, his father turned to his father's trade and began preaching in Congregational churches. His father died when Parker was in third grade. Stories became important to him when he listened to "The Old Squire," the poetic ramblings of poet/storyteller Lloyd Squier over Waterbury's WDEV-radio. Parker recalls, "There was a traditional Vermont voice ... that I grew up hearing. I loved that, and I wanted to use that voice to tell contemporary stories" (Granstrom, 1997, 105). In high school, Parker began writing stories; in his twenties, he performed them for the first time in the basement of a church in Barre, Vermont. Writing

remained a focus in his years at Hampshire College and the University of Vermont.

Like most storytellers, Parker possesses a blend of talents and interests. His life experiences include working the family tree farm and dairy farm, teaching junior high and high school English, composition, and drama, as well as carpentering, overseeing a construction crew, and training teachers. In writing and storytelling, he prefers the environmental and cultural issues that are meaningful to Vermonters and progresses to more controversial issues, such as one girl's dismay at the defeat of the Equal Rights Amendment. More than a stress on farming and earth values, he finds the connecting threads that unite humanity — the observations of barn swallows, walks in the woods, berry picking, and commonalities that form his monologues and reminiscences. A memorable piece, "Eulogy for a Living Farmer," resulted from the request of Earl Bessette, a forward-thinking friend, that Parker speak at his funeral.

Parker comes from a tradition of New England humorists and storytellers and made his big break into the profession at the 1986 Burlington's First Night celebration. One of his early performance starters was "Arnie's Hay Truck," a humorous anecdote about a young farm lad driving a decrepit hay truck. He disdains folksy humor that belittles Vermonters. His goal is to bring tradition to the present with stories of everyday life. To present a realistic glimpse of his state, he writes dialect poems, dialogues, and stories that form humorous, touching, reverent, and true portraits of his native milieu, neighbors, and landscape. His venue takes him to town hall gatherings, folk festivals, annual meetings, as well as radio and television. He has performed for a strange blend of audiences: the High Ridge Folk Festival in Stamford, Connecticut, American Academy of Nuclear Medicine, trade shows for auto dealers, National Folk Festival, Clearwater Storytelling Festival, Philadelphia Folk Festival, St. Louis Storytelling Festival, and the National Storytelling Festival in Jonesborough, Tennessee. Currently, he is working on a novel, *Foxes and Friends*, the story of a child's hard life in the country.

Bibliography
"Changes," *AudioFile Magazine*, August 1994, 13.

Videography
Let's Go to the Farm, Vermont Story Works, 1994. Covers all four seasons and describes livestock, haying, making maple syrup, harvesting, and performing chores; filmed at a farm near his house.

Audiography
Changes: More Tales of Rural Living (audio-cassette), self-produced, 1989. Contains "What Do Peepers Talk About?," "Father and Daughter," "Arnie's Hay Truck," "Fallen Apple," "Young One," "Farm Girl," and the title story.

Eulogy for a Living Farmer (audiocassette), self-produced, projected for Fall 1997.

The Givin' War: Tales of Vermont and Vermonters (audiocassette), self-produced, 1987. Contains "Fall Foliage," "Right of Way," "The Government Program," "Love Poem," "The Interstate," "Turds," "Springtime," and the title story; taped before a live audience in Middlebury, Vermont.

Wild Woods: New Tales of Rural Living (audio-cassette), self-produced, 1992. Contains "The Wagon Wheel," "Bird Trilogy," "Vermont Department of Demotion," "The Family Farm," "Bob's Development," "The War on Vermont," "Foxes and Friend," "Discretion," and the title story.

Awards
1994 Oppenheim Toy Portfolio Platinum Award for *Let's Go to the Farm*.

1994 American Library Association Award for *Let's Go to the Farm*.

1994 *AudioFile* Magazine Earphones Award for *Changes* and *Wild Woods*.

1994 Parents' Choice Award for *Let's Go to the Farm*.

1991 Vermont Council on the Arts Fiction Fellowship to write *Foxes and Friends*.

Source
Alarik, Scott, "Lowell Folk Fest: A Perfect 10," *Boston Globe*, July 29, 1996.

Bohjalian, Chris, "Books, Tapes, & Videos of Vermont Interest," *Vermont Life*, 1995, 70.

Granstrom, Chris, "Mac Parker: Storyteller," *Vermont Life*, Fall 1997, 74, 105–106.

"Keepers of the Lore: Storytelling for Adults," *AudioFile Magazine*, August 1994, 1, 12–13.

Marquard, B. K., "Mac Parker: Teller of Tales," *Vermont*, July 29, 1990, 1–2, 14–15.

ABBI PATRIX

Address   Compagnie du Cercle
99, Rue de Vaugirard
Paris, France 75006
phone 1-44-39-85-55
fax 2-45-49-41-19

Focus: myth; epic tales in a contemporary setting; New Testament stories from the life of Christ; Irish pirate lore; Arthurian legends; stories adapted from the Arabian Nights, Hindu religious texts, and French opera and history.

Audience: all ages.

Style: troubadour; tandem performance with storyteller Bernard Chèze.

Instruments/Props: violin and percussion background.

A bilingual performer in French and English, influenced by a French/Norwegian background, Abbi Patrix derived his reputation for storytelling from a decade of work in radio, film, and theater. He received training in masking, mime, and acting at the Jacques Lecoq School in Paris, but began to question his role in theater. To evolve a personal style of narrative, in 1980 he formed La Compagnie du Cercle, the troupe he currently manages. Like the *commedia dell'arte* of the Italian Renaissance, the company draws on individual creativity to feed group performances and has spent three years in residence in the National Theater of Evry, south of Paris. The group's combination of storytellers, musicians, actors, singers, and writers has attained a reputation for unique, creative programming. On his own, Patrix has toured France, Canada, Sweden, Norway, Guyana, Switzerland, England, and Wales and conducts workshops throughout Europe. His solo performances include "Death of a Hero," a mélange of epic tales with original music and dance, "Three Stories for a Cathedral: The Passion and the Resurrection," a biography of Christ; "Le Compagnon," a solo adapted from *Tales from Norway*; "The War of the Crows and the Owls," Indian stories from the 12th-century *Panchantantra*; "The French Revolution," a tandem performance with Yannick Jaulin at France's bicentenary; "The Legend of Joseph in Egypt," "The One-Eyed Man," and "Possible-Impossible," a tandem performance of African stories with Bernard Chèze. He has directed performances of "The Boy Without a Name," an original tale by Philippe Raulet; "Voilà-Voilà," a two-man recreation of musical history illustrated by stories, and "The Wanderings of Graïnné," the epic story of Grace O'Malley, Ireland's Elizabethan-era pirate.

Audiography

Abbi Patrix Tells of Jesus: The Passion, the Resurrection (audiocassette) Audivis/Jeunesse. Family entertainment from age five and above.

Possible-Impossible (audiocassette), Audivis/Jeunesse. For age five and above.

Stories of Norway: The Companion (audiocassette), Audivis/Jeunesse. Family entertainment for age five and above.

Stories of Norway: Trolls (audiocassette), Audivis/Jeunesse. Family entertainment for age five and above.

The War of the Crows and the Owls (audiocassette), Audivis/Jeunesse. For age ten and above.

The Zebra Does Not Cast a Shadow (audiocassette), Audivis/Jeunesse. For age five and above.

MAGGI PEIRCE
[purs]

Address 330 Huttleston Avenue
Fairhaven, Massachusetts 02719
phone 508-996-5295

Focus: Ulster rhymes, chants, legends, songs, and yarns from northern Ireland; stories and recitations from both countryside and Victorian drawing room; Finn McCool giant legends.

Audience: general.

Style: conversational tone and wry, witty presentation of song, story, recitation, reminiscences, vignettes, verse, and ballad.

As affable and charming in person as on stage, Maggi Peirce, a native of Belfast, Ireland, became a professional storyteller while doing a good deed — she took the place of an absent performer at a 1972 performance. Still telling after a quarter century of stage appearances, she maintains the rhythms and dialect of her youth. In a 1997 issue of *Storytelling Magazine*, she claims, "I like to be typical of Ulster, my homeland — kindly, brusque, telling it like it is." An ebullient, strong-minded Northern Irelander, she grew up in a milieu of skipping and counting rhymes, recitations, traditional *a capella* singing, and ballads, which influenced her appeal as a knowledgeable and spirited teller. In childhood, she recalls learning to whisper from her mother because children were expected to keep silent around grownups. She claimed to have "imbibed" her style from looking, listening,

and mimicking the hand gestures and tones of her father and Aunt Aileen. A consummate performer, she believes in making contact with her audience from the beginning and moving slowly into stories to cement the bond.

Once a clerk in a Belfast hem-stitching company, Peirce has lived and worked in Stockholm, Sweden; Amsterdam, Holland; London, England; and Edinburgh, Scotland. Since marrying an American, Kenneth Peirce, in 1964 and settling in Fairhaven, Massachusetts in 1965, she has raised their twins, Henry and Cora-Dorothy, and enjoyed the company of grandchildren. A lover of action and humor, Peirce has evolved a repertoire of ball-game rhymes, parody, schoolyard dialogue, and political and street chants. These bits of Irelandiana from childhood form the text of her book, *Keep the Kettle Boiling*, a best-seller in her native land. In addition, she has published verse in *World Without Violence, The Inquirer, Spinner,* and *Women and Language* and has contributed articles to the *Belfast Telegraph*, the *New Bedford Standard Times*, and *Northwest Folklore*. With frequent visits to Ireland, she maintains her ties with the Kerr and

Walker clans and visits her sister Dorothy, with whom she has a lasting bond.

Peirce directed the Try Works Coffee House in New Bedford, Massachusetts, from 1967 to 1987 and has served as artist-in-residence in Bonner County, Idaho. She is a veteran of many performances for libraries, women's clubs, staged events, and festivals, including Stone Soup Festival, The Ark, Augusta Festival, Boston Gaelic League, Sierra Storytelling Festival, Clearwater Revival, Long Island Storytelling Festival, Christmas Revels, Burlington Storytelling Festival, First Night Boston, Eisteddfod Folk Festival, Humboldt State, Illinois Storytelling Festival, Lincoln Center Summer Festival Middfest, and the National Storytelling Festival in Jonesborough, Tennessee, where she first performed in 1980. Her tellings have enlivened gatherings at Wolf Trap, the Smithsonian Campus on the Mall, Harvard University Irish League, University of Wyoming, Vassar College, and Lincoln Center, and have been heard on BBC Radio in Belfast, *A Christmas Celtic Sojourn* on WGBH-Boston, and the *Prairie Home Companion* from St. Paul, Minnesota.

Bibliography

Christmas Mince, self-published, 1983.
"Cousin Norman," in *Homespun: Tales from America's Favorite Storytellers*, Crown, 1988.
"The Half Blanket," in *Ready to Tell Tales*, August House, 1994.
Keep the Kettle Boiling, Appletree Press, Belfast, 1983.
"The Large Stuffed Rabbit," in *Homespun: Tales from America's Favorite Storytellers*, Crown, 1988.
"The Lucky Package," in *Homespun: Tales from America's Favorite Storytellers*, Crown, 1988.
"The Three Reeds," in *Investigating Cultures and Their Stories*, Frank Schaffer Publications, 1996.

Videography

Three Apples Festival (contributor), Wave, Inc., 1993.
"Why the Dog Has a Cold Wet Nose," in *American Storytelling Series, Vol. 1*, H. W. Wilson, 1987.

Audiography

Cream o' the Crop (audiocassette), Miracle Records, 1984.
For Younger I've Been: Stories of a Belfast Childhood (audiocassette), Yellow Moon, 1993. Contains anecdotes from the 1930s and 1940s, featuring "Lucky Package," "The Haunted House on Evelyn Avenue," and "Awakening."
"A Friend of My Father," in *Best Loved Stories Told at the National Storytelling Festival* (audiocassette), August House, 1991.
Maggi Peirce Live (audiocassette), Yellow Moon, 1982. A collection of Irish folktales, stories, skipping rhymes, recitations, and jokes.
An Ulster Christmas (audiocassette), Yellow Moon. 1986. Recorded live in concert; contains "Uncle Nelson, Belfast," "Lest We Forget," and other childhood memories.
Wicked and Wonderful (audiocassette).

Awards

1997 National Storytelling Association Circle of Excellence.
1988 Massachusetts Arts and Humanities Award for excellence in storytelling.

1974 Eisteddfod Award from Southwestern Massachusetts University for dedication to traditional Irish music.

Source

Braun, Linda W., "Audiovisual Review: Recordings," *School Library Journal*, November 1993, 70.
"A Brief Look at This Year's Storytellers," Jonesborough, Tennessee *Herald & Tribune*, September 30, 1992, 4C–8C.
Carey, Kim, "McConnell Receives NSA's Lifetime Achievement Award," *Tale Trader*, August 1997, 1, 4.
"Five Storytellers Receive Honors," *Storytelling Magazine*, May 1997, 41.
Mooney, Bill, and David Holt. *The Storyteller's Guide*. Little Rock, Ark.: August House, 1996.

ANNE PELLOWSKI

Address   819 West Broadway
           Winona, Minnesota 55987
507-454-7584

Focus: world folktales.
Audience: children and families.
Style: traditional narration.

Anne Pellowski is a proponent of pure narration, which she characterizes as an exercise for the ear and the mind. One of her memorable experiences in teaching children through stories involved taping tales of violence for use with disturbed and abused patients at a school associated with the Menninger Clinic. In the privacy of a listening booth, each child could respond to the story and to an individual history of mistreatment. From childhood, Pellowski has excelled at using her talents to solve problems. The sixth of the nine children of Anna Dorava and Alexander Pellowski, she was born on a Wisconsin farm in Pine Creek outside the town of Dodge and learned Polish as a natural part of living in the immigrant community. Her maternal grandfather bore the reputation of storyteller, but died when Pellowski was a toddler. For yarning, she

turned to her maternal uncle, a teller of ghost and devil stories, and her oldest sister Angie, who made up dog stories. In her early years, she had five sisters to read to her and entered school with a ready-made love of books con-taining myths, fairy tales, and biographies and a yen to travel.

At the College of St. Teresa, Pellowski com-pleted her grounding in literature and lan-guage and remembers her delight in the

French biography of Marie Curie written by Curie's daughter Eve. An honor graduate of Columbia University with a master's degree in library science, she studied on a Fulbright Fellowship at the University of Munich, where she determined to study children's literature and storytelling. With subsequent graduate study at the universities of Minnesota and Munich and the New School for Social Research, she remained at the forefront of studies in children and reading. Her work experience has advanced from senior children's librarian, storyteller, and group work specialist for the New York Public Library to researcher at the International Youth Library in Munich, to founder of the Information Center on Children's Cultures for UNICEF, to fifteen years as freelance writer, lecturer, consultant, and raconteur. In 1969, she served on the international jury of the Hans Christian Andersen Award. Consultancies and performances have carried her across the United States and to Venezuela, Japan, Mauritius, Korea, Netherlands, New Guinea, France, Germany, Cyprus, Belgium, India, Indonesia, Poland, Thailand, and Senegal and generate an impressive list of advisory boards and publications: *World Book, Children's Catalog, Childcraft, Phaedrus: An International Journal of Children's Literature Research, World Folktale Series, Parents' Choice, National Storytelling Journal*, and *Ediciones Ekare*. She has appeared at schools and colleges across the United States and in 100 countries. Her lectures cover children's library services, mass media and children's reading, designing play materials for children, writing and illustrating young adult literature, making cloth books, books for children with special needs, multicultural literature, and storytelling. Television credits include *Today Show, Mr. Roger's Neighborhood, A United Nations Christmas*, and Japan's *Today Show*.

Bibliography

"Culture and Developing Countries," *International Companion Encyclopedia of Children's Literature*, Routledge, 1996, 663–675.

The Family Storytelling Handbook (illustrator Lynn Sweat), Macmillan, 1987. Contains stories for the very young, handkerchief stories, origami stories, paper cutting or tearing stories, a finger story, stories with objects, drawing stories in sand, snow, or mud, and a Buddhist story from India.

First Farm in the Valley, St. Mary's Press, 1997.

Have You Seen a Comet?, John Day, 1971.

Hidden Stories in Plants (illustrator Lynn Sweat), Macmillan, 1989. Contains ornaments, disguises, playthings, dolls for a day, and musical instruments.

How to Make Cloth Books for Children, Chilton, 1992.

Joining In — An Anthology of Audience Participation Stories and How to Tell Them (contributor), Yellow Moon, 1988. Eighteen participation stories for all ages.

Made to Measure: Children's Books in Developing Countries, UNESCO, 1980.

The Nine Crying Dolls, Putnam, 1979.

Stairstep Farm, St. Mary's Press, 1997.

The Storytelling Handbook for Young Children (illustrator Martha Stoberock), Simon & Schuster, 1995. Contains cumulative tales, stories that use dramatic devices or objects, stories that are enhanced by costume, stories for holidays and celebrations, stories to memorize, and stories composed or improved by young people.

The Story Vine (illustrator Lynn Sweat), Macmillan, 1984. Contains string stories, cat's cradle, picture-drawing stories, sand stories, picture-drawing stories, stories with dolls or figurines, finger-play stories, riddling, and stories using musical instruments.

Willow Wind Farm, St. Mary's Press, 1997.

Winding Valley Farm, St. Mary's Press, 1997.

The World of Children's Literature, R. R. Bowker, 1968.

A World of Children's Stories, H. W. Wilson, 1990.

The World of Storytelling, H. W. Wilson, 1990. A discussion of historical traditions, storytelling as art, craft, heritage, and expression of world view plus types of storytelling and format and style.

Audiography

Nine audiocassettes, CMS Records, 1965–1975.

Awards

1996 *Storytelling World* Award for *The Storytelling Handbook*.

1995 *Storytelling World* Award for *The World of Storytelling.*

1983 Wisconsin State Historical Society Book Award.

1980 Women's National Book Association Constance Lindsay Skinner Award.

1979 American Library Association Grolier Foundation Award.

1969 College of St. Teresa Alumnae Award.

1965 Council on Library Resources Fellowship, Library of Congress.

1955 Fulbright Scholarship.

Source

Contemporary Authors. Vol. 23–24. Detroit: Gale Research, 1988.

Fifth Book of Junior Authors & Illustrators. New York: H. W. Wilson, 1983.

Nutter, Barbara, "Once Upon a Time There Was... ," *Honolulu Advertiser,* C1, C3.

Something About the Author. Vol. 20. Detroit: Gale Research, 1980.

Ward, Martha E., and Dorothy A. Marquardt. *Authors of Books for Young People.* Scarecrow, 1990.

LEE PENNINGTON

Address   11905 Lilac Way
        Middletown, Kentucky 40243
    phone 502-245-1629 or 502-245-0643

Focus: folktales; Jack tales; ghost stories and tales of premature burial; Kentucky lore; tall tales, beast fables, and yarns; poems and songs; personal anecdotes.

Audience: adults and children.

Style: rhythmic telling; idiomatic anecdotes.

Instruments/Props: bluegrass and folk music.

Lee Pennington, a favorite at poetry readings, folk concerts, and storytelling festivals, expends much of his time and energy promoting the art of oral narration. The ninth of eleven children of Mary Ellen Lawson and Andrew Virgil Pennington, Pennington was born May 1, 1939, on a 32-acre Kentucky farm. His parents told riddles and read stories from McGuffey Readers; neighbors prized anecdotes about a two-headed snake and a water witch who could divine for water. The extended family retained the oral lore of Granny Sued, the biblical parables of his grandfather, Andrew Madison Pennington, and yarns about his telekinetic grandmother, Laura Lawson, who could make tables walk and beds levitate. He attended a one-room mountain school and was inspired by the principal, poet and novelist Jesse Stuart, who helped him find a job reporting sports and school news for a local paper. In an interview for *Tale Trader,* Pennington declared that he has always been a storyteller, but realized it officially a quarter century ago at the National Storytelling Festival. He believes that the best tellers are honest, unaffected, and obsessed with their art heart and soul, and he determines his success by looking the audience in the eyes. To support and buoy the art of platform narrative, he has influenced the careers of many professional tellers and serves as editor and columnist for E.A.R.S., a voice for performers and clearinghouse in the storytelling world.

Pennington, a teacher, reporter, folksinger, video producer, and storyteller from White Oak, Kentucky, graduated first in his class from

Greenup County schools and attended Bald-win-Wallace College and Berea College on a journalism scholarship; he graduated in 1962 with a B.A. in English. He attended San Diego State and earned an M.A. in English from the University of Iowa in 1965. He has pursued postgraduate studies at the University of Kentucky, World University, from which he holds an honorary doctorate in literature, and the Academy of Southern Arts and Letters, which in 1993 conferred on him an honorary doctorate in philosophy in arts. His employment record is as diverse as his stories, covering fourteen years in farming, teaching English at Jefferson Community College, and writing for the *Portsmouth Times, Ashland Daily Independent, Huntington Herald Dispatch,* and *Greenup News.* He has served as professor of poetry at Morehead State University, Western Kentucky University, Defiance College, East Tennessee State University, Ball State University, and the Central Indiana Writers' Conference. He currently represents his home state as poet laureate and has earned 28 honors and awards for proficiency in verse. In addition to the filming of ten documentaries, singing in 1,000 concerts, and publishing over 1,300 poems and 16 novels, plus drama, criticism, and a textbook on composition, he has published 50 stories in *Bluegrass Woman, Laurel Review, Snowy Egret, Hoosier Challenger, Mountain Life and Work, Appalachian Review, Mountain Review,* and *Hearthstone* and 100 articles in such magazines as *Playgirl, Foreign Car Guide, California Writer, Sing Out!, Writer's Digest,* and *National Storytelling Journal.*

Bibliography

Appalachian Quartet, Aran Press, 1980. A drama about joy and despair in the Kentucky hills.

"The Calico Coffin," in *Homespun: Tales from America's Favorite Storytellers,* Crown, 1988.

Creative Composition (textbook), Jefferson Community College, 1976.

The Dark Hills of Jesse Stuart (criticism), Harvest Press, 1967.

I Knew a Woman, Love Street Books, 1977. Compendium of verse lauding the beauty and grace of women.

The Moonshine War (screenplay), MGM, 1970.

A feature film starring Richard Widmark and Alan Alda.

The Porch, Love Street Books, 1976.

"Rejection? Rejoicing!," *Writer's Digest,* August 1981, 64, 83.

The Scotian Women, Aran Press, 1981. An historical drama about a mine explosion.

Songs of Bloody Harlan, Westburg Associates, 1976.

"Time Upon a Place," *National Storytelling Journal,* Summer 1985, 14–17.

Awards

1996 National Storytelling Association Circle of Excellence.

1994 Pulitzer Prize nomination for *Thigmotropism.*

1992 International Order of E.A.R.S. Special Merit Award.

1992 National Association for the Preservation and Perpetuation of Storytelling Appreciation Award.

1983 Mildred A. Daughterty Award for contribution to literature.

1979 Central Indiana Writers' Association Outstanding Achievement and Dedication to Writers Award.

1978 Kentucky State Poetry Society Jesse Stuart Award.

1977 Pulitzer Prize nomination for *I Knew a Woman.*

1971 2000 Men of Achievement award.

1969 Outstanding Young Man in America.

Source

Beattie, L. Elisabeth, "A Teller of Tales," *Kentucky Living,* May 1989.

Boneham, Emile, "What Storytelling Means to Me," *Tale Trader,* August 1996, 4.

"A Brief Look at This Year's Storytellers," Jonesborough, Tennessee *Herald & Tribune,* September 30, 1992, 4C–8C.

Brown, Fred, "The Restoration of Our Senses," *Memphis Press-Scimitar,* October 5, 1982, B1.

Contemporary Authors, Vols. 69–72. Detroit: Gale Research, 1978.

Dictionary of Literary Biography Yearbook. Detroit: Gale Research, 1982.

Hicks, Jack, "Louisville Festival's Stories Long, Tall and Handsome," *Kentucky Today,* September 4, 1981, B1.

Hill, Jennifer, "Storytellers Recall Festival's First Years in Jonesborough," Jonesborough, Tennessee *Herald and Tribune*, September 30, 1992, 2C, 4C.

Hilliker, J. Marie, "Storyteller Extraordinary," *Louisville Magazine*, August 1979.

Jones, Michael L., "Poet Lee Pennington Whispers While Everyone Else Is Screaming," *Independent*, August 10, 1994, 4.

"The Multi-Talented Lee Pennington," *Entertainer*, February 1–12, 1983.

Reed, Billy, "He's a Storyteller, and Proud of It," *Lousville Courier-Journal*, October 1, 1975.

Rosen, Jackie, "Rattlesnakes Under His Bed," *Anderson Sunday Herald*, April 16, 1978, 13–14.

Ruiz, Ben, "NSA Presents 1996 Awards in Storytelling," *Tale Trader*, November 1996, 1, 7.

"Time Upon a Place," *National Storytelling Journal*, Summer 1985.

UTAH PHILLIPS

Address   No Guff Records
　　　　　P. O. Box 1235
　　　　　Nevada City, California 95959
phone 916-265-2855
email utah@nccn.net
fax 916-265-0197
website www.hidwater.com/utah/

Focus: radical yarning; whoppers and tall tales; shaggy dog stories; Southwestern humor; labor history; personal opinion and reflection; political jests and folk songs.

Audience: general.

Style: folksy; whimsical.

Instruments/Props: red flannel shirt, baggy trousers, suspenders, beard; guitar.

The son of labor organizers, Bruce "U. Utah" Phillips, born in 1935 in Cleveland, Ohio, is the fundamental pragmatist who makes stories of any raw material that finds its way into his experience. Whether miner, revivalist, revolutionary, or visionary, all have received Phillips's polite attention. A former warehouseman in Salt Lake City, he learned yarning from Earl M. Lyman, an elder of the Latter Day Saints and Phillips's employer, who interrupted the morning's wrapping and shipping to tell anecdotes and stories of events of Mormon pioneer days. At the end of a workday, Phillips went to the library to read territorial history to find questions to ask Lyman the next day. Thus Phillips learned the art of storytelling as a way to avoid work. Zuñi chants and Navaho songs and lore from Father Liebler, a San Juan priest, plus conversations with hobos and cowboys, lectures by anarchist and pacifist Ammon Hennacy, and a performance by Marian Anderson during the Korean War augmented Phillips's store of eyewitness accounts, anecdotes, tales, and philosophy.

Phillips ran away from home in his teens to gain an education on the road, riding the rails, and bumming along with tramps. He taught himself to play the ukulele and guitar and began writing songs about the hobo life while supporting himself as a printer, dishwasher, and stock clerk. His experience as a soldier during the Korean War convinced him that nonviolence is the only sane way to live. During the 1960s, Utah worked as a state archivist and founded the Poor People's Party in Utah. In 1968, he ran for the U.S. Senate on the Peace and Freedom ticket. A leave of absence from state service turned into permanent dismissal and an opportunity to try his luck as a platform entertainer. In 1972 and every four years since, he has run for the presidency on the Sloth and Indolence ticket. An adherent of Everyman, he has garnered a store of tales in the style of Mark Twain and Will Rogers and relates the adventures of labor heroes Mother Jones and Big Bill Haywood.

A promoter of the IWW and a national treasure of wit and humor, Phillips, dubbed the "Golden Voice of the Great Southwest," has earned a small, but devoted following for his tales, guitar music, and songs, which he shares among the folk family in the style of a Celtic bard. He is known for researching a town to learn landmarks, anecdotes, and local minutiae before appearing on-stage or at a festival. His programs extol self-reliance and encourage people to stop depending on government and to toss their televisions out the window. A heart condition prevents him from his usual circuit of 120 cities a year, but he continues to perform his history-based blarney about eccentrics and heroes of the road. Friends and fans of Phillips have rallied to his support since his disability. Beloved as a rabble rouser and individualist, he remains true to unionism in the tradition of Woody Guthrie, Pete Seeger, and the strikers of the 1930s.

Bibliography

"Moose Call," http://www.hidwater.com/utah/utahstory1.html.

"The Old Man and the Mule," *Entertainment Twin Cities*, May 14–20, 1987, 13D.

Audiography

All Used Up (audiocassette), Rounder Records. Songs about street people.

El Capitan (audiocassette), Rounder Records. Songs about the new and old West.

Good Though (audiocassette and CD), Rounder Records. Original and traditional songs about hobos and steam railroads; contains "Moose Turd Pie."

Heart Songs (CD), Rounder Records, 1997. Utah's songs performed by Jody Stecher and Kate Brislin.

I've Got to Know (audiocassette and CD), Alcazar. Songs, poems, and stories about peace, war, pacifism, and anarchy.

Legends of Folk (audiocassette and CD), Red House Records. Performed with Ramblin' Jack Elliott and Spider John Koerner.

Loafers Glory (music by Mark Ross) (CD), Red House Records, 1997. Features songs and tales about the traveling life.

The Long Memory (co-producer Rosalie Sorrels) (CD), Red House Records, 1996. Features songs and tales about work in the West and the American labor movement.

The Past Didn't Go Anywhere (audiocassette and CD), Righteous Babe, 1996. Traditional stories accompanied by punk-folksinger Ani DiFranco; recorded live.

The Telling Takes Me Home (CD), Rounder Records, 1997. An anthology of Utah's songs about the old and new West.

We Have Fed You All a Thousand Years (audiocassette and CD), Rounder Records. Songs and stories of the Industrial Workers of the World and working class culture.

Awards

1997 Folk Alliance Lifetime Achievement Award.

1997 NAIRD Award for best traditional recording.

1997 American Federation of Musicians' Lifetime Service to Labor Award from Traveling Musicians Local 1000.

1982 Proclaimed Grand Duke of Hoboes.

Source

Ainsworth, Bill, "Anarchy in Song," *Sacramento News & Review*, July 25, 1991.

Alarik, Scott, "Utah Phillips and Sabia," *Boston Globe*, March 28, 1988.

DiFranco, Ani, "The Seductive Tyranny of Youth Culture," *Musician*, August 1996.

Harrar, Paul, "Phillips Joins the Ranks of Guthrie, Seeger," Grass Valley-Nevada City, California *Union*, February 12, 1997, A3.

"Idiot's Delight Archive," http://www.planet.net/id/archive.

Kelp, Larry, "Utah's Tour of the Heart," *San Francisco Chronicle*, December 3, 1995.

Pariser, Emanuel, "Utah Phillips Sings of Real Life," *Camden Herald*, July 18, 1991.

Ray, Amy, "The Untouchable," *Advocate*, May 28, 1996.

Rayburn, Heather, "Famed Storyteller to Make Rare Local Appearance," *Asheville Citizen-Times*, May 2, 1997, D1, D3, D7.

Tarbox, James M., "Tall Tales Are Sooooo True," *Entertainment Twin Cities*, May 14–20, 1987, 13D.

"Utah Phillips," http://www.hidwater.com/utah.

Washburn, Jim, "The Fine State of Utah," *Los Angeles Times*, March 11, 1992.

Young, Charles M., "Review," *Musician*, August 1996.

JACKSON GERSHOM "PAW-PAW" PINKERTON

Address   11 Short Trail
Stamford, Connecticut 06903
home phone 203-322-2284
work phone 203-968-8318
email PawPawP@aol.com

Focus: a Santa Claus look-alike grandfather who tells old and original stories for all occasions; stories from all lands, including Texas, the Bible, and life in general; mainly stories he loves because they have something to say, even the funny ones.

Audience: all ages.

Style: traditional, rural Texas dialect softened by years of working overseas.

More familiar to storytelling fans as Pawpaw, J. G. Pinkerton began late in the business, but made up for lost time with dedication to promoting the art as the world's best teaching tool for transmitting values, faith, and wisdom. The founder of TELLABRATION! The Worldwide Evening of Storytelling for Grownups, he has seen his vision of worldwide story sessions encircle the globe each Saturday preceding Thanksgiving. He intends to remain a teller as long as he can find breath to power his stories. To him, the task of teller is like a new skin that has changed him from an administrative manager to a platform performer. His personal philosophy urges him to replace the mechanized modern existence with more humanity through direct communication with listeners.

Pinkerton comes from a family that told stories. He treasures the diaries of his great grandfather and his grandmother and the writings of his parents. In "HearSay" [stet], a magazine article detailing his construction of a personal story, he outlines how his family matched a problem with a story containing a solution. Pinkerton recalls staying with his paternal grandmother when he was ten years old and being allowed to sleep late. At breakfast, his grandmother offered him ten brands of cereal and told him to choose his favorite and return the other nine boxes to the store. The refund he would receive was to be his spending money. He was too shy to carry out her plan. In response to his immaturity, she told him the story of her own fear when her mother was about to give birth and needed help with the delivery. To calm her daughter's fears, the mother urged her to take the situation one stage at a time. The young Pinkerton realized the difference between his fear and his grandmother's more frightening situation and applied the advice of the story by taking his own challenge step by step.

The story of Pinkerton's odyssey began eight years before he retired from his corporate executive job as an administrative manager for a U.S. natural resource mining company. With a degree in accounting and management from the University of Texas, his career spanned 37 years, and he worked in Texas, Utah, Australia, and Panama before returning to the United States and settling with his wife Joann, two sons, and a daughter in Stamford, Connecticut, where he still resides. A life-long storyteller who got whippings in childhood for yarning, he never considered telling as a career possibility until 1982, when he read an article about Jay O'Callahan in *American Way*, an American Airlines magazine that introduced him to the profession of storytelling. Three years later, while recovering from a heart attack and losing weight to improve his health, he made himself a promise to begin performing his reminiscences of growing up with a mischievous brother in Turkey, Texas, where his father, Lewis Pinkerton, a former

J.G. "Paw-paw" Pinkerton

oilfield roughneck, worked as a plumber, tin-smith, and mechanic during the Depression. To better prepare for the challenge, Pinkerton studied improvisational acting and gained the help of Kate McClelland, assistant director and head of children's services at Perrot Memorial Library in Old Greenwich, Connecticut. He also studied the techniques of Peg O'Sullivan, Lorna Stengel, Carol Birch, Robert Bela Wilhelm, Jay O'Callahan, and Donald Davis.

After Pinkerton's first venture at telling "Itsy Bitsy Spider" at the Turn of River Library with grandson Trevor, he started researching the profession of platform telling and joined the National Association for the Preservation and Perpetuation of Storytelling. With a suspenseful account of a trip to the island of Fiji, he ventured before other tellers at the 1986 Connecticut Storytelling Festival. Other tellers applauded his professional technique without knowing that Pinkerton had neither training nor experience. He retired from office work and advanced to board membership of his local organization, the Connecticut Storytelling Center at Connecticut College. To suit his wire rims, white hair, and suspenders-and-bowtie style, he chose Paw-paw as a grandfatherly stage name, which precedes him on community stages and at libraries, schools,

youth rallies, juvenile halls, colleges, churches and synagogues, retirement villages, hospitals, conventions, retreats, and private and corporate gatherings as well as radio and television and the National Storytelling Festival in Jonesborough, Tennessee. His jobs include voice-overs and commercials. More comfortable with live audiences, he has enjoyed appearing at the Rainbow Gathering Festival in Perth, Australia, and at Cape Clear Island Storytelling Festival in County Cork, Ireland.

After wearying of corporate demands, Pinkerton is pleased to have found an outlet for the talents that had long endeared him to family and office workers. His signature stories recount the experiences of Sod Durst, a stuttering sheriff, and of Mister Barney and Mis' Mattie, Pinkerton's employers at a service station and quick stop in Kimble County, Texas. Mis' Mattie was the benefactor who loaned him $300 to begin his college education. He puts his vernacular best into stories of Elijah confronting Baal worshipers and of Saul's walk to Emmaus, a pivotal event in Christian history. These religious tales display faith in everyday life and testify to Pinkerton's Christian beliefs. To extend the use of stories, he encourages all churches to stop preaching at people and learn to tell biblical events in a more agreeable oral form of storytelling.

Bibliography

"HearSay," [stet], *Connecticut Storytelling Center Magazine*, Fall 1997.

Audiography

The Perfect Wedding ... and Other Moments of Mirth (audiocassette) self-published, 1997.

Pickins' from Paw-paw's Patch (audiocassette), self-published, 1993. Frequently requested personal and family stories.

Taste the New Wine (audiocassette), self-published, 1993. Stories based on New and Old Testament texts and teachings.

Source

Christoffersen, John, "In the Telling: Storytellers Use Tales to Break Down Barriers, Teach," *The* [Stamford, Connecticut] *Advocate*, April 26, 1997, A1, A7.

Eftimades, Maria, "The Story of Paw-paw," *The* [Stamford, Connecticut] *Advocate*, June 6, 1988.

Lee, Bernadette, "Once Upon a Time: Tales Woven by Teller Enchant Students," Abilene Christian University *Optimist*, September 22, 1993.

FRANKIE AND DOUG QUIMBY

Address   2428 Cleburne Street
Brunswick, Georgia 31520
phone 912-265-9545
fax 912-264-5368
website www.gacoast.com/navigator/
quimbys.html

Focus: work and game songs and chants; call-and-response participation songs; slave plaints and spirituals; hymns; jump songs; Sea Island lore.

Audience: all ages.

Style: traditional Gullah minstrelsy, including hamboning.

Instruments/Props: Nigerian dashikis; tambourine and woodblocks.

The Quimbys, Frankie and Doug, are a Southern coastal phenomenon—a source of genuine West African tradition and dialect that is more than a museum piece. Still thrumming with life, passion, and humor, the Quimbys' art combines body rhythms, shouting, call and response, oral history, and folk narrative with music, rhyme, and the jingle of the tambourine. Their *a cappella* renderings of such ebullient slave game songs as "Miss Frog," "Sally Walker," "Hambone," "Raggy Levy," "Old Bill Rolling Pin," and the slave chantey "Peh Me Ma Munie Doun [Pay Me My Money Down]" make them a favorite at gatherings, where they perform the songs, hymns, shouts, games, coded slave messages, and dances that entertained slave culture in the American South centuries ago.

Born into an Americanized West African tradition, Frankie Sullivan Quimby absorbed the Atlantic Coast atmosphere of St. Simons Island, Georgia, and its sassy slave frolics. A scion of the Foulah Tribe in Kianah on the Niger River, she traces her ancestry beyond slavery to African roots. Doug, also a survivor of servitude and hardship, is the son of cotton and rice sharecroppers of Beaconton near Albany, Georgia. He began singing "My Mother's Dead and Gone" and other gospel songs for his overseer's mother, who paid him a quarter or rewarded him with biscuits and syrup. He was discovered for the Georgia Sea Island Singers by founder Bessie Jones and collaborated with composer Walter Robinson, author of the folk opera, *Look What a Wonder Jesus Has Done.*

Both Frankie and Doug are the last of an isolated black population who speak Gullah dialect and share a common musical heritage, which they began performing at prisons, rest homes, colleges, churches, and museums in 1984. Their presentations, which include "Down by the Riverside," "All God's Children Got Shoes," "Amen," and "Wade in the Water," serve an educative purpose by preserving African-American history. Presentations include "The Ibo Landing Story" and Doug's singing of "Freedom, Freedom Over Me" in honor of eighteen Ibo tribesmen who chose death over capture by slavers. For children, the duo sings such participation songs as "Raggy Levy," and "Little Sally Walker" and performs "Shoo Turkey" and "Knock Jim Crow," both nineteenth-century minstrel stage acts. The Quimbys have been most successful with adult audiences by leading "Amazing Grace," John Newton's slave-era hymn that aroused a French audience during the duo's 1997 European tour.

The Quimbys have told at the National Storytelling Conference, Bay Area Storytelling Festival, Smithsonian Institution's Sesquicentennial, Mariposa Folk Festival, National Association for Music Therapy, Hunter Museum, Gamble Rogers Storytelling Festival, Harvard University, Hudson River Revival Festival, Hollywood Bowl, Winter Games in Lillehammer, Norway, Olympic Games in Mexico and Atlanta, Artists on the Green, the White House, Carnegie Hall, Music Education Association, Garrison Keillor's *Prairie Home Companion* radio show, and numerous times at the National Black Storytelling Festival and National Storytelling Festival. A 1997 tour took them to Greece, Spain, Germany, and France. They have been selected as represen-

tatives of Georgia and the United States to perform in Sierra Leone and at the Statue of Liberty Centennial, Philadelphia Folk Festival, and the International Children's Festival in Vancouver, Canada, and were keynote speakers at the 1997 National Storytelling Conference. Billed as the Georgia Sea Island Singers, they present "Revelations of African-American Culture," a lively performance of stories and songs with tambourine accompaniment, featuring tales of slave abuse, coded messages in song, and warnings to slaves in flight.

Bibliography

"The Ibo Landing Story," in *Talk That Talk*, Simon & Schuster, 1989.

Awards

1988 National Black Storytelling Festival's Zora Neale Hurston Award.

Source

Barnes, Marian E., "The Georgia Sea Island Singers: Frankie and Doug Quimby," *Talk That Talk*. New York: Simon & Schuster, 1989.

"A Brief Look at This Year's Storytellers," Jonesborough, Tennessee *Herald & Tribune*, September 30, 1992, 4C–8C.

"Georgia Sea Island Singers Deliver Message of Dignity," Jacksonville *Times-Union*, March 3, 1996.

Gewertz, Daniel, "Black History Alive in Singers Act," *Boston Herald*, April 12, 1991, S22.

Grogan, David, "Frankie and Doug Quimby Sing Songs of Slavery to Keep Alive the Lore of Their Forebears," *People*, October 12, 1987.

Hanson, Trudy Lewis, "United in Story and Song: The Power of Music in Storytelling," *Storytelling Magazine*, May 1997, 14–15.

Morgan, Bruce, "In Georgia: Through the Gospel Grapevine," *Time*, September 12, 1988, 12–13.

Ogunleye, Tolagbe, "Afro-American Folklore," *Journal of Black Studies*, March 1997, 435–456.

Young, Dianne, "They Sing of the South," *Southern Living*, November 1988, 168–170.

CONNIE REGAN-BLAKE

Address Storyteller
P. O. Box 2898
Asheville, North Carolina 28802
phone 704-258-1113
fax 704-253-0100

Focus: Appalachian mountain stories; grandfather tales; ghost stories; Western European traditional stories; literary, true life, and original stories.

Audience: all ages.

Style: concerts meshing intense, dynamic, thought-provoking, funny, and tender stories; has performed solo as well as in tandem with Barbara Freeman and with the Kandinsky Trio, a piano chamber group.

Instruments/Props: sound makers, ocarina, and autoharp.

One of America's most celebrated storytellers and a co-founder of the National Storytelling Association, Connie Regan-Blake maintains the sacred trust of narrative, a portal to wellness and wholeness. She has perpetuated and preserved the Southern legacy of the spoken word in performances across the United States and in twelve foreign countries in Europe and Asia. Born January 20, 1947, in Mobile, Alabama, she credits her father, John Regan, as her first mentor. His delight in language and ease with words, along with a scattering of Irish folktales, set her on the path to a lifetime of listening and telling. She was a good listener. After she graduated from Loyola University of the South with a degree in political science and math, she traveled in Europe and developed an interest in people from other cultures. She dreamed of traveling around the world, especially to Australia. On her return to the states, she worked as a waitress in Atlanta to earn money for more travels. In 1971, her cousin Barbara Freeman suggested that she investigate an opening for storyteller at the Chattanooga Public Library, a new position as storytelling ambassador that set the direction of her lifetime career. As a part of her involvement in the National Orga-

nization of Women, she visited organizations to talk about women's rights and equality for all, a theme that recurs in her stories.

After hearing of the first storytelling gathering in Jonesborough, Tennessee, Regan-Blake wrote to Jimmy Neil Smith and told a story there. Already a seasoned performer, she read a tattered manuscript of a ghost tale, "Two White Horses," which influenced her material for adults. The power of the story fueled her desire to tell to adults and children. She was involved at folk music festivals before she was named a featured teller at the second National Storytelling Festival. She served on the founding board of directors and joined Smith in outlining the annual festival, which she directed for ten years. In 1975, she and first cousin Barbara Freeman quit their library jobs to form The Folktellers and began making their living as freelance tellers in the days preceding the storytelling renaissance. As pathfinders in a new venue of folk culture, they pooled $2,000 in start-up money and christened their yellow Datsun truck and camper "D'Put." On alternate nights, they billed themselves as "Connie and Barbara"

and "Barbara and Connie." A flood at the Fox Hollow Folk Festival in Petersburg, New York, forced them to move D'Put to the only available space — in the performer's area, where they drew others to their campfire by telling stories. From a parking lot experience in Hartford, Connecticut, they improvised a Ping-Pong style of tandem telling for performances of "Three Billy Goats Gruff" and Maurice Sendak's *Where the Wild Things Are*, a story requested by a child.

A ransacking of D'Put robbed the duo of clothes, money, keepsakes, and tapes, leaving them entirely dependent on their art. The event assured them that their popular act was a functional career that brought requests for storytelling performances and offers to conduct workshops and credit courses. They have appeared with UNICEF, Rocky Mountain Healing Arts Festival, National Folk Festival in Washington, D.C., military bases in Okinawa, Philippines, Korea, and Japan, Lincoln Center, the World's Fair, Old Faithful in Yellowstone National Park, Belle Cher Celebration, Washington, D.C. Ethical Society, and the San Diego Folk Festival. The duo earned raves on main stage at festivals in Chicago, Vancouver, Winnipeg, Ithaca, Michigan, Knoxville, Alaska, Long Island, St. Louis, Charlotte, Philadelphia, Maine, Connecticut, Lincoln, England, and Monterey. With friend Jimmy Neil-Smith, Regan-Blake helped organize the National Association for the Preservation and Perpetuation of Storytelling and served for a decade as director and shaper of annual festivals. Along the way, The Folktellers nurtured new talent and earned from Ed Stivender perpetual thanks for being missionaries of storytelling and his personal fairy godmothers. For their two-act play, *Mountain Sweet Talk*, they joined writer-storyteller and director John Basinger and his daughter Savannah Basinger to create two strong mountain characters, Sarah and Jenny Rose, both outgrowths of family stories. Playing at the Folk Art Center near Asheville, the show ran from 1986 to 1994 and earned strong support from reviewers for *Southern Living, Good Housekeeping,* and *Good Morning America.*

Regan-Blake has been lauded on *Good Morning America,* Canadian National Radio, and

National Public Radio's *All Things Considered* and in cover stories in *School Library Journal* and *New Age Magazine*. Appearances at North Carolina's *Mountain Dance & Folk Festival,* Charleston's *Piccolo Spoleto*, National Folklife Festival at the Smithsonian Institution, Wolf Trap, National Council of Teachers of English, and festivals in Chicago, Philadelphia, Edmonton, New Zealand, and Vancouver have supplied audiences with her charm and wit. On home ground, she directs "Tell It in the Mountains," an annual storytelling festival held in North Carolina. A recent venture — the performance of "Tales of Appalachia: Cantankerous Blacksmith" with the Kandinsky Trio — is a collaboration of platform narration with classical chamber selections and an original composition by Grammy-winner Mike Reid. The pairing of the arts was well received at Penn State, Appalachian State University, Columbia University, Interlochen Michigan, and the universities of Maryland, North Carolina, and Pittsburgh, and has introduced storytelling to a new audience.

Bibliography

"No News," in *Best-Loved Stories Told at the National Storytelling Festival*, August House, 1991.

"No News," in *Homespun: Tales from America's Favorite Storytellers*, Crown, 1988.

"Old Drye Frye," in *Homespun: Tales from America's Favorite Storytellers*, Crown, 1988.

"Santa Visits the Moes," in *Ready-to-Tell Tales*, August House, 1994.

Stories for the Telling (bibliography), self-published, 1977.

"The Two Old Women's Bet," *Laughter in Appalachia*, August House, 1987.

"Two White Horses," in *Homespun: Tales from America's Favorite Storytellers*, Crown, 1988.

Videography

"No News," in *American Storytelling Series, Vol. 5*, H. W. Wilson, 1987.

Pennies, Pets & Peanut Butter: Stories for Children, The Folktellers, 1994. Contains "The Judge," "A Penny a Look," "Peanut Butter," "Crictor," "The Jazzy Three Bears," and "I Know an Old Lady"; for children; public performance rights.

Storytelling: Tales and Techniques, The Folktellers, 1994. Idea-packed workshop video for teachers, librarians, and parents; public performance rights.

Audiography

The Cantankerous Blacksmith (CD), De Note Records, projected 1998. Performed with the Kandinsky Trio.

Chillers (audiocassette), Mama T Artists, 1983. Scary stories blended with humor for teenagers through adults.

Christmas at the Homeplace (audiocassette), Mama T Artists, 1992. Old-time stories and songs for the holiday.

"The Foolish Bet," in *Homespun Tales* (audiocassette), National Association for the Preservation and Perpetuation of Storytelling, 1986.

"The Ghoul," in *Graveyard Tales* (audiocassette), National Association for the Preservation and Perpetuation of Storytelling, 1989.

Mountain Sweet Talk (two audiocassettes), Mama T Artists, 1988.

Stories for the Road (audiocassette), Mama T Artists, 1992. Family stories for car travel and rainy afternoons, including "Peanut Butter," "The Sneakout Mountain Diary," "Yellow Ribbon," "Jazzy Three Bears," "The Dancing Man," and "Come Again in the Spring"; for all ages.

Tales to Grow On (audiocassette), Mama T Artists, 1983. Mountain tales and participation stories, including "Wicked John and the Devil"; for kindergarten through sixth grade.

White Horses and Whippoorwills (audiocassette), Mama T Artists 1983. Powerful and moving mountain tales with lots of laughs, including "The Three Bears" and "Two White Horses"; for fifth grade through adult.

Awards

1996 National Storytelling Association Circle of Excellence.

1994 Parents' Choice Silver Honor Award for *Pennies, Pets & Peanut Butter: Stories for Children*.

1994 *Storytelling World* Award for *Pennies, Pets & Peanut Butter: Stories for Children*.

1993 American Library Association Notable Record Award for *Tales to Grow On*.

1992 American Library Association Notable Record Award for *Stories for the Road*.

1992 Parents' Choice Award for *Christmas at the Homeplace*.

1985 Mountain Dance and Folk Festival Performer of the Year.

1983 American Library Association Notable Record Award for *Chillers*.

Source

Brown, Tony, "Two Tell Tall Tales: Storytelling Cousins Blend Differing Perspective of Their Appalachian Heritage As They Spread Joy from Asheville to Asia," *Charlotte Observer*, March 1, 1989, 1D.

"Catching Up with Connie Regan-Blake," *Journal of Tar Heel Tellers*, December 1995, 1, 7.

"Chamber Trio and Teller Create New Genre," *Storytelling*, January 1997, 4–5.

DuBois, Lisa A., "Kandinsky Trio Warms Chilly Metro Night with Folk Music Penned by Ex-Grid Great," *Nashville Banner*, February 5, 1996.

Gelfand, Janelle, "Reid's 'Appalachia' Fresh Take on Old Yarn," *Cincinnati Enquirer*, March 19, 1996.

Gibbons, Cathy, "The Folktellers," *Laugh Makers Variety Arts Magazine*, Vol. 12, 1994, 272–274.

Greenwood, Jean, "Story to Music," *Arts and Entertainment*, March 21–27, 1997.

Hill, Jennifer, "Storytellers Recall Festival's First Years in Jonesborough," Jonesborough, Tennessee *Herald and Tribune*, September 30, 1992, 2C, 4C.

"In Touch," *Second Story Review*, June 1996.

"The Kandinsky Trio and Connie Regan-Blake," http://www.martechsys. com/paf/mikereid.htm, May 28, 1997.

LaPrise, Ann West, "Review," *School Library Journal*, July 1993.

Mendell, Phyllis Levy, "1995 Award-Winning Films and Videos: Language Arts," *School Library Journal*, April 1996, 54.

Mitnick, Fritz, "Audiovisual Review: Recordings," *School Library Journal*, July 1993, 52.

Mooney, Bill, and David Holt. *The Storyteller's Guide*. Little Rock, Ark.: August House, 1996.

Oxendine, Jill, "An Interview with Connie Regan-Blake," *National Storytelling Journal*, Winter 1986, 4–7.

"Review," *Booklist*, March 15, 1993.

"Review," *National Storytelling Journal*, Winter 1987.

Sanborn, LaVonne, "Review," *School Library Journal*, April 1995.

Sellen, Betty-Carol. *What Else You Can Do with a College Degree*. Gaylord, 1980.

Stein, Rachel, "Review," *The Arts Journal*, October 1985.

Stewart, Barbara Home, "The Folktellers: Scheherazades in Denim," *School Library Journal*, November 1978, 17–21.

_____, "The Mountain Sweet Sound of Success: Folktellers '89," *School Library Journal*, January 1989, 17.

Thomas, Dr. James L., Carol Lawrence, and Jennabeth Hutcherson. *Storytelling for Teachers and Media Specialists*. T. S. Denison & Co., 1980.

Timeless Voices: Images of the National Storytelling Festival. Jonesborough, Tenn.: National Storytelling Press, 1997.

Weyler, Rex, "On the Road with the Folktellers," *New Age*, July 1980, 26–33, 62–63.

White, Barb, "Review of 'Storytelling: Tales & Techniques,'" *School Library Journal*, April 1995.

See also John Basinger; Barbara Freeman.

ROBERT REISER
[ry'•suhr]

Address   15 Oak Avenue
Tarrytown, New York 10591
phone 914-422-1156
email Breiser@aol.com

Focus: legends from around the world; humorous and sad tales; healing and inspiring stories; nature lore about birds, plants, and humans; traditional and original work.

Audience: all people, all ages.

Style: conversational and dramatic, with a dash of music.

Instruments/Props: Native American flute,

drums, and an assortment of rhythm and percussion instruments.

Bob Reiser swears that storytelling was one of the last professions he could have imagined himself entering. His family had plans for him to become a doctor, while he pictured himself as a world-class playwright. It was medicine's loss that he gave up on pre-med courses in college and opted for the humanities. Born in April 1941, in Brooklyn, New York, Reiser just missed being a baby boomer. He claims that it has been like that for most of his life — "My parents were outspoken radicals while the rest of the country tiptoed through the conservative 1950s; I grew up Jewish while everyone on TV celebrated Christmas. I was too young to be a beatnik and too old to be a hippie." He says that his perch on the edge of things helped give him perspective and helped him develop a talent for writing and storytelling.

After graduating from the University of Chicago with a B.A. in English literature and completing an M.A. in theater from the New York University Drama School, he worked at Chicago's Second City Improvisational group, wrote off–Broadway theater, and composed comedy sketches for some now nearly forgotten television shows. He toured with his own comedy troupe, the Portable Radio Circus, until 1980, when he settled into full-time writing, including a collaboration on two books with folksinger and raconteur Pete Seeger.

The turn to storytelling came as a result of an encounter in Taos Pueblo, New Mexico. While wandering around the square, he noticed a hand-made "dream catcher" almost ten feet in diameter standing in front of a shop. Curious, he struck up a conversation with the proprietor and asked about the little seated clay figures he had seen all over New Mexico. "You mean storytellers?" asked the woman. She told Reiser about the Pueblo tradition where each winter the elders are welcomed into homes with their stories. "Each day they sit with the family, close their eyes and dream the stories of long ago— stories of how we came to be, stories of the sky and earth and the spirits and the animals. The children grow quiet and listen; even the adults who have heard the stories listen." Reiser was so moved

that he told his wife, "When I grow old, I want to be a storyteller!" His wife replied, "Why wait until you are old?"

Reiser began collecting stories from different cultures — Native American, South American, Australian Aboriginal, Tibetan, and Jewish — and adding his own original tales. By 1994 he had begun to perform professionally. Along the way, he worked with mentors Nancy Mellon, Joseph Bruchac, and Jackson Gillman, and found musical inspiration from flute maker Hawk Littlejohn and musician Carlos Nakai. Reiser's programs for schools, libraries, parents, and children focus on nature, music, and celebration of life. They include theme titles like *This Little Light of Mine, Flute Song,* and *Listen to the Trees.* For adult and high school events, and for conferences and workshops, he tells tales that help people recapture the "magical connection they once felt between themselves and all of the beings of this earth." His *Healing Story Circles* use the power of stories to transform and heal.

Bibliography

Carry It On (co-author Pete Seeger), Simon & Schuster, 1984. Songs and stories of working people.

David's Got His Drum (co-author David Panama Francis), Cobblehill Press, 1998. For children 4–7

Everybody Says Freedom (co-author Pete Seeger), W. W. Norton, 1990. Songs and stories of the Civil Rights movement, with an introduction by Jesse Jackson.

PJ (co-author Andrea Balis), Dell, 1983. Young adult novel.

Audiography

Carry It On (audiocassette), Rounder Records, 1987. Twenty stories and songs performed by artists including Holly Near and Pete Seeger.

Songs and Stories of Working People (audiocassette), Flying Fish, 1989. More stories and songs; performed with composer and musician Earl Robinson.

Awards

1991 Humanitas Award for *Everybody Says Freedom*.

J. J. RENEAUX
[rih•noh']

Address   P. O. Box 7782
Athens, Georgia 30604

phone and fax 706-549-7212
email jjreneaux@athensnet.com
website www.redhouse.com/jjreneaux/

Focus: traditional and contemporary multicultural folklore and music from the American South with emphasis on Deep South, Cajun, and Choctaw cultures; humor, ghost lore, trickster stories; animal folktales; Native American myths; wry commentary on Southern "characters" and "redneck" culture; adult satire; original contemporary music drawn from traditional Southern styles, including Cajun, country, jazz, gospel, and blues.

Audience: adapts performances to all ages.

Style: blends native Southern music and storytelling; songs support storytelling, create mood, and provide transition; music and vocals also produce sound effects.

Instruments/Props: guitar and vocals.

A storytelling author and musician, J. J. Reneaux weaves Cajun folklore and superstition into such signature tellings as "Knock, Knock, Who's There?," a tale of greed rewarded by terror and death. A native of southern Louisiana with influence from a childhood residence in Texas, she draws on childhood memories and true-life events in her telling of folktales. One of Reneaux's most successful tales pits M'su Cocodrie, the alligator, against Bullet, the family dog, a pair who parallel the efforts of a neighborhood child to outwit a schoolyard bully. Along with platform narration, Reneaux is an award-winning singer in English and Cajun-French. A former ambassador for the United States Information Service, she has performed internationally, bringing her characteristic mélange of superstition, customs, lore, and music of the multicultural South to diverse audiences, including concerts for the 1996 Olympics and the Disney Institute, as well as extensive touring in Europe as a performer and educator. A third-generation singer and songwriter, Reneaux is a recording artist on the Swiss Brambus label. Her first CD release, *Cajun, Country and Blue*, in 1996 received critical acclaim in Europe. Her second CD, *Life Line*, is scheduled for release in early 1997.

Bibliography

Cajun Fairytales, August House, 1996. Contains "The Magic Gifts," "Jean Malin and the Bull-Man," "King Peacock," "Marie Jolie," and "Catafo."

Cajun Folktales, August House, 1992. Twenty-seven stories featuring Cajun humor, animal folktales, fairytales, and ghost stories, including "'Po Boy and the $10,000 Egg," "The Killer Mosquitoes," "St. Antoine," "Roclore and His Bag of Tricks," "Why Grease Lives in the Kitchen," "Pierre and the Angel of Death," "An Honest Man," and "M'su Carencro and Manguer."

"Gold Discovered at Bubba's Bait, Beer and Barbeque," http://www.redhouse.com/jjreneaux/story. An essay.

Haunted Bayou and Other Cajun Ghost Stories, August House, 1994. A ghost lore collection of 51 ghost stories about Z'Onion Joe, Rufus, and the Werewolf Bridegroom.

"Knock, Knock, Who's There?" in *More Best-Loved Stories Told at the National Storytelling Festival*, August House, 1992.

"Kudzu: Stealth Weapon of the South," http://www.redhouse.com/jjreneaux/story.

"The Magic Gifts," http://www.redhouse.com/jjreneaux/story.

"Redneckonicks Spoken Here," http://www.redhouse.com/jjreneaux/story.

"The Toilets of Madison County" http://www.redhouse.com/jjreneaux/story.

Why Alligator Hates Dog (illustrator Donnie Lee Green), August House, 1995. An animal folktale from Cajun Louisiana tradition; for young children.

Audiography

Cajun, Country and Blue (CD), Brambus. A musical potpourri of twelve original songs, featuring "Raise Your Window High," "Every Now and Then," and original material in English and French.

Cajun Fairytales (audiocassette), August House, 1996. Five Cajun tales enhanced by fiddle music; includes "The Magic Gifts," "Jean Malin and the Bull-Man," "King Peacock," "Marie Jolie," and "Catafo."

Cajun Folktales (audiocassette), August House, 1995. Eight tales of foibles, folly, and fancy, including "'Po Boy and the $10,000 Egg," "The Killer Mosquitoes," "St. Antoine," "Roclore and His Bag of Tricks," "Why Grease Lives in the Kitchen," "Pierre and the Angel of Death," "An Honest Man," and "M'su Carencro and Manguer."

Cajun Ghost Stories (audiocassette), August House, 1992. Contains "The Half-Man," "The Ghost of Jean Lafitte," "Superstition or Caution?" "Rapadeen," "Knock, Knock, Who's There," stories about pirate ghosts, bayou spirits, and Fifolet, the evil swamp gas.

LifeLine (CD), projected for 1998. Contemporary adult alternative country-blues originals and covers.

"Marie Jolie," in *Best Loved Stories Told at the National Storytelling Festival, Vol. 2* (audiocassette), August House, 1992.

Saints and Sinners (audiocassette), self-published. Folk tradition of the Creole and Cajun; for all ages.

Wake, Snake! (audiocassette), self-published, 1997. Original and traditional stories and songs of the South, including "Why Alligator Hates Dog," "Ol'John the Rabbit," "Miss Mary Mac," "Gator Trouble," "The Possum Song," "How Animals Saved the People," "What Was That," "Summer in the South Stories," "Lapin's Sweet Tooth," "Lost Indian," "Mess of Trouble," "Why Possum Has a Bare Tail," and the title story; for young children.

"Wish Sandwiches," on *Rainbow Tales* (CD), Rounder Records, 1997.

Awards

1996 American Folklore Society's Aesop Accolade for *Why Alligator Hates Dog*.

1996 *AudioFile* Magazine Earphones Award for *Cajun Fairytales*.

1995 Anne Izard Storyteller's Choice Award for *Cajun Folktales*.

1994 Public Library Association Lifelong Learning's Best New Book for New Readers for *Haunted Bayou and Other Cajun Tales*.

1992 Parents' Choice Award for *Cajun Ghost Stories*.

Source

"A Brief Look at This Year's Storytellers," Jonesborough, Tennessee *Herald & Tribune*, September 30, 1992, 4C–8C.

Osborne, Linda, "The Wisdom of Nations," *World & I*, May 1993.

"Review," *AudioFile*, June 1996.

"Review," *Invisible Ink*, Fall/Winter 1994.

"Review," *Parent Review Council*, Spring 1995.

Richardson, Peggy Hemlich, "The Texas Storytelling Festival, 1997," http://members.aol.com/storypage/news/97texas.htm.

Woodard, Josef, "Tales — and Tunes — From the Swamp," *Los Angeles Times*, February 6, 1997, 3.

GAYLE ROSS

Address P. O. Box 761
            Fredericksburg, Texas 78624
      phone 210-997-3661

Focus: native American lore and tribal traditions; creation myths and nature lore; Texas ghost stories; Jack tales; call and response songs.

Audience: general.

Style: traditional stories and some songs and Cherokee melodies as well as Zuñi and Hopi music to reinforce stories.

A storytelling advocate and recipient of storytelling's highest award, Gayle Ross believes that human beings developed speech because of their urge to communicate and share stories. She concludes that the truly attuned raconteur locates stories by staying alert to tidbits of history, tradition, and lore that surface in everyday affairs. Her description of a good story features universal human emotions that transcend race, geography, and cultural boundaries. She trusts the material to guide her over unfamiliar ground and puts herself second to the story itself. For her warmth, humility, and intrinsic humanism, she has become a model of platform success and one of the storytelling industry's key spokespersons.

Ross is an opinionated teller with strong loyalties to her people and past. She dislikes hearing Anglo tellers profit from inferior tellings of native American stories and considers their performances an exploitation of sacred lore. A proud native American, she shares the genealogy of Chief John Ross, who led the Cherokee during their forced removal from the Appalachian Mountains to Oklahoma over a shameful path known as the Trail of Tears and who established the Tennessee River trading post that became Chattanooga. A native Texan, Ross got her start almost from birth by absorbing native American heritage through her grandmother, a local storyteller. Under the influence of genealogy and family lore, Ross began telling at an early age out of joy in communicating stories. Her first job in radio and television lacked the involvement she got from her career in storytelling, which was influenced by Elizabeth Ellis, a children's librarian and veteran performer who told stories at the Dallas Public Library. A professional platform teller since 1979, Ross joined Ellis in a traveling duo, performing as the Twelve Moons Storytellers, before going solo in 1982. She has published stories in *Family Reading* and *Mother Earth News*. Her workshop topics suit the needs of teachers, librarians, child-care professionals, parents, and beginning storytellers and cover "Stimulating the Storyteller in Everyone" and "Multiculturalism and Storytelling — One Native American Point of View."

A strong conservationist, Ross is pleased to have a job that is satisfying and productive rather than destructive to the earth. In an interview she said, "There's a difference between a career and a life's work for me. This is something that encompasses everything that I do best. It also satisfies all the needs that I have to make a contribution." (McGann 1996, 1) Another aspect of her career is the rescue of a native culture that was once threatened by governmental extermination, alcoholism, and missionaries who shamed native Americans into abandoning their lore. She concludes, "We have to stand again as Indian people and for many, many tribes that means recovering a lot of things that were lost" (McGann, 1996, 1).

Ross values traditional creation myths and nature lore, which she has published in collaboration with Abenaki narrator Joseph Bruchac, and tells Chippewa Cree stories derived from her adopted brother, Ron Evans, who is also a teller. She was featured teller and workshop leader at Mansfield University's Storytelling '96 and the only American teller at the First International Storytelling Festival in Copenhagen, Denmark. For *500 Nations*, an epic stage performance based on a CBS-TV miniseries, she was featured with Douglas Spotted Eagle, Chief Hawk Pope, Peter Buffett, and the New World Ensemble. She collaborated with John Spelman and Charlotte Blake-Alston for *American Storyfest* and shared heritage stories at the home of Vice President Al Gore and Tipper Gore, who hosted "Taste of Tennessee." College and university lectures have taken Ross to Southern Methodist University, Texas A & M, Boston College, Frostburg State College, Texas Tech, and the universities of Texas, Arkansas, and Wisconsin. She has appeared at the Philadelphia Folk Festival, Fall Festival of Tales, Southbank Theatre in London, Summer Stars Concert Series, Beyond the Borders Festival, A Celebration of Books, Kerrville Folk Festival, Festival of the Eagle, A Taste of Tennessee, Cultural Olympiad in Atlanta, Georgia, and the National Storytelling Festival, and in San Francisco in conjunction with the 1997 American Library Association conference.

Bibliography

"The Bird That Was Ashamed of Its Feet," in *Best Stories from Texas Storytelling Festival*, August House, 1995.

Dat-so-la-lee, Artisan, Modern Curriculum Press, 1995.

"Daughter of the Sun," in *More Best-Loved Stories Told at the National Storytelling Festival*, August House, 1992.

The Girl Who Married the Moon (co-author Joseph Bruchac), Bridgewater Books, 1995.

How Rabbit Tricked Otter and Other Cherokee Trickster Stories (illustrator Murv Jacob; foreword by Chief Wilma Mankiller), HaperCollins, 1994. Features stories from the time that people shared a common language, including "Flint Visits Rabbit," "Why Possum's Tail Is Bare," "Rabbit Escapes from the Wolves," "How Deer Won His Antlers," "Why Deer's Teeth Are Blunt," "Rabbit Helps Wildcat Hunt Turkeys," "Rabbit Goes Duck Hunting," "Rabbit and the Tar Wolf," "Bear Dines with Rabbit," "Rabbit Steals from Fox," "Rabbit Sends Wolf to the Sunset," "Rabbit Dances with the People," and the title story.

How Turtle's Back Was Cracked: A Traditional Cherokee Tale (illustrator Murv Jacob), Dial, 1995. A beast fable about a turtle's run-in with a pack of angry wolves.

The Legend of Windigo: A Tale from Native North America (illustrator Murv Jacob), Viking, 1996. A blend of humor and horror in the story of a stone monster.

"Rabbit and Possum Hunt for a Wife," in *Ready-to-Tell Tales*, August House, 1994.

The Story of the Milky Way: A Cherokee Tale (co-author Joseph Bruchac, illustrator Virginia Stroud), Dial, 1995. Explains the great path of stars.

"Strawberries," in *Homespun: Tales from America's Favorite Storytellers*, Crown 1988.

Videography

"Mosquitoes," in *American Storytelling Series, Vol. 1*, H. W. Wilson, 1987.

Audiography

How Rabbit Tricked Otter (audiocassette), Harper Children's Audio, 1994. A collection of traditional Cherokee stories recorded with flute. Music by Cherokee musician Eddie Bushyhead.

"Obedient Jack" (co-producer Elizabeth Ellis), in *Tales of Wit and Humor* (audiocassette), National Association for the Preservation and Perpetuation of Storytelling, 1992.

"The Skeleton Woman," in *Graveyard Tales* (audiocassette), National Association for the Preservation and Perpetuation of Storytelling, 1989.

"Strawberries" on *Rainbow Tales* (CD), Rounder Records, 1997.

To This Day: Native American Stories (audiocassette), self-published. A collection of creation, trickster, and monster tales recorded at a fireside gathering.

Awards

1997 National Storytelling Association Circle of Excellence.

1996 American Folklore Society Aesop Accolade for *The Story of the Milky Way* and *How Turtle's Back Was Cracked.*

1996 Anne Izard Storytellers' Choice Book Award for *How Rabbit Tricked Otter and Other Cherokee Trickster Stories.*

1995 National Association of Social Studies Teachers Award for contribution to multicultural literature for *The Girl Who Married the Moon.*

1995 Bank Street Child Study Children's Book Committee Children's Book of the Year for *How Turtle's Back Was Cracked.*

1995 Skipping Stones Honor Book for *The Girl Who Married the Moon.*

1994 Benjamin Franklin Award for *How Rabbit Tricked Otter and Other Cherokee Trickster Stories.*

1994 Oklahoma State Association of School Librarians Sequoyah Master List for *How Rabbit Tricked Otter and Other Cherokee Trickster Stories.*

1989 Tejas Storytelling Association's John Henry Faulk Award.

Source

"A Brief Look at This Year's Storytellers," Jonesborough, Tennessee *Herald & Tribune*, September 30, 1992, 4C–8C.

Carey, Kim, "McConnell Receives NSA's Lifetime Achievement Award," *Tale Trader*, August 1997, 1, 4.

"Featured Storytellers," Jonesborough, Tennessee *Herald & Tribune*, September 29, 1993, 9C–10C.

"Five Storytellers Receive Honors," *Storytelling Magazine*, May 1997, 41.

"Forecasts: Children's Books," *Publishers Weekly*, October 2, 1995, 74.

Green, Patricia Dooley, "Book Review: Preschool and Primary," *School Library Journal*, April 1995, 128.

Henderson, Van, "Gayle Ross Shares Cherokee Story in Folk Fest," *Chattanooga News-Free Press*, October 10, 1993, C7.

Hutt, Karen, "Books for Youth — Books for the Young — Nonfiction," *Booklist*, September 1, 1995, 79.

Jasper, Suzanne, "The Call of the Story," *Parabola*, Spring 1994, 89–92.

Knoth, Maeve Visser, "Booklist," *Horn Book*, March/April 1995, 208.

McGann, Chris, "An Interview with Gayle Ross, Native American Storyteller," http://www.mnstid.edu/depts/storytel/page6.htm, 1996.

Mooney, Bill, and David Holt. *The Storyteller's Guide.* Little Rock, Ark.: August House, 1996.

Moore, Susan M., "Preschool and Primary Grades: Nonfiction," *School Library Journal*, November 1996, 100–101.

Morgan, Karen, "Mosquito Lore," *Booklist*, September 15, 1996, 235.

Morrison, Philip, and Phyllis Morrison, "The Scientific American Young Readers Book Awards," *Scientific American*, December 1995, 108.

"'96 Izard Awards Named," *Tale Trader*, November 1996, 1.

Oothoudt, Sharon E. Johnson, "Books on Native-American History," *Book Report*, Mar/April 1996, 26–29.

Perkins, Linda, "Caught Between," *Wilson Library Bulletin*, March 1995, 105–106.

Stover, Lois, "Young Adult Literature," *English Journal*, January 1996, 87.

LYNN RUBRIGHT

Address 719 Craigwoods Drive
St. Louis, Missouri 63122
home phone 314-966-2382
work phone 314-968-7057
email LYNNTELLS@AOL.com

Focus: St. Louis and American history; Mississippi River lore; Ozark tales; Anansi myths; traditional British folktales; Norse mythology; American Indian lore; family folklore.

Audience: general.

Style: one-woman shows; kinetic tellings enhanced with vocalizations, animal noises, and gestures; collaboration with Ted Rubright, her husband.

Recalling hearing her grandmother Pickett tell "Jack and the Beanstalk," Lynn Rubright began relating the story out of exasperation in the 1970s, and her two boys stopped their squabbling to listen. Wrapped up in episodes of domestic narrative, in 1971, she continued teaching while completing an M.A.T. with emphasis on creative drama from Webster University. One of her first professional visits was to the Storytelling Festival in Jonesborough, Tennessee, where she became friends with tellers Jackie Torrence, Jay O'Callahan, Connie Regan-Blake, and Barbara Freeman and with Jimmy Neil Smith, founder of the National Association for the Preservation and Perpetuation of Storytelling. Over repeated visits to the annual gathering, she was featured as a teller and served on the board of the National Storytelling Association. For three decades, she has flourished in a host of appearances: National Folklore Conference in Budapest, Hungary, as well as keynote addresses, inspirational talks, concerts, teacher workshops, health-care facilities, school assemblies and classrooms, and universities.

Skilled in writing and performance, Rubright has taught by example. Her book *Beyond the Beanstalk* contains thirty years of philosophical and anecdotal material about using storytelling in the K–6 curriculum to motivate students to develop oral, writing, and reading skills across the curricula. A highly praised compendium of advice on storytelling in the classroom, the book advocates collaborative learning through oral expression and creative drama. Rubright celebrates the inspirational methods by which her colleagues have used stories in interdisciplinary thematic application. In an interview, she comments, "All of this helps children realize that they have a past, and they may be part of a rich heritage... It also helps them connect with older people and to visualize what the past was like for others" (Corrigan, 1997, 11).

Rubright's interest in oral tradition powered two influential venues for platform art: the award-winning Metro Theater Circus, a children's company, and the St. Louis Storytelling Festival, co-founded by Dr. Ron Turner. In 1979, she superintended Project TELL [Teaching English through Living Language] in the Kirkwood school district, a federally-funded literacy program founded on the amalgamation of storytelling with art, dance, and music. On her own, she performs "Mirrors: Reflections of St. Louis Past," a one-woman multimedia show based on Thomas M. Easterly's daguerreotypes, and "Missouri Bittersweet," a solo performance reflecting Missouri history, lore, and legend. In 1990, she researched and performed for the Missouri Historical Society the show "Oh, Freedom After While," a dramatic recitation based on the life of Reverend Owen Whitfield, an African-American sharecropper and labor leader. Whitfield led 1,300 sharecroppers down a highway in southeastern Missouri to protest unfair farm labor practices. St. Louis social activist and writer Fannie Cook aided the workers in finding housing after the protest. Presently, Rubright is co-producing a video documentary of the show for public television with writer Candace O'Connor and award-winning filmmaker Steve Ross.

Rubright's platform tellings have entranced the President of Iceland and her opera, "Little Red, the Folktale Hen — a Musical Circus," premiered at Northwestern University's Department of Theater and toured to 12,000 Chicago school children in 1990. The production features music composed by her sons, Ted and Daniel Rubright. In addition, she has presented seminars and workshops in Tennessee, Washington, Connecticut, Louisiana, Florida, Alaska, Kentucky, Illinois, Missouri, Kansas, Utah, Hungary, and Denmark. She has served Northwestern University's theater department and Drake University's education department as visiting professor. In 1971, she designed and implemented the course "Storytelling Across the Curriculum," now in its 26th consecutive year in the Masters of Teaching program at Webster University in St. Louis. Rubright began the course as an adjunct professor; since 1990, she has worked full time in the university's school of education. In addition to her work as an associate professor, she directs a summer institute on storytelling for the University of Missouri and serves as visiting professor for Northwestern University's department of drama.

Bibliography

Beyond the Beanstalk: Interdisciplinary Learning Through Storytelling, Heinemann, 1996. Reflects thirty years of Rubright's use of storytelling and the expressive arts across the curriculum.

"In the Land of Fire and Ice," *National Storytelling Journal*, Spring/Summer 1988, 22–26.

Little Red, the Folktale Hen, a Musical Circus (co-author Ted Rubright), Rodgers and Hammerstein, 1991.

"Mike Fink: Last of the Great Mississippi Keelboatmen," *National Storytelling Journal*, Fall 1986.

"The Seal Skin," in *Best Loved Stories Told at the Festival*, National Storytelling Press, 1996.

"Storytelling and 'Storybuilding' Promote Many Language Skills," *Missouri Schools*, December-January 1981, 31–32.

"Work Is Work" in *More Best-Loved Stories*, August House, 1992.

Videography

"Baked Potatoes," in *American Storytelling Series, Vol. 3*, H. W. Wilson, 1987.

Bally Sally Cato, Kaw Valley Films, 1989. Features an Ozark giant.

How Woodpeckers Came to Be, BARR Entertainment, 1989.

Rosie's Walk, Kaw Valley Films, 1989.

Six Wishes, BARR Entertainment, 1989.

Tell Me a Story (contributor), BARR Entertainment, 1986. Contains "How Woodpeckers Came to Be" and "Six Wishes."

Audiography

Mike Fink: Last of the Great Mississippi River Keelboatmen (audiocassette), self-published, 1988. Interdisciplinary teaching guide.

Rabbit's Tale and Other Native American Myths and Legends (audiocassette), self-published, 1989. Features "Bally Sally Cato," an Ozark folktale, and an interdisciplinary teaching guide.

Awards

1996 National Circle of Excellence Award for storytelling in education.

1996 Kemper Award for Excellence in Teaching nomination.

1994 Kemper Award for Excellence in Teaching nomination.

1991 Missouri Arts Council Creative Artist Grant.

1983 Webster University Distinguished Alumnus Award.

1978 St. Louis Young Audiences Award for "Bingham's Missouri."

1974 Winifred Ward Award for Best New Children's Theatre in America.

Source

Baker, Martha, "Old-Fashioned Way to Teach and Learn," St. Louis *Post-Dispatch*, February 9, 1997.

_____, "Storytelling as Learning," *St. Louis Times*, February 1997.

Breckenridge, D. P., "Storytelling Serves as a Teaching Tool," *Northeast Johnson County Star*, April 30, 1986.

Corrigan, Don, "Rubright Gets Animated, Takes Chances," *Webster Times*, April 18, 1997, 11, 13.

Harrison, Mary M., "Sparking Imagination and Kindling Learning Through Stories," *Education St. Louis*, January/February 1992.

Johnston, Laura, "Storyteller Enthralls Audiences," *Southeast Missourian*, August 20, 1995.

King, Louise, "1939 Sharecroppers' Plight Is the Focus of June 29-30 Performance," *St. Louis Post-Dispatch*, June 27, 1991.

Lybarger, Joan, "Children Become Part of Her Story," LaCrosse, Wisconsin, *Tribune*, April 20, 1988.

Lyon, Linda, "Heart-Shaped Gabadians, Rain Eyes Populate World of Young Storytellers," *St. Louis Globe Democrat*, April 9, 1980, 3–4.

Nufer, Kathy Walsh, "Magic of Storytelling Can Liberate the Spirit," Appleton-Neenah-Menasha, Wisconsin *Post-Crescent*, February 22, 1991.

_____. "Stories: Teachers Urged to Make Learning Exciting," Appleton-Neenah-Menasha, Wisconsin *Post-Crescent*, July 25, 1988.

Paquin, Tom, "Ancient Art Form Is Used to Teach Students of Today," *Marinette Eagle-Star*, December 9, 1988.

Pollack, Joe, "Actress and Storyteller Lynn Rubright Brings History to Sparkling Life," *St. Louis Post-Dispatch*, July 4, 1991.

"Review," *Second Story Review*, March 1997.

Stallings, Fran, "Book and Tape Reviews," *Territorial Tattler*, Summer 1997.

Williams, Dennis A., and Frank Maier, "Storyteller as Teacher," *Newsweek*, November 9, 1981.

ANTONIO SACRE
[sah'·kray]

Address P. O. Box 478075
Chicago, Illinois 60647
phone 773-296-2296
email Tonysacre@aol.com

Focus: Latin American stories about travel and emigration; Southwestern tall tales; stories from the Arabian Nights; folktales; autobiographical incidents.
Audience: all ages.
Style: lively, humorous bilingual telling in English and Spanish; performs with teller/magician Derek Hughes.

Antonio Bernardo Sacre's repertory of stories places him in a teeter-totter milieu — an Anglo in a Latino world and a Latino in an Anglo world. His multiple views of growing up in dual cultures and races has made his stories doubly useful. At mask-making workshops and residencies, his advice to parents, librarians, and educators is for non–English speaking citizens to learn English, but to preserve their heritage by asking grandparents for stories and by becoming storytellers themselves. Whether in park, school, library, stage, or lecture hall, Sacre encourages beginning tellers to find, develop, share, and preserve their personal and community heritage by telling their store of tales. Taking his own advice, he performs popular bilingual programs: *All My Wanderings/Todos Mis Viajes*, *The Weeping Woman/La Llorona*, *Conjuring Cubans, Twice*, and *Rafters and Runners/ Balseros y Corredores*, all Latin American stories, and *Tall Tales of the American West*, *Super Scary and Merry Tales*, and *Amazing Arabian Nights*. Among his tellings are outlandish recreations of his family's emigration from Cuba. On the move north to the United States, his father steals five boats from the Cuban navy, but has to swim through shark-infested waters to Miami because there is no room for him in the boats.

With a grant from the National Endowment for the Arts, Sacre served Savanna, Illinois, as storyteller-in-residence, for which he con-

ducted community story swaps, and writes and directs children's theater. His background is a model for storytelling magic. Born in 1968 in Boston, Massachusetts, to a Cuban father and Irish-American mother, Sacre grew up in New Castle, Maryland, where his classmates changed his nickname Papito to Dorito, a pejorative taken from a TV advertisement for corn chips. In self-defense, he tried to rid himself of his Latin heritage by changing his name to Tony and speaking only English. While summering in Miami's Little Havana in his teens, he relearned Spanish with help from his grandmother Mimi, who filled his imagination with tales, family stories, and fables. Intent on a professional career expressing the variety in Hispanic culture, Sacre earned a B.A. in English from Boston College and an M.A. in theater arts from Northwestern University. As a storyteller, he chose as models Jim May, Michael Meade, Carmen Deedy, Nancy Donoval, Donald Davis, Joe Hayes, Sarah Ransome, Paulette Atencio, Olga Loya, Dovie Thomason, and Susan Klein. To help bicultural children like him, he fills his stories with the doings of his Uncle Tito, Aunt

Nina, and Grandmother Mimi to build pride in Hispanic-American heritage. In addition to acting in *Frankenstein* and *Moby Dick*, he has worked with Red Moon Theater's artistic staff in training children in mask making, and he operates a youth-at-risk after-school acting class at Roberto Clemente High School. Because of his talent in stage, film, television, lecture, and platform narration, he appears on the Illinois Arts Council Residency Roster. After making a niche for himself in the Chicago area, Sacre has begun multimedia publication by Univision and Telemundo for Latin American television networks, and has appeared at Wild Onion Storytelling Festival, the National Storytelling Festival Exchange Place, Ottawa Fine Arts Festival, Navy Pier Grand Opening, Magic City Festival, and the Illinois Storytelling Festival.

Audiography

Looking for Papito ... Family Stories from Latin America (audiocassette), Woodside Avenue Music, 1996.

Awards

1996 Parents' Choice Gold Award for *Look-

ing for Papito ... Family Stories from Latin America.

1995 National Endowment for the Arts Grant.

Source

Garza, Melita Marie, "Teller of Tall Tales Turns His Verbal Skills into an Art Form," *Chicago Tribune*, June 22, 1995, section 5, page 5.

Ojito, Mirta, "Latin Storyteller Speaks Kids' Language," *Miami Herald*, November 2, 1995.

Reddick, Tracie, "Stories Students Can Share," *Tampa Tribune*, February 19, 1996.

Weiss, Hedy, "'Moby-Dick' Rides Theatrical Waves with Epic Daring," *Chicago Sun-Times*, February 23, 1995.

STEVE SANFIELD

Address   2200 Lost River Road
Nevada City, California 95959
phone 916-292-3353

Focus: Jewish and Hasidic tales and legends; stories from the vanished world of Eastern European Yiddish culture; world tales of serious laughter; personal reflections.
Audience: all ages.
Style: traditional.

One of America's foremost Jewish storytellers, Steve Sanfield believes stories are a blessing and a life-giving force — a touch of grace that the true storyteller must pass on to others. He has practiced his art by writing story books and picture books, serving residencies, and founding and directing the Sierra Storytelling Festival and the Sierra Storytelling Institute in Nevada City, California. He has performed at the major festivals in the United States, including several appearances at the National Storytelling Festival. Other venues include the University of Judaism, National Public Radio, Montalvo Center for the Arts, Jemez Bodhi Mandala Zen Center, and colleges and universities in Nebraska, Nevada, California, New York, Michigan, Washington,

and Colorado. He has educated other tellers at the Bremerton Educational Media District, Conference on Alternatives in Jewish Education, American Library Association, International Reading Association, Centrum Foundation Workshops for Creatively Gifted Children, Arts Are Basic, San Francisco Bay Area Book Festival, and Southern Festival of Books.

A pioneer of the national storyteller-in-residence programs, in 1977 Sanfield came under the sponsorship of the California Arts Council to perform, lecture, and conduct workshops throughout North America. His path to his career took him circuitously from stories to poems and back to stories. Born in the late 1930s in Lynn, Massachusetts, in childhood he was a solitary comber of beaches and purveyor of tides and storms. He derived his love of books from Elsie Grubb, a local librarian who introduced him to Mark Twain and inspired him to become a writer. He garnered a stock of Jewish and Lithuanian stories from his grandfather, a baker who immigrated to the United States at the beginning of the twentieth century. Sanfield began retelling the family's stock of lore at age eight as a means of survival. To elude anti–Semitic bullies, he shared his store of Jewish and Hasidic stories, but missed the irony until he grew wiser in the ways of bigotry. He studied English at the University of Massachusetts and moved to Hollywood in hopes of breaking into the film industry.

After working as a gossip columnist, publicist, news editor, scriptwriter, and book store manager, Sanfield moved to the Greek islands to complete his first novel. He lived and worked in the Mediterranean, North Africa, and the Middle East for three years; there, among other things, he acquired a life-long interest in Buddhism. Upon his return to the United States, he began an intensive four-year study of Zen Buddhism. Next came marriage and the building of his home in the mountains of northern California. He began working in the Poetry-in-the-Schools program and discovered that children had little interest in poetry unless it was narrative poetry. Much to the consternation of proponents of poetry in the classroom, he rejected the notion that chil-

dren can produce great verse. He saw that most children had a deep-seated and unsatisfied need for story in their lives, so he began to introduce more and more stories in his school appearances until he was blackballed from the poetry program. The California Arts Council intervened and made Sanfield the first storyteller-in-residence in the United States. He also began touring the country and appearing at festivals with a synergistic approach of gauging the audience from the platform and choosing his program accordingly.

Sanfield's stock of African-American hero lore such as John Henry and High John the Conqueror tales are always favorites of children who consider themselves underdogs. After hearing him tell some of them, a New York editor urged him to turn these stories into books. Thus began Sanfield's new career of writing books for young people. In his work both on and off the stage, he tries to combine the best of the written and the oral — poetry and prose to promote wholeness and to touch both the hearts and minds of listeners.

Articles

"Across Cultures: Stories That Say L'Chaim," *Sitting at the Feet of the Past: Retelling the*

North American Folktale for Children, Greenwood, 1992, 69–76.

"How to Spin a Tall Tale," *Parenting*, April 1997.

"Openings and Closings" in *Writing Across Cultures*, Blue Heron, 1994.

"Stories in Clay," in *National Storytelling Journal*, Summer 1987, 9.

"The Story Is Not Ended," in *National Storytelling Journal*, Winter 1985.

"Voices from a Vanished World" *Storytelling Magazine*, Summer 1989, 26.

Bibliography

The Adventures of High John the Conqueror, August House, 1991. African-American hero stories for young adult readers.

American Zen by a Guy Who Tried It, Larkspur Press, 1994.

Backlog, Nail Press, 1975.

Bit by Bit (illustrated by Paula Gaber), Philomel, 1995. Based on a Yiddish folk song "If I Had a Little Coat."

Chasing the Cranes (co-author Dale Pendell), Exiled-in-America Press, 1985.

Circling (co-author John Brandi), Exiled-in-America Press, 1988.

The Confounding, Larkspur Press, 1981. A Paiute tale to be told aloud.

"Could This Be Paradise?" in *Best-Loved Stories Told at the National Storytelling Festival*, August House, 1991.

"Could This Be Paradise?" in *Chosen Tales: Stories Told by Jewish Storytellers*, Jason Aronson, 1995, 261–264.

"Eros and Death," in *Death: An Anthology of Ancient Texts, Songs, Prayers, and Stories*, North Point Press, 1985, 72.

A Fall from Grace, Aldebaran Review, 1976.

The Feather Merchants and Other Tales of the Fools of Chelm, Orchard Books, 1991. Stories from the legendary town of fools and simpletons.

"The Fools of Chelm," in *Stories on Stage*, H. W. Wilson, 1993.

"The Founding Fathers," in *Because God Loves Stories*, Simon & Schuster, 1997, 72–73.

The Girl Who Wanted a Song (illustrator Stephen T. Johnson), Harcourt Brace, 1996. A tale of the redeeming power of friendship; for ages 5 and up.

The Great Turtle Drive (illustrated by Dirk Zimmer), Alfred A. Knopf, 1996. A twisted American tall tale.

He Smiled to Himself, Shakti Press, 1990.

"High John the Conqueror," in *From Sea to Shining Sea: A Treasury of Folklore and American Folk Songs*, Scholastic 1993, 134.

"John's Memory," *Storytelling Magazine*, May 1996, 22–23.

Just Rewards or Who Is That Man in the Moon and What Is He Doing Up There Anyway! (illustrator Emily Lisker), Orchard Books, 1996. A humorous tale explaining why there's a man in the moon.

A Natural Man: The True Story of John Henry (illustrator Peter J. Thornton), David R. Godine, 1988. The saga of one of America's greatest folk heroes.

A New Way, Truth of Time Books, 1983.

No Reason at All (co-author John Brandi), Yoo-Hoo Press, 1996. A call and response of short poems.

"Not Alone," in *More Best-Loved Stories Told at the National Storytelling Festival*, August House, 1992.

Only the Ashes, Tooth of Time, 1981.

"The Rabbi," *Storytelling World*, Summer-Fall 1993, 9–10.

Snow (illustrator Jeanette Winter), Philomel 1995. A collection of haiku verse for all ages.

Strudel, Strudel, Strudel (illustrator Emily Lisker), Orchard Books, 1995. An illustrated tale of the Fools of Chelm.

Wandering, Shaman Drum, 1977.

Water Before and Water After, Blackberry, 1974.

"What He Could Have Been" in *Ready-to-Tell Tales*, August House, 1994.

Audiography

"A Bull's-Eye Every Time," in *A Storytelling Treasury* (audiocassette), National Storytelling Press, 1993.

"Could This Be Paradise?" in *Best Loved Stories Told at the National Storytelling Festival* (audiocassette), August House, 1991.

"Could This Be Paradise?" in *Tales of Sages and Fools from the Jewish Tradition* (audiocassette), Backlog, 1984.

The Great Turtle Drive and Other Stories (audiocassette), Backlog, 1996. Oral versions of Sanfield's illustrated children's books: *Bit by Bit, The Girl Who Wanted a Song, The Great Turtle Drive, Strudel, Strudel, Strudel*.

Singing Up the Mountain (audiocassette), Nita, 1981. Native American tales.

Steve Sanfield Live at the Sierra Storytelling Festival (audiocassette), Backlog, 1992. Includes "True Love," "The Bakery Imps," "Just Rewards," "The Holy Demon," and "The Sabbath Fish."

Awards

1997 Young Hoosier Book Award finalist for *Bit by Bit*.

1997 *Storytelling World* Award for *The Great Turtle Drive*.

1997 *Storytelling World* Award for *Just Rewards*.

1996 National Storytelling Association Service and Leadership Award.

1996 Children's Book Committee Book of the Year for *Bit by Bit*.

1996 Children's Libraries Distinguished Book of the Year for *The Great Turtle Drive*.

1995 Junior Library Guild Book of the Month for *Bit by Bit*.

1995 Bank Street College Children's Committee Book of the Year for *Bit by Bit*.

1991 American Library Association Notable Children's Book for *The Adventures of High John the Conqueror*.

1991 Children's Book Council Book of the Year for *The Adventures of High John the Conqueror*.

1991 National Council for Social Studies Book of the Year for *The Adventures of High John the Conqueror*.

1991 Chicago Public Library Best of the Best for *The Adventures of High John the Conqueror*.

1991 International Reading Association Young Adults' Choice for *The Adventures of High John the Conqueror*.

1991 Parents' Choice What-Kids-Who-Don't-Like-to-Read Program for *The Adventures of High John the Conqueror*.

1991 Children's Catalog recommendation for *The Adventures of High John the Conqueror*.

1991 American Booksellers' Pick of the List for *The Feather Merchants and Other Tales of the Fools of Chelm*.

1991 Bay Area Book Reviewers' Award finalist for *The Feather Merchants and Other Tales of the Fools of Chelm*.

1991 Dorothy Canfield Fisher award finalist for *The Adventures of High John the Conqueror*.

1991 Parents' Choice Honor Book for *The Feather Merchants and Other Tales of the Fools of Chelm*.

1987 Society of Children's Book Writer and Illustrator Work-in-Progress Grant for *The Adventures of High John the Conqueror*.

1985 Haiku Zasshi Zo annual haiku contest grand prize.

1976–1979 California Arts Council Writer-in-Residence Grant.

Source

Arens, Karla, "An Interview: Steve Sanfield," *Wild Duck Review*, July/August 1995, 18, 19, 27.

Couzens, Jean, "Bookmarks," *Sierra Heritage*, October 1995.

Devereux, Pat, "Stories 'a Blessing Beyond Yourself,'" Grass Valley-Nevada City, California *Union*, May 23, 1994.

Gluck, Peggy Issak, "Storyteller Keeps Jewish Culture Alive with His Tales," *North-*

ern California Jewish Bulletin, October 19, 1984.

Hutchens, Kathleen, "Master Storyteller Weaves Tales Like Magic," Paradise, California *Post*, January 17, 1986.

"Interviews with Jimmy Neil Smith and Steve Sanfield," *Opera for Youth News*, 1989.

"Interviews with Steve Sanfield and Gary Snyder," *Poet News*, October/November 1989.

Lawler, Roxanne, "Tale Spinning," Port Angeles, Washington *Daily News*, April 4, 1986.

Lourie, Iven, "The Sierra Storytelling Festival," Auburn, California *Sierra Heritage*, August 1994.

Melton, Wayne, "Sanfield Speaks Up for Dying Art of Storytelling," *Reno Gazette-Journal*, March 29, 1996.

Mooney, Bill, and David Holt. *The Storyteller's Guide*. Little Rock, Ark.: August House, 1996.

Pigg, Sheryl, "Storyteller Entertains and Teaches," Lodi, California *News Sentinel*, January 31, 1985.

"Storytellers to Weave Their Special Magic During the First Week of October," *Herald & Tribune*, October 2, 1993, 3C–5C.

Wade, Gerald, "Poet Finds Audience Through Storytelling," *Omaha World-Herald*, June 16, 1996.

Wolgamott, L. Kent, "Storyteller Loves, Lives to Share Gift," *Lincoln* (Nebraska) *Journal Star*, October 18, 1996.

NANCY SCHIMMEL

Address 1639 Channing Way
Berkeley, California 94703
phone and fax 510-843-0533

Focus: tales from many countries, often with active heroines; personal, original, and family stories and songs; workshops and classes for beginning and experienced tellers.

Audience: general.

Style: witty, wise, conversational telling for adult audiences; participation stories, songs, chants, and movement for family audiences.

Instruments/Props: guitar, thumb piano, origami paper.

Born in 1935, Nancy Schimmel grew up in Berkeley and Long Beach, California, hearing her carpenter father tell guests stories of working on a sailing ship carrying freight to Australia during World War I and organizing the unemployed during the Depression. When she was in junior high school, her mother, Malvina Reynolds, composer of "Little Boxes" and "What Have They Done to the Rain," often introduced songs with stories. With her parents' example and encouragement, Schimmel felt at home on stage. She danced in high school and college productions and sang at summer camp. She also inherited her parents' love of words and reading.

Always a good listener, Schimmel worked briefly as a social worker, then entered library school at the University of California at Berkeley, where she found a vocation with room for her many skills and interests. She worked in school and public libraries for nine years, helping to organize peace marches in her spare time. In the early seventies, she began to find other venues for storytelling at local Renaissance fairs and art festivals. She taught storytelling in the library and at home.

In 1975, Guy and Candie Carawan of the Highlander Folk School brought Schimmel to her first National Storytelling Festival, where Guy was performing. Seeing professional tellers for the first time, she immediately quit her library job to go on the road and bought a van with her retirement funds. After she and librarian Carole Leita fixed up the van, they began touring to tell stories and organize women library workers. They received good advice on traveling and telling from Barbara Freeman and Connie Regan-Blake, an itinerant duo known as The Folktellers, who helped launch the storytelling renaissance.

Two years later, Schimmel began teaching storytelling at the graduate library school in Madison, Wisconsin. Her class outlines and handouts grew into *Just Enough to Make a Story*, a practical handbook now in its third edition, covering story selection, practice, and delivery and including annotated story lists such as "Active Heroines in Folk Tales." She also taught at the University of California at Berkeley and UCLA. One of her Berkeley students, Gay Ducey, has become a valued colleague, helping her shape a program of traditional stories about adoption set in a frame story of Schimmel's reunion with the daughter she gave up for adoption in 1955. Schimmel and Ducey occasionally perform and teach together.

With singer/songwriter Judy Fjell, Schimmel presents "An Evening of Malvina Spirit," telling family stories and introducing songs as Malvina did. They perform elementary school assemblies as well. Programs featuring Bonnie Lockhart and Ann Hershey as the Plum City Players take Schimmel to schools, libraries, storytelling festivals, and nature programs in parks. She occasionally performs women's stories with Olga Loya and Sandra MacLees.

Among Schimmel's favorite tellers are Angela Lloyd, Katy Rydell, Kathryn Windham, Ed Stivender, Luisah Teish, Bill Harley, Rosalie Sorrels, Johnny Moses, Milbre Burch, and David Holt. She also likes performing at local storytelling clubs where she can hear not-so-well-known tellers. Among her favorite performances she names the 1978 National Storytelling Festival, the Clearwater Festival organized by Pete and Toshi Seeger, and presentations at museums in conjunction with exhibits on Japan, feminist art, and dinosaurs. Her popular stories — "The Tailor," "The Rainhat," "The Handsome Prince," and "The Lionmakers"— are available in the third edition of *Just Enough to Make a Story*.

When Schimmel turned fifty, she began a songwriting/producing collaboration with Candy Forest that has earned them three Parents' Choice Gold awards. Schimmel used her life-long interest in science to write lyrics on such environmental themes as soil enrichment in "The Earthworm Dance" which she performed for the 1997 American Library Association Conference in San Francisco. A current project is her work with composer Fran Avni on a set of songs to help children become reading ready.

Articles
"Books on Adoption for Young Children: Looking at Language" (co-author Susan Love), *School Library Journal*, July 1997, 32–33.

"Telling Stories to Your Kids," *Whole Earth Review*, Summer 1991, 68–69.

Bibliography
Just Enough to Make a Story: A Sourcebook for Storytelling, Sisters' Choice, 1978, 1992.

"The Lionmakers," in *More Best-Loved Stories Told at the National Storytelling Festival*, August House, 1992.

Save My Rainforest (English version of a story by Monika Zak), Volcano Press, 1992. The true story of a Mexican eight-year-old trying to save a rain forest in Mexico.

"The Tailor," in *Spinning Tales, Weaving Hope: Stories of Peace, Justice, and the Environment*, New Society, 1992.

"The Woodcutter's Story," in *Best-Loved Stories Told at the National Storytelling Festival*, August House, 1991.

Videography
Tell Me a Story: Nancy Schimmel, BARR Entertainment, 1986. Contains "The Handsome Prince," "Clever Monka," "The Peddler of Swaftham," and "The Lionmakers."

Audiography
All in This Together: 15 Ecology Songs for the Whole Family (audiocassette), Sisters' Choice, 1990. Children's songs with a conservation theme.

Dinosaur and Other Stories from Plum City (audiocassette), Plum City, 1986. Features songs by Nancy Schimmel, Bonnie Lockhart, and Ann Hershey.

Head First and Belly Down (audiocassette), Sisters' Choice, 1992. Children's songs.

Plum Pudding: Stories and Songs with Nancy Schimmel and the Plum City Players (LP), Sisters' Choice, 1982. Music and tales, featuring "The Tailor" and "The Woodcutter's Story."

Awards

1992 Parents' Choice Gold Award for *Head First and Belly Down*.

1992 American Library Association Notable Recording for *Head First and Belly Down*.

1990 Parents' Choice Gold Award for *All in This Together: 15 Ecology Songs for the Whole Family*.

Source

"Art and Magic of Storytelling," *San Francisco Chronicle*, July 17, 1991.

Barnard, Kathy, "Storyteller Helps Inspire Imaginations," Lewiston, Idaho, *Morning Tribune*, February 16, 1987.

"A Brief Look at This Year's Storytellers," Jonesborough, Tennessee *Herald & Tribune*, September 30, 1992, 4C–8C.

Martin, Suzanne, "Green Grow the Stories," *Storytelling Magazine*, Spring 1992, 18–20.

Osborne, Linda, "The Wisdom of the Nations," *World & I*, May 1, 1993.

Weir, Joette Dignan, "Storyteller Travels into the Minds of Children," *Argus*, July 7, 1982, 14.

PENINNAH SCHRAM

Address   525 West End Avenue, 8C
New York, New York 10024
phone 212-787-0626 or 914-962-9387
fax 914-962-1714

Focus: legends, parables, and folktales from biblical, Talmudic, Midrashic, Hasidic, Sephardic, Yiddish, and Israeli sources; wit and wisdom stories in the fool and trickster mode; holiday and celebratory stories; personal and generational stories; episodes in the life of Elijah the Prophet; world culture.

Audience: all ages.

Style: dynamic facial expressions, words, and songs, such as a nigun, lullaby, or love song.

Instruments/Props: teams with guitarist/singer Gerard Edery.

One of Judaism's strongest voices, Peninnah Schram tells stories that relate practical human knowledge about how to live and die. She derives her trove of narrative from Lithuania on her father's side and White Russia from her mother's people. For these earth-based homilies, Schram has no difficulty naming her muse. Schooled in biblical and Midrashic lore by her father, a cantor in New London, Connecticut, and regaled with her mother's didactic Jewish proverbs and folktales, Schram formed a narrative technique in the Hebraic tradition. She credits her mother with oral warnings that women should give in more than 50 percent of the time, but that they should defy patriarchy by listening and questioning. Her mother declared that women can accomplish their aims by being *klug* (smart/wise) and applying *hob sekhl* (common sense).

Schram's strongest childhood memories are of tales of Elijah the Prophet, the master of miracles who disguised himself in rags and wandered the earth comforting and aiding Jews in need. In the early 1970s, she debuted at the 92nd Street Y, where the education director accepted her proposal for a storytelling program. From that point on, she has

told at museums and synagogues; two radio series, *A Bundle of Rainbows* and *Let's Tell Tales*, preceded a cable television pilot, *Conversations Over a Glass Tea*, taped in 1982. She took as mentors her father's example and the dignity and style of Yiddish folksinger/ethnomusicologist Ruth Rubin and philosopher and humanitarian Elie Wiesel. To prepare each story thoroughly, she adopted a tradition found in Kabbala: read the literal sequence of events, learn the lesson or moral, shape the events in personal language, interpret the story as it applies to life, and understand why the totality appeals to the teller.

Currently an associate professor of speech and drama at Stern College of Yeshiva University, Schram travels the United States and other countries to tell Jewish stories. As keynoter, storyteller-in-residence, festival performer, promoter of the Coalition for the Advancement of Jewish Education, and founder of the Jewish Storytelling Center, she remains dedicated to the preservation and perpetuation of folklore. Her programs include *Yiddish Tales: Mostly English, Sacred Stories for Shabbat, The Voice of the Woman in Jewish Folktales, Sephardic Love Stories,* and *A Table with People.* Her workshops offer two choices: *Kernels of a Pomegranate*, a participatory training for educators, clergy, and parents, and *Traveling in Time*, a participatory training in collecting and telling personal and family lore.

A consummate professional, Schram, called the Queen of Jewish Storytellers, calls herself a "*shelihah tzibur*, a messenger of the people." An individualist with an ear to the competition, she admires the work of Cherie Karo Schwartz, Heather Forest, Gerald Fierst, Roslyn Bresnick-Perry, Arthur Strimling, Laura Simms, Joel ben Izzy, Syd Lieberman, Judith Black, and Lisa Lipkin, and was featured teller at the 1997 Tell It in the Mountains and at several National Storytelling Festivals. She was also keynote speaker at the 1995 National Storytelling Conference. Schram's signature style involves connection with the audience by walking among them and by altering rhythms and texts to reflect new insights and meanings.

Articles

"The Art of Storytelling," *Reform Judaism*, Summer 1990, 36.

"A Cantor's Legacy," *Journal of Jewish Music and Liturgy*, Vol. 7, 1984-1985, 22–26.

"Collections from the People of the Story," in *Tales as Tools: The Power of Story in the Classroom*, National Storytelling Press, 1994, 176–178.

"Current Collections of Jewish Storytelling," *Jewish Book World*, Summer 1990, 28–29, 31.

"The Ethical and Folk Components of Jewish Storytelling," in *Creative Jewish Education*, Rossel Books, 1985.

"A Gracious Retelling: Jewish Fairy Tales Collected," *The Melton Journal*, Summer 1984.

"Jewish Models for Adapting Folktales for Telling Aloud," *Who Says?: Essays on Pivotal Issues in Contemporary Storytelling*, August House, 1996.

"Jewish Stories One Generation Tells Another," *National Storytelling Journal*, Summer 1987, 12–14.

"Jewish Storytelling," *Reconstructionist*, January-February 1988, 19–23.

"The Joys of Jewish Storytelling," *Jewish Book World*, Summer 1990, 2, 4, 23–24.

"Kernels of a Pomegranate," *Jewish Community Center Program Aids*, Summer 1975, 2–5, 12.

"Let Us Tell Tales," *Alternatives in Religious Education Journal*, Spring 1978, 8–9.

"On Storytelling," *Religion and Theatre Newsletter*, Spring 1978.

"One Generation Tells Another: The Transmission of Jewish Values Through Storytelling," *Literature in Performance*, April 1984, 33–45.

"Oriental-Sephardic Folktales," *Jewish Education News*, Summer 1990, 28–29, 31.

"Participatory Storytelling: A Partnership Between Storyteller and Listener," in *Tales as Tools: The Power of Story in the Classroom*, National Storytelling Press, 1994, 95–98.

"Perspective: Interweaving Threads — Influences in My Life," *United Synagogue Review*, Fall 1992.

"Producing Grown-Up Plays for Children," *Theatre Crafts Magazine*, July/August 1967.

"Storytelling: A Practical Approach to Life Review," *The Journal of Aging and Judaism*, Spring 1988, 187–190.

"Storytelling: Creative Sharing, Listening, Teaching," *The Pedagogic Reporter*, January 1985, 20–23.

"Storytelling: Five Steps to Teaching Others," *Ten Da'at*, Fall 1987, 14–17.

"Storytelling: Role and Technique," *Jewish Teacher's Handbook*, Vol. 2, 1981, 79–91.

"Telling Tales," *Jewish Frontier*, December 1972, 19–21.

"There Is a Time to Tell Tales," *The Melton Journal*, Winter 1982, 3–4, 19, 24.

"Where Are Storytellers Today?," *The Educational Forum*, January 1979, 175–183.

Bibliography

"The Artist's Search," in *Spinning Tales, Weaving Hope: Stories of Peace, Justice, and the Environment*, New Society, 1992.

The Big Sukkah, Kar-Ben Copies, 1986. Children's story on the theme of hospitality.

Chosen Tales: Stories Told by Jewish Storytellers (editor), Jason Aronson Inc., 1995. Sixty-eight favorite stories of Jewish storytellers; foreword by Rabbi Avraham Weiss.

"The Czar's Army" and "The Czarina's Dress," in *Because God Loves Stories: An Anthology of Jewish Storytelling*, Simon & Schuster, 1997.

Eight Tales for Eight Nights: Stories for Chanukah (co-author Steven M. Rosman; paper cut illustrations by Tsirl Waletzky), Jason Aronson Inc., 1990. Eight stories reflecting Ashkenazi and Sephardic traditions; appendixes of Chanukah music, the ancient legend, and suggestions for retrieving family stories.

Elijah the Prophet Study Guide/Instant Lesson, Torah Aura Productions, 1994.

Elijah's Mysterious Ways: An Instant Lesson, Torah Aura Productions, 1993. A study guide for Elijah the Prophet stories.

"The Great Debate," *Parabola*, Fall 1995, 24–25.

"The Innkeeper's Wise Daughter," in *Best-Loved Stories Told at the National Storytelling Festival*, August House, 1991.

Jewish Stories One Generation Tells Another, Jason Aronson, 1987. Sixty-four stories and folktales from Jewish oral and written traditions with source-filled introductions and index; foreword by Elie Wiesel.

"The Magic Pomegranate," in *Ready-to-Tell Tales*, August House, 1994.

The Storyteller's Companion to the Bible: Old Testament Wisdom (contributor to Volume V), Abingdon Press, 1994.

Tales of Elijah the Prophet, Jason Aronson Inc., 1991. Thirty-six stories gathered from varied sources and centuries; introduction and endnotes; foreword by Dov Noy.

A Teaching Guide to "Elijah's Violin & Other Jewish Fairy Tales, Coalition for Advancement in Jewish Education, 1985.

"The Three Brothers," in *More Best-Loved Stories Told at the National Storytelling Festival*, August House, 1992.

Videography

The Rooster Who Would Be King and Other Jewish Folktales, The Telling Tale, 1987.

Audiography

Elijah's Violin & Other Jewish Fairy Tales (audiocassette), POM Records, 1985.

"The Innkeeper's Daughter," in *Best Loved Stories Told at the National Storytelling Festival, Vol. 2* (audiocassette), August House, 1992.

A Storyteller's Journey (two audiocassettes), POM Records, 1977, 1982. Contains ten stories illustrating the Ten Commandments from Molly Cone's book *Who Knows Ten?*

"The Ten Sons" on *Celebrating Jewish Storytelling* (audiocassette), B'nai B'rith Women, 1988.

"Welcome to Clothes," *More Best-Loved Stories* (contributor) (audiocassette), August House, 1992.

Zlateh the Goat (audiocassette), Jewish Braille Institute, 1970. Features stories by Jewish folklorist and Nobel Prize winner Isaac Bashevis Singer.

Awards

1997 National Storytelling Association Leadership Award.

1996 *Storytelling World* Honor Award for Best Anthology for *Chosen Tales: Stories Told by Jewish Storytellers*.

1995 Covenant Foundation Outstanding Jewish Educator.

1995 National Jewish Book Award in Folklore for *Chosen Tales: Stories Told by Jewish Storytellers*.

Source

"A Brief Look at This Year's Storytellers," Jonesborough, Tennessee *Herald & Tribune*, September 30, 1992, 4C–8C.

Craft, C., "Book Reviews: Arts & Humanities," *Library Journal*, January 1991, 110.

Glatt, Carol R., "Book Reviews: Social Sciences," *Library Journal*, April 15, 1995, 85.

"Interview with Peninnah Schram," http://www.aronson.com/Judaica/chosint.html, May 29, 1997.

"National Storytelling Association's Service and Leadership Awards," *Storytelling Magazine*, July 1997, 42–43.

"Peninnah Schram," *Telling Tales*, June-July 1997, 1.

Schneider, Susan Weidman, "Eureka!," *Lilith*, September 30, 1994.

Stone, Amy, "The Rebirth of Jewish Storytelling: Not Just for Kids," *The Reporter*, Spring 1996, 6–10.

BARBARA SCHUTZ-GRUBER

Address   2855 Kimberly
            Ann Arbor, Michigan 48104
    phone 313-761-5118

Focus: world folklore; ghost stories; trickster tales; Michigan and Great Lakes legends; medieval ballads; string figures and games; stories of female protagonists and antagonists; family anecdotes; epic adult stories.

Audience: children and adults.

Style: spontaneous, animated, and imaginative tales with an informal, conversational delivery.

Instruments/Props: gesture, voice, string finger games.

A native of Brighton, Michigan, and a descendant of German and Irish immigrants, Barbara G. Schutz-Gruber grew up sur-

rounded by storytellers. She and her brothers, sisters, cousins, and friends listened in at family gatherings as three generations of adults shared with each other their adventures and misadventures and remembered people and places of their past. Thus storytelling became second nature to her. She began telling ghost stories to her friends at sleep-overs and summer campouts. In school, she was drawn to the narrative in history and geography lessons as she learned about diverse cultures and places. Her father, a physics teacher at the local high school, added to her growing interest as he shared stories of alchemists and inventors. She formalized her understanding of story with coursework in content, structure, and theme and received a B.A. in literature, language, speech, and drama from Eastern Michigan University. While earning an M.A. in children's literature with an emphasis in folklore from the same university, she studied comparative folklore under Dr. Gilbert B. Cross, co-author of *World Folktales*.

Schutz-Gruber's experience in teaching elementary and middle school preceded time at home rearing her children, Tristan and Andrea, with whom the multigenerational storytelling tradition continues. The combination of the flexibility of performance hours and a desire to be home with her young fam-

ily allowed her to launch a professional career as freelance platform storyteller in 1987. Early in her career, she sought other storytellers for support and inspiration and joined local and national storytelling organizations, including the Detroit Story League and the National Storytelling Association.

Over the years, Schutz-Gruber has developed a continually growing repertoire of over 75 stories from around the world. She is at ease before preschoolers or senior citizens, and has performed in schools, libraries, festivals, correctional facilities, hospitals, psychiatric wards, group homes, and family reunions. She is experienced at performing for both small groups of three or four and festival gatherings as large as four thousand. She was commissioned to design and perform programs on medieval Arthurian lore, complete with costume, and epic adult stories to accompany special exhibits in a museum setting. She conducts workshops for school children, teachers, librarians, and other tellers featuring multicultural folktales, studies in selecting and presenting trickster tales, string stories, and innovative strategies for adult storytelling. Her national workshops include "A Trickster Up Your Sleeve," "Tying It All Together: Using String Stories in the Ann Arbor Schools," and "Woven Splendor: Storytelling at the Detroit Institute of Arts."

Bibliography

Trickster Tales from Around the World: An Interdisciplinary Guide for Teachers (co-author Barbara Frates Buckley), self-published, 1991. Contains teaching activities for social studies, language arts, art and drama, music, and science to accompany four stories: "Coyote and the Blackbirds," "Maui's Gifts," "Jack Visits the Queen," and "Tortoise and Hyena."

Videography

String Things: Stories, Games and Fun!, self-published 1995. Contains "House in the Woods," "Frog Fable," "Maui's Gift," "St. Ives Riddle," "Anansi the Spider," and "Rag Doll"; activities for children from ages 4–10 feature string art for a broom, bowl, cat and mouse, and dancing ghost as well as cat's cradle.

Audiography

Little Sugar and a Lot of Spice: Stories of Gutsy Girls and Wise Women (audiocassette), self-published 1993. Contains "Shahrazad," "The Devil and the Farmer's Wife," "The Three Spinners," "The Farmer's Daughter," "Dancing Kate," "Chang Fa," "The Old Woman and Her Pig," "Lady Isabel," and "Cherry's Adventure"; hammered dulcimer accompaniment.

Trickster Tales (audiocassette), self-published, 1991. Contains "Coyote and the Blackbirds," "Maui's Gifts," "Jack Visits the Queen," and "Tortoise and Hyena"; hammered dulcimer accompaniment.

Voices on the Wind (audiocassette), self-published, 1993. Contains "The Mysterious Rider," "Harry Bail," "Wall of Fire," "The Handkerchief," "The Three Wishes," and "Moss Island."

Awards

1995 *Storytelling World* Honor for *String Things: Stories, Games and Fun!*

1993 American Library Association Notable Recording for *Voices on the Wind*.

1991 Parents' Choice Gold Award for *Trickster Tales from Around the World*.

Source

Alexa, Cynthia, "Review," *Booklist*, December 15, 1991.

Clark, Terry, "Review," *Tale Trader*, November 1994.

"Do Tell: SFC Hosts Festival," Sioux Falls *Argus Leader*, June 2, 1994, 11.

Elders, Ann, "Review," *School Library Journal*, December 1995, 55.

Gupta, Joy Das, "Once Upon a Time There Was a Storyteller Who…," *Michigan Journalist*, 11.

Maliszewski, Joanne, "Kids Party with Books," *Observer*, May 2, 1996.

Martineau, Janet I., "Storyteller Spins Michigan Yarns," *Saginaw News*, March 3, 1994, C-1, C-2.

"Review," *Booklist*, November 15, 1995.

"Review," *Michigan Reading Journal*, Summer 1995.

"Review," *Parents' Choice*, awards issue, 1991.

Rogers, Tom, "Not the Tale But the Teller," *Ann Arbor News*, October 14, 1989, B1.

Torgow, Joan, "Review," *Audiovisual Media*, November/December 1995, 9.

SHANTA

Address   P. O. Box 199311
Chicago, Illinois 60619
phone 708-557-2742
email storywiz@aol.com

Focus: traditional African and African-American folktales and chants; feminist stories; creation myths; spiritualism, motivation, and healing; personal experiences.
Audience: all ages.
Style: a genial, rhythmic exchange with the audience.
Instruments/Props: mbira, agogo, toa, wood block and stick, reed zither, sitar, shakere, and percussion instruments from Africa.

A Chicago-based teller, Shanta works under a stage name meaning peace. With a variety of narrative material, she entertains, teaches, and inspires groups at literacy training centers, job reentry programs, women's shelters,

Girl Scouts, at-risk teens, and Jack-and-Jill clubs. From her parents, she learned to revere music and strength of character. Shanta's introduction to platform narrative was extensive writing of poems and stories for children. For "Oral Traditions: Storytelling," the course she taught for six years at Columbia College, she drew on training at the Women's Self-Employment Project, a poverty prevention program which she serves as board member. For further instruction, in 1969, while completing her education at Carleton College, she traveled on an exchange program to India to study sitar, an experience that taught her the transforming power of art. On the journey, she began a collection of over fifty exotic musical instruments. She is also an active mentor in a teen outreach, An Income of Her Own, which supports empowerment through entrepreneurial skills. A success story in her own right, she was featured in *Inc.* magazine and has advanced the careers of other tellers.

With an impressive repertoire of 150 stories and songs, Shanta has been a musician, writer, and platform performer for twenty years. Telling in the griot tradition, she incorporates West African tales, chants, and verse in performances entitled *Stories and Songs of African People*, an exaltation of pride, respect, and understanding. Her *Women of Spirit, Women of Power* is a collection of tales and music that explores energy, resilience, strength, love, and courage in a variety of examples, from queens and goddesses to homeless women and bag ladies. To express woman's enduring qualities, she draws on folk heroes, leaders, spiritual seekers, and ordinary folk, including the fictional child Shedoobee and Nzinga, a seventeenth-century Angolan queen who created an African asylum for escaped slaves. Shanta's *In a World of Stories* presentation interweaves tales from three countries and ethnic groups. A holiday performance, *Kwanzaa: An African-American Celebration*, uses folktales to explain the seven Islamic principles of unity, self-determination, collective work and responsibility, cooperative economics, purpose, creativity, and faith.

Shanta has produced *Light Worker*, a collection of tales, music, meditation, and channeling. One of her works is on permanent display at the Brookfield Zoo's Habitat Africa. She helped establish a six-member African-American women's band, Samana, named for an acronym of the founders, Shanta, Maia, and Niki Mitchell. Shanta plays bass, sitar, mbira, and percussion for powerful musical numbers that merge African musical tradition with experimental jazz. The group also uses vibraharp, flute, cello, piccolo, clarinet, conga, djuni djuni, and Ghanaian peg drum. Shanta's published works include articles for *Ebony Jr., Black Books Bulletin, Hot Wire, Black News,* and *Cadence.* Her itinerary has taken her to the National Storytelling Festival, National Women's Music Festival, Yukon International Storytelling Festival, Illinois Storytelling Festival, Adler Planetarium, Augusta Baker's Dozen Storytelling Festival, Shedd Aquarium, Oxfam, Children's Memorial Hospital, Field Museum, Great River Traditional Music and Crafts Festival, and National Festival of Black Storytelling as well as libraries, schools, and colleges. The media have featured Shanta on the *Oprah Winfrey Show, WBEZ* and *WBBM Radio Chicago, WGN with Bill Campbell,* and *WTVS Detroit* and in feature articles for *Today's Chicago Woman, Chicago Sun-Times, Chicago Tribune, Chicago Reader,* and *St. Paul Dispatch.*

Bibliography

"Brother Blue," *Bloomsbury Review,* Winter 1996.

"Storytellers' Views on Blending Narrative and Song," *Storytelling Magazine,* May 1997, 16–20.

"A Village of Women," in *Jump Up and Say; Anthology of African-American Storytelling,* Simon & Schuster, 1995.

Videography

African Storytelling, Chicago Children's Museum, 1989. Contains "Why the Sun and Moon Are in the Sky" and "Leopard, Goat, and Yam."

Arts of Africa, Art Institute of Chicago, 1990.

Audiography

The Adventures of Shedoobee: Searching for the Good Life (audiocassette), Storywiz, 1988. The fictional story of a nine-year-old Swedish girl, including "Searching for the Good Life, Parts 1–4," "The Squash Story," "Exercise Game," "Breathe with Me," "The Rusty Crusties," "Kay," "Love Yourself," and "For My Friends."

Light Worker: Stories with Music (audiocassette and CD), Storywiz, 1994. A collection of stories and music synthesizing art and spirituality, including "Friendship," "Ekha and the Desert," "Gertrude's Lie," "A Village of Women," "The Boy and the River," "The Mamba," and "The Loving Ones."

Samana (audiocassette), Storywiz, 1996. Features "Time ta Boogie South Africa," "Real Blue," and a four-part suite, "Samana 1—Journey to Spirit."

A Village of Women (audiocassette). Stories and music by Samana.

Awards

1989 Metropolitan Chicago Minority Enterprise "Minority Service Firm of the Year."

1988 Carleton College's Distinguished Woman Visitor.

1981 Women's Jazz Festival Combo Winner.

1980 Northwestern University's Young Elders Award.

Source

Lackey, Mike, "Storyteller's Tales Teach and Enchant," *Lima News,* March 3, 1993.

"Shanta Maintains an Oral Tradition," *Northfield News,* January 19, 1994.

"Sharing a Touch of Africa," *Storytelling Magazine,* May 1997.

"South Side Jazz Women," *Chicago Music Awards,* February 1, 1997.

LAURA SIMMS

Address 814 Broadway
New York, New York 10003
phone 212-674-3479

Focus: ancient myths and fairy tales; world tales from Africa, Siberia, Hawaii, and Persia; true life stories; feminist material.

Audience: children and adults.

Style: dramatic presentation; has performed with Steve Gorn.

Instruments/Props: accompaniment by composer Steven Bansuri on the bamboo flute.

A vivid and intelligent performer, teacher, and scholar of oral traditions, Laura Simms, a native New Yorker, was one of the first in the United States to develop storytelling as a fine art to bridge the traditions of the past with contemporary theater and literature in the present. She has been called a "whirling dervish" and a "contemporary vaudevillian"; Maori elders have described her "as good as grandparents." Drawing on the influence of a great grandmother who was both linguist and mystic, a mother who played concert piano, and a poet father, Simms treasured childhood magic. She was blessed with a household that sheltered Eastern European immigrants and Asian and South American musicians, and a multicultural neighborhood, all valuable inspirations for her art. She began constructing stories and dance dramas in her backyard at age seven, and at age sixteen met renowned anthropologist Margaret Mead. By 1968, she began exploring the ritual art of solo storytelling. Platform experiences have taken her to venues as varied as Bryant Park in New York City, Philippine rain forests, Nepalese temples, and schools, festivals, theaters, and events around the world. She served seven years as consultant to the National Storytelling Association and has directed the National Festival. Her skills and energies have boosted the Storytelling Center in Oneonta, which she founded in 1977, and the New York City Storytelling Center, which she co-founded in 1985. Presently, she is part of the faculty of Naropa Institute in Boulder, Colorado, and teaches regularly at the University of Oslo and the New York Open Center. She is on the board of directors of the Humanity Foundation, sponsors New York's Rare Events Series, and, since 1995, has directed Medicine of the Heart, a storytelling and healing program at Beth Israel Hospital.

Named one of America's best teachers of storytelling, Simms has developed her talents through study with Tibetan Buddhists, Maori orators, Native American tellers, Central Asian epic singers, and African griots. Her writings and presentations influence folklorists, narrative researchers, and traditional storytellers. She is a contributing editor for *Parabola* magazine and *The Journal for Cultures and Traditions*. Her articles appear in *The Shambhala Sun, Parabola, Organica, Horn Book, Humanity, Tale Trader,* and *Storytelling World*. Her stories appear in numerous collections. For sixteen years she has directed the Storytelling Residency currently held at the Wellspring Renewal Center, where participants work together to discover their inner strengths. She presents full-length concerts entitled *Women and Wild Animals, A Woman in the Garden,* and *The Dream Merchant.* Her signature epic tale is "Demeter and Persephone," which focuses on the divine feminine. Additional feminist stories express such aspects of women's lives as the sacred youth, the crone, and the shamaness. She leads storytelling tours to Greece, Turkey, Morocco, Mexico, and Nepal and is currently creating interviews interwoven with stories to preserve and illumine the last living epic singers and traditional storytellers. In 1997, Simms was chosen to be an artist-in-residence for the Lincoln Center Arts and Education Institute in New York and the co-creator of Carnegie Kids. Working internationally, she dedicates herself to *Children at War, Children's Voices,* and *International Games.*

Articles

"Another Way of Knowing: The World of an Epic Singer," *Organica,* Winter 1996, 8–9.

"Arising Compassion: An Interview," *Parabola,* September 1997.

"Children's Voices: The First International Children's Parliament," *Organica,* Spring 1997, 4–5.

"In the Realms of Dreams," *Storytelling,* Fall 1996.

"In This World of Bones," *Parabola,* April 1997.

"Journey to Jerusalem," *Shambala Sun,* July 1995, 50–53.

"The Lamplighter: The Storyteller in the Modern World," *National Storytelling Journal,* Winter 1984, 8–11.

"Marrying the World by Story," *Tale Trader,* August 1996, 1, 9.

"Seeing the Invisible," *Humanity*, July 1996, 31.

"Storytelling and Tradition," *Journal of Traditions and Culture*, July 1997.

"Storytelling, Children, and Imagination," *Texas Library Journal*, Winter 1983.

"Summoning the Realm of Dream," *Storytelling World*, September 1996, 16–19.

"T'Boli Dreaming," *Organica*, March 1996, 22–23.

"What Storytelling Means to Me," *Tale Trader*, August 1995, 5.

"Words in Our Hearts: The Experience of Story," *Horn Book*, June 1983, 344–349.

Bibliography

"The Black Prince," in *Ready-to-Tell Tales*, August House, 1994.

The Bone Man (illustrator Michael McCurdy), Hyperion, 1997.

The Ghost and I: Scary Stories for Participatory Telling (contributor), Yellow Moon Press, 1992. Features 20 funny and scary stories and songs for ages 5–14.

"The Girl and the Ghost," in *Best-Loved Stories Told at the National Storytelling Festival*, August House, 1991.

Moon and Otter and Frog (illustrator Clifford Brycelea), Hyperion, 1995.

"Moon Dreaming," *Storytelling Magazine*, September 1996, 20–21.

Rotten Teeth (illustrator David Catrow), Houghton-Mifflin, projected 1998.

"Savitri," in *Homespun: Tales from America's Favorite Storytellers*, Crown, 1988.

"The Seal Maiden," in *Homespun: Tales from America's Favorite Storytellers*, Crown, 1988.

Storytelling and Tradition, regular column for *Journal of Traditions and Culture*, Boulder, Colorado.

Videography

"The Woodcutter," in *American Storytelling Series, Vol. 3*, H. W. Wilson, 1987.

Audiography

Dance Without End: Creation Myths (two audiocassettes), Northword Press.

An Incredible Journey (audiocassette), Gentle Winds Press. Features two African stories plus "Delgadina" from Chile, "Sunman,"a Bushman tale, and "Little Burned Face," a native American tale.

Making Peace: Heart Up Rising (audiocassette), Earwig, 1994. A combination of true street stories and ancient myth and fairy tale accompanied by world music, rap, and jazz.

Moon on Fire: Calling Forth the Power of the Feminine (music by Steve Gorn) (audiocassette), Yellow Moon, 1987. Feminist stories from around the world; for ages 8 and up.

Nightwalkers (two audiocassettes), Northword Press.

Stories Just Right for Kids (audiocassette), Warner Music.

Stories: Old as the World, Fresh as the Rain (audiocassette), Warner Music. Features rare stories for all ages.

There's a Horse in My Pocket (audiocassette), Warner Music.

Women and Wild Animals (audiocassette), Northword Press.

"The Woodcutter" (co-performer Steve Gorn), in *Graveyard Tales* (audiocassette), National Association for the Preservation and Perpetuation of Storytelling, 1989.

Awards

1996 National Storytelling Association Circle of Excellence.

1996 *Scientific American* Best Reader Award for *Moon and Otter and Frog*.

1986 American Library Association Notable Book for *Just Right for Kids*.

1988 *Choice* Magazine Outstanding Audio Award for *Moon on Fire: Calling Forth the Power of the Feminine*.

Source

"A Brief Look at This Year's Storytellers," Jonesborough, Tennessee *Herald & Tribune*, September 30, 1992, 4C–8C.

Burgos, Rowena C., "Laura Simms Gives Manila's Kids 1001 Nights of Wonder," *Malaya Living*, August 23, 1995.

Delatiner, Barbara, "Stories to Pique a Listener's Imagination," *New York Times*, July 11, 1982.

"Interview," *The Twentieth Anniversary of the National Storytelling Festival*, Hometown Entertainment, 1994.

"Laura Simms: Myth in Mendocino," *Mendocino County Entertainment*, July 31–August 14, 1991.

Mooney, Bill, and David Holt. *The Storyteller's Guide*. Little Rock, Ark.: August House, 1996.

"Simms Residency Set at Wellspring," *Tale Trader*, May 1997, 2.

"Simms Takes Audience on a Magical Journey," *Cazenovia Republican*, April 6, 1994, 17.

"Six Tellers at Wailing Wall in Jerusalem," *Tale Trader*, February 1997, 9.

Timeless Voices: Images of the National Storytelling Festival. Jonesborough, Tenn.: National Storytelling Press, 1997.

MARY CARTER SMITH

Address   P. O. Box 11484
             Baltimore, Maryland 21239
phone 410-323-4458

Focus: African-American songs, poems, dramatic sketches, jokes, and stories; restructured fairy tales; tales of justice, affirmation, and humanity; historical stories of Chaka, the Zulu warrior-king; Aesop's fables.

Audience: all ages.

Style: traditional griot; call and response.

Instruments/Props: African robes and headdress, cowtail switch.

Billed by Morgan State University as a "mighty mythopoet," Mary Carter Smith derives her gift for telling from a background in reading, poetry, and drama. In a statement of purpose in her résumé, she claims: "Misunderstanding abounds. It has no special reading place. Rich and poor, majority and minority, young and old. Black and white — all feel the sting of being misunderstood." As a warrior against confusion and misinformation, she chooses stories, drama, songs, poetry, and laughter as her weapons. Born February 10, 1919, in Birmingham, Alabama, to Rogers Ward and Eartha Nowden, a domestic worker, she had almost no knowledge of her father and was left motherless at age four when her second stepfather shot her 22-year-old mother. Coached and nurtured by her grandmother, Mary Deas Nowden, and her aunt Sallie Lou

Nowden Coleman, Smith learned to read in early childhood through regular Bible stories and daily visits to the public library. During summer vacations, she visited aunts in Kentucky, Ohio, Pennsylvania, and West Virginia and gathered stories in each locale.

Although deprived of natural parents, Smith's youth was lively and varied with extracurricular involvement in speech and drama, dance parties where she gyrated to the Charleston, and volunteer efforts to help the Scottsboro boys, black youths who were falsely charged with rape, for whom she made and sold paper flowers. She graduated from Frederick Douglass High School and, in 1942, completed her formal education at Coppin Teacher's College, where she enjoyed theater and concerts and first entertained groups with storytelling. To earn tuition that led to a B.S. degree in elementary education, she worked as a domestic and became one of the first blacks to obtain clerical work with Baltimore's Social Security office. She completed graduate study in drama, speech, stage lighting, directing, oral literature, and oral narration at New York University, Johns Hopkins University, Rutgers University, Queens College, Catholic University, University of Maryland, and Temple Buell University. For 31 years, she served the Baltimore public school system as elementary teacher and librarian. A focus of her pedagogy was addition of African verse, art, dance, music, cuisine, and tales to a curriculum that ignored black accomplishments and culture. To bolster discussions of Africana, she dressed in native jewelry, turbans, and dashikis in African colors of gold, red, and green and brandished a beaded cow switch, a traditional fringed goad carried by herders.

After retirement in 1978 — the year her only son, Ricardo Rogers Carter, was murdered — Smith once more dedicated herself to public service, her method of healing an aching heart. In 1953, she was one of several founding members of the Arena Players, America's oldest black acting troupe, and played the part of Essie in a stage adaptation of Langston Hughes's *Tambourines to Glory*. She began boosting African heritage with a series of media appearances: host of *Black Is*, a public television program; appearances on *Maryland*

Connections: Preserving the Past and NBC's *Three Stories Tall;* performance on talk radio for *The Mary Carter Smith Studio;* and production and presentation of *The Children's Hour* from WHUR at Howard University. In 1996, she received public tribute for two decades of producing *The Griot for the Young and the Young at Heart,* a radio program broadcast to the Virgin Islands from Morgan State University.

Since her shift in careers in 1969, Smith has adopted the mission of protecting stories and songs from the African diaspora and performing tales of justice and humanity. Her altruism has taken her seven times to Africa as well as across the United States and to the Caribbean, England, and France to collect and disseminate stories. She has enjoyed telling at the Detention Center in Baltimore, Kent State University, and Monrovia High School in Liberia in 1971, and has performed at the Smithsonian Festival of American Folk Life, Kennedy Center for the Performing Arts, First Night Annapolis, Joseph Meyerhoff Sym-

phony Hall, Charleston's Piccolo Spoleto, Baltimore Symphony Orchestra, Artpark in Lewiston, New York, Japanese-American Methodist Church in San Jose, California, Walters Art Gallery, University of Miami, John Henry Folklife Festival, and numerous schools, colleges, and churches. As one of the founders of Big Sisters International and the co-founder (with Linda Goss) of the National Association of Black Storytellers, she has helped to perpetuate the oral tradition among young storytellers. She is also founder-president of Aframa, her own agency, and of Citizens' Coalition for Urban Survival, a public withdrawal from commerce to honor the peaceful boycotts of Dr. Martin Luther King, Jr.

Smith's selflessness, skillful dialect telling, and witty recreations — particularly her signature story, "Cindy Ellie," an updated version of Cinderella — have earned numerous awards, notably, a likeness in the Great Blacks in Wax Museum in Baltimore, installed in 1989. She has served both Howard University and Morgan State University as griot-in-residence. In 1994, the National Association of Black Storytellers named her "America's Mother Griot." President Bill Clinton applauded her caring for others and commended her for concern for betterment of the future. A treasured compliment came from Alex Haley in 1975, when he proclaimed her his personal American griot.

Articles

"What Storytelling Means to Me," *The Tale Trader*, February 1996, 3.

Bibliography

"Cindy Ellie," in *Best-Loved Stories Told at the National Storytelling Festival*, August House, 1991.

"Cindy Ellie, a Modern Fairy Tale," in *Talk That Talk*, Simon & Schuster, 1989.

The Griot's Cookbook: Rare and Well-Done (co-authored with Alice McGill and Elmira M. Washington), C. H. Fairfax, 1985.

Heart to Heart, C. H. Fairfax, 1980. Autobiographical photos, poetry, and prose.

Merry Christmas, Baby (contributor), 1996.

"Moseatunyaa," in *Homespun: Tales from America's Favorite Storytellers*, Crown, 1988.

Opinionated, Beacon Press, 1966.

Poetry of the Negro (contributor), Doubleday, 1970.

Town Child, Nordika, 1976. Children's poetry.

Vibes (contributor), C. H. Fairfax, 1980. Illustrated by Wes Yamaka, John Levering, and Sten Nordh.

Videography

"Cindy Ellie," in *American Storytelling Series*, Vol. 5, H. W. Wilson, 1987.

Tell Me a Story (contributor), BARR Entertainment, 1986. Contains "John Henry," "Moseoatunya," "The Cowtail Switch," "The Talking Skull," "Zunn Gali Gali," and "Can of Corn Colors."

Audiography

"Cindy Ellie," in *Best Loved Stories Told at the National Storytelling Festival, Vol. 2*, August House, 1992.

"Dead Aaron," in *Graveyard Tales* (audiocassette), National Association for the Preservation and Perpetuation of Storytelling, 1989.

Mary Carter Smith Presents (audiocassette), Aframa Agency, 1984. Contains songs, poetry, and stories—"Moseoatunya, an African Folk Tale," "The Signifying Monkey," "A Street Poem Town Child," "Cindy Ellie, A Modern Fairy Tale," and "John Henry."

Mary Carter Smith—Nearing Seventy-Five (audiocassette), 1993. Contains "The Ragman," "Open the Door Richard," "Two Little Birds," "The Two Wives," "A Funeral," and "Tales of Aesop from Jamal Koram."

Awards

1996 National Storytelling Association Lifetime Achievement Award.

1996 National Storytelling Association Circle of Excellence.

1994 National Association of Black Storytellers's Mother Griot.

1991 Maryland State Governor's Proclamation of Griot of Maryland.

1990 Morgan State University Cultural Heritage Award.

1990 *Best of Baltimore Magazine* Certificate of Excellence in Storytelling.

1985 Association of Black Storytellers Zora Neale Hurston Folklore Award.

1985 Towson State University Beautiful Black Woman Award.

1983 African-American Women's Political Caucus Woman of Distinction.

1983 Named Griot of Baltimore.

1983 Maryland Writers' Council Keeper of the Flame Award.

1976 Phi Delta Kappa National Citation.

1974 Left Bank Jazz Society Award.

1973 Griot-in-Residence at Morgan State College.

1973 Delta Theta Sigma Distinguished Woman Award.

1969 *Guidepost* Writers Fellowship.

1968 Temple Buell College Juvenile Writers Fellowship.

1968 *Afro-American* Newspaper Award.

1968 National Council of Negro Women's Distinguished Teacher Award.

1967 Outstanding Soror Award.

1967 National Council of Jewish Women's Community Service Award.

1967 Delta Theta Sigma Distinguished Woman Award.

1966 Coppin State College Distinguished Alumni Citation.

1965 Sojourner Truth Award.

Source

Carlton, William, "Interview," Fort Wayne, Indiana, *News-Sentinel*, June 17, 1993.

Crockett, Sandra, "A Tale of Love and Loss," *Baltimore Sun*, December 19, 1995.

Current Biography. H. W. Wilson, 1996.

"From One Storyteller to Another: A Tribute to Mary Carter Smith," *Nashville Pride*, April 14, 1989.

Goss, Linda, and Marian E. Barnes, eds. *Talk That Talk: An Anthology of African-American Storytelling*, Simon & Schuster, 1989.

Hajdusiewicz, Babs Bell. *Mary Carter Smith: African-American Storyteller*, Enslow, 1995.

Hodges, Betty, "Interview," Durham, North Carolina *Herald Sun*, May 8, 1994.

"Mary Carter Smith's Performance at Arena Players Is Priceless," *Baltimore Afro-American*, March 8, 1987.

"Maryland Connections: Preserving the Past," *Baltimore Sun*, February 19–25, 1995.

"NSA Recognizes Lifetime Achievers," *Inside Story*, September 1996, 33–34.

Pike, Larry, "Profiles: A Modern Griot," *Storytelling Magazine,* Summer 1993, 28.

Reckley, Ralph. *Twentieth Century Black Women in Print*. Acton, Mass.: Copley, 1991.

Shatzkin, Kate, "Freeing the Soul on Wings of Words," *Baltimore Sun*, February 20, 1997, 1A, 10A.

Waldron, Thomas W., "Interview," *Baltimore Sun*, October 10, 1994.

Wynter, Leon E., "Tale of Cindie Ellie, Voodoo Godmother and White Cadillac: Black Storytellers Carry on a Rich, Tribal Tradition," *Wall Street Journal*, January 22, 1990.

JON SPELMAN

Address   1612 Ballard Street
Silver Springs, Maryland 20910
phone 800-585-5784 or 301-585-5784
fax 301-585-5786
email JSpelman@juno.com

Focus: family stories; stories from English literature; fractured fairy tales; tall tales from American folklore; monster lore; multicultural stories; urban folklore and contemporary fables.

Audience: families with children, adults.

Style: traditional narrative art; one-man shows accompanied by musician Andy Tierstein.

An artist in theater and platform narrative, Jon Spelman is billed as "six-and-a-half feet and has tales." A seventeen-year veteran of storytelling, he has mastered over twenty hours of material and regularly appears at colleges, schools, service clubs, prisons, museums, community centers, professional meetings, veterans' and senior centers, and theaters. A graduate of Cincinnati schools, he completed an honors degree in American history and literature from Williams College and an M.A. in theatre from Purdue University. For seven years, he taught speech and drama at the University of Tennessee and Florida State University. While directing the Asolo State Theater in Sarasota, Florida, he consulted on theater in curriculum for the Florida Department of Education and represented the American theater at the Fourth World Conference of the International Association of Theatre for Children and Young People. Simultaneously, he taught at New College and Manatee Junior College and founded the Florida Studio Theatre, which he directed until his shift to platform narration in 1980.

A native Missourian reared in Ohio, Spelman lives in Washington, D.C., with his wife, choreographer Liz Lerman, and daughter, Anna Clare. He has traveled to the Kennedy Center Terrace Theatre, Wolf Trap, National Storytelling Festival, Colloquium on the Revival of Storytelling in Paris, Florida Studio Theatre, Madison-Morgan Cultural Center, International Folkfair Society, Duplin County Arts Council, and Smithsonian Institution National Portrait Gallery. He has hosted NBC's *Three Stories Tall* and told on National Public Radio, off–Broadway, across the United States, and in Holland, Sweden, Denmark, England, and France. His performances feature updated stories: "Sleeping

Beauty in the Giant Briar Patch," "Little Cherry Red Cap," "Your Name Is Rumple-what?," "Raven Lights the World," "Br'er Panther Eats It All," and "The Mermaid in the Cow Pond," a retelling of a Grimm's fairy tale, plus "Some Good Old Tales," "Myths and Legends," "Three Stories Tall," "Once There Was a War: From Beowulf to World War II," "War Stories: Nam," "Frankenstein: The Beauty of the Beast," and "Canterbury Tales: A Comic Class Reunion at Canterbury School." In concert he presents "On the Bedpost Overnight," "I Was in America But I Didn't Know It," and "Grease Heat: Tales from the American Landscape." The programs reflect adult humor about conception and birth, popular psychology, native American and African-American legend and lore, and off-beat stories. His workshops and master classes cover storytelling and community, storytelling and curriculum, and storytelling as art, and express his skill at story building and collecting, solo performance, acting, and writing for the stage.

Bibliography

"The Old Giant" in *Ready-to-Tell Tales*, August House, 1994.

Videography

"Grass Cape," on *The American Storytelling Series, Vol. 4*, H. W. Wilson, 1987. A light-hearted blend of Cinderella and King Lear.

Storytellers (four cassettes), Acorn Media, 1991. Contains stories by Alice McGill, Joseph Bruchac, and Olga Loya. Cassettes are labeled "Tall Tales, Yarns, and Whoppers," "Animal Stories," "Magic Tales," and "Scary Stories."

Audiography

Jon Spelman Live at the Smithsonian (audiocassette), self-published, 1988. Includes "Yancey Register"; for families with children 8 and older.

Jon Spelman Tells Tales (audiocassette), self-published, 1988. Eleven stories, including radical versions of "Cinderella" and "King Lear"; suitable for families with small children.

Awards

1989 National Endowment for the Arts Distinguished Solo Performance Artist's Fellowship.

1988 Achievement in Children's Television Award.

1987, 1988 three Emmies for *Three Stories Tall.*

1985 Children's Radio Award.

1964 Gilbert W. Gabriel Award for Contributions to Theater.

Source

"A Brief Look at This Year's Storytellers," Jonesborough, Tennessee *Herald & Tribune*, September 30, 1992, 4C–8C.

Mooney, Bill, and David Holt. *The Storyteller's Guide.* Little Rock, Ark.: August House, 1996.

Parks, Steve, "Flash! The Lastest Entertainment News and More," *Newsday*, March 4, 1996.

Zad, Martie, "'Storytellers' Captives Kids of All Ages," *Washington Post*, October 20–26, 1991.

expression. A native of the Bronx, she began learning storytelling in infancy from her father, Martin Grayson, a raconteur, and her mother, Laura Borim Holtz, who told family stories. Her grandmother, Ethel Borim, passed along wisdom, which sweetened the mix. In the eighth grade in Tulsa, Oklahoma, Stavish loved mythology, which opened her mind to literature and history. She completed undergraduate degrees in theater and English at the University of Illinois at Urbana/Champaign and an M.A. in speech and performing arts at Northeastern Illinois University. She gained additional training at Hunter College, Chicago State College, and Body Politic. Through the guidance of mentor Robin Goldberg, she blended these four disciplines into a career in storytelling.

With no formal training in folklore, Stavish taught herself the narrative art and practiced on her children, Nicole and Scott. Her basis for self-study in Jewish and comparative literature were the writings of folklorists: Howard Schwartz's *Gates to the New City*, Peninnah Schram's *Jewish Stories One Generation Tells Another*, Jane Yolen's *Favorite Folktales*

CORINNE STAVISH

Address   26150 West 12 Mile Road #C-54
            Southfield, Michigan 48034
    phone (home) 248-356-8721
    phone (office) 248-204-3656
    fax 248-204-3518
    email STAVISH@LTU.com

Focus: Jewish and Hasidic stories; Jewish mysticism; world culture; Cinderella across cultures; Scotch-Irish stories; African-American stories; aging around the world.

Audience: general, often with the elderly.

Style: becomes a backdrop for the story.

Instruments/Props: dresses in black.

Storyteller, theater specialist, and humanities professor Corinne Stavish believes that stories are the collective conscience of a community and that storytelling is the medium of

from Around the World, and Joanna Cole's *Best-Loved Folktales.* These enlarged Stavish's teaching in humanities and comparative world folklore at Lawrence Technological University in Southfield, Michigan. She has also taught speech at Wayne State University, Jewish folklore at Midrasha College of Jewish Studies, speech, acting, and literature at Oakton Community College, and speech at Loyola University. From 1982 to 1984, further study with Joyce Piven at the Piven Theatre Workshop helped refine Stavish's artistry. Syd Lieberman was helpful and encouraging to her career. In 1986, she began promoting storytelling in Detroit's Jewish community with the help of Harlene Appelman, an innovator in Jewish family education for toddlers through adults. Encouragement from Donald and Merle Davis, Barbara McBride-Smith, Celia Goodman, Peninnah Schram, Howard Schwartz, Fred Boyce, Jim May, Michael Parent, and Lee Pennington has undergirded her career in myriad ways.

Stavish has had a wide acceptance in public tellings as well as the media. She has been endorsed by Michigan Touring Arts, Michigan Humanities Council, and Young Audiences of Michigan. Traveling from Massachusetts to California, Wisconsin to Florida, throughout the midwest and to Canada and Israel, she has appeared at Detroit Institute of Arts, Conference for Alternatives in Jewish Education, Mid-Atlantic Storyteller's Conference, Illinois Storytelling Festival, Michigan Reading Association, Ark Storytelling Festival, Michigan Storyhouse, and Renaissance Storytelling Festival. She particularly enjoyed telling at the 1996 Corn Island Festival in Louisville, Kentucky, and presenting a workshop at the 1997 National Storytelling Conference in Indianapolis. She served on the advisory board of Ellen A. Hay's *Speech Resources: Exercises and Activities* (Roxbury, 1992) and was chosen to join twelve tellers for "Michigan Storyhouse" on Michigan Public Radio. She has published articles and stories in *Storytelling World, Apple Tree, Jewish Family,* and *Jewish Parenting Today.* Her lecture material covers Jewish and comparative world folklore with emphasis on the Cinderella cycle, Jewish wit and wisdom, Jewish mysticism through story, Yiddish the-

ater and literature, and Hasidic folklore and history. Her workshops cover the importance of parents, grandparents, and teachers in storytelling as well as the legacy of family stories, storytelling coaching, training student tellers, creating new stories from old tales, creative dramatics and theater games, and the theme of justice in folklore.

Bibliography

"Breaking Idols," *Jewish Parenting Today,* November 1995.

"Forbidden Friendship," *Storytelling World,* Spring/Summer 1994, 25. An excerpt from *Women: Willful, Witty, Wise.*

Jewish Stories for Family Dialogue (editor), B'nai B'rith Center for Jewish Identity, Fall 1997.

"The Promise of the Promised Land," *The Apple Tree,* April 18, 1997.

Seeds from the Past (editor), B'nai B'rith, 1997.

"Slinging Stories," *Storytelling World,* Winter/Spring 1994, 26.

Speech Resources: Exercises and Activities (adviser), 2nd edition, Roxbury, 1992.

Story Seeds: Planting for Our Future (editor), B'nai B'rith, 1997.

"Who Can Retell?: Making Hanukkah a Time for Family History," *Jewish Family,* December 1993, 6–7. Presents preparation for the holiday through the lighting of eight candles.

Audiography

I'd Rather Be Me! (audiocassette), self-published, 1996. Contains six stories about self-esteem: "The Stonecutter," "The Apple Tree's Discovery," "Little Crow," "Grandpa Sam," "Baba the Baker from Boiberick," and "There's No Such Thing as a Chanukah Bush, Sandy Goldstein."

Tales Through the Ages for All Ages (audiocassette), self-published, 1992. Contains six stories from many cultures: "The Bear's Short Tail," "Sir Gawaine and the Hideous Hag," "Chelm Tales," "Things Couldn't Possibly Be Worse," "Trying to Please Everybody," and "Just Enough to Make a ...."; recorded live at the Trowbridge Senior Residence.

Women: Willful, Witty, Wise (audiocassette), self-published, 1994. Contains "Lilith,"

"Judith the Bold," "Saykhl the Wise," "Shmutzie — the Jewish Cinderella," "Forbidden Friendship," and "A Football for Grandma."

Source

Chu, Nancy L., "Review," *School Library Journal*, May 1997.

Crew, Hilary, "Audiovisual Review," *School Library Journal*, June 1993, 62.

Harris, Ellen, "Spinner of Tales Weaves Magic," *Cleveland Jewish News*, October 1994, 16.

Heinlein, Gary, "Jews Celebrate War of Deliverance," *Detroit News*, December 5, 1996, 3E.

McClear, Mary-Eileen, "Review," *Second Story Review*, June 1997, 9.

Rabinowitz, Renee, "Audiovisual Review," *School Library Journal*, February 1995, 64.

ED STIVENDER

Address   Nancy Clancy, agent
5138 Whitehall Drive
Clifton Heights, California 19018
phone 215-843-4350 or 610-259-8825

Focus: Old and New Testament stories, parables, and original Catholic stories; lives of saints and heroes; religious vignette; fractured fairy tales; participatory stories.

Style: humor and satire; nostalgia; improvisation, morris dancing, miming, and mummery.

Instruments/Props: costume of St. Francis of Assisi; banjo, harmonica, puppetry.

A native of Springfield, Pennsylvania, Edward Patrick Stivender demonstrated his skill as neighborhood *jongleur* in childhood backyard performances with his sister Nancy, now his manager. The firstborn son of an Irish Catholic mother and Protestant naval veteran, Stivender showed early promise with general excellence and religion awards at Holy Cross Elementary School and was earmarked for the priesthood. Added to his appeal were First

Class Scout, Lieutenant of the Safeties, and altar boy, all tendencies that pointed to seminary. He debuted on-stage at age eight in the Holy Cross Grammar School's St. Patrick's Day play in 1955, in which he played the virtuous shamrock seller. From musicals and comedies at Monsignor Bonner High School, he advanced to Shakespearean roles at St. Joseph's College in Philadelphia and the 1966 Shakespeare Festival. Following an M.A. in theology from Notre Dame, for five years he taught religion at Northwest Catholic High school in West Hartford, Connecticut, a platform from which he launched a career in storytelling.

Like other tellers, Stivender received advice and camaraderie from The Folktellers, two of the storytelling world's most devoted mentors. A year after Stivender joined Hartford's Plum Cake Players Children's Theatre, he saw the duo — Connie Regan-Blake and Barbara Freeman — who invited him to perform at the Storytelling Festival in Jonesborough, Tennessee. Among the founders of the movement, he observed the solo style of classic folksayer Ray Hicks, Doc McConnell, David Holt, and Kathryn Windham. In 1985, veteran teller Jim May challenged Stivender to narrate his signature stories of a Catholic boyhood, including the tale about a first kiss. Telling together with May at the Great Lakes Pastoral Gathering in Chicago, Stivender premiered "Altar Boy" and "Diane Tasca," two of his best-loved stories.

Taking as mentors Ray Gray, Brother Blue, and sacred clown Ken Feit, Stivender began semiannual performances at the University of Connecticut, playing a wide range of original creations from St. Francis of Assisi to Mr. Atom, and was frequently voted "Favorite Lecturer." For Art-O-Rama, he performed two satires: "Where Do They Keep the Insurance?" and "Send in the Clones," two spoofs of the corporate world. For WWUH-FM, he produced and hosted *Myth America Radio Half-Hour,* and he joined the Peace Train, a traveling arts festival. Advanced to featured performer at the National Storytelling Festival, he met two additional mentors, Heather Forest and Jay O'Callahan, from whom he learned more about refining style and tech-

nique. Subsequent performances took Stivender to sacred clowning conferences, Great Lakes Pastoral Gathering, and the National Storytelling Conference, where he met Jackie Torrence, Bill Harley, Len Cabral, Milbre Burch, Michael Parent, Gwenda LedBetter, Syd Lieberman, Chuck Larkin, George Goldman, Laura Simms, and Diane Wolkstein. With some original Catholic stories, he initiated Sacred Telling in 1981, a regular feature at the Jonesborough gathering, and served on the board of the National Association for the Preservation and Perpetuation of Storytelling.

Recent appearances have placed him at the Jakarta International School in Indonesia and the 1996 National Storytelling Conference, where he performed all twelve roles of Act V of William Shakespeare's *A Midsummer Night's Dream*. He has made a one-man show of Will Kemp's *Nine Daies Wonder*, composed in 1600, appeared as the "Vatican-American String Band" in the Philadelphia Mummers' Day Parade, and regularly lectures on children's literature and storytelling at colleges and universities. His original stories have been anthologized and appeared in *Reader's Digest*. Lauded as "the Robin Williams of storytelling" and "the Catholic Garrison Keillor," Stivender is always in demand for storylab workshops, artist-in-school residencies, Elderhostels, and comic presentations.

Bibliography

"Honey Bunny," in *Ready-to-Tell Tales*, August House, 1994.

"Jack and the Magic Boat," in *More Best-Loved Stories Told at the National Storytelling Festival*, August House, 1992.

"Jack and the Robbers," in *Homespun: Tales from America's Favorite Storytellers*, Crown, 1988.

Raised Catholic (Can You Tell?), August House, 1992. Stories of growing up Catholic in the 1950s and 1960s, including "First Communion," "First Confession," "Christmas Rapport," "Camp Columbus," "The Ocarina," "The Virtuous Shamrock Grower," "Diane Tasca," "Altar Boy," "The Privet Hedge," "Jersey Cousins," "Marian Callahan" and "The Bonner Junior Prom."

Still Catholic After All These Fears, August House. 1995. Sequel to his first book, featuring a cycle of twelve autobiographical stories filled with wit, humor, nostalgia, and adolescent difficulties.

Videography

"Br'er Possum," in *Tell Me a Story, Vol. 1*, Hometown Entertainment, 1995.

The Christopher's Story Laboratory (contributor), 1982. A children's series hosted by Stivender.

"Hansel and Gretel," in *American Storytelling Series, Vol. 6*, H. W. Wilson, 1987.

The Kingdom of Heaven Is Like a Party, Chesapeake Audio-Video Communications, 1988. Recorded live at the East Coast Educational Conference; covers religious history from creation through Pentecost.

Raised Catholic, Can You Tell?, White Star Video, 1996. Coming-of-age stories about parochial school, serving mass, and falling in love, including "First Communion," "First Confession," "Christmas Rapport," "Camp Columbus," "The Ocarina," "The Virtuous Shamrock Grower," "Diane Tasca," "Altar Boy," "The Privet Hedge," "Jersey Cousins," "Marian Callahan" and "The Bonner Junior Prom."

Audiography

Ed Stivender Live at the University of Connecticut (audiocassette), Les Jongleurs de Notre Dame, 1983. Contains "Jack and the Robbers," "The Princess and the Frog," "Goats: A New Improved Musical," "The Kingdom of Heaven Is Like a Party," and "The Creation According to Francis of Assisi."

The Kingdom of Heaven Is Like a Party (audiocassette), Clancy Agency, 1987.

Once ... Stories for Kids (audiocassette), Clancy Agency, 1990. Includes "Clap Your Hands," "The Giant Who Was More Than a Match," "Ode to Joy," "King's Cat," "Johnny Appleseed Song," "Little Scarface," "Simple Gifts," "50 Ways to Fool Your Mother," "Br'er Possum," "Stories Everywhere," "Harvey's Hideout," "Happy," and "Close Your Eyes."

Raised Catholic, Can You Tell? (audiocassette), August House, 1993. Nostalgia and humor.

Some of My Best Friends Are KIDS! (audiocassette), Clancy Agency, 1987. Contains "Banjo Quiz," "Sody Solaraitis," "Bear Hunt," "David and Goliath," "Foolish Frog," "Honey Bunny," "School Bus Song," and "Hansel & Gretel"; recorded live at the United Friends School, Quakertown, Pennsylvania.

Tales of Wit and Humor (contributor) (audiocassette), National Association for the Preservation and Perpetuation of Storytelling, 1992. Features "Cinderella."

Yankee Come Home ... Ed Stivender Live (audiocassette), Clancy Agency, 1990. Contains the title song plus "Sir Gawain and Lady Ragnall," "Pretty Polly," "Improvised Fairy Tale," "Winnebago," "Mud Miner," "Dueling Banjos," "Acres of Diamonds," "The Squire's Bride," "Jack and the Robbers," "Cinderella," "The Train," and a reprise of "Yankee Come Home."

Awards

1996 National Storytelling Association Circle of Excellence.
1982 Philadelphia Mummers' Day Parade Most Original Character.

Source

"The Barter Storytellers," *Storytelling Magazine*, July 1997, 5.
"A Brief Look at This Year's Storytellers," Jonesborough, Tennessee *Herald & Tribune*, September 30, 1992, 4C–8C.
Delatiner, Barbara, "Stories to Pique a Listener's Imagination," *New York Times*, July 11, 1982.
Flocken, Corinne, "Getting into the Holiday Spirit," *Los Angeles Times*, November 30, 1995.
King, Susan, "Home Entertainment," *Los Angeles Times*, October 4, 1996.
Michie, Dana, "A Storytelling Chat with Ed Stivender," *HearSay*, April 1997, 1–3.
Mooney, Bill, and David Holt. *The Storyteller's Guide*. Little Rock, Ark.: August House, 1996.
Stotter, Ruth, and William Bernard McCarthy, "Tellers and Their Tales: Revivalist Storytelling," *About Story: Writing on Stories and Storytelling 1980–1994*. Stotter Press, 1994; second edition 1996.
Timeless Voices: Images of the National Storytelling Festival. Jonesborough, Tenn.: National Storytelling Press, 1997.

RUTH STOTTER

Address 2244 Vistazo East
          Tiburon, California 94920
  phone 415-435-3568
  fax 415-435-9923
  email r.stotter@worldnet.att.net

Focus: California history; folktales from around the world.
Audience: children, families, adults.
Style: traditional.
Instruments/Props: origami, string, puppets, masks.

A professional storyteller and director of the Dominican College certificate-in-storytelling program in San Rafael, California, Ruth Stotter is known for workshops conducted in the United States, Australia, Canada, France, England, and Portugal and from her numerous publications. In the 1980s she produced and hosted *International Folkfest* for KUSF-FM in San Francisco and, since 1988, has published *The Storyteller's Calendar*. A storyteller from childhood, Stotter dates her title to a summer at Phantom Lake Camp in Mineral Point, Wisconsin, when she regaled fellow bunkmates with scary tales. She got into trouble because her stories were so frightening that the other campers were too terrified to go to the bathroom and opted to cower under the covers and wet their bunks.

Stotter comes to platform narrative with adequate preparation. She earned a B.A. in speech therapy from Ohio State University, an M.A. in speech pathology from Stanford University, and an M.A. in storytelling from an interdisciplinary psychology, anthropology, and English program at Sonoma State University. Her favorite lore came from original stories and Edgar Allan Poe's tales gained secondhand from her cousin. Certain that narration was her life's work, she chose folklorist Hector Lee as a mentor and recorded California history on a series of audiocassettes. As an instructor of storytelling, she teaches a beginning level course, story adaptation, analyzing tales, preschool storytelling, critique clinic, and workshops in tandem telling and enhancing the sending, as well as a folklore course for the extended education department of Sonoma State University. She has served on the Aesop Prize Committee of the American Folklore Society and has consulted on storytelling with puppets for Puppeteers of America. Her favorite telling experiences were at the Australian Bar Association in Melbourne, University of the Algarve in Portugal, "Folk Tales for the Fifties" at Rutgers University, and

Three Apple Festival, Bay Area Festival, Edmonton and Lethbridge Festivals, and Northern California Renaissance Faire, which she served as resident teller from 1978 to 1988. Other travels include visits to Bali, Burma, Canada, China, Corsica, Egypt, England, Fiji, France, Guatemala, Greece, India, Ireland, Italy, Japan, Norway, Mexico, Peru, Scotland, and Thailand. She has trained other professionals at the Puppeteers of America National Festival, National Association for the Perpetuation and Preservation of Storytelling Conference, London College of Storytellers, and Wellspring Renewal Center.

Articles

"Adaptation or Betrayal," in *Stories: A Western Storytelling Newsletter,* Spring 1994.

"Coyote, Hermes and the Knight Errant," *Stories: A Western Storytelling Newsletter,* 1991.

"Everybody Knows Old Dry Frye," *Stories: A Western Storytelling Newsletter,* 1993.

"Finding Tellable Tales," *Yarnspinner,* 1982.

"The Importance of Interdisciplinary Research," *Stories,* 1992.

"Interpreting Stories from Other Cultures: A Coyote Model," *National Storytelling Journal,* Winter 1988.

"The Kinesic Component of Storytelling," *Yarnspinner,* 1984, 1–2.

"Less Is More," *National Storytelling Journal,* Spring 1987, 13.

"Seeing the World Through Others' Lenses," *National Storytelling Magazine,* Spring 1993, 38–39.

"Spinning Tales from Corn Silk," *National Storytelling Journal,* Summer 1985.

"Spirituality and Storytelling," *Story Bag Newsletter,* April/May 1994.

"Story Openings and Closings," *Story Bag Newsletter,* Spring/Summer 1997.

"Storytelling," in *American Folklore: An Encyclopedia,* Garland, 1996, 690–691.

"Storytelling as a Cooperative Learning Experience," *California Reader,* Fall 1993.

"Storytelling: Bridge Between Cultures," *National Storytelling Journal,* Fall 1985.

"Storytelling Is Performance," *Stories,* 1990.

"Storytelling with Puppets," *Consultants Notebook,* Puppeteers of America, 1989, 53–54.

"Survey of Storytellers," *Yarnspinner,* 1986.

"The Tellers and the Tales: Revivalist Storytelling" (co-author William Bernard McCarthy), *Jack in Two Worlds.* University of North Carolina Press, 1994.

"Thirty-Five Recommended Books for the Storyteller's Library," *Yarnspinner,* February 1992.

"Truth and Lies: Manipulation of Story," *Marvels and Tales,* Spring 1996, 53–67.

"Try Them on for Size," *Yarnspinner,* 1982.

Bibliography

About Story: Writings on Story and Storytelling, Stotter Press, 1994; second edition, 1996. Contains "Spinning Tales from Corn Silk," "Everybody Knows Old Dry Frye," "Seeing the World Through Others' Lenses," "The Storyteller: Bridge Between Cultures," "Interpreting Stories from Other Cultures: A Coyote Model," "Storytelling as a Cooperative Learning Experience," "The Kinesic Component of Storytelling Performance," and "Tellers and Their Tales: Revivalist Storytelling."

"Agaboogawa, xnay snasznay," *Joining In: Participation Stories.* Yellow Moon Press, 1988.

Celebrating the World of Storytelling, Stotter

Press, 1995. Twenty-four color postcards of story artifacts from around the world.

"A Finger Story," "The Hungry Stranger," and "The Water Cup," in *The Family Storytelling Handbook*, Macmillan, 1987.

Little Acorns: an Introduction to Marin County Plants, Stotter Press, 1993.

"A Love Story—1806" in *Many Voices: True Tales from America's Past*. National Storytelling Association, 1995.

One Hundred Memorable Quotes About Storytelling, Stotter Press, 1995.

"The Storyteller's Calendar," Stotter Press, 1988–1997.

Videography

Origami Stories, Chip Taylor Communications, 1995.

String Stories, Chip Taylor Communications, 1995. Features "The Hole in My Neck," "Spider's Lunch," "The Earth Day Story," "The Siberian House," and "The Ladder Story."

Audiography

"The Shoes of Abu Kasan," in *Stories from the Hearth, Vol. 2* (audiocassette), GlassWing Media, 1995.

True Tales from California; There's Gold in Them There Hills! (two audiocassettes), Stotter Press, 1991. Ten stories about state characters, including poet outlaw Black Bart, mail carrier Snowshoe Thompson, the state president William B. Ide, stagecoach driver Charlie Parkhurst, miner Bill Wilson, Mormon millionaire Sam Brannar, gambler Jersey Ray, physician John Marsh, and prospector Malay Pete.

Women of the West: Four True Stories from California History (audiocassette), Stotter Press, 1995. Contains "A Love Story," "Fourth of July in Downeville, 1851," "The Irish Lace Shawl," and "Beauty Is as Beauty Does."

Awards

1996 National Storytelling Association Service and Leadership Award.

Source

"Claudia Gitelman," *Village Voice*, October 24–30, 1990.

Foster, Juanita R., "Review," *Video Rating Guide for Libraries*, Vol. 6, No. 2, 118.

Goldman, Phyllis, "Claudia Gitelman Dance Theater," *Back Stage*, November 30, 1990.

Jones, Gwendolyn, "Review," *Story Art*, April/May/June 1997, 8–9.

_____, "Tips & Tales," *Here & There*, June 1996.

"Origami Stories," http://www.chiptaylor.com/tellers.htm, June 2, 1997.

Peasley, Rosie, "Review," *Audiovisual Review*, November 1990, 72.

"Ruth Stotter," http://www.clever.net/stotterstorytelling, May 30, 1997.

FOLKE TEGETTHOFF
[fohl'•kuh nteh'•geht•tahv]

Address A8413 St. Georgen, Kloster
Austria
phone 03183 74 23 or 43-316-820620
fax 03183 74 00
website www.graz.tales.org

United States translator and distributor:
The New Fairy Tale Inc.
Milton Grimes
Martin Chapel Road
Murray, Kentucky 42071
phone 502-753-8215
fax 502-762-3434
email mgrimes@msumusik.mersuky.edu

Focus: contemporary fairy tales that display tolerance, humor, heart, morality, and truth.

Audience: primarily children.

Style: traditional Märchenerzähler (fairy tale teller).

Instruments/Props: costumes as Captain Canoe.

As fairy tale writer and organizer of Europe's largest festival of storytelling, Tegetthoff, a charismatic pioneer of international young adult literature, has filled a slot once occupied by Aesop, the brothers Grimm, and Hans Christian Andersen. Tegetthoff was born February 13, 1954, in Graz, Austria. After several years studying medicine and education theory, he left Austria in 1977 and spent a year

In the next two decades, Tegetthoff married Astrid, fathered four children, and settled into a former convent in St. Georgen, south of Styria, Austria. He has published 28 children's books, which are available in the United States, China, Japan, Mexico, and Russia, and has written seven television movies and performed 3500 times in 37 countries. In 1986, Kentucky's Murray State University opened the "Folke Tegetthoff Collection." Two years later, he inaugurated the international Graz Erzählt Festival, a prestigious gathering that draws performers from around the world. To facilitate his publications, in 1990 he established his own publishing house, Edition Neues Märchen.

Bibliography

Fairy Tales (Märchen), New Fairy Tale, 1989.

Fairy Stories of Love, New Fairy Tale, 1982.

in Ibiza, Spain, searching for a calling that suited his talents. While working as a songwriter, publicist, and manager in Hamburg, Germany, he discovered a fairy tale that gave him new direction. For a year, he researched theory and sources of fairy tales. In 1978, he wrote his first original fairy tale and initiated his career as a storyteller.

To activate his intent to spread tales worldwide, Tegetthoff proposed to the Austrian Foreign Minister that he travel the globe in exchange for food and lodging, just as Andersen had wanted to do. Tegetthoff received an immediate turndown, but proposed the idea to fifty Austrian ambassadors and received 29 invitations. Sponsored by the Austrian Tourist Board from 1982 to 1984, he appeared 500 times in 31 countries. Of his travels, he treasures performances at Sophia University in Tokyo, Al-Ahzar University in Cairo, Jerusalem University in Israel, Academy of Science in St. Petersburg, Russia, University of California at Los Angeles, Seoul University in Korea, University of Beijing in China, University of Istanbul in Turkey, University of Budapest in Hungary, Bangkok University in Thailand, and Corn Island Storytelling Festival in Louisville, Kentucky.

Awards

1994 Ygdrasil, the LEGO Prize, worth $100,000.

1982 *Fairy Stories of Love* tops the Austrian bestseller list.

Source

Cannarozzi, Sam Yada, "Lange Nacht Enchanting Enchanted," *Tale Trader*, August 1997, 9.

"Graz Erzählt," http://www.iicm.edu/graz/high-lights1997;internal&sk=ROBOT, May 30, 1997.

"Graz to Feature Tellers from Eleven Nations," *Tale Trader*, May 1997, 5.

"International Storytelling Events," *Storytelling Magazine*, July 1997, 5.

"LEGO Award," http://www.lego.com/press/press_15.html, October 8, 1996.

"Tegetthoff Is Austria's Correspondent," *Tale Trader*, February 1996, 6.

EVE WATTERS

Address   P. O. Box 1792
Charlottesville, Virginia 22902
phone 804-823-8600
email 76022.3035@compuserv.com

Focus: singalongs; tall tales; true stories and toe ticklers; traditional lore; history performances; Virginia fireside music and tales; group participation; riddles, tongue-twisters, and rhymes.

Audience: all ages.

Style: energetic, musical, humorous.

Instruments/Props: Celtic harp, Anglo concertina, 5-string banjo, lap dulcimer, autoharp, hurdy-gurdy, melodeon, pennywhistle, recorders, dumbek, guitar.

Eve Watters's art springs from a life-long appreciation for the dynamics of the oral tradition. She devotes her work to noteworthy entertainments that span cultures and generations. A seasoned professional, she is self-schooled folk style and has collected an impressive treasure of finely tuned material from around the world. Watters plays ten instruments and sings over three hundred songs in Welsh, German, French, Yiddish, Hebrew, Spanish, Russian, Persian, Ladino, and English. She performs over fifty tales from as far away as Burma, Ethiopia, Kenya, Japan, Korea, and Russia. Her English material derives from the British Isles, Australia, Canada, and the United States.

While living in Burma and eleven years in England, Watters acquired material from many influential folk artists, as well as from neighbors in village and town, and from her Irish in-laws. She has studied harp and oral tradition in Ireland and in workshops with Ed Stivender, Robin Williamson, Donald Davis, Elizabeth Ellis, Michael Parent, The Folktellers, and Jackie Torrence. In addition to a busy touring schedule, she was for many years originator and presenter of popular weekly radio programs of storytelling and music for WTJU-FM, appeared on the PBS-TV series "Inn Country," and produced numerous concerts, as well as the Charlottesville Fall Festival of Tales.

Watters took up the harp last of all, but passion for its mysterious beauty has become her instrumental focus. The harp is the ideal accompaniment for vocals and, as in African and European cultures of old, is well suited to storytelling. She uses the harp for portrayals of oral literature from the late eighteenth century and early nineteenth century. She bases programs on the American Federalist period on years of original research, much of it with such primary data as diaries, letters, and private collections, which she brings to light the domestic amusements of all classes. Her program entitled "Virginia Fireside" reveals the hand-made amusements of past centuries and sparkles with rhyme, riddles, songs, and tales; "Ladies of the Little Mountain," drawn from documentation at Monticello, reflects the African and European influences on the household of Thomas Jefferson.

Watters's schedule keeps her on the road over 200 days per year. She has performed throughout Virginia and the East Coast and in the United Kingdom and Australia, where she was featured performer at the annual conference of the Institute for Celtic Studies. She has been featured teller at the Virginia State

Storytelling Festival, Spring Festival, Annual Homecoming on St. Simon's Island, Virginia State Fair, Schiele Museum, Shenandoah Valley Storytelling Festival, and Monticello and at colleges, schools, libraries, and private and community events. She is currently storyteller-in-residence at the Museum of American Frontier Culture and resident musician on Sundays at the Boar's Head Inn.

Audiography

My Ship Sailed from China: International Songs and Stories for Children (audiocassette), Heartworks Music, 1992. Contains the title song plus "Merry Green Fields," "Era Una Vez," "John the Rabbit," "Kye Kye Kole," "Counting the Goats," "Melodeon Medley," "Waterbound," "Dance Thumbkin, Dance," "Ho, Ho, the Rattlin' Bog," "Grey Goose and Gander," "Little Fishes," "The Kingdom Lost for a Drop of Honey," "Grandfather's Son," "Three Gold Coins," and "Do', Do'"; for ages 3 and up.

Awards

1998–1999 Virginia Commission for the Arts Touring Grant.

1995 First Place in the Richmond Celtic Games Harp Competition.

1995 Third Place in the National Scottish Harp Competition.

1993 Parents' Choice Award for *My Ship Sailed from China*.

Source

"Review," *Parents' Choice*, Spring 1993.

TOM WEAKLEY

Address   RR 1, Box 1160
           Arlington, Vermont 05250
    phone 802-375-6934

Focus: literary stories; jocular tales; tall tales and trickster lore; local events; personal and family anecdotes and stories.
   Audience: general.
   Style: comic.

Tom Weakley, a candlemaker at Candle Mill Village in East Arlington, Vermont, retired from his cottage industry in 1990 to devote himself to writing and performing stories. A native of Jamestown, New York, he learned stories in childhood from his father, a jovial teller who was a master of timing and delivery. The addition of a journalism degree from Syracuse University prepared him for work on the editorial staff of a New York magazine. Drafted into the Marines, he was spared combat and spent two years routing soldiers about the United States. His decision to go to the West Coast to study Japanese and visit Japan met with serendipity. He encountered his future wife Barbara on the train, corresponded with her for six months, and decided to marry her. Wearied of commuting to Manhattan from Long Island, they established their candlemaking business as the outgrowth of a hobby, set up shop in a 200-year-old grist mill in 1958, and remained in business until 1990. In the interim, they produced two children and plenty of material to fuel Tom's second career as storyteller.

A popular after-dinner speaker and workshop leader, Weakley got his start in storytelling in 1982 through teaching Sunday school. When his class began passing Matchbox cars during the lesson, Weakley halted their squirming by recounting the story of Joseph's coat of many colors, how his brothers sold him into slavery in Egypt, and how Joseph predicted a famine. The eager response was so gratifying that Weakley decided to carry telling to larger audiences. Never satisfied with his stock, he continues to develop old stories with an individualized twist, as in his program, "Stories for a Southern Vermont Summer," designed for a library gathering. He names Jeannine Laverty as his teacher and coach and credits professional tellers Jay O'Callahan, Donald Davis, Milbre Burch, and Judith Black with giving him practical advice. One of his projects is researching the story of the St. Albans Raid, the northernmost Civil War battle, which occurred in northern Vermont. He intends to perform the story in concert and record it. In May 1997 he took part in a research team who interviewed and recorded native tellers in mountain villages of Dominica in the Caribbean for use by the Dominican National Cultural Library.

A second career in storytelling has carried Weakley far from home. A native of Chautauqua County, New York, he has traveled with his stories through New England and as far south as Georgia and west to Michigan to give workshops entitled "Our Stories, Ourselves: Finding and Telling Our Family and Personal Stories," "Bringing Home the Folktale: How to Make Your Town the Center of the Universe," and a unique and humane application of his art, "Saying Goodbye, Saying Hello: How to Use Stories to Help the Terminally Ill and Their Survivors," which he taught at the 18th National Storytelling Conference to express the worth of individual lives. He has appeared at Interfaith Council of Manchester, First Night, Good Sam Club Samboree, Clever Gretchen Conference, Union College, Conference of Catholic Educators, Michigan Storytelling Festival, Three Apples Storytelling Festival, Bennington College, Jonnycake Storytelling Festival, Vermont Law School, and Vermont Hospice Council Conference, for which he works as an organizer and volunteer.

Weakley, a believer in eye contact, enjoys telling because of its one-to-one communication with the listener. His signature tall tale, "The Lake Dunmore Whopper," brings out the actor in him because it calls for precise movements and exaggeration. Among his many performances, he enjoyed an invitation to tell at Exchange Place at the 1993 National Storytelling Festival, at the 1995 Doggone Storytelling Festival in Chester, Connecticut, and at a Veterans' Day performance of stories from Studs Terkel's *The Good War* with tellers Sue Spivack and Jeannine Laverty.

Bibliography

"The Ecstasy and the Agony," Bennington, Vermont *Banner*, April 25, 1996, 9.

"The Gift" and "On Hearing Loch Lomond," *Storytelling World*, Summer 1995.

"The Lake Dunmore Whopper" and "Mule Goes to Court," *Storytelling World*, Summer-Fall 1993, 8.

"Mommy Water," in *Who's Afraid ... ? Facing Children's Fears with Folktales*, Teacher Ideas Press, 1994.

"Mr. Furlong," *Storytelling World*, Winter/ Spring 1994, 13.

"Waiting on the Lord," *Storytelling World*, Winter 1997.

Audiography

Harry and the Texaco Boys (audiocassette), Highland Publications, 1992. Autobiographical stories about coming of age during the Depression, featuring the ballgame on Prendergast Street, lies about Mary Olson's bra, and the title story.

R. F. D. Vermont (audiocassette), Highland Publications, 1990. Vermont stories and original material, taped live at East Arlington Federated Church.

White Mules and Hoop Snakes (audiocassette), Highland Publications 1994. Featuring Bucky Grimm, the Green Mountain undertaker, Worthless the guard dog, Fenetre La Chienne's pie recipe, the heifer accident, Thurston Hulet's rabbit dog, and the wrestling champ.

Awards

1993 American Library Association Notable Recording Award for *Harry and the Texaco Boys*.

Source

"Arlington Storyteller Honored," Manchester, Vermont *Journal*, May 8, 1991, 15.

"Doggone Festival," *New York Times*, June 4, 1995.

"The Faces and Stories of Tom Weakley," Jamestown, New York *Post-Journal*, December 12, 1992.

"A Fete for Tom Weakley," Manchester, Vermont *Journal*, November 16, 1994.

"'The Good War' Comes to Vermont," Manchester, Vermont *Journal*, November 8, 1995, 8.

"Harry and the Texaco Boys," Manchester, Vermont *Journal*, March 18, 1992, 14.

Kirkendoll, Shantell M., "Once Upon a Time," Flint, Michigan *Journal*, July 13, 1997, E-1, E-3.

"Local Storyteller Brings War Memories to Life," Bennington, Vermont *Banner*, November 5, 1992.

"Local Storyteller Honored," Bennington, Vermont *Banner*, February 18, 1993.

McDonald, Christine, "WWII Revived," Glens Falls, New York *Chronicle*, November 21, 1985, 17.

Mengucci, Mary Ellen, "Once Upon a Time," *Syracuse University Magazine*, March 1990, 46, 47.

Paine, Maggie, "The Narrative Magic of Tom Weakley," Manchester, Vermont *Journal*, May 11, 1994.

_____, "Spinners of Stories, Tellers of Tales," Manchester, Vermont *Journal*, November 6, 1991, 13, 20.

Severinghaus, Wendy, "For the Blind, Stories Can Be Especially Compelling," Bennington, Vermont *Banner*, May 11, 1989, 13.

"Stories for Healing," (Manchester)*Vermont News Guide*, November 3, 1987, 1, 8.

"Storyteller at Arts Center," Bennington, Vermont *Banner*, September 15, 1994.

"Storyteller on the Loose," Bennington, Vermont *Banner*, September 12, 1987, 8.

"Storyteller Performs for Hospice," Littleton, New Hampshire *Courier*, January 6, 1993.

"Storyteller Returns," Bennington, Vermont *Banner*, September 12, 1996.

"Storytellers Bring 'The Good War' to Life," Schenectady, New York *Gazette*, March 31, 1987.

"Storytelling Festival," Glens Falls, New York *Post-Star*, September 20, 1993.

"Tom Weakley Spins Magic Tales," Bennington, Vermont *Banner*, October 13, 1996.

"Tom Weakley, Storyteller," Bennington, Vermont *Area Arts Guide 1997*, 8.

"Tom Weakley's Vermont Stories," Manchester, Vermont *Journal*, January 30, 1991, 14.

"Vermont Stories for United Way," Manchester *Vermont News Guide*, February 5, 1991, 1, 20.

"Voices from 'The Good War,'" Bennington, Vermont *Banner*, November 9, 1995.

JIM WEISS

Address   Greathall Productions
               P. O. Box 813
               Benicia, California 94510
        phone 800-477-6234 or 707-745-6234
        fax 707-745-5820

Focus: Greek mythology; works of William Shakespeare, Geoffrey Chaucer, Jonathan Swift, Alexandre Dumas, Sir Arthur Conan Doyle, and Washington Irving; classic fables and fairy tales of Aesop and Charles Perrault; mystery stories; multicultural lore; Bible stories; holiday stories of Charles Dickens, Bret Harte, and O. Henry; heroic tales of King Arthur and Robin Hood; historical figures and events.

Audience: children, families, adults; theaters, schools, festivals, homeschool groups, libraries; keynote speaker at educational conferences.

Style: intense characterization through gesture, facial expression, and multiple voicing.

Successful storyteller Jim Weiss, who heard King Arthur and Three Musketeers stories from his father, aims to make a full range of classic literature accessible and enjoyable to a wide audience. To an audience of students, he once claimed, "There isn't a greater gift than imagination. It is a short-sighted society that does not value creativity" (Jacobs, 1995). Weiss and his wife Randy have made a family business of activating his beliefs and packaging and marketing his stories on the Greathall label. His media performances include hosting and performing on PBS-TV's *Short Stories and Tall Tales*. He has earned 24 national awards from the American Library Association, Parents' Choice, Parents' Council, Oppenheim Toy Portfolio, *AudioFile*, *Storytelling World*, and Film Advisory Board and received thirteen recommendations from *Booklist* and seven from *School Library Journal*. A 1966 graduate of Highland Park High School in Highland Park, Illinois, Weiss returned to perform for classes and was surprised by a public acclamation of Jim Weiss Day in honor of his triumph as a platform narrator and publisher of moral literature for families and classes.

Weiss began his career with a B.A. in speech and communication from the University of Wisconsin and a teaching job in a Los Angeles elementary school. There, remembering his father's stories, he found he could interest students in any subject with an appropriate tale. From there he moved to selling printing in northern California, but found little real satisfaction in it. In 1989, he left and turned his natural bent for telling bedtime stories into an award-winning profession. By combining his talents with those of his wife, Randy, a nationally known education consultant, writer, and teacher, Jim began to produce and distribute recordings of his facile voice telling classic stories and singing songs. Underwritten by their life's savings, the first five titles — *Good Night, The Three Musketeers/Robin Hood, Greek Myths, Arabian Nights*, and *Tales from the Old Testament* — soon grew into a full catalog of products for home, school, church or synagogue, travel, and after-school entertainment. With Jim recording and performing and Randy running the corporate side of their company, Greathall Productions, the Weisses have sold hundreds of thousands of cassettes and CDs through distributors, stores, catalogs, and direct marketing. Jim performs across the country and speaks on literacy at education conferences. In workshops for parents, students, and classroom teachers of history, science, literature, and the arts, he offers techniques to structure stories, create characters, and motivate learning. He applies building confidence and offering insight into oral language and learning through storytelling and insists that he himself continues to learn from stories.

Audiography

Animal Tales (audiocassette and CD), Greathall Productions, 1990. Featuring Aesop's "The Crow and the Pitcher," "The Lion and the Mouse," and "The Tortoise and the Hare," plus Geoffrey Chaucer's "Chanticleer and the Rooster" and Horace's "City Mouse and the Country Mouse," plus "Giggly Biggly and the Invitation," "Goat Gets Away," and "The Cat Who Went to Church"; for ages 3 and up.

Arabian Nights (audiocassette), Greathall Productions, 1990. Contains "The Bird Who Speaks," "Ali Baba and the Forty Thieves," "Scheherazade," and "The Fisherman and the Genie"; for ages 5 to adult.

Best Loved Stories in Song and Dance (audiocassette and CD), Greathall Productions, 1997. Featuring Grimms' "The Twelve Dancing Princesses" and "Snow White and Rose Red," Perrault's "Sleeping Beauty," and original songs; for ages 5 to adult.

A Christmas Carol and Other Favorites (audiocassette and CD), Greathall Productions, 1996. Featuring O. Henry's "The Gift of the Magi," Bret Harte's "Dick Spindler's Family Christmas," and the title story, by Charles Dickens; for ages 5 to adult.

Fairytale Favorites in Story and Song (audiocassette and CD), Greathall Productions, 1993. Includes "Stone Soup," "Puss in Boots," "The Shoemaker and the Elves," and "Rapunzel" plus two songs, "Stone Soup" and "The Pussycat Rag"; for ages 5 to adult.

Giants! A Colossal Collection of Tales and Tunes (audiocassette and CD), Greathall Productions 1997. Featuring "Jack and the Beanstalk," "The Selfish Giant," and "The Giant of Grabbist," "The Fantastical Tale of Finn MacCoul," and the songs "In the Garden" and "If I Were a Giant"; for ages 5 to adult.

Good Night (audiocassette and CD), Greathall Productions, 1990. Includes "Tropical Island," "The Unicorn," "Mountain Cabin," "The Farm," "Treehouse in the Forest," and "Mermaid's Lagoon"; for ages 3 and up.

Greek Myths (audiocassette and CD), Greathall Productions, 1990. Featuring "Adventures of Hercules," "Arachne," "Perseus and Medusa," and "King Midas and the Golden Touch"; for ages 5 to adult.

The Jungle Book (audiocassette and CD), Greathall Productions, 1995. Featuring four of Rudyard Kipling's stories — "Mowgli's Brothers," "Red Dog," "Tiger, Tiger," and "The Spring Running"; for ages 7 to adult.

King Arthur and His Knights (audiocassette), Greathall Productions, 1990. Featuring "Sir Bedivere," "The Sword in the Stone," "King Arthur, Guinevere," "Sir Percival Meets a Lady," "The Round Table," "Sir Lancelot's Journey," "A Queen," and "Merlin's Magic"; for ages 5 to adult.

Mystery! Mystery! for Children (audiocassette and CD), Greathall Productions, 1994. Features Edgar Allan Poe's "The Purloined Letter," G. K. Chesterton's "The Blue Cross," and Sir Arthur Conan Doyle's "The Red-Headed League"; for ages 7 to adult.

Rip Van Winkle/Gulliver's Travels (audiocassette), Greathall Productions 1993. Includes Washington Irving's "Rip Van Winkle," Jonathan Swift's "Gulliver's Travels," and a folktale, "Fool's Gold" plus an original song, "Rip's Rap"; for grades 3–8.

Shakespeare for Children (audiocassette and CD), Greathall Productions, 1996. Featuring *A Midsummer Night's Dream* and *The Taming of the Shrew;* for ages 7 to adult.

She and He: Adventures in Mythology (audiocassette), Greathall Productions, 1991. Including "Psyche and Cupid," "Pygmalion and Galatea," "Echo and Narcissus," "Baucis and Philemon," and "Atalanta and the Golden Apples"; for ages 5 to adult.

Sherlock Holmes for Children (audiocassette and CD), Greathall Productions, 1991. Featuring "The Adventure of the Speckled Band," "The Mazarin Stone," "The Musgrave Ritual," and "The Blue Carbuncle"; for ages 7 to adult.

Spooky Classics (audiocassette and CD), Greathall Productions, 1997. Featuring Oscar Wilde's "The Canterville Ghost," Nathaniel Hawthorne's "Dr. Heidegger's Experiment," and Rudyard Kipling's "The Sending of Dana Da"; for ages 5 to adult.

Tales from Cultures Far and Near (audiocassette), Greathall Productions, 1990. Includes stories from Africa, Japan, China, Arabia, Spain, and native America: "A Guest Who Ran," "Two Monks," "The Three Friends of Manuel," "Djuha: Two Stories," "Courting the Wind," and "The Secret Weapon"; for ages 5 to adult.

Tales from the Old Testament (audiocassette), Greathall Productions, 1990. Featuring "Abraham and the Idols," "The Story of Ruth," "Noah and the Ark," "Queen Esther," "David and Goliath," "David's Dance," and "Wise King Solomon"; for ages 5 to adult.

The Three Musketeers/Robin Hood (audiocassette), Greathall Productions, 1989. Featuring "Our Hero," "Duel," "Athos, Porthos and Aramis," "The Queen's Diamonds," "Robin and Little John," "Lady Marion," "The Archery Contest," and "Robin and the King"; for ages 5 to adult.

Awards

1997 *AudioFile* Earphones Award for *Giants! A Colossal Collection of Tales and Tunes.*

1996 Film Advisory Board Award of Excellence for *A Christmas Carol and Other Favorites.*

1996 Film Advisory Board Award of Excellence for *Shakespeare for Children.*

1996 NAIRD Indie finalist for *A Christmas Carol and Other Favorites.*

1995 Parents' Choice Silver Award for *The Jungle Book.*

1995 NAIRD Indie finalist for *The Jungle Book.*

1995 American Library Association Notable Children's Recording for *The Jungle Book.*

1995 Oppenheim Toy Portfolio Best Audio for *The Jungle Book.*

1994 HarperCollins Best Toys, Books and Videos.

1994 American Library Association Notable Children's Recording for *Mystery! Mystery! for Children.*

1994 NAIRD Indie finalist for *Mystery! Mystery! for Children.*

1994 Oppenheim Toy Portfolio Best Audio for *Mystery! Mystery! for Children.*

1993 Parents' Choice Gold Award for *Fairytale Favorites in Story and Song.*

1993 NAIRD Indie finalist for *Fairytale Favorites in Story and Song.*

1993 Oppenheim Toy Portfolio Best Audio for *Fairytale Favorites in Story and Song.*

1992 Random House/The American Library Association Best of the Best for Children.

1991 *Booklist* Annual Editor's Choice for *Sherlock Holmes for Children.*

1991 NAIRD Indie finalist for *She and He: Adventures in Mythology.*

1991 American Library Association Notable Children's Recording for *King Arthur and His Knights.*

1991 Parents' Choice Gold Award for *Sherlock Holmes for Children.*

1991 American Library Association Notable Children's Recording for *Sherlock Holmes for Children.*

1990 *Booklist* Annual Editor's Choice for *Greek Myths.*

1990 Parents' Choice Gold Award for *Arabian Nights.*

Source

Balesnan, Teresa, "Review," *School Library Journal*, February 1994.

Bevin, Kristi, "Review," *Booklist*, May 15, 1991.

Duffy, Cathy, *Curriculum Manual Elementary Grades*, Homerun Enterprises, 1995.

Furber, Gretchen, "Review," *Booklist*, March 15, 1990.

Gordh, Bill, "A Storyteller's Favorites from Around the World," *Sesame Street Parents*, November 1993.

Gross, Margaret, "Review," *School Library Journal*, February 1994.

Hartshorn, Laurie, "Review," *Booklist*, May 15, 1993.

Heffley, Lynee, "A Taste of Holmes from a Master Storyteller," *Los Angeles Times*, March 20, 1993.

Holdren, John, and E. D. Hirsch, *Books to Build On: The Core Knowledge Series*. New York: Bantam/Doubleday Dell, 1996.

Jacobs, Jodie, "And They Lived Happily Ever After," *Chicago Tribune*, July 30, 1995.

Kepple, Joseph, "Review," *Booklist*, January 15, 1991.

Long, Pam, "Beyond Books: Kids' Sidelines," *American Bookseller*, March 1993.

Mitnck, Fritz, "Review," *School Library Journal*, May 1995.

Mooney, Bill, and David Holt. *The Storyteller's Guide*. Little Rock, Ark.: August House, 1996.

Peck, Penny, "Review," *School Library Journal*, October 1992.

Reid, Rob, "Review," *School Library Journal*, March 1996.

Reisner, Susan, "Review," *Booklist*, May 15, 1990.

"Review," *AudioFile*, February 1993.

"Review," *California Homeschool Network News*, August/September 1996.

"Review," *Contra Costa Times*, June 6, 1996.

"Review," *Entertainment Weekly*, June 17, 1994.

"Review," *Los Angeles Times,* November 27, 1994; December 10, 1996.

"Review," *National Homeschool Journal*, December 1996-January 1997.

"Review," *Parenting*, December/January 1997.

"Review," *Parents' Choice*, December 1994.

"Review," *Publishers Weekly*, November 21, 1994.

"Review," *Wilson Library Bulletin*, January 1995.

Rupp, Becky, "Good Stuff," *Home Education Magazine*, September-October 1992.

Sanborn, LaVonne, "Review," *School Library Journal*, May 1993.

Schackman, Paul, "Review," *Booklist*, February 15, 1996.

Sherouse, Vicki, "Review," *Booklist*, May 15, 1991.

Wotipka, Julia, "Tape Talk," *The Oregonian*, September 9, 1993.

MARY JO KELLY WILHELM AND ROBERT BÉLA WILHELM

Address   Storyfest Journeys
18934 Rolling Road
Hagerstown, Maryland 21742-2659
phone 301-791-9153 or 800-277-7035
fax 301-739-2779
email bob@storyfest.com
email kelly@storyfest.com
web site www.storyfest.com

Mary Jo Kelly Wilhelm's Focus: Scottish, Irish, and Welsh stories and the lives of female saints; homemade stories.

Audience: all ages.

Style: teams with her husband to listen and tell stories.

Born in Pittsburgh, Pennsylvania, Mary Jo Kelly Wilhelm grew up in an extended Irish clan who loved to talk. From her father, a captain in the U.S. Navy, she heard stories from around the world. She was educated at Dunbaron College and San Francisco State University. After settling on the West Coast with her husband, Robert Béla Wilhelm, she worked with children as a therapeutic recreator. She worked with young hospital patients, delinquent youth, and retarded children, and as a youth minister. While completing a Ph.D.

at the University of Maryland, she studied pilgrimage travel under Dr. Fred Humphrey and Dr. Daniel Huden.

Currently, Wilhelm offers "Telling the Stories of Women Saints," a one-day workshop for women that covers the lives of St. Etheldreda of Ely, St. Bridget of Kildare, St. Margaret of Scotland, St. Theresa of Avila, Blessed Kateri Tekawitha, St. Elizabeth Bayley Seton, and Our Lady of Walsingham. In April 1997, she joined her husband for a storyteller's journey to the Scottish borders, featuring history, myth, ballads, and tales in the land of Mary Queen of Scots, and in October conducted a tour to Assisi, Italy, to focus on St. Francis and St. Clare.

Bibliography

Camelot Sketch Book (co-author Joseph Paul Kelly, Jr., and Robert Béla Wilhelm), Storyfest, 1995. Images of a storyfest journey to Camelot featuring 17 pen and ink drawings from Devon, Somerset, and Cornwall.

Resource Guide to the Quest for Camelot, Part 2, Storyfest, 1995. Features Arthurian children's literature and historical romance; contains an annotated bibliography.

Storyfest Journeys Cookbook, Storyfest, 1993. Tour of past and present journeys and pilgrimages across America and Europe through stories, recipes, and line drawings, featuring Della's New Orleans Bread Pudding, Nigel Headley's Bermuda Fish Cakes, Rafael Auñon's lamb Alhambra, Jim Sullivan's Derryinver Salmon, and Linda Cisnero's Chicken Fajitas.

Storytelling in Youth Ministry, Storyfest, 1995. Includes personal narratives about stories and audiences, technique, and a rationale for telling and guide to use in youth ministry.

Robert Béla Wilhelm's Focus: sacred stories.

Audience: pastors, ministers, youth directors, and religious tour groups.

Style: pastoral.

For a quarter century, Robert Béla Wilhelm has served as pastor, storyteller, trainer in ministerial education, and lecturer in pastoral theology. Born December 28, 1943, in New York City, he derives an interest in world folklore from immigrant parents—a Hungarian grandmother and Slovak mother. Education at St. Stephen of Hungary School, St. Ann's School, and Holy Trinity High School preceded a B.A. from Seton Hall University and an M.A. from Catholic University of America. He earned a doctorate in religion and the arts from the Graduate Theological Union at Berkeley, specializing in pastoral use of stories, and completed post-doctoral studies at Cambridge University in England and the Gestalt Institute of Toronto under the direction of Jorge Rosner. He has held posts at the College of St. Catherine, Niagara University, and the Jesuit School of Theology at Berkeley.

As a Catholic artist and pastoral theologian, Wilhelm applies Gestalt psychology to narrative. He founded and directs the only professional apprenticeship training program in sacred storytelling, which has graduated sixteen people since its founding in 1994. Since 1967, he has visited over 150 dioceses in North America to conduct programs in religious education, spirituality, homiletics, and professional development. His concert performances include "Choices: The Way of Death or the Way of Life?," "Gospel Quest: For the Paradise of God's Blessing," "Art of Biblical Storytelling," "Eucharist and Bread: Stories of St. Francis and St. Clare," "Treasures Hidden: In the Kingdom of God," and "Images of Reconciliation: In Baptism, Penance and Eucharist." His seasonal lore includes Advent and Christmas material and Irish stories for St. Patrick's Day. He leads seminars with his wife on "Storytelling Celebration of Family Life" and "Storytelling Retreat for Youth Groups or Youth Ministers." He publishes four weekly journals, *Lectionary Storybook*, *Tradewinds and Pilgrim Paths*, *Tales for Pilgrims*, and *Sacred Passages*, which can be faxed or mailed to subscribers. The format includes homilies for sermon preparation and illuminates the Gospels.

Bibliography

Apples of Paradise: Armenian Folktales and Spirituality, Storyfest, 1993.

More Than the Blarney Stone (co-author Mary Jo Kelly Wilhelm), Storyfest, 1990. A study of the storytelling of Mark Coyne, Eddie Lenihan, and Michael O'Flaherty and of Irish-Americans returning to Ireland to find their storytelling roots.

Pagan Babies: Stories for 4 to 8-year-olds, Storyfest, 1985, 1993. Ten traditional world folktales plus full-page coloring pictures; introductory essay for parents and teachers.

Resource Guide to the Art of Biblical Storytelling, Storyfest, 1992. Contains an explanation of sacred narrative, oral roots of storytelling in ancient Israel, retelling old stories, and biblical characters.

Resource Guide to the Quest for Camelot, Part I, Storyfest, 1992. Contains a comprehensive resource guide to Arthurian lore.

Videography

Breaking Bread with St. Francis and St. Clare, Storyfest, 1992. Contains the story of Francis's miracles and the visit of Pope Gregory IX to Clare; filmed in Italy.

The Perfect Joy of St. Francis, Storyfest, 1992. A classic tale found in the medieval *Little Flowers of St. Francis*; set on Mount La Verna, the site of St. Francis's transformation; filmed in Italy.

Seagull and the Coming of Light: Native American Tale for Children, Storyfest, 1991. A creation myth from the Pacific Northwest; recorded live in the Washington National Cathedral, Washington, D.C.

St. Francis and His First Companions, Storyfest, 1992. The story of Brother Bernard, Brother Peter, Brother Giles, and Brother John the Simple; filmed in Italy.

Wolf of Gubbio: A Story of St. Francis, Storyfest, 1991. St. Francis talks with Brother Wolf; recorded in concert at Washington National Cathedral, Washington, D.C.

Audiography

Bermuda Longtales (two audiocassettes), Storyfest, 1995. Contains an original story and a retelling of the wreck of the Sea Venture, the kernel of William Shakespeare's *The Tempest*; based on eyewitness accounts published in early seventeenth century London.

Christmas Parables (four audiocassettes),

Storyfest, 1995. A collection of stories; an introduction of the Advent season and stories of St. Nicholas's Day and St. Lucy; meditations on Advent themes of light and hope.

Generous or Stingy? (two audiocassettes), Storyfest, 1995. Features four of George Bird Grinnell's Western Indian stories — "Punishment of the Stingy," "Thunder Maker," "Blind Piwapok," and "Little Friend Coyote."

More Lenten Stories (audiocassette), Storyfest, 1995. Contains "The Scots Tale of the Traveling People," "Jack and the Silken Purse," and a Haitian tale, "The Clever Doctor and Papa Death."

Our Lady Saint Mary (audiocassette), Storyfest, 1995. Medieval legends and miracles retold as short stories written by Evelyn Underhill; contains "The Ring of Roses," "Bread of Angels," "Knight of the Costrel," "Window of Paradise," "Our Lady of the Tournament," "Minstrel of Roc Amadour," and "Our Lady of the Lintel."

Pagan Babies: Stories for 4 to 8-year-olds (four audiocassettes), Storyfest, 1995. Contains thirty stories and a tape for parents and teachers on the place of storytelling in early childhood development.

Parsifal's Quest for the Holy Grail (audiocassette), Storyfest, 1995. Live performance of the Parsifal story at the Washington National Cathedral in Washington, D.C.

Sacred Stories from Celtic Lands (four audiocassettes), Storyfest, 1995. Compiles Irish, Scottish, and Welsh stories and an introductory tape on the history of sacred story in the Celtic tradition.

St. Francis at Christmastide (audiocassette), Storyfest, 1995. Features the story of the birth of St. Francis of Assisi, "Birth in a Stable," "The Wolf of Gubbio," and "Perfect Joy."

Stories for the Christmas Season (audiocassette), Storyfest, 1995. Features "St. Anthony's Light," a Sicilian folktale, and "Brother Lamb," an Armenian wonder tale.

Stories for the Lenten Journey (four audiocassettes), Storyfest, 1995. A retelling of "Two Friends," a story by Leo Tolstoy and of "The Apples of Eden," an Armenian wonder tale.

Stories for the Twelve Nights of Christmas (audiocassette), Storyfest, 1995. Features two women's tales: "Rachel's Cave" and "The Wedding Feast of Sir Gawain and Dame Ragnel" plus "Herod's Slaughter of the Holy Innocents" and "The Martyrdom of St. Thomas Becket of Canterbury."

Stories from the Hebrides (audiocassette), Storyfest, 1995. Features island stories, "The White Sword of Light" from the Isle of Jura and "Waterbull of Benbecula," from the Isle of Benbecula.

Tales of Bread and Peace (audiocassette), Storyfest, 1995. Contains Leo Tolstoy's "Pahom's Wish" and a medieval Icelandic saga, "Audun's Gift."

Tales of Old Ireland (audiocassette), Storyfest, 1995. Contains "The Harp," a mystery tale from Donegal, "Dermot's Love," a wonder tale from Galway, and "Rory's Story," a tall tale from Cork.

The Welsh Mabinogion (two audiocassettes), Storyfest, 1995. Contains two tales from the Welsh national epic, "Rhiannon" and "Manawyddan."

Source

Asch, Amy, "King Arthur's Realm," *New York Magazine*, March 11, 1991.

Beirne, Steve, "A Family Tradition Began with a Stranger's Visit," *Church World*, December 8, 1994.

DeCuir, Belinda, "Storytelling Workshop Helps Area Religious Educators," Lafayette, Louisiana *Morning Star*, June 2, 1982.

Dias, Lynn, "Storyteller: A Lost Art Is Coming Back, Thanks to Robert Wilhelm," Baton Rouge, Louisiana *State Times*, May 26, 1982.

Gearey, Amelia, "Storyteller's Tapes Share Tales, Insight," *Episcopal Teacher*, January 1989, 7.

Jacawy, Taffy, "Irish Stories Have a Sense of Mystery," Gig Harbor, Washington *Gateway*, March 13, 1985.

Johnson, Maryfran, "Sacred Art of Storytelling," Pasco, Washington *Tri-City Herald*, November 30, 1982.

Propp, Wren, "Cultivating Storytellers," *Albuquerque Journal*, June 29, 1996, 1, 3.

Roberts, Sherry, "Storyteller Says His Tales

Created for Entire Family," *Burlington* (Vermont) *Free Press*, October 10, 1981.

Shelby, Joyce, "Church Has Storied Visitor," *New York Daily News*, November 5, 1995.

Stillwell, Mary Jo, "Sacred Storyteller Comes to Maria Stein Center," *Catholic Telegraph*, August 16, 1996.

"Storytelling: A Dialogue of Growth," Orlando *Florida Catholic*, January 24, 1975.

"Tipp Priest Welcomes Fellow Storytellers," Carlow, Ireland *Nationalist Newspaper*, August 17, 1991.

Voelpel, Dan, "The Storyteller: His Voice Gives Old Yarns New Life," Tacoma, Washington *News Tribune*, March 30, 1985, A-4.

Wall, Peggy, "Once Upon a Time ... A Storyteller Came to Town for Two Lectures," Anderson South Carolina *Independent-Mail*, October 3, 1992, 1C.

DIANE WILLIAMS

Address   P. O. Box 825
Madison, Mississippi 39130

phone 601-856-6384
email DWTELLER@aol.com

Focus: literary tales; folktales; fables; participation stories; holiday celebrations; Bible stories; personal anecdotes; black history programs; personal stories.

Audience: children, teens, adults.

Style: dramatic characterization.

Instruments/Props: authentic African dress and musical instruments; illustrated story stick.

Skilled at gesture, music, dance, and telling, Diane Williams regales her audience with stories that come alive at her telling. In African dress and smooth Southern accent, she invites children to participate in the creation of characters and to participate in the narrative thread. In stories from other cultures and countries, she provides a sense of place as a teaching tool and an invitation to literacy. Her methods include storyweaving, thematic development, and imparting the storyteller's art to young would-be tellers. She has performed in Germany and Hawaii and at the Blueberry Storytelling Festival, Smith Robertson Museum and Cultural Center, Mississippi Museum of Archives and History, Pioneer and Indian Festival, Montgomery City Fest, Aliamalo Military Base, Flora Fest, Margaret Walker-Alexander Research Center's African American Bazaar, National Storytelling Festival Swapping Ground, Jubilee Jam, Blue Bluff River Festival, and Strawberry Storytelling Festival, and at clubs, parties, churches, libraries, schools, and universities and with the Mississippi Symphony.

A skilled raconteur who treasures stories that appeal to ear and heart, Williams began telling over a decade ago with the birth of her son. A native of New Jersey, she imparts a favorite memory in "The Best Gift of All," a reflection on Grandpa Walker, a widower who bought a sewing machine for her, and the gifts she made for him, including a dashiki. She recalls a 1992 meeting in Baltimore with veteran teller Mary Carter Smith, a mentor who has helped Williams expand her aims and horizons. Recounting her recent background from Madison, Mississippi, Williams guides listeners to other times and places, blending movement with songs and accent. In an original show, *Annie Mae Jumps the Broom*, she tells the story of a young man and woman and of Aunt Minnie, the older wisewoman they consult for advice on marriage. Williams's dedication to platform narrative led her to join the National Storytelling Association, International Platform Society, National Association of Black Storytellers, and Poplarville Storytelling Guild and to serve as president of the Mississippi Storyweavers Guild and director of the Good News Gospel Storytellers. In addition to a storytelling career, she has worked as executive secretary of Proffitt's, Inc., has told at many of their store openings, and performs voice-overs for Video Works in Jackson, Mississippi.

Bibliography

Annie Mae Jumps the Broom, Rendezvous with the Storyteller Press, 1994. An original story from African-American history about the marriage of Annie Mae and Buster, slaves who seek guidance from Aunt Minnie.

"The Best Gift of All," *Today in Mississippi*, December 1996, 4–6.

"Nature Love," in *Seasons to Come*, National Library of Poetry 1995.

Awards

1997 National Association of Black Storytellers Featured Performer.

1997 Mississippi Arts Commission Touring Artist Grant.

1994 National Storytelling Conference Scholarship.

1994 ArtSeen (RAPPS) Grant.

1994 Mississippi Arts Commission Fellowship nominee.

Source

Inman, Ed, "Stories Animate Black History," *Clarion-Ledger*, February 7, 1997.

"Storytellers Tell in Germany," Picayune, Mississippi *Item*, April 17, 1996, 3B.

"Storyteller to Come to Ole Miss," *Oxford Eagle*, November 11, 1996.

Stringer, Debbie, "Once Upon a Time," *Today in Mississippi*, December 1996, 4–6.

"Williams Spins Tales with Style," *Aberdeen Examiner*, October 11, 1995, 19C.

KATHRYN WINDHAM

Address   2004 Royal Street
Selma, Alabama 36701
phone 334-872-3398

Focus: ghost stories; Southern superstition and folklore; biography; family reminiscence.

Style: compassionate telling in Southern dialect.

Audience: all ages.

A newspaper reporter by profession, Kathryn Tucker Windham was surprised to be invited to tell stories at the 1973 National Storytelling Festival in Jonesborough, Tennessee. Although she grew up with stories ("All Southerners tell stories," she says), Windham never knew she was a storyteller. Listening to her father, James Wilson Tucker, a banker in the small town of Thomasville, Alabama, tell stories at the family dinner table, or on the front porch and around the fireplace, taught her all she knows about the art. She liked the role and has been doing it ever since.

Windham's newspaper career began when she was twelve, after a cousin let her write movie reviews for his weekly paper in exchange for a pass to the local theater. The job continued after her 1939 graduation from Huntingdon College in Montgomery, when she worked on the staffs of the *Alabama Journal*, the *Birmingham News*, and the *Selma Times-Journal*. Her career in print media stretches from the Great Depression through the Civil Rights movement and she won Associated Press awards for news stories and photographs over three decades. In 1946, she married Amasa Benjamin Windham and moved to Selma, where their children, Kitti, Dilcy, and Ben were born. After her husband's death in 1956, she and the children remained in Selma, where she currently shares a home with a ghost named Jeffrey.

Over the years, Windham collected folklore, superstitions, family tales, and local history, all of which she has woven into her stories, both written and oral. Readers and listeners appreciate her understanding and love of the South and its people, and enjoy the touches of humor that are her trademark. She has also told stories in pictures with a collection of Southern scenes dating to 1930, when she got her first Brownie Kodak. The photographs of rural baptisms, basketmaking, deserted tenant houses, country stores, and plain people are a part of the permanent collection at the Huntsville Museum of Art, and have been exhibited throughout Alabama.

For two years, Windham's informal commentaries were broadcast on National Public Radio's *All Things Considered*, and she is still heard weekly on Alabama Public Radio. In addition to telling stories at the National Storytelling Festival and the annual Alabama Tale Tellin' Festival in her home town, she has performed from Maine to California and in Canada and Germany. She has published nineteen books and narrated ten audio tapes and nine videos.

Bibliography

Alabama: One Big Front Porch, University of Alabama Press, 1991. An assortment of local lore, family stories, history sidelights, humor and folktales that have been told for generations on Alabama porches.

Count Those Buzzards! Stamp Those Grey Mules!, Strode, 1979. A collection of superstitions recalled from a Southern childhood.

Encounters, Black Belt Press, 1997. Photographs and stories of Southern scenes spanning a half century.

The Ghost in the Sloss Furnaces, Birmingham Historical Society, 1987. An account of the fiery death of Theophilus Calvin Jowers and his ghost's subsequent haunting of Birmingham's iron ore furnaces.

"The Hole That Will Not Stay Filled," in *Best-Loved Stories Told at the National Storytelling Festival*, August House, 1991.

Jeffrey Introduces Thirteen More Southern Ghosts, University of Alabama Press, 1987. A collection of thirteen tales of the supernatural collected from eight Southern states; for grades six and up.

Jeffrey's Latest Thirteen: More Alabama Ghosts, University of Alabama Press, 1987. Companion volume to the original Alabama collection.

"The Locket," in *Homespun: Tales from America's Favorite Storytellers*, Crown, 1988.

My Name Is Julia, Birmingham Public Library Press, 1991. A one-act play about the life of Julia Tutwiler, social reformer and humanitarian.

Odd-Egg Editor, University Press of Mississippi, 1990. Reflections on newspaper reporting from the Great Depression through the Civil Rights movement.

A Sampling of Selma Stories, Selma Printing Service, 1991. A light-hearted telling of stories that have helped local people retain their sense of humor and their sanity.

"The Selma Tourists," in *More Best-Loved Stories Told at the National Storytelling Festival*, August House, 1992.

A Serigamy of Stories, University Press of Mississippi, 1988. A collection of reminiscences about growing up in the small town of Thomasville, Alabama, in the 1920s and 1930s.

Southern Cooking to Remember, University Press of Mississippi, 1994. Traditional Southern recipes with an introductory essay for each group of foods.

Thirteen Alabama Ghosts and Jeffrey (co-author Margaret G. Figh) University of Alabama Press, 1987. The first of a series of ghost story collections; includes thirteen of the state's best documented ghost tales; for grade six and up.

Thirteen Georgia Ghosts and Jeffrey, University of Alabama Press, 1987. For grade six and up.

Thirteen Mississippi Ghosts and Jeffrey, University of Alabama Press, 1987. Tales of strange hauntings from Mississippi's Gulf Coast to its Delta; for grade six and up.

Thirteen Tennessee Ghosts and Jeffrey, University of Alabama Press, 1987. A collection of ghostly happenings from all across Tennessee, including an account of the Bell Witch of Adams; for grade six and up.

Treasured Alabama Recipes, Strode, 1964. Windham's first book, in its 29th printing.

Twice Blessed, Black Belt Press, 1996. Autobiographical snatches of memory from a long and happy life.

Videography

Alabama Ghosts and Jeffrey, New Frontier Media, 1995. Stories from the book filmed on the sites where the supernatural events occurred; narration by Windham.

Cooking Up Stories, New Frontier Media, 1996. Filmed live at the Birmingham Public Library as Windham cooks on hot plates while telling stories about food.

Let Her Own Works Praise Her, University of Alabama Center for Public Television, 1993. Windham portrays the life of Julia S. Tutwiler.

A Sampling of Southern Superstitions, New Frontier Media, 1996. Windham talks about and demonstrates some basic Southern superstitions.

The Spirited Life of Kathryn Tucker Windham, University of Alabama Center for Public Television, 1989. Windham visits her home town of Thomasville, Alabama, and reminisces about growing up there.

Audiography

Alabama Folk Tales (audiocassette), self-published, 1983. Contains "Hoop Snake," "The Rabbit," "The Vanishing Hitch-hiker," "Cry-Baby Bridge," "Marengo County Booger," and "Family Tales."

"The Farmer Who Vanished," in *Homespun*

Tales (audiocassette), National Association for the Preservation and Perpetuation of Storytelling, 1986.

"The Hole That Will Not Stay Filled," in *Graveyard Tales* (audiocassette), National Association for the Preservation and Perpetuation of Storytelling, 1989.

Jeffrey, Vol. 3 (audiocassette), self-produced, 1979. Contains "The Girl Nobody Knew," "The Dancing Ghost of Grancer Harrison," "Outracing the Devil," "The Lovely Afternoon," and "Jeffrey's Story."

Jeffrey, Vol. 4 (audiocassette), self-produced, 1979. Contains "Nellie," "Robert, I'll Never Leave You," "Snake Charmer," "Tidbits and Superstitions," and "Jeffrey's Story."

Jeffrey, Vol. 5 (audiocassette), self-produced, 1983. Contains "Paint the Gallows Red," "The University of Alabama Ghosts," and "Boyington Oak."

Kathryn Windham Tells Ghost Stories, Vol. 1 (audiocassette), self-produced, 1977. Contains "The Hole That Won't Stay Filled," "The Face in the Courthouse Window," "Ghost of the Eliza Battle," and "Jeffrey's Story."

Kathryn Windham Tells Ghost Stories, Vol. 2 (audiocassette), self-produced, 1978. Contains "The Eternal Dinner Party," "Long Dog," "Tidbits and Superstition," "Spirit of the Spindles," "Ghost of Gaineswood," "The Farmer Who Vanished," and "Jeffrey's Story."

Recollections, 1986–1989 (audiocassette), Charlie and Company, 1989. Commentaries on things Southern on Windham's public radio broadcasts.

Awards

1996 National Storytelling Association Circle of Excellence.

1996 National Storytelling Association Lifetime Achievement Award.

1996 *Storytelling World* Award for Best Video Recording for *Thirteen Alabama Ghosts and Jeffrey*.

1995 Governor's Award for the Arts.

1990 Alabama Business and Professional Women's Foundation's Women's Academy of Honor.

1990 Society for the Fine Arts' Alabama Arts Award.

1979 Honorary Doctor of Literature from Huntingdon College.

1975 Alabama Library Association Nonfiction Award for *Alabama: One Big Front Porch*.

Source

"A Brief Look at This Year's Storytellers," Jonesborough, Tennessee *Herald & Tribune*, September 30, 1992, 4C–8C.

"Featured Storytellers," Jonesborough, Tennessee, *Herald & Tribune*, September 29, 1993.

Ford, Gary D., "Travel Journal," *Southern Living*, September 1995, 46.

Hill, Jennifer, "Storytellers Recall Festival's First Years in Jonesborough," Jonesborough, Tennessee *Herald and Tribune*, September 30, 1992, 2C, 4C.

Mooney, Bill, and David Holt. *The Storyteller's Guide*. Little Rock, Ark.: August House, 1996.

"NSA Recognizes Lifetime Achievers," *Inside Story*, September 1996, 33–34.

Something About the Author. Detroit: Gale Research, 19.

"Storytellers to Weave Their Special Magic During the First Week of October," *Herald & Tribune*, October 2, 1996, 3C–5C.

Timeless Voices: Images of the National Storytelling Festival. Jonesborough, Tenn.: National Storytelling Press, 1997.

DIANE WOLKSTEIN

[wohlk'·steen]

Address   Cloudstone
10 Patchin Place
New York, New York 10011-8342
phone and fax 212-929-6871
fax 212-924-5469
email philipda@li.net

Focus: Hebraic lore; epic love poems; classic myths; world folktales; Taoist stories; parables and cautionary tales; trickster stories; native American and Caribbean lore.

Audience: all ages.

Style: kinetic and passionate with emphasis on logic, character, humanism, and family values.

After her first performance in February 1977, mythologist and self-taught anthropologist Diane S. Wolkstein took as her mission statement a line from the medieval Persian romance *Layla and Majnun:* "Let me not be cured of love, but let my passion grow! Make my love a hundred times greater than it is today" (Montague, 1996). The line has proved prophetic of nearly two decades of researching and recasting stories to perform, which she has savored in faraway climes to get a feel for their individualized milieus.

Wolkstein was born on November 11, 1942, in Maplewood, New Jersey, and currently resides in Greenwich Village. She recalls the stories of childhood, which she heard from her mother and the local rabbi. The plots and themes raised questions that set her on a lifetime of pondering human situations, as in "The Red Lion," a parable about fear. Joining the storytelling renaissance in the 1960s, she earned a B.A. in drama and music from Smith College and M.A. in education from Bank State College, and studied pantomime in Paris with mimemaster Etienne Decroux. From teaching Bible stories in French and English to European children in 1965, she realized that storytelling was her artistic forte. One of her early stories is the biography of Esther, a Hebrew queen and biblical matriarch, whom Wolkstein introduced to an audience at Temple Copernic in Paris. After her return to the United States in 1967, she told ecumenical stories at a Unitarian church. She convinced New York park officials to let her tell stories by the statue of Hans Christian Andersen in Central Park. The tradition has continued for three decades.

At first, Wolkstein concentrated on the epic of a Sumerian deity, Inanna, Queen of Heaven and Earth, and her consort, Dumuzi, the shepherd-king. Identified as the world's oldest love story, the narrative poem was composed 2,000 years before the Bible. With the help of Samuel Noah Kramer, an expert on Sumer, she established the text from shards of cuneiform tablets that date to Abraham, a biblical patriarch, before he migrated west from ancient Ur. After intense study, translation, and interpretation, she performed the Cycle of Inanna in June 1980 for the Mother Goddess Conference in Maine. One listener reported shivers of recognition from the universal themes of love, mating, personal trials, separation, loss, and rebirth. In 1983, Wolkstein published a scholarly reading of the frail, tattered remnants of Sanskrit lore, complete with illustrations taken from authentic Sumerian sculpture, bas-relief, and artistic patterns. She taught mythology and the results of her research at Sarah Lawrence College in 1984.

In 1991, Wolkstein presented Inanna's enduring love story as the predecessor of *The Song of Songs*, which she translated for her collection, *The First Love Stories*, a life's work that required fourteen years of research and visits to Egypt, Israel, Greece, Turkey, and India. She also features the Hindu mates Shiva and Sati, the Egyptian Isis and Osiris, the Graeco-Roman Psyche and Eros, the Arabic-Persian Layla and Majnun, the Celtic-European Tristan and Iseult, and an extensive glossary of terms and place names. Inspired by her rabbi, Shlomo Carlebach, she began with his stories and carried them on her travels, which have taken her to Australia, Ireland, England, France, Egypt, Israel, Greece, and Turkey, and as close to home as Central Park. In the 1970s, her research in Haiti produced over 500 tales from hovels where telling was an inexpensive form of entertainment.

Wolkstein has taught storytelling at Bank State College of Education and The New School for Social Research; she has entranced audiences at Lincoln Center, Smithsonian Institution, University of Judaism, United Nations, The Cloisters, Brooklyn Museum, Avignon Festival, Spoleto, Smothers Brothers Theater, Arlington Theater, and at museums, parks, universities, and synagogues throughout the United States, Canada, Australia, and Europe. She has been featured on *CBC Midday*, *CBS Sunday Morning*, *CNN*, and *20/20* and hosted *Stories with Diane Wolkstein* on WNYC-FM from 1968 to 1980. Her contributions to the narrative arts include establishing the New York City Storytelling Center,

National Storytelling Association's Summer Workshops, and the New York City Storytelling Festival.

Articles

"Beyond the Seer of Lublin" and "The Master Thief," *Parabola*, February 1979.

"An Interview with Harold Courlander," *School Library Journal*, May 1974.

"The Master Play Puppeteer," *Parabola*, December 1979.

"Old and New Sexual Messages in Fairy Tales," *Wilson Library Bulletin*, October 1971.

"On Storytelling and Religion: A Conversation with James Wiggins," *Horn Book*, June 1983, 350–357.

"Psyche Is Not a Wimp," *Anima*, Spring 1991.

"The Stories Behind the Stories: An Interview with Isaac Bashevis Singer," *Children's Literature in Education*, Fall 1975.

"Storytelling at the Hans Christian Andersen Storytelling Center, *Storytelling Magazine*, Summer 1985.

"Storytelling Classic Gets Fresh Start," *Storytelling Magazine*, January 1997, 10.

"Telling Stories," *Parabola*, 1977, 82–91.

"Twenty-Five Years of Storytelling: The Spirit of the Art," *Horn Book*, December 1992, 702–708.

"Tzaddik of Our Time" in *Parabola*, Summer 1995, 88–90.

"Why Tell Stories?," *New Era*, May/June 1981.

Bibliography

The Banza: A Haitian Folk Tale (illustrator Marc Brown), Dial, 1980, 1995. The story of a goat's friendship with a tiger.

"Bouki Dances the Kokioko," *Storytelling Magazine*, May 1997, 11–13.

Bouki Dances the Kokioko: A Haitian Story (illustrator Jessie Sweetwater), Harcourt, 1997.

The Cool Ride in the Sky (illustrator Paul Galdone), Knopf, 1973. A clever monkey outsmarts a greedy buzzard who takes other animals for a flight, then eats them.

Dreamsongs/Abulafia, Part of My Heart, Cloudstone, 1991. Contains eighteen dreams and nine songs influenced by 13th-century Kabbalist Abraham Abulafia.

8,000 Stone: A Chinese Folktale (illustrator Ed Young), Doubleday, 1972. A prince who discovers how to weigh an elephant.

Esther's Story (illustrator Juan Wijngaard), William Morrow, 1996. Adapted from Midrash and the Bible to cover events celebrated at Purim and the life of Esther; told in diary form; for ages 11 and up.

The First Love Stories: From Isis and Osiris to Tristan and Iseult, HarperCollins, 1991. Contains "Psyche and Eros," a Graeco-Roman myth, "Isis and Dumuzi," a Sumerian story, "Shiva and Sati" from Hindu lore, "The Song of Songs" from the Bible, "Layla and Majnun" from Arabic-Persian stories, and "Tristan and Iseult," a Celtic romance from the Arthurian cycle; contains notes and glossary.

The Grass Slipper: A Chinese Cinderella, Harcourt, 1997.

Inanna: Queen of Heaven and Earth, Her Stories and Hymns from Sumer (co-author Samuel Noah Kramer), HarperCollins, 1983. A myth dating to 2800 B. C.; contains "Inanna and Dumuzi" and original Sumer artwork; for mature readers.

Joining In — An Anthology of Audience Participation Stories and How to Tell Them (contributor), Yellow Moon, 1988. Eighteen participation stories for all ages.

Lazy Stories (illustrator James Marshall), Seabury, 1976. Three fanciful tales from Japan, Mexico, and Laos.

The Legend of Sleepy Hollow (illustrator R. W. Alley), William Morrow, 1987. A retelling of Washington Irving's ghost story about the headless horseman; for ages four and up.

Little Mouse's Painting (illustrator Mary Jane Begin), William Morrow, 1992. A story of friendship, art, and perspective.

The Magic Orange Tree and Other Haitian Folktales (illustrator Elsa Henriquez and D. M. Maurice), Schocken, 1997. Twenty-seven folktales, including "I'm Tipingee, She's Tipingee, We're Tipingee, Too," "Bouki Dances the Kokioko," songs, and commentary.

The Magic Wings (illustrator Robert Andrew Parker), E. P. Dutton, 1983. A Chinese folktale.

"The Nightingale," in *Homespun: Tales from America's Favorite Storytellers*, Crown, 1988.

Oom Razoom: Go I Know Not Where, Bring Back I Know Not What (illustrator Dennis McDermott), William Morrow, 1991. A Russian fairy tale about the comeuppance inflicted on an evil king.

"Owl," in *Homespun: Tales from America's Favorite Storytellers*, Crown, 1988.

The Red Lion: A Persian Sufi Tale (illustrator Ed Young), Thomas Y. Crowell, 1977. How Prince Azgid overcomes his fear of lions and wins a throne.

"The Red Lion," in *More Best-Loved Stories Told at the National Storytelling Festival*, August House, 1992.

Squirrel's Song: A Hopi-Indian Story (illustrator Lillian Hoban), Alfred A. Knopf, 1975.

Step by Step (illustrator Joseph Smith), William Morrow, 1994. The story of an ant's adventure.

Sun Mother Wakes the World, William Morrow, 1996.

The Visit (illustrator Lois Ehlert), Alfred A. Knopf, 1974.

"White Wave," in *Homespun: Tales from America's Favorite Storytellers*, Crown, 1988.

White Wave: A Tao Tale (illustrator Ed Young), Thomas Y. Crowell, 1979. The story of a poor farm boy aided by a goddess.

Videography

Inanna, Cloudstone, 1988. Wolkstein's story of a 4,000-year-old epic; slides of art and Sumer landscapes; for adults.

"White Wave," in *American Storytelling Series, Vol. 2*, H. W. Wilson, 1987.

Audiography

The Banza (audiocassette and book), Listening Library, 1991. A Haitian story accompanied by Shirley Keller on banjo; for ages three and up.

California Fairy Tales (audiocassette), Spoken Arts, 1972.

The Cool Ride in the Sky (audiocassette), Miller-Brody, 1975.

Diane Wolkstein Tells Eskimo Stories: Tales of Magic (audiocassette), Spoken Arts, 1974. Three shamanic stories from Kiethan's *Igloo Tales*; including "A Tale of Two Old Women," "A Brother and a Sister," and "The Man Who Became a Caribou"; accompaniment by Avraham Qanai and L. S. Messina on flute, bells, rattles, and drum; for ages 7 and up.

Diane Wolkstein Tells Fairy Tales from Estonia (audiocassette), Cloudstone, 1988. A compendium of stories from Wolkstein's radio program, *Stories from Many Lands*, featuring "The Wood of Tontla" and "The Magic Mirror"; accompaniment by Lilian Esop on the kennel; for ages four and up.

Diane Wolkstein Tells Tales of the Hopi Indians (audiocassette), Spoken Arts, 1985. Three stories from Harold Courlander's *People of the Short Blue Corn*; including "The Sun Callers," "Sikakokuh and the Hunting Dog," and "Coyote and the Crying Song"; for ages six and up.

The Epic of Inanna (audiocassette), Cloudstone, 1986. Recorded live at the United Nations with Geoffrey Gordon's accompaniment on harp, drums, flute, conch, and bells; for high school to adult.

Hans Christian Andersen in Central Park (LP), Weston Woods, 1982. Six classic Andersen stories, including "The Emperor's New Clothes," "Hans Clodhopper," "Dance, Dance, Dolly Mine," "The Ugly Duckling," "The Nightingale," and "The Goblin and the Grocer"; accompanied by Shirley Keller

on kazoo, kalimba, and guitar and Janet
Stuart on recorder; for ages five and up.
Psyche and Eros (audiocassette), Cloudstone,
1988. Stories of the god of love; for ages
eleven and up.
Romping (accompanied by musician Shirley
Keller) (audiocassette), Cloudstone, 1985.
Five playful stories of the seasons, including "Frog and Toad Are Friends," "Toad
and Frog," "My Crazy Sister," "The Kid-
napping of the Coffee Pot," and "Time for
Jody," from Wolkstein's radio show *Story
from Many Lands;* Shirley Keller accompanies on guitar, banjo, autoharp, alarm
clocks, pots and pans and plays "Just a Letter from Someone," "Freight Train," and
"The Marvelous Toy"; for ages 2–6.
The Story of Joseph (audiocassette), Cloudstone, 1986. Oral legends from the Midrash
and biblical text from Genesis 37:50; for
ages seven and up.
Tales from Estonia (audiocassette), Cloudstone, 1988.

Awards

1996 National Storytelling Association Circle of Excellence.
1996 Syndey Taylor Award runner-up for
Esther's Story.
1994 Banff Action Poets.
1992 Bologna Children's Book Fair/Critica
in Erba honorable mention for *Little Mouse's
Painting.*
1991 Smith College Centennial Award: Women Who Make a Difference in New York.
1991 American Library Association Social
Studies Award for *Oom Razoom: Go I Know
Not Where, Bring Back I Know Not What.*
1986 Parents' Choice Gold Seal Award for
Romping.
1985 Parents' Choice Gold Seal Award for
The Story of Joseph.
1983 Reading Rainbow Selection for *The
Magic Wings.*
1982 Parents' Choice Gold Seal Award for
Hans Christian Andersen in Central Park.
1982 American Library Association Notable
Recording for *Hans Christian Andersen in
Central Park.*
1981 Reading Rainbow Selection for *The
Banza.*

1979 American Library Association Notable
Book Award for *White Wave: A Tao Tale.*
1979 Marshall Grant.
1978 New York Academy of Sciences Award
for *The Magic Orange Tree.*
1978 American Library Association Notable
Book Award for *The Magic Orange Tree and
Other Haitian Folktales.*
1977 American Institute of Graphic Arts
Award for *The Red Lion: A Persian Sufi Tale.*
1976 Lithgow-Osborne Fellowship.
1972 New York Academy of Sciences Children's Science Book honorable mention for
8,000 Stones: A Chinese Folktale.
1969 Marshall Grant.

Source

Bezrudczyk, Joan E., "Review," *Library Jour-
nal,* September 1976, 127.
"A Brief Look at This Year's Storytellers,"
Jonesborough, Tennessee *Herald & Tri-
bune,* September 30, 1992, 4C–8C.
Burns, Mary M, "Review," *Horn Book,* April
1978, 157–158.
Dennis, Lisa, "Review," *School Library Jour-
nal,* June 1992, 105.
Elleman, Barbara, "Review," *Booklist,* July 15,
1978, 1738; October 15, 1987, 404.
Hanst, Anne, "Review," *School Library Jour-
nal,* April 1979, 64–65.
"Interview," *Stories and Mythology,* National
Public Radio 1979.
Lane, Belden, "Review," *National Storytelling
Journal,* Summer 1987.
MacCann, Donnarae, and Olga Richard, "Pic-
ture Books for Children," *Wilson Library
Bulletin,* February 1978, 496.
Maguire, Gregory, "Review," *Horn Book,* De-
cember 1983, 729.
Martin, Douglas, "Celebrating 25 Years as a
Teller of Mythic Tales," *New York Times,*
June 3, 1992.
McDonald, Margaret Read, "Review," *Yarn-
spinner,* May 1992.
Montague, Tony, "Tales That Stand the Test
of Time," *Georgia Straight,* March 28–
April 4, 1996, 53.
Mooney, Bill, and David Holt. *The Storyteller's
Guide.* Little Rock, Ark.: August House,
1996.
Morgan, Philip David, "This Is Diane Wolk-

stein," http://www.li.net/~philpda/diana2.htm, May 14, 1997.

O'Connell, Margaret R., "Review," *New York Times Book Review*, September 30, 1973, 8.

Osborne, Linda, "The Wisdom of the Nations," *World & I*, May 1, 1993.

"Review," *Bulletin of the Center for Children's Books*, January 1974, 88.

"Review," *Kirkus Reviews*, June 1, 1973, 621; July 1, 1973, 682–683; July 1, 1991, 862.

"Review," *Publishers Weekly*, May 24, 1976, 60; October 9, 1981, 67; November 4, 1983, 65.

Seaman, Donna, "Review," *Booklist*, January 15, 1991, 999.

Shannon, George, "Review," *School Library Journal*, December 1981, 58.

Shapiro, Carol, "Review," *Yarnspinner*, December 1989.

Something About the Author, Vol. 82. Detroit: Gale Research, 1996.

Stone, Amy, "The Rebirth of Jewish Storytelling: Not Just for Kids," *The Reporter*, Spring 1996, 6–10.

Sutherland, Zena, "Review," *Bulletin of the Center for Children's Books*, November 1979, 64.

Warwick, Ellen D., "Review," *School Library Journal*, October 1983, 154.

ELAINE WYNNE

Address   Circle of Cranes Psychology Center
315 Georgia N
Golden Valley, Minnesota 55427
phone (home) 612-546-1074
phone (work) 612-546-1662
fax (work) 612-512-0344

Box 27314
Minneapolis, Minnesota 55427-0314

Focus: stories of humor and healing for earth and everyone; therapeutic storytelling.

Audience: all ages.

Style: individual workshops on "The Healing Art of Storytelling," a study that covers numerous healing and therapeutic traditions to help professional healers develop storytelling in their work.

Instruments/Props: piano, keyboard, rhythm instruments.

Psychologist Elaine Wynne, a professional freelance storyteller for twenty years, is a practitioner of healing through telling. For over a quarter century, she has applied dreams, myths, and fairy tales to therapy and has used relaxation and mental imagery as a healing mechanism for children and adults. Her first application of video to therapy came in 1973, when she joined the Women's Film Collective to tape life stories of women. Since that time, she earned degrees from St. Mary's College and Metropolitan State University and obtained consultant status with the American Society for Clinical Hypnosis. Using narrative as oral therapy, she has applied her talents to a video that won the grand prize at the Tokyo Video Festival. She has also produced "Storytelling as a Healing Art" for Wisconsin Public Radio and discussed storytelling and grief counseling for *All Things Considered* on National Public Radio. In addition to workshops for the Minnesota Art Therapy Association, National Hospice Movement, Minnesota Society for Clinical Hypnosis, and group homes for chemical dependency and senior citizens, she has collected oral history in the Twin City area. She was a national advisory council member and coordinator for the National Association for the Preservation and Perpetuation of Storytelling. Her in-service presentations have taken her to the University of Wisconsin, National Hospice Conference, Janus Treatment Program, Minnesota Psychosynthesis Institute, Minneapolis Children's Medical Center, American Cancer Society, High Pointe Psychiatric Facility for Adolescents, St. Cloud University, Minnesota Society for Clinical Hypnosis, Sioux Falls State College, Metropolitan State University Conference on Storytelling in Growth and Development, and the University of New Mexico. She has presented workshops on metaphor and storytelling in psychotherapy for the National Folklore Association, Northlands Storytelling Network Conference, and National Storytelling Conference.

Wynne and her husband, storyteller Larry Johnson, form a duo performing as Key of See Storytellers and pair stories with emotional wellness, a philosophy of counseling that encourages young people to tell community-based stories and share them on video. Lifetime members of the National Story League and founders of the Northland Storytelling Network, they have traveled to Ecuador, Japan, England, Scandinavia, and across the United States. The pair supports children's gardening and the Cultural Environment Movement, a coalition that makes story distribution fair and equitable. On a family journey to Wynne and Johnson's Scandinavian roots in Sweden and Norway, they held a workshop at Skansen, a folk museum in Stockholm, and they performed at the Cric Crac Cafe. Wynne presented a therapeutic workshop for psychiatrists, social workers, and family therapists at Modum Bod Psychiatric Center. Other tandem tellings include "Cold Hands, Warm Heart" at Borders Book Shop and "The Great Groundhog Day Get Together" on children's television. Wynne also consulted with the Johnson Institute in Minneapolis, Minnesota, on a series of story videos on domestic violence, living in a family with chemical dependency, and divorce and separation, and has contributed articles to *Utne Reader, In Context,* and the *National Storytelling Journal.*

Bibliography

"Applying Hypnosis in a Preschool Asthma Education Program: Uses of Storytelling, Imagery, and Relaxation" (co-author Daniel P. Kohen), *American Journal of Clinical Hypnosis,* January 1997.

Betwixt and Between: Feminine and Masculine Rites of Passage (contributor), Open Court, 1987.

Children, Constipation and Soiling (co-author), Minneapolis Children's Medical Center, 1986.

"Encouraging Children's Personal Stories," in *Tales as Tools: The Power of Story in the Classroom,* National Storytelling Press, 1994, 156–158.

"The Legend of Sadako," *Storytelling Magazine,* July 1997, 28–29.

"Storytelling in Counseling and Therapy," *Children Today,* 1987.

Audiography

In the Beginning: Birth and Creation Stories (audiocassette), self-published, 1995.

The Rainbow Dream (audiocassette), Children's Hospital, 1980.

Running Scared and Flying High (co-author Larry Johnson) (audiocassette), Heritage Productions, 1986.

Videography

The Land of Many Shapes, (consultant), Johnson Institute 1990–1993. Animated story for children who are coping with separation and divorce.

My People Are My Home, Femme Films, 1976. Biography of Minnesota writer Meridel LeSeuer.

Tulip Doesn't Live Here Anymore, (consultant), Johnson Institute, 1990–1993. Animated story for children 5–9 who cope with domestic violence in the home.

Twee Fiddle and Huff (consultant), Johnson Institute, 1990–1993. Animated story for children 5–9 whose parents are alcoholic or drug dependent; includes guide for facilitators.

Video Letter Exchange, self-published, 1986.

Awards

1986 Tokyo Video Festival Grand Prize for *Video Letter Exchange.*

Source

"Cultural Environment Movement Holds Convention," *Storytelling Magazine,* July 1996, 6.

"Key of See: Tellers, Teachers, Activists," *Storytelling Magazine,* July 1997, 29.

Mizui, Yoko, "A Touching Tale of Kids Wows Video Fest Judges," Tokyo *Daily Yomiuri,* November 21, 1986.

See also Larry Johnson.

DAN YASHINSKY

Address   19 Kenwood Avenue
Toronto, Canada M6C2R8

phone 416-654-1542
fax 416-651-2910
email Dan_Yashinsky@tvo.org

Focus: traditional wonder tales; Medieval satire; stories of the wise and foolish; life stories and stories-within-stories.
Audience: all ages.
Style: Scheherajazz.
Instruments/Props: a "puny tune" (resembles a sawed-off ocarina) and talking stick; for "The Storyteller at Fault," illuminated masks and a granny puppet, with original fiddle score performed by Oliver Schroer.

A native of Detroit, Michigan, storyteller Dan Yashinsky lived in Santa Barbara, California, for many years before settling in Canada in 1972. He is a crossroads person, with Jewish, Romanian, Turkish, and French ancestry mixed into his American fifties background. He grew up surrounded by people who had survived the Holocaust, including his Bucharest-born mother. Their stories, half-stories, and silences turned him into a keen and attentive listener.

Yashinsky stepped into storytelling via *The Canterbury Tales*. The late Professor Marvin Mudrick at the University of California at

Santa Barbara, who was an enthusiastic guide to Chaucer, convinced Yashinsky that literature — particularly the oral branch of storytelling — was the most noble, romantic, and necessary line of work he could get into. The road to Canterbury led Yashinsky on a pilgrimage to the Arabian Nights, Boccaccio's *Decameron*, and further back to Homer. Odysseus describes storytelling as the "flower of life," a belief which Yashinsky found to be true after working for a summer as counselor at Bolton Camp. The inner-city boys in his cabin loved to listen to traditional fairy tales, ghost stories, epic adventures — anything that began with "Once upon a time." These kids were so hungry for beauty and wonder that Yashinsky, remembering what he'd learned about Chaucer and Homer, determined to make storytelling his livelihood.

Toronto was a hospitable place for a young storyteller. Yashinsky met the great Irish-Canadian storyteller Alice Kane at the beginning of his career, and their friendship and artistic partnership has been the foundation of his work. Among his other heroes are the storyteller/writer Joan Bodger, the late Yukon Indian elder Angela Sidney, Cree oral historian Louis Bird, and French troubadour Bruno de la Salle. In 1978, Yashinsky founded "1,001 Friday Nights of Storytelling," North America's longest-running weekly adult open session. He also founded the Toronto Festival of Storytelling in 1979 and co-founded the Storytellers School of Toronto. All of these activities came out of his belief that storytelling is first and foremost an art of and for the community. In 1997, he founded the Tellery, a mobile celebration of Canadian and international storytelling. He has also created the Telling Bee, a storytelling/book creation project that has been widely used in Canadian schools, and the Day of Stories at Toronto's Hospital for Sick Children.

Yashinsky has taken his storytelling to many places around the world, including the Israeli International Storytelling Festival, Yukon International Storytelling Festival, New Brunswick's Storyfest, Vancouver Storytelling Festival, Quebec's Festival interculturel de conte du Montréal, Lincoln Center Out-of-Doors Festival, Labrador Arts Festival, Long

Night of the Storytellers and Graz Erzahlt! in Austria, Corn Island Storytelling Festival, and many others. Besides a repertoire of traditional wonder tales, Yashinsky tells "The Miller's Tale" in Chaucer's English as well as "Seven Stories and a Puny Tune" and "The Listener's Tale." He performs "Screw in Your Ear!" with teller Itah Sadu and "The Storyteller at Fault" with composer/musician Oliver Schroer. In addition to four books of stories, he has published numerous articles in *The Globe and Mail, Wilson Library Bulletin, This Magazine, Paperplates, Tale Trader, Appleseed Quarterly*, and *Storytelling Magazine*. Works in progress include *The Listener's Tale — a Book of Scheherajazz* and *Hunting/Gathering*, an ongoing series of essays exploring contemporary storytelling.

Articles

"Hodja Nasrudin: Hunting/Gathering #3," *Tale Trader*, February 1997, 7.

"Magic Spoken Here," *The Tale Trader*, May 1996, 7.

"A Speakable Feast," *The Globe and Mail*, February 22, 1997.

"Tellingware: A Headful of Stories," in *Tales as Tools: The Power of Story in the Classroom*, National Storytelling Press, 1994, 15.

"What Crow Said That Day," *Tale Trader*, August 1997, 7.

Bibliography

Ghostwise, A Book of Midnight Stories (editor), August House, 1997. Ghost stories and spirit tales from many lands.

Next Teller: A Book of Canadian Storytelling (editor), Ragweed, 1994. A collection of stories celebrating Canada's multicultural storytellers.

"Stewart Cameron," *Appleseed*, Fall 1989, 5.

The Storyteller at Fault (illustrator Nancy Cairine Pitt), Ragweed, 1992. Stories-within-stories spun by a teller who must save his life with his words; contains "The Last Story," "The Master of the Tea Ceremony," "Ali the Persian's Bag," and other traditional and original tales.

Tales for an Unknown City (editor), McGill-Queen's University Press, 1990. Fifty stories from Quebec, the Maritimes, the Prairies, Trinidad, China, Italy, the Ukraine, Tan-zania, and Salem, Massachusetts, collected from tellers at Toronto's "1,001 Friday Nights of Storytelling."

Videography

Dan Yashinsky: A Storyteller's Story (director Paul Caulfield), Mirus Films, 1985.

Audiography

Banana Split (audiocassette), Mariposa in the Schools, 1987. Contains Yashinsky's bebop telling of "The Johnnycake."

Awards

1990 City of Toronto Book Prize for *Tales for an Unknown City*.

Grants from the Ontario Arts Council and the Canada Council for Artistic Projects.

Source

Dan Yashinsky: A Storyteller's Story (documentary), CBC-TV, Kinetic 1985.

Ouderkirk, Sharon, "The Storyteller and the Power of Imagination," *Varsity Review*, November 1992.

Rodriguez, Robert, "Canada's Ghosts," *Tale Trader*, August 1997, 18.

JUDY DOCKREY YOUNG AND RICHARD YOUNG

Address P. O. Box 1300B
          Kimberling City, Missouri 65686-
          1300B
phone 417-739-2947
email stories@yawp.com
website yawp.com

Focus: early American and Southwest history and local lore; ghost stories.

Audience: all ages.

Style: dramatic tellings.

Judy Young's Instruments/Props: period costume.

Judy Young's Bio

The offshoot of Irish, German, and Chickasaw bloodlines, Judy Elaine Dockrey Young has thrived in areas where storytelling is honored and perpetuated. She gives back to local

ing certificate. After two years as a high school speech and drama teacher in Republic, Missouri, she became a character actress and the official storyteller of Silver Dollar City theme park outside Branson, Missouri. Well known for three published cassettes of stories, she married raconteur Richard Alan Young in 1982, with whom she has published nine books of stories. Her heavy performance schedule includes radio performances for National Public Radio's "The Story Tree" and has taken her to the Texas Storytelling Festival as well as on tours of the Midwest and Southwest. She appeared in Pat Boone's film, *Old-Fashioned Christmas*, in 1984 and *Pass the Ammo* for PTA Films in 1985. With her husband, she conducts workshops for librarians, educators, and storytellers on oral narrative in the classroom, family histories and the at-risk child, beginning storytelling for professional candidates, self-produced tapes, professional tips on the business of storytelling, copyright law, and creating historic characters.

culture her tall tales from the Ozark Mountains and pioneers' bittersweet reminiscences of the Old Country. A native of Muskogee, Oklahoma, she was born June 25, 1949, to one of the state's original farm families. She first heard tales from her father, farmer Lewin Haden Dockrey, who served as an early mentor. Reading became an escape from the family's isolation in the country. Education took her from a two-room school on the Verdigris River to Miller High School in Rescue, Missouri. At Southwest Missouri State University, where she earned a B.A. in speech and theater, she received professional training from Dr. Leslie Irene Coger, the creator of Readers' Theater. Voice lessons from Arthur Lessac at the Dallas Theater Center of Trinity University in San Antonio, Texas, rounded out her narrative skills. Before becoming a platform narrator, she completed graduate courses in children's theater with an emphasis on creative dramatics and the role of storytelling in child development.

Young's ambitions took second place to her father's illness in 1974, when she returned to the family farm, then earned a lifetime teach-

Richard Young's Instruments/Props: period costume.

Richard Young's Bio

Of Spanish, French, Scotch, English, and Seneca ancestry, Richard Alan Young recreates the mystery and glamour of the American West in his specialty — ghost tales and Hispanic stories. He has toured the American Southwest in costume as Padre Bernardo, a Franciscan monk of the 1760s. Young was born March 1, 1946, in Huntsville, Texas, the great-grandson of pioneer stock, the Farines of La Réunion near Dallas. Young heard stories with an Hispanic flair from his father, Professor Morgan Martin Young, whom he claims as his early inspiration and mentor. When his father moved to teach education at a university in Siloam Springs, Arkansas, in 1959, Young completed high school there. While training under Norman DeMarco at the University of Arkansas, he developed technique by telling urban legends. He earned a B.A. in Spanish and French and completed an M.A. in humanities. He taught high school Spanish in Harrison, Arkansas, from 1968 to 1993 and worked summers at Dogpatch, USA, in Jasper, where he rose to character director. In subsequent summers, he worked in the *Great Passion Play* in Eureka Springs and the Silver Dollar City theme park outside Branson, Missouri, and has appeared at Rawhide in Scottsdale, Arizona.

Young has focused on the interaction of culture and tradition, with emphasis on performing and storytelling. Marriage to an actress-storyteller increased his involvement in platform narrative, which supplanted teaching as his full-time career. In performances at schools, churches, libraries, universities, museums, symposia, and festivals since 1983, he has developed a sizable story repertoire, and, in 1992, he represented Arkansas at the Regional Concert of the National Storytelling Conference in San Antonio, Texas. In 1993, he joined Judy on Storytellers' Theater on the Americana network.

Bibliography

African-American Folktales (introduction by Rex Ellis), August House, 1993. Collected stories in the black oral tradition for young readers.

Favorite Scary Stories of American Children, August House, 1990. Twenty-three spooky stories for children ages 5–10.

Ghost Stories from the American Southwest, August House, 1991. Twenty-three horror tales of vengeful spirits.

Outlaw Tales from America's Middle Border, August House, 1992. American stories about desperadoes.

Ozark Ghost Stories, August House, 1995. Ghostlore for all ages, featuring "Blood Red Cedar," "Mary Calhoun," "Vanishing Rider," and "Old Wall-Eye."

Ozark Tall Tales, August House, 1989. Seventy authentic mountain stories, tall tales, and jokes.

Race with Buffalo, August House, 1994. Thirty stories and legends from eighteen tribes.

The Scary Story Reader, August House, 1993. Forty-one macabre tales for young readers.

Stories from the Days of Christopher Columbus, August House, 1992. History tales of people living on both sides of the Atlantic in 1492; for young readers.

Videography

Andes to the Amazon, Premiere Video/Branson, 1997. Featuring stories of the Shuar, Waorani, and Quichua peoples.

Branson's Storytellers, Premiere Video/Branson, 1995. Five multicultural stories from the Youngs' most requested list.

This Here Story ... Video, Premiere Video, 1996. Ozark tall tales and mountain memories, with demonstrations of local crafts and toys.

Audiography

Favorite Scary Stories, Vols. 1 & 2 (audiocassette), August House, 1991. Twenty-three spooky stories for children ages 5–10.

Ghost Stories from the American Southwest (audiocassette), August House, 1991. Twenty-three horror tales of vengeful spirits.

Head on the High Road (audiocassette), August House, 1993. Contains "The Big Thicket," "La Llorona," and sixteen more Southwestern ghost stories from Arizona, Texas, California, and New Mexico.

Ozark Ghost Stories (audiocassette), August House, 1992. Seven eerie stories, including "Old Raw Head," "Mary Calhoun," and "Pennywinkle."

Ozark Tall Tales (audiocassette), August House, 1992. Twenty-two authentic mountain stories, tall tales, and jokes, including "Cloverine Salve," "Jack and the Gowerow," and "The Great Hog Meat Swindle."

Spinnin' Yarns (audiocassette), Young Stories, 1987. Ten bittersweet Ozark yarns including "Rex's Teacher" and "The Legend of the Three Trees."

There's No Such Thing As Ghosts (audiocassette), August House, 1993. Contains "The Bell Witch," "The Black Dog of the Blue Ridge," "Blackbeard's Lights," and eleven more Southeastern ghost stories.

This Here Story (audiocassette), Young Stories, 1985. Twelve Ozark yarns, featuring "The Old Woman and Her Pig" and "The Cold-Trailin' Coon Dog."

Awards

1996 *Storytelling World* Magazine Honor Award for the video *This Here Story*.

1995 *Storytelling World* Magazine Honor Award for "Br'er Rabbit and the Frogs" in *African-American Folktales*.

1994 Parents' Choice recommendation for *The Head on the High Road: Ghost Stories from the Southwest*.

Source

Branson's Country Review, Winter 1994, 34.

Country America, October/November 1996, 134.

Something About the Author, Vol. 72. Detroit: Gale Research, 1993.

Storytelling Magazine, September 1995, 18–19.

"Tall Tales in the Ozarks," *Los Angeles Times*, October 20, 1988.

Storytellers by
State or Country

O'Callahan, Jay
Papa Joe
Sacre, Antonio
Sanfield, Steve

Michigan
Schutz-Gruber, Barbara
Yashinsky, Dan

Minnesota
Johnson, Larry

Mississippi
Bias-Davis, LaDoris

Missouri
Horner, Beth
Mooney, Bill
Norfolk, Bobby
Rubright, Lynn
Spelman, Jon

Montana
Bandelier, Linda

New Jersey
Coggswell, Gladys
Fang, Linda
Greene, Ellin
Williams, Diane
Wolkstein, Diane

New York
Bankole, Adisa
Bruchac, Joseph
Forest, Heather
Gillman, Jackson
Gonzalez, David
Larkin, Chuck
Martin, Rafe
Reiser, Robert
Simms, Laura
Stavish, Corinne
Weakley, Tom
Wilhelm, Robert Béla

North Carolina
Arneach, Lloyd
Davis, Donald
Freeman, Barbara
Haven, Kendall

Hicks, Ray
Jenkins, Bob
McGill, Alice

Ohio
Brother Blue (Dr. Hugh
    Morgan Hill)
Harley, Bill
Phillips, Utah

Oklahoma
Edmonds, Dayton
Young, Judy Dockery

Oregon
Dashney, John

Pennsylvania
Alston, Charlotte Blake
Hayes, Joe
Livo, Norma
Moore, Robin
Stivender, Ed
Wilhelm, Mary Jo Kelly

Tennessee
Goss, Linda McNear
Massengill, David
McConnell, Doc

Texas
Beekman, Jeannine Passini
Ellaraino
Holt, David
McBride-Smith, Barbara
Pinkerton, J. G. "Paw-Paw"
Ross, Gayle
Young, Richard

Utah
Aoki, Brenda Wong

Vermont
Parker, Mac

Virginia
Ellis, Rex
Goodman, Linda
Gordh, Bill
LedBetter, Gwenda
Watters, Eve

Washington
DeSpain, Pleasant

West Virginia
Greenberg, Bonnie

Wisconsin
Pellowski, Anne

OUTSIDE THE UNITED STATES

Iraq
Goren, Shosha

Ireland
Peirce, Maggie

Australia
Dargin, Peter

Scotland
Campbell, David

Guyana
Corsbie, Ken

Austria
Tegetthoff, Folke

Cuba
Deedy, Carmen

South Africa
Condra, Estelle

Norway
Patrix, Abbi

England
Freeman, Mara

Ontario
Barton, Bob

Trinidad
Hallworth, Grace
Keens-Douglas, Paul

British Columbia
Moses, Johnny

Glossary

Ananse (also Anancy, Anansi, Ananzi) [uh • nahn' see] a spider who is said to have been the first storyteller; a trickster character in West African, Caribbean, and African-American tales who deceives animals, humans, and God.

anecdote fairly short account of a specific amusing or interesting incident or personal experience or event.

animism religious belief that every natural object has life and is endowed with a soul.

anthology a compendium or collection of stories or literary pieces from different sources.

The Arabian Nights (also called *The Thousand and One Nights*) a collection of 264 Middle Eastern stories dating to the tenth century and completed around 1450. The body of stories was supposedly told to Sultan Shahriaran, a jealous husband who married a new wife each day and killed her the next morning. His cleverest wife, Sheherazade, saved herself by stretching alluring stories of magic, seduction, ecstasies, and enchantment over 1,001 nights. The most famous stories in the collection are "Sinbad the Sailor," "Aladdin and the Magic Lamp,"

"The Magic Horse," and "Ali Baba and the Forty Thieves."

Ashkenazic tradition cultural derivations of Yiddish-speaking Jews of central and eastern Europe.

autoharp a trademark name for a zither, a musical instrument provided with hand-operated dampers which deaden some strings, leaving others free to form a chord. The autoharp is usually held on the lap or placed horizontally on a table, but can also be held vertically for strumming.

ballad a popular narrative poem, sentimental romance, or folk story told rhythmically or set to music.

bard a Celtic minstrel, singer, lyric poet, and storyteller skilled in music and recitation of heroic deeds.

bardic lore epic tales of historical impact declaimed or sung by a bard or minstrel poet.

beast fable an allegorical or moralistic story using animals acting like humans to point out or ridicule human foibles.

bones two thin strips or clappers of ivory, wood, or bone that are held between the fingers of one hand, and struck together in time to a rhythm or music.

309

box drum a simple African percussion instrument made from animal skins pulled over a wooden frame.

call and response a traditional back-and-forth recitation between a caller or leader and the audience, in which the teller calls out a phrase and the audience responds with a fixed refrain or emotional outcry.

cartoon storyboard an illustrated script, including sketches or a series of panels showing sequential character action and dialogue.

Celtic harp harp made of a hardwood, such as maple, with solid brass strings, which are plucked or strummed with the fingernails to give a clear, resonating sound.

chant a short, rhythmic melody characterized by repetition of an indefinite number of syllables on one tone.

Chuki stories [choo'•kee] stories of the Chukchi, people of the far eastern reaches of Russia. The Chukchi are divided into two groups — the nomadic reindeer herders and the fishing/seal hunting group of the Pacific coast.

clog dancing an Appalachian dance emphasizing the feet, which beat in time to lively music. Clogging shoes normally are equipped with taps to enhance the sound of the beat.

coming-of-age motif a pattern of behavior displaying or acting out the issues and problems posed by leaving childhood behind and/or entering adulthood.

commedia dell'arte [kohm•may'•dee•uh dehl•ahr'•tay] a tradition of the Italian Renaissance of improvised comedies relying on stereotypical characters, masks, broad physical gestures, seemingly unrehearsed dialogue, musical interludes, and clowning.

concert setting a public performance in which one or more storytellers or musicians entertains or displays a skill.

confessional mode a style of storytelling that emphasizes explicit references to personal anxieties, guilt, or disabilities.

contra dance (also contredanse) a traditional form of folk dancing from the British Isles, characterized by patterns or figures executed by squares or parallel lines of couples.

counting and game rhymes educational or illustrative rhymes which help children learn specific skills or bodies of language, sometimes used to set the rhythm for jump rope, hand-clapping games, or hop scotch.

dance percussion theater a combination of the music of drums and gongs with movement, mime, and other theatrical elements.

demotic recreation a simplified form of entertainment stressing everyday themes and colloquial speech.

diaphragm breathing inhaling and exhaling low on the torso through movement of the diaphragm, thus changing the tone and depth of the voice.

didactic story a story meant to teach a lesson or reveal a moral.

dilemma story a story presenting the protagonist with two or more alternatives, none of which are appealing or totally satisfactory.

ditze flute [diht'•zee] a bamboo flute with six holes used to vary notes. Performers often carry several ditze flutes to cover the range of keys.

docu-drama a drama for television, motion pictures, or theatre dealing freely with historical events, especially of a recent and controversial nature.

dream play a drama or scenario in which the character or characters act out mystical or dream-like sequence of events.

dreamscape a fanciful or unreal setting, like something dreamed or imagined.

Druidic lore prophetic or magical sagas, legends, and stories from the tradition of the Celtic philosopher-priests of ancient Britain.

dulcimer [duhl'•sih•muhr] a musical instrument made of metal strings stretched over a hollow sound board and played by being struck with leather-covered hammers; also, an Appalachian instrument which is laid across the lap and played with a pick.

dumbek [duhm'•behk] a Middle Eastern drum made of metal shaped like an hourglass and topped with goatskin heads.

dynamic monologue a long speech delivered by one person to produce drama or intense emotion.

eclectic mix a medley or blend of different or contrasting styles or types.

erotica works dealing with sensual themes, sexual love, and desire and often intended to arouse a physical or emotional response.

ethical theme an idea or motif appealing to or advocating moral actions, characters, or duties and modeling or teaching a prescribed standard of conduct.

Europeanized altered from a non–European form or motif to encompass characters and actions that would be readily understood by white Anglo-Saxon audiences.

expressionism the depiction of emotions and responses that objects and events arouse in the artist or performer.

fairy tale a story involving the adventurous or mysterious pranks and antics of fantastic forces and beings, such as fairies, witches, and goblins.

fantasy imaginative, fanciful literature featuring strange settings, unreal atmosphere, and grotesque or whimsical characters.

folk humor jokes, droll anecdotes, and funny stories emanating from ordinary people and commonplaces situations.

fool story a tale depicting a protagonist who acts stupidly or absurdly, usually with the foolish person prevailing in the end.

framework narrative an action or series of narratives that reside within a greater story or dramatic situation; for example, *The Arabian Nights* or *The Canterbury Tales*, in which the telling of stories is paramount to the overall plot.

freelance a career style that is not controlled by a particular body of authority, such as a company or agency.

Grammy an award given by the National Academy of Recording Arts and Sciences.

Grandfather Tales a traditional body of lore or stories collected by Richard Chase in the Appalachian Mountains.

grant a monetary allotment issued by a government agency or philanthropic or educational foundation to further some specific objective.

griot [gree'•oh] an African storyteller or tribal historian, who holds an honored position among villagers. The griot style of storytelling employs African instruments, chants, and other devices common to African storytellers to educate, enlighten, or preserve history, ritual, morals, or genealogy.

Gullah [guh'•luh] the language of the Georgia Sea Islands which blends West African and English dialects spoken quickly with unusual inflections, elision, or dropped endings.

gut strings strands derived from the preserved entrails of animals for use on harps, guitars, fiddles, and other stringed musical instruments.

haiku [hy'•koo] an unrhymed, three-line Japanese poem containing five, seven, and five syllables respectively and expressing a distinct emotion, image, or insight.

hambone a form of dance-song, accompanied by elaborate hand clapping and slapping of thighs, knees, chest, and hips. Hambone was practiced first by slaves and later imitated by vaudeville performers and minstrels.

humanistic concentrating on human tendencies and interests, rather than the natural or religious world.

hunting horn a bugle originally used to give signals to hunters on horseback.

idiom a colloquial way of speaking that derives from a specific dialect preferred by an identifiable body of speakers or members of a social class, profession, or team, such as the characteristic speech patterns of cowboys, sailors, or slaves.

imagery a phrase or series of phrases that creates a mental picture based on sight, sound, taste, feel, or smell.

inclusive story a narrative that draws in and includes all parts of a diverse audience.

Indian Kathakali [kath'•uh•kah•lee] a dance-drama characterized by complex language or mime and highly stylized and colorful makeup that resembles masks.

Indo-European tradition the customs and stories from Europe, Iran, the Indian subcontinent, and other parts of Asia.

Indonesian masked dance theater a stage style portraying episodes from Hindu epics and featuring brightly-colored, fantastic masks and exaggerated or expressive arm and hand movements.

intuitive interpretation the presentation of narrative derived from internal insight or feeling rather than from reasoning or deductive logic.

Jack Tale cycle a body of stories which present a trickster or adventurer named Jack as Everyman.

Jataka tale [juh•tah'•kuh] a birth story or narration of one of the former incarnations of the Buddha.

jaw harp (also Jew's harp or juice harp) a small metal harp-shaped device centered with a metal tongue. The harp is held against the teeth and played by strumming the metal tongue with the finger.

journeyman a reliable, experienced performer who has learned a craft, as compared to a student or apprentice.

Judaic lore [joo•day'•ihk] a body of stories and tales pertaining to Jewish history and culture.

jump story a scary oral narrative ending with a loud "boo" or similar stimulus intended to make the listener jump.

Kabbala (also Cabbala or Kabbalah) a medieval and modern system of Jewish belief marked by a cipher method of interpreting godhood, scripture, prophecy and visions, wisdom, numerology, and sacred mystery. The term derives from occult practices of the Essenes, the ascetic Jews from Jericho, which scholars recorded in the Zohar, a text composed in southern France and northern Spain during the twelfth and thirteenth centuries.

kabuki [kuh•boo'•kee] a Japanese drama or spectacle involving music and dance to traditional instruments and melodies, brilliantly colored settings and costumes, heavy makeup applied over a white base, and rigidly stylized acting that emulates the jerky motions and gestures of puppets.

kalimba [kuh•lihm'•buh] an African instrument consisting of a series of metal or bamboo strips mounted on a board or box, played by plucking the free ends of the strips.

kinetic style the use of movement, body language, and gesture to enhance a story.

koto [koh'•toh] a Japanese stringed instrument with thirteen silk strings placed over a shallow sound board and played with pick and fingers.

klezmer [klehz'•muhr] in the style of a wandering Jewish folk musician of eastern Europe who performed with a small band.

kulintang gongs a series of eight bronze gongs placed horizontally in a frame and played by a single performer.

kupuna [kuh•poo'•nuh] the Hawaiian word for ancestors; also, a term that honors senior citizens.

Kwanzaa [kwahn'•zuh] an African-American holiday based on the traditional African festival of the first harvest. The holiday focuses on the seven principles of black culture unity, self-determination, collective work and responsibility, cooperative economics, purpose, creativity, and faith.

kyogen [kyoh'•gihn] Japanese farces or interludes written in colloquial or informal language and performed without makeup or masks.

legend a traditional, popular history-based narrative which cannot be verified.

limberjack a hand-carved human figure with movable, jointed arms and legs, attached to a board with strings that move the figure to emulate a dance.

malong scarf a multipurpose, unisex article of clothing of the Maranao. The fabric is usually 72 inches long and 65 inches wide. Actors use the scarf as backdrop or a stage prop.

mantra a word or motto that embodies a principle, moral, or spiritual guide for an individual or group.

mbira [muh•bee'•ruh] an African thumb piano used as an enhancement to the story by some tellers. The mbira is made from a gourd that resonates the vibrations from metal keys plucked by the fingers.

medicine show a stylized performance of stories and music originally staged in a public area to attract or amuse an audience. Once the people gathered, hucksters offered various remedies for sale.

mentor a counselor, teacher, guide, or role model.

mime a form of theater which requires the acting out of a scene with no verbalization.

moralistic tale a story told to teach proper conduct, behavior, or social mores.

motivational story a story or parable intended to move a listener or audience toward personal development or improvement.

multicultural relating to, reflecting, or adapted to diverse groups of people

multidisciplinary applying to or containing elements of two or more studies, fields, or disciplines.

NAPPS acronym for the National Association for the Preservation and Perpetuation of Storytelling, which was founded in Jonesborough, Tennessee, in 1975. The association was formed to support storytelling and storytellers and continues today under the name, National Storytelling Association.

National Endowment for the Arts a part of an independent agency in the executive department of the federal government, the NEA provides grants to individuals and non-profit groups to encourage the growth of the arts in the United States.

National Public Radio a non-commercial satellite-delivered radio system serving more than 450 radio stations in the U.S.

National Storytelling Association *see* NAPPS.

National Theatre of the Deaf a professional international touring drama group, partially funded by the U.S. Department of Education, presenting stage performances through a combination of sign language and spoken word.

Native American renaissance the "rebirth" of interest in Native American arts, said to have begun with Scott Momaday's receipt of the Pulitzer Prize in 1969 for *House Made of Dawn.*

noh classic Japanese dance drama based on an heroic theme, chorus, and highly stylized action, costuming, and scenery.

nonsense song a ditty or jingle spoken, sung, or chanted for the sake of rhythm and composed of isolated sounds and syllables bearing no meaning.

olio a storytelling session at festivals and other multi-show performances, which features a short story or song from each featured teller. This is usually the first session, allowing attendees to get a "taste" of each performer.

organic style a mode of interconnected stories, where all parts are essential to a single theme or impression.

Ossian [uh'•zyihn] a legendary Gaelic warrior bard of the third century A.D., supposedly the son of Finn Mac Cumhail, a great Irish hero.

outdoor historical pageant a grandly staged production or tableau of some specific historical event, involving many costumed participants, and held in an outdoor amphitheater. An example is *Unto These Hills*, presented in Cherokee, North Carolina.

pa ndau [pan'•dow] a Hmong embroidered storycloth displaying elements or events of a narrative in the style of a storyboard or cartoon.

Panchatantra [pahn•chah•tahn'•truh] a collection of animal fables from India compiled around 500 B.C. by fablist Vishnusharma. The work is thought to have influenced the stories of Aesop.

participation story a narrative requiring members of the audience to join the teller in telling the story by rising in place, clapping on cue, repeating a refrain, or playing a part in the action.

patois [pah•twah'] a local form of speech or idiom confined to a small area or to one national or linguistic group.

period dialect a pattern of speech and pronunciation from a specific place and historic era.

picaro [pee•kah'•roh] the Spanish term for a rogue, trickster, bohemian, or wanderer living an unconventional or risqué life.

platform narrative a story performed before a large audience or from a dais or rostrum.

pourquoi story [poo•kwah'] a narrative explaining how something came to be, i.e., why a chipmunk has stripes, how the elephant got his trunk, how music was first created.

Rabelaisian [rahb•lay' zee•uhn] marked by gross robust humor, extravagance of character, fantasy, coarseness, and crude exhibitionism.

raconteur a person skilled in telling stories and anecdotes.

rap a rhythmic chanting often in unison of rhymed couplets to a music accompaniment to express a comic or satiric point of view or to express outrage, hatred, or contempt.

recorder a wooden wind instrument characterized by a conical tube, a whistle mouthpiece, and finger holes to alter the vibrating tones.

regionalist a performer whose work is associated with a particular geographic or linguistic area.

repertoire a stock of stories or performance material which the teller has mastered and can perform at any time.

santur [sahn•toor'] a stringed instrument from India composed of a finely finished triangular box with metal strings attached to the top across small wooden bridges. The pattern of strings groups three to each note. The player sounds each group of three by the strike of a pair of light wooden mallets.

Scheherazade [shuh•heh'•ruh•zahd] *see The Arabian Nights.*

seanachie [sihn' uh•shee] the Gaelic term for a reciter or a recorder of tales.

shakere [shay'•kuh•ray] a dried gourd covered by a loose netting strung with beads, bone, and other items that rattle when the device is shaken.

sho a Japanese mouth organ similar to a bagpipe and consisting of seventeen reeds inserted in a globular wind chest with a mouth hole.

slave narrative an autobiographical recitation of the history and experiences of a slave.

slide guitar a steel or Hawaiian guitar placed on a tripod in front of the player. The sound is produced by means of a slide which alters the sound of the strings.

spoons two common household eating implements held between the fingers of one hand, and played by rhythmically beating between the thigh and other hand.

squeeze box a concertina or accordion.

stand-up comedy a humorous monologue delivered typically in nightclubs or on television before an audience.

storykeeper the Native American term for a specific person who is selected by tribal elders to memorize the history and genealogies of the tribe.

storytelling renaissance the "rebirth" of storytelling begun in the late 1970s and continuing today.

storytelling therapist a trained counselor who uses narrative to help patients overcome trauma in their lives.

story-theatrics an elaborate form of narrative involving props, sets, and more elaborate costuming. Story-theatrics is done in a controlled environment, as opposed to a festival setting.

stretcher a very short story, joke, or song used as filler to make the storytelling session fit a specific time length.

taiko drums a set of Japanese drums mounted

in a frame and played by a single drummer.

tall tale an extravagant, unbelievable story told for the sake of humor.

tandem performance two tellers working together to tell one story, each having specific lines or a portion of the narrative to tell.

thematic bridging short stories, poems, songs, or anecdotes used to lead the listener from one long story to another by linking similar subjects or ideas contained in the two.

tin whistle an end-blown flute made of tin, with finger holes to change the pitch.

traditional lore a body of stories and tales that have been handed down from generation to generation, such as folktales and fairy tales.

traditional style performance which involves no props, music, or special setting and focuses on unadorned narration.

trickster a character dominating a series of stories who use wit and intelligence to overcome bigger opponents. Some examples are Anansi, Br'er Rabbit, and Coyote. Jack is sometimes a trickster figure.

troubadour a lyric poet and musician.

Uncle Remus a character created by Joel Chandler Harris. Uncle Remus was a free slave who told stories about animals who behave like humans.

UNESCO an acronym for the United Nations Educational, Scientific, and Cultural Organization.

urban lore a body of stories which are told as the truth, usually involving "I know someone who knows someone...," and which can never be proven as fact.

vocal characterization a method of altering the voice to personify specific characters.

washboard a corrugated rectangular surface used for scrubbing clothes or as a percussion instrument, such as the Cajun chink-a-chink.

wisdom lore a body of stories used to pass along the accumulated experience of humanity.

wonder tale a story containing magical elements that could not occur in real life.

yarn an exaggerated story or tall tale.

Bibliography

Aarne, Antti, and Stitt Thompson. *The Types of the Folktale.* Helsinki, Finland: Suomalainen Tiedeakatemia, 1973.

Baker, Augusta, and Ellin Greene. *Storytelling: Art and Technique.* New York: R. R. Bowker, 1977.

Barchers, Suzanne I. *Storybook Stew.* New York: Fulcrum, 1996.

Barton, Bob. *Tell Me Another: Storytelling and Reading Aloud at Home, at School and in the Community.* Portsmouth, N.H.: Heinemann, 1986.

Bauer, Caroline Feller. *Handbook for Storytellers.* Chicago: American Library Association, 1977.

Breneman, Lucille N., and Bren Breneman. *Once Upon a Time: A Storytelling Handbook.* Nelson-Hall, 1983.

Brody, Ed, *et al.*, eds. *Spinning Tales, Weaving Hope: Stories of Peace, Justice, and the Environment.* Philadelphia: New Society, 1992.

Champlin, Connie, and Nancy Renfro. *Storytelling with Puppets.* Chicago: American Library Association, 1985.

Crosson, Vicky L., and Jay C. Stailey. *Spinning Stories: An Introduction to Storytelling Skills.* Austin: Texas State Library, 1988.

Cullinan, Bernice E., and Lee Galda. *Literature and the Child.* New York: Harcourt Brace, 1994.

Dailey, Sheila, proj. dir. *Tales as Tools: The Power of Story in the Classroom.* Jonesborough, Tenn.: National Storytelling Press, 1994.

Farrell, Catharine. *Storytelling: A Guide for Teachers.* New York: Scholastic Professional, 1993.

Gantz, Jeffrey. *Early Irish Myths and Sagas.* London: Penguin, 1981.

Geisler, Harlynne. *Storytelling Professionally: The Nuts and Bolts of a Working Performer.* Englewood, Colo.: Libraries Unlimited, 1997.

Greene, Ellin. *Storytelling: Art and Technique*, Third Edition. New York: Bowker, 1996.

Hamilton, Martha, and Mitch Weiss. *Children Tell Stories: A Teaching Guide.* Katonah, N.Y.: Richard C. Owen, 1990.

Holt, David, and Bill Mooney. *Ready-to-Tell Tales: Sure-Fire Stories from America's Favorite Storytellers.* Little Rock, Ark.: August House, 1994.

Jagendorf, M. *New England Bean-Pot: American Folk Stories to Read and to Tell.* New York: Vanguard Press, 1948.

Landor, Lynn. *Children's Own Stories; A Literature-Based Language Arts Program*. San Francisco: San Francisco Study Center, 1990.

Lipke, Barbara. *Figures, Facts & Fables: Telling Tales in Science and Math*. Portsmouth, N.H.: Heinemann, 1996.

Lipman, Doug. *The Storytelling Coach: How to Listen, Praise, and Bring Out People's Best,* introduction by Jay O'Callahan. Little Rock, Ark.: August House, 1995.

Livo, Norma J., and Sandra A. Rietz. *Storytelling: Process and Practice*. Englewood, Colo.: Libraries Unlimited, 1986.

Lomax, Alan, and John Lomax. *American Ballads and Folk Songs*. New York: Macmillan, 1972.

MacDonald, Margaret Read. *The Storyteller's Sourcebook: A Subject, Title, and Motif-Index to Folklore Collections for Children*. Detroit: Gale, 1982.

_____. *The Storyteller's Start-Up Book: Finding, Learning, Performing, and Using Folktales*. Little Rock, Ark.: August House, 1993.

Maguire, Jack. *Creative Storytelling*. Cambridge, Mass.: Yellow Moon Press, 1992.

McCarthy, William Bernard, Cheryl Oxford, and Joseph Daniel Sobol, eds. *Jack in Two Worlds: Contemporary North American Tales and Their Tellers*. North Carolina: University of North Carolina Press, 1994.

McLeod, Michael, "Once Upon a Time," *Reader's Digest*, May 1997, 172-178.

Meade, Erica Helm. *Tell It by Heart: Women and the Healing Power of Story*. Chicago: Open Court, 1995.

Meyerhoff, Barbara. *Number Our Days*. New York: E. P. Dutton, 1978.

Miller, Teresa, and Norma Livo. *Joining In: An Anthology of Audience Participation Stories and How to Tell Them*. Cambridge, Mass.: Yellow Moon Press, 1988.

Mooney, Bill, and David Holt. *The Storyteller's Guide*. Little Rock, Arkansas: August House, 1996.

Moore, Robin. *Awakening the Hidden Storyteller: How to Build a Storytelling Tradition in Your Family*. Boston: Shambhala, 1991.

O'Rahilly, Thomas F. *Early Irish History and Mythology*. Dublin: Dublin Institute for Advanced Studies, 1976.

Paley, Vivian Gussin. *The Boy Who Would Be a Helicopter: The Uses of Storytelling in the Classroom*. Cambridge, Mass.: Harvard University Press, 1990.

Pellowski, Anne. *The Story Vine: A Source Book of Unusual and Easy-to-Tell Stories from Around the World*. Riverside, N.J.: Macmillan, 1984.

_____. *The World of Storytelling*. Bronx, N.Y.: H. W. Wilson, 1990.

Rees, Alwyn, and Brinley Rees. *Celtic Heritage*. London: Thames and Hudson, 1961.

Ross, Anne. *The Folklore of the Scottish Highlands*. London: B. T. Batsford, 1976.

Sawyer, Ruth. *The Way of the Storyteller*. New York: Viking, 1977.

Schimmel, Nancy. *Just Enough to Make a Story: A Sourcebook for Storytelling*. Berkeley, Calif.: Sisters' Choice Press, 1978.

Shedlock, Marie. *The Art of the Storyteller*. New York: Dover, 1951.

Sierra, Judy, and Robert Kaminski. *Twice Upon a Time: Stories to Tell, Retell, Act Out, and Write About*. New York: H. W. Wilson, 1989.

Stone, Richard. *The Healing Art of Storytelling: A Sacred Journey of Personal Discovery*. New York: Hyperion, 1996.

Stotter, Ruth. *About Story: Writings on Story and Storytelling*. Tiburon, Calif.: Stotter Press, 1996.

Tales as Tools: The Power of Story in the Classroom. Jonesboro, Tenn.: National Storytelling Press, 1994.

Thompson, Stith. *Motif-Index of Folk-Literature*. Bloomington: Indiana University Press, 1966.

Tooze, Ruth. *Storytelling*. Englewood Cliffs, N.J.: Prentice Hall, 1959.

Wolkstein, Diane. *The Magic Orange Tree and Other Haitian Folktales*. New York: Schocken, 1997.

Woodard, Jim. *The Storyteller's Challenge*. Venture, Calif.: self-produced, 1996.

Index

*Numbers in **boldface** refer to pages with photographs.*

321